THE

POETICAL WORKS

OF

WILLIAM WORDSWORTH

THE

Poetical Works

OF

WILLIAM WORDSWORTH

POEMS FOUNDED ON THE AFFECTIONS
POEMS ON THE NAMING OF PLACES
POEMS OF THE FANCY
POEMS OF THE IMAGINATION

Edited from the manuscripts
with
textual and critical notes
by
E. DE SELINCOURT

SECOND EDITION

OXFORD
AT THE CLARENDON PRESS

Oxford University Press, Ely House, London W.1

GLASGOW NEW YORK TORONTO MELBOURNE WELLINGTON
CAPE TOWN SALISBURY IBADAN NAIROBI LUSAKA ADDIS ABABA
BOMBAY CALCUTTA MADRAS KARACHI LAHORE DACCA
KUALA LUMPUR SINGAPORE HONG KONG TOKYO

821.7
W936po
v.2

FIRST EDITION 1944
SECOND EDITION 1952
REPRINTED LITHOGRAPHICALLY IN GREAT BRITAIN
AT THE UNIVERSITY PRESS, OXFORD
BY VIVIAN RIDLER, PRINTER TO THE UNIVERSITY
FROM SHEETS OF THE SECOND EDITION
1965, 1969

PREFACE

This volume, the second of my edition of Wordsworth's Poetical Works, contains the Poems of the Affections, on the Naming of Places, of the Fancy, and of the Imagination, which occupy pp. 187–299 of Volume I, and pp. 1–259 of Volume II of Wordsworth's final edition of 1849–50. In order to effect a more convenient division of material between my volumes I have added the Prefaces &c., which in 1850 were placed, after the great Ode, at the end of Volume V.

The manuscripts upon which I draw in my *apparatus criticus* are for the most part in the Wordsworth Museum at Grasmere: very few of them have hitherto been made available to the student. A further valuable source of information on the earlier text of those poems which first appeared in the *Lyrical Ballads*, 1800–5, and in *Poems in Two Volumes*, 1807, is to be found in *A Description of the Wordsworth and Coleridge Manuscripts in the possession of Mr. T. Norton Longman*, edited by W. Hale White, London, 1897. For permission to quote from this book I gratefully acknowledge my debt to the publishers, Messrs. Longmans, Green & Co. I have not seen the manuscript of the *Lyrical Ballads*, but Mr. Hale White was a scholar whose findings can be implicitly trusted; the manuscript of the *Poems* of 1807 I have examined for myself, through the kindness of Mr. E. H. W. Meyerstein, its present owner.

It should, perhaps, be noted that the punctuation of Wordsworth's manuscripts, even when they are fair copies, is as a rule deficient, and in his earlier drafts it is often entirely wanting: in my *apparatus criticus* I have added such stops as seemed necessary in order to make the lines easily intelligible. The *Longman MSS.*, being copy prepared for press, are naturally more adequately punctuated, but Wordsworth was not himself responsible for this, for in July 1800 he had sent the manuscript to Humphry Davy, confessing that he was 'no adept' at punctuation, and asking him to undertake it, and many of the stops are inserted in a different ink from the rest of the copy. At what date Wordsworth began to interest himself in the question, and undertake full responsibility for the punctuation of his printed text, we cannot tell. The general punctuation of his poems calls for little remark, except that he had a tendency to introduce a comma, where it is not required by logic or syntax, in order to suggest a metrical pause or emphasis. Mr. Thomas Hutchinson has often omitted such commas from the text of his *Oxford Wordsworth*: I have everywhere retained them except where they seemed to confuse the sense.

E. DE S.

GRASMERE,
January 1943

NOTE TO SECOND EDITION

THE re-issue of this volume gives me the opportunity to correct some textual and other errors and omissions in the volume issued in 1944, and to add in an Appendix (p. 535 *infra*) an account of a transcript, made by Sara Hutchinson, of very interesting first drafts of a number of Wordsworth's poems composed in the first six months of 1802, the majority of which appear in this volume: viz. *To a Butterfly* (p. 22); *A Farewell* (p. 23); *Stanzas* written in . . . Thomson's *Castle of Indolence* (p. 25); *Repentance* (p. 46); *The Sailor's Mother* (p. 54); *The Emigrant Mother* (p. 56); *To a Skylark* (p. 141); *The Redbreast chasing the Butterfly* (p. 149); *To a Cuckoo* (p. 207); *Written in March* (p. 220); *Beggars* (p. 222); *Resolution and Independence* (p. 235); "Among all lovely things" (p. 466).

Some of the other poems transcribed appear in Vols. I, III, and IV of the present edition, viz. "My heart leaps up" (I, p. 226); *To a Butterfly* (I, p. 226); *The Sparrow's Nest* (I, p. 227); *Foresight* (I, p. 227); *Alice Fell* (I, p. 232); "I griev'd for Buonaparte" (III, p. 110); "The Sun has long been set" (IV, p. 9); "These Chairs they have no words to utter" (IV, p. 365); *The Tinker* (IV, p. 366); *Travelling* (IV, p. 423).

The notebook was known in the family as "Sara Hutchinson's Poets". It now belongs to Miss Joanna Hutchinson, who has kindly allowed me to study it, and to publish what it reveals.

H. DARBISHIRE

OXFORD,
September 1951

CONTENTS

CONTENTS ix

POEMS OF THE IMAGINATION

TABLE OF ABBREVIATIONS ETC. USED IN THE *APPARATUS CRITICUS* AND NOTES

W. *or* W. W. William Wordsworth.

D. W. Dorothy Wordsworth.

Dora W. Dora Wordsworth.

M. H. or M. W. Mary Wordsworth (*née* Hutchinson).

S. H. Sara Hutchinson.

M. *The Memoirs of W. W.*, by Christopher Wordsworth, 1851.

E.L. The Early Letters of W. W. and D. W. Oxford, 1935.

M.Y. The Letters of W. W. and D. W. Middle Years (1806–20), 2 vols. Oxford, 1937.

L.Y. The Letters of W. W. and D. W. Later Years (1821–50), 3 vols. Oxford, 1939.

I. F. The notes dictated by W. W. to Isabella Fenwick in 1843.

O.E.D. the *Oxford English Dictionary*.

K. Professor William Knight, editor of W. W.'s *Poetical Works*, 8 vols. 1896.

C. Variants, quoted by K., from a copy of W.'s Works formerly in the possession of Lord Coleridge.

Dowden. Professor Edward Dowden, editor of W. W.'s *Poetical Works*, 7 vols. 1892–3.

Hutchinson. Mr. Thomas Hutchinson, editor of the Oxford Wordsworth, *The Lyrical Ballads* (1798), 1898, and the *Poems in two volumes* (1807), 1897.

Longman MSS. Manuscripts of the *Lyrical Ballads*, 1800–5, and of *Poems in Two Volumes*, 1807, formerly in the possession of Mr. T. Norton Longman.

MS. M. A Manuscript of Poems probably composed 1800–4 and described in my edition of *The Prelude*, pp. xx–xxi.

MS. 1, MS. 2, &c., in *App. Crit.* indicate variants from first draft, second draft, &c., of manuscript text of the particular poem.

[ ] a word or words missing from the manuscript.

[?] a word or words illegible in the manuscript.

A word or words inserted within square brackets and preceded by a ? indicate an editorial conjecture.

70/71 lines found in a manuscript or text between lines 70 and 71.

References to the several manuscripts of each poem are explained in the notes thereto at the end of the volume.

POEMS FOUNDED ON THE AFFECTIONS

I

THE BROTHERS

[Composed (in or about) February, 1800.—Published 1800]

"THESE Tourists, heaven preserve us! needs must live
A profitable life: some glance along,
Rapid and gay, as if the earth were air,
And they were butterflies to wheel about
Long as the summer lasted: some, as wise,   5
Perched on the forehead of a jutting crag,
Pencil in hand and book upon the knee,
Will look and scribble, scribble on and look,
Until a man might travel twelve stout miles,
Or reap an acre of his neighbour's corn.   10
But, for that moping Son of Idleness,
Why can he tarry *yonder?*—In our church-yard
Is neither epitaph nor monument,
Tombstone nor name—only the turf we tread
And a few natural graves."

      To Jane, his wife,   15
Thus spake the homely Priest of Ennerdale.
It was a July evening; and he sate
Upon the long stone-seat beneath the eaves
Of his old cottage,—as it chanced, that day,
Employed in winter's work. Upon the stone   20
His wife sate near him, teasing matted wool,
While, from the twin cards toothed with glittering wire,
He fed the spindle of his youngest child,
Who, in the open air, with due accord
Of busy hands and back-and-forward steps,   25
Her large round wheel was turning. Towards the field
In which the Parish Chapel stood alone,
Girt round with a bare ring of mossy wall,
While half an hour went by, the Priest had sent

6-8 *so* 1827: Upon the forehead of a jutting crag
    Sit perch'd with book and pencil on their knee
    And look   1800-20
24-6 *so* 1836: Who turn'd her large round wheel in the open air
    With back and forward steps   1800-32

Many a long look of wonder: and at last,   30
Risen from his seat, beside the snow-white ridge
Of carded wool which the old man had piled
He laid his implements with gentle care,
Each in the other locked; and down the path,
That from his cottage to the church-yard led,   35
He took his way, impatient to accost
The Stranger, whom he saw still lingering there.

'Twas one well known to him in former days,
A Shepherd-lad; who ere his sixteenth year
Had left that calling, tempted to entrust   40
His expectations to the fickle winds
And perilous waters; with the mariners
A fellow-mariner;—and so had fared
Through twenty seasons; but he had been reared
Among the mountains, and he in his heart   45
Was half a shepherd on the stormy seas.
Oft in the piping shrouds had Leonard heard
The tones of waterfalls, and inland sounds
Of caves and trees;—and, when the regular wind
Between the tropics filled the steady sail,   50
And blew with the same breath through days and weeks,
Lengthening invisibly its weary line
Along the cloudless Main, he, in those hours
Of tiresome indolence, would often hang
Over the vessel's side, and gaze and gaze;   55
And, while the broad blue wave and sparkling foam
Flashed round him images and hues that wrought
In union with the employment of his heart,
He, thus by feverish passion overcome,
Even with the organs of his bodily eye,   60
Below him, in the bosom of the deep,
Saw mountains; saw the forms of sheep that grazed
On verdant hills—with dwellings among trees,
And shepherds clad in the same country grey
Which he himself had worn.[1]

[1] This description of the Calenture is sketched from an imperfect recollection of an admirable one in prose, by Mr. Gilbert, author of the *Hurricane*.

31 snow-white] snowy 1800, *corr. in errata*   39 sixteenth 1815: thir-
teenth 1800–5   40 left that 1815:   changed his 1800–5   40–2 tempted
. . . waters *not in* 1800–5   56 blue 1840: green 1800–36

And now, at last,   65
From perils manifold, with some small wealth
Acquired by traffic 'mid the Indian Isles,
To his paternal home he is returned,
With a determined purpose to resume
The life he had lived there; both for the sake   70
Of many darling pleasures, and the love
Which to an only brother he has borne
In all his hardships, since that happy time
When, whether it blew foul or fair, they two
Were brother-shepherds on their native hills.   75
—They were the last of all their race: and now,
When Leonard had approached his home, his heart
Failed in him; and, not venturing to enquire
Tidings of one so long and dearly loved,
He to the solitary church-yard turned;   80
That, as he knew in what particular spot
His family were laid, he thence might learn
If still his Brother lived, or to the file
Another grave was added.—He had found
Another grave,—near which a full half-hour   85
He had remained; but, as he gazed, there grew
Such a confusion in his memory,
That he began to doubt; and even to hope
That he had seen this heap of turf before,—
That it was not another grave; but one   90
He had forgotten. He had lost his path,
As up the vale, that afternoon, he walked
Through fields which once had been well known to him:
And oh what joy this recollection now
Sent to his heart! he lifted up his eyes,   95
And, looking round, imagined that he saw
Strange alteration wrought on every side
Among the woods and fields, and that the rocks,
And everlasting hills themselves were changed.

By this the Priest, who down the field had come,   100
Unseen by Leonard, at the church-yard gate

79 *so* 1836: whom he so dearly loved 1800–32   80 *so* 1836: Towards
the church-yard he had turn'd aside, 1800–32   88 even to hope 1836:
he had hopes 1800–27: hope was his 1832   92 *so* 1815: he came that
afternoon 1800–5   96 *so* 1815: he thought that he perceiv'd 1800–5   99
everlasting 1827: the eternal 1800–15: the everlasting 1820

Stopped short,—and thence, at leisure, limb by limb
Perused him with a gay complacency.
Ay, thought the Vicar, smiling to himself,
'Tis one of those who needs must leave the path   105
Of the world's business to go wild alone:
His arms have a perpetual holiday;
The happy man will creep about the fields,
Following his fancies by the hour, to bring
Tears down his cheek, or solitary smiles   110
Into his face, until the setting sun
Write fool upon his forehead.—Planted thus
Beneath a shed that over-arched the gate
Of this rude church-yard, till the stars appeared
The good Man might have communed with himself,   115
But that the Stranger, who had left the grave,
Approached; he recognised the Priest at once,
And, after greetings interchanged, and given
By Leonard to the Vicar as to one
Unknown to him, this dialogue ensued.   120
    Leonard. You live, Sir, in these dales, a quiet life:
Your years make up one peaceful family;
And who would grieve and fret, if, welcome come
And welcome gone, they are so like each other,
They cannot be remembered? Scarce a funeral   125
Comes to this church-yard once in eighteen months;
And yet, some changes must take place among you:
And you, who dwell here, even among these rocks,
Can trace the finger of mortality,
And see, that with our threescore years and ten   130
We are not all that perish.——I remember,
(For many years ago I passed this road)
There was a foot-way all along the fields
By the brook-side—'tis gone—and that dark cleft!
To me it does not seem to wear the face   135
Which then it had!
    Priest.   Nay, Sir, for aught I know,
That chasm is much the same—
    Leonard.   But, surely, yonder—
    Priest. Ay, there, indeed, your memory is a friend

103 Perused 1815: He scann'd 1800–5
136–7 That rock for aught I know
      Is much the same. *Leon.* But that huge eminence MS.

That does not play you false.—On that tall pike
(It is the loneliest place of all these hills)   140
There were two springs which bubbled side by side,
As if they had been made that they might be
Companions for each other: the huge crag
Was rent with lightning—one hath disappeared;
The other, left behind, is flowing still.   145
For accidents and changes such as these,
We want not store of them;—a waterspout
Will bring down half a mountain; what a feast
For folks that wander up and down like you,
To see an acre's breadth of that wide cliff   150
One roaring cataract! a sharp May-storm
Will come with loads of January snow,
And in one night send twenty score of sheep
To feed the ravens; or a shepherd dies
By some untoward death among the rocks: 155
The ice breaks up and sweeps away a bridge;
A wood is felled:—and then for our own homes!
A child is born or christened, a field ploughed,
A daughter sent to service, a web spun,
The old house-clock is decked with a new face;   160
And hence, so far from wanting facts or dates
To chronicle the time, we all have here
A pair of diaries,—one serving, Sir,
For the whole dale, and one for each fire-side—
Yours was a stranger's judgment: for historians,   165
Commend me to these valleys!
    Leonard.   Yet your Church-yard
Seems, if such freedom may be used with you,
To say that you are heedless of the past:
An orphan could not find his mother's grave:
Here's neither head nor foot-stone, plate of brass,   170
Cross-bones nor skull,—type of our earthly state
Nor emblem of our hopes: the dead man's home
Is but a fellow to that pasture-field.

140 A solitary place among the clouds MS.
143–4 *so* 1827: Companions for each other: ten years back
             Close to those brother fountains, the huge crag
             Was rent with lightning—one is dead and gone, 1800–20.
           So MS., *but* split *for* rent
147 *so* 1815: Why, we have store of them! 1800–5   169 *not in* 1800 *text,*
but given in errata

Priest. Why, there, Sir, is a thought that's new to me!
The stone-cutters, 'tis true, might beg their bread   175
If every English church-yard were like ours;
Yet your conclusion wanders from the truth:
We have no need of names and epitaphs;
We talk about the dead by our fire-sides.
And then, for our immortal part! *we* want   180
No symbols, Sir, to tell us that plain tale:
The thought of death sits easy on the man
Who has been born and dies among the mountains.
    Leonard. Your Dalesmen, then, do in each other's thoughts
Possess a kind of second life: no doubt   185
You, Sir, could help me to the history
Of half these graves?
    Priest.   For eight-score winters past,
With what I've witnessed, and with what I've heard,
Perhaps I might; and, on a winter-evening,
If you were seated at my chimney's nook,   190
By turning o'er these hillocks one by one,
We two could travel, Sir, through a strange round;
Yet all in the broad highway of the world.
Now there's a grave—your foot is half upon it,—
It looks just like the rest; and yet that man   195
Died broken-hearted.
    Leonard.   'Tis a common case.
We'll take another: who is he that lies
Beneath yon ridge, the last of those three graves?
It touches on that piece of native rock
Left in the church-yard wall.
    Priest.   That's Walter Ewbank.   200
He had as white a head and fresh a cheek
As ever were produced by youth and age
Engendering in the blood of hale four-score.
Through five long generations had the heart
Of Walter's forefathers o'erflowed the bounds   205
Of their inheritance, that single cottage—
You see it yonder! and those few green fields.
They toiled and wrought, and still, from sire to son,
Each struggled, and each yielded as before
A little—yet a little,—and old Walter,   210

187 For eight-score winters past] *not in* 1800 *text, but given in errata*
189 winter-evening 1827: winter's evening 1800–20

They left to him the family heart, and land
With other burthens than the crop it bore.
Year after year the old man still kept up
A cheerful mind,—and buffeted with bond,
Interest, and mortgages; at last he sank,   215
And went into his grave before his time.
Poor Walter! whether it was care that spurred him
God only knows, but to the very last
He had the lightest foot in Ennerdale:
His pace was never that of an old man: 220
I almost see him tripping down the path
With his two grandsons after him:—but you,
Unless our Landlord be your host to-night,
Have far to travel,—and on these rough paths
Even in the longest day of midsummer—   225
    Leonard. But those two Orphans!
    Priest.   Orphans!—Such they were—
Yet not while Walter lived:—for, though their parents
Lay buried side by side as now they lie,
The old man was a father to the boys,
Two fathers in one father: and if tears,   230
Shed when he talked of them where they were not,
And hauntings from the infirmity of love,
Are aught of what makes up a mother's heart,
This old Man, in the day of his old age,
Was half a mother to them.—If you weep, Sir,   235
To hear a stranger talking about strangers,
Heaven bless you when you are among your kindred!
Ay—you may turn that way—it is a grave
Which will bear looking at.
    Leonard.   These boys—I hope
They loved this good old Man?—
    Priest.   They did—and truly: 240
But that was what we almost overlooked,
They were such darlings of each other. Yes,
Though from the cradle they had lived with Walter,
The only kinsman near them, and though he
Inclined to both by reason of his age,   245

213 kept up 1802: preserv'd 1800   242 Yes, 1836: For 1800–32
244–7 *so* 1836: *so* 1815–32, *but* them *for* both:
  The only Kinsman near them in the house,
  Yet he being old, they had much love to spare, 1800–5

With a more fond, familiar, tenderness;
They, notwithstanding, had much love to spare,
And it all went into each other's hearts.
Leonard, the elder by just eighteen months,
Was two years taller: 'twas a joy to see,   250
To hear, to meet them!—From their house the school
Is distant three short miles, and in the time
Of storm and thaw, when every watercourse
And unbridged stream, such as you may have noticed
Crossing our roads at every hundred steps,   255
Was swoln into a noisy rivulet,
Would Leonard then, when elder boys remained
At home, go staggering through the slippery fords,
Bearing his brother on his back. I have seen him,
On windy days, in one of those stray brooks,   260
Ay, more than once I have seen him, mid-leg deep,
Their two books lying both on a dry stone,
Upon the hither side: and once I said,
As I remember, looking round these rocks
And hills on which we all of us were born,   265
That God who made the great book of the world
Would bless such piety—
      Leonard.   It may be then—
      Priest. Never did worthier lads break English bread;
The very brightest Sunday Autumn saw,
With all its mealy clusters of ripe nuts,   270
Could never keep those boys away from church,
Or tempt them to an hour of sabbath breach.
Leonard and James! I warrant, every corner
Among these rocks, and every hollow place
That venturous foot could reach, to one or both   275
Was known as well as to the flowers that grow there.
Like roe-bucks they went bounding o'er the hills;
They played like two young ravens on the crags:
Then they could write, ay, and speak too, as well
As many of their betters—and for Leonard!   280
The very night before he went away,
In my own house I put into his hand

257–8 *so* 1836: when elder boys perhaps Remain'd at home, go staggering
through the fords 1800–32   259 I have 1832: I've 1800–27   269 *so*
1836: The finest Sunday that the Autumn saw 1800–32 .   275 *so* 1836:
Where foot could come, to one or both of them 1800–32

A Bible, and I'd wager house and field
That, if he be alive, he has it yet.
    Leonard. It seems, these Brothers have not lived to be   285
A comfort to each other—
    Priest.   That they might
Live to such end is what both old and young
In this our valley all of us have wished,
And what, for my part, I have often prayed:
But Leonard—
    Leonard. Then James still is left among you!   290
    Priest. 'Tis of the elder brother I am speaking:
They had an uncle;—he was at that time
A thriving man, and trafficked on the seas:
And, but for that same uncle, to this hour
Leonard had never handled rope or shroud: 295
For the boy loved the life which we lead here;
And though of unripe years, a stripling only,
His soul was knit to this his native soil.
But, as I said, old Walter was too weak
To strive with such a torrent; when he died,   300
The estate and house were sold; and all their sheep,
A pretty flock, and which, for aught I know,
Had clothed the Ewbanks for a thousand years:—
Well—all was gone, and they were destitute,
And Leonard, chiefly for his Brother's sake,   305
Resolved to try his fortune on the seas.
Twelve years are past since we had tidings from him.
If there were one among us who had heard
That Leonard Ewbank was come home again,
From the Great Gavel,[1] down by Leeza's banks,   310
And down the Enna, far as Egremont,
The day would be a joyous festival;
And those two bells of ours, which there you see—

---

[1] The Great Gavel, so called, I imagine, from its resemblance to the gable
end of a house, is one of the highest of the Cumberland mountains. It stands
at the head of the several vales of Ennerdale, Wastdale, and Borrowdale.
    The Leeza is a river which flows into the Lake of Ennerdale: on issuing
from the Lake, it changes its name, and is called the End, Eyne, or Enna.
It falls into the sea a little below Egremont.

---

283 house and field 1827: twenty pounds 1800–20   297 *so* 1815: And,
though a very Stripling, twelve years old ; 1800–5   307 *so* 1827: 'Tis now
twelve years 1800–20   312 joyous 1836: very 1800–32

Hanging in the open air—but, O good Sir!
This is sad talk—they'll never sound for him—   315
Living or dead.—When last we heard of him,
He was in slavery among the Moors
Upon the Barbary coast.—'Twas not a little
That would bring down his spirit; and no doubt,
Before it ended in his death, the Youth   320
Was sadly crossed.—Poor Leonard! when we parted,
He took me by the hand, and said to me,
If e'er he should grow rich, he would return,
To live in peace upon his father's land,
And lay his bones among us.
    Leonard.   If that day   325
Should come, 'twould needs be a glad day for him;
He would himself, no doubt, be happy then
As any that should meet him—
    Priest.   Happy! Sir—
    Leonard. You said his kindred all were in their graves,
And that he had one Brother—
    Priest.   That is but   330
A fellow-tale of sorrow. From his youth
James, though not sickly, yet was delicate;
And Leonard being always by his side
Had done so many offices about him,
That, though he was not of a timid nature,   335
Yet still the spirit of a mountain-boy
In him was somewhat checked; and, when his Brother
Was gone to sea, and he was left alone,
The little colour that he had was soon
Stolen from his cheek; he drooped, and pined, and pined—   340
    Leonard. But these are all the graves of full-grown men!
    Priest. Ay, Sir, that passed away: we took him to us;
He was the child of all the dale—he lived
Three months with one, and six months with another;
And wanted neither food, nor clothes, nor love: 345
And many, many happy days were his.
But, whether blithe or sad, 'tis my belief
His absent Brother still was at his heart.

320 Youth 1815: Lad 1800–5
323–5 *so* 1832: If ever the day came when he was rich,
         He would return, and on his Father's Land
         He would grow old among us.   1800–27

And, when he dwelt beneath our roof, we found
(A practice till this time unknown to him)   350
That often, rising from his bed at night,
He in his sleep would walk about, and sleeping
He sought his brother Leonard.—You are moved!
Forgive me, Sir: before I spoke to you,
I judged you most unkindly.
  Leonard.   But this Youth,   355
How did he die at last ?
  Priest.   One sweet May-morning,
(It will be twelve years since when Spring returns)
He had gone forth among the new-dropped lambs,
With two or three companions, whom their course
Of occupation led from height to height   360
Under a cloudless sun—till he, at length,
Through weariness, or, haply, to indulge
The humour of the moment, lagged behind.
You see yon precipice ;—it wears the shape
Of a vast building made of many crags ;   365
And in the midst is one particular rock
That rises like a column from the vale,
Whence by our shepherds it is called, THE PILLAR.
Upon its aëry summit crowned with heath,
The loiterer, not unnoticed by his comrades,   370
Lay stretched at ease ; but, passing by the place
On their return, they found that he was gone.

349 dwelt 1827: liv'd 1800–20
359–63 *so* 1820:   Companions whom it chanced
    Some further business summoned to a house
    Which stands at the Dale-head. James, tired perhaps,
    Or from some other cause, remain'd behind. 1800–15
364–5 *so* 1820: it almost looks Like some vast 1800–15
369–74 *so* 1827: James, pointing to its summit, over which
    They all had purposed to return together,
    Informed them that he there would wait for them ;
    They parted, and his Comrades passed that way
    Some two hours after, but they did not find him
    At the appointed place—a circumstance
    Of which they took no heed ; but one of them,
    Going by chance at night, into the house 1800. *So* 1802–5
     but pointed *for* pointing, And told *for* Informed, *and* find
     him Upon the Pillar at the appointed place. Of this *etc.*
    Upon the Summit at the appointed place 1815: 1820
    as 1827, *but* ll. 373–4. From this no ill was feared ; but
    one of them, Entering by chance, at eventide, the house

No ill was feared; till one of them by chance
Entering, when evening was far spent, the house
Which at that time was James's home, there learned   375
That nobody had seen him all that day:
The morning came, and still he was unheard of:
The neighbours were alarmed, and to the brook
Some hastened; some ran to the lake: ere noon
They found him at the foot of that same rock   380
Dead, and with mangled limbs. The third day after
I buried him, poor Youth, and there he lies!
    Leonard. And that then *is* his grave!—Before his death
You say that he saw many happy years?
    Priest. Ay, that he did—
    Leonard.   And all went well with him?—   385
    Priest. If he had one, the Youth had twenty homes.
    Leonard. And you believe, then, that his mind was easy?—
    Priest. Yes, long before he died, he found that time
Is a true friend to sorrow; and unless'
His thoughts were turned on Leonard's luckless fortune,   390
He talked about him with a cheerful love.
    Leonard. He could not come to an unhallowed end!
    Priest. Nay, God forbid!—You recollect I mentioned
A habit which disquietude and grief
Had brought upon him; and we all conjectured   395
That, as the day was warm, he had lain down
On the soft heath,—and, waiting for his comrades,
He there had fallen asleep; that in his sleep
He to the margin of the precipice
Had walked, and from the summit had fallen headlong: 400
And so no doubt he perished. When the Youth
Fell, in his hand he must have grasp'd, we think,
His shepherd's staff; for on that Pillar of rock
It had been caught mid-way; and there for years
It hung;—and mouldered there.

                        The Priest here ended—   405
The Stranger would have thanked him, but he felt

379 *so* 1836: Some went, and some towards the Lake; 1800–15: Some
hastened; some towards the Lake; 1820   382, 386 Youth 1815: Lad
1800–5   397 On the soft heath 1836: Upon the grass 1800–32   401–2
so 1836: at the time, We guess, that in his hands he must have had 1800–20;
so 1827–32 *but* held *for* had   403–4 *so* 1836: for midway in the cliff
It had been caught; and there for many years 1800–32

A gushing from his heart, that took away
The power of speech. Both left the spot in silence;
And Leonard, when they reached the church-yard gate,
As the Priest lifted up the latch, turned round,—   410
And, looking at the grave, he said, "My Brother!"
The Vicar did not hear the words: and now,
He pointed towards his dwelling-place, entreating
That Leonard would partake his homely fare:
The other thanked him with an earnest voice;   415
But added, that, the evening being calm,
He would pursue his journey. So they parted.

It was not long ere Leonard reached a grove
That overhung the road: he there stopped short,
And, sitting down beneath the trees, reviewed   420
All that the Priest had said: his early years
Were with him:—his long absence, cherished hopes,
And thoughts which had been his an hour before,
All pressed on him with such a weight, that now,
This vale, where he had been so happy, seemed   425
A place in which he could not bear to live:
So he relinquished all his purposes.
He travelled back to Egremont: and thence,
That night, he wrote a letter to the Priest,
Reminding him of what had passed between them;   430
And adding, with a hope to be forgiven,
That it was from the weakness of his heart
He had not dared to tell him who he was.
This done, he went on shipboard, and is now
A seaman, a grey-headed Mariner.   435

407–8 *so* 1815: Tears rushing in: both left the spot in silence; 1800–5
413 *so* 1836: Pointing towards the Cottage, he entreated 1800–32   415
an earnest . . . a fervent 1800–32   422 *so* 1836: Were with him in his
heart: his cherished hopes 1800–32   429 he wrote 1802: address'd
1800

II
ARTEGAL AND ELIDURE
(SEE THE CHRONICLE OF GEOFFREY OF MONMOUTH, AND
MILTON'S HISTORY OF ENGLAND)

[Composed 1815.—Published 1820]

WHERE be the temples which in Britain's Isle,
For his paternal Gods, the Trojan raised?
Gone like a morning dream, or like a pile
Of clouds that in cerulean ether blazed!
Ere Julius landed on her white-cliffed shore,   5
     They sank, delivered o'er
To fatal dissolution; and, I ween,
No vestige then was left that such had ever been.

Nathless, a British record (long concealed
In old Armorica, whose secret springs   10
No Gothic conqueror ever drank) revealed
The marvellous current of forgotten things;
How Brutus came, by oracles impelled,
     And Albion's giants quelled,
A brood whom no civility could melt,   15
"Who never tasted grace, and goodness ne'er had felt."

By brave Corineus aided, he subdued,
And rooted out the intolerable kind;
And this too-long-polluted land imbued
With goodly arts and usages refined;   20

1-8   Sunk are the Temples which as stories tell
        In Britain's isle the Trojan Brutus reared
        For his transplanted Gods therein to dwell,
        Ere Julius landed on the white-cliffed shore
        The sacred structures were delivered o'er
        To utter dissolution whence I ween
        A general doubt prevails if such have ever been MS.
1-4   Where be the Temples which in Britain's isle
        As legends tell the Trojan Founder reared?
        Gone like a dream of morning; or a pile
        Of gorgeous clouds that in the East appeared MS.
Another MS. omits stanza 1, *and begins with l.* 9. A British Record that had
lain concealed.
9-12 Yet in the wilds of Cambria lay concealed
        By *Snowdon's* forests or by Voga's springs
        A Book whose leaves to later time revealed
        The wondrous course of long-forgotten things; MS.
12   marvellous 1836: wondrous 1820-32

Whence golden harvests, cities, warlike towers,
     And pleasure's sumptuous bowers;
Whence all the fixed delights of house and home,
Friendships that will not break, and love that cannot roam.

O, happy Britain! region all too fair   25
For self-delighting fancy to endure
That silence only should inhabit there,
Wild beasts, or uncouth savages impure!
But, intermingled with the generous seed,
     Grew many a poisonous weed;   30
Thus fares it still with all that takes its birth
From human care, or grows upon the breast of earth.

Hence, and how soon! that war of vengeance waged
By Guendolen against her faithless lord;
Till she, in jealous fury unassuaged,   35
Had slain his paramour with ruthless sword:
Then into Severn hideously defiled,
     She flung her blameless child,
Sabrina,—vowing that the stream should bear
That name through every age, her hatred to declare.   40

So speaks the Chronicle, and tells of Lear
By his ungrateful daughters turned adrift.
Ye lightnings, hear his voice!—they cannot hear,
Nor can the winds restore his simple gift.
But One there is, a Child of nature meek,   45
     Who comes her Sire to seek;
And he, recovering sense, upon her breast
Leans smilingly, and sinks into a perfect rest.

There too we read of Spenser's fairy themes,
And those that Milton loved in youthful years;   50
The sage enchanter Merlin's subtle schemes;
The feats of Arthur and his knightly peers;

22 And, for soft pleasure, bowers
     And pleasure's peaceful bowers MSS.
26 self-delighting fancy] fondly favouring Nature MS.   30 Grew] Lurked MS
33 war of vengeance] uncouth warfare MS. *After l.* 40 *one* MS. *places*
ll. 194–201   41 Who has not wept the wrongs of aged Lear MS.   43
Hear him ye elements MS.   48 perfect] happy passing blissful MSS.
49–56 Praised be this book, and honour'd be the page
     Where England's Darling found a basis laid
     To those dread scenes which on the tragic stage
     To trembling multitudes his art displayed

Of Arthur,—who, to upper light restored,
    With that terrific sword
Which yet he brandishes for future war,   55
Shall lift his country's fame above the polar star!

What wonder, then, if in such ample field
Of old tradition, one particular flower
Doth seemingly in vain its fragrance yield,
And bloom unnoticed even to this late hour?   60
Now, gentle Muses, your assistance grant,
    While I this flower transplant
Into a garden stored with Poesy;
Where flowers and herbs unite, and haply some weeds be,
That, wanting not wild grace, are from all mischief free!   65

    A KING more worthy of respect and love
Than wise Gorbonian ruled not in his day;
And grateful Britain prospered far above
All neighbouring countries through his righteous sway;
He poured rewards and honours on the good;   70
    The oppressor he withstood;
And while he served the Gods with reverence due,
Fields smiled, and temples rose, and towns and cities grew.

He died, whom Artegal succeeds—his son;
But how unworthy of that sire was he!   75
A hopeful reign, auspiciously begun,
Was darkened soon by foul iniquity.
From crime to crime he mounted, till at length
    The nobles leagued their strength
With a vexed people, and the tyrant chased;   80
And on the vacant throne his worthier Brother placed.

> And to that chronicle be praise decreed
> For this, that there we read
> Of Merlin's insight into future years
> And all the mighty feats of Arthur and his peers MS.

55 *so* 1836: Which yet he graspeth, meditating war MS.: Which yet he
wields in subterranean war 1820–32   56 Shall spread his country's fame
in conquest wide and far MS.
57–60 What wonder then if 'mid the vast domain
    Of that rich volume one particular Flower
    Hath breathed its fragrance seemingly in vain MS.
61 Now, gentle] Ye gentle Ye bounteous MSS.   63 stored with] of pure,
stocked with, pure of MSS.   64–5 Small garden which I tend in (I
have tended long with, hath been tended long with) all humility MSS.
75 that 1836: such MS., 1820–32   77 foul iniquity] vilest tyranny MS.

From realm to realm the humbled Exile went,
Suppliant for aid his kingdom to regain;
In many a court, and many a warrior's tent,
He urged his persevering suit in vain.   85
Him, in whose wretched heart ambition failed,
    Dire poverty assailed;
And, tired with slights his pride no more could brook,
He towards his native country cast a longing look.

Fair blew the wished-for wind—the voyage sped;   90
He landed; and by many dangers scared,
"Poorly provided, poorly followèd,"
To Calaterium's forest he repaired.
How changed from him who, born to highest place,
    Had swayed the royal mace,   95
Flattered and feared, despised yet deified,
In Troynovant, his seat by silver Thames's side!

From that wild region where the crownless king
Lay in concealment with his scanty train,
Supporting life by water from the spring,   100
And such chance food as outlaws can obtain,
Unto the few whom he esteems his friends
    A messenger he sends;
And from their secret loyalty requires
Shelter and daily bread,—the sum of his desires.   105

88 his pride 1836: which he MS., 1820–32   89 *so* 1836: Towards his
native soil he MS., 1820–32
90–3 The winds and waves have aided him to reach
    That coast the object of his heart's desire;
    But while the crownless Sovereign trod the beach
    His eyeballs kindle with revengeful ire,
    As if incensed with all that he beholds
    The fields, the naked wolds,
    And those ten Followers, a helpless band
    That to his fortunes cleave and wait on his command.
    Bear with me, friends, said Artegal, ashamed;
    Then with quick steps they dive into a wood
    And from its shady boughs protection claimed
    For light he feared, and open neighbourhood. MS.
98–101 Oft by imaginary terrors scared
    And sometimes into real danger brought
    To Calaterium's forest he repaired
    And in its depth secure a refuge sought MS.
105 sum 1836: amount MS., 1820–32

While he the issue waits, at early morn
Wandering by stealth abroad, he chanced to hear
A startling outcry made by hound and horn,
From which the tusky wild boar flies in fear;
And, scouring toward him o'er the grassy plain,   110
    Behold the hunter train!
He bids his little company advance
With seeming unconcern and steady countenance.

The royal Elidure, who leads the chase,
Hath checked his foaming courser:—can it be!   115
Methinks that I should recognise that face,
Though much disguised by long adversity!
He gazed rejoicing, and again he gazed,
    Confounded and amazed—
"It is the king, my brother!" and, by sound   120
Of his own voice confirmed, he leaps upon the ground.

Long, strict, and tender was the embrace he gave,
Feebly returned by daunted Artegal;
Whose natural affection doubts enslave,
And apprehensions dark and criminal.   125
Loth to restrain the moving interview,
    The attendant lords withdrew;
And, while they stood upon the plain apart,
Thus Elidure, by words, relieved his struggling heart.

"By heavenly Powers conducted, we have met;   130
—O Brother! to my knowledge lost so long,
But neither lost to love, nor to regret,
Nor to my wishes lost;—forgive the wrong,
(Such it may seem) if I thy crown have borne,
    Thy royal mantle worn: 135
I was their natural guardian; and 'tis just
That now I should restore what hath been held in trust."

A while the astonished Artegal stood mute,
Then thus exclaimed: "To me, of titles shorn,
And stripped of power! me, feeble, destitute,   140
To me a kingdom! spare the bitter scorn:

106 With his attendants here MS.   109 *so* 1836: From which the tusky
boar hath fled MS., 1820–32   123 daunted] trembling, wondering MSS.
130–1 Heir of Gorbonian, Brother, gladly met,
    Whence comest thou *etc.* MS.

If justice ruled the breast of foreign kings,
    Then, on the wide-spread wings
Of war, had I returned to claim my right;
This will I here avow, not dreading thy despite."   145

"I do not blame thee," Elidure replied;
"But, if my looks did with my words agree,
I should at once be trusted, not defied,
And thou from all disquietude be free.
May the unsullied Goddess of the chase,   150
    Who to this blessed place
At this blest moment led me, if I speak
With insincere intent, on me her vengeance wreak!

"Were this same spear, which in my hand I grasp,
The British sceptre, here would I to thee   155
The symbol yield; and would undo this clasp,
If it confined the robe of sovereignty.
Odious to me the pomp of regal court,
    And joyless sylvan sport,
While thou art roving, wretched and forlorn,   160
Thy couch the dewy earth, thy roof the forest thorn!"

Then Artegal thus spake: "I only sought
Within this realm a place of safe retreat;
Beware of rousing an ambitious thought;
Beware of kindling hopes, for me unmeet!   165
Thou art reputed wise, but in my mind
    Art pitiably blind:
Full soon this generous purpose thou may'st rue,
When that which has been done no wishes can undo.

"Who, when a crown is fixed upon his head,   170
Would balance claim with claim, and right with right?
But thou—I know not how inspired, how led—
Wouldst change the course of things in all men's sight!
And this for one who cannot imitate
    Thy virtue, who may hate: 175
For, if, by such strange sacrifice restored,
He reign, thou still must be his king, and sovereign lord;

142 Had justice ruled in breasts *etc.* MS.   150 the unsullied 1827:
spotless Dian MSS., 1820   166 Thou bear'st the name of wise MS.
172 how inspired] whence inspired MS.

"Lifted in magnanimity above
Aught that my feeble nature could perform,
Or even conceive; surpassing me in love   180
Far as in power the eagle doth the worm:
I, Brother! only should be king in name,
      And govern to my shame;
A shadow in a hated land, while all
Of glad or willing service to thy share would fall."   185

"Believe it not," said Elidure; "respect
Awaits on virtuous life, and ever most
Attends on goodness with dominion decked,
Which stands the universal empire's boast;
This can thy own experience testify: 190
      Nor shall thy foes deny
That, in the gracious opening of thy reign,
Our father's spirit seemed in thee to breathe again.

"And what if o'er that bright unbosoming
Clouds of disgrace and envious fortune passed!   195
Have we not seen the glories of the spring
By veil of noontide darkness overcast?
The frith that glittered like a warrior's shield,
      The sky, the gay green field,
Are vanished; gladness ceases in the groves,   200
And trepidation strikes the blackened mountain-coves.

"But is that gloom dissolved? how passing clear
Seems the wide world, far brighter than before!
Even so thy latent worth will re-appear,
Gladdening the people's heart from shore to shore;   205
For youthful faults ripe virtues shall atone;
      Re-seated on thy throne,
Proof shalt thou furnish that misfortune, pain,
And sorrow, have confirmed thy native right to reign.

193 breathe] rule MS.   195 Clouds of disgrace] A cloud of time MS.
197–8   By noontide darkness veiled and overcast?
        The Lake that glittered like a sunbright shield MS.
200–1   All vanish in a moment, as if night
        Were sister to the sun, and darkness born of light MS.
202–5   But should the sun victorious glimmer forth
        Far brighter seems the wide world than before;
        Such power is latent in thy native worth
        To spread delight and joy from shore to shore MS.
208 Give proof that long adversity and pain MS.   209 native] inborn MS.

"But, not to overlook what thou may'st know,   210
Thy enemies are neither weak nor few;
And circumspect must be our course, and slow,
Or from my purpose ruin may ensue.
Dismiss thy followers;—let them calmly wait
    Such change in thy estate   215
As I already have in thought devised;
And which, with caution due, may soon be realized."

The Story tells what courses were pursued,
Until king Elidure, with full consent
Of all his peers, before the multitude,   220
Rose,—and, to consummate this just intent,
Did place upon his brother's head the crown,
    Relinquished by his own;
Then to his people cried, "Receive your lord,
Gorbonian's first-born son, your rightful king restored!"   225

218–41 The story tells that Artegal straitway
    Was by his Brother privily convey'd
    To a far distant city (at that day
    Alcwyd named) whose fortress undismayed
    By the hostility of mortals, stood
    In sight of land and flood,
    Obnoxious only on the lofty Rock
    To the careering storm, and perilous lightning's stroke.

When this impregnable retreat was gained
    In prudent furtherance of first intent
    King Elidure a mortal sickness feigned
    And to his mightiest Lords a summons sent.
    Softly and one by one, into such gloom
    As suits a sick man's room,
    The attendants introduced each potent peer
    There, singly and alone, his Sovereign's will to hear.

Said Elidure, Behold our rightful King
    The banished Artegal before thee stands
    Kneel, and renew to him the offering
    Of thy allegiance: Justice this demands,
    Immortal justice speaking through my voice.
    Accept him and rejoice.
    [?   ] he will prove
    Worthier than I have been of reverence and love.

If firm command and mild persuasion failed
    To change the temper of an adverse mind,
    With such by other engines he prevailed,
    Threatening to fling their bodies to the wind

The people answered with a loud acclaim:
Yet more;—heart-smitten by the heroic deed,
The reinstated Artegal became
Earth's noblest penitent; from bondage freed
Of vice—thenceforth unable to subvert   230
    Or shake his high desert.
Long did he reign; and, when he died, the tear
Of universal grief bedewed his honoured bier.

Thus was a Brother by a Brother saved;
With whom a crown (temptation that hath set   235
Discord in hearts of men till they have braved
Their nearest kin with deadly purpose met)
'Gainst duty weighed, and faithful love, did seem
    A thing of no esteem;
And, from this triumph of affection pure,   240
He bore the lasting name of "pious Elidure!"

III

TO A BUTTERFLY

[Composed April 20, 1802.—Published 1807.]

I'VE watched you now a full half-hour,
Self-poised upon that yellow flower;
And, little Butterfly! indeed
I know not if you sleep or feed.

From the dread summit of the lonely block,
    That castle-crested rock,
Alcwyd then, but now Dumbarton named
A memorable fort through spatious Albion famed.

Departing thence to York their way they bent
While the glad people flowers before them strewed;
And there King Elidure with full consent
Of all his peers before the multitude
Upon his brother's head replaced the crown
    Relinquished by his own,
Triumph of justice and affection pure
Whence he the title gained of "pious" Elidure. MS.
227 Through admiration of, And through strong feeling of MS.
229–33 "A true converted Man" from bondage freed,
    Of vice—henceforth unable to controul
    The motion of his soul
    And when he died the worthy and the brave
    Shed tears of fond regret upon his honoured grave MS.
III 1 full MS., 1807–32, 1845: short 1836.

How motionless!—not frozen seas   5
More motionless! and then
What joy awaits you, when the breeze
Hath found you out among the trees,
And calls you forth again!

This plot of orchard-ground is ours;   10
My trees they are, my Sister's flowers;
Here rest your wings when they are weary;
Here lodge as in a sanctuary!
Come often to us, fear no wrong;
Sit near us on the bough!   15
We'll talk of sunshine and of song,
And summer days, when we were young;
Sweet childish days, that were as long
As twenty days are now.

IV

A FAREWELL

[Finished May 29, 1802.—Published 1815.]

FAREWELL, thou little Nook of mountain-ground,
Thou rocky corner in the lowest stair
Of that magnificent temple which doth bound
One side of our whole vale with grandeur rare;
Sweet garden-orchard, eminently fair,   5
The loveliest spot that man hath ever found,
Farewell!—we leave thee to Heaven's peaceful care,
Thee, and the Cottage which thou dost surround.

Our boat is safely anchored by the shore,
And there will safely ride when we are gone;   10
The flowering shrubs that deck our humble door
Will prosper, though untended and alone:

8–9 Hath found . . . calls 1807: Shall find . . . call MS.
12–13 *so* 1815: Stop here whenever you are weary
           And rest as in a sanctuary MS., 1807
IV. A FAREWELL *so* 1827: COMPOSED IN THE YEAR 1802 1815–20
5–6 . . . of all spots that are The loveliest, surely, man *etc.* MS.   10
there will safely 1836: safely she will MS., 1815–27: safely will she 1832
11 deck our humble 1836: decorate our 1815–32
11–12 And ye few things that lie about our door
        Shall have our best protection, every one; MS.

Fields, goods, and far-off chattels we have none:
These narrow bounds contain our private store
Of things earth makes, and sun doth shine upon;   15
Here are they in our sight—we have no more.

Sunshine and shower be with you, bud and bell!
For two months now in vain we shall be sought;
We leave you here in solitude to dwell
With these our latest gifts of tender thought;   20
Thou, like the morning, in thy saffron coat,
Bright gowan, and marsh-marigold, farewell!
Whom from the borders of the Lake we brought,
And placed together near our rocky Well.

We go for One to whom ye will be dear;   25
And she will prize this Bower, this Indian shed,
Our own contrivance, Building without peer!
—A gentle Maid, whose heart is lowly bred,
Whose pleasures are in wild fields gatherèd,
With joyousness, and with a thoughtful cheer,   30
Will come to you; to you herself will wed;
And love the blessed life that we lead here.

Dear Spot! which we have watched with tender heed,
Bringing thee chosen plants and blossoms blown
Among the distant mountains, flower and weed,   35
Which thou hast taken to thee as thy own,
Making all kindness registered and known;
Thou for our sakes, though Nature's child indeed,
Fair in thyself and beautiful alone,
Hast taken gifts which thou dost little need.   40

And O most constant, yet most fickle Place,
That hast thy wayward moods, as thou dost show
To them who look not daily on thy face;
Who, being loved, in love no bounds dost know,
And say'st, when we forsake thee, "Let them go!"   45
Thou easy-hearted Thing, with thy wild race
Of weeds and flowers, till we return be slow,
And travel with the year at a soft pace.

14 This is the place that holds MS.   29 Whose] Her MS.
31 Will 1820: She'll MS., 1815   42 thy wayward moods] a wayward
heart MS. *Letter*, MS.

Help us to tell Her tales of years gone by,
And this sweet spring, the best beloved and best;   50
Joy will be flown in its mortality;
Something must stay to tell us of the rest.
Here, thronged with primroses, the steep rock's breast
Glittered at evening like a starry sky;
And in this bush our sparrow built her nest,   55
Of which I sang one song that will not die.

O happy Garden! whose seclusion deep
Hath been so friendly to industrious hours;
And to soft slumbers, that did gently steep
Our spirits, carrying with them dreams of flowers,   60
And wild notes warbled among leafy bowers;
Two burning months let summer overleap,
And, coming back with Her who will be ours,
Into thy bosom we again shall creep.

V

STANZAS

WRITTEN IN MY POCKET-COPY OF THOMSON'S
"CASTLE OF INDOLENCE"

[Composed May 9–11, 1802.—Published 1815.]

WITHIN our happy Castle there dwelt One
Whom without blame I may not overlook;
For never sun on living creature shone
Who more devout enjoyment with us took:
Here on his hours he hung as on a book,   5
On his own time here would he float away,
As doth a fly upon a summer brook;
But go to-morrow, or belike to-day,
Seek for him,—he is fled; and whither none can say.

Thus often would he leave our peaceful home,   10
And find elsewhere his business or delight;
Out of our Valley's limits did he roam:
Full many a time, upon a stormy night,

51 flown] gone MS.   53 thronged with] with its MS. *Letter*
56 sang 1832: sung 1815–27
57–9 O happy Garden! lov'd for hours of sleep
          O quiet Garden! lov'd for waking hours
          For soft half slumber MS.
61 Belov'd for days of rest in fruit-tree bowers MS.

His voice came to us from the neighbouring height:
Oft could we see him driving full in view   15
At mid-day when the sun was shining bright;
What ill was on him, what he had to do,
A mighty wonder bred among our quiet crew.

Ah! piteous sight it was to see this Man
When he came back to us, a withered flower,—   20
Or like a sinful creature, pale and wan.
Down would he sit; and without strength or power
Look at the common grass from hour to hour:
And oftentimes, how long I fear to say,
Where apple-trees in blossom made a bower,   25
Retired in that sunshiny shade he lay;
And, like a naked Indian, slept himself away.

Great wonder to our gentle tribe it was
Whenever from our Valley he withdrew;
For happier soul no living creature has   30
Than he had, being here the long day through.
Some thought he was a lover, and did woo:
Some thought far worse of him, and judged him wrong;
But verse was what he had been wedded to;
And his own mind did like a tempest strong   35
Come to him thus, and drove the weary Wight along.

With him there often walked in friendly guise,
Or lay upon the moss by brook or tree,
A noticeable Man with large grey eyes,
And a pale face that seemed undoubtedly   40
As if a blooming face it ought to be;
Heavy his low-hung lip did oft appear,
Deprest by weight of musing Phantasy;
Profound his forehead was, though not severe;
Yet some did think that he had little business here: 45

Sweet heaven forefend! his was a lawful right;
Noisy he was, and gamesome as a boy;
His limbs would toss about him with delight,
Like branches when strong winds the trees annoy.

15 could] did MS.   30 creature] mortal MS.   43 A face divine of
heaven-born idiotcy   MS.

Nor lacked his calmer hours device or toy   50
To banish listlessness and irksome care ;
He would have taught you how you might employ
Yourself; and many did to him repair,—
And certes not in vain ; he had inventions rare.

Expedients, too, of simplest sort he tried: 55
Long blades of grass, plucked round him as he lay,
Made, to his ear attentively applied,
A pipe on which the wind would deftly play;
Glasses he had, that little things display,
The beetle panoplied in gems and gold,   60
A mailèd angel on a battle-day ;
The mysteries that cups of flowers enfold,
And all the gorgeous sights which fairies do behold.

He would entice that other Man to hear
His music, and to view his imagery: 65
And, sooth, these two were each to the other dear:
No livelier love in such a place could be:
There did they dwell—from earthly labour free,
As happy spirits as were ever seen ;
If but a bird, to keep them company,   70
Or butterfly sate down, they were, I ween,
As pleased as if the same had been a Maiden-queen.

50–1 He lacked not implement, device, or toy
       To cheat away the hours that silent were MS.
55 Instruments had he, playthings for the ear MS.
57–9 These served to catch the wind as it came near,
       Glasses he had with many colours gay
       Others that did all little things display MS.
60 *so* 1827: The beetle with his radiance manifold MS., 1815–20
62 *so* 1827: And cups [leaves MS.] of flowers, and herbage green and gold;
MS., 1815–20   63 gorgeous] glorious MS.
66–7 *so* 1836: And, sooth, these two did love each other dear,
               As far as love in such a place could be; MS., 1815–32
68 dwell] lie MS.   69 spirits] livers MS.

VI

LOUISA

AFTER ACCOMPANYING HER ON A MOUN-
TAIN EXCURSION

[Composed (probably) 1801.—Published 1807.]

I MET Louisa in the shade,
And, having seen that lovely Maid,
Why should I fear to say
That, nymph-like, she is fleet and strong,
And down the rocks can leap along   5
Like rivulets in May?

And she hath smiles to earth unknown;
Smiles, that with motion of their own
Do spread, and sink, and rise;
That come and go with endless play,   10
And ever, as they pass away,
Are hidden in her eyes.

She loves her fire, her cottage-home;
Yet o'er the moorland will she roam
In weather rough and bleak;   15
And, when against the wind she strains,
Oh! might I kiss the mountain rains
That sparkle on her cheek.

Take all that's mine "beneath the moon,"
If I with her but half a noon   20
May sit beneath the walls
Of some old cave, or mossy nook,
When up she winds along the brook
To hunt the waterfalls.

VI. 1–3 *so* 1807–32, 1845: Though by a sickly taste betrayed,
            Some will dispraise the lovely maid,
            With fearless pride I say   1836
4 *so* 1845: That she is ruddy, fleet, and strong 1807–32: 1836 healthful
for ruddy   7–12 *so* 1807–43: 1845, 49 *omit*   11 pass] go MS.
23 When she goes barefoot up the brook MS.

VII

[Composed 1799.—Published 1800.]

STRANGE fits of passion have I known:
And I will dare to tell,
But in the Lover's ear alone,
What once to me befell.

When she I loved looked every day   5
Fresh as a rose in June,
I to her cottage bent my way,
Beneath an evening-moon.

Upon the moon I fixed my eye,
All over the wide lea;   10
With quickening pace my horse drew nigh
Those paths so dear to me.

And now we reached the orchard-plot;
And, as we climbed the hill,
The sinking moon to Lucy's cot   15
Came near, and nearer still.

In one of those sweet dreams I slept,
Kind Nature's gentlest boon!
And all the while my eyes I kept
On the descending moon.   20

My horse moved on; hoof after hoof
He raised, and never stopped:
When down behind the cottage roof,
At once, the bright moon dropped.

What fond and wayward thoughts will slide   25
Into a Lover's head!
"O mercy!" to myself I cried,
"If Lucy should be dead!"

VII. 1–4 *not in* MS. 1799
5–6 *so* 1836: Once when my love was strong and gay
           And like a rose in June MS.1799
When she I loved *etc.* 1800–32   8 an 1836: the MS., 1800–32
11 *so* 1836: My horse trudg'd on, and we drew nigh MS.1799, 1800–32
15–16 *so* 1836: Towards the roof of Lucy's cot
           The moon descended still MS.1799, 1800–32
24 bright moon 1815 *etc.*: planet MS., 1800–5   28 MS.1799 *has this
additional stanza:*
           I told her this: her laughter light
           Is ringing in my ears:
           And when I think upon that night
           My eyes are dim with tears.

VIII

[Composed 1799.—Published 1800.]

SHE dwelt among the untrodden ways
    Beside the springs of Dove,
A Maid whom there were none to praise
    And very few to love:

A violet by a mossy stone   5
    Half hidden from the eye!
—Fair as a star, when only one
    Is shining in the sky.

She lived unknown, and few could know
    When Lucy ceased to be;   10
But she is in her grave, and, oh,
    The difference to me!

IX

[Composed 1801.—Published 1807.]

I TRAVELLED among unknown men,
    In lands beyond the sea;
Nor, England! did I know till then
    What love I bore to thee.

'Tis past, that melancholy dream!   5
    Nor will I quit thy shore
A second time; for still I seem
    To love thee more and more.

Among thy mountains did I feel
    The joy of my desire;   10
And she I cherished turned her wheel
    Beside an English fire.

VIII *Before stanza* 1 MS.1799 has:
        My hope was one, from cities far,
        Nursed on a lonesome heath;
        Her lips were red as roses are,
        Her hair a woodbine wreath.
1 dwelt] MS. lived   4 And very few MS., 1800 *etc.*: A very few 1802
8/9 And she was graceful as the broom
    That flowers by Carron's side;
    But slow distemper checked her bloom,
    And on the Heath she died. MS.1799
9–11 Long time before her head lay low
    Dead to the world was she:
    But now she's *etc.* MS.1799
IX. 10 joy of my] gladness of MS.

Thy mornings showed, thy nights concealed,
  The bowers where Lucy played;
And thine too is the last green field   15
  That Lucy's eyes surveyed.

X

[Composed 1826.—Published 1827.]

ERE with cold beads of midnight dew
  Had mingled tears of thine,
I grieved, fond Youth! that thou shouldst sue
  To haughty Geraldine.

Immoveable by generous sighs,   5
  She glories in a train
Who drag, beneath our native skies,
  An oriental chain.

Pine not like them with arms across,
  Forgetting in thy care   10
How the fast-rooted trees can toss
  Their branches in mid air.

The humblest rivulet will take
  Its own wild liberties;
And, every day, the imprisoned lake   15
  Is flowing in the breeze.

Then crouch no more on suppliant knee,
  But scorn with scorn outbrave;
A Briton, even in love, should be
  A subject, not a slave!   20

XI

TO ——

[Composed 1824.—Published 1827.]

LOOK at the fate of summer flowers,
Which blow at daybreak, droop ere even-song;
And, grieved for their brief date, confess that ours,
Measured by what we are and ought to be,
Measured by all that, trembling, we foresee,   5
  Is not so long!

15 thine too is 1836: thine is, too, MS., 1807–32
X. 3 fond] lost MS.   5–6 No care hath she for generous sighs But MS.
9–16 The humblest rill thro' bush and brake
    Meanders here and there;
    The rooted trees are free to shake
    Their leafy boughs in air. MS.
17 suppliant] faultering MS.

If human Life do pass away,
Perishing yet more swiftly than the flower,
If we are creatures of a *winter's* day;
What space hath Virgin's beauty to disclose   10
Her sweets, and triumph o'er the breathing rose?
Not even an hour!

The deepest grove whose foliage hid
The happiest lovers Arcady might boast,
Could not the entrance of this thought forbid: 15
O be thou wise as they, soul-gifted Maid!
Nor rate too high what must so quickly fade,
So soon be lost.

Then shall love teach some virtuous Youth
"To draw, out of the object of his eyes,"   20
The while on thee they gaze in simple truth,
Hues more exalted, "a refinèd Form,"
That dreads not age, nor suffers from the worm,
And never dies.

XII

THE FORSAKEN

[Dated 1804 (W.).—Probably composed earlier.—Published 1842.]

THE peace which others seek they find;
The heaviest storms not longest last;
Heaven grants even to the guiltiest mind
An amnesty for what is past;
When will my sentence be reversed?   5
I only pray to know the worst;
And wish, as if my heart would burst.

O weary struggle! silent years
Tell seemingly no doubtful tale;
And yet they leave it short, and fears   10
And hopes are strong and will prevail.
My calmest faith escapes not pain;
And, feeling that the hope is vain,
I think that he will come again.

XI. 9 *so* 1836: Whose frail existence is but of a day 1827–32   21 while
1836: whilst 1827–32
XII. 8–9 Oft-times it seems that silent years
          Bring an unquestionable tale, MS.

XIII

[Composed 1800.—Published 1800.]

'TIS said, that some have died for love:
And here and there a church-yard grave is found
In the cold north's unhallowed ground,
Because the wretched man himself had slain,
His love was such a grievous pain.   5
And there is one whom I five years have known;
He dwells alone
Upon Helvellyn's side:
He loved—the pretty Barbara died;
And thus he makes his moan: 10
Three years had Barbara in her grave been laid
When thus his moan he made:

"Oh, move, thou Cottage, from behind that oak!
Or let the aged tree uprooted lie,
That in some other way yon smoke   15
May mount into the sky!
The clouds pass on; they from the heavens depart:
I look—the sky is empty space;
I know not what I trace;
But when I cease to look, my hand is on my heart.   20

"O! what a weight is in these shades! Ye leaves,
That murmur once so dear, when will it cease?
Your sound my heart of rest bereaves,
It robs my heart of peace.
Thou Thrush, that singest loud—and loud and free,   25
Into yon row of willows flit,
Upon that alder sit;
Or sing another song, or choose another tree.

"Roll back, sweet Rill! back to thy mountain-bounds,
And there for ever be thy waters chained!   30
For thou dost haunt the air with sounds
That cannot be sustained;
If still beneath that pine-tree's ragged bough
Headlong yon waterfall must come,
Oh let it then be dumb!   35
Be anything, sweet Rill, but that which thou art now.

22 *so* 1836: When will that dying murmur be supprest! 1800–32
23 rest 1836: peace 1800–32   24 peace 1836: rest 1800–32

"Thou Eglantine, so bright with sunny showers,
Proud as a rainbow spanning half the vale,
Thou one fair shrub, oh! shed thy flowers,
And stir not in the gale.   40
For thus to see thee nodding in the air,
To see thy arch thus stretch and bend,
Thus rise and thus descend,—
Disturbs me till the sight is more than I can bear."

The Man who makes this feverish complaint   45
Is one of giant stature, who could dance
Equipped from head to foot in iron mail.
Ah gentle Love! if ever thought was thine
To store up kindred hours for me, thy face
Turn from me, gentle Love! nor let me walk   50
Within the sound of Emma's voice, nor know
Such happiness as I have known to-day.

XIV

A COMPLAINT

[Composed 1806.—Published 1807.]

THERE is a change—and I am poor;
Your love hath been, nor long ago,
A fountain at my fond heart's door,
Whose only business was to flow;
And flow it did; not taking heed   5
Of its own bounty, or my need.

What happy moments did I count!
Blest was I then all bliss above!
Now, for that consecrated fount
Of murmuring, sparkling, living love,   10
What have I? shall I dare to tell?
A comfortless and hidden well.

A well of love—it may be deep—
I trust it is,—and never dry:
What matter? if the waters sleep   15
In silence and obscurity.
—Such change, and at the very door
Of my fond heart, hath made me poor.

37-8 *so* 1836: Thou Eglantine whose arch so proudly towers
              (Even like a rainbow spanning half the vale) 1800–32
XIV. 9 that 1836: this 1807–32

XV

TO ——

[Composed 1824.—Published 1827.]

LET other bards of angels sing,
  Bright suns without a spot;
But thou art no such perfect thing:
  Rejoice that thou art not!

Heed not tho' none should call thee fair;   5
  So, Mary, let it be
If nought in loveliness compare
  With what thou art to me.

True beauty dwells in deep retreats,
  Whose veil is unremoved   10
Till heart with heart in concord beats,
  And the lover is beloved.

XVI

[Composed?.—Published 1845.]

YES! thou art fair, yet be not moved
  To scorn the declaration,
That sometimes I in thee have loved
  My fancy's own creation.

Imagination needs must stir;   5
  Dear Maid, this truth believe,
Minds that have nothing to confer
  Find little to perceive.

Be pleased that nature made thee fit
  To feed my heart's devotion,   10
By laws to which all Forms submit
  In sky, air, earth, and ocean.

XV. 4/5 Such if thou wert in all men's view,
      A universal show,
    What would my Fancy have to do,
      My Feelings to bestow ? MS., 1827–32
5 *so* 1832: The world denies that Thou art fair MS., 1827
9 dwells] lurks MS.   12 Till lovers are beloved MS.

XVII

[Composed 1824.—Published 1827.]

How rich that forehead's calm expanse!
How bright that heaven-directed glance!
—Waft her to glory, wingèd Powers,
Ere sorrow be renewed,
And intercourse with mortal hours   5
Bring back a humbler mood!
So looked Cecilia when she drew
An Angel from his station;
So looked; not ceasing to pursue
Her tuneful adoration!   10

But hand and voice alike are still;
No sound *here* sweeps away the will
That gave it birth: in service meek
One upright arm sustains the cheek,
And one across the bosom lies—   15
That rose, and now forgets to rise,
Subdued by breathless harmonies
Of meditative feeling;
Mute strains from worlds beyond the skies,
Through the pure light of female eyes   20
Their sanctity revealing!

XVIII

[Composed ?.—Published 1845.]

WHAT heavenly smiles! O Lady mine,
Through my very heart they shine;
And, if my brow gives back their light,
Do thou look gladly on the sight;
As the clear Moon with modest pride   5
    Beholds her own bright beams
Reflected from the mountain's side
    And from the headlong streams.

XIX

TO ——

[Composed 1824.—Published 1827.]

O DEARER far than light and life are dear,
Full oft our human foresight I deplore;
Trembling, through my unworthiness, with fear
That friends, by death disjoined, may meet no more!

Misgivings, hard to vanquish or control,   5
Mix with the day, and cross the hour of rest;
While all the future, for thy purer soul,
With "sober certainties" of love is blest.

That sigh of thine, not meant for human ear,
Tells that these words thy humbleness offend;   10
Yet bear me up—else faltering in the rear
Of a steep march: support me to the end.

Peace settles where the intellect is meek,
And Love is dutiful in thought and deed;
Through Thee communion with that Love I seek: 15
The faith Heaven strengthens where *he* moulds the Creed.

XX

LAMENT OF MARY QUEEN OF SCOTS

ON THE EVE OF A NEW YEAR

[Composed 1817.—Published 1820.]

I

Smile of the Moon!—for so I name
That silent greeting from above;
A gentle flash of light that came
From her whom drooping captives love;
Or art thou of still higher birth?   5
Thou that didst part the clouds of earth
My torpor to reprove!

II

Bright boon of pitying Heaven!—alas,
I may not trust thy placid cheer!
Pondering that Time to-night will pass   10
The threshold of another year;
For years to me are sad and dull;
My very moments are too full
Of hopelessness and fear.

XIX. 9 *so* 1836: If a faint sigh 1827–32   11 *so* 1836: Cherish me still
1827–32   12 support 1836: uphold 1827–32

III

And yet, the soul-awakening gleam,   15
That struck perchance the farthest cone
Of Scotland's rocky wilds, did seem
To visit me, and me alone;
Me, unapproached by any friend,
Save those who to my sorrows lend   20
Tears due unto their own.

IV

To-night the church-tower bells will ring
Through these wide realms a festive peal;
To the new year a welcoming;
A tuneful offering for the weal   25
Of happy millions lulled in sleep;
While I am forced to watch and weep,
By wounds that may not heal.

V

Born all too high, by wedlock raised
Still higher—to be cast thus low!   30
Would that mine eyes had never gazed
On aught of more ambitious show
Than the sweet flowerets of the fields!
—It is my royal state that yields
This bitterness of woe.   35

21/2 Meek effluence—that while I trod
With downcast eye, in narrow space
Did'st vivify the wintry sod,
As if an Angel filled the place
With softened light—thou wert a touch
Even to my heart of hearts—and such
Is every gift of grace.

Ah wherefore did it leave the sky,
And wherefore did it seem to speak
Of something bordering all too nigh
On what I seldom dare to seek,—
A happier order for my doom,
A favoured æra when the gloom
At length would cleave and break.   MS.

VI

Yet how ?—for I, if there be truth
In the world's voice, was passing fair;
And beauty, for confiding youth,
Those shocks of passion can prepare
That kill the bloom before its time;   40
And blanch, without the owner's crime,
The most resplendent hair.

VII

Unblest distinction! showered on me
To bind a lingering life in chains:
All that could quit my grasp, or flee,   45
Is gone;—but not the subtle stains
Fixed in the spirit; for even here
Can I be proud that jealous fear
Of what I was remains.

VIII

A Woman rules my prison's key;   50
A sister Queen, against the bent
Of law and holiest sympathy,
Detains me, doubtful of the event;
Great God, who feel'st for my distress,
My thoughts are all that I possess,   55
O keep them innocent!

IX

Farewell desire of human aid,
Which abject mortals vainly court!
By friends deceived, by foes betrayed,
Of fears the prey, of hopes the sport;   60
Nought but the world-redeeming Cross
Is able to supply my loss,
My burthen to support.

42/3 Man's foolish envy is a stream
Where Wisdom's eye reflected sees
The fuel of a painful dream,
The incitements of a dire disease;
Ah what is life but Powers let loose
And revelling in their own abuse
The giver to displease.   MS.
51 sister Queen] sovereign MS.   57 desire of 1827: for ever MS., 1820

X

> Hark! the death-note of the year
> Sounded by the castle-clock!   65
> From her sunk eyes a stagnant tear
> Stole forth, unsettled by the shock;
> But oft the woods renewed their green,
> Ere the tired head of Scotland's Queen
> Reposed upon the block!   70

XXI

THE COMPLAINT

OF A FORSAKEN INDIAN WOMAN

[Composed 1798.—Published 1798.]

[When a Northern Indian, from sickness, is unable to continue his journey
with his companions, he is left behind, covered over with deer-skins, and
is supplied with water, food, and fuel, if the situation of the place will
afford it. He is informed of the track which his companions intend to
pursue, and if he be unable to follow, or overtake them, he perishes alone
in the desert, unless he should have the good fortune to fall in with some
other tribes of Indians. The females are equally, or still more, exposed
to the same fate. See that very interesting work Hearne's "Journey
from Hudson's Bay to the Northern Ocean". In the high northern
latitudes, as the same writer informs us, when the northern lights vary
their position in the air, they make a rustling and a crackling noise, as
alluded to in the following poem.]

I

> BEFORE I see another day,
> Oh let my body die away!
> In sleep I heard the northern gleams;
> The stars, they were among my dreams;
> In rustling conflict through the skies,   5
> I heard, I saw the flashes drive,
> And yet they are upon my eyes,
> And yet I am alive;
> Before I see another day,
> Oh let my body die away!   10

XXI. 4 *so* 1798–1805, 1836: The stars were mingled with my dreams
1815–32   5 *so* 1820: In sleep did I behold the skies, 1798–1815   6 *so*
1827: I saw the crackling flashes drive; 1798–1815; I heard, and saw the
flashes drive, 1820

II

My fire is dead: it knew no pain;
Yet is it dead, and I remain:
All stiff with ice the ashes lie;
And they are dead, and I will die.
When I was well, I wished to live,   15
For clothes, for warmth, for food, and fire;
But they to me no joy can give,
No pleasure now, and no desire.
Then here contented will I lie!
Alone, I cannot fear to die.   20

III

Alas! ye might have dragged me on
Another day, a single one!
Too soon I yielded to despair;
Why did ye listen to my prayer?
When ye were gone my limbs were stronger;   25
And oh, how grievously I rue,
That, afterwards, a little longer,
My friends, I did not follow you!
For strong and without pain I lay,
Dear friends, when ye were gone away.   30

IV

My Child! they gave thee to another,
A woman who was not thy mother.
When from my arms my Babe they took,
On me how strangely did he look!
Through his whole body something ran,   35
A most strange working did I see;
—As if he strove to be a man,
That he might pull the sledge for me:
And then he stretched his arms, how wild!
Oh mercy! like a helpless child.   40

23-4 *so* 1815: Too soon despair o'er me prevailed,
          Too soon my heartless spirit failed 1798–1805
30 Dear 1845: My 1798–1836   36 working 1815: something 1798–
1805   40 helpless 1815: little 1798–1805

V

My little joy! my little pride!
In two days more I must have died.
Then do not weep and grieve for me;
I feel I must have died with thee.
O wind, that o'er my head art flying   45
The way my friends their course did bend,
I should not feel the pain of dying,
Could I with thee a message send;
Too soon, my friends, ye went away:
For I had many things to say.   50

VI

I'll follow you across the snow;
Ye travel heavily and slow;
In spite of all my weary pain
I'll look upon your tents again.
—My fire is dead, and snowy white   55
The water which beside it stood:
The wolf has come to me to-night,
And he has stolen away my food.
For ever left alone am I;
Then wherefore should I fear to die?   60

VII

Young as I am, my course is run,
I shall not see another sun;
I cannot lift my limbs to know
If they have any life or no.
My poor forsaken Child, if I   65
For once could have thee close to me,
With happy heart I then would die,
And my last thought would happy be;
But thou, dear Babe, art far away,
Nor shall I see another day.   70

61–70 1815–32 *omit*   61 *so* 1836: My journey will be shortly run 1798–1805
68 thought 1836: thoughts 1798–1805
69–70 *so* 1836: I feel my body die away,
            I shall not see another day. 1798–1805

XXII

THE LAST OF THE FLOCK

[Composed 1798.—Published 1798.]

I

In distant countries have I been,
And yet I have not often seen
A healthy man, a man full grown,
Weep in the public roads, alone.
But such a one, on English ground,   5
And in the broad highway, I met;
Along the broad highway he came,
His cheeks with tears were wet:
Sturdy he seemed, though he was sad;
And in his arms a Lamb he had.   10

II

He saw me, and he turned aside,
As if he wished himself to hide:
And with his coat did then essay
To wipe those briny tears away.
I followed him, and said, "My friend,   15
What ails you? wherefore weep you so?"
—"Shame on me, Sir! this lusty Lamb,
He makes my tears to flow.
To-day I fetched him from the rock;
He is the last of all my flock.   20

III

"When I was young, a single man,
And after youthful follies ran,
Though little given to care and thought,
Yet, so it was, an ewe I bought;
And other sheep from her I raised,   25
As healthy sheep as you might see;
And then I married, and was rich
As I could wish to be;
Of sheep I numbered a full score,
And every year increased my store.   30

XXII. 1 have I 1815: I have 1798–1805   13 *so* 1836: Then with
his coat he made essay 1798–1832

IV

"Year after year my stock it grew;
And from this one, this single ewe,
Full fifty comely sheep I raised,
As fine a flock as ever grazed!
Upon the Quantock hills they fed; 35
They throve, and we at home did thrive:
—This lusty Lamb of all my store
Is all that is alive;
And now I care not if we die,
And perish all of poverty. 40

V

"Six Children, Sir! had I to feed;
Hard labour in a time of need!
My pride was tamed, and in our grief
I of the Parish asked relief.
They said, I was a wealthy man; 45
My sheep upon the uplands fed,
And it was fit that thence I took
Whereof to buy us bread.
'Do this: how can we give to you,'
They cried, 'what to the poor is due?' 50

VI

"I sold a sheep, as they had said,
And bought my little children bread,
And they were healthy with their food;
For me—it never did me good.
A woeful time it was for me, 55
To see the end of all my gains,
The pretty flock which I had reared
With all my care and pains,
To see it melt like snow away—
For me it was a woeful day. 60

VII

"Another still! and still another!
A little lamb, and then its mother!
It was a vein that never stopped—
Like blood-drops from my heart they dropped.

34 fine 1836: sweet 1798–1832   35 *so* 1836: Upon the mountain did
they feed 1798–1832   41 Six 1800: Ten 1798   46 uplands 1836:
mountain 1798–1832

Till thirty were not left alive   65
They dwindled, dwindled, one by one;
And I may say, that many a time
I wished they all were gone—
Reckless of what might come at last
Were but the bitter struggle past.   70

VIII

"To wicked deeds I was inclined,
And wicked fancies crossed my mind;
And every man I chanced to see,
I thought he knew some ill of me:
No peace, no comfort could I find,   75
No ease, within doors or without;
And crazily and wearily
I went my work about;
And oft was moved to flee from home,
And hide my head where wild beasts roam.   80

IX

"Sir! 'twas a precious flock to me,
As dear as my own children be;
For daily with my growing store
I loved my children more and more.
Alas! it was an evil time;   85
God cursed me in my sore distress;
I prayed, yet every day I thought
I loved my children less;
And every week, and every day,
My flock it seemed to melt away.   90

X

"They dwindled, Sir, sad sight to see!
From ten to five, from five to three,
A lamb, a wether, and a ewe;—
And then at last from three to two;

69–70 *so* 1827: They dwindled one by one away;
                   For me it was a woeful day 1798–1820
79–80 *so* 1836: Oft-times I thought to run away
                   For me it was a woeful day 1798–1820
                   Bent oftentimes to flee from home *etc. as* 1836, 1827–32

And, of my fifty, yesterday   95
I had but only one:
And here it lies upon my arm,
Alas! and I have none;—
To-day I fetched it from the rock;
It is the last of all my flock."   100

XXIII

REPENTANCE

A PASTORAL BALLAD

[Composed 1804?.—Published 1820.]

The fields which with covetous spirit we sold,
Those beautiful fields, the delight of the day,
Would have brought us more good than a burthen of gold,
Could we but have been as contented as they.

When the troublesome Tempter beset us, said I,   5
"Let him come, with his purse proudly grasped in his hand;
But, Allan, be true to me, Allan,—we'll die
Before he shall go with an inch of the land!"

There dwelt we, as happy as birds in their bowers;
Unfettered as bees that in gardens abide;   10
We could do what we liked with the land, it was ours;
And for us the brook murmured that ran by its side.

But now we are strangers, go early or late;
And often, like one overburthened with sin,
With my hand on the latch of the half-opened gate,   15
I look at the fields, but I cannot go in!

XXIII. 1–3 O fools that we were—we had land which we sold
    Snug fields that together contentedly lay,
    They'd have done us more good than another man's gold   MSS. 1–2
1–2 . . . without virtue to hold The fields   MS. 3
5 When the fine Man came to us from London   MSS. 1–2 *corr. to* bribe of
the Tempter came to us   MS. 2   6 purse] bags   MSS.   7 Allan]
Thomas   MSS.
9–10 In seed time, in harvest, come sunshine, come showers,
    Where *now* is your bustle, your joy and your pride?   MS. 3
    Oh Thomas, oh Thomas *etc.*
    Where's your bustle, your business *etc.* MSS. 1–2
11 liked   MSS., 1836: chose 1820–27   12 It lay close to the door like
another fireside   MSS.   14 And often] Oh Thomas   MS. 3   15 When
my hand has half lifted the latch of a gate   MSS.   16 but 1827: and
MSS., 1820

When I walk by the hedge on a bright summer's day,
Or sit in the shade of my grandfather's tree,
A stern face it puts on, as if ready to say,
"What ails you, that you must come creeping to me!"   20

With our pastures about us, we could not be sad;
Our comfort was near if we ever were crost;
But the comfort, the blessings, and wealth that we had,
We slighted them all,—and our birthright was lost.

Oh, ill-judging sire of an innocent son   25
Who must now be a wanderer! but peace to that strain!
Think of evening's repose when our labour was done,
The sabbath's return; and its leisure's soft chain!

And in sickness, if night had been sparing of sleep,
How cheerful, at sunrise, the hill where I stood,   30
Looking down on the kine, and our treasure of sheep
That besprinkled the field; 'twas like youth in my blood!

Now I cleave to the house, and am dull as a snail;
And, oftentimes, hear the church-bell with a sigh,
That follows the thought—We've no land in the vale,   35
Save six feet of earth where our fore-fathers lie!

XXIV

THE AFFLICTION OF MARGARET ——

[Dated 1804 (W.).— Probably composed earlier (1801 ?).—Published 1807.]

I

WHERE art thou, my beloved Son,
Where art thou, worse to me than dead ?
Oh find me, prosperous or undone!
Or, if the grave be now thy bed,

17 bright summer's] sunshiny MSS.   19 Such a face it puts on I half
think it will say MSS.   21 pastures] birthright MSS.
23–4 But we traitorously gave the best Friend that we had
    For spiritless pelf—as we feel to our cost MS. 3
    But, Thomas, we sold etc.
    And little we knew what a friend we had lost MSS. 1–2
29–32 When my sick crazy body had lain without sleep
    What a comfort did sunrise bestow when I stood
    And looked down on the fields and the kine and the sheep
    From the top of the hill etc. MSS.; 30–32 corr. to How cheering the
sunshiny hill . . . treasure of sheep That besprinkled the field etc. MS. 3
33–5 Now I sit in the house etc. And often I hear etc. When I think to myself
etc. MSS.
XXIV. MARGARET—1845: Mary— of — MS.: Margaret— of — 1807–
15: Margaret 1820–36

Why am I ignorant of the same   5
That I may rest; and neither blame
Nor sorrow may attend thy name?

II

Seven years, alas! to have received
No tidings of an only child;
To have despaired, have hoped, believed,   10
And been for evermore beguiled;
Sometimes with thoughts of very bliss!
I catch at them, and then I miss;
Was ever darkness like to this?

III

He was among the prime in worth,   15
An object beauteous to behold;
Well born, well bred; I sent him forth
Ingenuous, innocent, and bold:
If things ensued that wanted grace,
As hath been said, they were not base;   20
And never blush was on my face.

IV

Ah! little doth the young-one dream,
When full of play and childish cares,
What power is in his wildest scream,
Heard by his mother unawares!   25
He knows it not, he cannot guess:
Years to a mother bring distress;
But do not make her love the less.

V

Neglect me! no, I suffered long
From that ill thought; and, being blind,   30
Said, "Pride shall help me in my wrong:
Kind mother have I been, as kind
As ever breathed:" and that is true;
I've wet my path with tears like dew,
Weeping for him when no one knew.   35

10 have hoped, 1836: and have 1807–32   11 been 1836: be 1807–32
24 is in 1832: hath even 1807–27

VI

My Son, if thou be humbled, poor,
Hopeless of honour and of gain,
Oh! do not dread thy mother's door;
Think not of me with grief and pain:
I now can see with better eyes;   40
And worldly grandeur I despise,
And fortune with her gifts and lies.

VII

Alas! the fowls of heaven have wings,
And blasts of heaven will aid their flight;
They mount—how short a voyage brings   45
The wanderers back to their delight!
Chains tie us down by land and sea;
And wishes, vain as mine, may be
All that is left to comfort thee.

VIII

Perhaps some dungeon hears thee groan,   50
Maimed, mangled by inhuman men;
Or thou upon a desert thrown
Inheritest the lion's den;
Or hast been summoned to the deep,
Thou, thou and all thy mates, to keep   55
An incommunicable sleep.

IX

I look for ghosts; but none will force
Their way to me: 'tis falsely said
That there was ever intercourse
Between the living and the dead;   60
For, surely, then I should have sight
Of him I wait for day and night,
With love and longings infinite.

X

My apprehensions come in crowds;
I dread the rustling of the grass;   65
The very shadows of the clouds
Have power to shake me as they pass:
I question things and do not find
One that will answer to my mind;
And all the world appears unkind.   70

60 Between 1832: Betwixt 1807–27

XI

Beyond participation lie
My troubles, and beyond relief:
If any chance to heave a sigh,
They pity me, and not my grief.
Then come to me, my Son, or send   75
Some tidings that my woes may end;
I have no other earthly friend!

XXV

THE COTTAGER TO HER INFANT

BY MY SISTER

[Composed 1805.—Published 1815.]

THE days are cold, the nights are long,
The north-wind sings a doleful song;
Then hush again upon my breast;
All merry things are now at rest,
    Save thee, my pretty Love!   5

The kitten sleeps upon the hearth,
The crickets long have ceased their mirth;
There's nothing stirring in the house
Save one *wee*, hungry, nibbling mouse,
    Then why so busy thou?   10

Nay! start not at that sparkling light:
'Tis but the moon that shines so bright
On the window pane bedropped with rain:
Then, little Darling! sleep again,
    And wake when it is day.   15

XXV. MY SISTER 1845: A FEMALE FRIEND 1815–36
15 *To D. W.'s poem W. W. added the following 2 stanzas:*
        Ah! if I were a lady gay
        I should not grieve with thee to play;
        Right gladly would I lie awake
        Thy lively spirits to partake
        And ask no better chear.

        But, babe, there's none to work for me,
        And I must rise to industry;
        Soon as the cock begin to crow
        Thy mother to the fold must go
        To tend the sheep and kine.   MS.

XXVI

MATERNAL GRIEF

[Composed 1812–13.—Published 1842.]

DEPARTED Child! I could forget thee once
Though at my bosom nursed ; this woeful gain
Thy dissolution brings, that in my soul
Is present and perpetually abides
A shadow, never, never to be displaced   5
By the returning substance, seen or touched.
Seen by mine eyes, or clasped in my embrace.
Absence and death how differ they! and how
Shall I admit that nothing can restore
What one short sigh so easily removed ?—   10
Death, life, and sleep, reality and thought,
Assist me, God, their boundaries to know,
O teach me calm submission to thy Will!

The Child she mourned had overstepped the pale
Of Infancy, but still did breathe the air   15
That sanctifies its confines, and partook
Reflected beams of that celestial light
To all the Little-ones on sinful earth
Not unvouchsafed—a light that warmed and cheered
Those several qualities of heart and mind   20
Which, in her own blest nature, rooted deep,
Daily before the Mother's watchful eye,
And not hers only, their peculiar charms
Unfolded,—beauty, for its present self,
And for its promises to future years,   25
With not unfrequent rapture fondly hailed.

Have you espied upon a dewy lawn
A pair of Leverets each provoking each

XXVI. 4–5 Perpetually a Shadow doth abide
    That never nevermore shall be displaced MSS.
12 Assist] Instruct MS.   12/13 And make my new condition fairly
mine. MS.   14 The Child she] She whom we MS. 1
16–21 partook etc.] did still
    With all the Little-ones on earth partake
    Reflected beams of that celestial light
    Whose universal influence warmed and cheared
    The individual qualities of mind
    That in her own blest nature took their birth,
    Daily to open and unfold their sweets MS. 1

To a continuance of their fearless sport,
Two separate Creatures in their several gifts   30
Abounding, but so fashioned that, in all
That Nature prompts them to display, their looks,
Their starts of motion and their fits of rest,
An undistinguishable style appears
And character of gladness, as if Spring   35
Lodged in their innocent bosoms, and the spirit
Of the rejoicing morning were their own ?

Such union, in the lovely Girl maintained
And her twin Brother, had the parent seen,
Ere, pouncing like a ravenous bird of prey,   40
Death in a moment parted them, and left
The Mother, in her turns of anguish, worse
Than desolate ; for oft-times from the sound
Of the survivor's sweetest voice (dear child,
He knew it not) and from his happiest looks,   45
Did she extract the food of self-reproach,
As one that lived ungrateful for the stay
By Heaven afforded to uphold her maimed
And tottering spirit. And full oft the Boy,
Now first acquainted with distress and grief,   50
Shrunk from his Mother's presence, shunned with fear
Her sad approach, and stole away to find,
In his known haunts of joy where'er he might,
A more congenial object. But, as time
Softened her pangs, and reconciled the child   55

31   Of sense and intellect, but note them well,
     Observe them nearly, and behold in all MS. 1
37/38 Mark what one is, the other is the same.
     Now should a ravenous bird, a fowl of strength
     Such as abide among these craggy rocks
     Before your eyes with sudden swoop descend
     And of these unoffending Playmates seize
     One, and for ever break their joint delight,
     Would ye not shriek at such a Spectacle ?
     Ah, but a Mother saw it—it was seen
     And by a Father felt MSS.
43   desolate] destitute MS. 1
43–5   . . . from the sight
     He knew it not—of the beloved survivor MS. 2
49–52 And tottering spirit weak and desolate.
     For he to trouble and distress unus'd
     Shrank from her presence, shunned her sad approach
     With timid heart, and stole etc. MS. 1
55 Softened] Mellowed MS. 1

To what he saw, he gradually returned,
Like a scared Bird encouraged to renew
A broken intercourse; and, while his eyes
Were yet with pensive fear and gentle awe
Turned upon her who bore him, she would stoop   60
To imprint a kiss that lacked not power to spread
Faint colour over both their pallid cheeks,
And stilled his tremulous lip. Thus they were calmed
And cheered; and now together breathe fresh air
In open fields; and when the glare of day   65
Is gone, and twilight to the Mother's wish
Befriends the observance, readily they join
In walks whose boundary is the lost One's grave,
Which he with flowers hath planted, finding there
Amusement, where the Mother does not miss   70
Dear consolation, kneeling on the turf
In prayer, yet blending with that solemn rite
Of pious faith the vanities of grief;
For such, by pitying Angels and by Spirits
Transferred to regions upon which the clouds   75
Of our weak nature rest not, must be deemed

58-67 intercourse *etc.*] fellowship. O blessed Child,
Thy pure and perfect excellence demands
An everlasting record, but I think
And speak of thee among wild rocks and stones,
Nor ask for other audience which this day
Provideth, not unthankfully received
Albeit soon to be resigned. Large space,
Full twenty years of memory doth lie
Between us, rolling like the stormy deep;
But oh, sweet Comforter, I can perceive,
As in the nearness and the perfect light
Of yesterday, thy beauty, see thine eyes
(Large eyes of liquid sweetness, 'ever full)
On her who bore thee turn'd with pensive fear
And gentle awe, who stooping doth imprint
A kiss of chearfulness and hopeful love
That hath recalled the colour to thy cheek
And stills thy tremulous lip. So both were cheared,
And I with them, and they together breathed
Fresh air in open fields, and when the day
Was gone, and twilight to the Mother's wish
Befriended that observance they would join MS. 1
68 was MS.   69 with snowdrops planted MS.
74–9 For vanities if not by men at least
By pitying Angels must be deemed the sighs
The tears and all those outbreaks of a sorrow
Which soothed by time and sweetened by Heaven's grace MSS.

Those willing tears, and unforbidden sighs,
And all those tokens of a cherished sorrow,
Which, soothed and sweetened by the grace of Heaven
As now it is, seems to her own fond heart   80
Immortal as the love that gave it being.

XXVII

THE SAILOR'S MOTHER

[Composed March 11, 12, 1802.—Published 1807.]

ONE morning (raw it was and wet—
A foggy day in winter time)
A Woman on the road I met,
Not old, though something past her prime:
Majestic in her person, tall and straight;   5
And like a Roman matron's was her mien and gait.

The ancient spirit is not dead;
Old times, thought I, are breathing there;
Proud was I that my country bred
Such strength, a dignity so fair: 10
She begged an alms, like one in poor estate;
I looked at her again, nor did my pride abate.

When from these lofty thoughts I woke,
"What is it," said I, "that you bear,
Beneath the covert of your Cloak,   15
Protected from this cold damp air?"
She answered, soon as she the question heard,
"A simple burthen, Sir, a little Singing-bird."

And, thus continuing, she said,
"I had a Son, who many a day   20
Sailed on the seas, but he is dead;
In Denmark he was cast away:
And I have travelled weary miles to see
If aught which he had owned might still remain for me.

XXVII. 14–16 *so* 1836: With the first word I had to spare
                        I said to her "Beneath your Cloak
                        What's that which on your arm you bear?"
                            MS., 1807–15
                        "What treasure," said I, "do you bear
                        Beneath the covert of your Cloak
                        Protected from the cold damp air?" 1820–32
  19–21 *so* 1807–15, 1832: I had a son—the waves might roar
                        He feared them not, a Sailor gay!
                        But he will cross the waves no more; 1820, *so* 1827
                        but in 21 deep *for* waves

"The bird and cage they both were his: 25
'Twas my Son's bird; and neat and trim
He kept it: many voyages
The singing-bird had gone with him;
When last he sailed, he left the bird behind;
From bodings, as might be, that hung upon his mind.   30

"He to a fellow-lodger's care
Had left it, to be watched and fed,
And pipe its song in safety;—there
I found it when my Son was dead;
And now, God help me for my little wit!   35
I bear it with me, Sir;—he took so much delight in it."

XXVIII
THE CHILDLESS FATHER
[Composed 1800.—Published 1800.]

"Up, Timothy, up with your staff and away!
Not a soul in the village this morning will stay;
The hare has just started from Hamilton's grounds,
And Skiddaw is glad with the cry of the hounds."

—Of coats and of jackets grey, scarlet, and green,   5
On the slopes of the pastures all colours were seen;
With their comely blue aprons, and caps white as snow,
The girls on the hills made a holiday show.

Fresh sprigs of green box-wood, not six months before,
Filled the funeral basin[1] at Timothy's door;   10
A coffin through Timothy's threshold had past;
One Child did it bear, and that Child was his last.

[1] In several parts of the North of England, when a funeral takes place, a basin full of sprigs of box-wood is placed at the door of the house from which the coffin is taken up, and each person who attends the funeral ordinarily takes a sprig of this box-wood, and throws it into the grave of the deceased.

XXVII. 23–4 *so* 1827: And I have been as far as Hull to see
                    What clothes he might have left, or other pro-
                        perty MS., 1807
                    And I have travelled far *etc.* 1815
28 The . . . had 1845: This . . . hath MS. 1807: His . . . hath 1815: This . . .
had 1820–36   30 *so* 1827: As it might be, perhaps, from bodings of his
mind MS., 1807–20   33 *so* 1827: Till he come back again; and there
1807–20   36 bear 1827: trail 1807 MS. 20
XXVIII 5 both grey, red and green 1800, *corr. in errata*
5–10 *so* 1827: The bason of box-wood, just six months before
                    Had stood on the table   1800–15
                    The bason had offered . . . Fresh sprigs of green box-wood 1820
12 One] *so* 1820 *errata list.* A 1800–20

Now fast up the dell came the noise and the fray,
The horse, and the horn, and the hark! hark away!
Old Timothy took up his staff, and he shut   15
With a leisurely motion the door of his hut.

Perhaps to himself at that moment he said;
"The key I must take, for my Ellen is dead."
But of this in my ears not a word did he speak;
And he went to the chase with a tear on his cheek.   20

XXIX

THE EMIGRANT MOTHER

[Composed March 16, 17, 1802.—Published 1807.]

ONCE in a lonely hamlet I sojourned
In which a Lady driven from France did dwell;
The big and lesser griefs with which she mourned,
In friendship she to me would often tell.

This Lady, dwelling upon British ground,   5
Where she was childless, daily would repair
To a poor neighbouring cottage; as I found,
For sake of a young Child whose home was there.

Once having seen her clasp with fond embrace
This Child, I chanted to myself a lay,   10
Endeavouring, in our English tongue, to trace
Such things as she unto the Babe might say:
And thus, from what I heard and knew, or guessed,
My song the workings of her heart expressed.

XXIX. THE EMIGRANT MOTHER *so* 1820: *no title* MS., 1807-15
5 Lady] Mother MS., British 1845: English 1807-36   6 would 1827:
did MS. 1807-20
8/9   Oft with this Babe she to a grove withdrew
             And her I there have overheard in part
             While with love looks and words of language new
             To help her foreign speech she eas'd her heart. MS.
9-13 *so* 1845: Once did I see her clasp the Child about,
             And take it to herself; and I, next day,
             Wish'd in my native tongue to fashion out
             Such things as she unto this Child might say:
             And thus, from what I knew, had heard, and guess'd, MS.,
                1807-15
             Once did I see her take with fond embrace
             This infant to herself: and I, next day,
             Endeavoured in my native tongue to trace *etc. as* 1807, 1820
             Once having seen her take with fond embrace
             This infant to herself, I framed a lay,
             Endeavouring *etc. as* 1820, 1827-36

I

"Dear Babe, thou daughter of another,   15
One moment let me be thy mother!
An infant's face and looks are thine
And sure a mother's heart is mine:
Thy own dear mother's far away,
At labour in the harvest field: 20
Thy little sister is at play;—
What warmth, what comfort would it yield
To my poor heart, if thou wouldst be
One little hour a child to me!

II

"Across the waters I am come,   25
And I have left a babe at home:
A long, long way of land and sea!
Come to me—I'm no enemy:
I am the same who at thy side
Sate yesterday, and made a nest   30
For thee, sweet Baby!—thou hast tried,
Thou know'st the pillow of my breast;
Good, good art thou:—alas! to me
Far more than I can be to thee.

III

"Here, little Darling, dost thou lie;   35
An infant thou, a mother I!
Mine wilt thou be, thou hast no fears;
Mine art thou—spite of these my tears.
Alas! before I left the spot,
My baby and its dwelling-place,   40
The nurse said to me, 'Tears should not
Be shed upon an infant's face,
It was unlucky'—no, no, no;
No truth is in them who say so!

IV

"My own dear Little-one will sigh,   45
Sweet Babe! and they will let him die.
'He pines,' they'll say, 'it is his doom,
And you may see his hour is come.'

48 hour] day MS.

Oh! had he but thy cheerful smiles,
Limbs stout as thine, and lips as gay,   50
Thy looks, thy cunning, and thy wiles,
And countenance like a summer's day,
They would have hopes of him;—and then
I should behold his face again!

V

"'Tis gone—like dreams that we forget;   55
There was a smile or two—yet—yet
I can remember them, I see
The smiles, worth all the world to me.
Dear Baby! I must lay thee down;
Thou troublest me with strange alarms;   60
Smiles hast thou, bright ones of thy own;
I cannot keep thee in my arms;
For they confound me;—where—where is
That last, that sweetest smile of his?

VI

"Oh! how I love thee!—we will stay   65
Together here this one half day.
My sister's child, who bears my name,
From France to sheltering England came;
She with her mother crossed the sea;
The babe and mother near me dwell: 70
Yet does my yearning heart to thee
Turn rather, though I love her well:
Rest, little Stranger, rest thee here!
Never was any child more dear!

VII

"—I cannot help it; ill intent   75
I've none, my pretty Innocent!
I weep—I know they do thee wrong,
These tears—and my poor idle tongue.

55–6 *so* 1820: 'Tis gone—forgotten—let me do
          My best—there was a smile or two   MS., 1807–15
61 bright 1827: sweet MS., 1807–20
63–4 *so* 1836: For they confound me; as it is
          I have forgot those smiles [MS. too] of his MS., 1807–15
          For they bewilder me—even now
          His smiles are lost—I know not how!   1820
          By those bewildering glances crost
          In which the light of his is lost   1827
68 to sheltering England 1827: across the Ocean MS., 1807–20
71–2 *so* 1845: My Darling, she is not to me What thou art MS., 1807–32.
But to my heart she cannot be *etc.* 1836

Oh, what a kiss was that! my cheek
How cold it is! but thou art good;   80
Thine eyes are on me—they would speak,
I think, to help me if they could.
Blessings upon that soft, warm face,
My heart again is in its place!

VIII

"While thou art mine, my little Love,   85
This cannot be a sorrowful grove;
Contentment, hope, and mother's glee,
I seem to find them all in thee:
Here's grass to play with, here are flowers;
I'll call thee by my darling's name;   90
Thou hast, I think, a look of ours,
Thy features seem to me the same;
His little sister thou shalt be;
And, when once more my home I see,
I'll tell him many tales of Thee."   95

XXX

VAUDRACOUR AND JULIA

[Composed probably 1804.—Published 1820.]

The following tale was written as an Episode, in a work from which its
length may perhaps exclude it. The facts are true; no invention as to
these has been exercised, as none was needed.

O HAPPY time of youthful lovers (thus
My story may begin) O balmy time,
In which a love-knot on a lady's brow
Is fairer than the fairest star in heaven!
To such inheritance of blessed fancy   5
(Fancy that sports more desperately with minds
Than ever fortune hath been known to do)

81–2 And I grow happy while I speak
    Kiss, kiss me, Baby, thou art good MS.
83 soft, warm MS., 1820: quiet 1807–15
86/7 A Joy, a Comforter thou art;
    Sunshine and pleasure to my heart MS.
87–8 And love and hope and mother's glee *etc.* MS.
    My yearnings are allayed by thee
    My heaviness is turned to glee MS. (K.)
XXX. *For MS. readings prior to* 1820 *v. Prelude IX, pp.* 336–58

The high-born Vaudracour was brought, by years
Whose progress had a little overstepped
His stripling prime. A town of small repute,   10
Among the vine-clad mountains of Auvergne,
Was the Youth's birth-place. There he wooed a Maid
Who heard the heart-felt music of his suit
With answering vows. Plebeian was the stock,
Plebeian, though ingenuous, the stock,   15
From which her graces and her honours sprung:
And hence the father of the enamoured Youth,
With haughty indignation, spurned the thought
Of such alliance.—From their cradles up,
With but a step between their several homes,   20
Twins had they been in pleasure; after strife
And petty quarrels, had grown fond again;
Each other's advocate, each other's stay;
And, in their happiest moments, not content,
If more divided than a sportive pair   25
Of sea-fowl, conscious both that they are hovering
Within the eddy of a common blast,
Or hidden only by the concave depth
Of neighbouring billows from each other's sight.

Thus, not without concurrence of an age   30
Unknown to memory, was an earnest given
By ready nature for a life of love,
For endless constancy, and placid truth;
But whatsoe'er of such rare treasure lay
Reserved, had fate permitted, for support   35
Of their maturer years, his present mind
Was under fascination;—he beheld
A vision, and adored the thing he saw.
Arabian fiction never filled the world
With half the wonders that were wrought for him.   40
Earth breathed in one great presence of the spring;
Life turned the meanest of her implements,
Before his eyes, to price above all gold;
The house she dwelt in was a sainted shrine;
Her chamber-window did surpass in glory   45
The portals of the dawn; all Paradise
Could, by the simple opening of a door,

24-5 *so* 1836: And strangers to content if long apart, Or more 1820-32

Let itself in upon him:—pathways, walks,
Swarmed with enchantment, till his spirit sank,
Surcharged, within him, overblest to move   50
Beneath a sun that wakes a weary world
To its dull round of ordinary cares;
A man too happy for mortality!

So passed the time, till, whether through effect
Of some unguarded moment that dissolved   55
Virtuous restraint—ah, speak it, think it, not!
Deem rather that the fervent Youth, who saw
So many bars between his present state
And the dear haven where he wished to be
In honourable wedlock with his Love,   60
Was in his judgment tempted to decline
To perilous weakness, and entrust his cause
To nature for a happy end of all;
Deem that by such fond hope the Youth was swayed,
And bear with their transgression, when I add   65
That Julia, wanting yet the name of wife,
Carried about her for a secret grief
The promise of a mother.
                    To conceal
The threatened shame, the parents of the Maid
Found means to hurry her away by night,   70
And unforewarned, that in some distant spot
She might remain shrouded in privacy,
Until the babe was born. When morning came,
The Lover, thus bereft, stung with his loss,
And all uncertain whither he should turn,   75
Chafed like a wild beast in the toils; but soon
Discovering traces of the fugitives,
Their steps he followed to the Maid's retreat.
Easily may the sequel be divined—
Walks to and fro—watchings at every hour;   80
And the fair Captive, who, whene'er she may,
Is busy at her casement as the swallow
Fluttering its pinions, almost within reach,
About the pendent nest, did thus espy
Her Lover!—thence a stolen interview,   85
Accomplished under friendly shade of night.

61–2 *so* 1827: Was inwardly prepared to turn aside From law and custom, and
1820   79 *so* 1836: The sequel may be easily divined 1820–32

I pass the raptures of the pair;—such theme
Is, by innumerable poets, touched
In more delightful verse than skill of mine
Could fashion; chiefly by that darling bard   90
Who told of Juliet and her Romeo,
And of the lark's note heard before its time,
And of the streaks that laced the severing clouds
In the unrelenting east.—Through all her courts
The vacant city slept; the busy winds,   95
That keep no certain intervals of rest,
Moved not; meanwhile the galaxy displayed
Her fires, that like mysterious pulses beat
Aloft;—momentous but uneasy bliss!
To their full hearts the universe seemed hung   100
On that brief meeting's slender filament!

They parted; and the generous Vaudracour
Reached speedily the native threshold, bent
On making (so the Lovers had agreed)
A sacrifice of birthright to attain   105
A final portion from his father's hand;
Which granted, Bride and Bridegroom then would flee
To some remote and solitary place,
Shady as night, and beautiful as heaven,
Where they may live, with no one to behold   110
Their happiness, or to disturb their love.
But *now* of this no whisper; not the less,
If ever an obtrusive word were dropped
Touching the matter of his passion, still,
In his stern father's hearing, Vaudracour   115
Persisted openly that death alone
Should abrogate his human privilege
Divine, of swearing everlasting truth,
Upon the altar, to the Maid he loved.

"You shall be baffled in your mad intent   120
If there be justice in the court of France,"
Muttered the Father.—From these words the Youth
Conceived a terror; and, by night or day
Stirred nowhere without weapons, that full soon

122 these words 1827: this time 1820
124-5 *so* 1827: Stirred nowhere without arms . . . To their rural seat
          Meanwhile, his Parents artfully withdrew
          Upon some feigned occasion, and the Son
          Remained with one attendant. At midnight 1820

Found dreadful provocation: for at night,   125
When to his chamber he retired, attempt
Was made to seize him by three armèd men,
Acting, in furtherance of the Father's will,
Under a private signet of the State.
One the rash Youth's ungovernable hand   130
Slew, and as quickly to a second gave
A perilous wound—he shuddered to behold
The breathless corse; then peacefully resigned
His person to the law, was lodged in prison,
And wore the fetters of a criminal.   135

Have you observed a tuft of wingèd seed
That, from the dandelion's naked stalk,
Mounted aloft, is suffered not to use
Its natural gifts for purposes of rest,
Driven by the autumnal whirlwind to and fro   140
Through the wide element? or have you marked
The heavier substance of a leaf-clad bough,
Within the vortex of a foaming flood,
Tormented? by such aid you may conceive
The perturbation that ensued;—ah, no!   145
Desperate the Maid—the Youth is stained with blood;
Unmatchable on earth is their disquiet!
Yet as the troubled seed and tortured bough
Is man, subjected to despotic sway.

For him, by private influence with the Court,   150
Was pardon gained, and liberty procured;
But not without exaction of a pledge,
Which liberty and love dispersed in air.
He flew to her from whom they would divide him—
He clove to her who could not give him peace—   155
Yea, his first word of greeting was,—"All right
Is gone from me; my lately-towering hopes,
To the least fibre of their lowest root,
Are withered; thou no longer canst be mine,
I thine—the conscience-stricken must not woo   160
The unruffled Innocent,—I see thy face,
Behold thee, and my misery is complete!"

130–1 *so* 1836: One, did the Youth's ungovernable hand Assault and slay,
and 1820–32   136 observed 1836: beheld 1820–32   145 that ensued
1836: of each mind 1820–32   147 *so* 1836: *not in* 1820–32

"One, are we not ?" exclaimed the Maiden—"One,
For innocence and youth, for weal and woe ?"
Then with the father's name she coupled words   165
Of vehement indignation; but the Youth
Checked her with filial meekness; for no thought
Uncharitable crossed his mind, no sense
Of hasty anger, rising in the eclipse
Of true domestic loyalty, did e'er   170
Find place within his bosom.—Once again
The persevering wedge of tyranny
Achieved their separation: and once more
Were they united,—to be yet again
Disparted, pitiable lot! But here   175
A portion of the tale may well be left
In silence, though my memory could add
Much how the Youth, in scanty space of time,
Was traversed from without; much, too, of thoughts
That occupied his days in solitude   180
Under privation and restraint; and what,
Through dark and shapeless fear of things to come,
And what, through strong compunction for the past,
He suffered—breaking down in heart and mind!

Doomed to a third and last captivity,   185
His freedom he recovered on the eve
Of Julia's travail. When the babe was born,
Its presence tempted him to cherish schemes
Of future happiness. "You shall return,
Julia," said he, "and to your father's house   190
Go with the child.—You have been wretched; yet
The silver shower, whose reckless burthen weighs
Too heavily upon the lily's head,
Oft leaves a saving moisture at its root.
Malice, beholding you, will melt away.   195
Go!—'tis a town where both of us were born;
None will reproach you, for our truth is known;
And if, amid those once-bright bowers, our fate
Remain unpitied, pity is not in man.

168–9 *so* 1845: Uncharitable, no presumptuous rising
            Of hasty censure, modelled in the eclipse 1820–36
            Undutifully harsh dwelt in his mind,
            No proud resentment cherished in the eclipse MS. C

With ornaments—the prettiest, nature yields 200
Or art can fashion, shall you deck our boy,
And feed his countenance with your own sweet looks,
Till no one can resist him.—Now, even now,
I see him sporting on the sunny lawn;
My father from the window sees him too; 205
Startled, as if some new-created thing
Enriched the earth, or Faery of the woods
Bounded before him;—but the unweeting Child
Shall by his beauty win his grandsire's heart,
So that it shall be softened, and our loves 210
End happily, as they began!"
                                    These gleams
Appeared but seldom; oftener was he seen
Propping a pale and melancholy face
Upon the Mother's bosom; resting thus
His head upon one breast, while from the other 215
The Babe was drawing in its quiet food.
—That pillow is no longer to be thine,
Fond Youth! that mournful solace now must pass
Into the list of things that cannot be!
Unwedded Julia, terror-smitten, hears 220
The sentence, by her mother's lip pronounced,
That dooms her to a convent.—Who shall tell,
Who dares report, the tidings to the lord
Of her affections? so they blindly asked
Who knew not to what quiet depths a weight 225
Of agony had pressed the Sufferer down:
The word, by others dreaded, he can hear
Composed and silent, without visible sign
Of even the least emotion. Noting this,
When the impatient object of his love 230
Upbraided him with slackness, he returned
No answer, only took the mother's hand
And kissed it; seemingly devoid of pain,
Or care, that what so tenderly he pressed
Was a dependant on the obdurate heart 235
Of one who came to disunite their lives
For ever—sad alternative! preferred,
By the unbending Parents of the Maid,
To secret 'spousals meanly disavowed.

201 our 1840: your 1820–36

—So be it!

In the city he remained   240
A season after Julia had withdrawn
To those religious walls. He, too, departs—
Who with him ?—even the senseless Little-one.
With that sole charge he passed the city-gates,
For the last time, attendant by the side   245
Of a close chair, a litter, or sedan,
In which the Babe was carried. To a hill,
That rose a brief league distant from the town,
The dwellers in that house where he had lodged
Accompanied his steps, by anxious love   250
Impelled;—they parted from him there, and stood
Watching below till he had disappeared
On the hill top. His eyes he scarcely took,
Throughout that journey, from the vehicle
(Slow-moving ark of all his hopes!) that veiled   255
The tender infant: and at every inn,
And under every hospitable tree
At which the bearers halted or reposed,
Laid him with timid care upon his knees,
And looked, as mothers ne'er were known to look,   260
Upon the nursling which his arms embraced.

This was the manner in which Vaudracour
Departed with his infant; and thus reached
His father's house, where to the innocent child
Admittance was denied. The young man spake   265
No word of indignation or reproof,
But of his father begged, a last request,
That a retreat might be assigned to him,
Where in forgotten quiet he might dwell,
With such allowance as his wants required;   270
For wishes he had none. To a lodge that stood
Deep in a forest, with leave given, at the age
Of four-and-twenty summers he withdrew;
And thither took with him his motherless Babe,
And one domestic for their common needs,   275
An aged woman. It consoled him here
To attend upon the orphan, and perform
Obsequious service to the precious child,

266 word 1836: words 1820–32   274 motherless 1836: infant 1820–32

Which, after a short time, by some mistake
Or indiscretion of the Father, died.—   280
The Tale I follow to its last recess
Of suffering or of peace, I know not which:
Theirs be the blame who caused the woe, not mine!

From this time forth he never shared a smile
With mortal creature. An Inhabitant   285
Of that same town, in which the pair had left
So lively a remembrance of their griefs,
By chance of business, coming within reach
Of his retirement, to the forest lodge
Repaired, but only found the matron there,   290
Who told him that his pains were thrown away,
For that her Master never uttered word
To living thing—not even to her.—Behold!
While they were speaking, Vaudracour approached;
But seeing some one near, as on the latch   295
Of the garden-gate his hand was laid, he shrunk—
And, like a shadow, glided out of view.
Shocked at his savage aspect, from the place
The visitor retired.
             Thus lived the Youth
Cut off from all intelligence with man,   300
And shunning even the light of common day;
Nor could the voice of Freedom, which through France
Full speedily resounded, public hope,
Or personal memory of his own deep wrongs,
Rouse him: but in those solitary shades   305
His days he wasted, an imbecile mind!

XXXI

THE IDIOT BOY
[Composed 1798.—Published 1798.]

'Tis eight o'clock,—a clear March night,
The moon is up,—the sky is blue,
The owlet, in the moonlight air,
Shouts from nobody knows where;
He lengthens out his lonely shout,   5
Halloo! halloo! a long halloo!

289-90 *so* 1827:   to the spot repaired
              With an intent to visit him. He reached
              The house and only 1820
295-6 *so* 1836: even as his hand Was stretched towards the garden gate, 1820-32
XXXI. 4 Shouts 1827: He shouts 1798-1820

—Why bustle thus about your door,
What means this bustle, Betty Foy?
Why are you in this mighty fret?
And why on horseback have you set　　　　10
Him whom you love, your Idiot Boy?

Scarcely a soul is out of bed;
Good Betty, put him down again;
His lips with joy they burr at you;
But, Betty! what has he to do　　　　15
With stirrup, saddle, or with rein?

But Betty's bent on her intent;
For her good neighbour Susan Gale,
Old Susan, she who dwells alone,
Is sick, and makes a piteous moan,　　　　20
As if her very life would fail.

There's not a house within a mile,
No hand to help them in distress;
Old Susan lies a-bed in pain,
And sorely puzzled are the twain,　　　　25
For what she ails they cannot guess.

And Betty's husband's at the wood,
Where by the week he doth abide,
A woodman in the distant vale;
There's none to help poor Susan Gale;　　　　30
What must be done? what will betide?

And Betty from the lane has fetched
Her Pony, that is mild and good;
Whether he be in joy or pain,
Feeding at will along the lane,　　　　35
Or bringing fagots from the wood.

11/12 Beneath the moon that shines so bright,
　　　Till she is tired, let Betty Foy
　　　With girt and stirrup fiddle-faddle;
　　　But wherefore set upon a saddle
　　　Him whom she loves, her idiot boy?　　1798–1820
12 *so* 1836: There's scarce a soul that's 1798–1832
16/17 The world will say 'tis very idle,
　　　Bethink you of the time of night;
　　　There's not a mother, no not one,
　　　But when she hears what you have done,
　　　O Betty, she'll be in a fright.　　1798–1820

And he is all in travelling trim,—
And, by the moonlight, Betty Foy
Has on the well-girt saddle set
(The like was never heard of yet)   40
Him whom she loves, her Idiot Boy.

And he must post without delay
Across the bridge and through the dale,
And by the church, and o'er the down,
To bring a Doctor from the town,   45
Or she will die, old Susan Gale.

There is no need of boot or spur,
There is no need of whip or wand;
For Johnny has his holly-bough,
And with a *hurly-burly* now   50
He shakes the green bough in his hand.

And Betty o'er and o'er has told
The Boy, who is her best delight,
Both what to follow, what to shun,
What do, and what to leave undone,   55
How turn to left, and how to right.

And Betty's most especial charge,
Was, "Johnny! Johnny! mind that you
Come home again, nor stop at all,—
Come home again, what'er befall,   60
My Johnny, do, I pray you, do."

To this did Johnny answer make,
Both with his head and with his hand,
And proudly shook the bridle too;
And then! his words were not a few,   65
Which Betty well could understand.

And now that Johnny is just going,
Though Betty's in a mighty flurry,
She gently pats the Pony's side,
On which her Idiot Boy must ride,   70
And seems no longer in a hurry.

39 *so* 1836: Has up upon the 1798–1832   43 and through 1820: that's
in 1798–1815

But when the Pony moved his legs,
Oh! then for the poor Idiot Boy!
For joy he cannot hold the bridle,
For joy his head and heels are idle,   75
He's idle all for very joy.

And, while the Pony moves his legs,
In Johnny's left hand you may see
The green bough motionless and dead:
The Moon that shines above his head   80
Is not more still and mute than he.

His heart it was so full of glee
That, till full fifty yards were gone,
He quite forgot his holly whip,
And all his skill in horsemanship: 85
Oh! happy, happy, happy John.

And while the Mother, at the door,
Stands fixed, her face with joy o'erflows,
Proud of herself, and proud of him,
She sees him in his travelling trim,   90
How quietly her Johnny goes.

The silence of her Idiot Boy,
What hopes it sends to Betty's heart!
He's at the guide-post—he turns right;
She watches till he's out of sight,   95
And Betty will not then depart.

Burr, burr—now Johnny's lips they burr,
As loud as any mill, or near it;
Meek as a lamb the Pony moves,
And Johnny makes the noise he loves,   100
And Betty listens, glad to hear it.

Away she hies to Susan Gale:
Her Messenger's in merry tune;
The owlets hoot, the owlets curr,
And Johnny's lips they burr, burr, burr,   105
As on he goes beneath the moon.

87–8 *so* 1827: And Betty's standing at the door And Betty's face 1798–1820
103 *so* 1820: And Johnny's in a 1798–1815   106 As 1827: And 1798–
1820

His steed and he right well agree;
For of this Pony there's a rumour,
That, should he lose his eyes and ears,
And should he live a thousand years,   110
He never will be out of humour.

But then he is a horse that thinks!
And when he thinks, his pace is slack;
Now, though he knows poor Johnny well,
Yet, for his life, he cannot tell   115
What he has got upon his back.

So through the moonlight lanes they go,
And far into the moonlight dale,
And by the church, and o'er the down,
To bring a Doctor from the town,   120
To comfort poor old Susan Gale.

And Betty, now at Susan's side,
Is in the middle of her story,
What speedy help her Boy will bring,
With many a most diverting thing,   125
Of Johnny's wit, and Johnny's glory.

And Betty, still at Susan's side,
By this time is not quite so flurried:
Demure with porringer and plate
She sits, as if in Susan's fate   130
Her life and soul were buried.

But Betty, poor good woman! she,
You plainly in her face may read it,
Could lend out of that moment's store
Five years of happiness or more   135
To any that might need it.

But yet I guess that now and then
With Betty all was not so well;
And to the road she turns her ears,
And thence full many a sound she hears,   140
Which she to Susan will not tell.

124 *so* 1836: What comfort Johnny soon 1798–1820: What comfort soon
her Boy 1827–32   127–8 *so* 1827: And Betty's still at Susan's side; By
this time she's 1798–1820

Poor Susan moans, poor Susan groans;
"As sure as there's a moon in heaven,"
Cries Betty, "he'll be back again;
They'll both be here—'tis almost ten—   145
Both will be here before eleven."

Poor Susan moans, poor Susan groans;
The clock gives warning for eleven;
'Tis on the stroke—"He must be near,"
Quoth Betty, "and will soon be here,   150
As sure as there's a moon in heaven."

The clock is on the stroke of twelve,
And Johnny is not yet in sight:
—The Moon's in heaven, as Betty sees,
But Betty is not quite at ease;   155
And Susan has a dreadful night.

And Betty, half an hour ago,
On Johnny vile reflections cast:
"A little idle sauntering Thing!"
With other names, an endless string;   160
But now that time is gone and past.

And Betty's drooping at the heart,
That happy time all past and gone,
"How can it be he is so late?
The Doctor, he has made him wait;   165
Susan! they'll both be here anon."

And Susan's growing worse and worse,
And Betty's in a sad *quandary*;
And then there's nobody to say
If she must go, or she must stay!   170
—She's in a sad *quandary*.

The clock is on the stroke of one;
But neither Doctor nor his Guide
Appears along the moonlight road;
There's neither horse nor man abroad,   175
And Betty's still at Susan's side.

146 Both will 1827: They'll both 1798–1820   149–50 *so* 1827: "If Johnny's near", Quoth Betty "he 1798–1820

And Susan now begins to fear
Of sad mischances not a few,
That Johnny may perhaps be drowned;
Or lost, perhaps, and never found;   180
Which they must both for ever rue.

She prefaced half a hint of this
With, "God forbid it should be true!"
At the first word that Susan said
Cried Betty, rising from the bed,   185
"Susan, I'd gladly stay with you.

"I must be gone, I must away:
Consider, Johnny's but half-wise;
Susan, we must take care of him,
If he is hurt in life or limb"—   190
"Oh God forbid!" poor Susan cries.

"What can I do?" says Betty, going,
"What can I do to ease your pain?
Good Susan tell me, and I'll stay;
I fear you're in a dreadful way,   195
But I shall soon be back again."

"Nay, Betty, go! good Betty, go!
There's nothing that can ease my pain."
Then off she hies; but with a prayer,
That God poor Susan's life would spare,   200
Till she comes back again.

So, through the moonlight lane she goes,
And far into the moonlight dale;
And how she ran, and how she walked,
And all that to herself she talked,   205
Would surely be a tedious tale.

In high and low, above, below,
In great and small, in round and square,
In tree and tower was Johnny seen,
In bush and brake, in black and green;   2:0
'Twas Johnny, Johnny, everywhere.

177 now 1827: she 1798–1820   197 Nay 1800: Good 1798

And while she crossed the bridge, there came
A thought with which her heart is sore—
Johnny perhaps his horse forsook,
To hunt the moon within the brook,   215
And never will be heard of more.

Now is she high upon the down,
Alone amid a prospect wide;
There's neither Johnny nor his Horse
Among the fern or in the gorse;   220
There's neither Doctor nor his Guide.

"Oh saints! what is become of him?
Perhaps he's climbed into an oak,
Where he will stay till he is dead;
Or sadly he has been misled,   225
And joined the wandering gipsy-folk.

"Or him that wicked Pony's carried
To the dark cave, the goblin's hall;
Or in the castle he's pursuing
Among the ghosts his own undoing;   230
Or playing with the waterfall."

At poor old Susan then she railed,
While to the town she posts away;
"If Susan had not been so ill,
Alas! I should have had him still,   235
My Johnny, till my dying day."

Poor Betty, in this sad distemper,
The Doctor's self could hardly spare:
Unworthy things she talked, and wild;
Even he, of cattle the most mild,   240
The Pony had his share.

But now she's fairly in the town,
And to the Doctor's door she hies;
'Tis silence all on every side;
The town so long, the town so wide,   245
Is silent as the skies.

212–3 *so* 1836: She's past the bridge that's in the dale
              And now the thought torments her sore,   1798–1815: far
     in the dale 1820: The bridge is past—far in the dale 1827
215 within 1827: that's in 1798–1820   217 Now is she 1827: And now
she's 1798–1820   242 *so* 1836: And now she's got into the town 1798–
1832

And now she's at the Doctor's door,
She lifts the knocker, rap, rap, rap;
The Doctor at the casement shows
His glimmering eyes that peep and doze!   250
And one hand rubs his old night-cap.

"Oh Doctor! Doctor! where's my Johnny?"
"I'm here, what is 't you want with me?"
"Oh Sir! you know I'm Betty Foy,
And I have lost my poor dear Boy,   255
You know him—him you often see;

"He's not so wise as some folks be:"
"The devil take his wisdom!" said
The Doctor, looking somewhat grim,
"What, Woman! should I know of him?"   260
And, grumbling, he went back to bed!

"O woe is me! O woe is me!
Here will I die; here will I die;
I thought to find my lost one here,
But he is neither far nor near,   265
Oh! what a wretched Mother I!"

She stops, she stands, she looks about;
Which way to turn she cannot tell.
Poor Betty! it would ease her pain
If she had heart to knock again;   270
—The clock strikes three—a dismal knell!

Then up along the town she hies,
No wonder if her senses fail;
This piteous news so much it shocked her,
She quite forgot to send the Doctor,   275
To comfort poor old Susan Gale.

And now she's high upon the down,
And she can see a mile of road:
"O cruel! I'm almost threescore;
Such night as this was ne'er before,   280
There's not a single soul abroad."

264 lost one 1827: Johnny 1798–1820

She listens, but she cannot hear
The foot of horse, the voice of man;
The streams with softest sound are flowing,
The grass you almost hear it growing,   285
You hear it now, if e'er you can.

The owlets through the long blue night
Are shouting to each other still:
Fond lovers! yet not quite hob nob,
They lengthen out the tremulous sob,   290
That echoes far from hill to hill.

Poor Betty now has lost all hope,
Her thoughts are bent on deadly sin,
A green-grown pond she just has past,
And from the brink she hurries fast,   295
Lest she should drown herself therein.

And now she sits her down and weeps;
Such tears she never shed before;
"Oh dear, dear Pony! my sweet joy!
Oh carry back my Idiot Boy!   300
And we will ne'er o'erload thee more."

A thought is come into her head:
The Pony he is mild and good,
And we have always used him well;
Perhaps he's gone along the dell,   305
And carried Johnny to the wood.

Then up she springs as if on wings;
She thinks no more of deadly sin;
If Betty fifty ponds should see,
The last of all her thoughts would be   310
To drown herself therein.

Oh Reader! now that I might tell
What Johnny and his Horse are doing!
What they've been doing all this time,
Oh could I put it into rhyme,   315
A most delightful tale pursuing!

Perhaps, and no unlikely thought!
He with his Pony now doth roam
The cliffs and peaks so high that are,
To lay his hands upon a star,   320
And in his pocket bring it home.

Perhaps he's turned himself about,
His face unto his horse's tail,
And, still and mute, in wonder lost,
All silent as a horseman-ghost,   325
He travels slowly down the vale.

And now, perhaps, is hunting sheep,
A fierce and dreadful hunter he;
Yon valley, now so trim and green,
In five months' time, should he be seen,   330
A desert wilderness will be!

Perhaps, with head and heels on fire,
And like the very soul of evil,
He's galloping away, away,
And so will gallop on for aye,   335
The bane of all that dread the devil!

I to the Muses have been bound
These fourteen years, by strong indentures:
O gentle Muses! let me tell
But half of what to him befell;   340
He surely met with strange adventures.

O gentle Muses! is this kind?
Why will ye thus my suit repel?
Why of your further aid bereave me?
And can ye thus unfriended leave me;   345
Ye Muses! whom I love so well?

Who's yon, that, near the waterfall,
Which thunders down with headlong force,
Beneath the moon, yet shining fair,
As careless as if nothing were,   350
Sits upright on a feeding horse?

Unto his horse—there feeding free,
He seems, I think, the rein to give;
Of moon or stars he takes no heed;
Of such we in romances read: 355
—'Tis Johnny! Johnny! as I live.

325 *so* 1836: All like a silent 1798–1832   326 slowly down 1836: on
along 1798–1832   327 is 1820: he's 1798–1815   329 now 1820:
that's 1798–1815   341 He surely 1802: For sure he 1798   345
unfriended 1798: unfriendly 1805 (*only*)   352 there 1827: that's
1798–1820

And that's the very Pony, too!
Where is she, where is Betty Foy?
She hardly can sustain her fears;
The roaring waterfall she hears,   360
And cannot find her Idiot Boy.

Your Pony's worth his weight in gold:
Then calm your terrors, Betty Foy!
She's coming from among the trees,
And now all full in view she sees   365
Him whom she loves, her Idiot Boy.

And Betty sees the Pony too:
Why stand you thus, good Betty Foy?
It is no goblin, 'tis no ghost,
'Tis he whom you so long have lost,   370
He whom you love, your Idiot Boy.

She looks again—her arms are up—
She screams—she cannot move for joy;
She darts, as with a torrent's force,
She almost has o'erturned the Horse,   375
And fast she holds her Idiot Boy.

And Johnny burrs, and laughs aloud;
Whether in cunning or in joy
I cannot tell; but while he laughs,
Betty a drunken pleasure quaffs   380
To hear again her Idiot Boy.

And now she's at the Pony's tail,
And now is at the Pony's head,—
On that side now, and now on this;
And, almost stifled with her bliss,   385
A few sad tears does Betty shed.

She kisses o'er and o'er again
Him whom she loves, her Idiot Boy;
She's happy here, is happy there,
She is uneasy everywhere;   390
Her limbs are all alive with joy.

383 is 1827: she's 1798–1820   389 is 1827: she's 1798–1820

She pats the Pony, where or when
She knows not, happy Betty Foy!
The little Pony glad may be,
But he is milder far than she,   395
You hardly can perceive his joy.

"Oh! Johnny, never mind the Doctor;
You've done your best, and that is all:"
She took the reins, when this was said,
And gently turned the Pony's head   400
From the loud waterfall.

By this the stars were almost gone,
The moon was setting on the hill,
So pale you scarcely looked at her:
The little birds began to stir,   405
Though yet their tongues were still.

The Pony, Betty, and her Boy,
Wind slowly through the woody dale;
And who is she, betimes abroad,
That hobbles up the steep rough road?   410
Who is it, but old Susan Gale?

Long time lay Susan lost in thought;
And many dreadful fears beset her,
Both for her Messenger and Nurse;
And, as her mind grew worse and worse,   415
Her body—it grew better.

She turned, she tossed herself in bed,
On all sides doubts and terrors met her;
Point after point did she discuss;
And, while her mind was fighting thus,   420
Her body still grew better.

"Alas! what is become of them?
These fears can never be endured;
I'll to the wood."—The word scarce said,
Did Susan rise up from her bed,   425
As if by magic cured.

412 *so* 1827: Long Susan lay deep lost 1798–1820

Away she goes up hill and down,
And to the wood at length is come;
She spies her Friends, she shouts a greeting;
Oh me! it is a merry meeting   430
As ever was in Christendom.

The owls have hardly sung their last,
While our four travellers homeward wend;
The owls have hooted all night long,
And with the owls began my song,   435
And with the owls must end.

For while they all were travelling home,
Cried Betty, "Tell us, Johnny, do,
Where all this long night you have been,
What you have heard, what you have seen: 440
And, Johnny, mind you tell us true."

Now Johnny all night long had heard
The owls in tuneful concert strive;
No doubt too he the moon had seen;
For in the moonlight he had been   445
From eight o'clock till five.

And thus, to Betty's question, he
Made answer, like a traveller bold,
(His very words I give to you,)
"The cocks did crow to-whoo, to-whoo,   450
And the sun did shine so cold!"
—Thus answered Johnny in his glory,
And that was all his travel's story.

XXXII

MICHAEL

A PASTORAL POEM

[Composed October 11–December 9, 1800.—Published 1800.]

IF from the public way you turn your steps
Up the tumultuous brook of Green-head Ghyll,
You will suppose that with an upright path
Your feet must struggle; in such bold ascent
The pastoral mountains front you, face to face.   5

427 goes 1836: posts 1798–1832

But, courage! for around that boisterous brook
The mountains have all opened out themselves,
And made a hidden valley of their own.
No habitation can be seen; but they
Who journey thither find themselves alone   10
With a few sheep, with rocks and stones, and kites
That overhead are sailing in the sky.
It is in truth an utter solitude;
Nor should I have made mention of this Dell
But for one object which you might pass by,   15
Might see and notice not. Beside the brook
Appears a straggling heap of unhewn stones!
And to that simple object appertains
A story—unenriched with strange events,
Yet not unfit, I deem, for the fireside,   20
Or for the summer shade. It was the first
Of those domestic tales that spake to me
Of Shepherds, dwellers in the valleys, men
Whom I already loved;—not verily
For their own sakes, but for the fields and hills   25
Where was their occupation and abode.
And hence this Tale, while I was yet a Boy
Careless of books, yet having felt the power
Of Nature, by the gentle agency
Of natural objects, led me on to feel   30
For passions that were not my own, and think
(At random and imperfectly indeed)
On man, the heart of man, and human life.
Therefore, although it be a history
Homely and rude, I will relate the same   35
For the delight of a few natural hearts;
And, with yet fonder feeling, for the sake
Of youthful Poets, who among these hills
Will be my second self when I am gone.

    Upon the forest-side in Grasmere Vale   40
There dwelt a Shepherd, Michael was his name;

6 aróund 1827: beside 1800–20   9–10 *so* 1827: there is seen; but such As
1800–20   17 Appears 1827: There is 1800–20
18–20 *so* 1836: And to that place a story appertains,
           Which, though it be ungarnished with events,
           Is   1800–32
22 Of those domestic 1827: The earliest of these 1800–20

An old man, stout of heart, and strong of limb.
His bodily frame had ḫeen from youth to age
Of an unusual strength: his mind was keen,
Intense, and frugal, apt for all affairs,   45
And in his shepherd's calling he was prompt
And watchful more than ordinary men.
Hence had he learned the meaning of all winds,
Of blasts of every tone; and oftentimes,
When others heeded not, He heard the South   50
Make subterraneous music, like the noise
Of bagpipers on distant Highland hills.
The Shepherd, at such warning, of his flock
Bethought him, and he to himself would say,
"The winds are now devising work for me!"   55
And, truly, at all times, the storm, that drives
The traveller to a shelter, summoned him
Up to the mountains: he had been alone
Amid the heart of many thousand mists,
That came to him, and left him, on the heights.   60
So lived he till his eightieth year was past.
And grossly that man errs, who should suppose
That the green valleys, and the streams and rocks,
Were things indifferent to the Shepherd's thoughts.
Fields, where with cheerful spirits he had breathed   65
The common air; hills, which with vigorous step
He had so often climbed; which had impressed
So many incidents upon his mind
Of hardship, skill or courage, joy or fear;
Which, like a book, preserved the memory   70
Of the dumb animals, whom he had saved,
Had fed or sheltered, linking to such acts
The certainty of honourable gain;

48 had he 1827: he had 1800–20
61–6 So had he lived till he at length was come
        Within short distance of his seventieth year
        The fields where he with a clear mind had breathed
        The common air *etc. as text*,   MS.
66–7 *so* 1836: the hills, which he so oft Had climbed with vigorous steps;
1800–32   69–70 Of danger or of hardship, doubt or fear, Or MS.
73–4 The . . . hills 1832: So grateful in themselves, the certainty
                        Of honourable gain: these fields, these hills,
                        Which were his living Being, even more
                        Than his own blood 1800–27 *so* MS., *but*
        Where all his forefathers had lived and died, *between* hills, *and* Which

Those fields, those hills—what could they less? had laid
Strong hold on his affections, were to him   75
A pleasurable feeling of blind love,
The pleasure which there is in life itself.

   His days had not been passed in singleness.
His Helpmate was a comely matron, old—
Though younger than himself full twenty years.   80
She was a woman of a stirring life,
Whose heart was in her house: two wheels she had
Of antique form; this large, for spinning wool;
That small, for flax; and if one wheel had rest,
It was because the other was at work.   85
The Pair had but one inmate in their house,
An only Child, who had been born to them
When Michael, telling o'er his years, began
To deem that he was old,—in shepherd's phrase,
With one foot in the grave. This only Son,   90
With two brave sheep-dogs tried in many a storm,
The one of an inestimable worth,
Made all their household. I may truly say,
That they were as a proverb in the vale
For endless industry. When day was gone,   95
And from their occupations out of doors
The Son and Father were come home, even then,
Their labour did not cease; unless when all
Turned to the cleanly supper-board, and there,
Each with a mess of pottage and skimmed milk,   100
Sat round the basket piled with oaten cakes,
And their plain home-made cheese. Yet when the meal
Was ended, Luke (for so the Son was named)
And his old Father both betook themselves
To such convenient work as might employ   105
Their hands by the fire-side; perhaps to card
Wool for the Housewife's spindle, or repair
Some injury done to sickle, flail, or scythe,
Or other implement of house or field.

   Down from the ceiling, by the chimney's edge,   110
That in our ancient uncouth country style

78–9 *so* 1815: He had not passed his days ... He had a wife 1800–5
99, 101, 103 the 1836: their 1800–32

With huge and black projection overbrowed
Large space beneath, as duly as the light
Of day grew dim the Housewife hung a lamp;
An aged utensil, which had performed   115
Service beyond all others of its kind.
Early at evening did it burn—and late,
Surviving comrade of uncounted hours,
Which, going by from year to year, had found,
And left the couple neither gay perhaps   120
Nor cheerful, yet with objects and with hopes,
Living a life of eager industry.
And now, when Luke had reached his eighteenth year,
There by the light of this old lamp they sate,
Father and Son, while far into the night   125
The Housewife plied her own peculiar work,
Making the cottage through the silent hours
Murmur as with the sound of summer flies.
This light was famous in its neighbourhood,
And was a public symbol of the life   130
That thrifty Pair had lived. For, as it chanced,
Their cottage on a plot of rising ground

112 *so* 1836: Did with a huge projection overbrow 1800–32
123 had reached 1827: was in 1800–20   125 far 1836: late 1800–32
128/9 Though in these occupations they would pass
      Whole hours with but small interchange of speech,
      Yet were there times in which they did not want
      Discourse both wise and prudent, shrewd remarks
      Of daily providence, clothed in images
      Lively and beautiful, in rural forms
      That made their conversation fresh and fair
      As is a landscape:—And the shepherd oft
      Would draw out of his heart the obscurities
      And admirations that were there, of God
      And of his works, or yielding to the bent
      Of his peculiar humour, would let loose
      The tongue and give it the wind's freedom,—then,
      Discoursing on remote imaginations, story,
      Conceits, devices, day-dreams, thoughts and schemes,
      The fancies of a solitary man. *Letter to Poole* April 9, 1801
      Not with a waste of words, but for the sake
      Of pleasure, which I know that I shall give
      To many living now, I of this Lamp
      Speak thus minutely: for there are no few
      Whose memories will bear witness to my tale.   1800–2
129 This 1815: The 1800–5   131 That 1832: The 1800–27

Stood single, with large prospect, north and south,
High into Easedale, up to Dunmail-Raise,
And westward to the village near the lake;   135
And from this constant light, so regular,
And so far seen, the House itself, by all
Who dwelt within the limits of the vale,
Both old and young, was named THE EVENING STAR.

Thus living on through such a length of years,   140
The Shepherd, if he loved himself, must needs
Have loved his Helpmate; but to Michael's heart
This son of his old age was yet more dear—
Less from instinctive tenderness, the same
Fond spirit that blindly works in the blood of all—   145
Than that a child, more than all other gifts
That earth can offer to declining man,
Brings hope with it, and forward-looking thoughts,
And stirrings of inquietude, when they
By tendency of nature needs must fail.   150
Exceeding was the love he bare to him,
His heart and his heart's joy! For often-times
Old Michael, while he was a babe in arms,
Had done him female service, not alone
For pastime and delight, as is the use   155
Of fathers, but with patient mind enforced
To acts of tenderness; and he had rocked
His cradle, as with a woman's gentle hand.

And in a later time, ere yet the Boy
Had put on boy's attire, did Michael love,   160
Albeit of a stern unbending mind,
To have the Young-one in his sight, when he
Wrought in the field, or on his shepherd's stool

144 Less from 1827: Effect which might perhaps have been produced By that
. . . 1800–20   145 so 1836 Blind Spirit, which is 1800–32
146 Than 1827: Or 1800–20   147 not in 1800–32
150/1 From such, and other causes, to the thoughts
          Of the old Man his only Son was now
          The dearest object that he knew on earth. 1800–20
155 pastime 1827: dalliance MS., 1800–20   158 as with 1836: with MS., 1800–
32   159 in a later time] afterwards MS.   161 unbending] and active MS.
163–6 so 1836: Had work by his own door, or when he sate
          With sheep before him on his Shepherd's stool,
          Beneath that large old Oak, which near their door
          Stood,—and, from its enormous breadth of shade 1800–32.
          So MS., but Shearer's for Shepherd's

Sate with a fettered sheep before him stretched
Under the large old oak, that near his door   165
Stood single, and, from matchless depth of shade,
Chosen for the Shearer's covert from the sun,
Thence in our rustic dialect was called
The CLIPPING TREE,[1] a name which yet it bears.
There, while they two were sitting in the shade,   170
With others round them, earnest all and blithe,
Would Michael exercise his heart with looks
Of fond correction and reproof bestowed
Upon the Child, if he disturbed the sheep
By catching at their legs, or with his shouts   175
Scared them, while they lay still beneath the shears.

And when by Heaven's good grace the boy grew up
A healthy Lad, and carried in his cheek
Two steady roses that were five years old;
Then Michael from a winter coppice cut   180
With his own hand a sapling, which he hooped
With iron, making it throughout in all
Due requisites a perfect shepherd's staff,
And gave it to the Boy; wherewith equipt
He as a watchman oftentimes was placed   185
At gate or gap, to stem or turn the flock;
And, to his office prematurely called,
There stood the urchin, as you will divine,
Something between a hindrance and a help;
And for this cause not always, I believe,   190
Receiving from his Father hire of praise;
Though nought was left undone which staff, or voice,
Or looks, or threatening gestures, could perform.

But soon as Luke, full ten years old, could stand
Against the mountain blasts; and to the heights,   195
Not fearing toil, nor length of weary ways,

[1] Clipping is the word used in the North of England for shearing.

168-9 In times that now had long been out of mind
     It [ ] the title of the Clipping Tree   MS.
172 looks] words MS.
174 Upon the Child if e'er he stretch'd his hand
     Towards the glittering shears, when they were laid
     Upon the herbage, or disturbed the sheep   MS.
177 by Heaven's good grace] in after years   MS.   192-206 *omitted from first issue of* 1800

He with his Father daily went, and they
Were as companions, why should I relate
That objects which the Shepherd loved before
Were dearer now ? that from the Boy there came   200
Feelings and emanations—things which were
Light to the sun and music to the wind ;
And that the old Man's heart seemed born again ?

Thus in his Father's sight the Boy grew up :
And now, when he had reached his eighteenth year,   205
He was his comfort and his daily hope.

While in this sort the simple household lived
From day to day, to Michael's ear there came
Distressful tidings. Long before the time
Of which I speak, the Shepherd had been bound   210
In surety for his brother's son, a man
Of an industrious life, and ample means ;
But unforeseen misfortunes suddenly
Had prest upon him ; and old Michael now
Was summoned to discharge the forfeiture,   215
A grievous penalty, but little less
Than half his substance. This unlooked-for claim,
At the first hearing, for a moment took
More hope out of his life than he supposed
That any old man ever could have lost.   220
As soon as he had armed himself with strength
To look his trouble in the face, it seemed
The Shepherd's sole resource to sell at once
A portion of his patrimonial fields.
Such was his first resolve ; he thought again,   225
And his heart failed him. "Isabel," said he,
Two evenings after he had heard the news,
"I have been toiling more than seventy years,
And in the open sunshine of God's love
Have we all lived ; yet if these fields of ours   230
Should pass into a stranger's hand, I think

207 *so* 1815 : While this good household thus were living on 1800
            While in the fashion which I have described
            This simple Household thus were living on,   1802-5   **and**
cancel leaf 1800 *but* household
221-3 *so* 1836 : As soon as he had gathered so much strength,
            That he could look his trouble in the face,
            It seemed that his sole refuge was to sell   1800-32

That I could not lie quiet in my grave.
Our lot is a hard lot; the sun himself
Has scarcely been more diligent than I;
And I have lived to be a fool at last   235
To my own family. An evil man
That was, and made an evil choice, if he
Were false to us; and, if he were not false,
There are ten thousand to whom loss like this
Had been no sorrow. I forgive him;—but   240
'Twere better to be dumb than to talk thus.

"When I began, my purpose was to speak
Of remedies and of a cheerful hope.
Our Luke shall leave us, Isabel; the land
Shall not go from us, and it shall be free;   245
He shall possess it, free as is the wind
That passes over it. We have, thou know'st,
Another kinsman—he will be our friend
In this distress. He is a prosperous man,
Thriving in trade—and Luke to him shall go,   250
And with his kinsman's help and his own thrift
He quickly will repair this loss, and then
He may return to us. If here he stay,
What can be done ? Where every one is poor,
What can be gained ?"
                          At this the old Man paused,   255
And Isabel sat silent, for her mind
Was busy, looking back into past times.
There's Richard Bateman, thought she to herself,
He was a parish-boy—at the church-door
They made a gathering for him, shillings, pence,   260
And halfpennies, wherewith the neighbours bought
A basket, which they filled with pedlar's wares;
And, with this basket on his arm, the lad
Went up to London, found a master there,
Who, out of many, chose the trusty boy   265
To go and overlook his merchandise
Beyond the seas; where he grew wondrous rich,
And left estates and monies to the poor,
And, at his birth-place, built a chapel floored

233 himself 1827: itself 1800-20   **253** He may return 1836: May come
again 1800-32

With marble, which he sent from foreign lands.   270
These thoughts, and many others of like sort,
Passed quickly through the mind of Isabel,
And her face brightened. The old Man was glad,
And thus resumed:—"Well, Isabel! this scheme
These two days has been meat and drink to me.   275
Far more than we have lost is left us yet.
—We have enough—I wish indeed that I
Were younger;—but this hope is a good hope.
Make ready Luke's best garments, of the best
Buy for him more, and let us send him forth   280
To-morrow, or the next day, or to-night:
—If he *could* go, the Boy should go to-night."

　　Here Michael ceased, and to the fields went forth
With a light heart. The Housewife for five days
Was restless morn and night, and all day long   285
Wrought on with her best fingers to prepare
Things needful for the journey of her son.
But Isabel was glad when Sunday came
To stop her in her work: for, when she lay
By Michael's side, she through the last two nights   290
Heard him, how he was troubled in his sleep:
And when they rose at morning she could see
That all his hopes were gone. That day at noon
She said to Luke, while they two by themselves
Were sitting at the door, "Thou must not go: 295
We have no other Child but thee to lose,
None to remember—do not go away,
For if thou leave thy Father he will die."
The Youth made answer with a jocund voice;
And Isabel, when she had told her fears,   300
Recovered heart. That evening her best fare
Did she bring forth, and all together sat
Like happy people round a Christmas fire.

　　With daylight Isabel resumed her work;
And all the ensuing week the house appeared   305
As cheerful as a grove in Spring: at length
The expected letter from their kinsman came,

282 *could* 1827: could 1800-20　　　299 Youth 1815: Lad 1800-5
304 With daylight 1820: Next morning 1800-15

With kind assurances that he would do
His utmost for the welfare of the Boy;
To which, requests were added, that forthwith   310
He might be sent to him. Ten times or more
The letter was read over; Isabel
Went forth to show it to the neighbours round;
Nor was there at that time on English land
A prouder heart than Luke's. When Isabel   315
Had to her house returned, the old Man said,
"He shall depart to-morrow." To this word
The Housewife answered, talking much of things
Which, if at such short notice he should go,
Would surely be forgotten. But at length   320
She gave consent, and Michael was at ease.

Near the tumultuous brook of Green-head Ghyll,
In that deep valley, Michael had designed
To build a Sheep-fold; and, before he heard
The tidings of his melancholy loss,   325
For this same purpose he had gathered up
A heap of stones, which by the streamlet's edge
Lay thrown together, ready for the work.
With Luke that evening thitherward he walked:
And soon as they had reached the place he stopped,   330
And thus the old Man spake to him:—"My son,
To-morrow thou wilt leave me: with full heart
I look upon thee, for thou art the same
That wert a promise to me ere thy birth,
And all thy life hast been my daily joy.   335
I will relate to thee some little part
Of our two histories; 'twill do thee good
When thou art from me, even if I should touch
On things thou canst not know of.——After thou
First cam'st into the world—as oft befalls   340
To new-born infants—thou didst sleep away
Two days, and blessings from thy Father's tongue
Then fell upon thee. Day by day passed on,
And still I loved thee with increasing love.
Never to living ear came sweeter sounds   345
Than when I heard thee by our own fire-side

327 by the streamlet's edge 1815: close to the brook side 1800-5
338-9 touch On 1836: speak Of 1800-32

First uttering, without words, a natural tune;
While thou, a feeding babe, didst in thy joy
Sing at thy Mother's breast. Month followed month,
And in the open fields my life was passed   350
And on the mountains; else I think that thou
Hadst been brought up upon thy Father's knees.
But we were playmates, Luke: among these hills,
As well thou knowest, in us the old and young
Have played together, nor with me didst thou   355
Lack any pleasure which a boy can know."
Luke had a manly heart; but at these words
He sobbed aloud. The old Man grasped his hand,
And said, "Nay, do not take it so—I see
That these are things of which I need not speak.   360
—Even to the utmost I have been to thee
A kind and a good Father: and herein
I but repay a gift which I myself
Received at others' hands; for, though now old
Beyond the common life of man, I still   365
Remember them who loved me in my youth.
Both of them sleep together: here they lived,
As all their Forefathers had done; and when
At length their time was come, they were not loth
To give their bodies to the family mould.   370
I wished that thou should'st live the life they lived,
But 'tis a long time to look back, my Son,
And see so little gain from threescore years.
These fields were burthened when they came to me;
Till I was forty years of age, not more   375
Than half of my inheritance was mine.
I toiled and toiled; God blessed me in my work,
And till these three weeks past the land was free.
—It looks as if it never could endure
Another Master. Heaven forgive me, Luke,   380
If I judge ill for thee, but it seems good
That thou shouldst go."
                          At this the old Man paused;
Then, pointing to the stones near which they stood,
Thus, after a short silence, he resumed:
"This was a work for us; and now, my Son,   385
It is a work for me. But, lay one stone—
       373 three score 1827: sixty 1800–20

Here, lay it for me, Luke, with thine own hands.
Nay, Boy, be of good hope;—we both may live
To see a better day. At eighty-four
I still am strong and hale;—do thou thy part;   390
I will do mine.—I will begin again
With many tasks that were resigned to thee:
Up to the heights, and in among the storms,
Will I without thee go again, and do
All works which I was wont to do alone,   395
Before I knew thy face.—Heaven bless thee, Boy!
Thy heart these two weeks has been beating fast
With many hopes; it should be so—yes—yes—
I knew that thou couldst never have a wish
To leave me, Luke: thou hast been bound to me   400
Only by links of love: when thou art gone,
What will be left to us!—But I forget
My purposes. Lay now the corner-stone,
As I requested; and hereafter, Luke,
When thou art gone away, should evil men   405
Be thy companions, think of me, my Son,
And of this moment; hither turn thy thoughts,
And God will strengthen thee: amid all fear
And all temptation, Luke, I pray that thou
May'st bear in mind the life thy Fathers lived,   410
Who, being innocent, did for that cause
Bestir them in good deeds. Now, fare thee well—
When thou return'st, thou in this place wilt see
A work which is not here: a covenant
'Twill be between us; but, whatever fate   415
Befall thee, I shall love thee to the last,
And bear thy memory with me to the grave."

      The Shepherd ended here; and Luke stooped down,
    And, as his Father had requested, laid
    The first stone of the Sheep-fold. At the sight   420
    The old Man's grief broke from him; to his heart
    He pressed his Son, he kissèd him and wept;

387/8 I for this purpose brought thee to this place 1800   390 hale
1827: stout 1800–20
406–10 *so* 1802: Be thy companions, let this sheep-fold be
                    Thy anchor and thy shield; amid all fear
                    And all temptation, let it be to thee
                    An emblem of the life *etc.* 1800

And to the house together they returned.
—Hushed was that House in peace, or seeming peace,
Ere the night fell:—with morrow's dawn the Boy   425
Began his journey, and when he had reached
The public way, he put on a bold face;
And all the neighbours, as he passed their doors,
Came forth with wishes and with farewell prayers,
That followed him till he was out of sight.   430

    A good report did from their Kinsman come,
Of Luke and his well-doing: and the Boy
Wrote loving letters, full of wondrous news,
Which, as the Housewife phrased it, were throughout
"The prettiest letters that were ever seen."   435
Both parents read them with rejoicing hearts.
So, many months passed on: and once again
The Shepherd went about his daily work
With confident and cheerful thoughts; and now
Sometimes when he could find a leisure hour   440
He to that valley took his way, and there
Wrought at the Sheep-fold. Meantime Luke began
To slacken in his duty; and, at length,
He in the dissolute city gave himself
To evil courses: ignominy and shame   445
Fell on him, so that he was driven at last
To seek a hiding-place beyond the seas.

    There is a comfort in the strength of love;
'Twill make a thing endurable, which else
Would overset the brain, or break the heart: 450
I have conversed with more than one who well
Remember the old Man, and what he was
Years after he had heard this heavy news.
His bodily frame had been from youth to age
Of an unusual strength. Among the rocks   455
He went, and still looked up to sun and cloud,
And listened to the wind; and, as before,
Performed all kinds of labour for his sheep,
And for the land, his small inheritance.

424–5 *so* 1815: Next morning, as had been resolved, the Boy 1800–5
450 *so* 1820: Would break the heart:—Old Michael found it *so* 1800–15
456 *so* 1836: up upon the sun 1800–27; up towards the sun 1832

And to that hollow dell from time to time   460
Did he repair, to build the Fold of which
His flock had need. 'Tis not forgotten yet
The pity which was then in every heart
For the old Man—and 'tis believed by all
That many and many a day he thither went,   465
And never lifted up a single stone.

  There, by the Sheep-fold, sometimes was he seen
Sitting alone, or with his faithful Dog,
Then old, beside him, lying at his feet.
The length of full seven years, from time to time,   470
He at the building of this Sheep-fold wrought,
And left the work unfinished when he died.
Three years, or little more, did Isabel
Survive her Husband: at her death the estate
Was sold, and went into a stranger's hand.   475
The Cottage which was named the EVENING STAR
Is gone—the ploughshare has been through the ground
On which it stood; great changes have been wrought
In all the neighbourhood:—yet the oak is left
That grew beside their door; and the remains   480
Of the unfinished Sheep-fold may be seen
Beside the boisterous brook of Green-head Ghyll.

XXXIII

THE WIDOW ON WINDERMERE SIDE

[Composed 1837 (?).—Published 1842.]

I

How beautiful when up a lofty height
Honour ascends among the humblest poor,
And feeling sinks as deep! See there the door
Of One, a Widow, left beneath a weight
Of blameless debt. On evil Fortune's spite   5
She wasted no complaint, but strove to make
A just repayment, both for conscience-sake
And that herself and hers should stand upright
In the world's eye. Her work when daylight failed
Paused not, and through the depth of night she kept   10

468 *so* 1836: with that his faithful Dog 1800–32
XXXIII. 3 Ne'er without reverence let me pass the door MS.

Such earnest vigils, that belief prevailed
With some, the noble Creature never slept;
But, one by one, the hand of death assailed
Her children from her inmost heart bewept.

II

The Mother mourned, nor ceased her tears to flow,   15
Till a winter's noon-day placed her buried Son
Before her eyes, last child of many gone—
His raiment of angelic white, and lo!
His very feet bright as the dazzling snow
Which they are touching; yea far brighter, even   20
As that which comes, or seems to come, from heaven,
Surpasses aught these elements can show.
Much she rejoiced, trusting that from that hour
Whate'er befell she could not grieve or pine;
But the Transfigured, in and out of season,   25
Appeared, and spiritual presence gained a power
Over material forms that mastered reason.
Oh, gracious Heaven, in pity make her thine!

III

But why that prayer? as if to her could come
No good but by the way that leads to bliss   30
Through Death,—so judging we should judge amiss.
Since reason failed want is her threatened doom,
Yet frequent transports mitigate the gloom:
Nor of those maniacs is she one that kiss
The air or laugh upon a precipice;   35
No, passing through strange sufferings towards the tomb,
She smiles as if a martyr's crown were won:
Oft, when light breaks through clouds or waving trees,
With outspread arms and fallen upon her knees
The Mother hails in her descending Son   40
An Angel, and in earthly ecstasies
Her own angelic glory seems begun.

14 inmost heart] heart of hearts MS.   17 eyes] sight MS.
23 trusting that] as one who MS.   24 Should not again be doomed to
pine and mourn MS.
26–8   such power
     Over the balances of things that reason
     Fled, nor will ever to her mind return. MS.

XXXIV

THE ARMENIAN LADY'S LOVE

[Composed 1830.—Published 1835.]

[The subject of the following poem is from the Orlandus of the author's
friend, Kenelm Henry Digby: and the liberty is taken of inscribing it
to him as an acknowledgment, however unworthy, of pleasure and
instruction derived from his numerous and valuable writings, illustrative
of the piety and chivalry of the olden time.]

I

You have heard "a Spanish Lady
    How she wooed an English man;"[1]
Hear now of a fair Armenian,
    Daughter of the proud Soldàn;
How she loved a Christian Slave, and told her pain   5
By word, look, deed, with hope that he might love again.

II

"Pluck that rose, it moves my liking,"
    Said she, lifting up her veil;
"Pluck it for me, gentle gardener,
    Ere it wither and grow pale."   10
"Princess fair, I till the ground, but may not take
From twig or bed an humbler flower, even for your sake!"

III

"Grieved am I, submissive Christian!
    To behold thy captive state;
Women, in your land, may pity   15
    (May they not?) the unfortunate."
"Yes, kind Lady! otherwise man could not bear
Life, which to every one that breathes is full of care."

IV

"Worse than idle is compassion
    If it ends in tears and sighs;   20
Thee from bondage would I rescue
    And from vile indignities;
Nurtured, as thy mien bespeaks, in high degree,
Look up—and help a hand that longs to set thee free."

[1] See in Percy's Reliques that fine old ballad, "The Spanish Lady's
Love"; from which Poem the form of stanza, as suitable to dialogue, is
adopted.

XXXIV. 12 an humbler] the meaner MS.: the meanest MS.

V

"Lady! dread the wish, nor venture   25
  In such peril to engage;
Think how it would stir against you
  Your most loving father's rage:
Sad deliverance would it be, and yoked with shame,
Should troubles overflow on her from whom it came."   30

VI

"Generous Frank! the just in effort
  Are of inward peace secure:
Hardships for the brave encountered
  Even the feeblest may endure:
If almighty grace through me thy chains unbind,   35
My father for slave's work may seek a slave in mind."

VII

"Princess, at this burst of goodness,
  My long-frozen heart grows warm!"
"Yet you make all courage fruitless,
  Me to save from chance of harm: 40
Leading such companion I that gilded dome,
Yon minarets, would gladly leave for his worst home."

VIII

"Feeling tunes your voice, fair Princess!
  And your brow is free from scorn,
Else these words would come like mockery,   45
  Sharper than the pointed thorn."
"Whence the undeserved mistrust? Too wide apart
Our faith hath been,—O would that eyes could see the heart!"

34 feeblest] weakest MS.   35 If with your good help thy chains I
may unbind MS.   39 fruitless] useless MS.   42 Yon] These MS.
48/49 "Weak I am and inexperienc'd
         Yet my reason shrinks from trust
         In a law to Man remorseless
         And to womanhood unjust;
         Shape for me a fairer course, which thou canst do
         How readily if to thyself, thyself be true."

         "Embryo of celestial promise
         Heaven that opened out this rose
         By his breath will in due season
         Gently thy sweet bud unclose
         Or by miracle will work." "And is it none
  That I { a Princess thus should please [?] be won?"
         { such boldness have put on, nor thou be won?" *added to* MS., *but del.*

IX

"Tempt me not, I pray; my doom is
   These base implements to wield;   50
Rusty lance, I ne'er shall grasp thee,
   Ne'er assoil my cobwebb'd shield!
Never see my native land, nor castle towers,
Nor Her who thinking of me there counts widowed hours."

X

"Prisoner! pardon youthful fancies,   55
   Wedded? If you *can*, say no!
Blessed is and be your consort;
   Hopes I cherished—let them go!
Handmaid's privilege would leave my purpose free,
Without another link to my felicity."   60

XI

"Wedded love with loyal Christians,
   Lady, is a mystery rare;
Body, heart, and soul in union,
   Make one being of a pair."
"Humble love in me would look for no return,   65
Soft as a guiding star that cheers, but cannot burn."

XII

"Gracious Allah! by such title
   Do I dare to thank the God,
Him who thus exalts thy spirit,
   Flower of an unchristian sod!   70
Or hast thou put off wings which thou in heaven dost wear!
What have I seen, and heard, or dreamt? where am I? where?"

XIII

Here broke off the dangerous converse:
   Less impassioned words might tell
How the pair escaped together,   75
   Tears not wanting, nor a knell
Of sorrow in her heart while through her father's door,
And from her narrow world, she passed for evermore.

77 in . . . through] from . . . from MS.

XIV

But affections higher, holier,
　Urged her steps; she shrunk from trust　　　　　80
In a sensual creed that trampled
　Woman's birthright into dust.
Little be the wonder then, the blame be none,
If she, a timid Maid, hath put such boldness on.

XV

Judge both Fugitives with knowledge:　　　　　85
　In those old romantic days
Mighty were the soul's commandments
　To support, restrain, or raise.
Foes might hang upon their path, snakes rustle near,
But nothing from their inward selves had they to fear.　　90

XVI

Thought infirm ne'er came between them,
　Whether printing desert sands
With accordant steps, or gathering
　Forest-fruit with social hands;
Or whispering like two reeds that in the cold moonbeam　　95
Bend with the breeze their heads, beside a crystal stream.

XVII

On a friendly deck reposing
　They at length for Venice steer;
There, when they had closed their voyage,
　One, who daily on the pier　　　　　100
Watched for tidings from the East, beheld his Lord,
Fell down and clasped his knees for joy, not uttering word.

79–84 *not in one* MS.
81–2 In a creed to man remorseless
　　And to woman hard, unjust　MS.
86 old romantic] unperverted MS.　　　88·To support] Whether to MS.
89 path] track MS.　　94 social] mingled MS.
97–101 Hills they crossed—then broad seas measured
　　Steadily as ship could steer,
　　And while in the port of Venice
　　They were landing on the pier,
　　One, who there for tidings watched, *etc.*　MS.

XVIII

Mutual was the sudden transport;
   Breathless questions followed fast,
Years contracting to a moment,   105
   Each word greedier than the last;
"Hie thee to the Countess, friend! return with speed,
And of this Stranger speak by whom her lord was freed.

XIX

"Say that I, who might have languished,
   Drooped and pined till life was spent,   110
Now before the gates of Stolberg
   My Deliverer would present
For a crowning recompense, the precious grace
Of her who in my heart still holds her ancient place.

XX

"Make it known that my Companion   115
   Is of royal eastern blood,
Thirsting after all perfection,
   Innocent, and meek, and good,
Though with misbelievers bred; but that dark night
Will holy Church disperse by beams of gospel-light."   120

XXI

Swiftly went that grey-haired Servant,
   Soon returned a trusty Page
Charged with greetings, benedictions,
   Thanks and praises, each a gage
For a sunny thought to cheer the Stranger's way,   125
Her virtuous scruples to remove, her fears allay.

XXII

And how blest the Reunited,
   While beneath their castle-walls
Runs a deafening noise of welcome!—
   Blest, though every tear that falls   130
Doth in its silence of past sorrow tell,
And makes a meeting seem most like a dear farewell.

127–32 *so* 1836: Fancy (while, to banners floating
        High on Stolberg's Castle walls,
        Deafening noise of welcome mounted,
        Trumpets, Drums, and Atabals,)
        The devout embraces still, while such tears fell
        As made *etc.* MS., 1835

XXIII

Through a haze of human nature,
   Glorified by heavenly light,
Looked the beautiful Deliverer   135
   On that overpowering sight,
While across her virgin cheek pure blushes strayed,
For every tender sacrifice her heart had made.

XXIV

On the ground the weeping Countess
   Knelt, and kissed the Stranger's hand;   140
Act of soul-devoted homage,
   Pledge of an eternal band:
Nor did aught of future days that kiss belie,
Which, with a generous shout, the crowd did ratify.

XXV

Constant to the fair Armenian,   145
   Gentle pleasures round her moved,
Like a tutelary spirit
   Reverenced, like a sister, loved.
Christian meekness smoothed for all the path of life,
Who, loving most, should wiseliest love, their only strife.   150

XXVI

Mute memento of that union
   In a Saxon church survives,
Where a cross-legged Knight lies sculptured
   As between two wedded Wives—
Figures with armorial signs of race and birth,   155
And the vain rank the pilgrims bore while yet on earth.

140 Knelt] Dropped MS.   149 smoothed] soothed MS.
149–50 Blest by God above all liv'd—a happy life
      Whose rule of heart should wisest be *etc.* MS., *corr. on proof sheet*

XXXV

LOVING AND LIKING
IRREGULAR VERSES
ADDRESSED TO A CHILD
(BY MY SISTER)
[Composed 1832.—Published 1835.]

THERE's more in words than I can teach:
Yet listen, Child!—I would not preach;
But only give some plain directions
To guide your speech and your affections.
Say not you *love* a roasted fowl,   5
But you may love a screaming owl,
And, if you can, the unwieldy toad
That crawls from his secure abode
Within the mossy garden wall
When evening dews begin to fall.   10
Oh! mark the beauty of his eye:
What wonders in that circle lie!
So clear, so bright, our fathers said
He wears a jewel in his head!
And when, upon some showery day,   15
Into a path or public way
A frog leaps out from bordering grass,
Startling the timid as they pass,
Do you observe him, and endeavour
To take the intruder into favour;   20
Learning from him to find a reason
For a light heart in a dull season.
And you may love him in the pool,
That is for him a happy school,
In which he swims as taught by nature,   25
Fit pattern for a human creature,
Glancing amid the water bright,
And sending upward sparkling light.

Nor blush if o'er your heart be stealing
A love for things that have no feeling: 30
The spring's first rose by you espied,
May fill your breast with joyful pride;

XXXV. 26 Fit 1845: A 1835-6

And you may love the strawberry-flower,
And love the strawberry in its bower;
But when the fruit, so often praised   35
For beauty, to your lip is raised,
Say not you *love* the delicate treat,
But *like* it, enjoy it, and thankfully eat.

   Long may you love your pensioner mouse,
Though one of a tribe that torment the house: 40
Nor dislike for her cruel sport the cat,
Deadly foe both of mouse and rat;
Remember she follows the law of her kind,
And Instinct is neither wayward nor blind.
Then think of her beautiful gliding form,   45
Her tread that would scarcely crush a worm,
And her soothing song by the winter fire,
Soft as the dying throb of the lyre.

   I would not circumscribe your love:
It may soar with the eagle and brood with the dove,   50
May pierce the earth with the patient mole,
Or track the hedgehog to his hole.
Loving and liking are the solace of life,
Rock the cradle of joy, smooth the death-bed of strife.
You love your father and your mother,   55
Your grown-up and your baby brother;
You love your sister and your friends,
And countless blessings which God sends:
And while these right affections play,
You *live* each moment of your day;   60
They lead you on to full content,
And likings fresh and innocent,
That store the mind, the memory feed,
And prompt to many a gentle deed:
But *likings* come, and pass away;   65
'Tis *love* that remains till our latest day:
Our heavenward guide is holy love,
And will be our bliss with saints above.

---

42 *so* 1845: That deadly foe of both 1835: both of 1836   46 scarcely
1836: not 1835   54 *so* 1840: They foster all joy, and extinguish all
strife 1835–6   68 will 1845: it will 1835–6

XXXVI

FAREWELL LINES

[Composed 1828 (?).—Published 1842.]

"HIGH bliss is only for a higher state",
But, surely, if severe afflictions borne
With patience merit the reward of peace,
Peace ye deserve; and may the solid good,
Sought by a wise though late exchange, and here   5
With bounteous hand beneath a cottage-roof
To you accorded, never be withdrawn,
Nor for the world's best promises renounced.
Most soothing was it for a welcome Friend,
Fresh from the crowded city, to behold   10
That lonely union, privacy so deep,
Such calm employments, such entire content.
So when the rain is over, the storm laid,
A pair of herons oft-times have I seen,
Upon a rocky islet, side by side,   15
Drying their feathers in the sun, at ease;
And so, when night with grateful gloom had fallen,
Two glow-worms in such nearness that they shared,
As seemed, their soft self-satisfying light,
Each with the other, on the dewy ground,   20
Where He that made them blesses their repose.—
When wandering among lakes and hills I note,
Once more, those creatures thus by nature paired,
And guarded in their tranquil state of life,
Even, as your happy presence to my mind   25
Their union brought, will they repay the debt,
And send a thankful spirit back to you,
With hope that we, dear Friends! shall meet again.

XXXVI. 4–7 may the good which here To you beneath your lowly
cottage roof Has been accorded *etc.* MS.   8 the world's] our life's MS.
10-11 to behold That lonely union] to forget Noise hurry and distraction in
the sight Of lonely Union MS.   14 sometimes may be seen MS.
22–24 When I once more, to lake and hill returned,
       Shall see those creatures thus by Nature paired   MS. (24 *not in* MS.)
25-7 Even as your presence led my thoughts to them
       They in their several haunts, though of such power
       Unconscious, will not fail to pay the debt,
       And mid a thousand images of peace
       Concord and love in Earth or Sky perceived,
       Will send   MS.

XXXVII

THE REDBREAST

(SUGGESTED IN A WESTMORELAND COTTAGE)

[Composed 1834.—Published 1835.]

DRIVEN in by Autumn's sharpening air
From half-stripped woods and pastures bare,
Brisk Robin seeks a kindlier home:
Not like a beggar is he come,
But enters as a looked-for guest,   5
Confiding in his ruddy breast,
As if it were a natural shield
Charged with a blazon on the field,
Due to that good and pious deed
Of which we in the Ballad read.   10
But pensive fancies putting by,
And wild-wood sorrows, speedily
He plays the expert ventriloquist;
And, caught by glimpses now—now missed,
Puzzles the listener with a doubt   15
If the soft voice he throws about
Comes from within doors or without!
Was ever such a sweet confusion,
Sustained by delicate illusion?
He's at your elbow—to your feeling   20
The notes are from the floor or ceiling;
And there's a riddle to be guessed,
Till you have marked his heaving chest,
And busy throat whose sink and swell
Betray the Elf that loves to dwell   25
In Robin's bosom, as a chosen cell.

Heart-pleased we smile upon the Bird
If seen, and with like pleasure stirred
Commend him, when he's only heard.
But small and fugitive our gain   30
Compared with *hers* who long hath lain,
With languid limbs and patient head
Reposing on a lone sick-bed;

XXXVII. 2 half-stripped woods] rustling leaves MS.   23–4 *so* 1836:
Until you've ... breast, Where tiny sinking, and faint swell, 1835   30–1
our ... *hers* 1836: *our ... his* 1835

Where now, she daily hears a strain
That cheats her of too busy cares,   35
Eases her pain, and helps her prayers.
And who but this dear Bird beguiled
The fever of that pale-faced Child;
Now cooling, with his passing wing,
Her forehead, like a breeze of Spring;   40
Recalling now, with descant soft
Shed round her pillow from aloft,
Sweet thoughts of angels hovering nigh,
And the invisible sympathy
Of "Matthew, Mark, and Luke, and John,   45
Blessing the bed she lies upon?' [1]
And sometimes, just as listening ends
In slumber, with the cadence blends
A dream of that low-warbled hymn
Which old folk, fondly pleased to trim   50
Lamps of faith, now burning dim,
Say that the Cherubs carved in stone,
When clouds gave way at dead of night
And the ancient church was filled with light,
Used to sing in heavenly tone,   55
Above and round the sacred places
They guard, with wingèd baby-faces.

Thrice happy Creature! in all lands
Nurtured by hospitable hands:
Free entrance to this cot has he,   60
Entrance and exit both *yet* free;

[1] The words—"Matthew, Mark, and Luke, and John,
              Bless the bed that I lie on,"
are part of a child's prayer, still in general use through the northern
counties.

34–6 she . . . her 1836: he . . . him 1835
39–42 Now cooling, like a breeze of Spring,
        Her cheeks and brow with passing wing
        Recalling, while his descant soft
        Fell on her pillow *etc.*   MS., *First proof*
47–9 Or haply of that earthly hymn MS., *First proof*
53–5 When stricken by a gleam of light
        From the full moon at dead of night
        Used to chant *etc.*   MS., *First proof*
60–1 Free entrance to this humble cot
        He finds, and happy is his lot   MS.

And, when the keen unruffled weather,
That thus brings man and bird together,
Shall with its pleasantness be past,
And casement closed and door made fast,   65
To keep at bay the howling blast,
He needs not fear the season's rage,
For the whole house is Robin's cage.
Whether the bird flit here or there,
O'er table *lilt*, or perch on chair,   70
Though some may frown and make a stir,
To scare him as a trespasser,
And he belike will flinch or start,
Good friends he has to take his part;
One chiefly, who with voice and look   75
Pleads for him from the chimney-nook,
Where sits the Dame, and wears away
Her long and vacant holiday;
With images about her heart,
Reflected from the years gone by,   80
On human nature's second infancy.

XXXVIII

HER EYES ARE WILD

[Composed 1798.—Published 1798.]

I

HER eyes are wild, her head is bare,
The sun has burnt her coal-black hair;
Her eyebrows have a rusty stain,
And she came far from over the main.
She has a baby on her arm,   5
Or else she were alone:
And underneath the hay-stack warm,
And on the greenwood stone,
She talked and sung the woods among,
And it was in the English tongue.   10

62 And when the respite of calm weather MS., *First proof*   64 Shall
like a pleasant dream be past MS., *First proof*   71 If some there be
that MS.: If some should MS., *First proof* 73 And] Though MS., *First
proof*   74 He wants not friends MS.
XXXVIII. HER EYES ARE WILD 1815: THE MAD MOTHER 1798–1805

II

"Sweet babe! they say that I am mad,
But nay, my heart is far too glad;
And I am happy when I sing
Full many a sad and doleful thing:
Then, lovely baby, do not fear!   15
I pray thee have no fear of me;
But safe as in a cradle, here
My lovely baby! thou shalt be:
To thee I know too much I owe;
I cannot work thee any woe.   20

III

"A fire was once within my brain;
And in my head a dull, dull pain;
And fiendish faces, one, two, three,
Hung at my breast, and pulled at me;
But then there came a sight of joy;   25
It came at once to do me good;
I waked, and saw my little boy,
My little boy of flesh and blood;
Oh joy for me that sight to see!
For he was here, and only he.   30

IV

"Suck, little babe, oh suck again!
It cools my blood; it cools my brain;
Thy lips I feel them, baby! they
Draw from my heart the pain away.
Oh! press me with thy little hand;   35
It loosens something at my chest;
About that tight and deadly band
I feel thy little fingers prest.
The breeze I see is in the tree:
It comes to cool my babe and me.   40

V

"Oh! love me, love me, little boy!
Thou art thy mother's only joy;
And do not dread the waves below,
When o'er the sea-rock's edge we go;

24 breast 1820: breasts 1798–1815

The high crag cannot work me harm, 45
Nor leaping torrents when they howl;
The babe I carry on my arm,
He saves for me my precious soul;
Then happy lie; for blest am I;
Without me my sweet babe would die. 50

VI

"Then do not fear, my boy! for thee
Bold as a lion will I be;
And I will always be thy guide,
Through hollow snows and rivers wide.
I'll build an Indian bower; I know 55
The leaves that make the softest bed:
And if from me thou wilt not go,
But still be true till I am dead,
My pretty thing! then thou shalt sing
As merry as the birds in spring. 60

VII

"Thy father cares not for my breast,
'Tis thine, sweet baby, there to rest;
'Tis all thine own!—and if its hue
Be changed, that was so fair to view,
'Tis fair enough for thee, my dove! 65
My beauty, little child, is flown,
But thou wilt live with me in love;
And what if my poor cheek be brown?
'Tis well for me, thou canst not see
How pale and wan it else would be. 70

VIII

"Dread not their taunts, my little Life;
I am thy father's wedded wife;
And underneath the spreading tree
We two will live in honesty.
If his sweet boy he could forsake, 75
With me he never would have stayed:
From him no harm my babe can take;
But he, poor man! is wretched made;
And every day we two will pray
For him that's gone and far away. 80.

52 will I 1832: I will 1798–1827   69 me, 1800: me; 1798

IX

"I'll teach my boy the sweetest things:
I'll teach him how the owlet sings.
My little babe! thy lips are still,
And thou hast almost sucked thy fill.
—Where art thou gone, my own dear child?   85
What wicked looks are those I see?
Alas! alas! that look so wild,
It never, never came from me:
If thou art mad, my pretty lad,
Then I must be for ever sad.   90

X

"Oh! smile on me, my little lamb!
For I thy own dear mother am:
My love for thee has well been tried:
I've sought thy father far and wide.
I know the poisons of the shade;   95
I know the earth-nuts fit for food:
Then, pretty dear, be not afraid:
We'll find thy father in the wood.
Now laugh and be gay, to the woods away!
And there, my babe, we'll live for aye."   100

POEMS ON THE NAMING OF PLACES
ADVERTISEMENT

By persons resident in the country and attached to rural objects, many places will be found unnamed or of unknown names, where little Incidents must have occurred, or feelings been experienced, which will have given to such places a private and peculiar interest. From a wish to give some sort of record to such Incidents, and renew the gratification of such feelings, Names have been given to Places by the Author and some of his Friends, and the following Poems written in consequence.

I

[Composed 1800.—Published 1800.]

It was an April morning: fresh and clear
The Rivulet, delighting in its strength,
Ran with a young man's speed; and yet the voice
Of waters which the winter had supplied
Was softened down into a vernal tone.   5
The spirit of enjoyment and desire,
And hopes and wishes, from all living things
Went circling, like a multitude of sounds.
The budding groves seemed eager to urge on
The steps of June; as if their various hues   10
Were only hindrances that stood between
Them and their object: but, meanwhile, prevailed
Such an entire contentment in the air
That every naked ash, and tardy tree
Yet leafless, showed as if the countenance   15
With which it looked on this delightful day
Were native to the summer.—Up the brook
I roamed in the confusion of my heart,
Alive to all· things and forgetting all.
At length I to a sudden turning came   20
In this continuous glen, where down a rock
The Stream, so ardent in its course before,
Sent forth such sallies of glad sound, that all
Which I till then had heard, appeared the voice

9–13 *so* 1845: The budding groves appear'd as if in haste
          To spur the steps of June: as if their shades
          Of *various* green were hindrances that stood
          Between them and their object: yet, meanwhile
          There was such deep *etc.*   1800–36
15 showed as if 1845: seemed as though 1800–36

Of common pleasure: beast and bird, the lamb,   25
The shepherd's dog, the linnet and the thrush,
Vied with this waterfall, and made a song,
Which, while I listened, seemed like the wild growth
Or like some natural produce of the air,
That could not cease to be. Green leaves were here;   30
But 'twas the foliage of the rocks—the birch,
The yew, the holly, and the bright green thorn,
With hanging islands of resplendent furze:
And, on a summit, distant a short space,
By any who should look beyond the dell,   35
A single mountain-cottage might be seen.
I gazed and gazed, and to myself I said,
"Our thoughts at least are ours; and this wild nook,
My EMMA, I will dedicate to thee."
——Soon did the spot become my other home,   40
My dwelling, and my out-of-doors abode.
And, of the Shepherds who have seen me there,
To whom I sometimes in our idle talk
Have told this fancy, two or three, perhaps,
Years after we are gone and in our graves,   45
When they have cause to speak of this wild place,
May call it by the name of EMMA'S DELL.

II

TO JOANNA

[Composed August, 1800.—Published 1800.]

AMID the smoke of cities did you pass
The time of early youth; and there you learned,
From years of quiet industry, to love
The living Beings by your own fire-side,
With such a strong devotion, that your heart   5
Is slow to meet the sympathies of them
Who look upon the hills with tenderness,
And make dear friendships with the streams and groves.
Yet we, who are transgressors in this kind,
Dwelling retired in our simplicity   10
Among the woods and fields, we love you well,
Joanna! and I guess, since you have been

II. 2 The 1827: Your 1800–20   6 to meet 1836: towards 1800–20:
toward 1827

So distant from us now for two long years,
That you will gladly listen to discourse,
However trivial, if you thence be taught   15
That they, with whom you once were happy, talk
Familiarly of you and of old times.

   While I was seated, now some ten days past,
Beneath those lofty firs, that overtop
Their ancient neighbour, the old steeple-tower,   20
The Vicar from his gloomy house hard by
Came forth to greet me; and, when he had asked,
"How fares Joanna, that wild-hearted Maid!
And when will she return to us?" he paused;
And, after short exchange of village news,   25
He with grave looks demanded, for what cause,
Reviving obsolete idolatry,
I, like a Runic Priest, in characters
Of formidable size had chiselled out
Some uncouth name upon the native rock,   30
Above the Rotha, by the forest-side.
—Now, by those dear immunities of heart
Engendered between malice and true love,
I was not loth to be so catechised,
And this was my reply:—"As it befell,   35
One summer morning we had walked abroad
At break of day, Joanna and myself.
—'Twas that delightful season when the broom,
Full-flowered, and visible on every steep,
Along the copses runs in veins of gold.   40
Our pathway led us on to Rotha's banks;
And when we came in front of that tall rock
That eastward looks, I there stopped short—and stood
Tracing the lofty barrier with my eye
From base to summit; such delight I found   45
To note in shrub and tree, in stone and flower,
That intermixture of delicious hues,
Along so vast a surface, all at once,
In one impression, by connecting force
Of their own beauty, imaged in the heart.   50
—When I had gazed perhaps two minutes' space,

15 be 1836: are 1800–32   33 between 1836: betwixt 1800–32
43–4 so 1836: Which looks towards the East, I there stopp'd short And
trac'd 1800–32

Joanna, looking in my eyes, beheld
That ravishment of mine, and laughed aloud.
The Rock, like something starting from a sleep,
Took up the Lady's voice, and laughed again;   55
That ancient Woman seated on Helm-crag
Was ready with her cavern; Hammar-scar,
And the tall Steep of Silver-how, sent forth
A noise of laughter; southern Loughrigg heard,
And Fairfield answered with a mountain tone: 60
Helvellyn far into the clear blue sky
Carried the Lady's voice,—old Skiddaw blew
His speaking-trumpet;—back out of the clouds
Of Glaramara southward came the voice;
And Kirkstone tossed it from his misty head.   65
—Now whether (said I to our cordial Friend,
Who in the hey-day of astonishment
Smiled in my face) this were in simple truth
A work accomplished by the brotherhood
Of ancient mountains, or my ear was touched   70
With dreams and visionary impulses
To me alone imparted, sure I am
That there was a loud uproar in the hills.
And, while we both were listening, to my side
The fair Joanna drew, as if she wished   75
To shelter from some object of her fear.
—And hence, long afterwards, when eighteen moons
Were wasted, as I chanced to walk alone
Beneath this rock, at sunrise, on a calm
And silent morning, I sat down, and there,   80
In memory of affections old and true,
I chiselled out in those rude characters
Joanna's name deep in the living stone:—
And I, and all who dwell by my fireside,
Have called the lovely rock, JOANNA'S ROCK."   85

NOTE.—In Cumberland and Westmoreland are several Inscriptions, upon the native rock, which, from the wasting of time, and the rudeness of the workmanship, have been mistaken for Runic. They are, without doubt Roman.

The Rotha, mentioned in this poem, is the River which, flowing through the lakes of Grasmere and Rydal, falls into Wynandermere. On Helm-crag that impressive single mountain at the head of the Vale of Grasmere, is a

72 *so* 1827: Is not for me to tell; but 1800–20   83 deep in 1845: upon 1800–36

rock which from most points of view bears a striking resemblance to an old
Woman cowering. Close by this rock is one of those fissures or caverns,
which in the language of the country are called dungeons. Most of the
mountains here mentioned immediately surround the Vale of Grasmere;
of the others, some are at a considerable distance, but they belong to the
same cluster.

III

[Composed 1800.—Published 1800.]

THERE is an Eminence,—of these our hills
The last that parleys with the setting sun;
We can behold it from our orchard seat;
And, when at evening we pursue our walk
Along the public way, this Peak, so high   5
Above us, and so distant in its height,
Is visible; and often seems to send
Its own deep quiet to restore our hearts.
The meteors make of it a favourite haunt:
The star of Jove, so beautiful and large   10
In the mid heavens, is never half so fair
As when he shines above it. 'Tis in truth
The loneliest place we have among the clouds.
And She who dwells with me, whom I have loved
With such communion, that no place on earth   15
Can ever be a solitude to me,
Hath to this lonely Summit given my Name.

IV

[Composed October 10, 1800.—Published 1800.]

A NARROW girdle of rough stones and crags,
A rude and natural causeway, interposed
Between the water and a winding slope
Of copse and thicket, leaves the eastern shore
Of Grasmere safe in its own privacy: 5
And there myself and two beloved Friends,
One calm September morning, ere the mist
Had altogether yielded to the sun,
Sauntered on this retired and difficult way.
——Ill suits the road with one in haste; but we   10
Played with our time; and, as we strolled along,

III. 5 Peak 1840: Cliff 1800–36   17 *so* 1815: Hath said, this lonesome
Peak shall bear my name 1800–5

It was our occupation to observe
Such objects as the waves had tossed ashore—
Feather, or leaf, or weed, or withered bough,
Each on the other heaped, along the line   15
Of the dry wreck. And, in our vacant mood,
Not seldom did we stop to watch some tuft
Of dandelion seed or thistle's beard,
That skimmed the surface of the dead calm lake,
Suddenly halting now—a lifeless stand!   20
And starting off again with freak as sudden;
In all its sportive wanderings, all the while,
Making report of an invisible breeze
That was its wings, its chariot, and its horse,
Its playmate, rather say, its moving soul.   25
——And often, trifling with a privilege
Alike indulged to all, we paused, one now,
And now the other, to point out, perchance
To pluck, some flower or water-weed, too fair
Either to be divided from the place   30
On which it grew, or to be left alone
To its own beauty. Many such there are,
Fair ferns and flowers, and chiefly that tall fern,
So stately, of the Queen Osmunda named;
Plant lovelier, in its own retired abode   35
On Grasmere's beach, than Naiad by the side
Of Grecian brook, or Lady of the Mere,
Sole-sitting by the shores of old romance.
—So fared we that bright morning: from the fields,
Meanwhile, a noise was heard, the busy mirth   40
Of reapers, men and women, boys and girls.
Delighted much to listen to those sounds,
And feeding thus our fancies, we advanced
Along the indented shore; when suddenly,

IV. 19–21 *so* 1815: Which, seeming lifeless half, and half impell'd
                    By some internal feeling, skimm'd along
                    Close to the surface of the lake that lay
                    Asleep in a dead calm, ran closely on
                    Along the dead calm lake, now here, now there,
                    1800–5
25 *so* 1820: Its very playmate and 1800–15
33 fern 1802: plant 1800   39 bright 1827: sweet 1800–20
43 *so* 1820: And in the fashion which I have described
             Feeding unthinking fancies, we advanc'd   1800–15

Through a thin veil of glittering haze was seen   45
Before us, on a point of jutting land,
The tall and upright figure of a Man
Attired in peasant's garb, who stood alone,
Angling beside the margin of the lake.
"Improvident and reckless," we exclaimed,   50
"The Man must be, who thus can lose a day
Of the mid harvest, when the labourer's hire
Is ample, and some little might be stored
Wherewith to cheer him in the winter time."
Thus talking of that Peasant, we approached   55
Close to the spot where with his rod and line
He stood alone; whereat he turned his head
To greet us—and we saw a Man worn down
By sickness, gaunt and lean, with sunken cheeks
And wasted limbs, his legs so long and lean   60
That for my single self I looked at them,
Forgetful of the body they sustained.—
Too weak to labour in the harvest field,
The Man was using his best skill to gain
A pittance from the dead unfeeling lake   65
That knew not of his wants. I will not say
What thoughts immediately were ours, nor how
The happy idleness of that sweet morn,
With all its lovely images, was changed
To serious musing and to self-reproach.   70
Nor did we fail to see within ourselves
What need there is to be reserved in speech,
And temper all our thoughts with charity.
—Therefore, unwilling to forget that day,
My Friend, Myself, and She who then received   75
The same admonishment, have called the place
By a memorial name, uncouth indeed
As e'er by mariner was given to bay
Or foreland, on a new-discovered coast;
And POINT RASH-JUDGMENT is the Name it bears.   80

45 was seen 1827: we saw 1800–20
50–1 *so* 1827: That way we turn'd our steps; nor was it long
        Ere, making ready comments on the sight
        Which then we saw, with one and the same voice
        We all cried out, that he must be indeed (Did all cry 1815–20)
        An idle man, who thus could lose a day 1800–5 (An idler
            he who 1815–20)

V

TO M. H.

[Composed after December 21, and before December 28, 1799.—Published 1800.]

OUR walk was far among the ancient trees:
There was no road, nor any woodman's path;
But a thick umbrage—checking the wild growth
Of weed and sapling, along soft green turf
Beneath the branches—of itself had made   5
A track, that brought us to a slip of lawn,
And a small bed of water in the woods.
All round this pool both flocks and herds might drink
On its firm margin, even as from a well,
Or some stone-basin which the herdsman's hand   10
Had shaped for their refreshment; nor did sun,
Or wind from any quarter, ever come,
But as a blessing to this calm recess,
This glade of water and this one green field.
The spot was made by Nature for herself;   15
The travellers know it not, and 'twill remain
Unknown to them; but it is beautiful;
And if a man should plant his cottage near,
Should sleep beneath the shelter of its trees,
And blend its waters with his daily meal,   20
He would so love it, that in his death-hour
Its image would survive among his thoughts:
And therefore, my sweet MARY, this still Nook,
With all its beeches, we have named from You!

VI

[Begun August 29, 30, 1800.—Finished 1802.—Published 1815.]

WHEN, to the attractions of the busy world
Preferring studious leisure, I had chosen
A habitation in this peaceful Vale,
Sharp season followed of continual storm
In deepest winter; and, from week to week,   5
Pathway, and lane, and public road, were clogged

24 beeches] poplars MS. (K)   from 1800, 1815: for 1802–5
VI. 1–6 When first I journey'd hither to a home
    And dwelling of my own, it was a cold
    Tempestuous [And stormy] season, and from week to week,
    The pathways of the public roads were clogg'd   MSS.

With frequent showers of snow. Upon a hill,
At a short distance from my cottage, stands
A stately Fir-grove, whither I was wont
To hasten, for I found, beneath the roof 10
Of that perennial shade, a cloistral place
Of refuge, with an unincumbered floor.
Here, in safe covert, on the shallow snow,
And, sometimes, on a speck of visible earth,
The redbreast near me hopped; nor was I loth 15
To sympathize with vulgar coppice birds
That, for protection from the nipping blast,
Hither repaired.—A single beech-tree grew
Within this grove of firs! and, on the fork
Of that one beech, appeared a thrush's nest; 20
A last year's nest, conspicuously built
At such small elevation from the ground
As gave sure sign that they, who in that house
Of nature and of love had made their home
Amid the fir-trees, all the summer long 25
Dwelt in a tranquil spot. And oftentimes
A few sheep, stragglers from some mountain-flock,
Would watch my motions with suspicious stare,
From the remotest outskirts of the grove,—
Some nook where they had made their final stand, 30
Huddling together from two fears—the fear
Of me and of the storm. Full many an hour
Here did I lose. But in this grove the trees
Had been so thickly planted, and had thriven
In such perplexed and intricate array, 35
That vainly did I seek, beneath their stems,
A length of open space, where to and fro

10–12   for within its shade I found
commodious harbour, a sequestered nook
A cloister with an unencumber'd floor   MSS.
17–18 That . . . repaired] That hither come   MSS.
22/23 That even an unbreech'd boy might look into it   MSS.
23 And I have guess'd } MSS.
   Sure sign, I thought }
26 tranquil spot] quiet place   MSS.   27–8 of a scatter'd flock Were
my companions and would stare [look] at me   MSS.
33–46 Here did I lose, if hours be lost that we
      Give to ourselves. But in this grove the trees
      Had by the planter been so crowded each
      Upon the other, and withal had thriven

My feet might move without concern or care;
And, baffled thus, though earth from day to day
Was fettered, and the air by storm disturbed,   40
I ceased the shelter to frequent,—and prized,
Less than I wished to prize, that calm recess.

   The snows dissolved, and genial Spring returned
To clothe the fields with verdure. Other haunts
Meanwhile were mine; till one bright April day,   45
By chance retiring from the glare of noon
To this forsaken covert, there I found
A hoary pathway traced between the trees,
And winding on with such an easy line
Along a natural opening, that I stood   50
Much wondering how I could have sought in vain
For what was now so obvious. To abide,

In such perplex'd array, that I in vain
Between their stems endeavour'd to find out
A length of open space where I might walk
With back and forward steps, each following each, ⎫
Backwards and forwards, long as I had liking,   ⎭
In easy and mechanic thoughtlessness.
And, for this cause, I loved that shady grove
Less than I wished to love a place so sweet.
   I have a Brother—many times the leaves
Have faded, many times the Spring has touch'd
The heart of bird and beast, since from the shores
Of Windermere, from Esthwaite's chearful lake
And her grey cottages, from all the life
And beauty of his native hills he went
To be a sea boy on the barren seas.
When we had been divided fourteen years
At length he came to sojourn a short while
Beneath my roof, nor had the Sun twice set
Before he made discovery of the grove
Whither from that time forward he repaired
With daily visitation. Other haunts
Meanwhile were mine, but from the sultry heat
One morning chancing to betake myself   MSS.

39-40 *so* 1836: And baffled thus, before the Storm relaxed, *etc.* 1815-32
51-66 Much wondering of my own simplicity
How I myself had ever failed in search
Of what was now so obvious—with a sense
Of lively joy did I behold this path
Beneath the fir-trees, for at once I knew
That by the seaman's [my Brother's] steps it had been traced.
My thoughts were pleased within me to perceive

For an allotted interval of ease,
Under my cottage-roof, had gladly come
From the wild sea a cherished Visitant;   55
And with the sight of this same path—begun,
Begun and ended, in the shady grove,
Pleasant conviction flashed upon my mind
That, to this opportune recess allured,
He had surveyed it with a finer eye,   60
A heart more wakeful; and had worn the track
By pacing here, unwearied and alone,
In that habitual restlessness of foot
That haunts the Sailor measuring o'er and o'er
His short domain upon the vessel's deck,   65
While she pursues her course through the dreary sea.

When thou hadst quitted Esthwaite's pleasant shore,
And taken thy first leave of those green hills
And rocks that were the play-ground of thy youth,

That hither he had brought a finer eye
A heart more wakeful, that more loth to part
From place so lovely he had worn the track
One of his own deep paths! by pacing here,
In that habitual restlessness of foot
Wherewith the Sailor measures o'er and o'er
His short domain upon the vessel's deck
While she is travelling through the dreary seas. MS. 1, *so* MS. 2, *but
omitting* One of his own *etc.* (5 ll. *from end*) *and reading in next line*
By *for* In
51–61 *so* 1827: *but* 54 Beneath *for* Under (1845) *and* newly *for* gladly 1840
Much wondering at my own simplicity
How I could e'er have made a fruitless search
For what was now so obvious. At the sight
Conviction also flashed upon my mind
That this same path (within the shady grove
Begun and ended) by my Brother's steps
Had been impressed.—To sojourn a short while
Beneath my roof He from the barren seas
Had newly come—a cherished Visitant!
And much did it delight me to perceive
That, to this opportune recess allured,
He had surveyed it with a finer eye,
A heart more wakeful; that, more loth to part
From place so lovely, he had worn the track   1815
64–6 *so* 1845: 1815–36 *as* MS.
67–9 When thou hadst gone away from Esthwaite's shore *etc. as text* MS. 1
When thou hadst gone away from these green hills
And rocks   MS. 2

Year followed year, my Brother! and we two, 70
Conversing not, knew little in what mould
Each other's mind was fashioned; and at length,
When once again we met in Grasmere Vale,
Between us there was little other bond
Than common feelings of fraternal love. 75
But thou, a School-boy, to the sea hadst carried
Undying recollections; Nature there
Was with thee; she, who loved us both, she still
Was with thee; and even so didst thou become
A *silent* Poet; from the solitude 80
Of the vast sea didst bring a watchful heart
Still couchant, an inevitable ear,
And an eye practised like a blind man's touch.
—Back to the joyless Ocean thou art gone;
Nor from this vestige of thy musing hours 85
Could I withhold thy honoured name,—and now
I love the fir-grove with a perfect love.
Thither do I withdraw when cloudless suns
Shine hot, or wind blows troublesome and strong;
And there I sit at evening, when the steep 90
Of Silver-how, and Grasmere's peaceful lake,
And one green island, gleam between the stems
Of the dark firs, a visionary scene!
And while I gaze upon the spectacle
Of clouded splendour, on this dream-like sight 95
Of solemn loveliness, I think on thee,
My Brother, and on all which thou hast lost.
Nor seldom, if I rightly guess, while Thou,
Muttering the verses which I muttered first
Among the mountains, through the midnight watch 100
Art pacing thoughtfully the vessel's deck
In some far region, here, while o'er my head,
At every impulse of the moving breeze,
The fir-grove murmurs with a sea-like sound,
Alone I tread this path;—for aught I know, 105
Timing my steps to thine; and, with a store
Of undistinguishable sympathies,

85–7 And now I call the pathway by thy name
      And love *etc.*   MSS.
88 withdraw] repair MSS.   91 peaceful] silent MSS.   93 dark]
close MSS.   101 thoughtfully] to and fro MSS.

Mingling most earnest wishes for the day
When we, and others whom we love, shall meet
A second time, in Grasmere's happy Vale.   110

NOTE.—This wish was not granted; the lamented Person not long after
perished by shipwreck, in discharge of his duty as Commander of the
Honourable East India Company's Vessel, the Earl of Abergavenny.

VII
[Composed 1845.—Published 1845.]

FORTH from a jutting ridge, around whose base
Winds our deep Vale, two heath-clad Rocks ascend
In fellowship, the loftiest of the pair
Rising to no ambitious height; yet both,
O'er lake and stream, mountain and flowery mead,   5
Unfolding prospects fair as human eyes
Ever beheld. Up-led with mutual help,
To one or other brow of those twin Peaks
Were two adventurous Sisters wont to climb,
And took no note of the hour while thence they gazed,   10
The blooming heath their couch, gazed, side by side,
In speechless admiration. I, a witness
And frequent sharer of their calm delight
With thankful heart, to either Eminence
Gave the baptismal name each Sister bore.   15
Now are they parted, far as Death's cold hand
Hath power to part the Spirits of those who love
As they did love. Ye kindred Pinnacles—
That, while the generations of mankind
Follow each other to their hiding-place   20
In time's abyss, are privileged to endure
Beautiful in yourselves, and richly graced
With like command of beauty—grant your aid
For MARY's humble, SARAH's silent claim,
That their pure joy in nature may survive   25
From age to age in blended memory.

POEMS OF THE FANCY

I

A MORNING EXERCISE

[Composed 1828.—Published 1832.]

FANCY, who leads the pastimes of the glad,
Full oft is pleased a wayward dart to throw;
Sending sad shadows after things not sad,
Peopling the harmless fields with signs of woe:
Beneath her sway, a simple forest cry   5
Becomes an echo of man's misery.

Blithe ravens croak of death; and when the owl
Tries his two voices for a favourite strain—
Tu-whit—Tu-whoo! the unsuspecting fowl
Forebodes mishap or seems but to complain;   10
Fancy, intent to harass and annoy,
Can thus pervert the evidence of joy.

Through border wilds where naked Indians stray,
Myriads of notes attest her subtle skill;
A feathered task-master cries, "WORK AWAY!"   15
And in thy iteration, "WHIP POOR WILL!"[1]
Is heard the spirit of a toil-worn slave,
Lashed out of life, not quiet in the grave.

What wonder? at her bidding, ancient lays
Steeped in dire grief the voice of Philomel;   20
And that fleet messenger of summer days,
The Swallow, twittered subject to like spell;
But ne'er could Fancy bend the buoyant Lark
To melancholy service—hark! O hark!

The daisy sleeps upon the dewy lawn,   25
Not lifting yet the head that evening bowed;
But *He* is risen, a later star of dawn,
Glittering and twinkling near yon rosy cloud;
Bright gem instinct with music, vocal spark;
The happiest bird that sprang out of the Ark!   30

[1] See Waterton's "Wanderings in South America".

20 grief 1836: griefs 1832

Hail, blest above all kinds!—Supremely skilled
Restless with fixed to balance, high with low,
Thou leav'st the halcyon free her hopes to build
On such forbearance as the deep may show;
Perpetual flight, unchecked by earthly ties,   35
Leav'st to the wandering bird of paradise.

Faithful, though swift as lightning, the meek dove;
Yet more hath Nature reconciled in thee;
So constant with thy downward eye of love,
Yet, in aërial singleness, so free;   40
So humble, yet so ready to rejoice
In power of wing and never-wearied voice.

To the last point of vision, and beyond,
Mount, daring warbler!—that love-prompted strain,
('Twixt thee and thine a never-failing bond),   45
Thrills not the less the bosom of the plain:
Yet might'st thou seem, proud privilege! to sing
All independent of the leafy spring.

How would it please old Ocean to partake,
With sailors longing for a breeze in vain,   50
The harmony thy notes most gladly make
Where earth resembles most his own domain!
Urania's self might welcome with pleased ear
These matins mounting towards her native sphere.

Chanter by heaven attracted, whom no bars   55
To daylight known deter from that pursuit,
'Tis well that some sage instinct, when the stars
Come forth at evening, keeps Thee still and mute;
For not an eyelid could to sleep incline
Wert thou among them, singing as they shine!   60

43–8 *so* 1845: *before that date the stanza was a part of* To a Skylark
("Ethereal Minstrel"), *between stanzas* 1 *and* 2   51 *so* 1836: **that thou
best lovest to make** 1832   52 **own** 1836: blank 1832

II

A FLOWER GARDEN

AT COLEORTON HALL, LEICESTERSHIRE.

[Composed 1824.—Published 1827.]

TELL me, ye Zephyrs! that unfold,
While fluttering o'er this gay Recess,
Pinions that fanned the teeming mould
Of Eden's blissful wilderness,
Did only softly-stealing hours   5
There close the peaceful lives of flowers?

Say, when the *moving* creatures saw
All kinds commingled without fear,
Prevailed a like indulgent law
For the still growths that prosper here?   10
Did wanton fawn and kid forbear
The half-blown rose, the lily spare?

Or peeped they often from their beds
And prematurely disappeared,
Devoured like pleasure ere it spreads   15
A bosom to the sun endeared?
If such their harsh untimely doom,
It falls not *here* on bud or bloom.

All summer-long the happy Eve
Of this fair Spot her flowers may bind,   20
Nor e'er, with ruffled fancy, grieve,
From the next glance she casts, to find
That love for little things by Fate
Is rendered vain as love for great.

Yet, where the guardian fence is wound,   25
So subtly are our eyes beguiled,
We see not nor suspect a bound,
No more than in some forest wild;
The sight is free as air—or crost
Only by art in nature lost.   30

II. *subtitle added* 1836   26-7 *so* 1836: is the eye . . . It sees . . . sus-
pects 1827-32   29 *so* 1836: Free as the light in semblance—crost
1827-32

And, though the jealous turf refuse
By random footsteps to be prest,
And feed on never-sullied dews,
Ye, gentle breezes from the west,
With all the ministers of hope   35
Are tempted to this sunny slope!

And hither throngs of birds resort;
Some, inmates lodged in shady nests,
Some, perched on stems of stately port
That nod to welcome transient guests;   40
While hare and leveret, seen at play,
Appear not more shut out than they.

Apt emblem (for reproof of pride)
This delicate Enclosure shows
Of modest kindness, that would hide   45
The firm protection she bestows;
Of manners, like its viewless fence,
Ensuring peace to innocence.

Thus spake the moral Muse—her wing
Abruptly spreading to depart,   50
She left that farewell offering,
Memento for some docile heart;
That may respect the good old age
When Fancy was Truth's willing Page;
And Truth would skim the flowery glade,   55
Though entering but as Fancy's Shade.

III

[Composed March 18, 1798.—Published 1800.]

A WHIRL-BLAST from behind the hill
Rushed o'er the wood with startling sound;
Then—all at once the air was still,
And showers of hailstones pattered round.
Where leafless oaks towered high above,   5
I sat within an undergrove

III. 1 A whirl-blast] The wind sent MS.   2 startling] rushing MS.

Of tallest hollies, tall and green;
A fairer bower was never seen.
From year to year the spacious floor
With withered leaves is covered o'er,   10
And all the year the bower is green.
But see! where'er the hailstones drop
The withered leaves all skip and hop;
There's not a breeze—no breath of air—
Yet here, and there, and every where
Along the floor, beneath the shade   15
By those embowering hollies made,
The leaves in myriads jump and spring,
As if with pipes and music rare
Some Robin Good-fellow were there,
And all those leaves, in festive glee,   20
Were dancing to the minstrelsy.

IV

THE WATERFALL AND THE EGLANTINE

[Composed 1800.—Published 1800.]

I

"BEGONE, thou fond presumptuous Elf,"
Exclaimed an angry Voice,
"Nor dare to thrust thy foolish self
Between me and my choice!"

10/11 You could not lay a hair between MS. 1800–15   11 And all
the] From year to MS.   12 See where the heavy hailstones drop MS.
13 all] they MS.   14 a breeze—no breath] single breeze of MS.
16–22 Along the smooth and spatious floor
      Beneath the thick and verdant bower
      The withered leaves jump up and spring
      As if each were a living thing.
      This long description why indite?
      Because it was a pleasant sight.   MS.
21–2 *so* 1815: And all the leaves, that jump and spring,
           Were each a joyous living thing. 1800–5. *After* 22 1800–5
                add:
      Oh! grant me Heaven a heart at ease,
      That I may never cease to find,
      Even in appearances like these,
      Enough to nourish and to stir my mind!
IV. 2 an angry *so* 1836: a thundering 1800–32

A small Cascade fresh swoln with snows   5
Thus threatened a poor Briar-rose,
That, all bespattered with his foam,
And dancing high and dancing low,
Was living, as a child might know,
In an unhappy home.   10

II

"Dost thou presume my course to block?
Off, off! or, puny Thing!
I'll hurl thee headlong with the rock
To which thy fibres cling."
The Flood was tyrannous and strong;   15
The patient Briar suffered long,
Nor did he utter groan or sigh,
Hoping the danger would be past;
But, seeing no relief, at last,
He ventured to reply.   20

III

"Ah!" said the Briar, "blame me not;
Why should we dwell in strife?
We who in this sequestered spot
Once lived a happy life!
You stirred me on my rocky bed—   25
What pleasure through my veins you spread
The summer long, from day to day,
My leaves you freshened and bedewed;
Nor was it common gratitude
That did your cares repay.   30

IV

"When spring came on with bud and bell,
Among these rocks did I
Before you hang my wreaths to tell
That gentle days were nigh!
And in the sultry summer hours,   35
I sheltered you with leaves and flowers;
And in my leaves—now shed and gone,
The linnet lodged, and for us two
Chanted his pretty songs, when you
Had little voice or none.   40

5-6 *so* 1820: A falling Water ... Thus spake to 1800-15   23 sequestered
1820: natal 1800-15

V

"But now proud thoughts are in your breast—
What grief is mine you see,
Ah! would you think, even yet how blest
Together we might be!
Though of both leaf and flower bereft,   45
Some ornaments to me are left—
Rich store of scarlet hips is mine,
With which I, in my humble way,
Would deck you many a winter day,
A happy Eglantine!"   50

VI

What more he said I cannot tell,
The Torrent down the rocky dell
Came thundering loud and fast;
I listened, nor aught else could hear;
The Briar quaked—and much I fear   55
Those accents were his last.

V

THE OAK AND THE BROOM

A PASTORAL

[Composed 1800.—Published 1800.]

I

His simple truths did Andrew glean
Beside the babbling rills;
A careful student he had been
Among the woods and hills.
One winter's night, when through the trees   5
The wind was roaring, on his knees
His youngest born did Andrew hold:
And while the rest, a ruddy quire,
Were seated round their blazing fire,
This Tale the Shepherd told.   10

52–3 *so* 1840: The stream came thundering down the dell And gallop'd *etc.*
1800; The Torrent thundered... With unabating haste 1815–20. . . . With
aggravated haste 1827–32; 1836 *has* l. 52 *as* 1800, 53 *as* 1832
V. 6 roaring 1820: thundering 1800–15

II

"I saw a crag, a lofty stone
As ever tempest beat!
Out of its head an Oak had grown,
A Broom out of its feet.
The time was March, a cheerful noon—   15
The thaw-wind, with the breath of June,
Breathed gently from the warm south-west:
When, in a voice sedate with age,
This Oak, a giant and a sage,
His neighbour thus addressed:—   20

III

" 'Eight weary weeks, through rock and clay,
Along this mountain's edge,
The Frost hath wrought both night and day,
Wedge driving after wedge.
Look up! and think, above your head   25
What trouble, surely, will be bred;
Last night I heard a crash—'tis true,
The splinters took another road—
I see them yonder—what a load
For such a Thing as you!   30

IV

" 'You are preparing as before,
To deck your slender shape;
And yet, just three years back—no more—
You had a strange escape:
Down from yon cliff a fragment broke;   35
It thundered down, with fire and smoke,
And hitherward pursued its way;
This ponderous block was caught by me,
And o'er your head, as you may see,
'Tis hanging to this day!   40

19 *so* 1815: half giant and half sage 1800–5   36 *so* 1820: It came,
you know, 1800–15   37 *so* 1820: hither did it bend 1800; hitherward
it bent 1802–15

V

"'If breeze or bird to this rough steep
Your kind's first seed did bear;
The breeze had better been asleep,
The bird caught in a snare:
For you and your green twigs decoy   45
The little witless shepherd-boy
To come and slumber in your bower;
And trust me, on some sultry noon,
Both you and he, Heaven knows how soon!
Will perish in one hour.   50

VI

"'From me this friendly warning take'—
The Broom began to doze,
And thus, to keep herself awake,
Did gently interpose:
'My thanks for your discourse are due;   55
That more than what you say is true,
I know, and I have known it long;
Frail is the bond by which we hold
Our being, whether young or old,
Wise, foolish, weak, or strong.   60

VII

"'Disasters, do the best we can,
Will reach both great and small;
And he is oft the wisest man,
Who is not wise at all.
For me, why should I wish to roam?   65
This spot is my paternal home,
It is my pleasant heritage;
My father many a happy year
Spread here his careless blossoms, here
Attained a good old age.   70

41–4 *so* 1836: The Thing had better been asleep,
                 Whatever thing it were,
                 Or Breeze, or Bird, or Dog, or Sheep,
                   That first did plant you there. 1802–32. *So* 1800 *but* fleece of
                     for Dog or
56 *so* 1820: That it is true, and more than true, 1800–15   59 whether
1827; be we 1800–20

VIII

"'Even such as his may be my lot.
What cause have I to haunt
My heart with terrors ? Am I not
In truth a favoured plant!
On me such bounty Summer pours,   75
That I am covered o'er with flowers;
And, when the Frost is in the sky,
My branches are so fresh and gay
That you might look at me and say,
This Plant can never die.   80

IX

"'The butterfly, all green and gold,
To me hath often flown,
Here in my blossoms to behold
Wings lovely as his own.
When grass is chill with rain or dew,   85
Beneath my shade, the mother-ewe
Lies with her infant lamb; I see
The love they to each other make,
And the sweet joy which they partake,
It is a joy to me.'   90

X

"Her voice was blithe, her heart was light;
The Broom might have pursued
Her speech, until the stars of night
Their journey had renewed;
But in the branches of the oak   95
Two ravens now began to croak
Their nuptial song, a gladsome air;
And to her own green bower the breeze
That instant brought two stripling bees
To rest, or murmur there.   100

XI

"One night, my Children! from the north
There came a furious blast;
At break of day I ventured forth,
And near the cliff I passed.

75–6 *so* 1815: The Spring for me a garland weaves
          Of yellow flowers and verdant leaves   1800–5
100 rest, or 1820: feed and 1800–5: rest and 1815   101–2 *so* 1815:
One night the Wind came from the North And blew 1800–5

The storm had fallen upon the Oak,   105
And struck him with a mighty stroke,
And whirled, and whirled him far away;
And, in one hospitable cleft,
The little careless Broom was left
To live for many a day."   110

VI

TO A SEXTON

[Composed 1799.—Published 1800.]

LET thy wheel-barrow alone—
Wherefore, Sexton, piling still
In thy bone-house bone on bone?
'Tis already like a hill
In a field of battle made,   5
Where three thousand skulls are laid;
These died in peace each with the other,—
Father, sister, friend, and brother.

Mark the spot to which I point!
From this platform, eight feet square   10
Take not even a finger-joint:
Andrew's whole fire-side is there.
Here, alone, before thine eyes,
Simon's sickly daughter lies,
From weakness now, and pain defended,   15
Whom he twenty winters tended.

Look but at the gardener's pride—
How he glories, when he sees
Roses, lilies, side by side,
Violets in families!   20
By the heart of Man, his tears,
By his hopes and by his fears,
Thou, too heedless, art the Warden
Of a far superior garden.

Thus then, each to other dear,   25
Let them all in quiet lie,
Andrew there, and Susan here,
Neighbours in mortality.

VI. 23 too heedless, 1845: old Grey-beard! 1800–36

And should I live through sun and rain
Seven widowed years without my Jane,   30
O Sexton, do not then remove her,
Let one grave hold the Loved and Lover!

VII

TO THE DAISY

[Composed 1802.—Published 1807.]

"Her[1] divine skill taught me this,
That from every thing I saw
I could some instruction draw,
And raise pleasure to the height
Through the meanest object's sight.
By the murmur of a spring,
Or the least bough's rustelling;
By a Daisy whose leaves spread
Shut when Titan goes to bed;
Or a shady bush or tree;
She could more infuse in me
Than all Nature's beauties can
In some other wiser man."   G. WITHER.

In youth from rock to rock I went,
From hill to hill in discontent
Of pleasure high and turbulent,
    Most pleased when most uneasy;
But now my own delights I make,—   5
My thirst at every rill can slake,
And gladly Nature's love partake
    Of Thee, sweet Daisy!

Thee Winter in the garland wears
That thinly decks his few grey hairs;   10
Spring parts the clouds with softest airs,
    That she may sun thee;

_____
[1] His Muse.

VII. *Quotation from Wither first prefixed* 1815   6 To gentle sympathies
awake, MS.   7–8 *so* 1807–32, 1840: And Nature's love of thee partake,
Her much loved 1836
9–12 *so* 1836: When soothed a while by milder airs,
            Thee Winter in the garland wears
            That thinly shades his few grey hairs;
                Spring cannot shun thee;   1807–20
        When e'er a milder day appears *etc. as* 1807, MS.

        When Winter decks his few grey hairs
        Thee in the scanty wreath he wears;
        Spring parts the clouds with softest airs,
            That she may sun thee;   1827–32

Whole Summer-fields are thine by right;
And Autumn, melancholy Wight!
Doth in thy crimson head delight   15
    When rains are on thee.

In shoals and bands, a morrice train,
Thou greet'st the traveller in the lane;
Pleased at his greeting thee again;
    Yet nothing daunted,   20
Nor grieved if thou be set at nought:
And oft alone in nooks remote
We meet thee, like a pleasant thought,
    When such are wanted.

Be violets in their secret mews   25
The flowers the wanton Zephyrs choose;
Proud be the rose, with rains and dews
    Her head impearling,
Thou liv'st with less ambitious aim,
Yet hast not gone without thy fame;   30
Thou art indeed by many a claim
    The Poet's darling.

If to a rock from rains he fly,
Or, some bright day of April sky,
Imprisoned by hot sunshine lie   35
    Near the green holly,
And wearily at length should fare;
He needs but look about, and there
Thou art!—a friend at hand, to scare
    His melancholy.   40

A hundred times, by rock or bower,
Ere thus I have lain couched an hour,
Have I derived from thy sweet power
    Some apprehension;
Some steady love; some brief delight;   45
Some memory that had taken flight;
Some chime of fancy wrong or right;
    Or stray invention.

19–20 *so* 1836: If welcome (welcom'd 1815–20) once thou count'st it gain
       Thou art not daunted MS., 1807–32
21 grieved 1836: car'st MS., 1807–32   24/5 MS. *here has* VIII. 33–40
29–31 Thou liv'st to follow humbler aims Yet shall not want thy tender
names . . . many claims MS.   41 A thousand times in *etc.* MS.   45
brief] chance MS.

If stately passions in me burn,
And one chance look to Thee should turn,   50
I drink out of an humbler urn
   A lowlier pleasure;
The homely sympathy that heeds
The common life our nature breeds;
A wisdom fitted to the needs   55
   Of hearts at leisure.

Fresh-smitten by the morning ray,
When thou art up, alert and gay,
Then, cheerful Flower! my spirits play
   With kindred gladness: 60
And when, at dusk, by dews opprest
Thou sink'st, the image of thy rest
Hath often eased my pensive breast
   Of careful sadness.

And all day long I number yet,   65
All seasons through, another debt,
Which I, wherever thou art met,
   To thee am owing;
An instinct call it, a blind sense;
A happy, genial influence,   70
Coming one knows not how, or whence,
   Nor whither going.

Child of the Year! that round dost run
Thy pleasant course,—when day's begun
As ready to salute the sun   75
   As lark or leveret,

50 one] some MS.   57–8 *so* 1836: When, smitten by the morning ray,
I see thee rise MS., 1807–32   59–60 cheerful . . . kindred] Daisy! do
. . . chearful MS.   60 gladness 1815: motion MS. 1807
61–4 *so* 1815: At dusk, I've seldom mark'd thee press
        The ground, as if in thankfulness,
        Without some feeling, more or less,
        Of true devotion.   MS. 1807
65–8 But more than all I number yet
   O bounteous flower! (The whole year long) another debt
   Which I to thee wherever met
   Am daily owing;   MS.
73–6 *so* 1836: Child of the Year! that round dost run
        Thy course, bold lover of the sun,
        And cheerful (jocund MS.) when the day's begun
        As morning Leveret MS., 1807–32

Thy long-lost praise thou shalt regain;
Nor be less dear to future men
Than in old time;—thou not in vain
Art Nature's favourite.[1]   80

VIII

TO THE SAME FLOWER

[Composed 1802.—Published 1807.]

WITH little here to do or see
Of things that in the great world be,
Daisy! again I talk to thee,
    For thou art worthy,
Thou unassuming Common-place   5
Of Nature, with that homely face,
And yet with something of a grace,
    Which love makes for thee!

Oft on the dappled turf at ease
I sit, and play with similes,   10
Loose types of things through all degrees,
    Thoughts of thy raising:
And many a fond and idle name
I give to thee, for praise or blame,
As is the humour of the game,   15
    While I am gazing.

A nun demure of lowly port;
Or sprightly maiden, of Love's court,
In thy simplicity the sport
    Of all temptations;   20
A queen in crown of rubies drest;
A starveling in a scanty vest;
Are all, as seems to suit thee best,
    Thy appellations.

---

[1] See, in Chaucer and elder Poets, the honours formerly paid to this flower.

77–9 *so* 1836: Thou long the Poet's praise shalt gain;
                Thou wilt be more belov'd by men
                In times to come; MS. 1807
                Thy long-lost praise thou shalt regain;
                Dear shalt thou be to future men
                As in old time; 1815–32
VIII. 3 *so* 1845: Sweet Daisy oft 1807–32; Yet once again I 1836   9–10
so 1820: Oft do I sit by thee at ease And weave a web of similes 1807–15

A little Cyclops with one eye   25
Staring to threaten and defy,
That thought comes next—and instantly
    The freak is over,
The shape will vanish—and behold
A silver shield with boss of gold,   30
That spreads itself, some faery bold
    In fight to cover!

I see thee glittering from afar—
And then thou art a pretty star;
Not quite so fair as many are   35
    In heaven above thee!
Yet like a star, with glittering crest,
Self-poised in air thou seem'st to rest;—
May peace come never to his nest,
    Who shall reprove thee!   40

Bright *Flower!* for by that name at last,
When all my reveries are past,
I call thee, and to that cleave fast,
    Sweet silent creature!
That breath'st with me in sun and air,   45
Do thou, as thou art wont, repair
My heart with gladness, and a share
    Of thy meek nature!

IX

THE GREEN LINNET

[Composed 1803.—Published 1807.]

BENEATH these fruit-tree boughs that shed
Their snow-white blossoms on my head,
With brightest sunshine round me spread
    Of spring's unclouded weather,

41 Bright *Flower so* 1836: Sweet Flower 1807–32
IX. 1–8 *so* 1815 (*but in* l. 7 Flowers and Birds 1815–20):
        The May is come again:—how sweet
        To sit upon my Orchard-seat!
        And Birds and Flowers once more to greet,
          My last year's Friends together:

In this sequestered nook how sweet   5
To sit upon my orchard-seat!
And birds and flowers once more to greet,
  My last year's friends together.

One have I marked, the happiest guest
In all this covert of the blest: 10
Hail to Thee, far above the rest
  In joy of voice and pinion!
Thou, Linnet! in thy green array,
Presiding Spirit here to-day,
Dost lead the revels of the May;   15
  And this is thy dominion.

While birds, and butterflies, and flowers,
Make all one band of paramours,
Thou, ranging up and down the bowers,
  Art sole in thy employment: 20
A Life, a Presence like the Air,
Scattering thy gladness without care,
Too blest with any one to pair;
  Thyself thy own enjoyment.

Amid yon tuft of hazel trees,   25
That twinkle to the gusty breeze,
Behold him perched in ecstasies,
  Yet seeming still to hover;
There! where the flutter of his wings
Upon his back and body flings   30
Shadows and sunny glimmerings,
  That cover him all over.

My dazzled sight he oft deceives,
A Brother of the dancing leaves;
Then flits, and from the cottage-eaves   35
  Pours forth his song in gushes;

My thoughts they all by turns employ;
A whispering Leaf is now my joy,
And then a Bird will be the toy
  That doth my fancy tether   MS., 1807
25 Amid 1845: Upon MS., 1807–36   29 where] while MS.
33–40 *so* 1845: While thus before my eyes he gleams,
  A Brother of the Leaves he seems;
  When in a moment forth he teems
    His little song in gushes:

As if by that exulting strain
He mocked and treated with disdain
The voiceless Form he chose to feign,
    While fluttering in the bushes.   40

X

TO A SKY-LARK

[Composed 1802 (?).—Published 1807.]

Up with me! up with me into the clouds!
    For thy song, Lark, is strong;
Up with me, up with me into the clouds!
        Singing, singing,
With clouds and sky about thee ringing,   5
    Lift me, guide me till I find
That spot which seems so to thy mind!

I have walked through wildernesses dreary,
And to-day my heart is weary;
Had I now the wings of a Faery,   10
Up to thee would I fly.
There is madness about thee, and joy divine
In that song of thine;
Lift me, guide me high and high
To thy banqueting place in the sky.   15

As if it pleas'd him to disdain
And mock the Form which he did feign,
While he was dancing with the train
    Of Leaves among the bushes. MS., 1807–15. *So* 1820
        but l. 38 The voiceless form he chose to feign
1827–43 *as text, but* ll. 33–4   My sight he dazzles, half deceives,
            A bird so like the dancing Leaves.   1827
            My dazzled sight the Bird deceives
            A Brother of the dancing leaves.   1832–36
            The Bird my dazzled sight deceives
            A Brother of the dancing leaves.   1840
X. 5 clouds and sky 1827: all the heav'ns 1807–20
5–7 With all the clouds about us ringing
    We two will sail along. MS.
8–25 1827 *omits: restored* 1832   10 wings 1815: soul MS., 1807
13/14 I would yoke myself to thee
    We will travel merrily   MS.
14 Up with me, up with me, 1807–20

Joyous as morning,
Thou art laughing and scorning;
Thou hast a nest for thy love and thy rest,
And, though little troubled with sloth,
Drunken Lark! thou would'st be loth   20
To be such a traveller as I.
Happy, happy Liver,
With a soul as strong as a mountain river
Pouring out praise to the almighty Giver,
Joy and jollity be with us both!   25

Alas! my journey, rugged and uneven,
Through prickly moors or dusty ways must wind:
But hearing thee, or others of thy kind,
As full of gladness and as free of heaven,
I, with my fate contented, will plod on,   30
And hope for higher raptures, when life's day is done.

XI

TO THE SMALL CELANDINE[1]

[Composed April 30, 1802.—Published 1807.]

PANSIES, lilies, kingcups, daisies,
Let them live upon their praises;
Long as there's a sun that sets,
Primroses will have their glory;
Long as there are violets,   5
They will have a place in story:
There's a flower that shall be mine,
'Tis the little Celandine.

Eyes of some men travel far
For the finding of a star;   10
Up and down the heavens they go,
Men that keep a mighty rout!

[1] Common Pilewort.

26–31 *so* 1827: Hearing thee, or else some other,
          As merry a Brother
          I on the earth will go plodding on,
          By myself chearfully, till the day is done.   1807–20. *So*
          MS. *but* be *for* go
TO THE SMALL CELANDINE] . . . LESSER MS.

I'm as great as they, I trow,
Since the day I found thee out,
Little Flower—I'll make a stir,   15
Like a sage astronomer.

Modest, yet withal an Elf
Bold, and lavish of thyself;
Since we needs must first have met
I have seen thee, high and low,   20
Thirty years or more, and yet
'Twas a face I did not know;
Thou hast now, go where I may,
Fifty greetings in a day.

Ere a leaf is on a bush,   25
In the time before the thrush
Has a thought about her nest,
Thou wilt come with half a call,
Spreading out thy glossy breast
Like a careless Prodigal;   30
Telling tales about the sun,
When we've little warmth, or none.

Poets, vain men in their mood!
Travel with the multitude:
Never heed them; I aver   35
That they all are wanton wooers;
But the thrifty cottager,
Who stirs little out of doors,
Joys to spy thee near her home;
Spring is coming, Thou art come!   40

Comfort have thou of thy merit,
Kindly, unassuming Spirit!
Careless of thy neighbourhood,
Thou dost show thy pleasant face

16 sage 1836: great MS., 1807–32   27 her 1832: its MS., 1807–27
40/41 Drawn by what peculiar spell,
    By what charm for sight or smell,
    Do those wingèd dim-eyed creatures,
    Labourers sent from waxen cells,
    Settle on thy brilliant features,
    In neglect of buds and bells
    Opening daily at thy side,
    By the season multiplied?   1836–43 (v. next poem 41–8)

On the moor, and in the wood,   45
In the lane;—there's not a place,
Howsoever mean it be,
But 'tis good enough for thee.

Ill befall the yellow flowers,
Children of the flaring hours!   50
Buttercups, that will be seen,
Whether we will see or no;
Others, too, of lofty mien;
They have done as worldlings do,
Taken praise that should be thine,   55
Little, humble Celandine.

Prophet of delight and mirth,
Ill-requited upon earth;
Herald of a mighty band,
Of a joyous train ensuing,   60
Serving at my heart's command,
Tasks that are no tasks renewing,
I will sing, as doth behove,
Hymns in praise of what I love!

XII

TO THE SAME FLOWER

[Composed May 1, 1802.—Published 1807.]

PLEASURES newly found are sweet
When they lie about our feet:
February last, my heart
First at sight of thee was glad;
All unheard of as thou art,   5
Thou must needs, I think, have had,
Celandine! and long ago,
Praise of which I nothing know.

I have not a doubt but he,
Whosoe'er the man might be,   10
Who the first with pointed rays
(Workman worthy to be sainted)

58 *so* 1836: Scorned and slighted MS., 1807–32   61 Serving 1836: Singing MS., 1807–32   62 *so* 1836: In the lanes my thoughts pursuing MS., 1807–32

Set the sign-board in a blaze,
When the rising sun he painted,
Took the fancy from a glance   15
At thy glittering countenance.

Soon as gentle breezes bring
News of winter's vanishing,
And the children build their bowers,
Sticking 'kerchief-plots of mould   20
All about with full-blown flowers,
Thick as sheep in shepherd's fold!
With the proudest thou art there,
Mantling in the tiny square.

Often have I sighed to measure   25
By myself a lonely pleasure,
Sighed to think I read a book
Only read, perhaps, by me;
Yet I long could overlook
Thy bright coronet and Thee,   30
And thy arch and wily ways,
And thy store of other praise.

Blithe of heart, from week to week
Thou dost play at hide-and-seek;
While the patient primrose sits   35
Like a beggar in the cold,
Thou, a flower of wiser wits,
Slip'st into thy sheltering hold;
Liveliest of the vernal train
When ye all are out again.   40

Drawn by what peculiar spell,
By what charm of sight or smell,
Does the dim-eyed curious Bee,
Labouring for her waxen cells,
Fondly settle upon Thee   45
Prized above all buds and bells
Opening daily at thy side,
By the season multiplied?

XII.   14 rising 1836: risen MS., 1807–32   38 sheltering 1836: shelter'd
1807–32   39 *so* 1845: Bright as any of the train MS., 1807–43   41–8
so 1845: *not in* MS., *transferred from preceding poem* (*v. app. crit.*)

Thou art not beyond the moon,
But a thing "beneath our shoon:"   50
Let the bold Discoverer thrid
In his bark the polar sea;
Rear who will a pyramid;
Praise it is enough for me,
If there be but three or four   55
Who will love my little Flower.

XIII

THE SEVEN SISTERS

OR,

THE SOLITUDE OF BINNORIE

[Composed before August 17, 1800.—Published 1807.]

I

SEVEN Daughters had Lord Archibald,
All children of one mother:
You could not say in one short day
What love they bore each other.
A garland of seven lilies wrought!   5
Seven Sisters that together dwell;
But he, bold Knight as ever fought,
Their Father, took of them no thought,
He loved the wars so well.
Sing, mournfully, oh! mournfully,   10
The solitude of Binnorie!

II

Fresh blows the wind, a western wind,
And from the shores of Erin,
Across the wave, a Rover brave
To Binnorie is steering: 15

51-3 *so* 1845: *So* 1827–43 *but* Adventurer *for* Discoverer;
          Let, as old Magellen [Magellan 1815] did,
          Others roam about the sea;
          Build who will a pyramid;   MS., 1807-15

          Let, with bold advent'rous skill,
          Others thrid the polar sea;
          Rear a pyramid who will;   1820
XIII. 3 You 1836: I 1807–32

Right onward to the Scottish strand
The gallant ship is borne;
The warriors leap upon the land,
And hark! the Leader of the band
Hath blown his bugle horn.   20
Sing, mournfully, oh! mournfully,
The solitude of Binnorie.

III

Beside a grotto of their own,
With boughs above them closing,
The Seven are laid, and in the shade   25
They lie like fawns reposing.
But now, upstarting with affright
At noise of man and steed,
Away they fly to left, to right—
Of your fair household, Father-knight,   30
Methinks you take small heed!
Sing, mournfully, oh! mournfully
The solitude of Binnorie.

IV

Away the seven fair Campbells fly,
And over hill and hollow,   35
With menace proud, and insult loud,
The youthful Rovers follow.
Cried they, "Your Father loves to roam:
Enough for him to find
The empty house when he comes home;   40
For us your yellow ringlets comb,
For us be fair and kind!"
Sing, mournfully, oh! mournfully,
The solitude of Binnorie.

V

Some close behind, some side by side,   45
Like clouds in stormy weather;
They run, and cry, "Nay, let us die,
And let us die together."

A lake was near; the shore was steep;
There never foot had been;   50
They ran, and with a desperate leap
Together plunged into the deep,
Nor ever more were seen.
Sing, mournfully, oh! mournfully,
The solitude of Binnorie.   55

VI

The stream that flows out of the lake,
As through the glen it rambles,
Repeats a moan o'er moss and stone,
For those seven lovely Campbells.
Seven little Islands, green and bare,   60
Have risen from out the deep:
The fishers say, those sisters fair
By faeries all are buried there,
And there together sleep.
Sing, mournfully, oh! mournfully,   65
The solitude of Binnorie.

XIV

[Composed 1803.—Published 1807.]

Who fancied what a pretty sight
This Rock would be if edged around
With living snow-drops? circlet bright!
How glorious to this orchard-ground!
Who loved the little Rock, and set   5
Upon its head this coronet?

Was it the humour of a child?
Or rather of some gentle maid,
Whose brows, the day that she was styled
The shepherd-queen, were thus arrayed?   10
Of man mature, or matron sage?
Or old man toying with his age?

51-2 The sisters ran like Mountain Sheep,
      And in together did they leap,   MS.
XIV. 8 gentle 1836: love-sick 1807-32

I asked—'twas whispered; The device
To each and all might well belong:
It is the Spirit of Paradise   15
That prompts such work, a Spirit strong,
That gives to all the self-same bent
Where life is wise and innocent.

XV

THE REDBREAST CHASING THE BUTTERFLY

⌈Composed April 18, 1802.—Published 1807.⌉

ART thou the bird whom Man loves best,
The pious bird with the scarlet breast,
          Our little English Robin;
The bird that comes about our doors
When Autumn-winds are sobbing?   5
Art thou the Peter of Norway Boors?
          Their Thomas in Finland,
          And Russia far inland?
The bird, that by some name or other
All men who know thee call their brother,   10
The darling of children and men?
Could Father Adam open his eyes[1]
And see this sight beneath the skies,
He'd wish to close them again.
—If the Butterfly knew but his friend,   15
Hither his flight he would bend;
And find his way to me,
Under the branches of the tree:
In and out, he darts about;
Can this be the bird, to man so good,   20
That, after their bewildering,
Covered with leaves the little children,
          So painfully in the wood?

[1] See "Paradise Lost," Book XI., where Adam points out to Eve the ominous sign of the Eagle chasing "two Birds of gayest plume," and the gentle Hart and Hind pursued by their enemy.

14 and 1827: or 1807–20
XV. THE REDBREAST AND THE BUTTERFLY 1807–20: AND
BUTTERFLY 1827–43   6 Peter of Norway] Charles of Sweedish MS.
9 that 1849: whom 1807–20: who 1827–45   12 note added 1815
19/20 His little heart is throbbing 1807
          Robin! Robin!
          His whole heart is throbbing   MSS.
20/1 Our consecrated Robin 1807   22 Covered 1832: Did cover MS., 1807–27

What ailed thee, Robin, that thou couldst pursue
    A beautiful creature,   25
That is gentle by nature ?
Beneath the summer sky
From flower to flower let him fly ;
'Tis all that he wishes to do.
The cheerer Thou of our in-door sadness,   30
He is the friend of our summer gladness :
What hinders, then, that ye should be
Playmates in the sunny weather,
And fly about in the air together !
His beautiful wings in crimson are drest,   35
A crimson as bright as thine own :
Would'st thou be happy in thy nest,
O pious Bird ! whom man loves best,
Love him, or leave him alone !

XVI

SONG FOR THE SPINNING WHEEL

FOUNDED UPON A BELIEF PREVALENT AMONG THE PASTORAL
VALES OF WESTMORELAND

[Composed 1812.—Published 1820.]

SWIFTLY turn the murmuring wheel !
Night has brought the welcome hour,
When the weary fingers feel
Help, as if from faery power ;
Dewy night o'ershades the ground ;   5
Turn the swift wheel round and round !

Now, beneath the starry sky,
Couch the widely-scattered sheep ;—
Ply the pleasant labour, ply !
For the spindle, while they sleep,   10
Runs with speed more smooth and fine,
Gathering up a trustier line.

33-4 weather ? Like thine own breast MSS.   34/5 Like the hues of thy
breast 1807   36 *so* 1815: As if he were bone of thy bone: MSS.; A
brother he seems of thine own; 1807   35-6 His beautiful bosom is
drest, In 1832   37 Would'st thou 1836: If thou would'st MSS., 1807-32
XVI. 8 Couch 1827: Rest 1820   11-12 *so* 1832: With a motion smooth
and fine Gathers 1820: Runs with motion . . . Gathering 1827

Short-lived likings may be bred
By a glance from fickle eyes;
But true love is like the thread   15
Which the kindly wool supplies,
When the flocks are all at rest,
Sleeping on the mountain's breast.

XVII

HINT FROM THE MOUNTAINS

FOR CERTAIN POLITICAL PRETENDERS

[Composed 1817.—Published 1820.]

"WHO but hails the sight with pleasure
When the wings of genius rise,
Their ability to measure
    With great enterprise;
But in man was ne'er such daring   5
As yon Hawk exhibits, pairing
His brave spirit with the war in
    The stormy skies!

"Mark him, how his power he uses,
Lays it by, at will resumes!   10
Mark, ere for his haunt he chooses
    Clouds and utter glooms!
There, he wheels in downward mazes;
Sunward now his flight he raises,
Catches fire, as seems, and blazes   15
    With uninjured plumes!"

ANSWER

"Stranger, 'tis no act of courage
Which aloft thou dost discern;
No bold *bird* gone forth to forage
'Mid the tempest stern;   20
But such mockery as the nations
See, when public perturbations
Lift men from their native stations,
    Like yon TUFT OF FERN;

XVII. PRETENDERS 1827: ASPIRANTS 1820   1 *so* 1827:
Stranger, 'tis a sight of 1820   17 Stranger, 1827: Traveller, 1820
22 *so* 1827: Commonwealth vexations 1820

"Such it is; the aspiring creature   25
Soaring on undaunted wing,
(So you fancied) is by nature
    A dull helpless thing,
Dry and withered, light and yellow;—
That to be the tempest's fellow!   30
Wait—and you shall see how hollow
    Its endeavouring!"

XVIII

ON SEEING A NEEDLECASE IN THE FORM OF A HARP

THE WORK OF E. M. S.

[Composed 1827.—Published 1827.]

FROWNS are on every Muse's face,
    Reproaches from their lips are sent,
That mimicry should thus disgrace
    The noble Instrument.

A very Harp in all but size!   5
    Needles for strings in apt gradation!
Minerva's self would stigmatize
    The unclassic profanation.

Even her *own* needle that subdued
    Arachne's rival spirit,   10
Though wrought in Vulcan's happiest mood,
    Such honour could not merit.

And this, too, from the Laureate's Child,
    A living lord of melody!
How will her Sire be reconciled   15
    To the refined indignity?

I spake, when whispered a low voice,
    "Bard! moderate your ire;
Spirits of all degrees rejoice
    In presence of the lyre.   20

25 *so* 1827: Such it is, and not a Haggard 1820
27–8 *so* 1827: 'Tis by nature dull and laggard,
    A poor helpless Thing,   1820
XVIII. 12 Such honour 1845: Like station 1827–36

"The Minstrels of Pygmean bands,
    Dwarf Genii, moonlight-loving Fays,
Have shells to fit their tiny hands
    And suit their slender lays.

"Some, still more delicate of ear,   25
    Have lutes (believe my words)
Whose framework is of gossamer,
    While sunbeams are the chords.

"Gay Sylphs this miniature will court,
    Made vocal by their brushing wings,   30
And sullen Gnomes will learn to sport
    Around its polished strings;

"Whence strains to love-sick maiden dear,
    While in her lonely bower she tries
To cheat the thought she cannot cheer,   35
    By fanciful embroideries.

"Trust, angry Bard! a knowing Sprite,
    Nor think the Harp her lot deplores;
Though 'mid the stars the Lyre shine bright,
    Love *stoops* as fondly as he soars."   40

XIX

TO A LADY

IN ANSWER TO A REQUEST THAT I WOULD WRITE HER A POEM
UPON SOME DRAWINGS THAT SHE HAD MADE OF FLOWERS IN
THE ISLAND OF MADEIRA

[Composed Jan. 1, 1843.—Published 1845.]

FAIR Lady! can I sing of flowers
    That in Madeira bloom and fade,
I who ne'er sate within their bowers,
    Nor through their sunny lawns have strayed?
How they in sprightly dance are worn   5
    By Shepherd-groom or May-day queen,
Or holy festal pomps adorn,
    These eyes have never seen.

XIX. 6 or] and 1843 (*v.* notes)

Yet tho' to me the pencil's art
  No like remembrances can give,   10
Your portraits still may reach the heart
  And there for gentle pleasure live ;
While Fancy ranging with free scope
  Shall on some lovely Alien set
A name with us endeared to hope,   15
  To peace, or fond regret.

Still as we look with nicer care,
  Some new resemblance we may trace
A *Heart's-ease* will perhaps be there,
  A *Speedwell* may not want its place.   20
And so may we, with charmèd mind
  Beholding what your skill has wrought,
Another *Star-of-Bethlehem* find,
  A new *Forget-me-not.*

From earth to heaven with motion fleet   25
  From heaven to earth our thoughts will pass,
A *Holy-thistle* here we meet
  And there a *Shepherd's weather-glass;*
And haply some familiar name
  Shall grace the fairest, sweetest, plant   30
Whose presence cheers the drooping frame
  Of English Emigrant.

Gazing she feels its power beguile
  Sad thoughts, and breathes with easier breath ;
Alas! that meek that tender smile   35
  Is but a harbinger of death :
And pointing with a feeble hand
  She says, in faint words by sighs broken,
Bear for me to my native land
  This precious Flower, true love's last token.   40

XX

[Composed 1842.—Published 1845.]

GLAD sight wherever new with old
Is joined through some dear homeborn tie ;
The life of all that we behold
Depends upon that mystery.

Vain is the glory of the sky,   5
The beauty vain of field and grove,
Unless, while with admiring eye
We gaze, we also learn to love.

XXI

THE CONTRAST

THE PARROT AND THE WREN

[Composed 1825.—Published 1827.]

I

WITHIN her gilded cage confined
I saw a dazzling Belle,
A Parrot of that famous kind
Whose name is NON-PAREIL.

Like beads of glossy jet her eyes;   5
And, smoothed by Nature's skill,
With pearl or gleaming agate vies
Her finely-curvèd bill.

Her plumy mantle's living hues
In mass opposed to mass,   10
Outshine the splendour that imbues
The robes of pictured glass.

And, sooth to say, an apter Mate
Did never tempt the choice
Of feathered Thing most delicate   15
In figure and in voice.

But, exiled from Australian bowers,
And singleness her lot,
She trills her song with tutored powers,
Or mocks each casual note.   20

No more of pity for regrets
With which she may have striven!
Now but in wantonness she frets,
Or spite, if cause be given;

Arch, volatile, a sportive bird   25
By social glee inspired;
Ambitious to be seen or heard,
And pleased to be admired!

II

THIS moss-lined shed, green, soft, and dry,
Harbours a self-contented Wren,   30
Not shunning man's abode, though shy,
Almost as thought itself, of human ken.

Strange places, coverts unendeared,
She never tried; the very nest
In which this Child of Spring was reared   35
Is warmed, thro' winter, by her feathery breast.

To the bleak winds she sometimes gives
A slender unexpected strain;
Proof that the hermitess still lives,
Though she appear not, and be sought in vain.   40

Say, Dora! tell me, by yon placid moon,
If called to choose between the favoured pair,
Which would you be,—the bird of the saloon,
By lady-fingers tended with nice care,
Caressed, applauded, upon dainties fed,   45
Or Nature's DARKLING of this mossy shed ?

XXII

THE DANISH BOY

A FRAGMENT

[Composed 1799.—Published 1800.]

I

BETWEEN two sister moorland rills
There is a spot that seems to lie
Sacred to flowerets of the hills,
And sacred to the sky.
And in this smooth and open dell   5
There is a tempest-stricken tree;
A corner-stone by lightning cut,
The last stone of a lonely hut;
And in this dell you see
A thing no storm can e'er destroy,   10
The shadow of a Danish Boy.

39 Proof that 1836: That tells 1827–32
XXII. THE DANISH BOY 1836: 1800–32 *no title but* A FRAGMENT
8 lonely 1836: cottage 1800–32

II

In clouds above, the lark is heard,
But drops not here to earth for rest;
Within this lonesome nook the bird
Did never build her nest.   15
No beast, no bird, hath here his home;
Bees, wafted on the breezy air,
Pass high above those fragrant bells
To other flowers:—to other dells
Their burdens do they bear;   20
The Danish Boy walks here alone:
The lovely dell is all his own.

III

A Spirit of noon-day is he;
Yet seems a form of flesh and blood;
Nor piping shepherd shall he be,   25
Nor herd-boy of the wood.
A regal vest of fur he wears,
In colour like a raven's wing;
It fears not rain, nor wind, nor dew;
But in the storm 'tis fresh and blue   30
As budding pines in spring;
His helmet has a vernal grace,
Fresh as the bloom upon his face.

IV

A harp is from his shoulder slung;
Resting the harp upon his knee,   35
To words of a forgotten tongue
He suits its melody.
Of flocks upon the neighbouring hill
He is the darling and the joy;
And often, when no cause appears,   40
The mountain-ponies prick their ears,
—They hear the Danish Boy,

13–15 *so* 1827: He sings his blithest and his best; But in . . . his 1800–15:
She sings regardless of her rest, Within . . . her 1820   17 *so* 1827:
The bees borne on 1800–20
19–20 *so* 1827: To other flowers, to other dells,
            Nor ever linger there.   1800–20
35–7 *so* 1836: He rests his . . . And there in . . . He warbles 1800–32   38
so 1820: Of flocks and herds both far and near 1800: 1802–15 *as* 1820 *but* hills

While in the dell he sings alone
Beside the tree and corner-stone.

V

There sits he; in his face you spy   45
No trace of a ferocious air,
Nor ever was a cloudless sky
So steady or so fair.
The lovely Danish Boy is blest
And happy in his flowery cove: 50
From bloody deeds his thoughts are far;
And yet he warbles songs of war,
That seem like songs of love,
For calm and gentle is his mien;
Like a dead Boy he is serene.   55

XXIII

SONG

FOR THE WANDERING JEW

[Composed 1800.—Published 1800.]

THOUGH the torrents from their fountains
Roar down many a craggy steep,
Yet they find among the mountains
Resting-places calm and deep.

Clouds that love through air to hasten,   5
Ere the storm its fury stills,
Helmet-like themselves will fasten
On the heads of towering hills.

43 sings 1845: sits 1800–43
44/5 When near this blasted tree you pass,
    Two sods are plainly to be seen
Close at its root, and each with grass
Is cover'd fresh and green.
Like turf upon a new-made grave
These two green sods together lie,
Nor heat, nor cold, nor rain, nor wind
Can these two sods together bind,
Nor sun, nor earth, nor sky,
But side by side the two are laid,
As if just sever'd by the spade.   1800 *only*
XXIII. 5–8 *added* 1827

What, if through the frozen centre
Of the Alps the Chamois bound,   10
Yet he has a home to enter
In some nook of chosen ground:

And the Sea-horse, though the ocean
Yield him no domestic cave,
Slumbers without sense of motion,   15
Couched upon the rocking wave.

If on windy days the Raven
Gambol like a dancing skiff,
Not the less she loves her haven
In the bosom of the cliff.   20

The fleet Ostrich, till day closes,
Vagrant over desert sands,
Brooding on her eggs reposes
When chill night that care demands.

Day and night my toils redouble,   25
Never nearer to the goal;
Night and day, I feel the trouble
Of the Wanderer in my soul.

9–16 Though almost with eagle pinion
     O'er the rocks the Chamois roam,
     Yet he has some small dominion
     Which no doubt he calls his home.

     Though the Sea-horse in the ocean
     Own no dear domestic cave;
     Yet he slumbers without motion
     On the calm and silent wave.   1800–5.   *So* 1815–20, *but* l. 9 *as if for*
        almost *and* l. 12 Whence he feels himself at home
13 And 1836: Though 1800–32
15–16 *so* 1836: Yet he slumbers, by the motion
        Rocked of many a gentle wave 1827–32
13–16, 17–20 *Before* 1836 *these stanzas are in reverse order*   19 She . . .
her 1827: He . . . his 1800–20   21–4 *added* 1827   27 *so* 1800–5,
1827: Never—never does the trouble 1815–20 (*with* leave *for* in *in* l. 28)

XXIV

STRAY PLEASURES

[Composed 1806.—Published 1807.]

"—Pleasure is spread through the earth
In stray gifts to be claimed by whoever shall find."

By their floating mill,
That lies dead and still,
Behold yon Prisoners three,
The Miller with two Dames, on the breast of the Thames!
The platform is small, but gives room for them all;   5
And they're dancing merrily.

From the shore come the notes
To their mill where it floats,
To their house and their mill tethered fast:
To the small wooden isle where, their work to beguile,   10
They from morning to even take whatever is given;—
And many a blithe day they have past.

In sight of the spires,
All alive with the fires
Of the sun going down to his rest,   15
In the broad open eye of the solitary sky,
They dance,—there are three, as jocund as free,
While they dance on the calm river's breast.

Man and Maidens wheel,
They themselves make the reel,   20
And their music's a prey which they seize;
It plays not for them,—what matter? 'tis theirs;
And if they had care, it has scattered their cares
While they dance, crying, "Long as ye please!"

They dance not for me,   25
Yet mine is their glee!
Thus pleasure is spread through the earth
In stray gifts to be claimed by whoever shall find;
Thus a rich loving-kindness, redundantly kind,
Moves all nature to gladness and mirth.   30

XXIV. 5 gives 1820: there's 1807-15

The showers of the spring
Rouse the birds, and they sing;
If the wind do but stir for his proper delight,
Each leaf, that and this, his neighbour will kiss;
Each wave, one and t'other, speeds after his brother;   35
They are happy, for that is their right!

XXV

THE PILGRIM'S DREAM;

OR, THE STAR AND THE GLOW-WORM

[Composed 1818.—Published 1820.]

A PILGRIM, when the summer day
Had closed upon his weary way,
A lodging begged beneath a castle's roof;
But him the haughty Warder spurned;
And from the gate the Pilgrim turned,   5
To seek such covert as the field
Or heath-besprinkled copse might yield,
Or lofty wood, shower-proof.

He paced along; and, pensively,
Halting beneath a shady tree,   10
Whose moss-grown root might serve for couch or seat,
Fixed on a Star his upward eye;
Then, from the tenant of the sky
He turned, and watched with kindred look
A Glow-worm, in a dusky nook,   15
Apparent at his feet.

The murmur of a neighbouring stream
Induced a soft and slumbrous dream,
A pregnant dream, within whose shadowy bounds
He recognised the earth-born Star,   20
And *That* which glittered from afar;
And (strange to witness!) from the frame
Of the ethereal Orb, there came
Intelligible sounds.

XXV. 3 castle's] convent's MS.   4 Warder]Abbot MS.   5 sump-
tuous gate he MS.   7–8 The heath or rocky holt . . . Or leafy
MS.   21 which glittered *etc.* 1827: whose radiance gleamed from far 1820
streamed MS.

Much did it taunt the humble Light   25
That now, when day was fled, and night
Hushed the dark earth, fast closing weary eyes,
A very reptile could presume
To show her taper in the gloom,
As if in rivalship with One   30
Who sat a ruler on his throne
Erected in the skies.

"Exalted Star!" the Worm replied,
"Abate this unbecoming pride,
Or with a less uneasy lustre shine;   35
Thou shrink'st as momently thy rays
Are mastered by the breathing haze;
While neither mist, nor thickest cloud
That shapes in heaven its murky shroud,
Hath power to injure mine.   40

"But not for this do I aspire
To match the spark of local fire,
That at my will burns on the dewy lawn,
With thy acknowledged glories;—No!
Yet, thus upbraided, I may show   45
What favours do attend me here,
Till, like thyself, I disappear
Before the purple dawn."

When this in modest guise was said,
Across the welkin seemed to spread   50
A boding sound—for aught but sleep unfit!
Hills quaked, the rivers backward ran;
That Star, so proud of late, looked wan;
And reeled with visionary stir
In the blue depth, like Lucifer   55
Cast headlong to the pit!

Fire raged: and, when the spangled floor
Of ancient ether was no more
New heavens succeeded, by the dream brought forth:
And all the happy Souls that rode   60

26-7 That now, while sleep to solemn Night
      Was offering gifts of duteous sacrifice,   MS.
45 *so* 1827: But it behoves that thou should'st know   MS., 1820

Transfigured through that fresh abode
Had heretofore, in humble trust,
Shone meekly 'mid their native dust,
The Glow-worms of the earth!

This knowledge, from an Angel's voice   65
Proceeding, made the heart rejoice
Of Him who slept upon the open lea:
Waking at morn he murmured not;
And, till life's journey closed, the spot
Was to the Pilgrim's soul endeared,   70
Where by that dream he had been cheered
Beneath the shady tree.

XXVI

THE POET AND THE CAGED TURTLEDOVE

[Composed early Dec. 1830.—Published 1835.]

As often as I murmur here
    My half-formed melodies,
Straight from her osier mansion near,
    The Turtledove replies:
Though silent as a leaf before,   5
    The captive promptly coos;
Is it to teach her own soft lore,
    Or second my weak Muse?

I rather think the gentle Dove
    Is murmuring a reproof,   10
Displeased that I from lays of love
    Have dared to keep aloof;
That I, a Bard of hill and dale,
    Have carolled, fancy free,
As if nor dove nor nightingale   15
    Had heart or voice for me.

If such thy meaning, O forbear,
    Sweet Bird! to do me wrong;
Love, blessed Love, is everywhere
    The spirit of my song: 20
'Mid grove, and by the calm fireside,
    Love animates my lyre—
That coo again!—'tis not to chide,
    I feel, but to inspire.

61 fresh] fair MS.
XXVI. 3, 7 her] his MS.   23–4 chide ... inspire] *chide ... inspire* MS.

XXVII

A WREN'S NEST

[Composed 1833.—Published 1835.]

AMONG the dwellings framed by birds
    In field or forest with nice care,
Is none that with the little Wren's
    In snugness may compare.

No door the tenement requires,   5
    And seldom needs a laboured roof;
Yet is it to the fiercest sun
    Impervious, and storm-proof.

So warm, so beautiful withal,
    In perfect fitness for its aim,   10
That to the Kind by special grace
    Their instinct surely came.

And when for their abodes they seek
    An opportune recess,
The hermit has no finer eye   15
    For shadowy quietness.

These find, 'mid ivied abbey-walls,
    A canopy in some still nook;
Others are pent-housed by a brae
    That overhangs a brook.   20

There to the brooding bird her mate
    Warbles by fits his low clear song;
And by the busy streamlet both
    Are sung to all day long.

XXVII. 1–2 Among the mansions built by birds
        In grove and woodland *etc.* MS. A
3 with] to MS. A   5–8 *not in* MS. A
6–8 Nor need the Builder frame a roof
    Yet baffled is the fiercest Sun,
    The dwellers tempest-proof. MS.
10 In . . . for] Through . . . to MS. A   13–28 *not in* MS. A
13–14 And what attractive Sites they chuse!
    The world-renouncing votaress, MS.
16/17 Some darkling, flitting to and fro,
    Betray that their abodes are nigh;
    But watch the Owners in and out,
    Else vainly shall you pry. MS.
17–18 Some in an Abbey's ivied wall
    Find for their nests a sheltering; MS.
21–2 To chear . . . There chaunts by fits his slender MS.

Or in sequestered lanes they build,   25
    Where, till the flitting bird's return,
Her eggs within the nest repose,
    Like relics in an urn.

But still, where general choice is good,
    There is a better and a best;   30
And, among fairest objects, some
    Are fairer than the rest;

This, one of those small builders proved
    In a green covert, where, from out
The forehead of a pollard oak,   35
    The leafy antlers sprout;

For She who planned the mossy lodge,
    Mistrusting her evasive skill,
Had to a Primrose looked for aid
    Her wishes to fulfil.   40

High on the trunk's projecting brow,
    And fixed an infant's span above
The budding flowers, peeped forth the nest
    The prettiest of the grove!

The treasure proudly did I show   45
    To some whose minds without disdain
Can turn to little things; but once
    Looked up for it in vain:

29–30 But oft, where judgments all are good
    Among the good is found a best;   MS. A
33–4 And this to me was proved by one
    Of those small Builders where, from out   MS. A
37 For] But   MS. A   42 an infant's span] three fingers' breadth
MS. A   43 budding flowers] yellowing buds   MS. A
45–8 But as I once approached the tree
    My greeting was a shock of pain;
    When for my treasure I looked up
    But looked for it in vain   MS. A
    To some who have a mind that turns (whose genial minds are born)
    To little things without disdain
    I pointed out the nest, but once
    We looked (Looked up) for it in vain   MS.

'Tis gone—a ruthless spoiler's prey,
  Who heeds not beauty, love, or song,   50
'Tis gone! (so seemed it) and we grieved
  Indignant at the wrong.

Just three days after, passing by
  In clearer light the moss-built cell
I saw, espied its shaded mouth;   55
  And felt that all was well.

The Primrose for a veil had spread
  The largest of her upright leaves;
And thus, for purposes benign,
  A simple flower deceives.   60

Concealed from friends who might disturb
  Thy quiet with no ill intent,
Secure from evil eyes and hands
  On barbarous plunder bent,

Rest, Mother-bird! and when thy young   65
  Take flight, and thou art free to roam,
When withered is the guardian Flower,
  And empty thy late home,

Think how ye prospered, thou and thine,
  Amid the unviolated grove   70
Housed near the growing Primrose-tuft
  In foresight, or in love.

49 'Tis gone, said I, some ruthless hand MS. A   51 we] I   MS. A
53 Just] But MS. A   57 How shaded ? By the Primrose spreading MS.
59–60 Bless, happy Bird, the simple course By which a flower   MS. A
61–4 *not in* MS. A
61–4 Hid her awhile from Friends that marred
      Her quiet with no ill intent,
      And save her still from evil eyes
      And hands on mischief bent.   MS.
65–7 And when the young have taken flight
      And thou art free and pleased to roam
      And   MS. A
66 Take flight] Are fledged   MS.   70 Amid] Within MS. A   71 grow-
ing] spreading   MS. A

XXVIII

LOVE LIES BLEEDING

[Composed 1842 (?).—Published 1842.]

You call it, "Love lies bleeding,"—so you may,
Though the red Flower, not prostrate, only droops,
As we have seen it here from day to day,
From month to month, life passing not away:
A flower how rich in sadness! Even thus stoops, 5
(Sentient by Grecian sculpture's marvellous power),
Thus leans, with hanging brow and body bent
Earthward in uncomplaining languishment,
The dying Gladiator. So, sad Flower!
('Tis Fancy guides me willing to be led, 10
Though by a slender thread,)
So drooped Adonis, bathed in sanguine dew
Of his death-wound, when he from innocent air
The gentlest breath of resignation drew;
While Venus in a passion of despair 15
Rent, weeping over him, her golden hair
Spangled with drops of that celestial shower.
She suffered, as Immortals sometimes do;
But pangs more lasting far, *that* Lover knew
Who first, weighed down by scorn, in some lone bower 20
Did press this semblance of unpitied smart
Into the service of his constant heart,
His own dejection, downcast Flower! could share
With thine, and gave the mournful name which thou wilt ever
    bear.

XXIX

COMPANION TO THE FOREGOING

[Composed 1842 (?).—Published 1842.]

Never enlivened with the liveliest ray
That fosters growth or checks or cheers decay,
Nor by the heaviest rain-drops more deprest,
This Flower, that first appeared as summer's guest,
Preserves her beauty 'mid autumnal leaves, 5
And to her mournful habits fondly cleaves.

XXVIII and XXIX. *For variants v. notes*, pp. 495, 6.
XXIX. 5 Preserved her beauty among summer [falling MS.] leaves 1842
    but corrected in erratum to text. 1842.

When files of stateliest plants have ceased to bloom,
One after one submitting to their doom,
When her coevals each and all are fled,
What keeps her thus reclined upon her lonesome bed ?　10

　The old mythologists, more impress'd than we
Of this late day by character in tree
Or herb, that claimed peculiar sympathy,
Or by the silent lapse of fountain clear,
Or with the language of the viewless air　　　　　　15
By bird or beast made vocal, sought a cause
To solve the mystery, not in Nature's laws
But in Man's fortunes. Hence a thousand tales
Sung to the plaintive lyre in Grecian vales.
Nor doubt that something of their spirit swayed　　20
The fancy-stricken Youth or heart-sick Maid,
Who, while each stood companionless and eyed
This undeparting Flower in crimson dyed,
Thought of a wound which death is slow to cure,
A fate that has endured and will endure,　　　　　25
And, patience coveting yet passion feeding,
Called the dejected Lingerer, *Love lies Bleeding*.

XXX

RURAL ILLUSIONS

[Composed 1832.—Published 1835.]

SYLPH was it ? or a Bird more bright
　Than those of fabulous stock ?
A second darted by ;—and lo !
　Another of the flock,
Through sunshine flitting from the bough　　　5
　To nestle in the rock.
Transient deception ! a gay freak
　Of April's mimicries !

XXX.　1–3 . . . or a dazzling bird
　　　　　Sprung from a foreign stock ?
　　　　　A brighter *etc.*　MS. 1
7–9　Soon was the pride of fancy tamed
　　　Conjecture set at ease, The *etc.*　MS. 1
　　　Illusion gay ! it passed away
　　　Those sporting companies Of *etc.*　MS. 2

Those brilliant strangers, hailed with joy
　　Among the budding trees,   10
Proved last year's leaves, pushed from the spray
　　To frolic on the breeze.

Maternal Flora! show thy face,
　　And let thy hand be seen,
Thy hand here sprinkling tiny flowers,   15
　　That, as they touch the green,
Take root (so seems it) and look up
　　In honour of their Queen.
Yet, sooth, those little starry specks,
　　That not in vain aspired   20
To be confounded with live growths,
　　Most dainty, most admired,
Were only blossoms dropped from twigs
　　Of their own offspring tired.

Not such the World's illusive shows;   25
　　Her wingless flutterings,
Her blossoms which, though shed, out-brave
　　The floweret as it springs,
For the undeceived, smile as they may,
　　Are melancholy things: 30

13–24 Maternal Flora, I exclaimed,
　　　Why is thy hand unseen
　　　So busy scattering full blown flowers
　　　Of various hue and mien,
　　　That fall through air and as they drop
　　　Take root upon the green?
　　　Bold words, yet those small flowers in sooth *etc. as text but* l. 22 By
Flora most admired *and* l. 24 That of their hues were tired   MS. 1
15 *so* 1836: Which sprinkles here these tiny flowers 1835:
　　　　Here sprinkling softly full-blown flowers   MS. 1, tiny   MS. 2
25–30 Vain heart of man, to thy false shows
　　　No fond remembrance clings,
　　　When withered joys by time cast off
　　　Make sport—as if on wings,
　　　And blooms of hope tho' shed to earth
　　　Would pass for thriving things;   MS. 1
　　　Vain world, from thy illusive shows
　　　If light amusement springs,
　　　Yet the shed blooms that mimic flowers
　　　And wingless flutterings
　　　Smile as we may, for afterthought
　　　Are but unwelcome things;   MS. 2

But gentle Nature plays her part
  With ever-varying wiles,
And transient feignings with plain truth
  So well she reconciles,
That those fond Idlers most are pleased   35
  Whom oftenest she beguiles.

XXXI

THE KITTEN AND FALLING LEAVES

[Composed 1804.—Published 1807.]

THAT way look, my Infant, lo!
What a pretty baby-show!
See the Kitten on the wall,
Sporting with the leaves that fall,
Withered leaves—one—two—and three—   5
From the lofty elder-tree!
Through the calm and frosty air
Of this morning bright and fair,
Eddying round and round they sink
Softly, slowly: one might think,   10
From the motions that are made,
Every little leaf conveyed
Sylph or Faery hither tending,—
To this lower world descending,
Each invisible and mute,   15
In his wavering parachute.
—But the Kitten, how she starts,
Crouches, stretches, paws, and darts!
First at one, and then its fellow,
Just as light and just as yellow;   20
There are many now—now one—
Now they stop and there are none:
What intenseness of desire
In her upward eye of fire!
With a tiger-leap half-way   25
Now she meets the coming prey,
Lets it go as fast, and then
Has it in her power again:

31–6 *not in* MS. 1
35–6 That undeceived we are not grieved
  Repent not of our smiles   MS. 2

Now she works with three or four,
Like an Indian conjurer;   30
Quick as he in feats of art,
Far beyond in joy of heart.
Were her antics played in the eye
Of a thousand standers-by,
Clapping hands with shout and stare,   35
What would little Tabby care
For the plaudits of the crowd ?
Over happy to be proud,
Over wealthy in the treasure
Of her own exceeding pleasure!   40

'Tis a pretty baby-treat;
Nor, I deem, for me unmeet;
Here, for neither Babe nor me,
Other playmate can I see.
Of the countless living things,   45
That with stir of feet and wings
(In the sun or under shade,
Upon bough or grassy blade)
And with busy revellings,
Chirp and song, and murmurings,   50
Made this orchard's narrow space,
And this vale, so blithe a place;
Multitudes are swept away
Never more to breathe the day:
Some are sleeping; some in bands   55
Travelled into distant lands;
Others slunk to moor and wood,
Far from human neighbourhood;
And, among the Kinds that keep
With us closer fellowship,   60
With us openly abide,
All have laid their mirth aside.

Where is he, that giddy Sprite,
Blue-cap, with his colours bright,
Who was blest as bird could be,   65
Feeding in the apple-tree;
Made such wanton spoil and rout,
Turning blossoms inside out:

Hung—head pointing towards the ground—
Fluttered, perched, into a round   70
Bound himself, and then unbound;
Lithest, gaudiest Harlequin!
Prettiest Tumbler ever seen!
Light of heart and light of limb;
What is now become of Him?   75
Lambs, that through the mountains went
Frisking, bleating merriment,
When the year was in its prime,
They are sobered by this time.
If you look to vale or hill,   80
If you listen, all is still,
Save a little neighbouring rill,
That from out the rocky ground
Strikes a solitary sound.
Vainly glitter hill and plain,   85
And the air is calm in vain;
Vainly Morning spreads the lure
Of a sky serene and pure;
Creature none can she decoy
Into open sign of joy: 90
Is it that they have a fear
Of the dreary season near?
Or that other pleasures be
Sweeter even than gaiety?

    Yet, whate'er enjoyments dwell   95
In the impenetrable cell
Of the silent heart which Nature
Furnishes to every creature;
Whatsoe'er we feel and know
Too sedate for outward show,   100
Such a light of gladness breaks,
Pretty Kitten! from thy freaks,—
Spreads with such a living grace
O'er my little Dora's face;
Yes, the sight so stirs and charms   105
Thee, Baby, laughing in my arms,

69 *so* 1836: Hung with head towards the ground 1807–32   104 Dora's
1849: Laura's 1807–45   105 sight] thought MS.   106 Thee, Baby]
Laura MS.

That almost I could repine
That your transports are not mine,
That I do not wholly fare
Even as ye do, thoughtless pair!   110
And I will have my careless season
Spite of melancholy reason,
Will walk through life in such a way
That, when time brings on decay,
Now and then I may possess   115
Hours of perfect gladsomeness.
—Pleased by any random toy:
By a kitten's busy joy,
Or an infant's laughing eye
Sharing in the ecstasy;   120
I would fare like that or this,
Find my wisdom in my bliss;
Keep the sprightly soul awake,
And have faculties to take,
Even from things by sorrow wrought,   125
Matter for a jocund thought,
Spite of care, and spite of grief,
To gambol with Life's falling Leaf.

110/11 But I'll take a hint from you, And to pleasure will be true;   MS.
111,12 *inverted in* MS., *omitting* And
112/13   Be it songs of endless spring
               Which the frolic Muses sing;
               Jest, and Mirth's unruly brood
               Dancing to the Phrygian mood;
               Be it love or be it wine,
               Myrtle wreath or ivy twine,
               Or a garland made of both
               Testifying double truth;
               Whether their philosophy
               That would fill us full of glee,
               Seeing that our breath we draw
               Under an unbending law,
               That our years are halting never,
               Quickly gone, and gone for ever,
               And would teach us thence to brave
               The conclusion in the grave;
               Whether it be these that give
               Strength and spirit so to live
               Or the conquest best be made
               By a sober course and stai'd,   MS.
113 I would walk in such a way   MS.   116 gladsomeness] joyousness
MS.

XXXII

ADDRESS TO MY INFANT DAUGHTER, DORA

ON BEING REMINDED THAT SHE WAS A MONTH OLD THAT
DAY, SEPTEMBER 16

[Composed September 16, 1804.—Published 1815.]

—————HAST thou then survived—
Mild Offspring of infirm humanity,
Meek Infant! among all forlornest things
The most forlorn—one life of that bright star,
The second glory of the Heavens?—Thou hast;   5
Already hast survived that great decay,
That transformation through the wide earth felt,
And by all nations. In that Being's sight
From whom the Race of human kind proceed,
A thousand years are but as yesterday;   10
And one day's narrow circuit is to Him
Not less capacious than a thousand years.
But what is time? What outward glory? Neither
A measure is of Thee, whose claims extend
Through "heaven's eternal year."—Yet hail to Thee,   15
Frail, feeble, Monthling!—by that name, methinks,
Thy scanty breathing-time is portioned out
Not idly.—Hadst thou been of Indian birth,
Couched on a casual bed of moss and leaves,
And rudely canopied by leafy boughs,   20
Or to the churlish elements exposed

XXXII. ADDRESS TO MY INFANT DAUGHTER, DORA: DORA *added* 1849
1 Dear Babe, whose age is marked, whose birthday told
   By the revolving Moon, and shall not cease
   Perchance to be so marked till thrice six times
   That orb have lost its brightness and resumed,
   Thereafter destined like all other gifts
   Become familiar, haply slighted too,
   To be less scrupulously registered
   By month at first and then by years, the span
   A little longer that metes out the Course   [MS. meets]
   Of man and Empires—hast thou then survived   MS. 1
   Dear Babe whose peaceful birthdays now begin
   To have their date from the revolving moon
   Destined hereafter *etc. as* MS. 1   MS. 2
4 bright] fair MS.   6 survived] outlived MS.   8 That Being's]
thy maker's MSS.   9 *not in* MS.   11 narrow] little MS. 1   circuit]
compass MSS.   21 churlish] open MS. 1

On the blank plains,—the coldness of the night,
Or the night's darkness, or its cheerful face
Of beauty, by the changing moon adorned,
Would, with imperious admonition, then   25
Have scored thine age, and punctually timed
Thine infant history, on the minds of those
Who might have wandered with thee.—Mother's love,
Nor less than mother's love in other breasts,
Will, among us warm-clad and warmly housed,   30
Do for thee what the finger of the heavens
Doth all too often harshly execute
For thy unblest coevals, amid wilds
Where fancy hath small liberty to grace
The affections, to exalt them or refine;   35
And the maternal sympathy itself,
Though strong, is, in the main, a joyless tie
Of naked instinct, wound about the heart.
Happier, far happier is thy lot and ours!
Even now—to solemnise thy helpless state,   40
And to enliven in the mind's regard
Thy passive beauty—parallels have risen,
Resemblances, or contrasts, that connect,
Within the region of a father's thoughts,
Thee and thy mate and sister of the sky.   45
And first;—thy sinless progress, through a world
By sorrow darkened and by care disturbed,
Apt likeness bears to hers, through gathered clouds
Moving untouched in silver purity,
And cheering oft-times their reluctant gloom.   50
Fair are ye both, and both are free from stain:
But thou, how leisurely thou fill'st thy horn
With brightness! leaving her to post along,
And range about, disquieted in change,
And still impatient of the shape she wears.   55
Once up, once down the hill, one journey, Babe,
That will suffice thee; and it seems that now
Thou hast foreknowledge that such task is thine;
Thou travellest so contentedly, and sleep'st
In such a heedless peace. Alas! full soon   60

34–6 fancy ... And *not in* MS.   33–71 *torn out of* MS. 2   37 joyless]
mournful MS.   43 Affinities ... unite MS.   46–52 thy sinless
... But thou *not in* MS.

Hath this conception, grateful to behold,
Changed countenance, like an object sullied o'er
By breathing mist; and thine appears to be
A mournful labour, while to her is given
Hope, and a renovation without end.   65
—That smile forbids the thought; for on thy face
Smiles are beginning, like the beams of dawn,
To shoot and circulate; smiles have there been seen;—
Tranquil assurances that Heaven supports
The feeble motions of thy life, and cheers   70
Thy loneliness: or shall those smiles be called
Feelers of love, put forth as if to explore
This untried world, and to prepare thy way
Through a strait passage intricate and dim?
Such are they; and the same are tokens, signs,   75
Which, when the appointed season hath arrived,
Joy, as her holiest language, shall adopt;
And Reason's godlike Power be proud to own.

XXXIII

THE WAGGONER

[Composed 1805.—Published 1819.]

"In Cairo's crowded streets
The impatient Merchant, wondering, waits in vain,
And Mecca saddens at the long delay." THOMSON.

TO CHARLES LAMB, ESQ.

MY DEAR FRIEND,

When I sent you, a few weeks ago, the Tale of Peter Bell, you asked "why THE WAGGONER was not added?"—To say the truth,—from the higher tone of imagination, and the deeper touches of passion aimed at in the former, I apprehended this little Piece could not accompany it without disadvantage. In the year 1806, if I am not mistaken, THE WAGGONER was read to you in manuscript, and, as you have remembered it for so long a time, I am the more encouraged to hope that, since the localities on which the Poem partly depends did not prevent its being interesting to you, it may prove acceptable to others. Being therefore in some measure the cause of its present appearance, you must allow me the gratification of inscribing it to you; in acknowledgment of the pleasure I have derived from your Writings, and of the high esteem with which

I am very truly yours,

RYDAL MOUNT, *May* 20, 1819.   WILLIAM WORDSWORTH.

66 forbids] dispels MS.   66/7 The first faint stir and promise of the east MS.   71 shall I call those smiles MS.   74 *not in* MS.
XXXIII. "In Cairo's *etc.* 1845; "What's in a Name? . . . Brutus will start a Spirit as soon as Cæsar!" 1819; *no motto* 1820-36

Canto First

'Tis spent—this burning day of June!
Soft darkness o'er its latest gleams is stealing;
The buzzing dor-hawk, round and round, is wheeling,—
That solitary bird
Is all that can be heard   5
In silence deeper far than that of deepest noon!

Confiding Glow-worms, 'tis a night
Propitious to your earth-born light!
But, where the scattered stars are seen
In hazy straits the clouds between,   10
Each, in his station twinkling not,
Seems changed into a pallid spot.

1–2 At last this loitering day of June
    This long long day is going out MSS. 1, 2, *corr. to*
    Its very twilight is gone out
3–5 The Night-hawk is singing his frog-like tune
    On restless pinion wheeling *etc.* MS. 3 (*for* MSS. 1, 2 *v.* W. W. *note* p. 498)
    The dor-hawk, solitary bird
    Round the dim crags on heavy pinions wheeling,
    Buzzes incessantly, a tiresome tune;
    That constant voice is all that can be heard   1819–32
    (With untired voice sings an unvaried tune
    Those burring notes are *etc.* 1836)
7–12 *so* 1819–32, 1845: Now that the children are a-bed
                The little glowworms nothing dread,
                Pretty playthings as they would be
                Forth they come (*corr. to* peep) in company
                And lift their fearless head.
                In the sky and on the hill
                Everything is hushed and still,
                The clouds show here and there a spot
                Of a star that twinkles not MSS. 1, 2
                Now that the children's busiest schemes
                Do all lie buried in blank sleep,
                Or only live in stirring dreams,
                The glow-worms fearless watch may keep;
                Rich prize as their bright lamps would be,
                They shine a quiet company,
                On mossy bank by cottage-door,
                As safe as on the loneliest moor.
                In hazy straits the clouds between,
                And in their stations twinkling not,
                Some thinly-sprinkled stars are seen,
                Each changed into a pallid spot. 1836: *text of*
            MS. 3 *between* MSS. 1, 2 *and* 1836

The mountains against heaven's grave weight
Rise up, and grow to wondrous height.
The air, as in a lion's den,   15
Is close and hot;—and now and then
Comes a tired and sultry breeze
With a haunting and a panting,
Like the stifling of disease;
But the dews allay the heat,   20
And the silence makes it sweet.

    Hush, there is some one on the stir!
'Tis Benjamin the Waggoner;
Who long hath trod this toilsome way,
Companion of the night and day.   25
That far-off tinkling's drowsy cheer,
Mixed with a faint yet grating sound
In a moment lost and found,
The Wain announces—by whose side
Along the banks of Rydal Mere   30
He paces on, a trusty Guide,—
Listen! you can scarcely hear!
Hither he his course is bending;—
Now he leaves the lower ground,
And up the craggy hill ascending   35
Many a stop and stay he makes,
Many a breathing-fit he takes;—
Steep the way and wearisome,
Yet all the while his whip is dumb!

    The Horses have worked with right good-will,   40
And so have gained the top of the hill;

13–14 The mountains rise to (are of MS. 1) wondrous height
       And in the heavens there hangs (is MS. 1, 1819–20) a weight MSS.,
         1819–32, *where the lines follow* l. 19
17 tired 1819 *etc.*: faint 1836 *only*   20 the dews 1819 *etc.*: welcome
dews 1836 *only*
24 The dark night's Fellow-traveller
    Long hath he trod this mountain way MS. 1 *corr.*
32–7 *so* 1819 *etc.*: . . . hardly hear!
            Now he has left the lower ground,
            And up the hill his course is bending,
            With many a stop and stay ascending; 1836–43 *only*
41 And now are up at the top *etc.* MSS. 1, 2

He was patient, they were strong,
And now they smoothly glide along,
Recovering breath, and pleased to win
The praises of mild Benjamin.   45
Heaven shield him from mishap and snare!
But why so early with this prayer?
Is it for threatenings in the sky?
Or for some other danger nigh?
No; none is near him yet, though he   50
Be one of much infirmity;
For at the bottom of the brow,
Where once the DOVE and OLIVE-BOUGH
Offered a greeting of good ale
To all who entered Grasmere Vale;   55
And called on him who must depart
To leave it with a jovial heart;
There, where the DOVE and OLIVE-BOUGH
Once hung, a Poet harbours now,
A simple water-drinking Bard;   60
Why need our Hero then (though frail
His best resolves) be on his guard?
He marches by, secure and bold;
Yet while he thinks on times of old,
It seems that all looks wondrous cold;   65
He shrugs his shoulders, shakes his head,
And, for the honest folk within,
It is a doubt with Benjamin
Whether they be alive or dead!

    Here is no danger,—none at all!   70
Beyond his wish he walks secure;
But pass a mile—and *then* for trial,—
Then for the pride of self-denial;
If he resist that tempting door,

44 Recovering 1836: Gathering MSS., 1819–32   45 mild] good MSS.
46 . . . and from all defend
   For he is their Father and their (never failing MS. 3) friend
   From all mishap and every snare! MSS.
50–1 *so* 1819 *etc.*: No; him infirmities beset,
           But danger is not near him yet 1836
61–2 Then why need Ben be on his guard? MSS. 1, 2   67 folk] folks
MSS. 1, 2   70 No danger's here, no, none at all MSS.   71 walks
1836: is MSS., 1819–32   74 he] thou MSS. 1, 2

Which with such friendly voice will call;   75
If he resist those casement panes,
And that bright gleam which thence will fall
Upon his Leaders' bells and manes,
Inviting him with cheerful lure:
For still, though all be dark elsewhere,   80
Some shining notice will be *there*,
Of open house and ready fare.

   The place to Benjamin right well
Is known, and by as strong a spell
As used to be that sign of love   85
And hope—the OLIVE-BOUGH and DOVE;
He knows it to his cost, good Man!
Who does not know the famous SWAN?
Object uncouth! and yet our boast,
For it was painted by the Host;   90
His own conceit the figure planned,
'Twas coloured all by his own hand;
And that frail Child of thirsty clay,
Of whom I sing this rustic lay,
Could tell with self-dissatisfaction   95
Quaint stories of the bird's attraction![1]

   Well! that is past—and in despite
Of open door and shining light.
And now the conqueror essays
The long ascent of Dunmail-raise;   100
And with his team is gentle here
As when he clomb from Rydal Mere;
His whip they do not dread—his voice
They only hear it to rejoice.

---

[1] This rude piece of self-taught art (such is the progress of refinement) has been supplanted by a professional production.

76–82 Look at thee with so bright a lure
    For surely if no other where
    Candle or lamp is burning there   MSS. 1, 2
83 right 1836: full MSS., 1819–32
89 Uncouth although the object be
    An image of perplexity;
    But what of that (Yet not the less MS. 1 *corr.*) it is our boast MSS.,
      1819–32
93–4 *not in* MSS.: sing 1827: frame 1819–20
95–6 And Ben with *etc.*
    Could tell long tales of its attraction MSS.
99 the conqueror] good Benjamin MSS.

To stand or go is at *their* pleasure;   105
Their efforts and their time they measure
By generous pride within the breast;
And, while they strain, and while they rest,
He thus pursues his thoughts at leisure.

   Now am I fairly safe to-night--   110
And with proud cause my heart is light:
I trespassed lately worse than ever—
But Heaven has blest a good endeavour;
And, to my soul's content, I find
The evil One is left behind.   115
Yes, let my master fume and fret,
Here am I—with my horses yet!
My jolly team, he finds that ye
Will work for nobody but me!
Full proof of this the Country gained;   120
It knows how ye were vexed and strained,

105, 6 *trs.* MSS.   107 He knows that each will do his best   MSS.
111 *so* 1836: And never was my heart more light   MSS., 1819–32
111/12 I've been a sinner, I avow,
     But better times are coming now   MSS.
112–13 A sinner lately . . . But God will bless . . . MSS.   113 will
bless 1819–32   114 content 1836: delight   MSS., 1819–32   115
left] cast MSS.
116 I'm here and let my master fret
    He makes a mighty noise about me
    And yet he cannot do without me   MSS. 1, 2, MS. 1 *corr. to*
    When I was gone he felt my lack
    And was right glad to have me back
120–138 Finds that with hills so steep and high
    This Monster at our heels must lie
    Dead as a cheese upon a shelf
    Or fairly learn to draw itself.
    When I was gone he felt his lack
    And was right glad to have me back   MSS. 1, 2 *corr to*
    Let Simon flog and Arthur curse
    He knows they only make bad worse
    That without me *etc. as* 136–7
    Let force and flattery both be tried
    This Monster at our heels must lie
    Midway upon the bleak Fell-side
    As dead as Bowder-stone, to stir
    No more till Ben be Waggoner.
    Then grieve not *etc.*
120 Full 1836: Good MS. 3, 1819–32
121–3 *so* 1836: One day when ye . . . Entrusted to . . .
      And forced (ll. 122 *and* 123 *transposed*) MS. 3, 1819–32

And forced unworthy stripes to bear,
When trusted to another's care.
Here was it—on this rugged slope,
Which now ye climb with heart and hope,   125
I saw you, between rage and fear,
Plunge, and fling back a spiteful ear,
And ever more and more confused,
As ye were more and more abused:
As chance would have it, passing by   130
I saw you in that jeopardy:
A word from me was like a charm;
Ye pulled together with one mind;
And your huge burthen, safe from harm,
Moved like a vessel in the wind!   135
—Yes, without me, up hills so high
'Tis vain to strive for mastery.
Then grieve not, jolly team! though tough
The road we travel, steep, and rough;
Though Rydal-heights and Dunmail-raise,   140
And all their fellow banks and braes,
Full often make you stretch and strain,
And halt for breath and halt again,
Yet to their sturdiness 'tis owing
That side by side we still are going!   145

      While Benjamin in earnest mood
His meditations thus pursued,
A storm, which had been smothered long,
Was growing inwardly more strong;

124–8 *so* 1830: Here was it—on this rugged spot
                    Which now contented with our lot
                    We climb—that piteously abused
                    Ye plung'd in anger and confused   MS. 3, 1819–32
131 that 1836: your   MS. 3, 1819–32   133 *so* 1836: The ranks were
taken with *etc.*   MS. 3, 1819–32   139 The road we travel 1819–32: Our
road be, narrow *etc.* 1836: Our road be sometimes   MSS.
140–5 But take your time, no more I ask,
          I know you're equal to your task,
          And for us all I'll sing the praise
          Of our good friend here Dunmail Raise
          And of his brother Banks and Braes,
          For plain it is that they're the tether
          By which we have been kept together.   MSS. 1, 2
MS. 3 *first 3 lines as above*, l. 4 Of Rydal-heights and, ll. 5–*end as text* 141–5,
but l. 142 For though full oft they make you strain

And, in its struggles to get free,   150
Was busily employed as he.
The thunder had begun to growl—
He heard not, too intent of soul;
The air was now without a breath—
He marked not that 'twas still as death.   155
But soon large rain-drops on his head
Fell with the weight of drops of lead;—
He starts—and takes, at the admonition,
A sage survey of his condition.
The road is black before his eyes,   160
Glimmering faintly where it lies;
Black is the sky—and every hill,
Up to the sky, is blacker still—
Sky, hill, and dale, one dismal room,
Hung round and overhung with gloom;   165
Save that above a single height
Is to be seen a lurid light,
Above Helm-crag[1]—a streak half dead,
A burning of portentous red;
And near that lurid light, full well   170
The ASTROLOGER, sage Sidrophel,
Where at his desk and book he sits,
Puzzling aloft his curious wits;
He whose domain is held in common
With no one but the ANCIENT WOMAN,   175
Cowering beside her rifted cell,
As if intent on magic spell;—
Dread pair that, spite of wind and weather,
Still sit upon Helm-crag together!

[1] A mountain of Grasmere, the broken summit of which presents two figures, full as distinctly shaped as that of the famous Cobbler near Arroquhar in Scotland.

---

156 soon large 1836: now some   MSS., 1819–32
158–9 *so* 1836: He starts—and at the admonition
            Takes a survey of his condition. MSS. 1819–32
164 *so* 1836: A huge and melancholy room MSS., 1819–32   169 por-
tentous] a sullen MSS. 1, 2   171 sage] dread MSS.   173 *so* 1836:
Puzzling his wicked wicked MSS. 1, 2, on high his wicked   MS. 3, 1819–32
174–8 He who from Quarter in the North
        For mischief looks or sends it forth
        Sharing his wild domain in common
        With southern Neighbour the old Woman
        A pair that *etc.*   MSS. 1, 2

The ASTROLOGER was not unseen   180
By solitary Benjamin;
But total darkness came anon,
And he and everything was gone:
And suddenly a ruffling breeze,
(That would have rocked the sounding trees,   185
Had aught of sylvan growth been there)
Swept through the Hollow long and bare:
The rain rushed down—the road was battered,
As with the force of billows shattered;
The horses are dismayed, nor know   190
Whether they should stand or go;
And Benjamin is groping near them,
Sees nothing, and can scarcely hear them.
He is astounded,—wonder not,—
With such a charge in such a spot;   195
Astounded in the mountain gap
With thunder-peals, clap after clap,
Close-treading on the silent flashes—
And somewhere, as he thinks, by crashes
Among the rocks; with weight of rain,   200
And sullen motions long and slow,
That to a dreary distance go—
Till, breaking in upon the dying strain,
A rending o'er his head begins the fray again.

Meanwhile, uncertain what to do,   205
And oftentimes compelled to halt,
The horses cautiously pursue
Their way, without mishap or fault;
And now have reached that pile of stones,
Heaped over brave King Dunmail's bones,   210
He who had once supreme command,
Last king of rocky Cumberland;

184–7 *not in* MSS., 1819: 185 sounded through the trees 1820–32
187 Was felt throughout that region bare 1820–32   190 The horses
scarcely seem to know MSS. 1, 2
197–9 *so* 1836: By peals of thunder clap on clap!
          And now and then a dismal flash
          And somewhere as it seems a crash   MSS., *but* MS. 3 And many a
              terror-striking flash   *so* 1819–32
201–4 *added to* MSS. 1, 2 *in place of illegible erasure*   210 brave] good
MSS. 1, 2   212 Our King in MSS. 1, 2

His bones, and those of all his Power,
Slain here in a disastrous hour!

When, passing through this narrow strait,   215
Stony, and dark, and desolate,
Benjamin can faintly hear
A voice that comes from some one near,
A female voice:—"Whoe'er you be,
Stop," it exclaimed, "and pity me!"   220
And less in pity than in wonder,
Amid the darkness and the thunder,
The Waggoner, with prompt command,
Summons his horses to a stand.

While, with increasing agitation,   225
The Woman urged her supplication,
In rueful words, with sobs between—
The voice of tears that fell unseen;
There came a flash—a startling glare,
And all Seat-Sandal was laid bare!   230
'Tis not a time for nice suggestion,
And Benjamin, without a question,

215 narrow] stony MSS. 1, 2   216 ('Tis little wider than a gate) MSS. 1, 2
219–20 A female voice, a voice of fear
        "Stop" says the voice "whoe'er ye be
        Stop, stop good friend and pity me"   MSS. 1, 2
223 The Waggoner] Good Benjamin MSS.
225–30 *so* 1836: "Now tell" says he "in honest deed
        Who you are and what you need."
        Careless of this adjuration
        The voice to move commiseration
        Still prolonged its supplication—
        "This storm that beats so furiously
        This dreadful place! oh pity me!"
        While this was said, with sobs between
        And many tears by one unseen,
        There came a flash and held a candle
        To the whole bosom of Seat Sandal.   MSS. 1, 2
        The voice, to move commiseration,
        Prolong'd its earnest supplication—
        "This storm that beats so furiously—
        This dreadful place! oh pity me!"
        While this was said, with sobs between,
        And many tears, by one unseen; *etc. as text,* 1819–32
232–3 And, kind to every way-worn rover
        Benjamin without a question 1836; 1819–32 *as text, but* further *for* a

Taking her for some way-worn rover,
Said, "Mount, and get you under cover!"

    Another voice, in tone as hoarse   235
As a swoln brook with rugged course,
Cried out, "Good brother, why so fast?
I've had a glimpse of you—*avast!*
Or, since it suits you to be civil,
Take her at once—for good and evil!"   240

    "It is my Husband," softly said
The Woman, as if half afraid:
By this time she was snug within,
Through help of honest Benjamin;
She and her Babe, which to her breast   245
With thankfulness the Mother pressed;
And now the same strong voice more near
Said cordially, "My Friend, what cheer?
Rough doings these! as God's my judge,
The sky owes somebody a grudge!   250
We've had in half an hour or less
A twelvemonth's terror and distress!"

    Then Benjamin entreats the Man
Would mount, too, quickly as he can:
The Sailor—Sailor now no more,   255
But such he had been heretofore—
To courteous Benjamin replied,
"Go you your way, and mind not me;
For I must have, whate'er betide,
My Ass and fifty things beside,—   260
Go, and I'll follow speedily!"

    The Waggon moves—and with its load
Descends along the sloping road;
And the rough Sailor instantly
Turns to a little tent hard by: 265

236 As Brook with steep and stony course MSS. 1, 2   239 Let go, or
since you must be civil MSS.   245–6 . . . for Babe she had No wonder
then if she was glad MSS. 1, 2
253/4 But Kate give thanks for this and ride
      In quiet (Contented MS. 3) and be pacified"   MSS.
264–5 *so* 1845: And to a little tent hard by
        Turns the Sailor instantly   MSS., 1819–32
        And to his tent-like domicile,
        Built in a nook with cautious skill,

For when, at closing-in of day,
The family had come that way,
Green pasture and the soft warm air
Tempted them to settle there.—
Green is the grass for beast to graze,   270
Around the stones of Dunmail-raise!

    The Sailor gathers up his bed,
Takes down the canvass overhead;
And, after farewell to the place,
A parting word—though not of grace,   275
Pursues, with Ass and all his store,
The way the Waggon went before.

Canto Second

IF Wytheburne's modest House of prayer,
As lowly as the lowliest dwelling,
Had, with its belfry's humble stock,
A little pair that hang in air,
Been mistress also of a clock,   5
(And one, too, not in crazy plight)
Twelve strokes that clock would have been telling
Under the brow of old Helvellyn—
Its bead-roll of midnight,
Then, when the Hero of my tale   10
Was passing by, and, down the vale
(The vale now silent, hushed, I ween,
As if a storm had never been)
Proceeding with a mind at ease;
While the old Familiar of the seas,   15
Intent to use his utmost haste,
Gained ground upon the Waggon fast,

      The Sailor turns, well pleased to spy
      His shaggy friend who stood hard by
      Drenched—and, more fast than with a tether,
      Bound to the nook by that fierce weather,
      Which caught the vagrants unaware: 1836
269 Tempted 1836: Had tempted MSS. 1819–32
II. 1 modest] lowly MSS.
14–15 *so* 1836: Proceeding with an easy mind
               And little thought of Him behind   MSS.
               While he who had been left behind 1819–32
16 Who having used MSS.   17/18 And now is almost at its heels
MSS. 1, 2

And gives another lusty cheer;
For, spite of rumbling of the wheels,
A welcome greeting he can hear;—   20
It is a fiddle in its glee
Dinning from the CHERRY TREE!

Thence the sound—the light is there—
As Benjamin is now aware,
Who, to his inward thoughts confined,   25
Had almost reached the festive door,
When, startled by the Sailor's roar,
He hears a sound and sees the light,
And in a moment calls to mind
That 'tis the village MERRY-NIGHT![1]   30

Although before in no dejection,
At this insidious recollection
His heart with sudden joy is filled,—
His ears are by the music thrilled,
His eyes take pleasure in the road   35
Glittering before him bright and broad;
And Benjamin is wet and cold,
And there are reasons manifold
That make the good, tow'rds which he's yearning,
Look fairly like a lawful earning.   40

Nor has thought time to come and go,
To vibrate between yes and no;
For, cries the Sailor, "Glorious chance
That blew us hither!—let him dance,
Who can or will!—my honest soul,   45
Our treat shall be a friendly bowl!"

[1] A term well known in the North of England, and applied to rural
Festivals where young persons meet in the evening for the purpose of
dancing.

25–7 *so* 1820: Who neither saw nor heard—no more
                 Than if he had been deaf or blind
                 Till, startled (rouz'd up MSS. 1, 2) by *etc.* MSS. 1819
32 He gladdens at the MSS.   37 And] For MSS. 1, 2   40 a lawful]
an honest MSS.
44–6 *so* 1819–32, 1845: dance boys dance
                 Rare luck for us! my honest soul
                 I'll treat thee to (with MSS. 1, 2) a friendly bowl.
                 MSS., 1836

He draws him to the door—"Come in,
Come, come," cries he to Benjamin!
And Benjamin—ah, woe is me!
Gave the word—the horses heard   50
And halted, though reluctantly.

  "Blithe souls and lightsome hearts have we
Feasting at the CHERRY TREE!"
This was the outside proclamation,
This was the inside salutation;   55
What bustling—jostling—high and low!
A universal overflow!
What tankards foaming from the tap!
What store of cakes in every lap!
What thumping—stumping—overhead!   60
The thunder had not been more busy:
With such a stir you would have said,
This little place may well be dizzy!
'Tis who can dance with greatest vigour—
'Tis what can be most prompt and eager;   65
As if it heard the fiddle's call,
The pewter clatters on the wall;
The very bacon shows its feeling,
Swinging from the smoky ceiling!

  A steaming bowl, a blazing fire,   70
What greater good can heart desire?
'Twere worth a wise man's while to try
The utmost anger of the sky:
To *seek* for thoughts of a gloomy cast,
If such the bright amends at last.   75
Now should you say I judge amiss,
The CHERRY TREE shows proof of this;
For soon, of all the happy there,
Our Travellers are the happiest pair;
All care with Benjamin is gone—   80
A Cæsar past the Rubicon!

74 *so* 1836: To seek even thoughts of painful cast MSS. 1, 2; 1819–32 *as* 1836,
but painful *for* a gloomy   75 If such be the amends at last MSS. 1819–32
80–84 *so* MSS., 1819–32, 1845: And happiest far is he the One
                      No longer with himself at strife,
                      A Caesar *etc.*
                      The Sailor *etc.*
                      Found not a scruple in *his* **way**   1836

He thinks not of his long, long, strife;—
The Sailor, Man by nature gay,
Hath no resolves to throw away;
And he hath now forgot his Wife,   85
Hath quite forgotten her—or may be
Thinks her the luckiest soul on earth,
Within that warm and peaceful berth,
        Under cover,
        Terror over,   90
Sleeping by her sleeping Baby.

    With bowl that sped from hand to hand,
The gladdest of the gladsome band,
Amid their own delight and fun,
They hear—when every dance is done,   95
When every whirling bout is o'er—
The fiddle's *squeak*[1]—that call to bliss,
Ever followed by a kiss;
They envy not the happy lot,
But enjoy their own the more!   100

    While thus our jocund Travellers fare,
Up springs the Sailor from his chair—
Limps (for I might have told before
That he was lame) across the floor—
Is gone—returns—and with a prize;   105
With what?—a Ship of lusty size;
A gallant stately Man-of-war,
Fixed on a smoothly-sliding car.

----

[1] At the close of each strathspey, or jig, a particular note from the fiddle
summons the Rustic to the agreeable duty of saluting his partner.

87–8 *so* 1836: Knows what is the truth I wis
                That she is better where she is   MSS. 1, 2
                Deems that she is happier, laid
                Within that warm and peaceful bed,   MS. 3, 1819–32
92–3 *so* 1845: With bowl in hand,
                (It may not stand)
                Gladdest of the gladsome band,   MSS. 1819–32
                With bowl that sped *etc.*
                Refreshed, brimful of hearty fun
                The gladdest *etc.*   1836
96 *so* 1836: They hear—when every fit is o'er—MSS., 1819–32
106/7 A Vessel following at his heels
      Upon a frame that goes by wheels   MSS.
108 Sliding on a sliding car MSS.

Surprise to all, but most surprise
To Benjamin, who rubs his eyes,   110
Not knowing that he had befriended
A Man so gloriously attended!

"This," cries the Sailor, "a Third-rate is—
Stand back, and you shall see her gratis!
This was the Flag-ship at the Nile,   115
The VANGUARD—you may smirk and smile,
But, pretty Maid, if you look near,
You'll find you've much in little here!
A nobler ship did never swim,
And you shall see her in full trim: 120
I'll set, my friends, to do you honour,
Set every inch of sail upon her."
So said, so done; and masts, sails, yards,
He names them all; and interlards
His speech with uncouth terms of art,   125
Accomplished in the showman's part;
And then, as from a sudden check,
Cries out—"'Tis there, the quarter-deck
On which brave Admiral Nelson stood—
A sight that would have roused your blood!—   130
One eye he had, which, bright as ten,
Burned like a fire among his men;
Let this be land, and that be sea,
Here lay the French—and *thus* came we!"

Hushed was by this the fiddle's sound,   135
The dancers all were gathered round,
And such the stillness of the house,
You might have heard a nibbling mouse;
While, borrowing helps where'er he may,
The Sailor through the story runs   140
Of ships to ships and guns to guns;
And does his utmost to display
The dismal conflict, and the might
And terror of that marvellous night!
"A bowl, a bowl of double measure,"   145
Cries Benjamin, "a draught of length,

113 Third-rate] first rate MS. 2   130 . . . done you good MSS. 1, 2
144 marvellous 1836: wondrous MSS., 1819–32

To Nelson, England's pride and treasure,
Her bulwark and her tower of strength!"
When Benjamin had seized the bowl,
The mastiff, from beneath the waggon,   150
Where he lay, watchful as a dragon,
Rattled his chain;—'twas all in vain,
For Benjamin, triumphant soul!
He heard the monitory growl;
Heard—and in opposition quaffed   155
A deep, determined, desperate draught!
Nor did the battered Tar forget,
Or flinch from what he deemed his debt:
Then, like a hero crowned with laurel,
Back to her place the ship he led;   160
Wheeled her back in full apparel;
And so, flag flying at mast head,
Re-yoked her to the Ass:—anon
Cries Benjamin, "We must be gone."
Thus, after two hours' hearty stay,   165
Again behold them on their way!

Canto Third

RIGHT gladly had the horses stirred,
When they the wished-for greeting heard,
The whip's loud notice from the door,
That they were free to move once more.
You think, those doings must have bred   5
In them disheartening doubts and dreads;
No, not a horse of all the eight,
Although it be a moonless night,
Fears either for himself or freight;
For this they know (and let it hide,   10
In part, the offences of their guide)
That Benjamin, with clouded brains,
Is worth the best with all their pains;
And, if they had a prayer to make,
The prayer would be that they may take   15
With him whatever comes in course,
The better fortune or the worse;

149/50 The mastiff gave a warning growl MSS. 1, 2
III. 3–4 The smack of greeting . . . The sign that they might move MSS.
10–11 . . . show full well And this in pleasure I may tell MSS. 1, 2   12
clouded] half his MSS.

That no one else may have business near them,
And, drunk or sober, he may steer them.

So forth in dauntless mood they fare,   20
And with them goes the guardian pair.

Now, heroes, for the true commotion,
The triumph of your late devotion!
Can aught on earth impede delight,
Still mounting to a higher height;   25
And higher still—a greedy flight!
Can any low-born care pursue her,
Can any mortal clog come to her ?
No notion have they—not a thought,
That is from joyless regions brought!   30
And, while they coast the silent lake,
Their inspiration I partake;
Share their empyreal spirits—yea,
With their enraptured vision, see—
O fancy—what a jubilee!   35
What shifting pictures—clad in gleams
Of colour bright as feverish dreams!
Earth, spangled sky, and lake serene,
Involved and restless all—a scene

23 triumph] blessing MSS. 1, 2   28/9 *for episode omitted here from text,*
v. note, p. 499.   30 Not one that is not highly wrought MSS. 1, 2
31 Beside the spring and silent lake   MSS. 1, 2
36–42 Behold the radiant imagery
          The many pictures and the gleams
          Of colour bright as feverish dreams
          Brave world for poet's eye to see
          O Fancy what a jubilee
          This sight *etc.*   MSS. 1, 2 (*with slight variants*). *The verso of* MS. 1 *has*
              several rough drafts of 38–41, *e.g.*:
          Commingling with the world that lies
          In peace before their outward eyes
          Rocks, clouds and stars a solemn show
          Repeated in the lake below
          The heavens the air the abyss serene
          Of waters all a restless scene
          But restless to their eyes alone
          Pregnant with rare imagination
          Rich change and multiplied creation:
      MS. 3 *between this and text*

Pregnant with mutual exaltation,   40
Rich change, and multiplied creation!
This sight to me the Muse imparts;—
And then, what kindness in their hearts!
What tears of rapture, what vow-making,
Profound entreaties, and hand-shaking!   45
What solemn, vacant, interlacing,
As if they'd fall asleep embracing!
Then, in the turbulence of glee,
And in the excess of amity,
Says Benjamin, "That Ass of thine,   50
He spoils thy sport, and hinders mine:
If he were tethered to the waggon,
He'd drag as well what he is dragging;
And we, as brother should with brother,
Might trudge it alongside each other!"   55

Forthwith, obedient to command,
The horses made a quiet stand;
And to the waggon's skirts was tied
The Creature, by the Mastiff's side,
The Mastiff wondering, and perplext   60
With dread of what will happen next;
And thinking it but sorry cheer
To have such company so near!

This new arrangement made, the Wain
Through the still night proceeds again;   65
No moon hath risen her light to lend;
But indistinctly may be kenned
The VANGUARD, following close behind,
Sails spread, as if to catch the wind!

5 6–7 *not in* MSS. 1, 2   58 So to the . . . they tied MSS. 1, 2
60–3 *so* 1836: The Mastiff not well pleased to be
                So very near such company   MSS., 1819–32
64–7 And stumbling (staggering MS. 2) to the Rock once more
        They drank as deeply as before
        Their burning faces they bedew'd
        And thus their journey all renew'd
        The vanguard following (do not blame
        The Poet for the unlucky name
        No, praise him, he makes no pretence
        To wit that deals in double sense)   MSS. 1, 2 (*v. note on* 28/9)

"Thy wife and child are snug and warm,   70
Thy ship will travel without harm:
I like," said Benjamin, "her shape and stature:
And this of mine—this bulky creature
Of which I have the steering—this,
Seen fairly, is not much amiss!   75
We want your streamers, friend, you know;
But, altogether as we go,
We make a kind of handsome show!
Among these hills, from first to last,
We've weathered many a furious blast;   80
Hard passage forcing on, with head
Against the storm, and canvass spread.
I hate a boaster; but to thee
Will say't, who know'st both land and sea,
The unluckiest hulk that stems the brine   85
Is hardly worse beset than mine,
When cross-winds on her quarter beat:
And, fairly lifted from my feet,
I stagger onward—heaven knows how;
But not so pleasantly as now: 90
Poor pilot I, by snows confounded,
And many a foundrous pit surrounded!
Yet here we are, by night and day
Grinding through rough and smooth our way;
Through foul and fair our task fulfilling;   95
And long shall be so yet—God willing!"

    "Ay," said the Tar, "through fair and foul—
But save us from yon screeching owl!"
That instant was begun a fray
Which called their thoughts another way: 100
The Mastiff, ill-conditioned carl!
What must he do but growl and snarl,

80 furious] stormy MSS. 1, 2
81–99 Aye long and long by night and day
        Together have we ground our way
        Through foul and fair our task fulfilling
        And long shall do so yet, God willing.
        "Plague on the whooping and the howl"
        Replies the Tar "of yon screech owl"
        But instantly began a fray   MSS. 1, 2
MS. 3 81–96 *as text*, 97–9 *as* MS. 1
85 stems 1836: sails MS. 3, 1819–32

Still more and more dissatisfied
With the meek comrade at his side!
Till, not incensed though put to proof,   105
The Ass, uplifting a hind hoof,
Salutes the Mastiff on the head;
And so were better manners bred,
And all was calmed and quieted.

"Yon screech-owl," says the Sailor, turning   110
Back to his former cause of mourning,
"Yon owl!—pray God that all be well!
'Tis worse than any funeral bell;
As sure as I've the gift of sight,
We shall be meeting ghosts to-night!"   115
—Said Benjamin, "This whip shall lay
A thousand, if they cross our way.
I know that Wanton's noisy station,
I know him and his occupation;
The jolly bird hath learned his cheer   120
Upon the banks of Windermere;
Where a tribe of them make merry,
Mocking the Man that keeps the ferry;
Hallooing from an open throat,
Like travellers shouting for a boat.   125
—The tricks he learned at Windermere
This vagrant owl is playing here—
That is the worst of his employment:
He's at the top of his enjoyment!"

This explanation stilled the alarm,   130
Cured the foreboder like a charm;
This, and the manner, and the voice,
Summoned the Sailor to rejoice;
His heart is up—he fears no evil
From life or death, from man or devil;   135
He wheels—and, making many stops,
Brandished his crutch against the mountain tops;
And, while he talked of blows and scars,
Benjamin, among the stars,

106 hind] fore MSS.   117 cross our] come this MSS. 1, 2   127
vagrant] lonely MSS. 1, 2   129 at the top 1836: in the height MSS.
1819–32   136 wheels 1836: wheel'd MSS., 1819–32   139–40 Ben
beheld . . . Such a MSS. 1, 2

Beheld a dancing—and a glancing;   140
Such retreating and advancing
As, I ween, was never seen
In bloodiest battle since the days of Mars!

Canto Fourth

Thus they, with freaks of proud delight,
Beguile the remnant of the night;
And many a snatch of jovial song
Regales them as they wind along;
While to the music, from on high,   5
The echoes make a glad reply.—

IV. 1–82 MSS. 1, 2 *have no break of canto here, but run straight on as follows*:
          Triumphant pair pursue your sport;
          But let us cut our story short.
          What is yon that glitters bright
          Like a cloud of Rainbow-light,
          Like—it *is* a purple cloud
          Or a rainbow-coloured shroud,
          Such as doth round Angels blaze
          Travelling along heavenly ways;
          Slowly slowly up the steep
          Of Castrigg doth the vapour creep,
          Neither melting nor dividing
          Ever high and higher gliding,
          Glorious as at first it show'd
          Winding with the winding road:
          If you never saw or heard
          Of such object, take my word
          That the Waggon, the dull care
          Of good Benjamin is there
          And there, though hidden by the gleam,
          Benjamin is with his Team,
          Faithful still whate'er betide
          Whether follower or guide,
          And with him goes his Sailor friend *etc. as text* 70–4
MS. 1 *deletes, and on verso gives* 1–56 *as text, followed by drafts of* 57–62, *of which the following is adopted in* MS. 3
          The mists that were of dusky grey
          Are smitten by the silver ray,
          But what is yon that glitters bright
          Like a cloud of rainbow light
          Like ? it is *etc. as* MS. 1 . . . winding road
          And with that bright empurpled steam
          And partly hidden by the gleam
          The slow-paced Waggon hath ascended
          By faithful Benjamin attended.

But the sage Muse the revel heeds
No farther than her story needs;
Nor will she servilely attend
The loitering journey to its end.   10
—Blithe spirits of her own impel
The Muse, who scents the morning air,
To take of this transported pair
A brief and unreproved farewell;
To quit the slow-paced waggon's side,   15
And wander down yon hawthorn dell,
With murmuring Greta for her guide.
—There doth she ken the awful form
Of Raven-crag—black as a storm—
Glimmering through the twilight pale;   20
And Ghimmer-crag,[1] his tall twin brother,
Each peering forth to meet the other:—
And, while she roves through St. John's Vale,
Along the smooth unpathwayed plain,
By sheep-track or through cottage lane,   25
Where no disturbance comes to intrude
Upon the pensive solitude,
Her unsuspecting eye, perchance,
With the rude shepherd's favoured glance,
Beholds the faeries in array,   30
Whose party-coloured garments gay
The silent company betray:
Red, green, and blue; a moment's sight!
For Skiddaw-top with rosy light
Is touched—and all the band take flight.   35
—Fly also, Muse! and from the dell
Mount to the ridge of Nathdale Fell;
Thence, look thou forth o'er wood and lawn
Hoar with the frost-like dews of dawn;
Across yon meadowy bottom look,   40
Where close fogs hide their parent brook;
And see, beyond that hamlet small,
The ruined towers of Threlkeld-hall,
Lurking in a double shade,
By trees and lingering twilight made!   45
There, at Blencathara's rugged feet,
Sir Lancelot gave a safe retreat

[1] The crag of the ewe lamb.

To noble Clifford; from annoy
Concealed the persecuted boy,
Well pleased in rustic garb to feed   50
His flock, and pipe on shepherd's reed
Among this multitude of hills,
Crags, woodlands, waterfalls, and rills;
Which soon the morning shall enfold,
From east to west, in ample vest   55
Of massy gloom and radiance bold.

The mists, that o'er the streamlet's bed
Hung low, begin to rise and spread;
Even while I speak, their skirts of grey
Are smitten by a silver ray;   60
And, lo!—up Castrigg's naked steep
(Where, smoothly urged, the vapours sweep
Along—and scatter and divide,
Like fleecy clouds self-multiplied)
The stately waggon is ascending,   65
With faithful Benjamin attending,
Apparent now beside his team—
Now lost amid a glittering steam:
And with him goes his Sailor-friend,
By this time near their journey's end;   70
And, after their high-minded riot,
Sickening into thoughtful quiet;
As if the morning's pleasant hour
Had for their joys a killing power.
And, sooth, for Benjamin a vein   75
Is opened of still deeper pain,
As if his heart by notes were stung
From out the lowly hedge-rows flung;
As if the warbler lost in light
Reproved his soarings of the night,   80
In strains of rapture pure and holy
Upbraided his distempered folly.

Drooping is he, his step is dull;
But the horses stretch and pull;

75–82 *not in* MSS., 1819–32: 1836 *so text but ll.* 75–6:
        Say more: for by that power a vein
        Seems opened of brow-saddening pain, *and* their hearts
        . . . their . . . their *in ll.* 76, 80, 82
83 *so* 1845. They are drooping, weak and dull: MSS., 1819–32
        Drooping they are, and weak and dull;   1836

With increasing vigour climb,   85
Eager to repair lost time;
Whether, by their own desert,
Knowing what cause there is for shame,
They are labouring to avert
As much as may be of the blame,   90
Which, they foresee, must soon alight
Upon *his* head, whom, in despite
Of all his failings, they love best;
Whether for him they are distrest;
Or, by length of fasting roused,   95
Are impatient to be housed:
Up against the hill they strain
Tugging at the iron chain,
Tugging all with might and main,
Last and foremost, every horse   100
To the utmost of his force!
And the smoke and respiration,
Rising like an exhalation,
Blend with the mist—a moving shroud
To form, an undissolving cloud;   105
Which, with slant ray, the merry sun
Takes delight to play upon.
Never golden-haired Apollo,
Pleased some favourite chief to follow
Through accidents of peace or war,   110
In a perilous moment threw
Around the object of his care
Veil of such celestial hue;

88 *so* 1836: Knowing that there's cause MSS., 1819–20
                Knowing there is cause 1827
90–1 *so* 1845: At least a portion of the blame
      Which full surely will alight MSS. 1819–32
      (Kind creatures!) something of the blame *etc. as text* 1836
93 *so* 1836: Of all his faults, they love the best; MSS., 1819–32
106 Which the merry merry Sun MSS. 1, 2
108–13 *so* 1845: Never, surely, old Apollo,
                He, or other God as old,
                Of whom in story we are told,
                Who had a favourite to follow
                Through a battle or elsewhere,
                Round the object of his care,
                In a time of peril, threw
                Veil of such celestial hue;   1819–27
                Never Venus or Apollo,
                Pleased a favourite chief to follow

Interposed so bright a screen—
Him and his enemies between!   115

   Alas! what boots it ?—who can hide,
When the malicious Fates are bent
On working out an ill intent ?
Can destiny be turned aside ?
No—sad progress of my story!   120
Benjamin, this outward glory
Cannot shield thee from thy Master,
Who from Keswick has pricked forth,
Sour and surly as the north;
And, in fear of some disaster,   125
Comes to give what help he may,
And to hear what thou canst say;
If, as needs he must forbode,
Thou hast been loitering on the road!
His fears, his doubts, may now take flight—   130
The wished-for object is in sight;
Yet, trust the Muse, it rather hath
Stirred him up to livelier wrath;
Which he stifles, moody man!
With all the patience that he can;   135
To the end that, at your meeting,
He may give thee decent greeting.

     Through accidents of peace or war,
     In a time of peril threw,
     Round the object of his care,
     Veil of such celestial hue;   1832
     Never golden-haired Apollo,
     Nor blue-eyed Pallas, nor the Idalian Queen,
     When each was pleased some favourite chief to follow
     Through accidents of peace or war,
     In a perilous moment threw
     Around the object of celestial care
     A veil so rich to mortal view.   1836
128 *so* MSS. 1819–32; If, as he cannot but forebode 1836   129 been
loitering 1836: loitered MSS., 1819–32
130–2 He is waiting on the height
    Of Castrigg, sees the vapour bright;
    Soon as he beheld he knew it
    And the Waggon glimmering through it,
    Glad sight and yet it rather hath   MSS. 1, 2
    Peace to his spirit, envious night
    For what he seeks is now in sight; Yet *etc*   MS. 3 *corr.*

There he is—resolved to stop,
Till the waggon gains the top;
But stop he cannot—must advance: 140
Him Benjamin, with lucky glance,
Espies—and instantly is ready,
Self-collected, poised, and steady:
And, to be the better seen,
Issues from his radiant shroud,   145
From his close-attending cloud,
With careless air and open mien.
Erect his port, and firm his going;
So struts yon cock that now is crowing;
And the morning light in grace   150
Strikes upon his lifted face,
Hurrying the pallid hue away
That might his trespasses betray.
But what can all avail to clear him,
Or what need of explanation,   155
Parley or interrogation?
For the Master sees, alas!
That unhappy Figure near him,
Limping o'er the dewy grass,
Where the road it fringes, sweet,   160
Soft and cool to way-worn feet;
And, O indignity! an Ass,
By his noble Mastiff's side,
Tethered to the waggon's tail:
And the ship, in all her pride,   165
Following after in full sail!
Not to speak of babe and mother;
Who, contented with each other,
And snug as birds in leafy arbour,
Find, within, a blessed harbour!   170

　　　With eager eyes the Master pries;
Looks in and out, and through and through;
Says nothing—till at last he spies

141–2 And Ben espies him by good chance,
　　In a moment he is ready　MSS. 1, 2
145 Issues forth from out his shroud MSS. 1, 2   149 As yon cock
that now is crowing MSS. 1, 2   151 Crimsons o'er his MSS. 1, 2
152–3 And some sober thoughts arise
　　To steal the wandering from his eyes　MSS. 1, 2
169 And as snug as birds in arbour MSS. 1, 2

A wound upon the Mastiff's head,
A wound where plainly might be read   175
What feats an Ass's hoof can do!
But drop the rest:—this aggravation,
This complicated provocation,
A hoard of grievances unsealed;
All past forgiveness it repealed;   180
And thus, and through distempered blood
On both sides, Benjamin the good,
The patient, and the tender-hearted,
Was from his team and waggon parted;
When duty of that day was o'er,   185
Laid down his whip—and served no more.—
Nor could the waggon long survive,
When Benjamin had ceased to drive:
It lingered on;—guide after guide
Ambitiously the office tried;   190
But each unmanageable hill
Called for *his* patience and *his* skill;—
And sure it is that through this night,
And what the morning brought to light,
Two losses had we to sustain,   195
We lost both WAGGONER and WAIN!

Accept, O Friend, for praise or blame,
The gift of this adventurous song;
A record which I dared to frame,
Though timid scruples checked me long;   200

176 hoof] paw MSS. 1, 2
177 But drop the rest and give the sense
    The sum of all the consequence
    'T was briefly, that this aggravation   MSS. 1, 2
187–92 Nor could the Waggon's self survive
    The want of Benjamin to drive;
    Each steep unmanageable hill
    Call'd *etc.*
    It lingered on a month or so
    What came of it I do not know   MSS.
197–207 A poor Catastrophe say you
    Adventure never worth a song,
    Be free to think so, for I too
    Have thought so many times and long;
    But what I have *etc.* MSS. 1, 2 (*with reading of text written in later*)

They checked me—and I left the theme
Untouched;—in spite of many a gleam
Of fancy which thereon was shed,
Like pleasant sunbeams shifting still
Upon the side of a distant hill: 205
But Nature might not be gainsaid;
For what I have and what I miss
·I sing of these;—it makes my bliss!
Nor is it I who play the part,
But a shy spirit in my heart,   210
That comes and goes—will sometimes leap
From hiding-places ten years deep;
Or haunts me with familiar face,
Returning, like a ghost unlaid,
Until the debt I owe be paid.   215
Forgive me, then; for I had been
On friendly terms with this Machine:
In him, while he was wont to trace
Our roads, through many a long year's space,
A living almanack had we;   220
We had a speaking diary,
That in this uneventful place,
Gave to the days a mark and name
By which we knew them when they came.
—Yes, I, and all about me here,   225
Through all the changes of the year,
Had seen him through the mountains go,
In pomp of mist or pomp of snow,
Majestically huge and slow:
Or, with a milder grace adorning   230
The landscape of a summer's morning;
While Grasmere smoothed her liquid plain
The moving image to detain;
And mighty Fairfield, with a chime
Of echoes, to his march kept time;   235

213 *so* 1827: Sometimes as in the present case
           Will show a more familiar face   MSS., 1819
           Or, proud all rivalship to chase
           Will haunt me *etc*.   1820
218–20 In him, a Chieftain of his race
           A living *etc*.   MSS. 1, 2
223 to the days] every day MSS. 1, 2   224 them . . . they] it . . . it
MSS. 1, 2

When little other business stirred,
And little other sound was heard;
In that delicious hour of balm,
Stillness, solitude, and calm,
While yet the valley is arrayed,   240
On this side with a sober shade;
On that is prodigally bright—
Crag, lawn, and wood—with rosy light.
—But most of all, thou lordly Wain!
I wish to have thee here again,   245
When windows flap and chimney roars,
And all is dismal out of doors;
And, sitting by my fire, I see
Eight sorry carts, no less a train!
Unworthy successors of thee,   250
Come straggling through the wind and rain:
And oft, as they pass slowly on,
Beneath my windows, one by one,
See, perched upon the naked height
The summit of a cumbrous freight,   255
A single traveller—and there
Another; then perhaps a pair—
The lame, the sickly, and the old;
Men, women, heartless with the cold;
And babes in wet and starveling plight;   260
Which once, be weather as it might,
Had still a nest within a nest,
Thy shelter—and their mother's breast!
Then most of all, then far the most,
Do I regret what we have lost;   265
Am grieved for that unhappy sin
Which robbed us of good Benjamin;—
And of his stately Charge, which none
Could keep alive when He was gone!

253 windows 1836: window MSS., 1819–32

POEMS OF THE IMAGINATION

I

THERE WAS A BOY

[Composed November or December, 1798. Published 1800.]

THERE was a Boy; ye knew him well, ye cliffs
And islands of Winander!—many a time,
At evening, when the earliest stars began
To move along the edges of the hills,
Rising or setting, would he stand alone,   5
Beneath the trees, or by the glimmering lake;
And there, with fingers interwoven, both hands
Pressed closely palm to palm and to his mouth
Uplifted, he, as through an instrument,
Blew mimic hootings to the silent owls,   10
That they might answer him.—And they would shout
Across the watery vale, and shout again,
Responsive to his call,—with quivering peals,
And long halloos, and screams, and echoes loud
Redoubled and redoubled; concourse wild   15
Of jocund din! And, when there came a pause
Of silence such as baffled his best skill:
Then, sometimes, in that silence, while he hung
Listening, a gentle shock of mild surprise
Has carried far into his heart the voice   20
Of mountain-torrents; or the visible scene
Would enter unawares into his mind
With all its solemn imagery, its rocks,
Its woods, and that uncertain heaven received
Into the bosom of the steady lake.   25

This boy was taken from his mates, and died
In childhood, ere he was full twelve years old.
Pre-eminent in beauty is the vale
Where he was born and bred: the church-yard hangs
Upon a slope above the village-school;   30
And, through that churchyard when my way has led
On summer-evenings, I believe, that there
A long half-hour together I have stood
Mute—looking at the grave in which he lies!

I. *For variants v. Prelude*, pp. 154–7, 530–1, 608 D.

II

TO THE CUCKOO

[Composed March 23–26, 1802.—Published 1807.]

O BLITHE New-comer! I have heard,
I hear thee and rejoice.
O Cuckoo! shall I call thee Bird,
Or but a wandering Voice?

While I am lying on the grass 5
Thy twofold shout I hear,
From hill to hill it seems to pass
At once far off, and near.

Though babbling only to the Vale,
Of sunshine and of flowers, 10
Thou bringest unto me a tale
Of visionary hours.

Thrice welcome, darling of the Spring!
Even yet thou art to me
No bird, but an invisible thing, 15
A voice, a mystery;

The same whom in my schoolboy days
I listened to; that Cry
Which made me look a thousand ways
In bush, and tree, and sky. 20

II. 5–8 *so* 1845: While I am lying on the grass,
 I hear thy restless [hollow MS.] shout:
 From hill to hill it seems to pass,
 About, and all about! 1807
 While I am lying on the grass
 Thy loud note smites my ear!—
 From hill to hill it seems to pass,
 At once far off and near! 1815: *so* 1820, *but l.* 7 It seems
  to fill the whole air's space:
 While I am lying on the grass,
 Thy two-fold shout I hear,
 That seems to fill the whole air's space,
 As loud far off as near. 1827–43
9 *so* 1827: To me, no Babbler with a tale MS., 1807; I hear thee babbling to
the Vale 1815–20 11 *so* 1827: Thou tellest, Cuckoo! in the vale MS.,
1807: And unto me thou bring'st a tale 1815; But *etc.* 1820 18–19
. . . whom I Look'd for a thousand thousand ways MS.

To seek thee did I often rove
Through woods and on the green;
And thou wert still a hope, a love;
Still longed for, never seen.

And I can listen to thee yet;   25
Can lie upon the plain
And listen, till I do beget
That golden time again.

O blessèd Bird! the earth we pace
Again appears to be   30
An unsubstantial, faery place;
That is fit home for Thee!

III

A NIGHT-PIECE

[Composed January 25, 1798.—Published 1815.]

————THE sky is overcast
With a continuous cloud of texture close,
Heavy and wan, all whitened by the Moon,
Which through that veil is indistinctly seen,
A dull, contracted circle, yielding light   5
So feebly spread that not a shadow falls,
Chequering the ground—from rock, plant, tree, or tower.
At length a pleasant instantaneous gleam
Startles the pensive traveller while he treads
His lonesome path, with unobserving eye   10
Bent earthwards; he looks up—the clouds are split
Asunder,—and above his head he sees
The clear Moon, and the glory of the heavens.
There, in a black-blue vault she sails along,
Followed by multitudes of stars, that, small   15
And sharp, and bright, along the dark abyss
Drive as she drives: how fast they wheel away,
Yet vanish not!—the wind is in the tree,

III. 1–7   The sky is overspread
     With a close veil of one continuous cloud
     All whitened by the moon that first appears
     A dim seen orb, yet chequers not the ground
     With any shadow—plant or tower or tree   MS.
8 At last . . . light MS.   9–10 . . . musing man whose eyes are bent
To earth; he looks around *etc.* MS.   12 sees] views MS.   16 dark
abyss] gloomy vault MS.

But they are silent;—still they roll along
Immeasurably distant; and the vault,   20
Built round by those white clouds, enormous clouds,
Still deepens its unfathomable depth.
At length the Vision closes; and the mind,
Not undisturbed by the delight it feels,
Which slowly settles into peaceful calm,   25
Is left to muse upon the solemn scene.

IV

AIREY-FORCE VALLEY

[Composed Sept. 1835.—Published 1842.]

————Not a breath of air
Ruffles the bosom of this leafy glen.
From the brook's margin, wide around, the trees
Are steadfast as the rocks; the brook itself,
Old as the hills that feed it from afar,   5
Doth rather deepen than disturb the calm
Where all things else are still and motionless.
And yet, even now, a little breeze, perchance
Escaped from boisterous winds that rage without,
Has entered, by the sturdy oaks unfelt,   10
But to its gentle touch how sensitive
Is the light ash! that, pendent from the brow
Of yon dim cave, in seeming silence makes
A soft eye-music of slow-waving boughs,
Powerful almost as vocal harmony   15
To stay the wanderer's steps and soothe his thoughts.

V

YEW-TREES

[Composed 1803 (?).—Published 1815.]

There is a Yew-tree, pride of Lorton Vale,
Which to this day stands single, in the midst
Of its own darkness, as it stood of yore:

22 unfathomable] interminable MS.   24 delight] deep joy MS.
IV. 4/5 Following, in patient solitude, a course MSS.
V. 1 In a small croft of Lorton's pleasant vale
     A venerable Yew-tree may be seen   MS.

Not loth to furnish weapons for the bands
Of Umfraville or Percy ere they marched   5
To Scotland's heaths; or those that crossed the sea
And drew their sounding bows at Azincour,
Perhaps at earlier Crecy, or Poictiers.
Of vast circumference and gloom profound
This solitary Tree! a living thing   10
Produced too slowly ever to decay;
Of form and aspect too magnificent
To be destroyed. But worthier still of note
Are those fraternal Four of Borrowdale,
Joined in one solemn and capacious grove;   15
Huge trunks! and each particular trunk a growth
Of intertwisted fibres serpentine
Up-coiling, and inveterately convolved;
Nor uninformed with Phantasy, and looks
That threaten the profane;—a pillared shade,   20
Upon whose grassless floor of red-brown hue,
By sheddings from the pining umbrage tinged
Perennially—beneath whose sable roof
Of boughs, as if for festal purpose decked
With unrejoicing berries—ghostly Shapes   25
May meet at noontide; Fear and trembling Hope,
Silence and Foresight; Death the Skeleton
And Time the Shadow;—there to celebrate,
As in a natural temple scattered o'er
With altars undisturbed of mossy stone,   30
United worship; or in mute repose
To lie, and listen to the mountain flood
Murmuring from Glaramara's inmost caves.

9/10 Obdurate and invincible appears MS.
After 33 Pass not the [? Place] unvisited—Ye will say
         That Mona's Druid Oaks composed a Fane
         Less awful than this grove: as Earth so long
         On its unwearied bosom has sustained
         The undecaying Pile; as Frost and Drought,
         The Fires of heaven have spared it, and the Storms,
         So for its hallowed uses may it stand
         For ever spared by Man!   MS. (*deleted*)

VI

NUTTING

[Composed 1798.—Published 1800.]

——————————It seems a day
(I speak of one from many singled out)
One of those heavenly days that cannot die;
When, in the eagerness of boyish hope,
I left our cottage-threshold, sallying forth   5
With a huge wallet o'er my shoulders slung,
A nutting-crook in hand; and turned my steps
Tow'rd some far-distant wood, a Figure quaint,
Tricked out in proud disguise of cast-off weeds
Which for that service had been husbanded,   10
By exhortation of my frugal Dame—
Motley accoutrement, of power to smile
At thorns, and brakes, and brambles,—and, in truth,
More ragged than need was! O'er path-less rocks,
Through beds of matted fern, and tangled thickets,   15
Forcing my way, I came to one dear nook
Unvisited, where not a broken bough
Drooped with its withered leaves, ungracious sign
Of devastation; but the hazels rose
Tall and erect, with tempting clusters hung,   20
A virgin scene!—A little while I stood,
Breathing with such suppression of the heart
As joy delights in; and, with wise restraint
Voluptuous, fearless of a rival, eyed
The banquet;—or beneath the trees I sate   25
Among the flowers, and with the flowers I played;

VI. 1–9 Among the autumnal woods a figure quaint
          Equipped with wallet and with crooked stick
          They led me, and I followed in their steps,
          Tricked out *etc.* MS.
2 *not in* 1800, *but added in errata*   4 *not in* MS., 1800–20   5 *so* 1827:
When forth I sallied from our cottage door 1800–20   6–7 *so* 1815: And
with a wallet . . . I turn'd 1800–5   8 *so* 1836: Towards the distant
woods 1800–32
9–11 *so* 1815:   of beggars weeds
          Put on for the occasion, by advice
          And exhortation *etc.* MS., 1800–5
14–16 *so* 1836:   Among the woods
          And o'er the pathless rocks, I forc'd my way
          Until at length I came *etc.* 1800–32
19 rose] towered MS.   20 tempting 1845: milk-white MS., 1800–36

A temper known to those who, after long
And weary expectation, have been blest
With sudden happiness beyond all hope.
Perhaps it was a bower beneath whose leaves   30
The violets of five seasons re-appear
And fade, unseen by any human eye;
Where fairy water-breaks do murmur on
For ever; and I saw the sparkling foam,
And—with my cheek on one of those green stones   35
That, fleeced with moss, under the shady trees,
Lay round me, scattered like a flock of sheep—
I heard the murmur and the murmuring sound,
In that sweet mood when pleasure loves to pay
Tribute to ease; and, of its joy secure,   40
The heart luxuriates with indifferent things,
Wasting its kindliness on stocks and stones,
And on the vacant air. Then up I rose,
And dragged to earth both branch and bough, with crash
And merciless ravage: and the shady nook   45
Of hazels, and the green and mossy bower,
Deformed and sullied, patiently gave up
Their quiet being: and, unless I now
Confound my present feelings with the past,
Ere from the mutilated bower I turned   50
Exulting, rich beyond the wealth of kings,
I felt a sense of pain when I beheld
The silent trees, and saw the intruding sky.—
Then, dearest Maiden, move along these shades
In gentleness of heart; with gentle hand   55
Touch—for there is a spirit in the woods.

VII

THE SIMPLON PASS

[Composed 1799 (? 1804).—Published 1845.]

————Brook and road
Were fellow-travellers in this gloomy Pass,
And with them did we journey several hours

35–7   upon the mossy stones
    That like a flock of sheep were fleeced with moss   MS.
36 under 1845: beneath 1800–36   50 *so* 1836: Even then, when from
the bower I turned away MS., 1800–32   53 and saw the 1836: and the
MS., 1800–32
VII. *For early variants v. Prelude* p. 206

At a slow step. The immeasurable height
Of woods decaying, never to be decayed,   5
The stationary blasts of waterfalls,
And in the narrow rent, at every turn,
Winds thwarting winds bewildered and forlorn,
The torrents shooting from the clear blue sky,
The rocks that muttered close upon our ears,   10
Black drizzling crags that spake by the wayside
As if a voice were in them, the sick sight
And giddy prospect of the raving stream,
The unfettered clouds and region of the heavens,
Tumult and peace, the darkness and the light—   15
Were all like workings of one mind, the features
Of the same face, blossoms upon one tree,
Characters of the great Apocalypse,
The types and symbols of Eternity,
Of first, and last, and midst, and without end.   20

VIII
[Composed 1804.—Published 1807.]

SHE was a Phantom of delight
When first she gleamed upon my sight;
A lovely Apparition, sent
To be a moment's ornament;
Her eyes as stars of Twilight fair;   5
Like Twilight's, too, her dusky hair;
But all things else about her drawn
From May-time and the cheerful Dawn;
A dancing Shape, an Image gay,
To haunt, to startle, and way-lay.   10

I saw her upon nearer view,
A Spirit, yet a Woman too!
Her household motions light and free,
And steps of virgin-liberty;
A countenance in which did meet   15
Sweet records, promises as sweet;
A Creature not too bright or good
For human nature's daily food;
For transient sorrows, simple wiles,
Praise, blame, love, kisses, tears, and smiles.   20

VIII. 8 From Maytime's brightest, liveliest dawn 1836 *only*   9 Shape]
sight MS.

And now I see with eye serene
The very pulse of the machine;
A Being breathing thoughtful breath,
A Traveller between life and death;
The reason firm, the temperate will,   25
Endurance, foresight, strength, and skill;
A perfect Woman, nobly planned,
To warn, to comfort, and command;
And yet a Spirit still, and bright
With something of angelic light.   30

IX

[Composed 1806.—Published 1807.]

O NIGHTINGALE! thou surely art
A creature of a "fiery heart":—
These notes of thine—they pierce and pierce;
Tumultuous harmony and fierce!
Thou sing'st as if the God of wine   5
Had helped thee to a Valentine;
A song in mockery and despite
Of shades, and dews, and silent night;
And steady bliss, and all the loves
Now sleeping in these peaceful groves.   10

I heard a Stock-dove sing or say
His homely tale, this very day;
His voice was buried among trees,
Yet to be come-at by the breeze:
He did not cease; but cooed—and cooed;   15
And somewhat pensively he wooed:
He sang of love, with quiet blending,
Slow to begin, and never ending;
Of serious faith, and inward glee;
That was the song—the song for me!   20

X

[Composed 1799.—Published 1800.]

THREE years she grew in sun and shower,
Then Nature said, "A lovelier flower
On earth was never sown;

24 between 1832: betwixt MS., 1807-27   30 angelic light 1845: an
angel light MS., 1807-32: an angel-light 1836
IX. 2 a "fiery heart" 1845: a fiery heart 1807, 1820-36: ebullient heart 1815

This Child I to myself will take;
She shall be mine, and I will make   5
A Lady of my own.

"Myself will to my darling be
Both law and impulse: and with me
The Girl, in rock and plain,
In earth and heaven, in glade and bower,   10
Shall feel an overseeing power
To kindle or restrain.

"She shall be sportive as the fawn
That wild with glee across the lawn
Or up the mountain springs;   15
And her's shall be the breathing balm,
And her's the silence and the calm
Of mute insensate things.

"The floating clouds their state shall lend
To her; for her the willow bend;   20
Nor shall she fail to see
Even in the motions of the Storm
Grace that shall mould the Maiden's form
By silent sympathy.

"The stars of midnight shall be dear   25
To her; and she shall lean her ear
In many a secret place
Where rivulets dance their wayward round,
And beauty born of murmuring sound
Shall pass into her face.   30

"And vital feelings of delight
Shall rear her form to stately height,
Her virgin bosom swell;
Such thoughts to Lucy I will give
While she and I together live   35
Here in this happy dell."

X. 7–8 Her teacher I myself will be,
         She is my darling—and with me   1802 *only*
23 *so* 1802: A beauty that shall mould her form 1800

Thus Nature spake—The work was done—
How soon my Lucy's race was run!
She died, and left to me
This heath, this calm, and quiet scene;   40
The memory of what has been,
And never more will be.

XI

[Composed 1799.—Published 1800.]

A SLUMBER did my spirit seal;
   I had no human fears:
She seemed a thing that could not feel
   The touch of earthly years.

No motion has she now, no force;   5
   She neither hears nor sees;
Rolled round in earth's diurnal course,
   With rocks, and stones, and trees.

XII

[Composed 1804.—Published 1807.]

I WANDERED lonely as a cloud
That floats on high o'er vales and hills,
When all at once I saw a crowd,
A host, of golden daffodils;
Beside the lake, beneath the trees,   5
Fluttering and dancing in the breeze.

Continuous as the stars that shine
And twinkle on the milky way,
They stretched in never-ending line
Along the margin of a bay: 10
Ten thousand saw I at a glance,
Tossing their heads in sprightly dance.

The waves beside them danced; but they
Out-did the sparkling waves in glee:
A poet could not but be gay,   15
In such a jocund company:
I gazed—and gazed—but little thought
What wealth the show to me had brought:

XII. 4 golden 1815: dancing 1807   5–6 Along . . . Ten Thousand
dancing . . . 1807   7–12 *added* 1815   16 jocund 1815: laughing 1807

For oft, when on my couch I lie
In vacant or in pensive mood, 20
They flash upon that inward eye
Which is the bliss of solitude;
And then my heart with pleasure fills,
And dances with the daffodils.

XIII

THE REVERIE OF POOR SUSAN

[Composed 1797.—Published 1800.]

At the corner of Wood Street, when daylight appears,
Hangs a Thrush that sings loud, it has sung for three years:
Poor Susan has passed by the spot, and has heard
In the silence of morning the song of the Bird.

'Tis a note of enchantment; what ails her? She sees 5
A mountain ascending, a vision of trees;
Bright volumes of vapour through Lothbury glide,
And a river flows on through the vale of Cheapside.

Green pastures she views in the midst of the dale,
Down which she so often has tripped with her pail; 10
And a single small cottage, a nest like a dove's,
The one only dwelling on earth that she loves.

She looks, and her heart is in heaven: but they fade,
The mist and the river, the hill and the shade:
The stream will not flow, and the hill will not rise, 15
And the colours have all passed away from her eyes!

XIV

POWER OF MUSIC

[Composed 1806.—Published 1807.]

An Orpheus! an Orpheus! yes, Faith may grow bold,
And take to herself all the wonders of old;—
Near the stately Pantheon you'll meet with the same
In the street that from Oxford hath borrowed its name.

XIII. 2 Hangs 1820: There's 1800–15 *After* l. 16, 1800 *has*:
Poor Outcast! return—to receive thee once more
The house of thy Father will open its door,
And thou once again, in thy plain russet gown,
May'st hear the thrush sing from a tree of its own.

His station is there; and he works on the crowd,   5
He sways them with harmony merry and loud;
He fills with his power all their hearts to the brim—
Was aught ever heard like his fiddle and him?

What an eager assembly! what an empire is this!
The weary have life, and the hungry have bliss;   10
The mourner is cheered, and the anxious have rest;
And the guilt-burthened soul is no longer opprest.

As the Moon brightens round her the clouds of the night,
So He, where he stands, is a centre of light;
It gleams on the face, there, of dusky-browed Jack,   15
And the pale-visaged Baker's, with basket on back.

That errand-bound 'Prentice was passing in haste—
What matter! he 's caught—and his time runs to waste;
The Newsman is stopped, though he stops on the fret;
And the half-breathless Lamplighter—he 's in the net!   20

The Porter sits down on the weight which he bore;
The Lass with her barrow wheels hither her store;—
If a thief could be here he might pilfer at ease;
She sees the Musician, 'tis all that she sees!

He stands, backed by the wall;—he abates not his din;   25
His hat gives him vigour, with boons dropping in,
From the old and the young, from the poorest; and there!
The one-pennied Boy has his penny to spare.

O blest are the hearers, and proud be the hand
Of the pleasure it spreads through so thankful a band;   30
I am glad for him, blind as he is!—all the while
If they speak 'tis to praise, and they praise with a smile.

That tall Man, a giant in bulk and in height,
Not an inch of his body is free from delight;
Can he keep himself still, if he would? oh, not he!   35
The music stirs in him like wind through a tree.

Mark that Cripple who leans on his crutch; like a tower
That long has leaned forward, leans hour after hour!—
That Mother, whose spirit in fetters is bound,
While she dandles the Babe in her arms to the sound.   40

XIV.   9 an empire] empire *Longman* MS.   13 the clouds] all the clouds
Longman MS.   15 browed 1815: faced 1807   37 Mark that 1827:
There 's a 1807–20   39 That 1827: A 1807–20

Now, coaches and chariots! roar on like a stream;
Here are twenty souls happy as souls in a dream:
They are deaf to your murmurs—they care not for you,
Nor what ye are flying, nor what ye pursue!

XV

STAR-GAZERS

[Composed 1806.—Published 1807.]

WHAT crowd is this? what have we here! we must not pass it by;
A Telescope upon its frame, and pointed to the sky:
Long is it as a barber's pole, or mast of little boat,
Some little pleasure-skiff, that doth on Thames's waters float.

The Show-man chooses well his place, 'tis Leicester's busy Square;
And is as happy in his night, for the heavens are blue and fair; 6
Calm, though impatient, is the crowd; each stands ready with
the fee,
And envies him that's looking;—what an insight must it be!

Yet, Show-man, where can lie the cause? Shall thy Implement
have blame,
A boaster that, when he is tried, fails, and is put to shame?   10
Or is it good as others are, and be their eyes in fault?
Their eyes, or minds? or, finally, is yon resplendent vault?

Is nothing of that radiant pomp so good as we have here?
Or gives a thing but small delight that never can be dear?
The silver moon with all her vales, and hills of mightiest fame,   15
Doth she betray us when they're seen? or are they but a name?

Or is it rather that Conceit rapacious is and strong,
And bounty never yields so much but it seems to do her wrong?
Or is it that, when human Souls a journey long have had
And are returned into themselves, they cannot but be sad?   20

Or must we be constrained to think that these Spectators rude,
Poor in estate, of manners base, men of the multitude,
Have souls which never yet have risen, and therefore prostrate lie?
No, no, this cannot be;—men thirst for power and majesty!

44 nor 1815: or 1807
XV. 6 is 1827: he's 1807–20   7 stands 1827: is 1807–20   8 *so*
1807–20, 1840: Impatient till his moment comes 1827–32, . . . come 1836
9 Yet,] Now, MS.   12 yon 1832: this MS., 1807–27   21–8 MS. *trans-*
poses these two stanzas, and for l. 21 *has* Or is it, last, unwelcome thought,
that *etc. for* l. 23–4 . . . lie, Not to be lifted up at once to *etc. and for* l. 25
Or does some deep and earnest joy *etc.*

Does, then, a deep and earnest thought the blissful mind employ
Of him who gazes, or has gazed ? a grave and steady joy,   26
That doth reject all show of pride, admits no outward sign,
Because not of this noisy world, but silent and divine!

Whatever be the cause, 'tis sure that they who pry and pore
Seem to meet with little gain, seem less happy than before: 30
One after One they take their turn, nor have I one espied
That doth not slackly go away, as if dissatisfied.

XVI

WRITTEN IN MARCH

WHILE RESTING ON THE BRIDGE AT THE FOOT OF BROTHER'S
WATER

[Composed April 16, 1802.—Published 1807.]

THE Cock is crowing,
The stream is flowing,
The small birds twitter,
The lake doth glitter,
The green field sleeps in the sun;   5
The oldest and youngest
Are at work with the strongest;
The cattle are grazing,
Their heads never raising;
There are forty feeding like one!   10

Like an army defeated
The snow hath retreated,
And now doth fare ill
On the top of the bare hill;
The Ploughboy is whooping—anon—anon: 15
There's joy in the mountains;
There's life in the fountains;
Small clouds are sailing,
Blue sky prevailing;
The rain is over and gone!   20

31 turn 1827: turns 1807–20
XVI. 6–7 The horse and his Marrow
       Drag the plow and the harrow, MS. *Letter*

XVII

[Composed ?—Published 1842.]

Lyre! though such power do in thy magic live
  As might from India's farthest plain
  Recall the not unwilling Maid,
    Assist me to detain
    The lovely Fugitive: 5
Check with thy notes the impulse which, betrayed
By her sweet farewell looks, I longed to aid.
Here let me gaze enrapt upon that eye,
The impregnable and awe-inspiring fort
Of contemplation, the calm port   10
By reason fenced from winds that sigh
Among the restless sails of vanity.
But if no wish be hers that we should part,
A humbler bliss would satisfy my heart.
    Where all things are so fair,   15
Enough by her dear side to breathe the air
    Of this Elysian weather;
And on or in, or near, the brook, espy
  Shade upon the sunshine lying
    Faint and somewhat pensively;   20
  And downward Image gaily vying
    With its upright living tree
'Mid silver clouds, and openings of blue sky
As soft almost and deep as her cerulean eye.

XVII. 1–2 Lyre that from India's farthest plain
      By powers that in thy magic live   MS. 2
3 my own beloved Maid MSS.   5 My would be fugitive MSS.   9 awe-
inspiring] tranquil MS. 1, awful MS. 2
11–12 That reason guards from winds that try ·
    The restless soul *etc.* MS. 2
13–17 Or could I stoop to gaze elsewhere
    Oh then what joy with her
    To sit in this Elysian weather   } MSS.
    Through this mild hour of sunny weather }
18–19 Aloft, and in the brook below espy
    Shade, sunbeam, substance, image all together
    Freaks of Nature's witchery
    Shade upon still water lying MSS.
22–33 With its type the living tree
    Or up the stream to cast a glance
    And note *etc. as* l. 33 MS. 2

Nor less the joy with many a glance   25
Cast up the Stream or down at her beseeching,
To mark its eddying foam-balls prettily distrest
By ever-changing shape and want of rest;
    Or watch, with mutual teaching,
    The current as it plays   30
    In flashing leaps and stealthy creeps
    Adown a rocky maze;
Or note (translucent summer's happiest chance!)
In the slope-channel floored with pebbles bright,
Stones of all hues, gem emulous of gem,   35
So vivid that they take from keenest sight
The liquid veil that seeks not to hide them.

XVIII

BEGGARS

[Composed March 13, 14, 1802.—Published 1807.]

She had a tall man's height or more;
Her face from summer's noontide heat
No bonnet shaded, but she wore
A mantle, to her very feet
Descending with a graceful flow,   5
And on her head a cap as white as new-fallen snow.

29–33 And ever and anon with mutual teaching
    Upon the stream to cast a glance
    And note *etc.*   MS. 1
34 The sloping channel floored with MSS.
XVIII. 1–6 *so* 1845:
        She had a tall Man's height, or more;
        No bonnet screen'd her from the heat;
        A long drab-colour'd Cloak she wore,
        A Mantle reaching to her feet:
        What other dress she had I could not know;
        Only she wore a Cap that was as white as snow.   MS., 1807–20
        Before me as the Wanderer stood,
        No bonnet screened her from the heat;
        Nor claimed she service from the hood
        Of a blue mantle, to her feet
        Depending with a graceful flow;
        Only she wore a cap pure as unsullied snow.   1827
        Before my eyes a Wanderer stood;
        Her face from summer's noon-day heat
        Nor [No 1836–43] bonnet shaded, nor the hood
        Of that [the 1836–43] blue cloak, which to her feet
        Depended with a graceful flow;
        Only she wore a cap as white as new-fallen snow.   1832–43

Her skin was of Egyptian brown:
Haughty, as if her eye had seen
Its own light to a distance thrown,
She towered, fit person for a Queen   10
To lead those ancient Amazonian files;
Or ruling Bandit's wife among the Grecian isles.

Advancing, forth she stretched her hand
And begged an alms with doleful plea
That ceased not; on our English land   15
Such woes, I knew, could never be;
And yet a boon I gave her, for the creature
Was beautiful to see—a weed of glorious feature.

I left her, and pursued my way;
And soon before me did espy   20
A pair of little Boys at play,
Chasing a crimson butterfly;
The taller followed with his hat in hand,
Wreathed round with yellow flowers the gayest of the land.

        She had a tall man's height or more;
        And while, 'mid April's noontide heat,
        A long blue cloak the vagrant wore,
        A mantle reaching to her feet
        No bonnet screened her lofty brow,
        Only she wore a cap as white as new fallen snow C
7–10 *so* 1827: In all my walks, through field or town,
        Such Figure had I never seen:
        Her face was of Egyptian brown:
        Fit person was she for a Queen,   MS., 1807–20
11 lead *so* 1836: head MS., 1807–32
13–16 Before me begging did she stand,
     Pouring out sorrows like a sea;
     Grief after grief:—on English land
     Such woes I knew could never be;   MS., 1807–20
     Her suit no faltering scruples checked;
     Forth did she pour, in current free,
     Tales that could challenge no respect
     But from a blind credulity;   1827
     She begged an alms; no scruple checked
     The current of her ready plea
     Words that could challenge, *etc.*   1832–43
14 And boldly urged a doleful plea, C   24 With yellow flowers around,
as with a golden band. C

The other wore a rimless crown   25
With leaves of laurel stuck about;
And while both followed up and down,
Each whooping with a merry shout,
In their fraternal features I could trace
Unquestionable lines of that wild Suppliant's face.   30

Yet *they*, so blithe of heart, seemed fit
For finest tasks of earth or air:
Wings let them have, and they might flit
Precursors to Aurora's car,
Scattering fresh flowers; though happier far, I ween,   35
To hunt their fluttering game o'er rock and level green.

They dart across my path—but lo,
Each ready with a plaintive whine!
Said I, "not half an hour ago
Your Mother has had alms of mine."   40
"That cannot be," one answered—"she is dead:"—
I looked reproof—they saw—but neither hung his head.

"She has been dead, Sir, many a day."—
"Hush, boys! you're telling me a lie;
It was your Mother, as I say!"   45
And, in the twinkling of an eye,
"Come! come!" cried one, and without more ado
Off to some other play the joyous Vagrants flew!

27 And while 1827: And they 1807–20
29–30 *so* 1820: Two Brothers seem'd they, eight and ten years old;
               And like that Woman's face as gold is like to gold   MS.,
               1807–15
31–6 *added* 1827   37 *so* 1827: They bolted on me thus, and lo! MS.
1807–20   42 *so* 1827: "Nay but I gave her pence, and she will buy you
bread." MS., 1807–20   44 *so* 1845: "Sweet boys, you're telling me a
lie; MS., 1807–20, 1836–40. "Sweet boys, Heaven hears that rash reply
1827–32   48 *so* 1827: they both together flew MS., 1807–20: the thoughtless vagrants flew C

XIX

SEQUEL TO THE FOREGOING

COMPOSED MANY YEARS AFTER ·

[Composed 1817.—Published 1827.]

WHERE are they now, those wanton Boys?
For whose free range the dædal earth
Was filled with animated toys,
And implements of frolic mirth;
With tools for ready wit to guide;   5
And ornaments of seemlier pride,
More fresh, more bright, than princes wear;
For what one moment flung aside,
Another could repair;
What good or evil have they seen   10
Since I their pastime witnessed here,
Their daring wiles, their sportive cheer?
I ask—but all is dark between!

They met me in a genial hour,
When universal nature breathed   15
As with the breath of one sweet flower,—
A time to overrule the power
Of discontent, and check the birth
Of thoughts with better thoughts at strife,
The most familiar bane of life   20
Since parting Innocence bequeathed
Mortality to Earth!
Soft clouds, the whitest of the year,
Sailed through the sky—the brooks ran clear;
The lambs from rock to rock were bounding;   25
With songs the budded groves resounding;

XIX. 13/14 Spirits of beauty and of grace!
              Associates in that eager chase;
              Ye, by a course to nature true,
              The sterner judgment can subdue;
              And waken a relenting smile
              When she encounters fraud or guile;
              And sometimes ye can charm away
              The inward mischief, or allay,
              Ye, who within the blameless mind,
              Your favourite seat of empire find! 1827-32

And to my heart are still endeared
The thoughts with which it then was cheered;
The faith which saw that gladsome pair
Walk through the fire with unsinged hair.   30
Or, if such faith must needs deceive—
Then, Spirits of beauty and of grace,
Associates in that eager chase;
Ye, who within the blameless mind
Your favourite seat of empire find—   ·35
Kind Spirits! may we not believe
That they, so happy and so fair
Through your sweet influence, and the care
Of pitying Heaven, at least were free
From touch of *deadly* injury?   40
Destined, whate'er their earthly doom,
For mercy and immortal bloom?

XX

GIPSIES

[Composed 1807.—Published 1807.]

YET are they here the same unbroken knot
Of human Beings, in the self-same spot!
　　Men, women, children, yea the frame
　　Of the whole spectacle the same!
Only their fire seems bolder, yielding light,   5
Now deep and red, the colouring of night;
　　That on their Gipsy-faces falls,
　　Their bed of straw and blanket-walls.
—Twelve hours, twelve bounteous hours are gone, while I
Have been a traveller under open sky,   10
　　Much witnessing of change and cheer,
　　Yet as I left I find them here!
The weary Sun betook himself to rest;—
Then issued Vesper from the fulgent west,
　　Outshining like a visible God   15
　　The glorious path in which he trod.
And now, ascending, after one dark hour
And one night's diminution of her power,

27–8 are . . . thoughts 1836: is . . . faith 1827–32   31 faith 1836:
thoughts 1827–32   32–5 *not in* 1827–32
XX. 1 here 1827 here? 1807–20

Behold the mighty Moon! this way
She looks as if at them—but they   20
Regard not her:—oh better wrong and strife
(By nature transient) than this torpid life;
Life which the very stars reprove
As on their silent tasks they move!
Yet, witness all that stirs in heaven or earth!   25
In scorn I speak not;—they are what their birth
And breeding suffer them to be;
Wild outcasts of society!

XXI

RUTH

[Composed 1799.—Published 1800.]

WHEN Ruth was left half desolate,
Her Father took another Mate;
And Ruth, not seven years old,
A slighted child, at her own will
Went wandering over dale and hill,   5
In thoughtless freedom, bold.

And she had made a pipe of straw,
And music from that pipe could draw
Like sounds of winds and floods;
Had built a bower upon the green,   10
As if she from her birth had been
An infant of the woods.

Beneath her father's roof, alone
She seemed to live; her thoughts her own;
Herself her own delight;   15
Pleased with herself, nor sad, nor gay;
And, passing thus the live-long day,
She grew to woman's height.

21-8 Regard her not:—oh better wrong and strife
Better vain deeds or evil than such life!
The silent Heavens have goings-on;
The stars have tasks—but these have none. 1807-15. *So* 1820 *but*
l. 22 (By nature transient) than such torpid life! *and adding ll.*
25-8: 1827 *as text but* such *for* this *in* l. 22.
XXI. 3. And Ruth 1802: And so 1800   4. A 1802: The 1800
8-9 *so* 1836: And from that oaten pipe could draw All 1800-32.   13-18
not in 1800   16-18 . . . gay, She passed her time; and in this way Grew
up 1802-20

There came a Youth from Georgia's shore—
A military casque he wore,   20
With splendid feathers drest;
He brought them from the Cherokees;
The feathers nodded in the breeze,
And made a gallant crest.

From Indian blood you deem him sprung: 25
But no! he spake the English tongue,
And bore a soldier's name;
And, when America was free
From battle and from jeopardy,
He 'cross the ocean came.   30

With hues of genius on his cheek
In finest tones the Youth could speak:
—While he was yet a boy,
The moon, the glory of the sun,
And streams that murmur as they run,   35
Had been his dearest joy.

He was a lovely Youth! I guess
The panther in the wilderness
Was not so fair as he;
And, when he chose to sport and play,   40
No dolphin ever was so gay
Upon the tropic sea.

Among the Indians he had fought,
And with him many tales he brought
Of pleasure and of fear;   45
Such tales as told to any maid
By such a Youth, in the green shade,
Were perilous to hear.

He told of girls—a happy rout!
Who quit their fold with dance and shout,   50
Their pleasant Indian town,
To gather strawberries all day long;
Returning with a choral song
When daylight is gone down.

26 But 1836: Ah, 1800–32   27 bore 1805: bare 1800–2

He spake of plants that hourly change   55
Their blossoms, through a boundless range
Of intermingling hues;
With budding, fading, faded flowers
They stand the wonder of the bowers
From morn to evening dews.   60

He told of the magnolia, spread
High as a cloud, high over head!
The cypress and her spire;
—Of flowers that with one scarlet gleam
Cover a hundred leagues, and seem   65
To set the hills on fire.

The Youth of green savannahs spake,
And many an endless, endless lake,
With all its fairy crowds
Of islands, that together lie   70
As quietly as spots of sky
Among the evening clouds.

"How pleasant," then he said, "it were
A fisher or a hunter there,
In sunshine or in shade   75

55–7 *so* 1836: . . . divine and strange
    That every hour their blossoms change,
    Ten thousand lovely hues   1800–32, *but* day *for* hour 1800
60/61 1802 *reads*:
    Of march and ambush, siege and fight,
    Then did he tell; and with delight
    The heart of Ruth would ache;
    Wild histories they were, and dear:
    But 'twas a thing of heaven to hear
    When of himself he spake. *followed by ll.* 163–8, 127–44 (*but*
      with change of he . . . his *to* I . . . my), 175–80, *and then*:
            It is a purer, better mind:
            O Maiden innocent and kind
            What sights I might have seen!
            Even now upon my eyes they break!
            And he again began to speak
            Of lands where he had been.
  1805 *restores* 127–44 *to their original* (1800) *and final position, and*
  adds 169–74; *thus reading* "Of march etc., 163–80, It is a purer", *etc.*
73 *so* 1836: And then he said "How sweet it were   1800–32
75–7 *so* 1845: A gardener in the shade,
        Still wandering with an easy mind
        To   1800–32: 1836 *as* 1845 *but* through shade

To wander with an easy mind;
And build a household fire, and find
A home in every glade!

"What days and what bright years! Ah me!
Our life were life indeed, with thee   80
So passed in quiet bliss,
And all the while," said he, "to know
That we were in a world of woe,
On such an earth as this!"

And then he sometimes interwove   85
Fond thoughts about a father's love:
"For there," said he, "are spun
Around the heart such tender ties,
That our own children to our eyes
Are dearer than the sun.   90

"Sweet Ruth! and could you go with me
My helpmate in the woods to be,
Our shed at night to rear;
Or run, my own adopted bride,
A sylvan huntress at my side,   95
And drive the flying deer!

"Beloved Ruth!"—No more he said.
The wakeful Ruth at midnight shed
A solitary tear:
She thought again—and did agree   100
With him to sail across the sea,
And drive the flying deer.

"And now, as fitting is and right,
We in the church our faith will plight,
A husband and a wife."   105
Even so they did; and I may say
That to sweet Ruth that happy day
Was more than human life.

Through dream and vision did she sink,
Delighted all the while to think   110
That on those lonesome floods,
And green savannahs, she should share
His board with lawful joy, and bear
His name in the wild woods.

79 bright 1836: sweet 1800–32   86 Fond 1832: Dear 1800–27
98 The wakeful Ruth 1820: Sweet Ruth alone 1800–15

But, as you have before been told,   115
This Stripling, sportive, gay, and bold,
And, with his dancing crest,
So beautiful, through savage lands
Had roamed about, with vagrant bands
Of Indians in the West.   120

The wind, the tempest roaring high,
The tumult of a tropic sky,
Might well be dangerous food
For him, a Youth to whom was given
So much of earth—so much of heaven,   125
And such impetuous blood.

Whatever in those climes he found
Irregular in sight or sound
Did to his mind impart
A kindred impulse, seemed allied   130
To his own powers, and justified
The workings of his heart.

Nor less, to feed voluptuous thought,
The beauteous forms of nature wrought,
Fair trees and gorgeous flowers;   135
The breezes their own languor lent;
The stars had feelings, which they sent
Into those favored bowers.

Yet, in his worst pursuits, I ween
That sometimes there did intervene   140
Pure hopes of high intent:
For passions linked to forms so fair
And stately, needs must have their share
Of noble sentiment.

But ill he lived, much evil saw,   145
With men to whom no better law
Nor better life was known;
Deliberately, and undeceived,
Those wild men's vices he received,
And gave them back his own.   150

133 voluptuous] unhallowed 1802   135 gorgeous 1845: lovely 1800–43
138 favored 1845: magic 1800–5: gorgeous 1815–43.   140 sometimes]
often 1802 *only*   142 linked to] amid 1802   143 needs must have]
wanted not 1802 *only*   145 Ill did he live 1802 *only*

His genius and his moral frame
Were thus impaired, and he became
The slave of low desires:
A Man who without self-control
Would seek what the degraded soul   155
Unworthily admires.

And yet he with no feigned delight
Had wooed the Maiden, day and night
Had loved her, night and morn:
What could he less than love a Maid   160
Whose heart with so much nature played?
So kind and so forlorn!

Sometimes, most earnestly, he said,
"O Ruth! I have been worse than dead;
False thoughts, thoughts bold and vain,   165
Encompassed me on every side
When I, in confidence and pride,
Had crossed the Atlantic main.

"Before me shone a glorious world—
Fresh as a banner bright, unfurled   170
To music suddenly:
I looked upon those hills and plains,
And seemed as if let loose from chains,
To live at liberty.

"No more of this; for now, by thee   175
Dear Ruth! more happily set free
With nobler zeal I burn;
My soul from darkness is released,
Like the whole sky when to the east
The morning doth return."   180

163–80 *not in* 1815   163–8 *not in* 1800   167–8 When I, a Boy
without a guide Had MS. . . . in thoughtlessness and pride Had 1802
When first in confidence and pride, I 1820–36
169–71 *so* 1840: It was a fresh and glorious world—
        A banner bright that was [shone 1836] unfurled
        Before me suddenly   1805–36 (*stanza not in* 1800–2)
175–80 *so* 1845:   So it was then, and so is now:
        For, Ruth! with thee I know not how
        I feel my spirit burn
        Even as the east when day comes forth;
        And to the west, and south, and north,
        The morning doth return.   1802 (not in 1800)
        But wherefore speak of this! For now
        Sweet [Dear 1836] Ruth *etc.* 1805–36

Full soon that better mind was gone:
No hope, no wish remained, not one,—
They stirred him now no more;
New objects did new pleasure give,
And once again he wished to live   185
As lawless as before.

Meanwhile, as thus with him it fared,
They for the voyage were prepared,
And went to the sea-shore,
But, when they thither came, the Youth   190
Deserted his poor Bride, and Ruth
Could never find him more.

God help thee, Ruth!—Such pains she had,
That she in half a year was mad,
And in a prison housed;   195
And there, with many a doleful song
Made of wild words, her cup of wrong
She fearfully caroused.

Yet sometimes milder hours she knew,
Nor wanted sun, nor rain, nor dew,   200
Nor pastimes of the May;
—They all were with her in her cell;
And a clear brook with cheerful knell
Did o'er the pebbles play.

When Ruth three seasons thus had lain,   205
There came a respite to her pain;
She from her prison fled;
But of the Vagrant none took thought;
And where it liked her best she sought
Her shelter and her bread.   210

Among the fields she breathed again:
The master-current of her brain
Ran permanent and free;

181 *so* 1845: But now the pleasant dream was gone 1800–15; Full soon the
purer mind *etc.* 1820–43
196–8 *so* 1836: And there, exulting in her wrongs,
                 Among the music of her songs,
                 She fearfully carouzed. 1800–15
                 And there she sang tumultuous songs,
                 By recollection of her wrongs
                 To fearful passion rouzed. 1820–32
203 clear 1836: wild 1800–32

And, coming to the Banks of Tone,
There did she rest; and dwell alone   215
Under the greenwood tree.

The engines of her pain, the tools
That shaped her sorrow, rocks and pools,
And airs that gently stir
The vernal leaves—she loved them still;   220
Nor ever taxed them with the ill
Which had been done to her.

A Barn her *winter* bed supplies;
But, till the warmth of summer skies
And summer days is gone,   225
(And all do in this tale agree)
She sleeps beneath the greenwood tree,
And other home hath none.

An innocent life, yet far astray!
And Ruth will, long before her day,   230
Be broken down and old:
Sore aches she needs must have! but less
Of mind, than body's wretchedness,
From damp, and rain, and cold.

If she is prest by want of food,   235
She from her dwelling in the wood
Repairs to a road-side;
And there she begs at one steep place
Where up and down with easy pace
The horsemen-travellers ride.   240

That oaten pipe of hers is mute,
Or thrown away; but with a flute
Her loneliness she cheers:
This flute, made of a hemlock stalk,
At evening in his homeward walk   245
The Quantock woodman hears.

214–5 *so* 1802: And to the pleasant Banks of Tone
          She took her way, to dwell alone   1800
217 pain 1802: grief 1800   226 *so* 1802: (And in this tale we all agree)1800
229–34 *not in* 1800 The neighbours grieve for her and say That she will
etc. 1802; 1805 *as text*

I, too, have passed her on the hills
Setting her little water-mills
By spouts and fountains wild—
Such small machinery as she turned   250
Ere she had wept, ere she had mourned,
A young and happy Child!

Farewell! and when thy days are told,
Ill-fated Ruth, in hallowed mould
Thy corpse shall buried be,   255
For thee a funeral bell shall ring,
And all the congregation sing
A Christian psalm for thee.

XXII

RESOLUTION AND INDEPENDENCE
[Composed May 3–July 4, 1802.—Published 1807.]

I

THERE was a roaring in the wind all night;
The rain came heavily and fell in floods;
But now the sun is rising calm and bright;
The birds are singing in the distant woods;
Over his own sweet voice the Stock-dove broods;   5
The Jay makes answer as the Magpie chatters;
And all the air is filled with pleasant noise of waters.

II

All things that love the sun are out of doors;
The sky rejoices in the morning's birth;
The grass is bright with rain-drops;—on the moors   10
The hare is running races in her mirth;
And with her feet she from the plashy earth
Raises a mist; that, glittering in the sun,
Runs with her all the way, wherever she doth run.

III

I was a Traveller then upon the moor;   15
I saw the hare that raced about with joy;
I heard the woods and distant waters roar;
Or heard them not, as happy as a boy:
The pleasant season did my heart employ:
My old remembrances went from me wholly;   20
And all the ways of men, so vain and melancholy.

IV

But, as it sometimes chanceth, from the might
Of joy in minds that can no further go,
As high as we have mounted in delight
In our dejection do we sink as low;   25
To me that morning did it happen so;
And fears and fancies thick upon me came;
Dim sadness—and blind thoughts, I knew not, nor could name.

V

I heard the sky-lark warbling in the sky;
And I bethought me of the playful hare: 30
Even such a happy Child of earth am I;
Even as these blissful creatures do I fare;
Far from the world I walk, and from all care;
But there may come another day to me—
Solitude, pain of heart, distress, and poverty.   35

VI

My whole life I have lived in pleasant thought,
As if life's business were a summer mood;
As if all needful things would come unsought
To genial faith, still rich in genial good;
But how can He expect that others should   40
Build for him, sow for him, and at his call
Love him, who for himself will take no heed at all?

VII

I thought of Chatterton, the marvellous Boy,
The sleepless Soul that perished in his pride;
Of Him who walked in glory and in joy   45
Following his plough, along the mountain-side:
By our own spirits are we deified:
We Poets in our youth begin in gladness;
But thereof come in the end despondency and madness.

XXII. 29 warbling 1820: singing MS., 1807–15   32 blissful] happy MS.
38–9 And they who lived in genial faith found nought
     That grew more willingly than genial good; MS.
44 his MS., 1815: its 1807   46 Following 1820: Behind MS., 1807–15

VIII

Now, whether it were by peculiar grace,   50
A leading from above, a something given,
Yet it befell that, in this lonely place,
When I with these untoward thoughts had striven,
Beside a pool bare to the eye of heaven
I saw a Man before me unawares: 55
The oldest man he seemed that ever wore grey hairs.

IX

As a huge stone is sometimes seen to lie
Couched on the bald top of an eminence;
Wonder to all who do the same espy,
By what means it could thither come, and whence;   60
So that it seems a thing endued with sense:
Like a sea-beast crawled forth, that on a shelf
Of rock or sand reposeth, there to sun itself;

X

Such seemed this Man, not all alive nor dead,
Nor all asleep—in his extreme old age: 65
His body was bent double, feet and head
Coming together in life's pilgrimage;
As if some dire constraint of pain, or rage
Of sickness felt by him in times long past,
A more than human weight upon his frame had cast.   70

XI

Himself he propped, limbs, body, and pale face,
Upon a long grey staff of shaven wood:
And, still as I drew near with gentle pace,
Upon the margin of that moorish flood
Motionless as a cloud the old Man stood,   75
That heareth not the loud winds when they call;
And moveth all together, if it move at all.

53-4 *so* 1820: When up and down my fancy thus was driven,
         And I with these untoward thoughts had striven MS., 1807–15
56/57   My course I stopped as soon as I espied
        The Old Man in that naked wilderness:
        Close by a Pond, upon the further side,
        He stood alone: a minute's space I guess
        I watch'd him, he continuing motionless:
        To the Pool's further margin then I drew;
        He being all the while before me full in view. MS.
67 life's 1820: their MS., 1807–15   70 frame] age MS.   71 *so* 1836:
his body, limbs, and face, 1807–32; both body *etc.* MS.   74 Beside the
little pond or MS.

XII

At length, himself unsettling, he the pond
Stirred with his staff, and fixedly did look
Upon the muddy water, which he conned,   80
As if he had been reading in a book:
And now a stranger's privilege I took;
And, drawing to his side, to him did say,
"This morning gives us promise of a glorious day."

XIII

A gentle answer did the old Man make,   85
In courteous speech which forth he slowly drew:
And him with further words I thus bespake,
"What occupation do you there pursue?
This is a lonesome place for one like you."
Ere he replied, a flash of mild surprise   90
Broke from the sable orbs of his yet-vivid eyes.

XIV

His words came feebly, from a feeble chest,
But each in solemn order followed each,
With something of a lofty utterance drest—
Choice word and measured phrase, above the reach   95
Of ordinary men; a stately speech;
Such as grave Livers do in Scotland use,
Religious men, who give to God and man their dues.

82 *so* 1820: And now such freedom as I could I took MS., 1807–15
84/85 He wore a Cloak, the same as women wear,
      As one whose blood did needful comfort lack:
      His face look'd pale as if it had grown fair:
      And, furthermore, he had upon his back,
      Beneath his cloak, a round and bulky Pack;
      A load of wool or raiment, as might seem;
      That on his shoulders lay as if it clave to him: *Longman* MS., MS.
88 *so* 1820: What kind of work is that which you MS., 1807–15
90–1 *so* 1836: He answer'd me with pleasure and surprize;
          And there was, while he spake, a fire about his eyes MS.,
            1807–15
          He answered, while a flash *etc.* 1820–32
95 Choice word] Pompous MS.

XV

He told, that to these waters he had come
To gather leeches, being old and poor: 100
Employment hazardous and wearisome!
And he had many hardships to endure:
From pond to pond he roamed, from moor to moor;
Housing, with God's good help, by choice or chance;
And in this way he gained an honest maintenance.   105

XVI

The old Man still stood talking by my side;
But now his voice to me was like a stream
Scarce heard; nor word from word could I divide;
And the whole body of the Man did seem
Like one whom I had met with in a dream;   110
Or like a man from some far region sent,
To give me human strength, by apt admonishment.

XVII

My former thoughts returned: the fear that kills;
And hope that is unwilling to be fed;
Cold, pain, and labour, and all fleshly ills;   115
And mighty Poets in their misery dead.
—Perplexed, and longing to be comforted,
My question eagerly did I renew,
"How is it that you live, and what is it you do?"

XVIII

He with a smile did then his words repeat;   120
And said that, gathering leeches, far and wide
He travelled; stirring thus about his feet
The waters of the pools where they abide.
"Once I could meet with them on every side;
But they have dwindled long by slow decay;   125
Yet still I persevere, and find them where I may."

99 *so* 1827: He told me that he to this pond had come MS., 1807–20
101–2   That 'twas his calling, better far than some
               Though he had *etc.*   MS.
112 by apt 1827: and strong MS., 1807–15: by strong 1820   114 And
1815: The 1807   117 *so* 1820: And now, not knowing what the Old Man
had said MS., 1807: But now, perplex'd by what the Old Man had said 1815
121–2   And said that, wheresoe'er they might be spied
               He gather'd Leeches, stirring at his feet   MS.
123 pools 1827 Ponds MS., 1807–20   124–6 Once he . . . But they had
. . . And few could now be found and fewer day by day MS.

XIX

While he was talking thus, the lonely place,
The old Man's shape, and speech—all troubled me:
In my mind's eye I seemed to see him pace
About the weary moors continually,   130
Wandering about alone and silently.
While I these thoughts within myself pursued,
He, having made a pause, the same discourse renewed.

XX

And soon with this he other matter blended,
Cheerfully uttered, with demeanour kind,   135
But stately in the main; and when he ended,
I could have laughed myself to scorn to find
In that decrepit Man so firm a mind.
"God," said I, " be my help and stay secure;
I'll think of the Leech-gatherer on the lonely moor!" 140

XXIII

THE THORN

[Composed March–April, 1798.—Published 1798.]

I

"THERE is a Thorn—it looks so old,
In truth, you'd find it hard to say
How it could ever have been young,
It looks so old and grey.
Not higher than a two years' child   5
It stands erect, this aged Thorn;

135 Which he delivered with *etc.* MS.
XXIII. 1–22 A [? On a] summit where the stormy gale
        Sweeps through the clouds from vale to vale,
        A thorn there is which like a stone
        With jagged lichens is o'ergrown,
        A thorn that wants its thorny points
        A toothless thorn with knotted joints;
        Not higher than a two years child
        It stands upon that spot so wild;
        Of leaves it has repaired its loss
        With heavy tufts of dark green moss,
        Which from the ground in plenteous crop
        Creep upward to its very top
        To bury it for evermore   MS.

No leaves it has, no prickly points;
It is a mass of knotted joints,
A wretched thing forlorn.
It stands erect, and like a stone   10
With lichens is it overgrown.

II

"Like rock or stone, it is o'ergrown,
With lichens to the very top,
And hung with heavy tufts of moss,
A melancholy crop: 15
Up from the earth these mosses creep,
And this poor Thorn they clasp it round
So close, you'd say that they are bent
With plain and manifest intent
To drag it to the ground;   20
And all have joined in one endeavour
To bury this poor Thorn for ever.

III

"High on a mountain's highest ridge,
Where oft the stormy winter gale
Cuts like a scythe, while through the clouds   25
It sweeps from vale to vale;
Not five yards from the mountain path,
This Thorn you on your left espy;
And to the left, three yards beyond,
You see a little muddy pond   30
Of water—never dry,
Though but of compass small, and bare
To thirsty suns and parching air.

IV

"And, close beside this aged Thorn,
There is a fresh and lovely sight,   35
A beauteous heap, a hill of moss,
Just half a foot in height.
All lovely colours there you see,
All colours that were ever seen;

7 prickly 1836: thorny 1798–1832   11 is it 1836: it is 1798–1832
18 are 1836: were 1798–1832
32–3 *so* 1820: I've measured it from side to side;
          'Tis three feet long, and two feet wide. 1798–1815.

And mossy network too is there,   40
As if by hand of lady fair
The work had woven been;
And cups, the darlings of the eye,
So deep is their vermilion dye.

V

"Ah me! what lovely tints are there   45
Of olive green and scarlet bright,
In spikes, in branches, and in stars,
Green, red, and pearly white!
This heap of earth o'ergrown with moss,
Which close beside the Thorn you see,   50
So fresh in all its beauteous dyes,
Is like an infant's grave in size,
As like as like can be:
But never, never any where,
An infant's grave was half so fair.   55

VI

"Now would you see this aged Thorn,
This pond, and beauteous hill of moss,
You must take care and choose your time
The mountain when to cross.
For oft there sits between the heap,   60
So like an infant's grave in size,
And that same pond of which I spoke,
A Woman in a scarlet cloak,
And to herself she cries,
'Oh misery! oh misery!   65
Oh woe is me! oh misery!'

VII

"At all times of the day and night
This wretched Woman thither goes;
And she is known to every star,
And every wind that blows;   70
And there, beside the Thorn, she sits
When the blue daylight's in the skies,

61 So 1827: That's 1798–1820

And when the whirlwind's on the hill,
Or frosty air is keen and still,
And to herself she cries,   75
'Oh misery! oh misery!
Oh woe is me! oh misery!'"

VIII

"Now wherefore, thus, by day and night,
In rain, in tempest, and in snow,
Thus to the dreary mountain-top   80
Does this poor Woman go?
And why sits she beside the Thorn
When the blue daylight's in the sky
Or when the whirlwind's on the hill,
Or frosty air is keen and still,   85
And wherefore does she cry?—
O wherefore? wherefore? tell me why
Does she repeat that doleful cry?"

IX

"I cannot tell; I wish I could;
For the true reason no one knows: 90
But would you gladly view the spot,
The spot to which she goes;
The hillock like an infant's grave,
The pond—and Thorn, so old and grey;
Pass by her door—'tis seldom shut—   95
And if you see her in her hut—
Then to the spot away!
I never heard of such as dare
Approach the spot when she is there."

X

"But wherefore to the mountain-top   100
Can this unhappy Woman go,
Whatever star is in the skies,
Whatever wind may blow?"

91 *so* 1827: But if you'd gladly 1798–1820   93 *so* 1820: The heap
that's like 1798–1815
103/104   Nay rack your brain—'tis all in vain,
                           I'll tell you every thing I know;
                           But to the Thorn, and to the Pond
                           Which is a little step beyond,

"Full twenty years are past and gone
Since she (her name is Martha Ray)   105
Gave with a maiden's true good-will
Her company to Stephen Hill;
And she was blithe and gay,
While friends and kindred all approved
Of him whom tenderly she loved.   110

XI

"And they had fixed the wedding day,
The morning that must wed them both;
But Stephen to another Maid
Had sworn another oath;
And, with this other Maid, to church   115
Unthinking Stephen went—
Poor Martha! on that woeful day
A pang of pitiless dismay
Into her soul was sent;
A fire was kindled in her breast,   120
Which might not burn itself to rest.

XII

"They say, full six months after this,
While yet the summer leaves were green,
She to the mountain-top would go,
And there was often seen.   ˎ   125

I wish that you would go:
Perhaps when you are at the place
You something of her tale may trace.

I'll give you the best help I can:
Before you up the mountain go,
Up to the dreary mountain top,
I'll tell you all I know.   1798–1815

104 *so* 1845: 'Tis now some two and twenty years 1798–1815; 'Tis known
that twenty years are pass'd 1820–36
109–110 *so* 1820: And she was happy, happy still
          Whene'er she thought of Stephen Hill   1798–1815
118–21 *so* 1815: A cruel, cruel fire, they say
          Into her bones was sent;
          It dried her body like a cinder,
          And almost turn'd her brain to tinder.   1798–1805

What could she seek ?—or wish to hide ?
Her state to any eye was plain ;
She was with child, and she was mad ;
Yet often was she sober sad
From her exceeding pain.   130
O guilty Father—would that death
Had saved him from that breach of faith !

XIII

"Sad case for such a brain to hold
Communion with a stirring child !
Sad case, as you may think, for one   135
Who had a brain so wild !
Last Christmas-eve we talked of this,
And grey-haired Wilfred of the glen
Held that the unborn infant wrought
About its mother's heart, and brought   140
Her senses back again :
And, when at last her time drew near,
Her looks were calm, her senses clear.

XIV

"More know I not, I wish I did,
And it should all be told to you ;   145
For what became of this poor child
No mortal ever knew ;
Nay—if a child to her was born
No earthly tongue could ever tell ;

126–7 *so* 1836:   'Tis said, a child was in her womb,
                As now to any eye was plain ;   1798–1815
                    So 1827–32, *but* Alas ! *for* 'Tis said.
                'Tis said, her lamentable state
                Even to a careless eye was plain ;   1820
131–2 *so* 1820:   Oh me ! ten thousand times I'd rather
                That he had died, that cruel father !   1798–1815
137–9 *so* 1820:   Last Christmas when we talk'd of this,
                Old Father Simpson did maintain
                That in her womb the infant wrought   1798–1815
144–51 *so* 1827: No more I know, I wish I did,
                And I would tell it all to you ;
                For what became of this poor child
                There's none that ever knew :
                And if a child was born or no,
                There's no one that could ever tell ;
                And if 'twas born alive or dead,
                There's no one knows, as I have said   1798–1820

And if 'twas born alive or dead,   150
Far less could this with proof be said ;
But some remember well,
That Martha Ray about this time
Would up the mountain often climb.

XV

"And all that winter, when at night   155
The wind blew from the mountain-peak,
'Twas worth your while, though in the dark,
The churchyard path to seek:
For many a time and oft were heard
Cries coming from the mountain head: 160
Some plainly living voices were ;
And others, I've heard many swear,
Were voices of the dead:
I cannot think, whate'er they say,
They had to do with Martha Ray.   165

XVI

" But that she goes to this old Thorn,
The Thorn which I described to you,
And there sits in a scarlet cloak,
I will be sworn is true.
For one day with my telescope,   170
To view the ocean wide and bright,
When to this country first I came,
Ere I had heard of Martha's name,
I climbed the mountain's height:—
A storm came on, and I could see   175
No object higher than my knee.

XVII

" 'Twas mist and rain, and storm and rain:
No screen, no fence could I discover ;
And then the wind! in sooth, it was
A wind full ten times over.   180
I looked around, I thought I saw
A jutting crag,—and off I ran,

179 sooth 1845: faith 1798–1836

Head-foremost, through the driving rain,
The shelter of the crag to gain;
And, as I am a man, 185
Instead of jutting crag, I found
A Woman seated on the ground.

XVIII

"I did not speak—I saw her face;
Her face!—it was enough for me;
I turned about and heard her cry, 190
'Oh misery! oh misery!'
And there she sits, until the moon
Through half the clear blue sky will go;
And when the little breezes make
The waters of the pond to shake, 195
As all the country know,
She shudders, and you hear her cry,
'Oh misery! oh misery!'"

XIX

"But what's the Thorn? and what the pond?
And what the hill of moss to her? 200
And what the creeping breeze that comes
The little pond to stir?"
"I cannot tell; but some will say
She hanged her baby on the tree;
Some say she drowned it in the pond, 205
Which is a little step beyond:
But all and each agree,
The little Babe was buried there,
Beneath that hill of moss so fair.

XX

"I've heard, the moss is spotted red 210
With drops of that poor infant's blood;
But kill a new-born infant thus,
I do not think she could!

189 Her face!] In truth, 1800–1805 *only*. 199–201 what's ... what
... what ... what 1827: what's ... what's ... what's ... what *s* 1798–
1820   210 *so* 1800: the scarlet moss is red 1798

Some say, if to the pond you go,
And fix on it a steady view,   215
The shadow of a babe you trace,
A baby and a baby's face,
And that it looks at you;
Whene'er you look on it, 'tis plain
The baby looks at you again.   220

XXI

"And some had sworn an oath that she
Should be to public justice brought;
And for the little infant's bones
With spades they would have sought.
But instantly the hill of moss   ·   225
Before their eyes began to stir!
And, for full fifty yards around,
The grass—it shook upon the ground!
Yet all do still aver
The little Babe lies buried there,   230
Beneath that hill of moss so fair.

XXII

"I cannot tell how this may be,
But plain it is the Thorn is bound
With heavy tufts of moss that strive
To drag it to the ground;   235
And this I know, full many a time,
When she was on the mountain high,
By day, and in the silent night,
When all the stars shone clear and bright,
That I have heard her cry,   240
'Oh misery! oh misery!
Oh woe is me! oh misery!'"

225 *so* 1845: But then the beauteous hill 1798–1820, 1832: It might not
be—the hill 1827: But then the speckled hill 1836

XXIV
HART-LEAP WELL
[Composed January or February, 1800.—Published 1800.]

Hart-Leap Well is a small spring of water, about five miles from Richmond in Yorkshire, and near the side of the road that leads from Richmond to Askrigg. Its name is derived from a remarkable Chase, the memory of which is preserved by the monuments spoken of in the second Part of the following Poem, which monuments do now exist as I have there described them.

THE Knight had ridden down from Wensley Moor
With the slow motion of a summer's cloud,
And now, as he approached a vassal's door,
"Bring forth another horse!" he cried aloud.

"Another horse!"—That shout the vassal heard   5
And saddled his best Steed, a comely grey;
Sir Walter mounted him; he was the third
Which he had mounted on that glorious day.

Joy sparkled in the prancing courser's eyes;
The horse and horseman are a happy pair;   10
But, though Sir Walter like a falcon flies,
There is a doleful silence in the air.

A rout this morning left Sir Walter's Hall,
That as they galloped made the echoes roar;
But horse and man are vanished, one and all;   15
Such race, I think, was never seen before.

Sir Walter, restless as a veering wind,
Calls to the few tired dogs that yet remain:
Blanch, Swift, and Music, noblest of their kind,
Follow, and up the weary mountain strain.   20

The Knight hallooed, he cheered and chid them on
With suppliant gestures and upbraidings stern;
But breath and eyesight fail; and, one by one,
The dogs are stretched among the mountain fern.

Where is the throng, the tumult of the race?   25
The bugles that so joyfully were blown?
—This chase it looks not like an earthly chase;
Sir Walter and the Hart are left alone.

XXIV. 3–4 *so* 1836: He turned aside towards *etc.* And, "Bring another
etc. 1800–32   19 Blanch 1827: Brach 1800–20   20 *so* 1802: and
weary up the 1800   21 cheered and chid 1827: chid and cheered
1800–20   25, 27 race . . . chase 1836: chace . . . race 1800–27

The poor Hart toils along the mountain-side;
I will not stop to tell how far he fled,   30
Nor will I mention by what death he died;
But now the Knight beholds him lying dead.

Dismounting, then, he leaned against a thorn;
He had no follower, dog, nor man, nor boy:
He neither cracked his whip, nor blew his horn,   35
But gazed upon the spoil with silent joy.

Close to the thorn on which Sir Walter leaned
Stood his dumb partner in this glorious feat;
Weak as a lamb the hour that it is yeaned;
And white with foam as if with cleaving sleet.   40

Upon his side the Hart was lying stretched:
His nostril touched a spring beneath a hill,
And with the last deep groan his breath had fetched
The waters of the spring were trembling still.

And now, too happy for repose or rest,   45
(Never had living man such joyful lot!)
Sir Walter walked all round, north, south, and west,
And gazed and gazed upon that darling spot.

And climbing up the hill—(it was at least
Four roods of sheer ascent) Sir Walter found   50
Three several hoof-marks which the hunted Beast
Had left imprinted on the grassy ground.

Sir Walter wiped his face, and cried, "Till now
Such sight was never seen by human eyes:
Three leaps have borne him from this lofty brow,   55
Down to the very fountain where he lies.

35 cracked 1820: smacked 1800–15   38 feat 1820: act 1800–15   40 *so*
1820: And foaming like a mountain cataract 1800–15   42 nostril
touched 1820: nose half-touched 1800–15   46 *so* 1820: (Was never
man in such a joyful case!) 1800–15   48 spot 1820: place 1800–15
49 climbing 1802: turning 1800   50 Four 1840: Nine 1800–36   51 *so*
1802: Three several marks which with his hoofs the beast 1800   52
grassy 1820: verdant 1800–15   54 human 1836; living 1800–32

"I'll build a pleasure-house upon this spot,
And a small arbour, made for rural joy;
'Twill be the traveller's shed, the pilgrim's cot,
A place of love for damsels that are coy.   60

"A cunning artist will I have to frame
A basin for that fountain in the dell!
And they who do make mention of the same,
From this day forth, shall call it HART-LEAP WELL.

"And, gallant Stag! to make thy praises known,   65
Another monument shall here be raised;
Three several pillars, each a rough-hewn stone,
And planted where thy hoofs the turf have grazed.

"And in the summer-time when days are long,
I will come hither with my Paramour;   70
And with the dancers and the minstrel's song
We will make merry in that pleasant bower.

"Till the foundations of the mountains fail
My mansion with its arbour shall endure;—
The joy of them who till the fields of Swale,   75
And them who dwell among the woods of Ure!"

Then home he went, and left the Hart, stone-dead,
With breathless nostrils stretched above the spring.
—Soon did the Knight perform what he had said;
And far and wide the fame thereof did ring.   80

Ere thrice the Moon into her port had steered,
A cup of stone received the living well;
Three pillars of rude stone Sir Walter reared,
And built a house of pleasure in the dell.

And, near the fountain, flowers of stature tall   85
With trailing plants and trees were intertwined,—
Which soon composed a little sylvan hall,
A leafy shelter from the sun and wind.

And thither, when the summer days were long,
Sir Walter led his wondering Paramour;   90
And with the dancers and the minstrel's song
Made merriment within that pleasant bower.

65 Stag! 1827: brute! 1800–20   79–80 *so* 1815: And soon the **Knight**
performed *etc*. The fame whereof through many a land *etc*. 1800–5   90
so 1820: journeyed with his 1800–15

The Knight, Sir Walter, died in course of time,
And his bones lie in his paternal vale.—
But there is matter for a second rhyme,   95
And I to this would add another tale.

PART SECOND

The moving accident is not my trade;
To freeze the blood I have no ready arts:
'Tis my delight, alone in summer shade,
To pipe a simple song for thinking hearts.   100

As I from Hawes to Richmond did repair,
It chanced that I saw standing in a dell
Three aspens at three corners of a square;
And one, not four yards distant, near a well.

What this imported I could ill divine: 105
And, pulling now the rein my horse to stop,
I saw three pillars standing in a line,—
The last stone-pillar on a dark hill-top.

The trees were grey, with neither arms nor head;
Half wasted the square mound of tawny green;   110
So that you just might say, as then I said,
"Here in old time the hand of man hath been."

I looked upon the hill both far and near,
More doleful place did never eye survey;
It seemed as if the spring-time came not here,   115
And Nature here were willing to decay.

I stood in various thoughts and fancies lost,
When one, who was in shepherd's garb attired,
Came up the hollow:—him did I accost,
And what this place might be I then inquired.   120

The Shepherd stopped, and that same story told
Which in my former rhyme I have rehearsed.
"A jolly place," said he, "in times of old!
But something ails it now: the spot is curst.

"You see these lifeless stumps of aspen wood—   125
Some say that they are beeches, others elms—
These were the bower; and here a mansion stood,
The finest palace of a hundred realms!

98 freeze 1800 *errata*: curl 1800

"The arbour does its own condition tell;
You see the stones, the fountain, and the stream; 130
But as to the great Lodge! you might as well
Hunt half a day for a forgotten dream.

"There's neither dog nor heifer, horse nor sheep,
Will wet his lips within that cup of stone;
And oftentimes, when all are fast asleep, 135
This water doth send forth a dolorous groan.

"Some say that here a murder has been done,
And blood cries out for blood: but, for my part,
I've guessed, when I've been sitting in the sun,
That it was all for that unhappy Hart. 140

"What thoughts must through the creature's brain have past!
Even from the topmost stone, upon the steep,
Are but three bounds—and look, Sir, at this last—
O Master! it has been a cruel leap.

"For thirteen hours he ran a desperate race; 145
And in my simple mind we cannot tell
What cause the Hart might have to love this place,
And come and make his death-bed near the well.

"Here on the grass perhaps asleep he sank,
Lulled by the fountain in the summer-tide; 150
This water was perhaps the first he drank
When he had wandered from his mother's side.

"In April here beneath the flowering thorn
He heard the birds their morning carols sing;
And he, perhaps, for aught we know, was born 155
Not half a furlong from that self-same spring.

"Now, here is neither grass nor pleasant shade;
The sun on drearier hollow never shone;
So will it be, as I have often said,
Till trees, and stones, and fountain, all are gone." 160

"Grey-headed Shepherd, thou hast spoken well;
Small difference lies between thy creed and mine:
This Beast not unobserved by Nature fell;
His death was mourned by sympathy divine.

142 *so* 1815: To this place from the stone upon the steep 1800; From the
stone upon the summit of the steep 1802   153 flowering 1836: scented
1800–32   157 Now, here is 1827: But now here's 1800–20

"The Being, that is in the clouds and air,   165
That is in the green leaves among the groves,
Maintains a deep and reverential care
For the unoffending creatures whom he loves.

"The pleasure-house is dust:—behind, before,
This is no common waste, no common gloom;   170
But Nature, in due course of time, once more
Shall here put on her beauty and her bloom.

"She leaves these objects to a slow decay,
That what we are, and have been, may be known;
But at the coming of the milder day   175
These monuments shall all be overgrown.

"One lesson, Shepherd, let us two divide,
Taught both by what she shows, and what conceals;
Never to blend our pleasure or our pride
With sorrow of the meanest thing that feels."   180

XXV

SONG AT THE FEAST OF BROUGHAM CASTLE

UPON THE RESTORATION OF LORD CLIFFORD, THE SHEPHERD, TO THE ESTATES AND HONOURS OF HIS ANCESTORS

[Composed 1807.—Published 1807.]

HIGH in the breathless Hall the Minstrel sate,
And Emont's murmur mingled with the Song.—
The words of ancient time I thus translate,
A festal strain that hath been silent long:—

"From town to town, from tower to tower,   5
The red rose is a gladsome flower.
Her thirty years of winter past,
The red rose is revived at last;
She lifts her head for endless spring,
For everlasting blossoming: 10
Both roses flourish, red and white:
In love and sisterly delight
The two that were at strife are blended,
And all old troubles now are ended.—

168 *so* 1815: For them the quiet creatures whom he loves 1800–5
XXV. 14 troubles 1815: sorrows 1807

Joy! joy to both! but most to her   15
Who is the flower of Lancaster!
Behold her how She smiles to-day
On this great throng, this bright array!
Fair greeting doth she send to all
From every corner of the hall;   20
But chiefly from above the board
Where sits in state our rightful Lord,
A Clifford to his own-restored!

    "They came with banner, spear, and shield;
And it was proved in Bosworth-field.   25
Not long the Avenger was withstood—
Earth helped him with the cry of blood:
St. George was for us, and the might
Of blessed Angels crowned the right.
Loud voice the Land has uttered forth,   30
We loudest in the faithful north:
Our fields rejoice, our mountains ring,
Our streams proclaim a welcoming;
Our strong-abodes and castles see
The glory of their loyalty.   35

    "How glad is Skipton at this hour—
Though lonely, a deserted Tower;
Knight, squire, and yeoman, page and groom:
We have them at the feast of Brough'm.
How glad Pendragon—though the sleep   40
Of years be on her!—She shall reap
A taste of this great pleasure, viewing
As in a dream her own renewing.
Rejoiced is Brough, right glad, I deem,
Beside her little humble stream;   45
And she that keepeth watch and ward
Her statelier Eden's course to guard;
They both are happy at this hour,
Though each is but a lonely Tower:—
But here is perfect joy and pride   50
For one fair House by Emont's side,

37/38   Silent, deserted of her best (Deserted, emptied of MS.)
         Without an Inmate or a Guest,   1807–15
         To vacancy and silence left;
         Of all her guardian sons bereft—1820–43

This day, distinguished without peer,
To see her Master and to cheer—
Him, and his Lady-mother dear!

"Oh! it was a time forlorn   55
When the fatherless was born—
Give her wings that she may fly,
Or she sees her infant die!
Swords that are with slaughter wild
Hunt the Mother and the Child.   60
Who will take them from the light?
—Yonder is a man in sight—
Yonder is a house—but where?
No, they must not enter there.
To the caves, and to the brooks,   65
To the clouds of heaven she looks;
She is speechless, but her eyes
Pray in ghostly agonies.
Blissful Mary, Mother mild,
Maid and Mother undefiled,   70
Save a Mother and her Child!

"Now Who is he that bounds with joy
On Carrock's side, a Shepherd-boy?
No thoughts hath he but thoughts that pass
Light as the wind along the grass.   75
Can this be He who hither came
In secret, like a smothered flame?
O'er whom such thankful tears were shed
For shelter, and a poor man's bread!
God loves the Child; and God hath willed   80
That those dear words should be fulfilled,
The Lady's words, when forced away
The last she to her Babe did say:
'My own, my own, thy Fellow-guest
I may not be; but rest thee, rest,   85
For lowly shepherd's life is best!'

"Alas! when evil men are strong
No life is good, no pleasure long.
The Boy must part from Mosedale's groves,
And leave Blencathara's rugged coves,   90

And quit the flowers that summer brings
To Glenderamakin's lofty springs;
Must vanish, and his careless cheer
Be turned to heaviness and fear.
—Give Sir Lancelot Threlkeld praise!   95
Hear it, good man, old in days!
Thou tree of covert and of rest
For this young Bird that is distrest;
Among thy branches safe he lay,
And he was free to sport and play,   100
When falcons were abroad for prey.

   "A recreant harp, that sings of fear
And heaviness in Clifford's ear!
I said, when evil men are strong,
No life is good, no pleasure long,   105
A weak and cowardly untruth!
Our Clifford was a happy Youth,
And thankful through a weary time,
That brought him up to manhood's prime.
—Again he wanders forth at will,   110
And tends a flock from hill to hill:
His garb is humble; ne'er was seen
Such garb with such a noble mien;
Among the shepherd-grooms no mate
Hath he, a Child of strength and state!   115
Yet lacks not friends for simple glee,
Nor yet for higher sympathy.
To his side the fallow-deer
Came, and rested without fear;
The eagle, lord of land and sea,   120
Stooped down to pay him fealty;
And both the undying fish that swim
Through Bowscale-tarn did wait on him;
The pair were servants of his eye
In their immortality;   125
And glancing, gleaming, dark or bright,
Moved to and fro, for his delight.

116 simple 1845: solemn 1807–43   117 *so* 1845: And a chearful company
1807–32: A spirit-soothing 1836–43
117/118   That learn'd of him submissive ways;
         And comforted his private days.   1807–43
126–7 *so* 1836:   They moved about in open sight,
         To and fro, for his delight.   1807–32

He knew the rocks which Angels haunt
Upon the mountains visitant;
He hath kenned them taking wing: 130
And into caves where Faeries sing
He hath entered; and been told
By Voices how men lived of old.
Among the heavens his eye can see
The face of thing that is to be;   135
And, if that men report him right,
His tongue could whisper words of might.
—Now another day is come,
Fitter hope, and nobler doom;
He hath thrown aside his crook,   140
And hath buried deep his book;
Armour rusting in his halls
On the blood of Clifford calls;—
'Quell the Scot,' exclaims the Lance—
Bear me to the heart of France,   145
Is the longing of the Shield—
Tell thy name, thou trembling Field;
Field of death, where'er thou be,
Groan thou with our victory!
Happy day, and mighty hour,   150
When our Shepherd in his power,
Mailed and horsed, with lance and sword,
To his ancestors restored
Like a re-appearing Star,
Like a glory from afar,   155
First shall head the flock of war!'"

Alas! the impassioned minstrel did not know
How, by Heaven's grace, this Clifford's heart was framed:
How he, long forced in humble walks to go,
Was softened into feeling, soothed, and tamed.   160

Love had he found in huts where poor men lie;
His daily teachers had been woods and rills,
The silence that is in the starry sky,
The sleep that is among the lonely hills.

129 Upon 1836: On 1807–32   131 And into 1836: And the 1807–32
135 The face 1836: Face 1807–32   136 if that 1836: if 1807–32   137
His tongue could 1840: He can 1807–20 He could 1827–36
157–9 so 1845: Alas! the fervent Harper did not know
              That for a tranquil Soul the Lay was framed,
              Who, long compelled in humble walks to go,   1807–36

In him the savage virtue of the Race,   165
Revenge, and all ferocious thoughts were dead:
Nor did he change; but kept in lofty place
The wisdom which adversity had bred.

Glad were the vales, and every cottage-hearth;
The Shepherd-lord was honoured more and more;   170
And, ages after he was laid in earth,
"The good Lord Clifford" was the name he bore.

XXVI

LINES

COMPOSED A FEW MILES ABOVE TINTERN ABBEY, ON REVISITING
THE BANKS OF THE WYE DURING A TOUR. JULY 13, 1798

[Composed July 13, 1798.—Published 1798.]

FIVE years have past; five summers, with the length
Of five long winters! and again I hear
These waters, rolling from their mountain-springs
With a soft inland murmur.[1]—Once again
Do I behold these steep and lofty cliffs,   5
That on a wild secluded scene impress
Thoughts of more deep seclusion; and connect
The landscape with the quiet of the sky.
The day is come when I again repose
Here, under this dark sycamore, and view   10
These plots of cottage-ground, these orchard-tufts,
Which at this season, with their unripe fruits,
Are clad in one green hue, and lose themselves
'Mid groves and copses. Once again I see
These hedge-rows, hardly hedge-rows, little lines   15
Of sportive wood run wild: these pastoral farms,
Green to the very door; and wreaths of smoke

[1] The river is not affected by the tides a few miles above Tintern.

XXVI. 4 soft: 1845: sweet 1798–1836
13–14 so 1845: Among the woods and copses lose themselves,
                Nor, with their green and simple hue, disturb
                The wild green landscape.   1798–1800
                Are clad in one green hue, and lose themselves
                Among the woods and copses, nor disturb
                The wild green landscape.   1802–43

Sent up, in silence, from among the trees!
With some uncertain notice, as might seem
Of vagrant dwellers in the houseless woods,   20
Or of some Hermit's cave, where by his fire
The Hermit sits alone.

                These beauteous forms,
Through a long absence, have not been to me
As is a landscape to a blind man's eye:
But oft, in lonely rooms, and 'mid the din   25
Of towns and cities, I have owed to them
In hours of weariness, sensations sweet,
Felt in the blood, and felt along the heart;
And passing even into my purer mind,
With tranquil restoration:—feelings too   30
Of unremembered pleasure: such, perhaps,
As have no slight or trivial influence
On that best portion of a good man's life,
His little, nameless, unremembered, acts
Of kindness and of love. Nor less, I trust,   35
To them I may have owed another gift,
Of aspect more sublime; that blessed mood
In which the burthen of the mystery,
In which the heavy and the weary weight
Of all this unintelligible world,   40
Is lightened:—that serene and blessed mood,
In which the affections gently lead us on,—
Until, the breath of this corporeal frame
And even the motion of our human blood
Almost suspended, we are laid asleep   45
In body, and become a living soul:
While with an eye made quiet by the power
Of harmony, and the deep power of joy,
We see into the life of things.
                      If this
Be but a vain belief, yet, oh! how oft—   50
In darkness and amid the many shapes
Of joyless daylight; when the fretful stir
Unprofitable, and the fever of the world,

18/19 And the low copses—coming from the trees 1798 *cancelled in errata*
22-3 *so* 1827: Though absent long These forms of beauty 1798–1820   32
so 1820: As may have had no trivial influence 1798–1815

Have hung upon the beatings of my heart—
How oft, in spirit, have I turned to thee,   55
O sylvan Wye! thou wanderer thro' the woods,
How often has my spirit turned to thee!

And now, with gleams of half-extinguished thought,
With many recognitions dim and faint,
And somewhat of a sad perplexity,   60
The picture of the mind revives again:
While here I stand, not only with the sense
Of present pleasure, but with pleasing thoughts
That in this moment there is life and food
For future years. And so I dare to hope,   65
Though changed, no doubt, from what I was when first
I came among these hills; when like a roe
I bounded o'er the mountains, by the sides
Of the deep rivers, and the lonely streams,
Wherever nature led: more like a man   70
Flying from something that he dreads than one
Who sought the thing he loved. For nature then
(The coarser pleasures of my boyish days,
And their glad animal movements all gone by)
To me was all in all.—I cannot paint   75
What then I was. The sounding cataract
Haunted me like a passion: the tall rock,
The mountain, and the deep and gloomy wood,
Their colours and their forms, were then to me
An appetite; a feeling and a love,   80
That had no need of a remoter charm,
By thought supplied, nor any interest
Unborrowed from the eye.—That time is past,
And all its aching joys are now no more,
And all its dizzy raptures. Not for this   85
Faint I, nor mourn nor murmur; other gifts
Have followed; for such loss, I would believe,
Abundant recompense. For I have learned
To look on nature, not as in the hour
Of thoughtless youth; but hearing oftentimes   90
The still, sad music of humanity,
Nor harsh nor grating, though of ample power
To chasten and subdue. And I have felt
A presence that disturbs me with the joy

Of elevated thoughts; a sense sublime   95
Of something far more deeply interfused,
Whose dwelling is the light of setting suns,
And the round ocean and the living air,
And the blue sky, and in the mind of man:
A motion and a spirit, that impels   100
All thinking things, all objects of all thought,
And rolls through all things. Therefore am I still
A lover of the meadows and the woods,
And mountains; and of all that we behold
From this green earth; of all the mighty world   105
Of eye, and ear,—both what they half create,[1]
And what perceive; well pleased to recognise
In nature and the language of the sense
The anchor of my purest thoughts, the nurse,
The guide, the guardian of my heart, and soul   110
Of all my moral being.
                              Nor perchance,
If I were not thus taught, should I the more
Suffer my genial spirits to decay:
For thou art with me here upon the banks
Of this fair river; thou my dearest Friend,   115
My dear, dear Friend; and in thy voice I catch
The language of my former heart, and read
My former pleasures in the shooting lights
Of thy wild eyes. Oh! yet a little while
May I behold in thee what I was once,   120
My dear, dear Sister! and this prayer I make,
Knowing that Nature never did betray
The heart that loved her; 'tis her privilege,
Through all the years of this our life, to lead
From joy to joy: for she can so inform   125
The mind that is within us, so impress
With quietness and beauty, and so feed
With lofty thoughts, that neither evil tongues,
Rash judgments, nor the sneers of selfish men,
Nor greetings where no kindness is, nor all   130
The dreary intercourse of daily life,
Shall e'er prevail against us, or disturb
Our cheerful faith, that all which we behold

---

[1] This line has a close resemblance to an admirable line of Young's, the exact expression of which I do not recollect.

Is full of blessings. Therefore let the moon
Shine on thee in thy solitary walk;   135
And let the misty mountain-winds be free
To blow against thee: and, in after years,
When these wild ecstasies shall be matured
Into a sober pleasure; when thy mind
Shall be a mansion for all lovely forms,   140
Thy memory be as a dwelling-place
For all sweet sounds and harmonies; oh! then,
If solitude, or fear, or pain, or grief,
Should be thy portion, with what healing thoughts
Of tender joy wilt thou remember me,   145
And these my exhortations! Nor, perchance—
If I should be where I no more can hear
Thy voice, nor catch from thy wild eyes these gleams
Of past existence—wilt thou then forget
That on the banks of this delightful stream   150
We stood together; and that I, so long
A worshipper of Nature, hither came
Unwearied in that service: rather say
With warmer love—oh! with far deeper zeal
Of holier love. Nor wilt thou then forget,   155
That after many wanderings, many years
Of absence, these steep woods and lofty cliffs,
And this green pastoral landscape, were to me
More dear, both for themselves and for thy sake!

XXVII

[Composed 1803.—Published 1807.]

It is no Spirit who from heaven hath flown,
And is descending on his embassy;
Nor Traveller gone from earth the heavens to espy!
'Tis Hesperus—there he stands with glittering crown,
First admonition that the sun is down!   5
For yet it is broad day-light: clouds pass by;
A few are near him still—and now the sky,
He hath it to himself—'tis all his own.

XXVII. 6 For] Even MS.   7 And now he is left single in the sky
MS.

O most ambitious Star! an inquest wrought
Within me when I recognised thy light;   10
A moment I was startled at the sight:
And, while I gazed, there came to me a thought
That I might step beyond my natural race
As thou seem'st now to do; might one day trace
Some ground not mine; and, strong her strength above,   15
My Soul, an Apparition in the place,
Tread there with steps that no one shall reprove!

XXVIII

FRENCH REVOLUTION

AS IT APPEARED TO ENTHUSIASTS AT ITS COMMENCEMENT.[1]
REPRINTED FROM "THE FRIEND"

[Composed 1804.—Published October 26, 1809 (*The Friend*); ed. 1815.]

OH! pleasant exercise of hope and joy!
For mighty were the auxiliars which then stood
Upon our side, we who were strong in love!
Bliss was it in that dawn to be alive,
But to be young was very heaven!—Oh! times,   5
In which the meagre, stale, forbidding ways
Of custom, law, and statute, took at once
The attraction of a country in romance!
When Reason seemed the most to assert her rights,
When most intent on making of herself   10
A prime Enchantress—to assist the work
Which then was going forward in her name!
Not favoured spots alone, but the whole earth,
The beauty wore of promise, that which sets

[1] This and the Extract, Vol. I, p. 248, and the first Piece of this Class, are
from the unpublished Poem of which some account is given in the Preface to
THE EXCURSION.

9–14 *So* MS., 1807, 1836–49 (*but* MS. *l.* 11 My mind was startled at the
unusual sight:)   thy Presence brought
            A startling recollection to the mind
            Of the distinguished few among mankind,
            Who dare to step beyond their natural race
            As thou seem'st now to do: nor was a thought
            Denied—that even I might one day trace
            Some ground *etc.*   1820–32: 1815 *as text but ll.* 13–14
            That even I beyond my natural race
            Might step as thou dost now:—might one day trace
XXVIII. *For variants v. Prelude*, pp. 400–3, 584

(As at some moment might not be unfelt   15
Among the bowers of paradise itself)
The budding rose above the rose full blown.
What temper at the prospect did not wake
To happiness unthought of ? The inert
Were roused, and lively natures rapt away!   20
They who had fed their childhood upon dreams,
The playfellows of fancy, who had made
All powers of swiftness, subtilty, and strength
Their ministers,—who in lordly wise had stirred
Among the grandest objects of the sense,   25
And dealt with whatsoever they found there
As if they had within some lurking right
To wield it;—they, too, who, of gentle mood,
Had watched all gentle motions, and to these
Had fitted their own thoughts, schemers more mild,   30
And in the region of their peaceful selves;—
Now was it that both found, the meek and lofty
Did both find, helpers to their heart's desire,
And stuff at hand, plastic as they could wish;
Were called upon to exercise their skill,   35
Not in Utopia, subterranean fields,
Or some secreted island, Heaven knows where!
But in the very world, which is the world
Of all of us,—the place where in the end
We find our happiness, or not at all!   40

XXIX

[Composed 1806.—Published 1807.]

YES, it was the mountain Echo,
Solitary, clear, profound,
Answering to the shouting Cuckoo,
Giving to her sound for sound!

XXIX. 1 *so* 1827: Yes full surely 'twas the Echo 1807–20   3–4 *so* 1827:
. . . thee, shouting . . . thee   1807–20
4/5   Whence the Voice ? from air or earth ?
                        This the Cuckoo cannot tell;
                        But a startling sound had birth,
                        As the Bird must know full well; 1807

Unsolicited reply   5
To a babbling wanderer sent;
Like her ordinary cry,
Like—but oh, how different!

Hears not also mortal Life?
Hear not we, unthinking Creatures!   10
Slaves of folly, love, or strife—
Voices of two different natures?

Have not *we* too?—yes, we have
Answers, and we know not whence;
Echoes from beyond the grave,   15
Recognised intelligence!

Such rebounds our inward ear
Catches sometimes from afar—
Listen, ponder, hold them dear;
For of God,—of God they are.   20

XXX

TO A SKYLARK

[Composed 1825.—Published 1827.]

ETHEREAL minstrel! pilgrim of the sky!
Dost thou despise the earth where cares abound?
Or, while the wings aspire, are heart and eye
Both with thy nest upon the dewy ground?
Thy nest which thou canst drop into at will,   5
Those quivering wings composed, that music still!

Leave to the nightingale her shady wood;
A privacy of glorious light is thine;
Whence thou dost pour upon the world a flood
Of harmony, with instinct more divine;   10
Type of the wise who soar, but never roam;
True to the kindred points of Heaven and Home!

5–6 *so* 1815:   Like the voice through earth and sky
                  By the restless Cuckoo sent;   1807
17–18 *so* 1836 Such within ourselves we hear
                  Oft-times, ours though sent from far; 1807–20
                  Such rebounds *etc.* Often catches   1827
                  Often as thy inward ear
                  Catches such rebounds, beware—   1832
19 Giddy mortals, hold them dear   1827 *only*
XXX. 6/7 1827–43 *have here ll.* 43–8 *of* A Morning Exercise *v.* p. 125
10 instinct 1832: rapture 1827

XXXI

LAODAMIA

[Composed 1814.—Published 1815.]

"WITH sacrifice before the rising morn
Vows have I made by fruitless hope inspired;
And from the infernal Gods, 'mid shades forlorn
Of night, my slaughtered Lord have I required;
Celestial pity I again implore;—   5
Restore him to my sight—great Jove, restore!"

So speaking, and by fervent love endowed
With faith, the Suppliant heavenward lifts her hands;
While, like the sun emerging from a cloud,
Her countenance brightens—and her eye expands;   10
Her bosom heaves and spreads, her stature grows;
And she expects the issue in repose.

O terror! what hath she perceived?—O joy!
What doth she look on?—whom doth she behold?
Her Hero slain upon the beach of Troy?   15
His vital presence? his corporeal mould?
It is—if sense deceive her not—'tis He!
And a God leads him, wingèd Mercury!

Mild Hermes spake—and touched her with his wand
That calms all fear; "Such grace hath crowned thy prayer, 20
Laodamía! that at Jove's command
Thy Husband walks the paths of upper air:
He comes to tarry with thee three hours' space;
Accept the gift, behold him face to face!"

XXXI. 2-4 *so* 1827: Performed, my slaughtered Lord have I required;
                And in thick darkness, amid shades forlorn,
                Him of the infernal Gods have I desired: MS. 1815–20
7–12 *not in* 1815 *Wel.*
12/13   That rapture failing, the distracted Queen
                Knelt and embraced the Statue of the God:
                "Mighty the boon I ask, but Earth has seen
                Effects as awful from thy gracious nod;
                All-ruling Jove, unbind the mortal chain,
                Nor let the force of prayer be spent in vain!"

                Round the high-seated Temple a soft breeze
                Along the columns sighed—all else was still—
                Mute, vacant as the face of summer seas,
                No sign accorded of a favouring will.
                Dejected she withdraws—her palace-gate
                Enters—and, traversing a room of state,
20   "Thy prayers such grace have won 1815 *Wel.*
22   Thy husband now revisits the bright sun 1815 *Wel*

Forth sprang the impassioned Queen her Lord to clasp;   25
Again that consummation she essayed;
But unsubstantial Form eludes her grasp
As often as that eager grasp was made.
The Phantom parts—but parts to re-unite,
And re-assume his place before her sight.   30

"Protesiláus, lo! thy guide is gone!
Confirm, I pray, the vision with thy voice:
This is our palace,—yonder is thy throne;
Speak, and the floor thou tread'st on will rejoice.
Not to appal me have the gods bestowed   35
This precious boon; and blest a sad abode."

"Great Jove, Laodamía! doth not leave
His gifts imperfect:—Spectre though I be,
I am not sent to scare thee or deceive;
But in reward of thy fidelity.   40
And something also did my worth obtain;
For fearless virtue bringeth boundless gain.

"Thou knowest, the Delphic oracle foretold
That the first Greek who touched the Trojan strand
Should die; but me the threat could not withhold: 45
A generous cause a victim did demand;
And forth I leapt upon the sandy plain;
A self-devoted chief—by Hector slain."

"Supreme of Heroes—bravest, noblest, best!
Thy matchless courage I bewail no more,   50
Which then, when tens of thousands were deprest
By doubt, propelled thee to the fatal shore;
Thou found'st—and I forgive thee—here thou art—
A nobler counsellor than my poor heart.

"But thou, though capable of sternest deed,   55
Wert kind as resolute, and good as brave;
And he, whose power restores thee, hath decreed
Thou should'st elude the malice of the grave:
Redundant are thy locks, thy lips as fair
As when their breath enriched Thessalian air.   60

27 Form 1815: air 1815 *Wel.*   45 could 1820: did 1815   58 *so* 1845:
That thou should'st cheat 1815–36

"No Spectre greets me,—no vain Shadow this;
Come, blooming Hero, place thee by my side!
Give, on this well-known couch, one nuptial kiss
To me, this day, a second time thy bride!"
Jove frowned in heaven: the conscious Parcæ threw   65
Upon those roseate lips a Stygian hue.

"This visage tells thee that my doom is past:
Nor should the change be mourned, even if the joys
Of sense were able to return as fast
And surely as they vanish. Earth destroys   70
Those raptures duly—Erebus disdains:
Calm pleasures there abide—majestic pains.

"Be taught, O faithful Consort, to control
Rebellious passion: for the Gods approve
The depth, and not the tumult, of the soul;   75
A fervent, not ungovernable, love.
Thy transports moderate; and meekly mourn
When I depart, for brief is my sojourn—"

"Ah wherefore?—Did not Hercules by force
Wrest from the guardian Monster of the tomb   80
Alcestis, a reanimated corse,
Given back to dwell on earth in vernal bloom?
Medea's spells dispersed the weight of years,
And Æson stood a youth 'mid youthful peers.

"The Gods to us are merciful—and they   85
Yet further may relent: for mightier far
Than strength of nerve and sinew, or the sway
Of magic potent over sun and star,
Is love, though oft to agony distrest,
And though his favourite seat be feeble woman's breast.   90

"But if thou goest, I follow—" "Peace!" he said,—
She looked upon him and was calmed and cheered;
The ghastly colour from his lips had fled;
In his deportment, shape, and mien, appeared
Elysian beauty, melancholy grace,   95
Brought from a pensive though a happy place.

68 *so* 1836: Know, virtue were not virtue if the joys 1815–32   76 *so*
1820: The fervor—not the impotence of love 1815   82 vernal 1827:
beauty's 1815- 20

He spake of love, such love as Spirits feel
In worlds whose course is equable and pure;
No fears to beat away—no strife to heal—
The past unsighed for, and the future sure;   100
Spake of heroic arts in graver mood
Revived, with finer harmony pursued;

Of all that is most beauteous—imaged there
In happier beauty; more pellucid streams,
An ampler ether, a diviner air,   105
And fields invested with purpureal gleams;
Climes which the sun, who sheds the brightest day
Earth knows, is all unworthy to survey.

Yet there the Soul shall enter which hath earned
That privilege by virtue.—"Ill," said he,   110
"The end of man's existence I discerned,
Who from ignoble games and revelry
Could draw, when we had parted, vain delight,
While tears were thy best pastime, day and night;

"And while my youthful peers before my eyes   115
(Each hero following his peculiar bent)
Prepared themselves for glorious enterprise
By martial sports,—or, seated in the tent,
Chieftains and kings in council were detained;
What time the fleet at Aulis lay enchained,   120

"The wished-for wind was given:—I then revolved
The oracle, upon the silent sea;
And, if no worthier led the way, resolved
That, of a thousand vessels, mine should be
The foremost prow in pressing to the strand,—   125
Mine the first blood that tinged the Trojan sand.

98 whose course is 1815: where all is 1815 *Wel.*
101–2 *so* 1827: Spake, as a witness, of a second birth
          For all that is most perfect upon earth; 1815–20
107–8 Climes which the Sun, who sheds the troubled day On earth *etc.*
1815 *Wel.*
112–14   Engrossed in pleasures, games and revelry;
          But a new course I took; and lofty thought,
          In act embodied, my deliverance wrought. 1815 *Wel.*
115–20 *not in* 1815 *Wel.*   120 enchained, MS. *Letter*: enchained. 1815–49
122 The oracle 1820: Our future course 1815

"Yet bitter, oft-times bitter, was the pang
When of thy loss I thought, belovèd Wife!
On thee too fondly did my memory hang,
And on the joys we shared in mortal life,—   130
The paths which we had trod—these fountains, flowers;
My new-planned cities, and unfinished towers.

"But should suspense permit the Foe to cry,
'Behold they tremble!—haughty their array,
Yet of their number no one dares to die?'   135
In soul I swept the indignity away:
Old frailties then recurred:—but lofty thought,
In act embodied, my deliverance wrought.

"And Thou, though strong in love, art all too weak
In reason, in self-government too slow;   140
I counsel thee by fortitude to seek
Our blest re-union in the shades below.
The invisible world with thee hath sympathised;
Be thy affections raised and solemnised.

"Learn, by a mortal yearning, to ascend—   145
Seeking a higher object. Love was given,
Encouraged, sanctioned, chiefly for that end;
For this the passion to excess was driven—
That self might be annulled: her bondage prove
The fetters of a dream opposed to love."—   150

Aloud she shrieked! for Hermes reappears!
Round the dear Shade she would have clung—'tis vain:
The hours are past—too brief had they been years;
And him no mortal effort can detain:
Swift, toward the realms that know not earthly day,   155
He through the portal takes his silent way,
And on the palace-floor a lifeless corse She lay.

Thus, all in vain exhorted and reproved,
She perished; and, as for a wilful crime,
By the just Gods whom no weak pity moved,   160
Was doomed to wear out her appointed time,
Apart from happy Ghosts, that gather flowers
Of blissful quiet 'mid unfading bowers.

146 Seeking 1836: Towards 1815–32   147 that 1827: this 1815–20
158–63 *so* 1845:
      Ah, judge her gently who so deeply loved!
      Her, who, in reason's spite, yet without crime,
      Was in a trance of passion thus removed;
      Delivered from the galling yoke of time

—Yet tears to human suffering are due;
And mortal hopes defeated and o'erthrown   165
Are mourned by man, and not by man alone,
As fondly he believes.—Upon the side
Of Hellespont (such faith was entertained)
A knot of spiry trees for ages grew
From out the tomb of him for whom she died;   170
And ever, when such stature they had gained
That Ilium's walls were subject to their view,
The trees' tall summits withered at the sight;
A constant interchange of growth and blight! [1]

XXXII

DION

[Composed 1816.—Published 1820.]

(SEE PLUTARCH)

I

SERENE, and fitted to embrace,
Where'er he turned, a swan-like grace
Of haughtiness without pretence,
And to unfold a still magnificence,

---

[1] For the account of these long-lived trees, see Pliny's "Natural History",
ib. xvi. cap. 44; and for the features in the character of Protesilaus, see the
"Iphigenia in Aulis" of Euripides. Virgil places the Shade of Laodamia in a
mournful region, among unhappy Lovers,

————His Laodamia
        It Comes.————

        And these frail elements—to gather flowers
        Of blissful quiet 'mid unfading bowers.   1815–1820
            By no weak pity might the Gods be moved;
        She who thus perished not without the crime
        Of Lovers that in Reason's spite have loved,
            Was doomed to wander in a grosser clime etc. as text 1827;
So 1832–36 but 161–3 as text,
        She—who though warned, exhorted, and reproved,
        Thus died, from passion desperate to a crime—etc. as text, 1840
        She perished thus, admonished and reproved
        In vain; and even as for a wilful crime
      · By the just gods   C
XXXII. 1–2   [I]
        FAIR is the Swan, whose majesty, prevailing
        O'er breezeless water, on Locarno's lake,
        Bears him on while proudly sailing
        He leaves behind a moon-illumined wake:
        Behold! the mantling spirit of reserve
        Fashions his neck into a goodly curve;

Was princely Dion, in the power 5
And beauty of his happier hour.
And what pure homage *then* did wait
On Dion's virtues, while the lunar beam
Of Plato's genius, from its lofty sphere,
Fell round him in the grove of Academe, 10
Softening their inbred dignity austere—
  That he, not too elate
  With self-sufficing solitude,
But with majestic lowliness endued,
Might in the universal bosom reign, 15
And from affectionate observance gain
Help, under every change of adverse fate.

II

Five thousand warriors—O the rapturous day!
Each crowned with flowers, and armed with spear and shield,
Or ruder weapon which their course might yield, 20
To Syracuse advance in bright array.

> An arch thrown back between luxuriant wings
> Of whitest garniture, like fir-tree boughs
> To which, on some unruffled morning, clings
> A flaky weight of winter's purest snows!
> —Behold!—as with a gushing impulse heaves
> That downy prow, and softly cleaves
> The mirror of the crystal flood,
> Vanish inverted (the dusky MS.) hill, and shadowy wood,
> And pendent rocks, where'er, in gliding state,
> Winds the mute Creature without visible Mate
> Or Rival, save the Queen of night
> Showering down a silver light,
> From heaven, upon her chosen Favourite!

[II]

So pure, so bright, so fitted to embrace
Where'er he turned, a natural grace   MS., 1820–32; *printed
  in notes* 1837 *etc.*
7–8 Nor less the homage that was seen to wait
  On Dion's virtues, when *etc.*   MS., 1820–32
12–17 If in thy path the world delight to gaze,
  Pride of the world, beware! for thou mayst live
  Like Dion, to behold the torch of Praise
  Inverted in thy presence, and to give
  Proof, for the historian's page and poet's lays
  That Peace, even Peace herself, is fugitive.   MS.
·18 rapturous] joyful MS.   20 such as chance might yield   MS.

Who leads them on?—The anxious people see
Long-exiled Dion marching at their head,
He also crowned with flowers of Sicily,
And in a white, far-beaming, corslet clad!   25
Pure transport undisturbed by doubt or fear
The gazers feel; and, rushing to the plain,
Salute those strangers as a holy train
Or blest procession (to the Immortals dear)
That brought their precious liberty again.   30
Lo! when the gates are entered, on each hand,
Down the long street, rich goblets filled with wine
    In seemly order stand,
On tables set, as if for rites divine;—
And, as the great Deliverer marches by,   35
He looks on festal ground with fruits bestrown;
And flowers are on his person thrown
    In boundless prodigality;
Nor doth the general voice abstain from prayer,
Invoking Dion's tutelary care,   40
As if a very Deity he were!

III

Mourn, hills and groves of Attica! and mourn
Ilissus, bending o'er thy classic urn!
Mourn, and lament for him whose spirit dreads
Your once sweet memory, studious walks and shades!   45
For him who to divinity aspired,
Not on the breath of popular applause,
But through dependence on the sacred laws
Framed in the schools where Wisdom dwelt retired,

35-7   And, wheresoe'er the great Deliverer passed,
          Fruits were strewn before his eye,
          And flowers upon his person cast   MS., 1820
39   doth 1827: did MS. 1820
42   Mourn, olive bowers of Attica and Thou
          Partake the sadness of the groves
          Famed Hill Hymettus, round whose fragrant brow
          Industrious bees, each seeking what she loves
          Or fraught with treasure which she best approves,
          Their murmurs blend in choral elevation,
          Not wholly lost upon the abstracted ears
          Of unambitious men who wander near
              Immersed in lonely contemplation;
              Mourn sunny hill and shady groves! and mourn MS.
47 breath] wings MS.

Intent to trace the ideal path of right   50
(More fair than heaven's broad causeway paved with stars)
Which Dion learned to measure with sublime delight;—
But He hath overleaped the eternal bars;
And, following guides whose craft holds no consent
With aught that breathes the ethereal element,   55
Hath stained the robes of civil power with blood,
Unjustly shed, though for the public good.
Whence doubts that came too late, and wishes vain,
Hollow excuses, and triumphant pain;
And oft his cogitations sink as low   60
As, through the abysses of a joyless heart,
The heaviest plummet of despair can go—
But whence that sudden check? that fearful start!

50   Meek Wisdom tracing with a sturdy hand
            The path which he alone hath scanned
            The ideal path of right   MS.
52   sublime *added* 1837: to gaze on with delight, MS.
            That path which Dion travelled with delight   MS. x.
53   But he hath] Now hath he   1837 *only*
57–9   Unjustly shed, albeit to prevent
            Manifold tumults and incessant strife
            That hang upon a single life,
            Ambitious fickle envious turbulent
            Ever aspiring to the topmost height,
            To whom the calm of general content,
            The steadfastness of public good,
            Was tiresome as the weight
            That presses down the mind of mariners
            When not a billow stirs
            On the wide surface of the ocean flood.
            Untractable disturber of the state,
            Repeated pardons make him more elate
            And bolder to transgress again;
            He hath provoked his fate.
            Deliberative sadness ratifies
            The offender's doom, and solemn be his obsequies,
            Yes, let him fall, decision slowly won
            From Dion's mind, to authorize a deed
            Which, when the word was uttered, with the speed
            Of lightning hurrying through the heavens is done.
            But since that fated word, the princely sage,
            Prime boast and envy of a glorious age,
            Droops under burthen of repentant sorrow,
            Depressed to-day and unrelieved to-morrow;   MS. x

He hears an uncouth sound—
Anon his lifted eyes   65
Saw, at a long-drawn gallery's dusky bound,
A Shape of more than mortal size
And hideous aspect, stalking round and round!
A woman's garb the Phantom wore,
And fiercely swept the marble floor,—   70
Like Auster whirling to and fro,
His force on Caspian foam to try;
Or Boreas when he scours the snow
That skins the plains of Thessaly,
Or when aloft on Mænalus he stops   75
His flight, 'mid eddying pine-tree tops!

IV

So, but from toil less sign of profit reaping,
The sullen Spectre to her purpose bowed,
Sweeping—vehemently sweeping—
No pause admitted, no design avowed!   80
"Avaunt, inexplicable Guest!—avaunt,"
Exclaimed the Chieftain—"let me rather see
The coronal that coiling vipers make;
The torch that flames with many a lurid flake,
And the long train of doleful pageantry   85
Which they behold, whom vengeful Furies haunt;
Who, while they struggle from the scourge to flee,
Move where the blasted soil is not unworn,
And, in their anguish, bear what other minds have borne!"

66–7 farthest bound A formidable shape MS. x   71 Like winged Auster
stooping low MS.
81–6   Long gazed the Chieftain ere he spake aloud
        With even voice and stern composure, wrought
        Into his brow by self-supporting thought;
        Avaunt, inexplicable guest, avaunt
        Intrusive Phantom, let me rather see
        What they behold *etc., corr. to*
        Breathless the Chieftain gazed—at length
        Endeavouring to collect his strength,
        With pallid cheek and rueful brow
        And a half pleading a half threatening eye,
        Such as the Fates exclusively allow
        For the behoof of suffering majesty,
        He rose and spoke aloud:
        Intrusive Phantom! let me rather see
        What they behold *etc.*   MS.
82 *so* 1827: Intrusive Presence! let me *etc.*   1820

V

But Shapes that come not at an earthly call,   90
Will not depart when mortal voices bid;
Lords of the visionary eye whose lid,
Once raised, remains aghast, and will not fall!
Ye Gods, thought He, that servile Implement
    Obeys a mystical intent!   95
Your Minister would brush away
The spots that to my soul adhere;
But should she labour night and day,
They will not, cannot disappear;
Whence angry perturbations,—and that look   100
Which no philosophy can brook!

VI

Ill-fated Chief! there are whose hopes are built
Upon the ruins of thy glorious name;
Who, through the portal of one moment's guilt,
Pursue thee with their deadly aim!   105
O matchless perfidy! portentous lust
Of monstrous crime!—that horror-striking blade
Drawn in defiance of the Gods, hath laid
The noble Syracusan low in dust!
Shuddered the walls—the marble city wept—   110
And sylvan places heaved a pensive sigh;
But in calm peace the appointed Victim slept,
As he had fallen in magnanimity;
Of spirit too capacious to require
That Destiny her course should change; too just   115
To his own native greatness to desire
That wretched boon, days lengthened by mistrust.
So were the hopeless troubles, that involved
The soul of Dion, instantly dissolved.
Released from life and cares of princely state,   120
He left this moral grafted on his Fate;

94 thought He] *not in MS. but inverted commas before* Ye
102–5   Away, for hark a rushing sound
        A conflict—and a groan profound   MS. *corr. to*
        Ill-fated Lord there are *etc. as text*
102 Afflicted Chief MS. x   103 Upon the basis of thy ruined name MS. x
110 Shuddered 1832: Shudder 1820–27   110–17 *added to* MS. x   116
native] inborn MS. x

"Him only pleasure leads, and peace attends,
Him, only him, the shield of Jove defends,
Whose means are fair and spotless as his ends."

XXXIII

THE PASS OF KIRKSTONE

[Composed June 27, 1817.—Published 1820.]

I

WITHIN the mind strong fancies work,
A deep delight the bosom thrills,
Oft as I pass along the fork
Of these fraternal hills:
Where, save the rugged road, we find   5
No appanage of human kind,
Nor hint of man; if stone or rock
Seem not his handy-work to mock
By something cognizably shaped;
Mockery—or model roughly hewn,   10
And left as if by earthquake strewn,
Or from the Flood escaped:
Altars for Druid service fit;
(But where no fire was ever lit,
Unless the glow-worm to the skies   15
Thence offer nightly sacrifice)
Wrinkled Egyptian monument;
Green moss-grown tower; or hoary tent;
Tents of a camp that never shall be raised—
On which four thousand years have gazed!   20

II

Ye ploughshares sparkling on the slopes!
Ye snow-white lambs that trip
Imprisoned 'mid the formal props
Of restless ownership!
Ye trees, that may to-morrow fall   25
To feed the insatiate Prodigal!
Lawns, houses, chattels, groves, and fields,
All that the fertile valley shields;

XXXIII. 26 So bids the careless Prodigal MS.   28 fertile] beauteous
MS.

Wages of folly—baits of crime,
Of life's uneasy game the stake,   30
Playthings that keep the eyes awake
Of drowsy, dotard Time;—
O care! O guilt!—O vales and plains,
Here, 'mid his own unvexed domains,
A Genius dwells, that can subdue   35
At once all memory of You,—
Most potent when mists veil the sky,
Mists that distort and magnify,
While the coarse rushes, to the sweeping breeze,
Sigh forth their ancient melodies!   40

III

List to those shriller notes!—*that* march
Perchance was on the blast,
When, through this Height's inverted arch,
Rome's earliest legion passed!
—They saw, adventurously impelled,   45
And older eyes than theirs beheld,
This block—and yon, whose church-like frame
Gives to this savage Pass its name.
Aspiring Road! that lov'st to hide
Thy daring in a vapoury bourn,   50
Not seldom may the hour return
When thou shalt be my guide:
And I (as all men may find cause,
When life is at a weary pause,
And they have panted up the hill   55
Of duty with reluctant will)
Be thankful, even though tired and faint,
For the rich bounties of constraint;
Whence oft invigorating transports flow
That choice lacked courage to bestow!   60

IV

My Soul was grateful for delight
That wore a threatening brow;
A veil is lifted—can she slight
The scene that opens now?

34 'mid] in MS.   48 this 1836: the MS.1820–32   53–5 *so* 1836, as
often we find . . . we MS., 1820–32   61 My Soul] The Song MS.

Though habitation none appear,   65
The greenness tells, man must be there;
The shelter—that the pérspective
Is of the clime in which we live;
Where Toil pursues his daily round;
Where Pity sheds sweet tears—and Love,   70
In woodbine bower or birchen grove,
Inflicts his tender wound.
—Who comes not hither ne'er shall know
How beautiful the world below;
Nor can he guess how lightly leaps   75
The brook adown the rocky steeps.
Farewell, thou desolate Domain!
Hope, pointing to the cultured plain,
Carols like a shepherd-boy;
And who is she?—Can that be Joy!   80
Who, with a sunbeam for her guide,
Smoothly skims the meadows wide;
While Faith, from yonder opening cloud,
To hill and vale proclaims aloud,
"Whate'er the weak may dread, the wicked dare,   85
Thy lot, O Man, is good, thy portion fair!"

XXXIV

TO ENTERPRISE

[Composed 1821.—Published 1822.]

KEEP for the Young the impassioned smile
Shed from thy countenance, as I see thee stand
High on that chalky cliff of Britain's Isle,
A slender volume grasping in thy hand—

66 tells us man is near MS.   68 clime] world MS.   70 Pity's tears are
shed MS.
73–86   Who comes not hither can he know
             How beautiful the world (*corr. to* Vale) below?
             Companion of the Brook that leaps
             And turns adown the rocky steeps
             As if impatient for the plain,
             I utter a repentant strain
             And this the burden—Cares enthral
             And troubles crush—but spite of all
             The weak are tempted to, the wicked dare,
             Our lot is good our portion fair.   MS.
XXXIV. 3 that 1837: a 1822–32   Britain's 1822–45: Briton's (*sic*)
1849

(Perchance the pages that relate   5
The various turns of Crusoe's fate)—
Ah, spare the exulting smile,
And drop thy pointing finger bright
As the first flash of beacon light;
But neither veil thy head in shadows dim,   10
Nor turn thy face away
From One who, in the evening of his day,
To thee would offer no presumptuous hymn!

I

Bold Spirit! who art free to rove
Among the starry courts of Jove,   15
And oft in splendour dost appear
Embodied to poetic eyes,
While traversing this nether sphere,
Where Mortals call thee ENTERPRISE.
Daughter of Hope! her favourite Child,   20
Whom she to young Ambition bore,
When hunter's arrow first defiled
The grove, and stained the turf with gore;
Thee wingèd Fancy took, and nursed
On broad Euphrates' palmy shore,   25
And where the mightier Waters burst
From caves of Indian mountains hoar!
She wrapped thee in a panther's skin;
And Thou, thy favourite food to win,
The flame-eyed eagle oft wouldst scare   30
From her rock-fortress in mid air,

26 And 1845: Or 1822–37
29–32 *so* 1837: And thou (if rightly I rehearse
      What wondering Shepherds told in verse)
      From rocky fortress in mid air
      (The food which pleased thee best to win)
      Didst oft the flame-eyed Eagle scare
      With infant shout,—as often sweep,   1822
      And thou, whose earliest thoughts held dear
      Allurements that were edged with fear,
      (The food that pleased thee best, to win)
      From rocky fortress in mid air
      The flame-eyed Eagle oft wouldst scare
      With infant shout,—as often sweep,   1827 *so* 1832, *but* 30–2
      With infant shout wouldst often scare
      From her rock-fortress in mid air
      The flame-eyed Eagle—often sweep,

With infant shout; and often sweep,
Paired with the ostrich, o'er the plain;
Or, tired with sport, wouldst sink asleep
Upon the couchant lion's mane!   35
With rolling years thy strength increased;
And, far beyond thy native East,
To thee, by varying titles known
As variously thy power was shown,
Did incense-bearing altars rise,   40
Which caught the blaze of sacrifice,
From suppliants panting for the skies!

                                II

What though this ancient Earth be trod
No more by step of Demi-god
Mounting from glorious deed to deed   45
As thou from clime to clime didst lead;
Yet still, the bosom beating high,
And the hushed farewell of an eye
Where no procrastinating gaze
A last infirmity betrays,   50
Prove that thy heaven-descended sway
Shall ne'er submit to cold decay.
By thy divinity impelled,
The Stripling seeks the tented field;
The aspiring Virgin kneels; and, pale   55
With awe, receives the hallowed veil,
A soft and tender Heroine
Vowed to severer discipline;
Inflamed by thee, the blooming Boy
Makes of the whistling shrouds a toy,   60
And of the ocean's dismal breast
A play-ground,—or a couch of rest;
'Mid the blank world of snow and ice,
Thou to his dangers dost enchain
The Chamois-chaser awed in vain   65
By chasm or dizzy precipice;
And hast Thou not with triumph seen
How soaring Mortals glide between

34 Or 1837: And 1822–32   63–4 *reverse order in* 1822–7   68–9 *so*
1837: glide serene From cloud to cloud 1822–32

Or through the clouds, and brave the light
With bolder than Icarian flight?   70
How they, in bells of crystal, dive—
Where winds and waters cease to strive—
For no unholy visitings,
Among the monsters of the Deep;
And all the sad and precious things   75
Which there in ghastly silence sleep?
Or, adverse tides and currents headed,
And breathless calms no longer dreaded,
In never-slackening voyage go
Straight as an arrow from the bow;   80
And, slighting sails and scorning oars,
Keep faith with Time on distant shores?
—Within our fearless reach are placed
The secrets of the burning Waste;
Egyptian tombs unlock their dead,   85
Nile trembles at his fountain head;
Thou speak'st—and lo! the polar Seas
Unbosom their last mysteries.
—But oh! what transports, what sublime reward,
Won from the world of mind, dost thou prepare   90
For philosophic Sage; or high-souled Bard

71 *so* 1832: Or, in their bells *etc.* 1822–7   77–82 *not in* 1822–7
77–82   Whither shall Solitude retreat,
                    Where, seat renouncing after seat,
                    Knows Silence an unbroken hour?
                    Urged on by some insatiate Power
                    Slow-climbing Man his foot hath set,   5
                    Proud Jungfrau, on thy coronet,
                    Hath pierced the deepest western wood
                    For secrets older than the flood,
                    Unquarried the surviving bones
                    Of monstrous fossil Skeletons,   10
                    Or tempted later Confidant
                    Of time and nature to disclose
                    The corse of uncorrupted Elephant
                    Enshrined amid Siberian snows;
                    Within *etc.*   MS.   *Another draft gives the lines* 4–5
                    Driven by thee, *etc. and* shall *for* hath,
followed by   To Himalayan crest will mount
                    And bend o'er *Amrah's* darkest fount,
                    Where Vishnu sleeps (as fables tell)
                    Within an [? ear-astounding] shell
                    To mortals inaccessible.

Who, for thy service trained in lonely woods,
Hath fed on pageants floating through the air,
Or calentured in depth of limpid floods;
Nor grieves—tho' doomed thro' silent night to bear   95
The domination of his glorious themes,
Or struggle in the net-work of thy dreams!

III

If there be movements in the Patriot's soul,
From source still deeper, and of higher worth,
'Tis thine the quickening impulse to control,   100
And in due season send the mandate forth;
Thy call a prostrate Nation can restore,
When but a single Mind resolves to crouch no more.

IV

Dread Minister of wrath!
Who to their destined punishment dost urge   105
The Pharaohs of the earth, the men of hardened heart!
Not unassisted by the flattering stars,
Thou strew'st temptation o'er the path
When they in pomp depart
With trampling horses and refulgent cars—   110
Soon to be swallowed by the briny surge;
Or cast, for lingering death, on unknown strands;
Or caught amid a whirl of desert sands—
An Army now, and now a living hill
That a brief while heaves with convulsive throes—   115
Then all is still;
Or, to forget their madness and their woes,
Wrapt in a winding-sheet of spotless snows!

V

Back flows the willing current of my Song:
If to provoke such doom the Impious dare,   120
Why should it daunt a blameless prayer?
—Bold Goddess! range our Youth among;

98–103 *not in* 1822   113 caught amid a whirl 1837: stifled under weight
1822–32
115–16 *so* 1845: Heaving with convulsive throes
              It quivers—and is still.   1822–32
              Raised in a moment; with convulsive throes
              It heaved—and all is still;   1837

Nor let thy genuine impulse fail to beat
In hearts no longer young;
Still may a veteran Few have pride   125
In thoughts whose sternness makes them sweet;
In fixed resolves by Reason justified;
That to their object cleave like sleet
Whitening a pine tree's northern side,
When fields are naked far and wide,   130
And withered leaves, from earth's cold breast
Up-caught in whirlwinds, nowhere can find rest.

VI

But if such homage thou disdain
As doth with mellowing years agree,
One rarely absent from thy train   135
More humble favours may obtain
For thy contented Votary.
She who incites the frolic lambs
In presence of their heedless dams,
And to the solitary fawn   140
Vouchsafes her lessons, bounteous Nymph
That wakes the breeze, the sparkling lymph
Doth hurry to the lawn;
She who inspires that strain of joyance holy
Which the sweet Bird, misnamed the melancholy,   145
Pours forth in shady groves, shall plead for me;
And vernal mornings opening bright
With views of undefined delight,
And cheerful songs, and suns that shine
On busy days, with thankful nights, be mine.   150

VII

But thou, O Goddess! in thy favourite Isle
(Freedom's impregnable redoubt,
The wide earth's storehouse fenced about
With breakers roaring to the gales
That stretch a thousand thousand sails)   155

129–32 *so* 1840; *so* 1832, *but* tall pine's *for* pine tree's *and* While *for* When
          Clothing a tall pine's northern side
          In rough November days when winds have tried
          Their force on all things else—left naked far and wide.   1837
131–2 *not in* 1822–7

Quicken the slothful, and exalt the vile!—
Thy impulse is the life of Fame;
Glad Hope would almost cease to be
If torn from thy society;
And Love, when worthiest of his name,   160
Is proud to walk the earth with Thee!

XXXV

TO ——

ON HER FIRST ASCENT TO THE SUMMIT OF HELVELLYN

[Composed 1816.—Published 1820.]

INMATE of a mountain-dwelling,
Thou hast clomb aloft, and gazed
From the watch-towers of Helvellyn;
Awed, delighted, and amazed!

Potent was the spell that bound thee   5
Not unwilling to obey;
For blue Ether's arms, flung round thee,
Stilled the pantings of dismay.

Lo! the dwindled woods and meadows;
What a vast abyss is there!   10
Lo! the clouds, the solemn shadows,
And the glistenings—heavenly fair!

And a record of commotion
Which a thousand ridges yield;
Ridge, and gulf, and distant ocean   15
Gleaming like a silver shield!

Maiden! now take flight;—inherit
Alps or Andes—they are thine!
With the morning's roseate Spirit
Sweep their length of snowy line;   20

160 his 1837: the 1822–32
XXXV. 6–7 *so* 1827: In the moment of display, While   MS., 1820
17 *so* 1845: Take thy flight, possess, inherit   MS., 1820–32
        Now—take flight; possess, inherit   1836

Or survey their bright dominions
In the gorgeous colours drest
Flung from off the purple pinions,
Evening spreads throughout the west!

Thine are all the choral fountains   25
Warbling in each sparry vault
Of the untrodden lunar mountains;
Listen to their songs!—or halt,

To Niphates' top invited,
Whither spiteful Satan steered;   30
Or descend where the ark alighted,
When the green earth re-appeared;

For the power of hills is on thee,
As was witnessed through thine eye
Then, when old Helvellyn won thee   35
To confess their majesty!

XXXVI

TO A YOUNG LADY

WHO HAD BEEN REPROACHED FOR TAKING LONG WALKS
IN THE COUNTRY

[Composed 1801 (?).—Published *Morning Post*, February 11, 1802; ed.
1807.]

DEAR Child of Nature, let them rail!
—There is a nest in a green dale,
A harbour and a hold;
Where thou, a Wife and Friend, shalt see
Thy own heart-stirring days, and be   5
A light to young and old.

There, healthy as a shepherd boy,
And treading among flowers of joy
Which at no season fade,

21–4   Or adopt the purple pinions
                Evening spreads throughout the west
                And survey thy new dominions
                In that bright reflection drest.   MS.
25 choral MS., 1820–27: coral 1832 *etc.*
XXXVI. 5 heart-stirring 1837: delightful 1807–32
8–9 *so* 1827 (*but* That *for* Which)
                As if thy heritage were joy,
                And pleasure were thy trade, 1807–20

Thou, while thy babes around thee cling,   10
Shalt show us how divine a thing
A Woman may be made.

Thy thoughts and feelings shall not die,
Nor leave thee, when grey hairs are nigh,
A melancholy slave;   15
But an old age serene and bright,
And lovely as a Lapland night,
Shall lead thee to thy grave.

XXXVII

WATER FOWL

[Composed March 1800.—Published 1823; ed. 1827.]

"Let me be allowed the aid of verse to describe the evolutions which these
visitants sometimes perform, on a fine day towards the close of winter."—
Extract from the Author's Book on the Lakes.

MARK how the feathered tenants of the flood,
With grace of motion that might scarcely seem
Inferior to angelical, prolong
Their curious pastime! shaping in mid air
(And sometimes with ambitious wing that soars   5
High as the level of the mountain-tops)
A circuit ampler than the lake beneath—
Their own domain; but ever, while intent
On tracing and retracing that large round,
Their jubilant activity evolves   10
Hundreds of curves and circlets, to and fro,
Upward and downward, progress intricate
Yet unperplexed, as if one spirit swayed
Their indefatigable flight. 'Tis done—
Ten times, or more, I fancied it had ceased;   15
But lo! the vanished company again
Ascending; they approach—I hear their wings,

16 serene 1815: alive 1807
XXXVII. 1–13: Behold them how they shape,
        Orb after orb, their course still round and round
        Above the area of the lake, their own
        Adopted region, girding it about
        In wanton repetition, yet therewith
        Hundreds of curves and circlets, high and low,
        Backwards and forwards, progress intricate
        As if one spirit was in all, and swayed   MS.
    7 they approach]—list! again MS.

Faint, faint at first; and then an eager sound,
Past in a moment—and as faint again!
They tempt the sun to sport amid their plumes;   20
They tempt the water, or the gleaming ice,
To show them a fair image; 'tis themselves,
Their own fair forms, upon the glimmering plain,
Painted more soft and fair as they descend
Almost to touch;—then up again aloft,   25
Up with a sally and a flash of speed,
As if they scorned both resting-place and rest!

XXXVIII

VIEW FROM THE TOP OF BLACK COMB[1]

[Composed 1813.—Published 1815.]

THIS Height a ministering Angel might select:
For from the summit of BLACK COMB (dread name
Derived from clouds and storms!) the amplest range
Of unobstructed prospect may be seen
That British ground commands:—low dusky tracts,   5
Where Trent is nursed, far southward! Cambrian hills
To the south-west, a multitudinous show;
And, in a line of eye-sight linked with these,
The hoary peaks of Scotland that give birth
To Tiviot's stream, to Annan, Tweed, and Clyde:—   10
Crowding the quarter whence the sun comes forth
Gigantic mountains rough with crags; beneath,

[1] Black Comb stands at the southern extremity of Cumberland: its base covers a much greater extent of ground than any other mountain in those parts; and, from its situation, the summit commands a more extensive view than any other point in Britain.

XXXVIII. 1–3: Let him who, having wandered by the side
                          Of Lakes and Rivers entertains a wish
                          By lofty place to elevate his soul
                          Ascend on some clear morning to the top
                          Of huge *Black Comb*, so named from brooding clouds
                          And storms that gather round the mountain's brow.
                          This Height *etc. as l.* 1 MS.
2–3 MS. 2 *as text.*   For 'tis the spot from which the amplest range   MS. 3
                          It is the spot from which the amplest range MS. 1.
6–7 *so* MS. 3:   and south west
                          A multitudinous show of Cambrian hills   MSS. 1, 2

Right at the imperial station's western base,
Main ocean, breaking audibly, and stretched
Far into silent regions blue and pale;—   15
And visibly engirding Mona's Isle
That, as we left the plain, before our sight
Stood like a lofty mount, uplifting slowly
(Above the convex of the watery globe)
Into clear view the cultured fields that streak   20
Her habitable shores, but now appears
A dwindled object, and submits to lie
At the spectator's feet.—Yon azure ridge,
Is it a perishable cloud ? Or there
Do we behold the line of Erin's coast ?   25
Land sometimes by the roving shepherd-swain
(Like the bright confines of another world)
Not doubtfully perceived.—Look homeward now!
In depth, in height, in circuit, how serene
The spectacle, how pure!—Of Nature's works,   30
In earth, and air, and earth-embracing sea,
A revelation infinite it seems;
Display august of man's inheritance,
Of Britain's calm felicity and power!

XXXIX

THE HAUNTED TREE

TO ——

[Composed 1819.—Published 1820.]

THOSE silver clouds collected round the sun
His mid-day warmth abate not, seeming less
To overshade than multiply his beams
By soft reflection—grateful to the sky,
To rocks, fields, woods. Nor doth our human sense   5
Ask, for its pleasure, screen or canopy
More ample than the time-dismantled Oak
Spreads o'er this tuft of heath, which now, attired

16–20 *so* MS. 3: Save where that lofty barrier Mona's Isle,
             Above the convex of that wat'ry globe,
             Lifts into view *etc*. MSS. 1, 2
21 Her 1827: Its MSS., 1815–20   21–3 but . . . feet MS. 3: *not in* MSS. 1, 2
23–30 Yon azure . . . pure MSS. 2, 3: *added to* MS. 1   25 line 1832: frame
MSS., 1815–27
XXXIX. 7 the 1827: that 1820

In the whole fulness of its bloom, affords
Couch beautiful as e'er for earthly use   10
Was fashioned; whether by the hand of Art,
That eastern Sultan, amid flowers enwrought
On silken tissue, might diffuse his limbs
In languor; or, by Nature, for repose
Of panting Wood-nymph, wearied with the chase.   15
O Lady! fairer in thy Poet's sight
Than fairest spiritual creature of the groves,
Approach;—and, thus invited, crown with rest
The noon-tide hour: though truly some there are
Whose footsteps superstitiously avoid   20
This venerable Tree; for, when the wind
Blows keenly, it sends forth a creaking sound
(Above the general roar of woods and crags)
Distinctly heard from far—a doleful note!
As if (so Grecian shepherds would have deemed)   25
The Hamadryad, pent within, bewailed
Some bitter wrong. Nor is it unbelieved,
By ruder fancy, that a troubled ghost
Haunts the old trunk; lamenting deeds of which
The flowery ground is conscious. But no wind   30
Sweeps now along this elevated ridge;
Not even a zephyr stirs;—the obnoxious Tree
Is mute; and, in his silence, would look down,
O lovely Wanderer of the trackless hills,
On thy reclining form with more delight   35
Than his coevals in the sheltered vale
Seem to participate, the while they view
Their own far-stretching arms and leafy heads
Vividly pictured in some glassy pool,
That, for a brief space, checks the hurrying stream!   40

10 *so* 1827: As beautiful a couch as e'er on earth 1820   15 wearied
with 1836: weary of 1820: wearied of 1827: wearied by 1832   29
the 1836: this 1820–27   34 *added* 1827   37 the while 1849: the
whilst 1820–45

XL

THE TRIAD

[Composed early in 1828.—Published 1829 (*The Keepsake*); ed. 1832.]

SHOW me the noblest Youth of present time,
Whose trembling fancy would to love give birth;
Some God or Hero, from the Olympian clime
Returned, to seek a Consort upon earth;
Or, in no doubtful prospect, let me see   5
The brightest star of ages yet to be,
And I will mate and match him blissfully.

I will not fetch a Naiad from a flood
Pure as herself—(song lacks not mightier power)
Nor leaf-crowned Dryad from a pathless wood,   10
Nor Sea-nymph glistening from her coral bower;
Mere Mortals, bodied forth in vision still,
Shall with Mount Ida's triple lustre fill
The chaster coverts of a British hill.

"Appear!—obey my lyre's command!   15
Come, like the Graces, hand in hand!
For ye, though not by birth allied,
Are Sisters in the bond of love;
Nor shall the tongue of envious pride
Presume those interweavings to reprove   20
In you, which that fair progeny of Jove
Learned from the tuneful spheres that glide
In endless union, earth and sea above."

—I sing in vain;—the pines have hushed their waving:
A peerless Youth expectant at my side,   25
Breathless as they, with unabated craving
Looks to the earth, and to the vacant air;
And, with a wandering eye that seems to chide,
Asks of the clouds what occupants they hide:—
But why solicit more than sight could bear,   30
By casting on a moment all we dare?
Invoke we those bright Beings one by one;
And what was boldly promised, truly shall be done.

XL. 3–5:   Or Demi God, if from the Olympian clime
       The immortalized return to visit earth;
       Here seeking what heaven wants—or let me see   MS.
19–21 *so* 1836:   And not the boldest tongue of envious pride
       In you those interweavings could reprove
       Which they, the progeny of Jove   MS., 1829–32
24 **sing** 1836: speak MS., 1829–32

"Fear not a constraining measure!
—Yielding to this gentle spell,   35
Lucida! from domes of pleasure,
Or from cottage-sprinkled dell,
Come to regions solitary,
Where the eagle builds her aery,
Above the hermit's long-forsaken cell!"   40
—She comes!—behold
That Figure, like a ship with snow-white sail!
Nearer she draws; a breeze uplifts her veil;
Upon her coming wait
As pure a sunshine and as soft a gale   45
As e'er, on herbage covering earthly mould,
Tempted the bird of Juno to unfold
His richest splendour—when his veering gait
And every motion of his starry train
Seem governed by a strain   50
Of music, audible to him alone.

"O Lady, worthy of earth's proudest throne!
Nor less, by excellence of nature, fit
Beside an unambitious hearth to sit
Domestic queen, where grandeur is unknown;   55
What living man could fear
The worst of Fortune's malice, wert Thou near,
Humbling that lily-stem, thy sceptre meek,
That its fair flowers may from his cheek
Brush the too happy tear?   60
—Queen, and handmaid lowly!
Whose skill can speed the day with lively cares,
And banish melancholy
By all that mind invents or hand prepares;
O Thou, against whose lip, without its smile   65
And in its silence even, no heart is proof;
Whose goodness, sinking deep, would reconcile
The softest Nursling of a gorgeous palace
To the bare life beneath the hawthorn-roof
Of Sherwood's Archer, or in caves of Wallace—   70

34 a 1836: this MS., 1829–32   35 *so* 1836: Drawn by a poetic spell MS.
1829–32   42 snow-white 1845: silver MS., 1829–36
59–60 *so* 1845: . . . may brush from off his cheek
         The too, too happy tear. MS., 1829–36

Who that hath seen thy beauty could content
His soul with but a *glimpse* of heavenly day ?
Who that hath loved thee, but would lay
His strong hand on the wind, if it were bent
To take thee in thy majesty away ?   75
—Pass onward (even the glancing deer
Till we depart intrude not here ;)
That mossy slope, o'er which the woodbine throws
A canopy, is smoothed for thy repose !"

Glad moment is it when the throng   80
Of warblers in full concert strong
Strive, and not vainly strive, to rout
The lagging shower, and force coy Phoebus out,
Met by the rainbow's form divine,
Issuing from her cloudy shrine ;—   85

79/80   The Heavens, whose aspect makes our mind as still
        As they themselves appear to be,
        Innumerable voices fill
        With everlasting harmony ;
        The towering headlands crowned with mist,
        Their feet among the billows, know
        That Ocean is a mighty harmonist.
        Thy pinions universal Air,
        For ever sweeping to and fro
        Are delegates of harmony and bear
        Accents that cheer the seasons in their round—
        Even winter loves a dirgelike sound ;
        With rapturous notes the vernal throng   MS. *corr. to*
        There is a world of spirit
        Whose motions by fit music are controlled,
        And glorious is their privilege who merit
        Initiation in that mystery old ;
        Glad moment is it *etc.*
80–99   Like notes of Birds that, after showers,
        In April concert try their powers,
        And with a tumult and a rout
        Of warbling force coy Phoebus out,
        Or bid some dark cloud's bosom show
        That form divine, the many-coloured Bow,
        Even so the thrillings of the Lyre
        Prevail to further our desire,
        While to these shades a Nymph I call
        The youngest of the lovely Three :—
        With glowing cheek, from pastimes virginal.
        Behold her hastening to the tents
        Of Nature, and the lonely elements !
        And, as if wishful to disarm *etc.*   MS. *Letter*

So may the thrillings of the lyre
Prevail to further our desire,
While to these shades a sister Nymph I call.

"Come, if the notes thine ear may pierce,
Come, youngest of the lovely Three,   90
Submissive to the might of verse
And the dear voice of harmony,
By none more deeply felt than Thee!"
—I sang; and lo! from pastimes virginal
She hastens to the tents   95
Of nature, and the lonely elements.
Air sparkles round her with a dazzling sheen;
But mark her glowing cheek, her vesture green!

And, as if wishful to disarm
Or to repay the potent Charm,   100
She bears the stringèd lute of old romance,
That cheered the trellised arbour's privacy,
And soothed war-wearied knights in raftered hall.
How vivid, yet how delicate, her glee!
So tripped the Muse, inventress of the dance;   105
So, truant in waste woods, the blithe Euphrosyne!

But the ringlets of that head
Why are they ungarlanded?
Why bedeck her temples less
Than the simplest shepherdess?   110
Is it not a brow inviting
Choicest flowers that ever breathed,
Which the myrtle would delight in
With Idalian rose enwreathed?
But her humility is well content   115
With *one* wild floweret (call it not forlorn)
FLOWER OF THE WINDS, beneath her bosom worn—
Yet more for love than ornament.

88–93 *so* 1836: While to these shades a Nymph I call
                             The youngest of the lovely Three,
                             Come if these notes thine ear may pierce
                             Submissive to the might of verse
                             By none more deeply felt than thee MS. *corr.*, 1829–32
                             While . . . Three,
                             Come with a shooting star's velocity   MS.
97–8 *added to* MS.   104 *so* 1836: How light her air, how delicate *etc.* MS., 1829–32
106 waste] wild MS.   118 Yet more 1836: Yet is it more MS., 1829–32

Open, ye thickets! let her fly,
Swift as a Thracian Nymph o'er field and height!   120
For She, to all but those who love her, shy,
Would gladly vanish from a Stranger's sight;
Though, where she is beloved and loves,
Light as the wheeling butterfly she moves;
Her happy spirit as a bird is free,   125
That rifles blossoms on a tree,
Turning them inside out with arch audacity.
Alas! how little can a moment show
Of an eye where feeling plays
In ten thousand dewy rays;   130
A face o'er which a thousand shadows go!
—She stops—is fastened to that rivulet's side;
And there (while, with sedater mien,
O'er timid waters that have scarcely left
Their birthplace in the rocky cleft   135
She bends) at leisure may be seen
Features to old ideal grace allied,
Amid their smiles and dimples dignified—
Fit countenance for the soul of primal truth;
The bland composure of eternal youth!   140

What more changeful than the sea?
But over his great tides
Fidelity presides;
And this light-hearted Maiden constant is as he.
High is her aim as heaven above,   145
And wide as ether her good-will;
And, like the lowly reed, her love
Can drink its nurture from the scantiest rill:
Insight as keen as frosty star
Is to *her* charity no bar,   150
Nor interrupts her frolic graces
When she is, far from these wild places,
Encircled by familiar faces.

123–6 *so* 1836: Though . . . loves, as free
                  As bird that rifles blossoms on a tree   MS., 1829–32
138/9   A face clear mirror of the ingenuous soul
                  Where not a thought stands single
                  But all things intermingle
                  To make a very wonder of the whole.   MS.
147 lowly 1832: lowliest MS., 1829

O the charm that manners draw,
Nature, from thy genuine law!   155
If from what her hand would do,
Her voice would utter, aught ensue
Untoward or unfit;
She, in benign affections pure,
In self-forgetfulness secure,   160
Sheds round the transient harm or vague mischance
A light unknown to tutored elegance:
Her's is not a cheek shame-stricken,
But her blushes are joy-flushes;
And the fault (if fault it be)   165
Only ministers to quicken
Laughter-loving gaiety,
And kindle sportive wit—
Leaving this Daughter of the mountains free
As if she knew that Oberon king of Faery   170
Had crossed her purpose with some quaint vagary,
And heard his viewless bands
Over their mirthful triumph clapping hands.

    "Last of the Three, though eldest born,
Reveal thyself, like pensive Morn   175
Touched by the skylark's earliest note,
Ere humbler gladness be afloat.
But whether in the semblance drest
Of Dawn—or Eve, fair vision of the west,
Come with each anxious hope subdued   180
By woman's gentle fortitude,
Each grief, through meekness, settling into rest.

155 thy] the 1836 *only*
156–63 *so* 1845: Through benign affections—pure,
        In the slight of self—secure;
        If from what her hand would do,
        Or tongue utter, there ensue
        Aught untoward or unfit,
        Transient mischief, vague mischance,
        Shunned by guarded elegance,
        Hers *etc.* MS. 1829; 1832–6 *as text but*
        157–8 there ensue Aught untoward
167–9 *so* MS. *corr.*: Sallies of instinctive wit,
           Unchecked in laughter-loving gaiety,
           In all the motions of her spirit, free MS. *Letter*
170 *so* 1832: Oberon the fairy MS., 1829

—Or I would hail thee when some high-wrought page
Of a closed volume lingering in thy hand
Has raised thy spirit to a peaceful stand   185
Among the glories of a happier age."

Her brow hath opened on me—see it there,
Brightening the umbrage of her hair ;
So gleams the crescent moon, that loves
To be descried through shady groves.   190
Tenderest bloom is on her cheek ;
Wish not for a richer streak ;
Nor dread the depth of meditative eye ;
But let thy love, upon that azure field
Of thoughtfulness and beauty, yield   195
Its homage offered up in purity.
What wouldst thou more ? In sunny glade,
Or under leaves of thickest shade,
Was such a stillness e'er diffused
Since earth grew calm while angels mused ?   200
Softly she treads, as if her foot were loth
To crush the mountain dew-drops—soon to melt
On the flower's breast ; as if she felt
That flowers themselves, whate'er their hue,
With all their fragrance, all their glistening,   205
Call to the heart for inward listening—
And though for bridal wreaths and tokens true
Welcomed wisely ; though a growth
Which the careless shepherd sleeps on,
As fitly spring from turf the mourner weeps on—   210
And without wrong are cropped the marble tomb to strew.
The Charm is over ; the mute Phantoms gone,
Nor will return—but droop not, favoured Youth ;
The apparition that before thee shone
Obeyed a summons covetous of truth.   215
From these wild rocks thy footsteps I will guide
To bowers in which thy fortune may be tried,
And one of the bright Three become thy happy Bride.

185 peaceful 1832: fearless MS., 1829   218 happy] joyful MS.

XLI

THE WISHING-GATE

[Composed 1828.—Published 1829 (*The Keepsake*); ed. 1832.]

In the vale of Grasmere, by the side of the old highway leading to Amble-side, is a gate, which, time out of mind, has been called the Wishing-gate, from a belief that wishes formed or indulged there have a favourable issue.

HOPE rules a land for ever green:
All powers that serve the bright-eyed Queen
 Are confident and gay;
Clouds at her bidding disappear;
Points she to aught ?—the bliss draws near,   5
 And Fancy smooths the way.

Not such the land of Wishes—there
Dwell fruitless day-dreams, lawless prayer,
 And thoughts with things at strife;
Yet how forlorn, should *ye* depart,   10
Ye superstitions of the *heart*,
 How poor, were human life!

When magic lore abjured its might,
Ye did not forfeit one dear right,
 One tender claim abate;   15
Witness this symbol of your sway,
Surviving near the public way,
 The rustic Wishing-gate!

Inquire not if the faery race
Shed kindly influence on the place,   20
 Ere northward they retired;
If here a warrior left a spell,
Panting for glory as he fell;
 Or here a saint expired.

Enough that all around is fair,   25
Composed with Nature's finest care,
 And in her fondest love—
Peace to embosom and content—
To overawe the turbulent,
 The selfish to reprove.   30

Yea! even the Stranger from afar,
Reclining on this moss grown bar,
     Unknowing, and unknown,
The infection of the ground partakes,
Longing for his Belov'd—who makes   35
     All happiness her own.

Then why should conscious Spirits fear
The mystic stirrings that are here,
     The ancient faith disclaim ?
The local Genius ne'er befriends   40
Desires whose course in folly ends,
     Whose just reward is shame.

Smile if thou wilt, but not in scorn,
If some, by ceaseless pains outworn,
     Here crave an easier lot ;   45
If some have thirsted to renew
A broken vow, or bind a true,
     With firmer, holier knot.

And not in vain, when thoughts are cast
Upon the irrevocable past,   50
     Some Penitent sincere
May for a worthier future sigh,
While trickles from his downcast eye
     No unavailing tear.

The Worldling, pining to be freed   55
From turmoil, who would turn or speed
     The current of his fate,
Might stop before this favoured scene,
At Nature's call, nor blush to lean
     Upon the Wishing-gate.   60

The Sage, who feels how blind, how weak
Is man, though loth such help to *seek*,
     Yet, passing, here might pause,
And thirst for insight to allay
Misgiving, while the crimson day   65
     In quietness withdraws ;

     64 thirst 1836: yearn MS. 1829–32

Or when the church-clock's knell profound
To Time's first step across the bound
    Of midnight makes reply;
Time pressing on with starry crest,   70
To filial sleep upon the breast
    Of dread eternity.

XLII

THE WISHING-GATE DESTROYED

[Composed?—Published 1842.]

'Tis gone—with old belief and dream
That round it clung, and tempting scheme
    Released from fear and doubt;
And the bright landscape too must lie,
By this blank wall, from every eye,   5
    Relentlessly shut out.

Bear witness ye who seldom passed
That opening—but a look ye cast
    Upon the lake below,
What spirit-stirring power it gained   10
From faith which here was entertained,
    Though reason might say no.

Blest is that ground, where, o'er the springs
Of history, Glory claps her wings,
    Fame sheds the exulting tear;   15
Yet earth is wide, and many a nook
Unheard of is, like this, a book
    For modest meanings dear.

It was in sooth a happy thought
That grafted, on so fair a spot,   20
    So confident a token
Of coming good;—the charm is fled;
Indulgent centuries spun a thread,
    Which one harsh day has broken.

Alas! for him who gave the word;   25
Could he no sympathy afford,
    Derived from earth or heaven,

To hearts so oft by hope betrayed;
Their very wishes wanted aid
　　Which here was freely given ?   30

Where, for the love-lorn maiden's wound,
Will now so readily be found
　　A balm of expectation ?
Anxious for far-off children, where
Shall mothers breathe a like sweet air   35
　　Of home-felt consolation ?

And not unfelt will prove the loss
'Mid trivial care and petty cross
　　And each day's shallow grief;
Though the most easily beguiled   40
Were oft among the first that smiled
　　At their own fond belief.

If still the reckless change we mourn,
A reconciling thought may turn
　　To harm that might lurk here,   45
Ere judgment prompted from within
Fit aims, with courage to begin,
　　And strength to persevere.

Not Fortune's slave is Man: our state
Enjoins, while firm resolves await   50
　　On wishes just and wise,
That strenuous action follow both,
And life be one perpetual growth
　　Of heaven-ward enterprise.

So taught, so trained, we boldly face   55
All accidents of time and place;
　　Whatever props may fail,
Trust in that sovereign law can spread
New glory o'er the mountain's head,
　　Fresh beauty through the vale.   60

42/3 When selfish interest rules her sway
　　　Fancy and feeling must obey;
　　　'Tis done but in this age (*corr. to* But in this sweeping age)
　　　At such mild injuries why repine (Why at a wrong like this repine)
　　　When throne and altar, tomb and shrine
　　　Have bowed to vulgar rage ?　MS.
44 reconciling] salutary MS.

That truth informing mind and heart,
The simplest cottager may part,
    Ungrieved, with charm and spell;
And yet, lost Wishing-gate, to thee
The voice of grateful memory   65
    Shall bid a kind farewell![1]

XLIII

THE PRIMROSE OF THE ROCK

[Composed 1831.—Published 1835.]

A Rock there is whose homely front
    The passing traveller slights;
Yet there the glow-worms hang their lamps,
    Like stars, at various heights;
And one coy Primrose to that Rock   5
    The vernal breeze invites.

What hideous warfare hath been waged,
    What kingdoms overthrown,
Since first I spied that Primrose-tuft
    And marked it for my own;   10
A lasting link in Nature's chain
    From highest heaven let down!

The flowers, still faithful to the stems,
    Their fellowship renew;
The stems are faithful to the root,   15
    That worketh out of view;
And to the rock the root adheres
    In every fibre true.

Close clings to earth the living rock,
    Though threatening still to fall;   20
The earth is constant to her sphere;
    And God upholds them all:
So blooms this lonely Plant, nor dreads
    Her annual funeral.

.   .   .   .   .   .

[1] See Note, p. 523.

XLIII. 1 homely MSS. 1845: lonely 1835-6

Here closed the meditative strain;   25
    But air breathed soft that day,
The hoary mountain-heights were cheered,
    The sunny vale looked gay;
And to the Primrose of the Rock
    I gave this after-lay.   30

I sang—Let myriads of bright flowers,
    Like Thee, in field and grove
Revive unenvied;—mightier far,
    Than tremblings that reprove
Our vernal tendencies to hope,   35
    Is God's redeeming love;

That love which changed—for wan disease,
    For sorrow that had bent
O'er hopeless dust, for withered age—
    Their moral element,   40
And turned the thistles of a curse
    To types beneficent.

Sin-blighted though we are, we too,
    The reasoning Sons of Men,
From one oblivious winter called   45
    Shall rise, and breathe again;
And in eternal summer lose
    Our threescore years and ten.

To humbleness of heart descends
    This prescience from on high,   50
The faith that elevates the just,
    Before and when they die;
And makes each soul a separate heaven,
    A court for Deity.

25–42 *not in* MS. 1   29 Primrose of the Rock] little central flower MS. 2
43 We also earth's most noble growth MS. 1   45 From . . . called] For
. . . doomed MS. 1   47 in . . . lose] for . . . change MS. 1
49–53   Else why was foresight given with love
               Deep as the roots of Being, and why
               That faith among the just and good
               Before and when they die
               That makes *etc.*   MS. 1 *corr. to*
               Bold speech, yet not more bold than words
               From lips that cannot lie

XLIV

PRESENTIMENTS

[Composed 1830.—Published 1835.]

PRESENTIMENTS! they judge not right
Who deem that ye from open light
  Retire in fear of shame;
All *heaven-born* Instincts shun the touch
Of vulgar sense,—and, being such,   5
  Such privilege ye claim.

The tear whose source I could not guess,
The deep sigh that seemed fatherless,
  Were mine in early days;
And now, unforced by time to part   10
With fancy, I obey my heart,
  And venture on your praise.

What though some busy foes to good,
Too potent over nerve and blood,
  Lurk near you—and combine   15
To taint the health which ye infuse;
This hides not from the moral Muse
  Your origin divine.

        Words whence the just derive a faith
        Before *etc. with* Hath made *etc. corr. to*
        Take to Thyself, my heart, the hope *etc.*
        From humbleness of heart proceeds
        Divine Philosophy,
        That faith *etc.* MS. 2
XLIV. 2–6   Who deem that all which shrinks from light
        Is false and merits shame
        If that poor Pleader, Common Sense
        Fail you, go deeper for defence
        Remembering your good name MS. 1
10 time] age MSS.   13 busy MSS. 2–4: subtle MS. 1
14–16   Walk near you in our human blood
        And mischief intertwine
        With benefit which ye infuse MS. 1
17   moral MSS. 2–4 thoughtful MS. 1
18/19   Alas for Man, upon whose eye
        Hangs such a world of mystery,
        Whose freedom's but a chain
        To struggle with, should he affect
        Your divinations to reject,
        Your alchemy disdain. MS. 1

How oft from you, derided Powers!
Comes Faith that in auspicious hours   20
    Builds castles, not of air:
Bodings unsanctioned by the will
Flow from your visionary skill,
    And teach us to beware.

The bosom-weight, your stubborn gift,   25
That no philosophy can lift,
    Shall vanish, if ye please,
Like morning mist: and, where it lay,
The spirits at your bidding play
    In gaiety and ease.   30

Star-guided contemplations move
Through space, though calm, not raised above
    Prognostics that ye rule;
The naked Indian of the wild,
And haply, too, the cradled Child,   35
    Are pupils of your school.

But who can fathom your intents,
Number their signs or instruments?
    A rainbow, a sunbeam,
A subtle smell that Spring unbinds,   40
Dead pause abrupt of midnight winds,
    An echo, or a dream.

The laughter of the Christmas hearth
With sighs of self-exhausted mirth
    Ye feelingly reprove;   45
And daily, in the conscious breast,
Your visitations are a test
    And exercise of love.

19 Whence but from you, misdeemed of Powers MS. 1
31–3   The sage whose contemplations move
                Starguided, breathes not raised above
                The province where ye rule.   MS. 3 *corr. to*
                Newtonian contemplations move
                Starguided, are they . . . rule?   *So* MS. 4
37–40   But who shall search that inner school
                Whence ye can mark your two-fold rule
                Even by a weather gleam,
                By a sweet smell that *etc.*   MS. 2
48/49   They fill with tears the Mother's eyes
                While in soft calm her Infant lies
                Asleep upon her knee;

When some great change gives boundless scope
To an exulting Nation's hope,   50
    Oft, startled and made wise
By your low-breathed interpretings,
The simply-meek foretaste the springs
    Of bitter contraries.

Ye daunt the proud array of war,   55
Pervade the lonely ocean far
    As sail hath been unfurled;
For dancers in the festive hall
What ghastly partners hath your call
    Fetched from the shadowy world.   60

'Tis said that warnings ye dispense,
Emboldened by a keener sense;
    That men have lived for whom,
With dread precision, ye made clear
The hour that in a distant year   65
    Should knell them to the tomb.

Unwelcome insight! Yet there are
Blest times when mystery is laid bare,
    Truth shows a glorious face,
While on that isthmus which commands   70
The councils of both worlds, she stands,
    Sage Spirits! by your grace.

God, who instructs the brutes to scent
All changes of the element,
    Whose wisdom fixed the scale   75
Of natures, for our wants provides
By higher, sometimes humbler, guides,
    When lights of reason fail.

      Ah! why this sadness? Let her trace
      Prognostics in that quiet face
      Of happy destiny. MSS. 3, 4
49–50   When public change in transport spreads
      That maddens even experienced heads MS. 3
58–60   Unboastful ministers of Faith
      Ye flutter through the shades of death
      To seek a brighter world. MS. 2

XLV

VERNAL ODE

[Composed April 17, 1817.—Published 1820.]

"Rerum Natura tota est nusquam magis quam in minimis." PLIN.
Nat. Hist.

I

BENEATH the concave of an April sky,
When all the fields with freshest green were dight,
Appeared, in presence of the spiritual eye
That aids or supersedes our grosser sight,
The form and rich habiliments of One   5
Whose countenance bore resemblance to the sun,
When it reveals, in evening majesty,
Features half lost amid their own pure light.
Poised like a weary cloud, in middle air
He hung,---then floated with angelic ease   10
(Softening that bright effulgence by degrees)

XLV. VERNAL ODE] ODE—1817. 1820
XLV. 1–47 Forsake me not, Urania, but when Ev'n
            Fades into night, resume the enraptur'd song
            That shadowed forth the immensity of Heaven
            In music—uttered surely without wrong
            (For 'twas thy work) though here the Listener lay
            Couched on green herbage mid the warmth of May
            —A parting promise makes a bright farewell:
               Empower'd to wait for thy return,
               Voice of the Heav'ns, I will not mourn;
            Content that holy peace and mute remembrance dwell
            Within the bosom of the chorded shell
            Tuned mid those seats of love and joy concealed,
               By day,
            By night imperfectly revealed;
            Thy native mansions that endure—
            Beyond their fondest seeming—pure
            From taint of dissolution or decay.
            —No blights, no wintry desolations
            Affect those blissful habitations
            Built such as hope might gather from the hue
            Profound of the celestial blue,
            And from the aspect of each radiant orb,
            Some fix'd, some wandering with no timid curb,
            Yet both permitted to proclaim
               Their Maker's glory with unaltered frame   MS. 1
3 I saw by virtue of that spiritual eye MS. 2   9 *so* 1827: Poised in the
middle region of the air MS. 2, 1820

Till he had reached a summit sharp and bare,
Where oft the venturous heifer drinks the noontide breeze.
Upon the apex of that lofty cone
Alighted, there the Stranger stood alone;   15
Fair as a gorgeous Fabric of the east
Suddenly raised by some enchanter's power,
Where nothing was; and firm as some old Tower
Of Britain's realm, whose leafy crest
Waves high, embellished by a gleaming shower!   20

II

Beneath the shadow of his purple wings
Rested a golden harp;—he touched the strings;
And, after prelude of unearthly sound
Poured through the echoing hills around,
He sang—
                "No wintry desolations,   25
Scorching blight or noxious dew,
Affect my native habitations;
Buried in glory, far beyond the scope
Of man's inquiring gaze, but to his hope
Imaged, though faintly, in the hue   30
Profound of night's ethereal blue;
And in the aspect of each radiant orb;—
Some fixed, some wandering with no timid curb;
But wandering star and fixed, to mortal eye,
Blended in absolute serenity,   35
And free from semblance of decline;—
Fresh as if Evening brought their natal hour,
Her darkness splendour gave, her silence power,
To testify of Love and Grace divine.

12 *so* 1827: Until he reached a rock, of summit bare, MS. 2, 1820
13 noontide 1827: summer MS. 2, 1820   23–4 *not in* MS. 2   25 He] And MS. 2
25–33   My native habitations
           Built such as Hope might gather from the hue
           And from the aspect of each radiant orb   MS. 3
27–30   Affect these mansions of celestial bliss
                My native habitations,
           Built such as Love might gather from the hue   MS. 2
29–30 *so* 1836: and (but 1827–32) imaged to his hope
                (Alas, how faintly!) in the hue 1820–32
34–9   Yet fixed or wandering suffered to proclaim
           Their Maker's glory with unaltered frame   MS. 2
34 star 1827: orb 1820   37–9 *so* 1827: So wills eternal Love, with Power
divine, 1820.

III

"What if those bright fires   40
Shine subject to decay,
Sons haply of extinguished sires,
Themselves to lose their light, or pass away
Like clouds before the wind,
Be thanks poured out to Him whose hand bestows,   45
Nightly, on human kind
That vision of endurance and repose.
—And though to every draught of vital breath,
Renewed throughout the bounds of earth or ocean,
The melancholy gates of Death   50
Respond with sympathetic motion;
Though all that feeds on nether air
Howe'er magnificent or fair,
Grows but to perish, and entrust
Its ruins to their kindred dust;   55
Yet, by the Almighty's ever-during care,
Her procreant vigils Nature keeps
Amid the unfathomable deeps;
And saves the peopled fields of earth
From dread of emptiness or dearth.   60
Thus, in their stations, lifting tow'rd the sky
The foliaged head in cloud-like majesty,
The shadow-casting race of trees survive:
Thus, in the train of Spring, arrive
Sweet flowers;—what living eye hath viewed   65
Their myriads?—endlessly renewed,
Wherever strikes the sun's glad ray;
Where'er the subtle waters stray;
Wherever sportive breezes bend
Their course, or genial showers descend!   70

40–7 *so* 1836: *not in* MSS., 1820–32
48–51 *so* 1827: And what if his presiding breath
                         Impart a sympathetic motion
                         Unto the gates of life and death
                         Throughout the bounds of earth and ocean: MSS., 1820
56 the Almighty's] this MS. 1   57 vigils] cradle MS 1   59 peopled]
changeful MS. 1   60 dread] fear MS. 1   66 myriads] numbers MS. 1
68 subtle 1827: joyous MSS. 1820   69 breezes 1849: zephyrs MSS.,
1820–45

Mortals, rejoice! the very Angels quit
Their mansions unsusceptible of change,
Amid your pleasant bowers to sit,
And through your sweet vicissitudes to range!"

IV

O, nursed at happy distance from the cares   75
Of a too-anxious world, mild pastoral Muse!
That, to the sparkling crown Urania wears,
And to her sister Clio's laurel wreath,
Prefer'st a garland culled from purple heath,
Or blooming thicket moist with morning dews;   80
Was such bright Spectacle vouchsafed to me?
And was it granted to the simple ear
Of thy contented Votary
Such melody to hear!
Him rather suits it, side by side with thee,   85
Wrapped in a fit of pleasing indolence,
While thy tired lute hangs on the hawthorn-tree,
To lie and listen—till o'erdrowsèd sense
Sinks, hardly conscious of the influence—
To the soft murmur of the vagrant Bee.   90
—A slender sound! yet hoary Time
Doth to the *Soul* exalt it with the chime
Of all his years;—a company
Of ages coming, ages gone;
(Nations from before them sweeping,   95
Regions in destruction steeping,)
But every awful note in unison
With that faint utterance, which tells
Of treasure sucked from buds and bells,
For the pure keeping of those waxen cells;   100
Where She—a statist prudent to confer
Upon the common weal; a warrior bold,
Radiant all over with unburnished gold,

71–4 *not in* MS. 1   71 Mortals, rejoice! 1827: Rejoice, O men! MS. 2,
1820   72 Fields insusceptible of wintry change MS. 2
81–6   Oft side by side with some lov'd Votary
          Wrapp'd like thyself in pleasing indolence   MS. 1
87 hangs] hung MS. 1   88–9 Hast thou sate listening till . . . Sank
MS. 1   88–*end not in* MS. 2   95–6 *not in* MS. 1   97 Yet each and all
in unison MS. 1   100 And stored with frugal care in waxen cells   MS. 1
101–9 *not in* MS. 1   102 common 1845: public 1820–36

And armed with living spear for mortal fight;
 A cunning forager   105
That spreads no waste; a social builder; one
In whom all busy offices unite
With all fine functions that afford delight—
Safe through the winter storm in quiet dwells!

V

And is She brought within the power   110
Of vision ?—o'er this tempting flower
Hovering until the petals stay
Her flight, and take its voice away!—
Observe each wing!—a tiny van!
The structure of her laden thigh,   115
How fragile! yet of ancestry
Mysteriously remote and high;
High as the imperial front of man;
The roseate bloom on woman's cheek;
The soaring eagle's curvèd beak;   120
The white plumes of the floating swan;
Old as the tiger's paw, the lion's mane
Ere shaken by that mood of stern disdain
At which the desert trembles.—Humming Bee!
Thy sting was needless then, perchance unknown, 125
The seeds of malice were not sown;
All creatures met in peace, from fierceness free,
And no pride blended with their dignity.
—Tears had not broken from their source;
Nor Anguish strayed from her Tartarean den; 130
The golden years maintained a course
Not undiversified though smooth and even;
We were not mocked with glimpse and shadow then,
Bright Seraphs mixed familiarly with men;
And earth and stars composed a universal heaven! 135

111 Of vision by this MS. 1 112–13 *not in* MS. 1 128 dignity]
majesty MS. 1 129–35 *not in* MS. 1

XLVI

DEVOTIONAL INCITEMENTS

[Composed 1832.—Published 1835.]

"Not to the earth confined,
Ascend to heaven."

WHERE will they stop, those breathing Powers,
The Spirits of the new-born flowers?
They wander with the breeze, they wind
Where'er the streams a passage find;
Up from their native ground they rise   5
In mute aerial harmonies;
From humble violet—modest thyme—
Exhaled, the essential odours climb,
As if no space below the sky
Their subtle flight could satisfy: 10
Heaven will not tax our thoughts with pride
If like ambition be *their* guide.

Roused by this kindliest of May-showers,
The spirit-quickener of the flowers,
That with moist virtue softly cleaves   15
The buds, and freshens the young leaves,
The birds pour forth their souls in notes
Of rapture from a thousand throats—
Here checked by too impetuous haste,
While there the music runs to waste,   20
With bounty more and more enlarged,
Till the whole air is overcharged;
Give ear, O Man! to their appeal,
And thirst for no inferior zeal,
Thou, who canst *think*, as well as feel.   25

Mount from the earth; aspire! aspire!
So pleads the town's cathedral quire,
In strains that from their solemn height
Sink, to attain a loftier flight;
While incense from the altar breathes   30
Rich fragrance in embodied wreaths;
Or, flung from swinging censer, shrouds
The taper-lights, and curls in clouds
Around angelic Forms, the still
Creation of the painter's skill,   35

That on the service wait concealed
One moment, and the next revealed.
—Cast off your bonds, awake, arise,
And for no transient ecstasies!
What else can mean the visual plea   40
Of still or moving imagery—
The iterated summons loud,
Not wasted on the attendant crowd,
Nor wholly lost upon the throng
Hurrying the busy streets along?   45

　　Alas! the sanctities combined
By art to unsensualise the mind
Decay and languish; or, as creeds
And humours change, are spurned like weeds:
The priests are from their altars thrust;   50
Temples are levelled with the dust;
And solemn rites and awful forms
Founder amid fanatic storms.
Yet evermore, through years renewed
In undisturbed vicissitude   55
Of seasons balancing their flight
On the swift wings of day and night,
Kind Nature keeps a heavenly door
Wide open for the scattered Poor.
Where flower-breathed incense to the skies   60
Is wafted in mute harmonies;
And ground fresh-cloven by the plough
Is fragrant with a humbler vow;
Where birds and brooks from leafy dells
Chime forth unwearied canticles,   65
And vapours magnify and spread
The glory of the sun's bright head—
Still constant in her worship, still
Conforming to the eternal Will,
Whether men sow or reap the fields,   70
Divine monition Nature yields,
That not by bread alone we live,
Or what a hand of flesh can give;

50–3 *so* 1836: 1835 *transposes* 50–1 *and* 52–3, *reading* The temples (51)
and The solemn rites (52)   69 eternal 1836: almighty 1835   71 Divine
monition 1845: Her admonitions 1835: Divine admonishment She yields
1836

That every day should leave some part
Free for a sabbath of the heart: 75
So shall the seventh be truly blest,
From morn to eve, with hallowed rest.

XLVII

THE CUCKOO-CLOCK

[Composed April 7, 1840.—Published 1842.]

WOULDST thou be taught, when sleep has taken flight,
By a sure voice that can most sweetly tell,
How far off yet a glimpse of morning light,
And if to lure the truant back be well,
Forbear to covet a Repeater's stroke,   5
That, answering to thy touch, will sound the hour;
Better provide thee with a Cuckoo-clock,
For service hung behind thy chamber-door;
And in due time the soft spontaneous shock,
The double note, as if with living power,   10
Will to composure lead—or make thee blithe as bird in bower.

List, Cuckoo—Cuckoo!—oft tho' tempests howl,
Or nipping frost remind thee trees are bare,
How cattle pine, and droop the shivering fowl,
Thy spirits will seem to feed on balmy air: 15
I speak with knowledge,—by that Voice beguiled,
Thou wilt salute old memories as they throng
Into thy heart; and fancies, running wild
Through fresh green fields, and budding groves among,
Will make thee happy, happy as a child;   20
Of sunshine wilt thou think, and flowers, and song,
And breathe as in a world where nothing can go wrong.

And know—that, even for him who shuns the day
And nightly tosses on a bed of pain;
Whose joys, from all but memory swept away,   25
Must come unhoped for, if they come again;
Know—that, for him whose waking thoughts, severe

XLVII.   4 be] were MS. 1   5 Forbear to] Thou needst not MS. 1 must
not MS. 2   8 behind] beside MSS.   15 spirits] spirit MS. 1   23 shuns
the] shrinks from MSS.

As his distress is sharp, would scorn my theme,
The mimic notes, striking upon his ear
In sleep, and intermingling with his dream,   30
Could from sad regions send him to a dear
Delightful land of verdure, shower and gleam,
To mock the *wandering* Voice beside some haunted stream.

O bounty without measure! while the grace
Of Heaven doth in such wise, from humblest springs,   35
Pour pleasure forth, and solaces that trace
A mazy course along familiar things,
Well may our hearts have faith that blessings come,
Streaming from founts above the starry sky,
With angels when their own untroubled home   40
They leave, and speed on nightly embassy
To visit earthly chambers,—and for whom?
Yea, both for souls who God's forbearance try,
And those that seek his help, and for his mercy sigh.

XLVIII

TO THE CLOUDS

[Composed 1808.—Published 1842.]

ARMY of Clouds! ye wingèd Host in troops
Ascending from behind the motionless brow
Of that tall rock, as from a hidden world,
Oh whither with such eagerness of speed?
What seek ye, or what shun ye? of the gale   5
Companions, fear ye to be left behind,
Or racing o'er your blue ethereal field
Contend ye with each other? of the sea
Children, thus post ye over vale and height
To sink upon your mother's lap—and rest?   10

33 *wandering* Voice] "wandering voice" MSS.   38 Well may we trust
that richer blessings come MS. 1
XLVIII.   1 Army of Clouds, equestrian flight of Clouds MS. 2: Legion of
Clouds, army of Earth and Air MS. 3
9–10   Children, bright Children of the distant sea
              Thus post ye over dale and mountain height
              To sink upon your Mother's joyous lap   MSS. 1,2
              Each panting for the foremost place to sink
              Upon your distant Mother's joyous lap   MS. 3

Or were ye rightlier hailed, when first mine eyes
Beheld in your impetuous march the likeness
Of a wide army pressing on to meet
Or overtake some unknown enemy ?—
But your smooth motions suit a peaceful aim;   15
And Fancy, not less aptly pleased, compares
Your squadrons to an endless flight of birds
Aerial, upon due migration bound
To milder climes; or rather do ye urge
In caravan your hasty pilgrimage   20
To pause at last on more aspiring heights
Than these, and utter your devotion there
With thunderous voice ? Or are ye jubilant,
And would ye, tracking your proud lord the Sun,
Be present at his setting; or the pomp   25
Of Persian mornings would ye fill, and stand
Poising your splendours high above the heads
Of worshippers kneeling to their up-risen God ?
Whence, whence, ye Clouds! this eagerness of speed ?
Speak, silent creatures.—They are gone, are fled,   30

11–30	Your motion is my own; my very blood
	Is quickened to your pace—a thousand thoughts
	Ten thousand wingèd fancies have ye raised
	And not a thought which is not fleet as ye are;
	Speak *etc.* MS. 1
12–19	I lifted, for ye still are sweeping on
	Like a wide Army in impetuous march
	Or like a never ending Flight of Birds
	Aerial, upon due migration bound,
	Embodied Travellers not blindly led
	To milder climes *etc.* MS. 2
15–17	But smooth your motion, smooth as keen and fleet
	Compared with things in character and aim
	Peaceful—a never ending flight of birds MS. 4
21–2	With hope to pause at last upon the tops
	Of some remoter mountains more belov'd
	Than these *etc.* MS. 2
26	Persian] Indian MSS. 2, 3
27–8	Yourselves apparell'd in the virgin garb
	Of radiance yet unknown, transcendent hues MSS. 1, 2
	Thronging like Cherubim what time they cower
	Before the insufferable throne of light
	With wings advanced to veil their timid eyes MS. 3
29/30	Sheer o'er the Rocks' gigantic brow Ye cut
	Your way, and thirsting to reveal himself, athirst
	The coming and the going to secure

Buried together in yon gloomy mass
That loads the middle heaven; and clear and bright
And vacant doth the region which they thronged
Appear; a calm descent of sky conducting
Down to the unapproachable abyss,   35
Down to that hidden gulf from which they rose
To vanish—fleet as days and months and years,
Fleet as the generations of mankind,
Power, glory, empire, as the world itself,
The lingering world, when time hath ceased to be.   40
But the winds roar, shaking the rooted trees,
And see! a bright precursor to a train
Perchance as numerous, overpeers the rock
That sullenly refuses to partake
Of the wild impulse. From a fount of life   45
Invisible, the long procession moves
Luminous or gloomy, welcome to the vale
Which they are entering, welcome to mine eye
That sees them, to my soul that owns in them,
And in the bosom of the firmament   50
O'er which they move, wherein they are contained,
A type of her capacious self and all
Her restless progeny.
                    A humble walk
Here is my body doomed to tread, this path,

Each for himself an unbelated course,
Ye Clouds, the very blood within my veins
Is quickened to your pace, a thousand thoughts
Ten thousand winged Fancies have ye rais'd
And not a thought that is not fleet as ye are   MS. 2
31 All buried in yon mighty mass of gloom MSS. 2, 3   33 which they
thronged] of the East MSS. 2, 3   34 conducting] that leads MSS. 2, 3
36 rose MS. 3 came. MS. 2   37–40 *so* MS. 3: *not in* MS. 2
41–3   Yet the winds roar and toss the rooted trees
            As if impatient of yon lofty seat (ridge)
            On which they stand enthralled from year to year.
            But lo! the pageant is renewed, behold
            Another bright precursor of a band
            Perhaps as numerous, from behind a rock   MS. 2
46 moves] streams MSS.   46/7 A multitude as rapid of like shapes   MS. 5
47 Glorious (radiant) or darksome MSS.
52–3 *so* MS. 3; An Image, a reflection palpable
            Of her capacious self, of what she is
            With all her restless Offspring, what she is
            And what she doth possess!   MSS. 1, 2

A little hoary line and faintly traced,   55
Work, shall we call it, of the shepherd's foot
Or of his flock ?—joint vestige of them both.
I pace it unrepining, for my thoughts
Admit no bondage and my words have wings.
Where is the Orphean lyre, or Druid harp,   60
To accompany the verse ? The mountain blast
Shall be our *hand* of music ; he shall sweep
The rocks, and quivering trees, and billowy lake,
And search the fibres of the caves, and they
Shall answer, for our song is of the Clouds,   65
And the wind loves them ; and the gentle gales—
Which by their aid re-clothe the naked lawn
With annual verdure, and revive the woods,
And moisten the parched lips of thirsty flowers—
Love them ; and every idle breeze of air   70
Bends to the favourite burthen. Moon and stars
Keep their most solemn vigils when the Clouds
Watch also, shifting peaceably their place
Like bands of ministering Spirits, or when they lie,
As if some Protean art the change had wrought,   75
In listless quiet o'er the ethereal deep
Scattered, a Cyclades of various shapes
And all degrees of beauty. O ye Lightnings !
Ye are their perilous offspring ; and the Sun—
Source inexhaustible of life and joy,   80
And type of man's far-darting reason, therefore
In old time worshipped as the god of verse,
A blazing intellectual deity—

55/6 Stony, or turf, or lost in withered leaves   MS. 1
59   See what they will and through their own wide world
      Go with the perfect freedom which is theirs   MS. 2, 3
61 verse MS. 3 : song MS. 2   67–9 *not in* MS. 2   70 of air] in heaven MSS.
71–9 Moon . . . offspring : not in MS. 2
75–8   Blank forms and listless thro' the azure deep
             Dispersed in island quiet. *corr. to*
             Scattered like Cyclades from hour to hour
             Islands in perfect quiet. *corr. to text*   MS. 5
80 That is the daily source of joyous thought   81 therefore] He
MSS.
82 Who therefore was esteemed in antient times
   The God of verse, and stood before men's sight   MSS.

Loves his own glory in their looks, and showers
Upon that unsubstantial brotherhood   85
Visions with all but beatific light
Enriched—too transient, were they not renewed
From age to age, and did not, while we gaze
In silent rapture, credulous desire
Nourish the hope that memory lacks not power   90
To keep the treasure unimpaired. Vain thought!
Yet why repine, created as we are
For joy and rest, albeit to find them only
Lodged in the bosom of eternal things ?

XLIX

SUGGESTED BY A PICTURE OF THE BIRD OF PARADISE

[Composed ?—Published 1842.]

THE gentlest Poet, with free thoughts endowed,
And a true master of the glowing strain,
Might scan the narrow province with disdain
That to the Painter's skill is here allowed.
This, this the Bird of Paradise! disclaim   5
The daring thought, forget the name;
This the Sun's Bird, whom Glendoveers might own
As no unworthy Partner in their flight
Through seas of ether, where the ruffling sway
Of nether air's rude billows is unknown;   10
Whom Sylphs, if e'er for casual pastime they
Through India's spicy regions wing their way,
Might bow to as their Lord. What character,
O sovereign Nature! I appeal to thee,
Of all thy feathered progeny   15
Is so unearthly, and what shape so fair ?
So richly decked in variegated down,
Green, sable, shining yellow, shadowy brown,

84–5   Loves in the clouds his own reflected glory.
        He from his throne, to sight impervious, showers
        And not without regard to human kind   MS. 5
84–6 ... the Sun
    Showers on that unsubstantial brotherhood
    A vision of beatitude and light.   MSS.
87–94 *not in* MSS. 1–4; *a rough draft in* MS. 5.

Tints softly with each other blended,
Hues doubtfully begun and ended;   20
Or intershooting, and to sight
Lost and recovered, as the rays of light
Glance on the conscious plumes touched here and there?
Full surely, when with such proud gifts of life
Began the pencil's strife,   25
O'erweening Art was caught as in a snare.

A sense of seemingly presumptuous wrong
Gave the first impulse to the Poet's song;
But, of his scorn repenting soon, he drew
A juster judgment from a calmer view;   30
And, with a spirit freed from discontent,
Thankfully took an effort that was meant
Not with God's bounty, Nature's love, to vie,
Or made with hope to please that inward eye
Which ever strives in vain itself to satisfy,   35
But to recall the truth by some faint trace
Of power ethereal and celestial grace,
That in the living Creature find on earth a place.

L

A JEWISH FAMILY

(IN A SMALL VALLEY OPPOSITE ST. GOAR, UPON THE RHINE)

[Composed July 1828.—Published 1835.]

GENIUS of Raphael! if thy wings
    Might bear thee to this glen,
With faithful memory left of things
    To pencil dear and pen,
Thou wouldst forego the neighbouring Rhine,   5
    And all his majesty—
A studious forehead to incline
    O'er this poor family.

XLIX. 35 Which loftiest fiction cannot satisfy, *corr. to* Which skill of
angels scarce could satisfy MS.
L. 3 With memory left of shapes and things MSS.   5–8 Thy studious forehead should incline *etc.* . . . . family And thou forget . . . majesty MS. 1
(*i.e.* 5–6 *and* 7–8 *transposed*).

The Mother—her thou must have seen,
  In spirit, ere she came   10
To dwell these rifted rocks between,
  Or found on earth a name;
An image, too, of that sweet Boy,
  Thy inspirations give—
Of playfulness, and love, and joy,   15
  Predestined here to live.

Downcast, or shooting glances far,
  How beautiful his eyes,
That blend the nature of the star
  With that of summer skies!   20
I speak as if of sense beguiled;
  Uncounted months are gone,
Yet am I with the Jewish Child,
  That exquisite Saint John.

I see the dark-brown curls, the brow,   25
  The smooth transparent skin,
Refined, as with intent to show
  The holiness within;
The grace of parting Infancy
  By blushes yet untamed;   30
Age faithful to the mother's knee,
  Nor of her arms ashamed.

Two lovely Sisters, still and sweet
  As flowers, stand side by side;
Their soul-subduing looks might cheat   35
  The Christian of his pride:
Such beauty hath the Eternal poured
  Upon them not forlorn,
Though of a lineage once abhorred,
  Nor yet redeemed from scorn.   40

13–14   A dawning, too, of this sweet Boy
          Might dream or vision give   MS. 1
16   Which yet in colours live   MS. 1
33–6   Two elder Innocents, as sweet
          Stand gazing side by side,
          Fair creatures in this lone retreat
          By happy chance espied   MS. 1;
          Fair Creatures . . . espied, Your soul-subduing *etc.*   MS. 2
37–8   Such . . . them] Your . . . you   MS. 1; Such . . . you MS. 2

Mysterious safeguard, that, in spite
Of poverty and wrong,
Doth here preserve a living light,
From Hebrew fountains sprung;
That gives this ragged group to cast   45
Around the dell a gleam
Of Palestine, of glory past,
And proud Jerusalem!

LI

ON THE POWER OF SOUND

[Composed 1828.—Published 1835.]

ARGUMENT

The Ear addressed, as occupied by a spiritual functionary, in communion with sounds, individual, or combined in studied harmony.—Sources and effects of those sounds (to the close of 6th Stanza).—The power of music, whence proceeding, exemplified in the idiot.—Origin of music, and its effect in early ages—how produced (to the middle of 10th Stanza).—The mind recalled to sounds acting casually and severally.—Wish uttered (11th Stanza) that these could be united into a scheme or system for moral interests and intellectual contemplation.—(Stanza 12th.)—The Pythagorean theory of numbers and music, with their supposed power over the motions of the universe—imaginations consonant with such a theory.—Wish expressed (in 11th Stanza) realized, in some degree, by the representation of all sounds under the form of thanksgiving to the Creator. —(Last Stanza) the destruction of earth and the planetary system—the survival of audible harmony, and its support in the Divine Nature, as revealed in Holy Writ.

I

THY functions are ethereal,
As if within thee dwelt a glancing mind,
Organ of vision! And a Spirit aërial
Informs the cell of Hearing, dark and blind;
Intricate labyrinth, more dread for thought   5
To enter than oracular cave;
Strict passage, through which sighs are brought,
And whispers for the heart, their slave;

41 Strange mystery that in despite MS. 1
LI. 1 *not in* MS. A, *which begins with* XII (*v. notes*)

And shrieks, that revel in abuse
Of shivering flesh ; and warbled air,   10
Whose piercing sweetness can unloose
The chains of frenzy, or entice a smile
Into the ambush of despair ;
Hosannas pealing down the long-drawn aisle,
And requiems answered by the pulse that beats   15
Devoutly, in life's last retreats!

II

The headlong streams and fountains
Serve Thee, invisible Spirit, with untired powers ;
Cheering the wakeful tent on Syrian mountains,
They lull perchance ten thousand thousand flowers.   20
That roar, the prowling lion's *Here I am*,
How fearful to the desert wide!
That bleat, how tender! of the dam
Calling a straggler to her side.
Shout, cuckoo!—let the vernal soul   25
Go with thee to the frozen zone ;
Toll from thy loftiest perch, lone bell-bird, toll
At the still hour to Mercy dear,
Mercy from her twilight throne
Listening to nun's faint throb of holy fear,   30
To sailor's prayer breathed from a darkening sea
Or widow's cottage-lullaby.

III

Ye Voices, and ye Shadows
And Images of voice—to hound and horn
From rocky steep and rock-bestudded meadows   35
Flung back, and, in the sky's blue caves, reborn—

10–16   Of shivering flesh, and blanch the hair,
         And artful concords that the chains unloose
         Of phrenzy *etc.* . . . despair ;
         Or caught from fear do of their speech beguile
         The wood-nymphs, in those eddies sway where move
         The dancing Dryads fann'd by hovering Love.   MS.
18 Tire not the day, nor waste by night their powers MS. A   19 on] and
(*sic*) MS. A   29 twilight] golden MS. A ; pensive MS.   30 Listening
to the Nun's soft sigh MS. A ; sob MS.   30–31 To . . . Or: The . . .
The MS. A
35–6   Flung back by woods, and rock-besprinkled meadows
          And in the clear crystalline sky reborn   MS. A
35 Flung back from rocky steep, o'er lakes and meadows MS.

On with your pastime! till the church-tower bells
A greeting give of measured glee;
And milder echoes from their cells
Repeat the bridal symphony.   40
Then, or far earlier, let us rove
Where mists are breaking up or gone,
And from aloft look down into a cove
Besprinkled with a careless quire,
Happy milk-maids, one by one   45
Scattering a ditty each to her desire,
A liquid concert matchless by nice Art,
A stream as if from one full heart.

IV

Blest be the song that brightens
The blind man's gloom, exalts the veteran's mirth;   50
Unscorned the peasant's whistling breath, that lightens
His duteous toil of furrowing the green earth.
For the tired slave, Song lifts the languid oar,
And bids it aptly fall, with chime
That beautifies the fairest shore,   55
And mitigates the harshest clime.
Yon pilgrims see—in lagging file
They move; but soon the appointed way
A choral *Ave Marie* shall beguile,
And to their hope the distant shrine   60
Glisten with a livelier ray:
Nor friendless he, the prisoner of the mine,
Who from the well-spring of his own clear breast
Can draw, and sing his griefs to rest.

V

When civic renovation   65
Dawns on a kingdom, and for needful haste
Best eloquence avails not, Inspiration
Mounts with a tune, that travels like a blast
Piping through cave and battlemented tower;
Then starts the sluggard, pleased to meet   70
That voice of Freedom, in its power
Of promises, shrill, wild, and sweet!

41 us] me MS. A   42 The mountain side if mists be gone MS. A: Some
pastoral hill if *etc.* MS.   43 aloft] its brow MS.   44–7 Frequented by
a scattered quire, Nymphlike . . . Chanting or warbling . . . A strange
wild concert MS. A   iv–v. *not in* MS. A

Who, from a martial *pageant*, spreads
Incitements of a battle-day,
Thrilling the unweaponed crowd with plumeless heads ?— 75
Even She whose Lydian airs inspire
Peaceful striving, gentle play
Of timid hope and innocent desire
Shot from the dancing Graces, as they move
Fanned by the plausive wings of Love.   80

VI

How oft along thy mazes,
Regent of sound, have dangerous Passions trod!
O Thou, through whom the temple rings with praises,
And blackening clouds in thunder speak of God,
Betray not by the cozenage of sense   85
Thy votaries, wooingly resigned
To a voluptuous influence
That taints the purer, better, mind ;
But lead sick Fancy to a harp
That hath in noble tasks been tried ;   90
And, if the virtuous feel a pang too sharp,
Soothe it into patience—stay
The uplifted arm of Suicide ;
And let some mood of thine in firm array
Knit every thought the impending issue needs,   95
Ere martyr burns, or patriot bleeds!

VII

As Conscience, to the centre
Of being, smites with irresistible pain,
So shall a solemn cadence, if it enter
The mouldy vaults of the dull idiot's brain,   100
Transmute him to a wretch from quiet hurled—
Convulsed as by a jarring din ;
And then aghast, as at the world
Of reason partially let in

82 Regent] Spirit MS. A   85 the cozenage] a charm MS. A   86 votaries
wooingly] youthful votaries MS. A
91–6 too sharp, *etc.*]   too sharp
            For patience, steal the pang away,
            Melt the gloom of Suicide ;
            And let some mood of thine in firm array
            Knit every feeling which the thoughtful need
            To triumph in some glorious deed.   MS. A
VII–X. *not in* MS. A

By concords winding with a sway   105
Terrible for sense and soul!
Or, awed he weeps, struggling to quell dismay.
Point not these mysteries to an Art
Lodged above the starry pole;
Pure modulations flowing from the heart   110
Of divine Love, where Wisdom, Beauty, Truth
With Order dwell, in endless youth?

VIII

Oblivion may not cover
All treasures hoarded by the miser, Time.
Orphean Insight! truth's undaunted lover,   115
To the first leagues of tutored passion climb,
When Music deigned within this grosser sphere
Her subtle essence to enfold,
And voice and shell drew forth a tear
Softer than Nature's self could mould.   120
Yet *strenuous* was the infant Age:
Art, daring because souls could feel,
Stirred nowhere but an urgent equipage
Of rapt imagination sped her march
Through the realms of woe and weal: 125
Hell to the lyre bowed low; the upper arch
Rejoiced that clamorous spell and magic verse
Her wan disasters could disperse.

IX

The GIFT to king Amphion
That walled a city with its melody   130
Was for belief no dream:—thy skill, Arion!
Could humanise the creatures of the sea,
Where men were monsters. A last grace he craves,
Leave for one chant;—the dulcet sound
Steals from the deck o'er willing waves,   135
And listening dolphins gather round.
Self-cast, as with a desperate course,
'Mid that strange audience, he bestrides
A proud One docile as a managed horse;
And singing, while the accordant hand   140
Sweeps his harp, the Master rides;
So shall he touch at length a friendly strand,

And he, with his preserver, shine starbright
In memory, through silent night.

X

The pipe of Pan, to shepherds   145
Couched in the shadow of Mænalian pines,
Was passing sweet; the eyeballs of the leopards,
That in high triumph drew the Lord of vines,
How did they sparkle to the cymbal's clang!
While Fauns and Satyrs beat the ground   150
In cadence,—and Silenus swang
This way and that, with wild-flowers crowned.
To life, to *life* give back thine ear:
Ye who are longing to be rid
Of fable, though to truth subservient, hear   155
The little sprinkling of cold earth that fell
Echoed from the coffin-lid;
The convict's summons in the steeple's knell;
"The vain distress-gun", from a leeward shore,
Repeated—heard, and heard no more!   160

XI

For terror, joy, or pity,
Vast is the compass and the swell of notes:
From the babe's first cry to voice of regal city,
Rolling a solemn sea-like bass, that floats
Far as the woodlands—with the trill to blend   165
Of that shy songstress, whose love-tale
Might tempt an angel to descend,
While hovering o'er the moonlight vale.
Ye wandering Utterances, has earth no scheme,
No scale of moral music—to unite   170

152 wild-flowers] roses MS.   161 joy] love MS. A   166 shy] sweet
MS. A   168 hovering] passing MS. A
169–74   What skill in soul-affecting scheme
        Of moral music, shall unite
        Those viewless Powers more fleeting than a dream,
        Shall bind those wanderers thro' loose air
        In the precious chains of sight
        That laboured minstrelsies thro' ages wear?
        Shall frame a balance *etc.*   MS. A

Powers that survive but in the faintest dream
Of memory?—O that ye might stoop to bear
Chains, such precious chains of sight
As laboured minstrelsies through ages wear!
O for a balance fit the truth to tell   175
Of the Unsubstantial, pondered well!

XII

By one pervading spirit
Of tones and numbers all things are controlled,
As sages taught, where faith was found to merit
Initiation in that mystery old.   180
The heavens, whose aspect makes our minds as still
As they themselves appear to be,
Innumerable voices fill
With everlasting harmony;
The towering headlands, crowned with mist,   185
Their feet among the billows, know
That Ocean is a mighty harmonist;
Thy pinions, universal Air,
Ever waving to and fro,
Are delegates of harmony, and bear   190
Strains that support the Seasons in their round;
Stern Winter loves a dirge-like sound.

XIII

Break forth into thanksgiving,
Ye banded instruments of wind and chords;
Unite, to magnify the Ever-living,   195
Your inarticulate notes with the voice of words!

169–71 O for some soul-affecting scheme
      Of moral music, to unite
      Wanderers, whose portion is the faintest dream   MS., 1835
172 ye 1836; they MS., 1835   XII: *i.e. Stanza* 1 *in* MS. A
177–9   There is a world of spirit
      By *etc.*
      And glorious privilege have they who merit   MS. A
      All things are ruled by spirit
      The Universe is guided and controlled
      By tuneful numbers, as they know who merit   MS.
192 Stern] Even MS. A   XIII *not in* MS. A

Nor hushed be service from the lowing mead,
Nor mute the forest hum of noon ;
Thou too be heard, lone eagle! freed
From snowy peak and cloud, attune　　　　　　　　200
Thy hungry barkings to the hymn
Of joy, that from her utmost walls
The six-days' Work by flaming Seraphim
Transmits to Heaven! As Deep to Deep
Shouting through one valley calls,　　　　　　　　205
All worlds, all natures, mood and measure keep
For praise and ceaseless gratulation, poured
Into the ear of God, their Lord!

XIV

A Voice to Light gave Being;
To Time, and Man his earth-born chronicler;　　　　210
A Voice shall finish doubt and dim foreseeing,
And sweep away life's visionary stir;
The trumpet (we, intoxicate with pride,
Arm at its blast for deadly wars)
To archangelic lips applied,　　　　　　　　215
The grave shall open, quench the stars.
O Silence! are Man's noisy years
No more than moments of thy life?
Is Harmony, blest queen of smiles and tears,
With her smooth tones and discords just,　　　　220
Tempered into rapturous strife,
Thy destined bond-slave? No! though earth be dust
And vanish, though the heavens dissolve, her stay
Is in the WORD, that shall not pass away.

210 To changeful Time, and Man his Chronicler MS. A　　　213 intoxicate
with] the puny sons of MS. A
220-4　　　Awakened thro' a world of dust
　　　　　Smoothly, or in rapturous strife,
　　　　　Thy destined Bond-slave? No—but where the trust?
　　　　　Not in the Earth or Heaven (how fleet are they)
　　　　　But in *etc.*　MS. A

PETER BELL
A TALE

[Composed 1798.—Published 1819.]

"What's in a *Name?*"

* * * * * * *

"Brutus will start a Spirit as soon as Cæsar!"

TO ROBERT SOUTHEY, Esq., P.L., etc., etc.

My Dear Friend,

The Tale of Peter Bell, which I now introduce to your notice, and to that of the Public, has, in its Manuscript state, nearly survived its *minority:* —for it first saw the light in the summer of 1798. During this long interval, pains have been taken at different times to make the production less unworthy of a favourable reception; or, rather, to fit it for filling *permanently* a station, however humble, in the Literature of our Country. This has, indeed, been the aim of all my endeavours in Poetry, which, you know, have been sufficiently laborious to prove that I deem the Art not lightly to be approached; and that the attainment of excellence in it may laudably be made the principal object of intellectual pursuit by any man, who, with reasonable consideration of circumstances, has faith in his own impulses.

The Poem of Peter Bell, as the Prologue will show, was composed under a belief that the Imagination not only does not require for its exercise the intervention of supernatural agency, but that, though such agency be excluded, the faculty may be called forth as imperiously, and for kindred results of pleasure, by incidents within the compass of poetic probability, in the humblest departments of daily life. Since that Prologue was written, *you* have exhibited most splendid effects of judicious daring in the opposite and usual course. Let this acknowledgment make my peace with the lovers of the supernatural; and I am persuaded it will be admitted that to you, as a Master in that province of the art, the following Tale, whether from contrast or congruity, is not an unappropriate offering. Accept it, then, as a public testimony of affectionate admiration from one with whose name yours has been often coupled (to use your own words) for evil and for good; and believe me to be, with earnest wishes that life and health may be granted you to complete the many important works in which you are engaged, and with high respect,

Most faithfully yours,

Rydal Mount,   WILLIAM WORDSWORTH.
April 7, 1819.

PROLOGUE

There's something in a flying horse,
There's something in a huge balloon;
But through the clouds I'll never float
Until I have a little Boat,
Shaped like the crescent-moon.   5

A TALE 1820: A TALE IN VERSE 1819   Mottoes *not in* 1819   2 There's
MSS. 1827 *etc.*: And 1819-20   5, 7 In shape just like the MSS. 2, 3, 5

And now I *have* a little Boat,
In shape a very crescent-moon:
Fast through the clouds my Boat can sail;
But if perchance your faith should fail,
Look up—and you shall see me soon!   10

The woods, my Friends, are round you roaring,
Rocking and roaring like a sea;
The noise of danger 's in your ears,
And ye have all a thousand fears
Both for my little Boat and me!   15

Meanwhile untroubled I admire
The pointed horns of my canoe;
And, did not pity touch my breast,
To see how ye are all distrest,
Till my ribs ached, I'd laugh at you!   20

Away we go, my Boat and I—
Frail man ne'er sate in such another;
Whether among the winds we strive,
Or deep into the clouds we dive,
Each is contented with the other.   25

Away we go—and what care we
For treasons, tumults, and for wars?
We are as calm in our delight
As is the crescent-moon so bright
Among the scattered stars.   30

Up goes my Boat among the stars
Through many a breathless field of light,
Through many a long blue field of ether,
Leaving ten thousand stars beneath her:
Up goes my little Boat so bright!   35

12 The woods are roaring MSS.   13 danger's in MSS., 1845: danger
fills 1819–36   16 Meanwhile I from the helm admire MSS., 1819
22 Sure never man had such another MSS. *corr. to* Triumphant o'er this
dreadful pother MS. 6, *corr. to text*
24 the clouds 1827: the heavens MSS., 1819; Or into massy clouds 1820
25   We're both contented with each other   MSS. 2, 3
            We're each . . . the . . . MSS. 4–6
31 among 1820: between MSS., 1819

The Crab, the Scorpion, and the Bull—
We pry among them all; have shot
High o'er the red-haired race of Mars,
Covered from top to toe with scars;
Such company I like it not!   40

The towns in Saturn are decayed,
And melancholy Spectres throng them;—
The Pleiads, that appear to kiss
Each other in the vast abyss,
With joy I sail among them.   45

Swift Mercury resounds with mirth,
Great Jove is full of stately bowers;
But these, and all that they contain,
What are they to that tiny grain,
That little Earth of ours?   50

Then back to Earth, the dear green Earth:—
Whole ages if I here should roam,
The world for my remarks and me
Would not a whit the better be;
I've left my heart at home.   55

See! there she is, the matchless Earth!
There spreads the famed Pacific Ocean!
Old Andes thrusts yon craggy spear
Through the grey clouds; the Alps are here,
Like waters in commotion!   60

36–40 *not in* MSS. 2, 3 These honest folks in Charles's wain
                    Jog forwards at a dreary trot;
                    They are a red-headed race in Mars *etc.*   MS. 4
                    The Crab, the Virgin and the Bear
                    We range among them all, God wot   MS. 5
                    The spangles of the milky way
                    We pry *etc.*   MS. 6
39 Covered] All seamed   MS 6
41–50   The towns in Saturn are ill-built
           But Jove has very pretty (is full of stately MSS. 5, 6) bowers,
           The evening star is not amiss
           But what are all of them to this,
           This little earth of ours?   MSS.
42   But proud let *him* be who has seen them   1819–20
45 among 1827: between 1819–20
50 little Earth MSS., 1827: darling speck 1819–20   51 Then back again to
our green Earth MSS. 2–5   52 What business had I here to roam? MSS.
56–69   And there it is, the dear green Earth
           And that's the dear Pacific Ocean
           And that's the Caucasus so dear,
           To think that I again am here
           Oh! my poor heart's commotion!

Yon tawny slip is Libya's sands;
That silver thread the river Dnieper;
And look, where clothed in brightest green
Is a sweet Isle, of isles the Queen;
Ye fairies, from all evil keep her!   65

And see the town where I was born!
Around those happy fields we span
In boyish gambols;—I was lost
Where I have been, but on this coast
I feel I am a man.   70

Never did fifty things at once
Appear so lovely, never, never;—
How tunefully the forests ring!
To hear the earth's soft murmuring
Thus could I hang for ever!   75

"Shame on you!" cried my little Boat,
"Was ever such a homesick Loon,
Within a living Boat to sit,
And make no better use of it;
A Boat twin-sister of the crescent-moon!   80

"Ne'er in the breast of full-grown Poet
Fluttered so faint a heart before;—
Was it the music of the spheres
That overpowered your mortal ears?
—Such din shall trouble them no more.   85

> And there is little Tartary
> And there's the famous river Dnieper
> And there amid the ocean green
> Is that sweet isle of isles *etc.*
> And there's the town *etc.*
> And that's the house of Parson Swan
> My heart is touch'd I must avow
> Consider where I've been, and now *etc.*   MSS. 2–4

73 The woods how sweetly do they ring MSS.   76 Oh shame upon you,
cruel shame MS. 3   77 homesick 1827: heartless MSS., 1819–20   78 In
such a lovely MSS.   80 twin-sister of] that's like MSS.
80/81   Out, out, and like a brooding hen
                        Beside your sooty hearthstone cower;
                        Go, creep along the dirt, and pick
                        Your way with your good walking stick,
                        Just three good miles an hour!   MSS., 1819–20.
81–5   Sure in the breast of full-grown poet
                        So faint a heart was ne'er before,
                        Come to the poet's wild delights,
                        I have ten thousand lovely sights,
                        Ten thousand sights in store   MSS.

"These nether precincts do not lack
Charms of their own;—then come with me;
I want a comrade, and for you
There's nothing that I would not do;
Nought is there that you shall not see.   90

"Haste! and above Siberian snows
We'll sport amid the boreal morning;
Will mingle with her lustres gliding
Among the stars, the stars now hiding,
And now the stars adorning.   95

"I know the secrets of a land
Where human foot did never stray;
Fair is that land as evening skies,
And cool, though in the depth it lies
Of burning Africa.   100

"Or we'll into the realm of Faery,
Among the lovely shades of things;
The shadowy forms of mountains bare,
And streams, and bowers, and ladies fair,
The shades of palaces and kings!   105

"Or, if you thirst with hardy zeal
Less quiet regions to explore,
Prompt voyage shall to you reveal
How earth and heaven are taught to feel
The might of magic lore!"   110

"My little vagrant Form of light,
My gay and beautiful Canoe,
Well have you played your friendly part;
As kindly take what from my heart
Experience forces—then adieu!   115

86–7   I am a pretty little Barge
              Then come I pray you *etc*.   MSS.
91 Come, and above the land of snow MSS.   93 Where thousand forms
of light are riding   MSS.
96–100   . . . a deep romantic land
                  A land that's deep and far away
                  And fair it is *etc*.
                  And in the farthest heart it lies
                  Of deepest Africa.   MSS.
101 realm MS. 5, 6: world MSS. 1–4   106–10 not in MSS. 1–4; *added to* 5
111–12   My pretty little . . . My sweet MSS.
113–15   Now though it grieves me to the heart
              I feel, I feel that we must part,
              I must take leave of you.   MSS.

"Temptation lurks among your words;
But, while these pleasures you're pursuing
Without impediment or let,
No wonder if you quite forget
What on the earth is doing.   120

"There was a time when all mankind
Did listen with a faith sincere
To tuneful tongues in mystery versed;
Then Poets fearlessly rehearsed
The wonders of a wild career.   125

"Go—(but the world's a sleepy world,
And 'tis, I fear, an age too late)
Take with you some ambitious Youth!
For, restless Wanderer! I, in truth,
Am all unfit to be your mate.   130

"Long have I loved what I behold,
The night that calms, the day that cheers;
The common growth of mother-earth
Suffices me—her tears, her mirth,
Her humblest mirth and tears.   135

"The dragon's wing, the magic ring,
I shall not covet for my dower,
If I along that lowly way
With sympathetic heart may stray,
And with a soul of power.   140

116 You are a pretty little (most delightful MSS. 5, 6) Barge   MSS.
119 *so* 1845: My little Barge MSS.; My radiant Pinnace 1819–36
121–5   a time indeed
                  A time when Poets lived in clover
                  —What boots it now to keep the key
                  Of Fairyland ? for, woe is me!
                  Those blessed days are over.   MSS. 1–5,
preceded in MS. 2 *by*
                  Suppose now in the land of Fairy
                  That we should play our sportive pranks
                  Above those shadowy streams, and there
                  Should make discovery rich and rare
                  The world would count us little thanks.
122–5   . . . submissive ear,
                  Then boldly might the trump of Fame
                  Blown by the Poet's breath proclaim
                  The wonders of this mortal sphere.   MS. 6
126–55 MS. 6: *not in* 1–4, *added to* 5

"These given, what more need I desire
To stir, to soothe, or elevate?
What nobler marvels than the mind
May in life's daily prospect find,
May find or there create?   145

"A potent wand doth Sorrow wield;
What spell so strong as guilty Fear!
Repentance is a tender Sprite;
If aught on earth have heavenly might,
'Tis lodged within her silent tear.   150

"But grant my wishes,—let us now
Descend from this ethereal height;
Then take thy way, adventurous Skiff,
More daring far than Hippogriff,
And be thy own delight!   155

"To the stone-table in my garden,
Loved haunt of many a summer hour,
The Squire is come: his daughter Bess
Beside him in the cool recess
Sits blooming like a flower.   160

"With these are many more convened;
They know not I have been so far;—
I see them there, in number nine,
Beneath the spreading Weymouth-pine!
I see them—there they are!   165

"There sits the Vicar and his Dame;
And there my good friend, Stephen Otter;
And, ere the light of evening fail,
To them I must relate the Tale
Of Peter Bell the Potter."   170

156–60   There is a party in the Bower
         Round the stone table in my garden
         The Squire is there, and as I guess
         His pretty little daughter Bess
         With Harry the Churchwarden   MSS. 2–5
         So MS. 6, *but* ll. 156–8 For me are homelier tasks prepared. To
         the stone . . . is come
161   They were to come this very evening   MSS. 2–5
         This was the appointed day and hour   MS. 6, *corr. to*
         O shield me, shield me from reproach
164 All in the bower of MSS.   166 *so* MS. 6: And there's the wife of
Parson Swan MSS. 1–5

Off flew the Boat—away she flees,
Spurning her freight with indignation!
And I, as well as I was able,
On two poor legs, toward my stone-table
Limped on with sore vexation.   175

"O, here he is!" cried little Bess—
She saw me at the garden-door;
"We've waited anxiously and long,"
They cried, and all around me throng,
Full nine of them or more!   180

"Reproach me not—your fears be still—
Be thankful we again have met;—
Resume, my Friends! within the shade
Your seats, and quickly shall be paid
The well-remembered debt."   185

I spake with faltering voice, like one
Not wholly rescued from the pale
Of a wild dream, or worse illusion;
But straight, to cover my confusion,
Began the promised Tale.   190

171 *so* 1845: Off flew my sparkling Boat in scorn   1819–36
                      pretty little Boat   MSS. 1, 4–6 (barge 2, 3)
172 *so* 1820: Yea, in a trance of indignation   1819,
                All in a . . . MSS. 2–6
175 sore 1845: some MSS., 1819–36
178–9 *so* MS. 5: "O! here he is" cried Mistress Swan,
                And all at once around me ran   MSS. 1–4
181–5   "Sit down, I beg you would be seated"
               Said I, no doubt with visage pale,
               "And if, my Friends, it pleases you,
               This instant, without more ado
               We'll have the promised Tale"   MSS. 1–4
               " Resume your seats within the Bower "
               I softly said with visage pale *etc.*   MSS. 5, 6
186–90 *so* 1827: And so though somewhat out of breath
                With lips, no doubt, and visage pale,
                And sore too from a slight contusion
                Did I, *etc.*
                Begin *etc.*   MSS.
                Breath failed me as I spake—but soon
                etc. as MSS., 1819–20

PART FIRST

ALL by the moonlight river-side
Groaned the poor Beast—alas! in vain;
The staff was raised to loftier height,
And the blows fell with heavier weight
As Peter struck—and struck again.   195

"Hold!" cried the Squire, "against the rules
Of common sense you're surely sinning;
This leap is for us all too bold;
Who Peter was, let that be told,
And start from the beginning."   200

————"A Potter,[1] Sir, he was by trade,"
Said I, becoming quite collected;
"And wheresoever he appeared,
Full twenty times was Peter feared
For once that Peter was respected.   205

"He, two-and-thirty years or more,
Had been a wild and woodland rover;
Had heard the Atlantic surges roar
On farthest Cornwall's rocky shore,
And trod the cliffs of Dover.   210

[1] In the dialect of the North, a hawker of earthenware is thus designated.

192–5 *so* 1820:   It gave three miserable groans
                    "'Tis come then to a pretty pass."
                    Said Peter to the groaning Ass,
                    "But I will bang your bones!"   MSS., 1819
195/6   "My dearest Sir," cried Mistress Swan
                    "You've got at once into the middle,"
                    And little Bess in accents sweeter
                    Cried "O dear Sir, but who is Peter?"
                    Said Harry "'Tis a downright riddle."   MSS.
196–200 *so* 1836: The Squire said "Sure as Paradise
                    Was lost to us by Adam's sinning
                    We all are wandering in a wood,
                    And therefore, Sir, I wish you would
                    Begin at the beginning"   MSS. 2–5
                    . . . This leap for us is all too bold
                    Who Peter was let that be told
                    And start . . .   MS. 6, 1819
                    Like winds that lash the waves, or smite
                    The woods (the 1820) autumnal foliage thinning—
                    "Hold!" said the Squire, "I pray you, hold!
                    Who Peter was *etc.*   1820–7
208–10 *so* MS. 6   Had been in farthest Pembroke, sir,
                    And he had been at Exeter
                    In Kent, Sir, and at Dover.   MSS. 1–5

"And he had seen Caernarvon's towers,
And well he knew the spire of Sarum;
And he had been where Lincoln bell
Flings o'er the fen that ponderous knell—
A far-renowned alarum.   215

"At Doncaster, at York, and Leeds,
And merry Carlisle had he been;
And all along the Lowlands fair,
All through the bonny shire of Ayr;
And far as Aberdeen.   220

"And he had been at Inverness;
And Peter, by the mountain-rills,
Had danced his round with Highland lasses;
And he had lain beside his asses
On lofty Cheviot Hills: 225

"And he had trudged through Yorkshire dales,
Among the rocks and winding *scars;*
Where deep and low the hamlets lie
Beneath their little patch of sky
And little lot of stars: 230

"And all along the indented coast,
Bespattered with the salt-sea foam;
Where'er a knot of houses lay
On headland, or in hollow bay;—
Sure never man like him did roam!   235

"As well might Peter, in the Fleet,
Have been fast bound, a begging debtor;—
He travelled here, he travelled there;—
But not the value of a hair
Was heart or head the better.   240

"He roved among the vales and streams,
In the green wood and hollow dell;
They were his dwellings night and day,—
But nature ne'er could find the way
Into the heart of Peter Bell.   245

211 *so* MS. 6:   And he had been at Nottingham   MSS. 1–5
214–15   To Shepherds in the distant dell
                     Rings out his loud alarum   MSS.
216   At York, and at the hill of Brough   MS. 3
                     At Doncaster, at York and Brough   MS. 4
231 indented MS. 6: winding MSS. 3–5   239–40 *so* MS. 6: But Peter
never was a hair In *etc.* MSS. 3–5

"In vain, through every changeful year,
Did Nature lead him as before;
A primrose by a river's brim
A yellow primrose was to him,
And it was nothing more.   250

"Small change it made in Peter's heart
To see his gentle panniered train
With more than vernal pleasure feeding,
Where'er the tender grass was leading
Its earliest green along the lane.   255

"In vain, through water, earth, and air,
The soul of happy sound was spread,
When Peter on some April morn,
Beneath the broom or budding thorn,
Made the warm earth his lazy bed.   260

"At noon, when, by the forest's edge
He lay beneath the branches high,
The soft blue sky did never melt
Into his heart; he never felt
The witchery of the soft blue sky!   265

"On a fair prospect some have looked
And felt, as I have heard them say,
As if the moving time had been
A thing as steadfast as the scene
On which they gazed themselves away.   270

"Within the breast of Peter Bell
These silent raptures found no place;
He was a Carl as wild and rude
As ever hue-and-cry pursued,
As ever ran a felon's race.   275

"Of all that lead a lawless life,
Of all that love their lawless lives,
In city or in village small,
He was the wildest far of all;—
He had a dozen wedded wives.   280

266 looked] gazed MS. 4
271-2 *so* 1820: With Peter Bell, I need not tell
          That this had never been the case; MSS., 1819

"Nay, start not!—wedded wives—and twelve!
But how one wife could e'er come near him,
In simple truth I cannot tell;
For, be it said of Peter Bell,
To see him was to fear him.   285

"Though Nature could not touch his heart
By lovely forms, and silent weather,
And tender sounds, yet you might see
At once that Peter Bell and she
Had often been together.   290

"A savage wildness round him hung
As of a dweller out of doors;
In his whole figure and his mien
A savage character was seen
Of mountains and of dreary moors.   295

"To all the unshaped half-human thoughts
Which solitary Nature feeds
'Mid summer storms or winter's ice,
Had Peter joined whatever vice
The cruel city breeds.   300

"His face was keen as is the wind
That cuts along the hawthorn-fence;
Of courage you saw little there,
But, in its stead, a medley air
Of cunning and of impudence.   305

"He had a dark and sidelong walk,
And long and slouching was his gait;
Beneath his looks so bare and bold,
You might perceive, his spirit cold
Was playing with some inward bait.   310

281–5 *so* MSS. 5, 6 *but in* 284 I must say *for* be it said
                    "Oh monster!" cried the Parson's lady
                    "Poor fellow!" echo'd Stephen Otter
                    "Poor fellow, say you!" "Mistress Swan
                    I do assure you such a man
                    Was Peter Bell the Potter." MSS. 3, 4
306–10 *added to* MS. 4

"His forehead wrinkled was and furred ;
A work, one half of which was done
By thinking of his '*whens*' and '*hows*';
And half, by knitting of his brows
Beneath the glaring sun.   315

"There was a hardness in his cheek,
There was a hardness in his eye,
As if the man had fixed his face,
In many a solitary place,
Against the wind and open sky!"   320

ONE NIGHT, (and now, my little Bess!
We've reached at last the promised Tale ;)
One beautiful November night,
When the full moon was shining bright
Upon the rapid river Swale,   325

Along the river's winding banks
Peter was travelling all alone ;—
Whether to buy or sell, or led
By pleasure running in his head,
To me was never known.   330

314	knitting] wrinkling MSS. 3, 4
326	Beside the rapid river Swale MS. 1
	It chanc'd that by the river's banks MSS. 3, 4
328	If in the way of trade MS. 1
330/1	Along the turf and through the grass
	And in the mire he travelled on,
	If he had left that night or day
	His wife or wives I cannot say
	But wife or comrade he had none.

As Peter was a lazy soul
And seldom walked when he could ride
I wonder he should trudge alone,
I wonder that he had not thrown
His legs on some poor asses hide.

Some love to travel with a dog,
And Peter had a savage elf
A lurcher, and he loved him well,
But sure it is that Peter Bell
That evening travelled by himself.   MSS.

He trudged along through copse and brake
He trudged along o'er hill and dale;
Nor for the moon cared he a tittle,
And for the stars he cared as little,
And for the murmuring river Swale. 335

But, chancing to espy a path
That promised to cut short the way;
As many a wiser man hath done,
He left a trusty guide for one
That might his steps betray. 340

To a thick wood he soon is brought
Where cheerily his course he weaves,
And whistling loud may yet be heard,
Though often buried like a bird
Darkling, among the boughs and leaves. 345

But quickly Peter's mood is changed,
And on he drives with cheeks that burn
In downright fury and in wrath;—
There's little sign the treacherous path
Will to the road return! 350

331-2 trudged along MS. 4 *etc.* travelled on MSS. 1, 3
336-45 Quoth Peter "here's a nearer cut
    'Twill save a mile as sure as day."
    He took the path, the path did lead
    Across a smooth and grassy mead
    And a tall wood before him lay.

    And Peter to the wood is gone
    And Peter now in whole cart-loads
    Is heaping curses on them all,
    Commissioners both great and small
    Who made the zig-zag roads MSS. 1, 3; *so* MS. 4 *but* those elbows
      in the *for* the zig-zag
MSS. 5, 6 *as* MS. 1 *down to* 341, *followed by*
        And with the path his way he weaves
        He whistles and *etc.*
        Though he is buried *etc.*
        Among the boughs *etc.*
342 cheerily 1836: cheerfully 1819-32
346-7   For while he drives among the boughs
        With head and hands and cheeks *etc.* MSS. 1, 3, 4
349 the treacherous] that Peter's MSS.

The path grows dim, and dimmer still;
Now up, now down, the Rover wends,
With all the sail that he can carry,
Till brought to a deserted quarry—
And there the pathway ends.   355

He paused—for shadows of strange shape,
Massy and black, before him lay;
But through the dark, and through the cold,
And through the yawning fissures old,
Did Peter boldly press his way   360

Right through the quarry;—and behold
A scene of soft and lovely hue!
Where blue and grey, and tender green,
Together make as sweet a scene
As ever human eye did view.   365

Beneath the clear blue sky he saw
A little field of meadow ground;
But field or meadow name it not;
Call it of earth a small green plot,
With rocks encompassed round.   370

The Swale flowed under the grey rocks,
But he flowed quiet and unseen:—
You need a strong and stormy gale
To bring the noises of the Swale
To that green spot, so calm and green!   375

355/6   "What back again, old Grimface? No
                 I'll grapple with the devil first,
                 Stretch like a yawning wolf your paws
                 But dam'me if by any laws
                 Of your's I'll ever be curs'd.   MS. 3
      . . . Back, think you when I've come so far
                 You stretch a pair of gloomy jaws
                 But I'm your man, nor care two straws
                 For lantern or for star.   MSS. 4, 5
                 What! would'st thou daunt me, grisly den?
                 Back must I, having (when I've MS.) come so far
                 Stretch as thou wilt thy gloomy jaws,
                 I'll on, nor would I give *etc.*   MS. 6, 1819
356–8 *so* 1820 And so where on the huge rough stones
                 The black and massy shadows lay
                 And through *etc.* MSS., 1819
361 MS. 5: And in a moment opened out MSS. 1, 3, 4   368 But oh! far
rather name it not, MSS.
375/6 Now you'll suppose that Peter Bell
                 Had some (Felt small MSS. 4–6, 1819) temptation here to tarry
                 And so it was, but I must add
                 His heart was not a little glad
                 That he was out of the old quarry.   MSS., 1819

And is there no one dwelling here,
No hermit with his beads and glass ?
And does no little cottage look
Upon this soft and fertile nook ?
Does no one live near this green grass ?   380

Across the deep and quiet spot
Is Peter driving through the grass—
And now has reached the skirting trees;
When, turning round his head, he sees
A solitary Ass.   385

"A prize!" cries Peter—but he first
Must spy about him far and near:
There's not a single house in sight,
No woodman's hut, no cottage light—
Peter, you need not fear!   390

There's nothing to be seen but woods,
And rocks that spread a hoary gleam,
And this one Beast, that from the bed
Of the green meadow hangs his head
Over the silent stream.   395

383 *so* 1836: And now he is among the trees   MSS. 1819–32
385/6   "No doubt I'm founder'd in these woods—
        "For once," quoth he, "I will be wise,
        "With better speed I'll back again—
        "And, lest the journey should prove vain,
        "Will take yon Ass, my lawful prize!"   5

        Off Peter hied,—"A comely beast!
        "Though not so plump as he might be;
        "My honest friend, with such a platter,
        "You should have been a little fatter,
        "But come, Sir, come with me!"   10

        But first doth Peter deem it fit
        To spy about him far and near;
        There's not a single house in sight,
        No woodman's hut, no cottage light—   14
        Peter, you need not fear! 1819 (1–10 *not in* 1827, 6–10 *not
        in* 1820)

So MSS., *but* ll. 4–5 And not to make the journey vain
        I'll take the Ass likewise.
followed by   So oft he goes as you'll suppose
        With thoughts as blithe as any dream
        To where the ass beside the bed
        Of that green meadow hung his head
        Over the silent stream.
        A pretty beast, though you'll allow
        Not quite so fat *etc.*
        Upon my soul with such *etc. to* l. 15

His head is with a halter bound;
The halter seizing, Peter leapt
Upon the Creature's back, and plied
With ready heels his shaggy side;
But still the Ass his station kept.   400

Then Peter gave a sudden jerk,
A jerk that from a dungeon-floor
Would have pulled up an iron ring;
But still the heavy-headed Thing
Stood just as he had stood before!   405

Quoth Peter, leaping from his seat,
"There is some plot against me laid;"
Once more the little meadow-ground
And all the hoary cliffs around
He cautiously surveyed.   410

396–400   Close to the river's brink he stood
His head was with a halter bound,
Now Peter's purpose did not alter
And so at once he seized the halter
And would have turned him round.

He pulled, the creature did not move,
Upon his back then Peter leapt
And with his staff and heels he plied
The little ass on either side,
But still the ass his station kept.

Quoth Peter "You're a beast of mettle
I see you'll suit me to an ace."
And now the ass through his left eye
On Peter turned most quietly
Looked quietly in his face.

"What's this," cries Peter, brandishing
A new-peeled sapling white as cream.
The ass knew well what Peter said
But as before hung down his head
Over the silent stream.   MSS. (*this stanza in* 1819)
    ... though, I deem
This threat was understood full well,
Firm, as before, the Sentinel
Stood by the silent stream 1827–32; 1836 *omits* (1820
between 1819 *and* 1827), *as text.*
401 a sudden] another MSS.
406–42   And still did Peter [ ] the ass
With blows that might have cracked the bone,
The ass as if he felt no ill
Beside the river stood stock still
As if he had been made of stone.   5

All, all is silent—rocks and woods,
All still and silent—far and near!
Only the Ass, with motion dull,
Upon the pivot of his skull
Turns round his long left ear.   415

Thought Peter, What can mean all this?
Some ugly witchcraft must be here!
—Once more the Ass, with motion dull,
Upon the pivot of his skull
Turned round his long left ear.   420

Quoth Peter, "By the devil's beard
I'll make you stir, you mongrel hound",
And both his arms did Peter pass
Beneath the belly of the ass
With both his arms he clasped him round.   10

"Now for it now you sturdy thief"
And desperately friend Peter heaves;
He might as well have tried to stir
The abbey huge of Westminster
Or twice five hundred head of beeves.   15

Quoth Peter, "there is witchcraft here
And damned tricks, but what care I?"
And so upon the ass's hide
Making the hair and dust fly wide
He beat most furiously.   20

At last the little harmless beast
Gently as if to take his ease,
The ass whom Peter thus had bruised
Whom he so cruelly had used
Dropped gently down upon his knees.   25

Cried Peter, "you'll be wise, I hope,
Before we're both five minutes older."
Upon the Ass his sapling rings
Each blow the arm of Peter stings
Up to the elbow and the shoulder.   30

At last, poor patient thing, at last
His sides they heaved, his belly stirred   MS. 1
MSS. 2, 3 *as text* 406–20, *but* 410/11
There's nothing, Peter, far or near
There's nothing with your purpose jars
Only the full moon's in the sky
And with her a fair company
The fairest of the stars.   *and for* 417
There is some ugly witchcraft here.

420 *is followed by* MS. 1, 6–10, 26–32; MS. 4 *drops added stanza, and* MS. 1
6–10; MSS. 5 *and* 6 *approximate more closely to text, but for* 421–2 (*as* 1819)
"I'll cure you of these desperate tricks."—And *etc.*

Suspicion ripened into dread;
Yet, with deliberate action slow,
His staff high-raising, in the pride
Of skill, upon the sounding hide
He dealt a sturdy blow.   425

The poor Ass staggered with the shock;
And then, as if to take his ease,
In quiet uncomplaining mood,
Upon the spot where he had stood,
Dropped gently down upon his knees;   430

As gently on his side he fell;
And by the river's brink did lie;
And, while he lay like one that mourned,
The patient Beast on Peter turned
His shining hazel eye.   435

'Twas but one mild, reproachful look,
A look more tender than severe;
And straight in sorrow, not in dread,
He turned the eye-ball in his head
Towards the smooth river deep and clear.   440

Upon the Beast the sapling rings;
His lank sides heaved, his limbs they stirred;
He gave a groan, and then another,
Of that which went before the brother,
And then he gave a third.   445

All by the moonlight river side
He gave three miserable groans;
And not till now hath Peter seen
How gaunt the Creature is,—how lean
And sharp his staring bones!   450

With legs stretched out and stiff he lay:—
No word of kind commiseration
Fell at the sight from Peter's tongue;
With hard contempt his heart was wrung,
With hatred and vexation.   455

434 *so* 1819–20, 1836: The Beast on his tormentor turned 1827–32.
448–50 *so* 1820: "'Tis come then to a pretty pass"
                   Said Peter to the groaning ass,
                   "But I will *bang* your bones." MSS., 1819
451–65   And Peter did as he had said
                   For Peter's anger now increased
                   And with his heels and with his toes
                   And with more fierce and furious blows
                   He fell upon the harmless beast.   5

The meagre beast lay still as death ;
And Peter's lips with fury quiver ;
Quoth he, "You little mulish dog,
I'll fling your carcass like a log
Head-foremost down the river!"   460

Again the Ass was still as death
"The devil's in him", Peter cried,
At length beneath the moonlight trees
Once more he stirred, and from his knees
Fell down upon his side.   10

Close by the moonlight river's brim
Upon his side the ass did lie *etc. as* 433–5   15
'Twas but one look, one patient look
For strait, as plainly did appear,
Whether in sorrow or in dread,
He turned the eyeball in his head
Towards the stream so deep and clear.   20

How could it be, how could it be
That while the poor ass thus did lie
On Peter's heart, on Peter's brain,
But one impression did remain
Of his large and shining eye ?   25

And Peter's more and more enraged
His lips with rage and *etc. as* 457–60   30
By God I will." When this was said
As stretched upon his side *etc.* 462–5, *but*
l. 465 A loud and horrible bray.   MS. 1
(1819–1832 A loud and piteous bray)

451–65 MSS. 2–4 *read here* MS. 1, 21–5 (*above*) *followed by*
The meagre beast lay still as death
No word *etc. as* 452–5, *followed by*
For Peter's merriment is flown
His lips with rage *etc. as*   MS. 1

but in MS. 4, MS. 1 21–5, *is preceded by*
And then upon his side he fell
And now to Peter's eye was shewn
What till this time he had not seen,
That the poor ass was gaunt and lean
And almost wasted to the bone.

So MS. 5, *but without* stanza MS. 1, 21–5
MS. 6, 1819–20 *read*:
And Peter halts to gather breath,
And now full clearly was it shewn
(What he before in part had seen)
How gaunt was the poor ass and lean,
Yea, wasted to a skeleton!   *etc.*

So 1827–32, *but* And while he halts, was clearly shewn,
and How gaunt the creature was *etc.*

An impious oath confirmed the threat—
Whereat from the earth on which he lay
To all the echoes, south and north,
And east and west, the Ass sent forth
A long and clamorous bray!   465

This outcry, on the heart of Peter,
Seems like a note of joy to strike,—
Joy at the heart of Peter knocks;
But in the echo of the rocks
Was something Peter did not like.   470

Whether to cheer his coward breast,
Or that he could not break the chain,
In this serene and solemn hour,
Twined round him by demoniac power,
To the blind work he turned again.   475

Among the rocks and winding crags;
Among the mountains far away;
Once more the Ass did lengthen out
More ruefully a deep-drawn shout,
The hard dry see-saw of his horrible bray!   480

462 *so* 1836:   But, while upon the ground he lay   1819–20
                 That instant, while outstretched he lay   1827–32
470/1   "Up, up." The ass brayed loud again
                 And Peter's heart far less rejoices,
                 He's now beginning to demur,
                 He thinks he hears a barking cur
                 And there's a sound of human voices.

                 Quoth Peter "is it come to this?"
                 Then kill or cure we must be brief
                 So he let fall a thundering smack
                 And heard a voice behind his back
                 From the old quarry cry "Thief, thief!"

                 As you'll suppose this ugly voice
                 His rage did not a little quell,
                 But as he did not hear again
                 The voice which he had heard so plain
                 To work again he fell.   MS. 1
472–4   Or that he felt a wicked chain
                 Twined round him like a magic spell
                 Upon my faith I cannot tell,
                 But to the work he fell again.   MSS.
479–80 *so* 1836: Just like a sounding trumpet's shout
                 The long   MSS. 2, 3
                 More ruefully an endless shout,
                 The long   MSS. 4–6, 1819–32

What is there now in Peter's heart!
Or whence the might of this strange sound?
The moon uneasy looked and dimmer,
The broad blue heavens appeared to glimmer,
And the rocks staggered all around—   485

From Peter's hand the sapling dropped!
Threat has he none to execute;
"If any one should come and see
That I am here, they'll think," quoth he,
"I'm helping this poor dying brute."   490

482   Or what's the power of that   MSS.
487–90   'Twas plain that he felt small temptation
            To play again the ruffian's part
            For by this time in Peter's heart
            There was a wondrous alteration.   MS. 1
486–8   And down he sits beside the ass
            Just under a tall alder root,
            "If any *etc. as text* MSS. 2, 4
490/1   His staff is in the grass, and look!
            With fainting heart and trembling knees
            And visage pale while both his hands
            Hung down against his thighs he stands
            Beneath the moonlight trees.

            Shall Peter go or shall he stay
            Or what is it that he must do?
            Whether from shame or tenderness
            Or from his coward heart's distress
            At length towards the ass he drew,

            The little ass still hung his head
             Over the stream so clear and deep,
            Over the stream his head he kept
            And like a human being wept,
            He wept as men and women weep.

            No doubt he was in piteous case;
            While on his side the ass was lying,
            From sorrow, weakness, or from pain
            The tears flowed down his cheeks amain,
            You would have thought that he was dying,

            And to the eye of Peter now
            To Peter's eye was clearly shewn
            What till this time he had not seen,
            That the poor ass was gaunt and lean
            And almost wasted to the bone.

            You often meet a poor man's horse
            Whose bones stare on you as you pass.
            Of such you will see many a one
            But never such a skeleton
            As this poor miserable ass. MS. 1

He scans the Ass from limb to limb,
And ventures now to uplift his eyes;
More steady looks the moon, and clear,
More like themselves the rocks appear
And touch more quiet skies.   495

His scorn returns—his hate revives;
He stoops the Ass's neck to seize
With malice—that again takes flight;
For in the pool a startling sight
Meets him, among the inverted trees.   500

Is it the moon's distorted face?
The ghost-like image of a cloud?
Is it a gallows there portrayed?
Is Peter of himself afraid?
Is it a coffin,—or a shroud?   505

491–500   "'Tis plain" quoth he "as plain can be
             That here has been some wicked dealing,
             No doubt the devil in me wrought,
             I'm not the man who could have thought
             An ass like this was worth the stealing."

             But now while he is thus employed
             The burthen of his soul relieving
             Ten thousand ugly apprehensions,
             Of eyes and ears the black inventions,
             The soul of Peter are deceiving.

             And closer to the ass he draws
             As if into the ass he'd creep.
             The ass no doubt in piteous case
             Just as before hangs down his face
             Over the stream so clear and deep.

             Yet in a fit of dastard rage
             He stoops the ass's neck to seize,
             And in the clear deep stream below
             He spies an ugly sight I trow
             Among the shadows of the trees.   MS. 2
             MSS. 3, 4 *omit all but the last stanza*
492 *so* 1836:   And Peter now uplifts his eyes   MSS. 5, 6, 1819–32
495 *so* 1836:   And quiet (tranquil 1819–32) are the skies   MSS. 5, 6
495/6   And Peter in a heartsome tone
             Cries out "your pipes are clear and shrill
             'Twas a rare peal, no doubt you meant
             To rouze your friends by Pennygent
             And far as Pendle Hill"   MSS. 5, 6.
496 *so* 1836:   Whereat in resolute mood once more   MS. 6, 1819–32
498–500   Foul purpose quickly put to flight
             . . . beneath the shadowy trees   MS. 6, 1819–32
501–2   shadow of the moon . . . shadow of a cloud   MSS. 2–4

A grisly idol hewn in stone?
Or imp from witch's lap let fall?
Perhaps a ring of shining fairies?
Such as pursue their feared vagaries
In sylvan bower, or haunted hall?   510

Is it a fiend that to a stake
Of fire his desperate self is tethering?
Or stubborn spirit doomed to yell
In solitary ward or cell,
Ten thousand miles from all his brethren?   515

Never did pulse so quickly throb,
And never heart so loudly panted;
He looks, he cannot choose but look;
Like some one reading in a book—
A book that is enchanted.   520

506–10 *not in* MSS. 2–5   512 Of red hot fire himself   MSS.
513–14   Some solitary ward or cell
                Where lies a damned soul in hell   MSS.
515/6   Is it a party in a parlour?
                Cramm'd just as they on earth were cramm'd—
                Some sipping punch, some sipping tea,
                But, as you by their faces see,
                All silent and all damn'd!   MSS., 1819

                'Tis no such thing I do assure you
                That Peter sees in the clear flood,
                It is no ugly apprehension,
                Of eyes and ears 'tis no invention,
                It is a thing of flesh and blood.

                It cannot be a water rat
                No, Peter is not such a noddy,
                The flesh and blood which Peter sees
                Among the shadows of the trees
                It is a dead man's body.   MS. 3
516–17   Poor Peter looks and looks again
                Even like a man whose brain is haunted   MSS.
                A throbbing pulse the Gazer hath—
                Puzzled he was, and now is daunted;   1819–20
519 *so* 1836:   Like one that's reading in MSS.   intent upon 1819–32
520/1   He grasps the poor Ass by the jaws
                His hands and body shake and shiver,
                And up and down, and to and fro
                The ass's head and mouth they go
                Dimpling the surface of the river.   MSS.

                Sure uglier sights were never seen
                By good or bad, by sad or simple
                Than Peter while he holds the ass
                Sees clearly in that watery glass
                Where the still moonlight waters dimple.   MS. 3 *only*

Ah, well-a-day for Peter Bell!
He will be turned to iron soon,
Meet Statue for the court of Fear!
His hat is up—and every hair
Bristles, and whitens in the moon!   525

He looks, he ponders, looks again;
He sees a motion—hears a groan;
His eyes will burst—his heart will break—
He gives a loud and frightful shriek,
And back he falls, as if his life were flown!   530

PART SECOND

WE left our Hero in a trance,
Beneath the alders, near the river;
The Ass is by the river-side,
And, where the feeble breezes glide,
Upon the stream the moonbeams quiver.   535

A happy respite! but at length
He feels the glimmering of the moon;
Wakes with glazed eye, and feebly sighing—
To sink, perhaps, where he is lying,
Into a second swoon!   540

523–5   Flesh, sinew, fibre, bone and gristle,
         His hat is up; his hairs they bristle,
         Bristle and whiten *etc.*   MSS.
525/6   And see him now fast bound like iron
         Head, joints, and hands and lips, and teeth,
         You'd think that he was looking at you
         But no, this uncouth iron statue
         Is looking at the stream beneath.

         And now poor Peter is convinced
         While still he holds the ass's head,
         That 'tis a fiend with visage wan,
         A live man-fiend, a living man
         That's lying in the river's bed.   MSS.
526 ponders, MS. 6   he looks, he MSS. 2–5
530 *so* 1836:   And back he falls, dead as a stone   MSS. 2–5
         And drops, a senseless weight, as if his
                  life were flown   1819–32
531 our Hero] poor Peter MSS.
536   And Peter wakes, he wakes at last   MSS.
536–7 *so* 1827: A happy respite! but he wakes   And   1819–20
538–40 And to stretch forth his hand is trying; Sure, when he knows
where *etc.*   He'll sink into MSS., 1819–20.

He lifts his head, he sees his staff;
He touches—'tis to him a treasure!
Faint recollection seems to tell
That he is yet where mortals dwell—
A thought received with languid pleasure!   545

His head upon his elbow propped,
Becoming less and less perplexed,
Sky-ward he looks—to rock and wood—
And then—upon the glassy flood
His wandering eye is fixed.   550

543–5   To find that he is not in hell
             As you'll suppose to Peter Bell
             Doth give a sweet and languid pleasure.   MSS.
546–60   And while upon his side he lies
             His head upon his elbow raised
             Almost you'd say as in a dream
             His eyes are settling on the stream
             Where he before had gazed.   5

             No dimple now disturbs the stream
             In Peter's brain there is no riot,
             His eye upon the stream he fixes
             And with the sight no terror mixes
             His heart is calm and quiet.   10

             Quoth he "that is a dead man's face
             Among the shadows of the trees,
             Those are no doubt a dead man's knuckles
             And there you see his brass shoe buckles
             And there his breeches' knees."   15

             At last he rises from his side
             And sits upright upon the ground,
             And o'er the stream he hangs his nose
             And points his staff as you'd suppose
             The river's depth to sound.   20

             This sees the ass while on the grass
             Close by the river's bank he lies
             And strait with a transition tragic
             As if he had been touched with magic
             (That seems just like the touch of magic   MS. 2)
             Up from the ground the ass doth rise.   MSS. 2–5
So MS. 6, but 13–15 A harmless body—nothing worse
             Like the [?] figure of the corse
             Head, trunk, feet, hands, and knees
and 18–19   . . . his head is bent
             . . . with plain intent

Thought he, that is the face of one
In his last sleep securely bound!
So toward the stream his head he bent,
And downward thrust his staff, intent
The river's depth to sound.   555

Now—like a tempest-shattered bark,
That overwhelmed and prostrate lies,
And in a moment to the verge
Is lifted of a foaming surge—
Full suddenly the Ass doth rise!   560

His staring bones all shake with joy,
And close by Peter's side he stands:
While Peter o'er the river bends,
The little Ass his neck extends,
And fondly licks his hands.   565

Such life is in the Ass's eyes,
Such life is in his limbs and ears;
That Peter Bell, if he had been
The veriest coward ever seen,
Must now have thrown aside his fears.   570

The Ass looks on—and to his work
Is Peter quietly resigned;
He touches here—he touches there—
And now among the dead man's hair
His sapling Peter has entwined.   575

553–5 *so* 1827:   So faltering not in *this* intent
                    He makes his staff an instrument
                    The river's *etc.*   1819
                    So toward the stream his head he bent
                    And downward thrust his staff, intent
                    To reach the Man who there lay drowned.   1820
561 staring] meagre MSS.
570/1   But 'tis not by the ass's eyes
         Or ass's ears that he 's protected,
         There is a weakness in his heart
         That may not readily depart,
         Peter in spirit is dejected.   MSS. 5, 6
         With caution Peter eyes the stream
         His sapling deep and deeper goes
         "The body is no doubt", quoth he,
         "The thing which it appears to be
         It moves not, neither limbs nor clothes." MSS. 2–6

He pulls—and looks—and pulls again ·
And he whom the poor Ass had lost.
The man who had been four days dead,
Head-foremost from the river's bed
Uprises like a ghost!   580

And Peter draws him to dry land;
And through the brain of Peter pass
Some poignant twitches, fast and faster;
"No doubt," quoth he, "he is the Master
Of this poor miserable Ass!"   585

The meagre shadow that looks on—
What would he now? what is he doing?
His sudden fit of joy is flown,—
He on his knees hath laid him down,
As if he were his grief renewing;   590

But no—that Peter on his back
Must mount, he shows well as he can:
Thought Peter then, come weal or woe,
I'll do what he would have me do,
In pity to this poor drowned man.   595

576   looks] pulls   MSS.
582-3   And lays him strait upon the grass
           And Peter feels some ugly pains
           Across his liver heart and reins
           Just like a weaver's shuttle pass.
           (In quick succession pass.   MS. 3)
           He sees the poor man's blue swoln face
           And through *etc. as text, but* ugly *for* poignant   MSS. 2-3
585/6   He scans the beast from limb to limb
           "I've played with you an ugly game"
           Quoth Peter to the ass, "but still
           I did not mean to use you ill
           You must allow you were to blame."   MSS.
586-7 *so* 1836:   But the poor Shadow all this while
           The little ass   MSS.
           The meagre shadow . . . What aim is his?   1819-32
591-5 *so* 1836:   That Peter on his back should mount
           He's shewing all the wish he can
           "I'll go, I'll go, if life forsake me
           No doubt he to his home will take me
           The cottage of this drowned man"   MSS.

           He shows a wish, well as he can
                   . . . what e'er betide
           He to his home my way will guide *etc.*   1819

With that resolve he boldly mounts
Upon the pleased and thankful Ass;
And then, without a moment's stay,
That earnest Creature turned away,
Leaving the body on the grass.   600

Intent upon his faithful watch,
The Beast four days and nights had past;
A sweeter meadow ne'er was seen,
And there the Ass four days had been,
Nor ever once did break his fast: 605

Yet firm his step, and stout his heart;
The mead is crossed—the quarry's mouth
Is reached; but there the trusty guide
Into a thicket turns aside,
And deftly ambles towards the south.   610

But no—his purpose and his wish
The Suppliant shews, well as he can;
Thought Peter, whatsoe'er betide
I'll go, and he my way *etc.* . . . . To the cottage *etc.*   1820–32
596–9 *so* 1836 This said, friend Peter mounts forthwith
Upon that good and faithful ass
And strait without a moment's stay
The ass turns quietly away   MSS.
596   This uttered (hoping 1820) Peter mounts forthwith 1819;
Encouraged by the hope he mounts, 1827;
This hoping Peter boldly mounts 1832
601–10   The little ass is strong at heart
And firm he walks and bolt upright,
But well may the poor beast be wasted
For four long days he has not tasted
Of food a single bite.
(No food these four days has he tasted
Not even a single bite   MSS. 4–6)

Amid that green and quiet spot
He four long days and nights had passed,
A sweeter meadow ne'er was seen
And there the ass four days had been
And never once had broke his fast.

Across the meadow they are gone
And now are at the quarry's mouth,
The little ass who is the guide
Into a thicket turns aside
And takes his way towards the South.   MSS.
610 *so* 1836: 1819–32 *as* MSS.

When hark a burst of doleful sound!
And Peter honestly might say,
The like came never to his ears,
Though he has been, full thirty years,
A rover—night and day!   615

'Tis not a plover of the moors,
'Tis not a bittern of the fen;
Nor can it be a barking fox,
Nor night-bird chambered in the rocks,
Nor wild-cat in a woody glen!   620

The Ass is startled—and stops short
Right in the middle of the thicket;
And Peter, wont to whistle loud
Whether alone or in a crowd,
Is silent as a silent cricket.   625

What ails you now, my little Bess?
Well may you tremble and look grave!
This cry—that rings along the wood,
This cry—that floats adown the flood,
Comes from the entrance of a cave: 630

611–15   But hark! among the woods they hear
          A cry of lamentable sort,
          Though there is nothing he should stick at
          Yet in the middle of the thicket
          The little ass stops short.
          And Peter hears the doleful sound
          And he in honest truth may say *etc.*   MSS.
618–19   Nor is it like . . . Nor like a night-bird in   MSS.
620/21   The cry grows loud and louder still
          The little ass who meant to climb
          That lofty mountain which you see
          Beneath the shadow of a tree
          Is listening all the time.   MSS.
621–5   And Peter's on the Ass's back,
          Is in . . . And though he's used . . . He's   MSS.
625/6   Now should it be a crazy ghost
          One who must sing in doleful pain
          Through a long vision to be broken
          When time shall snap the true love token
          To which she sings her doleful strain.   MSS. 2, 3
627   What is 't that makes you look so grave   MSS. 2–4
          Ah well indeed you may look grave   MSS. 5–6
628–30   This cry which sets your heart a throbbing
          It is a little boy that's sobbing
          Beside the *etc.*   MSS.

I see a blooming Wood-boy there,
And if I had the power to say
How sorrowful the wanderer is,
Your heart would be as sad as his
Till you had kissed his tears away!   635

Grasping a hawthorn branch in hand,
All bright with berries ripe and red,
Into the cavern's mouth he peeps;
Thence back into the moonlight creeps;
Whom seeks he—whom ?—the silent dead: 640

631–3 A blooming wood boy of the woods
       And, Bess, I will be bold to say
       If once you knew but where he is   MSS.
636   A branch of hawthorn in his hand MSS.
639   moonlight] moon he MSS.
640   And then (draws back MSS. 2, 3) cries out in fear and dread MSS.
640/1 He is bewitch'd by some strange hope
       And shews a wondrous self command,
       Yet though his heart be bold and staunch
       The berries on the hawthorn branch
       All rattle in his hand.

       Beneath the ivy now he creeps
       Upon his hands and knees, and then
       Like swans which pinch'd by hunger make
       Their moan beside a frozen lake
       He sobs and sobs and sobs again.   MSS. 2, 3

       And then his face is stained with blood,
       Well may he be in piteous plight,
       To his coat lap a bramble clings
       And both his hands with nettle stings
       Are blistered red and white.   MS. 2

       Ah well my pretty little Bess
       To hear that miserable sound
       The tears into your eyes may gather   MSS. 2–4
       And sure to see him at this time
       And hear him make this dolorous sound
       Sad thoughts round any heart may gather   MSS. 5, 6
       The boy is seeking his dead Father
       His Father dead and drown'd.

       Poor Robin loved his Father well
       For often by the hand he led
       Sweet Robin over hill and height
       And oft with his own hand at night
       He laid him on his bed.

His father!—Him doth he require—
Him hath he sought with fruitless pains,
Among the rocks, behind the trees;
Now creeping on his hands and knees,
Now running o'er the open plains.   645

And hither is he come at last,
When he through such a day has gone,
By this dark cave to be distrest
Like a poor bird—her plundered nest
Hovering around with dolorous moan!   650

Of that intense and piercing cry
The listening Ass conjectures well;
Wild as it is, he there can read
Some intermingled notes that plead
With touches irresistible.   655

He brought him playthings from the Fair
He told him tales, with nuts he fed
Sweet Robin in the wood, and he
Gave Robin many a half-penny
And many a crust of bread.   MS. 4 (MSS. 2 *and* 3 *with
     some variants*) in the woody bowers
And helped him oft to gather flowers
And wove rush bonnets for his head.   MSS. 5, 6
641–5   Since five o'clock hath Robin sought
O'er heath and hill, through copse and lane,
Through gipsey-scenes of rocks and woods
Sooth'd day and night by murmuring floods
And wild as any place in Spain.   MSS. 2, 3
(And Robin all day long hath sought
His father in the woods and lanes
Among the rocks, *etc. as text*.   MSS. 4–6)
649–50 *so* MS. 6: Where like a bird about its nest
                He flutters off and on.   MSS. 2–5
651–5   At last (both in despair MSS. 2, 3) in hopelessness and fear
Along the wood his road he takes,
And like a little child that's lost
And thinks he's follow'd by a ghost
A wild and doleful cry he makes.

The ass when first he caught the noise
Stopp'd short, and soon he knew it well
And towards the cave whence Robin sent
All through the wood that sad lament
He has been carrying Peter Bell.   MSS.
652 conjectures well 1836: doth rightly spell 1819–32

But Peter—when he saw the Ass
Not only stop but turn, and change
The cherished tenor of his pace
That lamentable cry to chase—
It wrought in him conviction strange;   660

A faith that, for the dead man's sake
And this poor slave who loved him well,
Vengeance upon his head will fall,
Some visitation worse than all
Which ever till this night befell.   665

Meanwhile the Ass to reach his home
Is striving stoutly as he may;
But, while he climbs the woody hill,
The cry grows weak—and weaker still;
And now at last it dies away.   670

So with his freight the Creature turns
Into a gloomy grove of beech,
Along the shade with footsteps true
Descending slowly, till the two
The open moonlight reach.   675

And there, along the narrow dell,
A fair smooth pathway you discern,
A length of green and open road—
As if it from a fountain flowed—
Winding away between the fern.   680

656–9   But soon as Peter saw the ass
His road all on a sudden change
And turn right upwards from the hollow
That lamentable noise to follow   MSS.
661–3   A sober and a firm belief
Is in the heart of Peter Bell
That something will to him befall   MSS. 2, 3
     MSS. 4–6 *as text but* 662   And this poor ass from heaven or hell
666 *so* 1836: . . . on Robin's track MSS.: to gain his end 1819–32
667 striving] following MSS.
670/1   Fain would he overtake the boy
For Robin is his dear delight,
But finding 'tis an idle hope
Down the close pathway's rugged slope
He gently turns towards the right.   MSS.
671   With Peter on his back he turns MSS.   678   A verdant and
an MSS. 2, 3
679–80 As any little river broad MSS.
The ass winds on among *etc.* MS. 2–4

The rocks that tower on either side
Build up a wild fantastic scene;
Temples like those among the Hindoos,
And mosques, and spires, and abbey-windows,
And castles all with ivy green!   685

And while the Ass pursues his way
Along this solitary dell,
As pensively his steps advance,
The mosques and spires change countenance,
And look at Peter Bell!   690

That unintelligible cry
Hath left him high in preparation,—
Convinced that he, or soon or late,
This very night will meet his fate—
And so he sits in expectation!   695

685/6   This smooth-green path, you know not how,
Winds upwards like a straggling chain;
And when you two good miles have pass'd
Between the rocks you come at last
Unto a high and level plain.   MS. 2

The verdant pathway, in and out,
Winds upwards like a straggling chain;
And, when two toilsome miles are past,
Up through the rocks it leads at last
Into a high and open plain.   1819–20: MSS. 5 and 6 between
MS. 2 and 1819

686   While Peter now is travelling on MS. 2

688–90   In truth I should be much inclined
To tell what's passing in his mind
If it would suit my tale as well.   MS. 2

694 very] luckless MSS.

695/6   The little ass makes no complaint
He feels not any want of strength
And slowly up the smooth-green track
He winds with Peter on his back
And to the top is come at length.   MSS.

And while together now they go
Across the open moonlight down,
To say the truth, they seem a pair
Come from some region of the air,
Some unknown region of their own   (MS. 2 only)

The strenuous Animal hath clomb
With the green path; and now he wends
Where, shining like the smoothest sea,
In undisturbed immensity
A level plain extends.   700

But whence this faintly-rustling sound
By which the journeying pair are chased?
—A withered leaf is close behind,
Light plaything for the sportive wind
Upon that solitary waste.   705

When Peter spied the moving thing,
It only doubled his distress;
"Where there is not a bush or tree,
The very leaves they follow me—
So huge hath been my wickedness!"   710

696–707 Right onward walks the trusty ass
Over the Down his way he bends
Where smooth and bare as any sea
Without a plant, without a tree
The level plain extends.

And ever where along the turf
They go with smooth and steady pace
You see driven forward by the wind
A dancing leaf that's close behind
Following them .o'er that lonely place.

And Peter hears the rustling leaf (stirring noise MSS. 5, 6)
And many a time he turns his face
Both here and there ere he can find
What 'tis that follows him behind
Along that lonely (solitary MSS. 5, 6) place.

At last he spies the withered leaf
And Peter is in sore distress   MS. 2; *so* MSS. 4–6 *with slight*
              variants
701–3 *so* 1836: How blank! but whence this (that 1820–32) rustling sound
Which, all too long, the pair hath chased!
—A dancing leaf *etc*. 1819–32
706–7 *so* 1836: When Peter spies the withered leaf,
It yields no cure to his distress— 1819–32
710/11 Along the [ ] down they go
And to a broad highway are come
They quit the turf and on the gravel
Upon the broad highway they travel
A pair both sad and dumb

To a close lane they now are come,
Where, as before, the enduring Ass
Moves on without a moment's stop,
Nor once turns round his head to crop
A bramble-leaf or blade of grass.   715

Between the hedges as they go,
The white dust sleeps upon the lane;
And Peter, ever and anon
Back-looking, sees, upon a stone,
Or in the dust, a crimson stain.   720

A stain—as of a drop of blood
By moonlight made more faint and wan;
Ha! why these sinkings of despair?
He knows not how the blood comes there—
And Peter is a wicked man.   725

For Peter Bell he looks I vow
With his dull face of ashy white
Just like a creature that pertains
To some strange world of silent pains
A creature of a moonlight night.   MS. 2

711–12   And now they to a lane are come
And still the little meagre ass   MSS.

717–20   The dusty road is white as bone,
And Peter casting down his eyes
Towards the moonlight road espies
A drop of blood upon a stone.   MSS.

721–3   Peter has little power to move
Upon the ass remain he must,
He travels on, and now and then
He sees that drop of blood again
Upon a stone or in the dust.

Did Peter e'er with club or stake
Smite some poor traveller on the head,
Or beat his father in a rage
And spill the blood of his old age,
Or kick a child till it was dead?

Did Peter ever kill his man
With fist or staff in single duel,
Or stab with some inhuman wound
A soldier bleeding on the ground?
No, Peter never was so cruel.

Then why to see this drop of blood
Doth Peter look so pale and wan?
Why is he in this sad despair?   MSS.

723 these sinkings of 1836: this comfortless 1819–32

At length he spies a bleeding wound,
Where he had struck the Ass's head;
He sees the blood, knows what it is,—
A glimpse of sudden joy was his,
But then it quickly fled;   730

Of him whom sudden death had seized
He thought,—of thee, O faithful Ass!
And once again those ghastly pains,
Shoot to and fro through heart and reins,
And through his brain like lightning pass.   735

PART THIRD

I've heard of one, a gentle Soul,
Though given to sadness and to gloom,
And for the fact will vouch,—one night
It chanced that by a taper's light
This man was reading in his room;   740

Bending, as you or I might bend
At night o'er any pious book,
When sudden blackness overspread
The snow-white page on which he read,
And made the good man round him look.   745

The chamber walls were dark all round,—
And to his book he turned again;
—The light had left the lonely taper,
And formed itself upon the paper
Into large letters—bright and plain!   750

The godly book was in his hand—
And on the page, more black than coal,
Appeared, set forth in strange array,
A *word*—which to his dying day
Perplexed the good man's gentle soul.   755

731–5   He thought he could not help but think
        Of that poor beast, that faithful ass,
        (Of the dead man and his poor ass   MSS. 5, 6)
        And once again those ugly pains
        Across his liver heart and reins
        Just like (Swift as MSS. 5, 6) a weaver's shuttle pass.   MSS.
733–5 *so* 1826:   darting pains
        As meteors shoot through heaven's wide plains,
        Pass through his bosom—and repass!   1819–32
738 will] I'll MSS.   741–2 Bending . . . bend . . . o'er] Reading . . . read
. . . in MSS., 1819–20
753–4   Those ghostly letters formed a word
        Which to his dying day, I've heard   MSS.

The ghostly word, thus plainly seen,
Did never from his lips depart;
But he hath said, poor gentle wight!
It brought full many a sin to light
Out of the bottom of his heart.   760

Dread Spirits! to confound the meek
Why wander from your course so far,
Disordering colour, form, and stature!
—Let good men feel the soul of nature,
And see things as they are.   765

Yet, potent Spirits! well I know,
How ye, that play with soul and sense,
Are not unused to trouble friends
Of goodness, for most gracious ends—
And this I speak in reverence!   770

But might I give advice to you,
Whom in my fear I love so well;
From men of pensive virtue go,
Dread Beings! and your empire show
On hearts like that of Peter Bell.   775

Your presence often have I felt
In darkness and the stormy night;
And with like force, if need there be,
Ye can put forth your agency
When earth is calm, and heaven is bright.   780

756 *so* 1836: The wondrous word which thus he saw   MSS.   The ghostly
. . . was framed 1819–20 . . . full plainly seen 1827–32
761–2   . . . thus to vex the good
        How can ye with your functions jar   MSS.
            to torment the good   1819–20
766–9 *so* 1836: I know you, potent Spirits! well,
            How, with the feeling and the sense,   MSS. –1832
            Ye play both with your foes and friends
            Most fearful work for fearful ends   MSS.
            Playing, ye govern foes or friends,
            Yok'd to your will, for fearful ends   1819–32
778 *so* 1836: And well I know MSS. –1832   780 Beneath the sweet
moonlight MSS.

Then, coming from the wayward world,
That powerful world in which ye dwell,
Come, Spirits of the Mind! and try,
To-night, beneath the moonlight sky,
What may be done with Peter Bell!   785

—O, would that some more skilful voice
My further labour might prevent!
Kind Listeners, that around me sit,
I feel that I am all unfit
For such high argument.   790

—I've played, I've danced, with my narration;
I loitered long ere I began:
Ye waited then on my good pleasure;
Pour out indulgence still, in measure
As liberal as ye can!   795

Our Travellers, ye remember well,
Are thridding a sequestered lane;
And Peter many tricks is trying,
And many anodynes applying,
To ease his conscience of its pain.   800

By this his heart is lighter far;
And, finding that he can account
So snugly for that crimson stain,
His evil spirit up again
Does like an empty bucket mount.   805

786   O would that any, friend or foe MSS.
788   On me it cannot easy sit   MSS. 2–4
        Aw'd am I when I think of it   MSS. 5, 6
792   A happy and a thoughtless man   MSS. 2, 3
793–5   I've moved to many a giddy measure
        But now, my Friends, for your good pleasure
        I'll do the best I can.   MSS.
796–7   The ass as you remember well
        Is travelling now along a lane   MSS.
800 conscience] stomach MSS.   801–5 *not in* MS. 3; *added to* MS. 2
803 snugly MSS., 1836: clearly 1819–32
805/6   Quoth Peter "wounds will bleed we know
        And blood is blood, and fools have fears"
        And yet that leaf, he can't deny,
        Dogg'd him, and still that doleful cry
        Is ringing in his ears.   MSS.

And Peter is a deep logician
Who hath no lack of wit mercurial;
"Blood drops—leaves rustle—yet," quoth he,
"This poor man never, but for me,
Could have had Christian burial.   810

"And, say the best you can, 'tis plain,
That here has been some wicked dealing;
No doubt the devil in me wrought;
I'm not the man who could have thought
An Ass like this was worth the stealing!"   815

So from his pocket Peter takes
His shining horn tobacco-box;
And, in a light and careless way,
As men who with their purpose play,
Upon the lid he knocks.   820

Let them whose voice can stop the clouds,
Whose cunning eye can see the wind,
Tell to a curious world the cause
Why, making here a sudden pause,
The Ass turned round his head and *grinned*.   825

Appalling process! I have marked
The like on heath, in lonely wood;
And, verily, have seldom met
A spectacle more hideous—yet
It suited Peter's present mood.   830

808 "Why, after all, 'tis plain" quoth he MSS.   811–15 *not in* MS. 3;
added to MS. 2, *but cf. app. crit. to* 491–500
818–19   And in a careless way as you,
         Or I, good Mr Swan, might do   MSS. 2–5
         (Or any of our friends *etc.* MS. 6)
820/1   There's some of you, my Friends, perhaps
         There's some of you in yawning weather
         Who may have seen an ass's grin
         'Tis uglier far than death and sin
         And all the devils together   MSS.
821–5   And just as Peter struck the box
         —It might be to recruit his wind
         Or from some more important cause—
         The quiet creature made a pause
         Turn'd round his head and grinn'd.   MSS.
826–30   You know that Peter is resolved
         His drooping spirits to repair,
         And though no doubt a sight like this
         To others might have come amiss
         It suited Peter to a hair.   MSS.

And, grinning in his turn, his teeth
He in jocose defiance showed—
When, to upset his spiteful mirth,
A murmur, pent within the earth,
In the dead earth beneath the road,   835

Rolled audibly!—it swept along,
A muffled noise—a rumbling sound!—
'Twas by a troop of miners made,
Plying with gunpowder their trade,
Some twenty fathoms underground.   840

Small cause of dire effect! for, surely,
If ever mortal, King or Cotter,
Believed that earth was charged to quake
And yawn for his unworthy sake,
'Twas Peter Bell the Potter.   845

But, as an oak in breathless air
Will stand though to the centre hewn;
Or as the weakest things, if frost
Have stiffened them, maintain their post;
So he, beneath the gazing moon!—   850

831-4   And Peter grinning with the joke
        His teeth in approbation shewed
        When, cruel blow to Peter's mirth,
        He heard a murmur in the earth   MSS.
833   upset 1836: confound 1819-32
836-7   Beneath the ass's feet it pass'd
        A murmur and *etc.*   MSS.
840   Some twenty MS. 6: Some hundred MSS. 2-4: A score of MS. 5
841-4   And I will venture to affirm
        If ever any, King or Cotter,
        Did think as sure as five is five
        That he'd be swallow'd up alive   MSS.
846-53 And while the little silent ass
        Requiring neither rein nor goad
        Moves on beneath the moonlight skies
        And the grey dust in silence lies
        Upon the moonlight road.   MSS. 2-4

        But still he keeps upon his seat,
        The ass moves slowly with his load
        Peter is busy with his ears
        And now and then he thinks he hears
        A murmuring noise beneath the road.   MS. 5

The Beast bestriding thus, he reached
A spot where, in a sheltering cove,
A little chapel stands alone,
With greenest ivy overgrown,
And tufted with an ivy grove;   855

Dying insensibly away
From human thoughts and purposes,
It seemed—wall, window, roof and tower—
To bow to some transforming power,
And blend with the surrounding trees.   860

Poor Peter by an ugly fiend (fancy MS. 5)
Is troubled more and more, quoth he
"I know the truth, I know it well
Through meadowy ground and rock and dell
A devil is following me."

At this poor Peter gave a groan,
And straightway from a cottage door
A little cur came barking out
Barking and making such a rout
As never cur had made before.

This barking cur as you suppose
Must needs have been a joyful sight,
You think no doubt it must have cut
The thread of Peter's trance and put
The subterraneous devil to flight.

The barking cur he might have been
A roaring lion just as well
For any good that he has wrought,
For any comfort he has brought
To poor unhappy Peter Bell.   MSS. 2, 3

Upon the ass's back he sits
Like one that's riding in a swoon
Or as a ghost that cannot see,
Whose face, if any such there be,
Is like the eyeless moon.   MSS. (*with slight variants*)

And every twenty yards or less
Poor Peter, well may he look grim,
Whether on rising ground or level
Still feels the subterraneous devil
Heave up the little ass and him.   MSS. 2-5

And now the patient ass is come
To where beneath a mountain cove
A little chapel *etc.*   MSS. (*with slight variants*)

856 *so* MS. 6: A building dying half (all MS. 5) away MSS. 2-5
858 *so* 1836: . . . both wall and roof MSS. 2-5; The building seems, wall, roof, and tower MS. 6—1832

As ruinous a place it was,
Thought Peter, in the shire of Fife
That served my turn, when following still
From land to land a reckless will
I married my sixth wife!   865

The unheeding Ass moves slowly on,
And now is passing by an inn
Brim-full of a carousing crew,
That make, with curses not a few,
An uproar and a drunken din.   870

I cannot well express the thoughts
Which Peter in those noises found;—
A stifling power compressed his frame,
While-as a swimming darkness came
Over that dull and dreary sound.   875

For well did Peter know the sound;
The language of those drunken joys
To him, a jovial soul, I ween,
But a few hours ago, had been
A gladsome and a welcome noise.   880

861-4 *so* 1836: Deep sighing as he passed along
          Quoth Peter "In the shire of Fife,
          'Twas just in such a place as that
          Not knowing what I should be at   MSS.
861-2 1819-32 *as above*
863-4   Mid such a ruin, following still
          From land to land a lawless will,   1819-32
865/6   Thus Peter commun'd with himself;
          By this time he is somewhat wean'd,
          I think, from his delirious notion
          That the road's giddy with commotion
          Made by some subterraneous fiend.   5

          Yet ever and anon sad thoughts
          And woeful apprehensions gall him,
          Believing in his own despite
          That soon or late this very night
          Some cruel judgment will befal him.   MSS. 4, 5   10
          (*added to* MSS. 2, 3); MS. 6 *has ll.* 1, *and* 7-10
866   unheeding] little MSS.
874 *so* 1836: 'Twas just as if a MSS.; As if (And a 1832) confusing 181 ̄ 32

Now, turned adrift into the past,
He finds no solace in his course;
Like planet-stricken men of yore,
He trembles, smitten to the core
By strong compunction and remorse.   885

But, more than all, his heart is stung
To think of one, almost a child;
A sweet and playful Highland girl,
As light and beauteous as a squirrel,
As beauteous and as wild!   890

Her dwelling was a lonely house,
A cottage in a heathy dell;
And she put on her gown of green,
And left her mother at sixteen,
And followed Peter Bell.   895

But many good and pious thoughts
Had she; and, in the kirk to pray,
Two long Scotch miles, through rain or snow,
To kirk she had been used to go,
Twice every Sabbath-day.   900

881-5   But now 'tis plain that Peter's thoughts
        Have taken a far different course,
        Whate'er he sees, whate'er he hears
        Gives him new sorrow and new fears,
        Deepens his anguish and remorse.   MSS.
885/6   And passing by a twisted elm
        Again poor Peter thus began
        "'Twas just by such another tree
        I robb'd of sixpence halfpenny
        A boy that led a poor blind man.

        "And close by such a gate (stile MSS. 4, 5) as that
        Did I by a most heinous murther
        Destroy my good dog Ruffian, he
        Who gladly would have gone for me
        To the world's end and further.

        "A faithful beast like this poor ass
        Whom I have bruis'd so cruelly,
        Just such another animal
        Made by the God that made us all,
        And fitter far to live than I.   MSS. 2-5
891 *so* 1836: A lonely house her dwelling was MSS., 1819-32

And, when she followed Peter Bell,
It was to lead an honest life;
For he, with tongue not used to falter,
Had pledged his troth before the altar
To love her as his wedded wife.   905

A mother's hope is hers;—but soon
She drooped and pined like one forlorn;
From Scripture she a name did borrow;
Benoni, or the child of sorrow,
She called her babe unborn.   910

For she had learned how Peter lived,
And took it in most grievous part;
She to the very bone was worn,
And, ere that little child was born,
Died of a broken heart.   915

And now the Spirits of the Mind
Are busy with poor Peter Bell;
Upon the rights of visual sense
Usurping, with a prevalence
More terrible than magic spell.   920

Close by a brake of flowering furze
(Above it shivering aspens play)
He sees an unsubstantial creature,
His very self in form and feature,
Not four yards from the broad highway: 925

And stretched beneath the furze he sees
The Highland girl—it is no other;
And hears her crying as she cried,
The very moment that she died,
"My mother! oh my mother!"   930

906   A child was in her womb   MSS.
918–20 *so* 1820: And from the ass's back he sees
       I think as ugly images
       As ever eye did see in hell.   MSS.
       Distraction reigns in soul and sense,
       And reason drops in impotence
       From her deserted pinnacle!   1819
922–4 He sees himself as plain as day
       He sees himself a man in figure
       Even like himself nor less nor bigger   MSS. *but* MS. 6 (924)
       His very self.
925   four MS. 6: five MSS. 2–5

The sweat pours down from Peter's face,
So grievous is his heart's contrition;
With agony his eye-balls ache
While he beholds by the furze-brake
This miserable vision!   935

Calm is the well-deserving brute,
His peace hath no offence betrayed;
But now, while down that slope he wends,
A voice to Peter's ear ascends,
Resounding from the woody glade: 940

The voice, though clamorous as a horn
Re-echoed by a naked rock,
Comes from that tabernacle—List!
Within, a fervent Methodist
Is preaching to no heedless flock!   945

"Repent! repent!" he cries aloud,
"While yet ye may find mercy;—strive
To love the Lord with all your might;
Turn to him, seek him day and night,
And save your souls alive!   950

"Repent! repent! though ye have gone,
Through paths of wickedness and woe,
After the Babylonian harlot;
And, though your sins be red as scarlet,
They shall be white as snow!"   955

Even as he passed the door, these words
Did plainly come to Peter's ears;
And they such joyful tidings were,
The joy was more than he could bear!—
He melted into tears.   960

936–7   The ass is pacing down a hill
         By this he has not far to go   MSS.
940   From the deep woody dell below   MSS.
941 *so* 1836: It is a voice just like a voice   MSS. 2–4
         The voice he hears is   MSS. 5, 6
         Though clamorous as a hunter's horn   1819–27
         The voice, though clamorous as a horn   1832
943 *so* 1836: It comes from that low chapel   MSS. 2, 3
         'Tis (Is 1832) from that Tabernacle   MSS. 4–6, 1819–32
944 It is a pious MSS. 2–4 Within a pious MSS. 5, 6   945 That's . . .
his pious MSS. 2–4; Is . . . his pious MSS. 5, 6   949 Do that which
lawful is and right MSS. 2, 3   951 My friends! my brethren, though
you've gone MSS.   956 Even] Just MSS.

Sweet tears of hope and tenderness!
And fast they fell, a plenteous shower!
His nerves, his sinews seemed to melt;
Through all his iron frame was felt
A gentle, a relaxing, power!   965

Each fibre of his frame was weak;
Weak all the animal within;
But, in its helplessness, grew mild
And gentle as an infant child,
An infant that has known no sin.   970

'Tis said, meek Beast! that, through Heaven's grace,
He not unmoved did notice now
The cross upon thy shoulder scored,
For lasting impress, by the Lord
To whom all human-kind shall bow;   975

Memorial of his touch—that day
When Jesus humbly deigned to ride,
Entering the proud Jerusalem,
By an immeasurable stream
Of shouting people deified!   980

Meanwhile the persevering Ass
Turned towards a gate that hung in view
Across a shady lane; his chest
Against the yielding gate he pressed
And quietly passed through.   985

And up the stony lane he goes;
No ghost more softly ever trod;
Among the stones and pebbles he
Sets down his hoofs inaudibly,
As if with felt his hoofs were shod.   990

966–8   Each nerve each fibre of his frame
        And all *etc.*
      Was weak, perhaps, but it was mild   MSS.
971–80 *so* 1819–20, *not in* MSS. *or* 1827; *restored* 1832   971 *so* 1836:
'Tis said, that through prevailing grace 1819, 1832   974 Meek beast!
in memory of 1819–20, 1832   976 *so* 1836: In memory of that solemn
1819–20, 1832   981 But now the little patient ass MSS.
982–3 *so* 1836: Towards a gate in open (that's full in MSS. 2–4) view
        Turns (Turn'd MSS.) up a narrow lane *etc.* MSS., 1819–32

Along the lane the trusty Ass
Went twice two hundred yards or more,
And no one could have guessed his aim,—
Till to a lonely house he came,
And stopped beside the door.   995

Thought Peter, 'tis the poor man's home!
He listens—not a sound is heard
Save from the trickling household rill;
But, stepping o'er the cottage-sill,
Forthwith a little Girl appeared.   1000

She to the Meeting-house was bound
In hopes some tidings there to gather:
No glimpse it is, no doubtful gleam;
She saw—and uttered with a scream,
"My father! here's my father!"   1005

The very word was plainly heard,
Heard plainly by the wretched Mother—
Her joy was like a deep affright:
And forth she rushed into the light,
And saw it was another!   1010

And, instantly, upon the earth,
Beneath the full moon shining bright,
Close to the Ass's feet she fell;
At the same moment Peter Bell
Dismounts in most unhappy plight.   1015

991 trusty] little MSS.
992–5 *so* 1836: Had gone two hundred yards, not more;
              When to a lonely house he came;
              He turn'd aside towards the same
              And stopp'd before the door.   MSS., 1819–32
998–1000 But ere you could count half a score
              It chanced that at the cottage door
              A little girl appeared.   MSS.
1001 bound] going MSS.
1002–4   With hopes that she some news might gather:
              She saw the pair, and with a scream
              Cried out like one that's in a dream   MSS.
1009 rushed MS. 6: ran MS. 2–5   1012 Close to] Just at MSS.
1014 And from the ass poor MSS.

As he beheld the Woman lie
Breathless and motionless, the mind
Of Peter sadly was confused;
But, though to such demands unused,
And helpless almost as the blind,   1020

He raised her up; and while he held
Her body propped against his knee,
The Woman waked—and when she spied
The poor Ass standing by her side,
She moaned most bitterly.   1025

"Oh! God be praised—my heart's at ease—
For he is dead—I know it well!"
—At this she wept a bitter flood;
And, in the best way that he could,
His tale did Peter tell.   1030

He trembles—he is pale as death;
His voice is weak with perturbation;
He turns aside his head, he pauses;
Poor Peter from a thousand causes
Is crippled sore in his narration.   1035

At length she learned how he espied
The Ass in that small meadow-ground;
And that her Husband now lay dead,
Beside that luckless river's bed
In which he had been drowned.   1040

A piercing look the Widow cast
Upon the Beast that near her stands;
She sees 'tis he, that 'tis the same;
She calls the poor Ass by his name,
And wrings, and wrings her hands.   1045

1016–20 What could he do? the Woman lay
        Dead as it seem'd both breath and limb
        Poor Peter *etc.*
        To scenes like this he was not us'd
        'Twas altogether new to him.   MSS.
1016 *so* 1832: 1819–27 *as* MSS.   1028 Of tears she poured   MSS. 2, 3
1038–40 And that beside the river bed
        Her husband now was lying dead
        That he was dead and drowned.   MSS.
1041   The wretched mother looks and looks   MSS.
        widow 1836: sufferer 1819–32

"O wretched loss—untimely stroke!
If he had died upon his bed!
He knew not one forewarning pain;
He never will come home again—
Is dead, for ever dead!"　　　　　　　　　　1050

Beside the Woman Peter stands;
His heart is opening more and more;
A holy sense pervades his mind;
He feels what he for human-kind
Has never felt before.　　　　　　　　　　1055

At length, by Peter's arm sustained,
The Woman rises from the ground—
"Oh, mercy! something must be done,
My little Rachel, you must run,—
Some willing neighbour must be found.　　　　1060

"Make haste—my little Rachel—do,
The first you meet with—bid him come,
Ask him to lend his horse to-night,
And this good Man, whom Heaven requite,
Will help to bring the body home."　　　　　1065

Away goes Rachel weeping loud;—
An Infant, waked by her distress,
Makes in the house a piteous cry;
And Peter hears the Mother sigh,
"Seven are they, and all fatherless!"　　　　1070

And now is Peter taught to feel
That man's heart is a holy thing;
And Nature, through a world of death,
Breathes into him a second breath,
More searching than the breath of spring.　　1075

Upon a stone the Woman sits
In agony of silent grief—
From his own thoughts did Peter start;
He longs to press her to his heart,
From love that cannot find relief.　　　　　1080

1046 Oh woe is me, he was so stout MSS.　　　1048 . . . no sickness, knew
no pain MSS.　　　1053 pervades] is in MSS.　　　1060 Across the meadow
by the pound MSS.　　　1062 Bid Matthew (farmer MSS. 4–6) Simpson
hither come MSS.　　　1070 Poor thing, 'tis fatherless MSS.
1071–2　And now does Peter deeply feel
　　　　　The heart of man's a holy thing　MSS. 2–4
1075 Just (MSS. 2, 3) Even like the breath of spring MSS.　　　1080 find
MS. 6: give MSS. 2–5

But roused, as if through every limb
Had past a sudden shock of dread,
The Mother o'er the threshold flies,
And up the cottage stairs she hies,
And on the pillow lays her burning head.   1085

And Peter turns his steps aside
Into a shade of darksome trees,
Where he sits down, he knows not how,
With his hands pressed against his brow,
His elbows on his tremulous knees.   1090

There, self-involved, does Peter sit
Until no sign of life he makes,
As if his mind were sinking deep
Through years that have been long asleep!
The trance is passed away—he wakes;   1095

He lifts his head—and sees the Ass
Yet standing in the clear moonshine;
"When shall I be as good as thou?
Oh! would, poor beast, that I had now
A heart but half as good as thine!"   1100

But *He*—who deviously hath sought
His Father through the lonesome woods,
Hath sought, proclaiming to the ear
Of night his grief and sorrowful fear—
He comes, escaped from fields and floods;—   1105

1081-2   At last upspringing from her seat
             As with a sudden fear and dread   MSS.
1085 *so* 1836: And flings herself upon the bed   MSS.
             And to the pillow gives her burning head   1819-32
1087 darksome] alder MSS.
1090 *so* 1827: And his head fix'd between his knees   MSS.
             And resting on his tremulous knees   1819-20
1091-2 In silence there . . . Not any . . . MSS.   1095 At last as from a
trance MSS.   1096 lifts 1827: turns MSS., 1819-20
1101-6   But hark! that doleful cry again
             'Tis travelling up the woody slope,
             Once more while Peter hears the sound
             With stifling pain his heart is bound.
             He feels like one that has no hope.

With weary pace is drawing nigh;
He sees the Ass—and nothing living
Had ever such a fit of joy
As hath this little orphan Boy,
For he has no misgiving!   1110

Forth to the gentle Ass he springs,
And up about his neck he climbs;
In loving words he talks to him,
He kisses, kisses face and limb,—
He kisses him a thousand times!   1115

This Peter sees, while in the shade
He stood beside the cottage-door;
And Peter Bell, the ruffian wild,
Sobs loud, he sobs even like a child,
"Oh! God, I can endure no more!"   1120

—Here ends my Tale: for in a trice
Arrived a neighbour with his horse;
Peter went forth with him straightway;
And, with due care, ere break of day,
Together they brought back the Corse.   1125

And many years did this poor Ass,
Whom once it was my luck to see
Cropping the shrubs of Leming-Lane,
Help by his labour to maintain
The Widow and her family.   1130

And Peter Bell, who, till that night,
Had been the wildest of his clan,
Forsook his crimes, renounced his folly,
And, after ten months' melancholy,
Became a good and honest man.   1135

'Tis little Robin he who sought
His father with such grief and pain
And after many perils past
Has found his way safe home at last
And now is coming up the lane.
He's coming towards the door, and now   MSS.
1104 *so* 1836: Of night his inward grief and fear MSS., 1819–32   1111
Forth to 1836: Towards MSS., 1819–32   1122 Came Matthew (Farmer
MSS. 4–6) Simpson with his horse MSS.   1123 went forth] set out
MSS.   1124 And two hours ere the break of day MSS.   1128 Not many
miles from MSS.   1133 renounced 1832; forsook MSS; repressed 1819–27

PREFACES

ETC., ETC.

MUCH the greatest part of the foregoing Poems has been so long before the Public that no prefatory matter, explanatory of any portion of them, or of the arrangement which has been adopted, appears to be required; and had it not been for the observations contained in those Prefaces upon the principles of Poetry in general they would not have been reprinted even in an Appendix in this Edition.—W. W. 1849–50.

ADVERTISEMENT[1]

TO THE LYRICAL BALLADS, 1798

It is the honourable characteristic of Poetry that its materials are to be found in every subject which can interest the human mind. The evidence of this fact is to be sought, not in the writings of Critics, but in those of Poets themselves.

The majority of the following poems are to be considered as experiments. They were written chiefly with a view to ascertain how far the language of conversation in the middle and lower classes of society is adapted to the purposes of poetic pleasure. Readers accustomed to the gaudiness and inane phraseology of many modern writers, if they persist in reading this book to its conclusion, will perhaps frequently have to struggle with feelings of strangeness and aukwardness: they will look round for poetry, and will be induced to enquire by what species of courtesy these attempts can be permitted to assume that title. It is desirable that such readers, for their own sakes, should not suffer the solitary word Poetry, a word of very disputed meaning, to stand in the way of their gratification; but that, while they are perusing this book, they should ask themselves if it contains a natural delineation of human passions, human characters, and human incidents; and if the answer be favourable to the author's wishes, that they should consent to be pleased in spite of that most dreadful enemy to our pleasures, our own pre-established codes of decision.

Readers of superior judgment may disapprove of the style in which many of these pieces are executed; it must be expected that many lines and phrases will not exactly suit their taste. It will perhaps appear to them, that wishing to avoid the prevalent fault of the day, the author has sometimes descended too low, and that many of his expressions are too familiar, and not of sufficient dignity. It is apprehended, that the more conversant the reader is with our elder

[1] This "Advertisement" was never reprinted by W. It is placed here, rather than in my Appendix, for the reader's convenience.

writers, and with those in modern times who have been the most successful in painting manners and passions, the fewer complaints of this kind will he have to make.

An accurate taste in poetry, and in all the other arts, Sir Joshua Reynolds has observed, is an acquired talent, which can only be produced by severe thought, and a long continued intercourse with the best models of composition. This is mentioned not with so ridiculous a purpose as to prevent the most inexperienced reader from judging for himself; but merely to temper the rashness of decision, and to suggest that if poetry be a subject on which much time has not been bestowed, the judgment may be erroneous, and that in most cases it necessarily will be so.

The tale of Goody Blake and Harry Gill is founded on a well-authenticated fact which happened in Warwickshire. Of the other poems in the collection it may be proper to say that they are either absolute inventions of the author, or facts which took place within his personal observation or that of his friends. The poem of the Thorn, as the reader will soon discover, is not supposed to be spoken in the author's own person: the character of the loquacious narrator will sufficiently shew itself in the course of the story. The Rime of the Ancyent Marinere was professedly written in imitation of the *style*, as well as of the spirit of the elder poets; but with a few exceptions the Author believes that the language adopted in it has been equally intelligible for these three last centuries. The lines entitled Expostulation and Reply, and those which follow, arose out of conversation with a friend who was somewhat unreasonably attached to modern books of moral philosophy.

PREFACE TO THE SECOND EDITION OF SEVERAL OF THE FOREGOING POEMS, PUBLISHED, WITH AN ADDITIONAL VOLUME, UNDER THE TITLE OF "LYRICAL BALLADS"

[*Note*.—In succeeding Editions, when the Collection was much enlarged and diversified, this Preface was transferred to the end of the Volumes as having little of a special application to their contents.]

THE first Volume of these Poems has already been submitted to general perusal. It was published, as an experiment, which, I hoped, might be of some use to ascertain, how far, by fitting to metrical arrangement a selection of the real language of men in a state of vivid sensation, that sort of pleasure and that quantity of pleasure may be imparted, which a Poet may rationally endeavour to impart.

I had formed no very inaccurate estimate of the probable effect of those Poems: I flattered myself that they who should be pleased with them would read them with more than common pleasure: and, on the other hand, I was well aware, that by those who should dislike them, they would be read with more than common dislike. The result has differed from my expectation in this only, that a greater number have been pleased[1] than I ventured to hope I should please.[2]

.   .   .   .

Several of my Friends are anxious for the success of these Poems, from a belief, that, if the views with which they were composed were indeed realised, a class of Poetry would be produced, well adapted to interest mankind permanently, and not unimportant in the quality, and in the multiplicity of its moral relations: and on this account they have advised me to prefix a systematic defence of the theory upon which the Poems were written. But I was unwilling to undertake the task, knowing that on this occasion the Reader would look coldly upon my arguments, since I might be suspected of having been principally influenced by the selfish and foolish hope of *reasoning* him into an approbation of these particular Poems: and I was still more unwilling to undertake the task, because, adequately to display the opinions, and fully to enforce the arguments, would require a space wholly disproportionate to a preface. For, to treat the subject with the clearness and coherence of which it is susceptible, it would be necessary to give a full account of the present state of the public taste in this country, and to determine how far this taste is healthy or depraved; which, again, could not be determined, without pointing out in what manner language and the human mind act and re-act on each other, and without retracing the revolutions, not of literature alone, but likewise of society itself. I have therefore altogether declined to enter regularly upon this defence; yet I am sensible, that there would be something like impropriety in abruptly obtruding upon the Public, without a few words of introduction, Poems so materially different from those upon which general approbation is at present bestowed.

It is supposed, that by the act of writing in verse an Author makes a formal engagement that he will gratify certain known habits of association; that he not only thus apprises the Reader that certain classes of ideas and expressions will be found in his book, but that

---

[1] *so* 1836: 1 have pleased a greater number 1800–32 (*so throughout, edd.* 1800–32, *generally have first person for third*)

[2] please./Several] For the sake of variety and from a consciousness of my own weakness I was induced to request the assistance of a Friend, who furnished me with the Poems of the ANCIENT MARINER, the FOSTER-MOTHER'S TALE, the NIGHTINGALE, the DUNGEON, and the Poem entitled LOVE. I should not, however, have requested this assistance, had I not believed that the poems of my Friend would in a great measure have the same tendency as my own, and that, though there would be found a difference, there would be found no discordance in the colours of our style; as our opinions on the subject of poetry do almost entirely coincide. 1800–5; *but* 1802–5 *omit* the DUNGEON.

others will be carefully excluded. This exponent or symbol held forth by metrical language must in different eras of literature have excited very different expectations: for example, in the age of Catullus, Terence, and Lucretius, and that of Statius or Claudian; and in our own country, in the age of Shakspeare and Beaumont and Fletcher, and that of Donne and Cowley, or Dryden, or Pope. I will not take upon me to determine the exact import of the promise which, by the act of writing in verse, an Author in the present day makes to his reader: but it will undoubtedly appear to many persons that I have not fulfilled the terms of an engagement thus voluntarily contracted. They[1] who have been accustomed to the gaudiness and inane phraseology of many modern writers, if they persist in reading this book to its conclusion, will, no doubt, frequently have to struggle with feelings of strangeness and awkwardness: they will look round for poetry, and will be induced to inquire by what species of courtesy these attempts can be permitted to assume that title.[1] I hope therefore the reader will not censure me for attempting to state what I have proposed to myself to perform; and also (as far as the limits of a preface will permit) to explain some of the chief reasons which have determined me in the choice of my purpose: that at least he may be spared any unpleasant feeling of disappointment, and that I myself may be protected from one of the most dishonourable accusations which can be brought against an Author; namely, that of an indolence which prevents him from endeavouring to ascertain what is his duty, or, when his duty is ascertained, prevents him from performing it.

The principal object, then, proposed in these Poems was[2] to choose incidents and situations from common life, and to relate or describe them, throughout, as far as was possible in a selection of language really used by men, and, at the same time, to throw over them a certain colouring of imagination, whereby ordinary things should be presented to the mind in an unusual aspect; and, further, and above all, to make these incidents and situations[2] interesting by tracing in them, truly though not ostentatiously, the primary laws of our nature: chiefly, as far as regards the manner in which we associate ideas in a state of excitement. Humble[3] and rustic life was generally chosen, because, in that condition[4], the essential passions of the heart find a better soil in which they can attain their maturity, are less under restraint, and speak a plainer and more emphatic language; because in that condition of life our elementary feelings co-exist[5] in a state of greater simplicity, and consequently, may be more

---

[1] They who have ... title: *not in* 1800

[2] to choose ... to make these incidents and situations 1802: to make the accidents of common life 1800

[3] Humble 1832: Low 1800–27

[4] condition 1836: situation 1800–32   [5] coexist 1802: exist 1800

accurately contemplated, and more forcibly communicated; because
the manners of rural life germinate from those elementary feelings,
and, from the necessary character of rural occupations, are more
easily comprehended, and are more durable; and, lastly, because in
that condition the passions of men are incorporated with the beautiful and permanent forms of nature. The language, too, of these men
has been adopted (purified indeed from what appear to be its real
defects, from all lasting and rational causes of dislike or disgust)
because such men hourly communicate with the best objects from
which the best part of language is originally derived; and because,
from their rank in society and the sameness and narrow circle of their
intercourse, being less under the influence[1] of social vanity, they
convey their feelings and notions in simple and unelaborated expressions. Accordingly, such a language, arising out of repeated experience and regular feelings, is a more permanent, and a far more
philosophical language, than that which is frequently substituted for
it by Poets, who think that they are conferring honour upon themselves and their art, in proportion as they separate themselves from
the sympathies of men, and indulge in arbitrary and capricious habits
of expression, in order to furnish food for fickle tastes, and fickle
appetites, of their own creation.[2]

I cannot, however, be insensible to the present outcry against the
triviality and meanness, both of thought and language, which some
of my contemporaries have occasionally introduced into their metrical
compositions; and I acknowledge that this defect, where it exists, is
more dishonourable to the Writer's own character than false refinement or arbitrary innovation, though I should contend at the same
time, that it is far less pernicious in the sum of its consequences.
From such verses the Poems in these volumes will be found distinguished at least by one mark of difference, that each of them has
a worthy *purpose*. Not that I[3] always began to write with a distinct
purpose formally conceived; but habits of meditation have, I trust,
so prompted and regulated my feelings,[4] that my descriptions of such
objects as strongly excite those feelings, will be found to carry along
with them a *purpose*. If this opinion be erroneous, I can have little
right to the name of a Poet. For all good poetry is the spontaneous
overflow of powerful feelings: and though this be true, Poems to which
any value can be attached were never produced on any variety of
subjects but by a man who, being possessed of more than usual

[1] influence 1802: action 1800
[2] It is worth while here to observe, that the affecting parts of Chaucer are
almost always expressed in language pure and universally intelligible even
to this day.—W. W.
[3] *so* 1836: Not that I mean to say, I 1800–32
[4] *so* 1836: but I believe that my habits of meditation have so formed my
feelings, as 1800–32

organic sensibility, had also thought long and deeply. For our continued influxes of feeling are modified and directed by our thoughts, which are indeed the representatives of all our past feelings; and, as by contemplating the relation of these general representatives to each other, we discover what is really important to men, so, by the repetition and continuance of this act, our feelings will be connected with important subjects, till at length, if we be originally possessed of much sensibility, such habits of mind will be produced, that, by obeying blindly and mechanically the impulses of those habits, we shall describe objects, and utter sentiments, of such a nature, and in such connection with each other, that the understanding of the Reader must necessarily be in some degree enlightened, and his affections strengthened and purified.

It[1] has been said that each of these poems has a purpose. Another circumstance must be mentioned which distinguishes these Poems from the popular Poetry of the day; it is this, that the feeling therein

---

[1] It has been said . . . feeling *so* 1845: I have said that each of these poems has a purpose. I have also informed my Reader what this purpose will be found principally to be: namely to illustrate the manner in which our feelings and ideas are associated in a state of excitement. But speaking in less general language [language somewhat more appropriate 1802–36], it is to follow the fluxes and refluxes of the mind when agitated by the great and simple affections of our nature. This object I have endeavoured in these short essays to attain by various means; by tracing the maternal passion through many of its more subtle windings, as in the poems of the IDIOT BOY and the MAD MOTHER; by accompanying the last struggles of a human being at the approach of death, cleaving in solitude to life and society, as in the Poem of the FORSAKEN INDIAN; by shewing, as in the stanzas entitled WE ARE SEVEN, the perplexity and obscurity which in childhood attend our notion of death, or rather our utter inability to admit that notion; or by displaying the strength of fraternal, or to speak more philosophically, of moral attachment when early associated with the great and beautiful objects of nature, as in THE BROTHERS; or, as in the Incident of SIMON LEE, by placing my Reader in the way of receiving from ordinary moral sensations another and more salutary impression than we are accustomed to receive from them. It has also been part of my general purpose to attempt to sketch characters under the influence of less impassioned feelings, as in the OLD MAN TRAVELLING, THE TWO THIEVES, &c., characters of which the elements are simple, belonging rather to nature than to manners, such as exist now and will probably always exist, and which from their constitution may be distinctly and profitably contemplated. I will not abuse the indulgence of my Reader by dwelling longer upon this subject; but it is proper that I should mention another circumstance . . . feeling. My meaning will be rendered perfectly intelligible by referring my Reader to the Poems entitled POOR SUSAN and the CHILDLESS FATHER, particularly the last stanza of the latter Poem. 1800–32. *So* 1836, *but with third person for first, and for* MAD MOTHER *W. writes* and the one beginning "Her eyes are wild".

developed gives importance to the action and situation, and not the action and situation to the feeling.[1]

A sense of false modesty[2] shall not prevent me from asserting, that the Reader's attention is pointed to this mark of distinction, far less for the sake of these particular Poems than from the general importance of the subject. The subject is indeed important! For the human mind is capable of being excited[3] without the application of gross and violent stimulants; and he must have a very faint perception of its beauty and dignity who does not know this, and who does not further know, that one being is elevated above another, in proportion as he possesses this capability. It has therefore appeared to me, that to endeavour to produce or enlarge this capability is one of the best services in which, at any period, a Writer can be engaged; but this service, excellent at all times, is especially so at the present day. For a multitude of causes, unknown to former times, are now acting with a combined force to blunt the discriminating powers of the mind, and, unfitting it for all voluntary exertion, to reduce it to a state of almost savage torpor. The most effective of these causes are the great national events which are daily taking place, and the increasing accumulation of men in cities, where the uniformity of their occupations produces a craving for extraordinary incident, which the rapid communication of intelligence hourly gratifies. To this tendency of life and manners the literature and theatrical exhibitions of the country have conformed themselves. The invaluable works of our elder writers, I had almost said the works of Shakspeare and Milton, are driven into neglect by frantic novels, sickly and stupid German Tragedies, and deluges of idle and extravagant stories in verse.— When I think upon this degrading thirst after outrageous stimulation I am almost ashamed to have spoken of the feeble endeavour made in these volumes to counteract it; and, reflecting upon the magnitude of the general evil, I should be oppressed with no dishonourable melancholy, had I not a deep impression of certain inherent and indestructible qualities of the human mind, and likewise of certain powers in the great and permanent objects that act upon it, which are equally inherent and indestructible; and were there not added to this impression a belief, that the time is approaching when the evil will be systematically opposed, by men of greater powers, and with far more distinguished success.

Having dwelt thus long on the subjects and aim of these Poems, I shall request the Reader's permission to apprise him of a few circumstances relating to their *style*, in order, among other reasons, that he may not censure me for not having performed what I never

---

[1] See footnote, p. 388.

[2] A sense of false modesty . . . pointed to *so* 1805: I will not suffer a sense of false modesty to prevent me from asserting, that I point my Reader's attention to 1800–2.   [3] being excited *so* 1800–2: excitement 1805

attempted. The Reader[1] will find that personifications of abstract ideas rarely occur in these volumes; and are utterly rejected, as an ordinary device to elevate the style, and raise it above prose. My purpose was to imitate, and, as far as is possible, to adopt the very language of men; and assuredly such personifications do not make any natural or regular part of that language. They are, indeed, a figure of speech occasionally prompted by passion, and I have made use of them as such; but have endeavoured utterly to reject them as a mechanical device of style, or as a family language which Writers in metre seem to lay claim to by prescription.[1] I have wished to keep the Reader in the company of flesh and blood, persuaded that by so doing I shall interest him. Others who pursue a different track will interest him likewise; I do not interfere with their claim, but wish to prefer a claim of my own. There will also be found in these volumes little of what is usually called poetic diction; as much pains has been taken to avoid it as is ordinarily taken to produce it; this has been done for the reason already alleged, to bring my language near to the language of men; and further, because the pleasure which I have proposed to myself to impart, is of a kind very different from that which is supposed by many persons to be the proper object of poetry. Without being culpably particular, I do not know how to give my Reader a more exact notion of the style in which it was my wish and intention to write, than by informing him that I have at all times endeavoured to look steadily at my subject; consequently, there is I hope in these Poems little falsehood of description, and my ideas are expressed in language fitted to their respective importance. Something must have been gained by this practice, as it is friendly to one property of all good poetry, namely, good sense: but it has necessarily cut me off from a large portion of phrases and figures of speech which from father to son have long been regarded as the common inheritance of Poets. I have also thought it expedient to restrict myself still further, having abstained from the use of many expressions, in themselves proper and beautiful, but which have been foolishly repeated by bad Poets, till such feelings of disgust are connected with them as it is scarcely possible by any art of association to overpower.

If in a poem there should be found a series of lines, or even a single line, in which the language, though naturally arranged, and according to the strict laws of metre, does not differ from that of prose, there is a numerous class of critics, who, when they stumble upon these

---

[1] The Reader . . . prescription *so* 1802: Except in a very few instances tho Reader will find no personifications of abstract ideas in these volumes, not that I mean to censure such personifications; they may well be fitted for certain sorts of composition, but in these Poems I propose to myself to imitate, and, as far as possible, to adopt the very language of men, and I do not find that such personifications make any regular or natural part of that language. 1800

prosaisms, as they call them, imagine that they have made a notable discovery, and exult over the Poet as over a man ignorant of his own profession. Now these men would establish a canon of criticism which the Reader will conclude he must utterly reject, if he wishes to be pleased with these volumes. And it would be a most easy task to prove to him, that not only the language of a large portion of every good poem, even of the most elevated character, must necessarily, except with reference to the metre, in no respect differ from that of good prose, but likewise that some of the most interesting parts of the best poems will be found to be strictly the language of prose when prose is well written. The truth of this assertion might be demonstrated by innumerable passages from almost all the poetical writings, even of Milton himself. To illustrate[1] the subject in a general manner, I will here adduce a short composition of Gray, who was at the head of those who, by their reasonings, have attempted to widen the space of separation betwixt Prose and Metrical composition, and was more than any other man curiously elaborate in the structure of his own poetic diction.

> "In vain to me the smiling mornings shine,
> And reddening Phoebus lifts his golden fire:
> The birds in vain their amorous descant join,
> Or cheerful fields resume their green attire.
> These ears, alas! for other notes repine;
> *A different object do these eyes require;*
> *My lonely anguish melts no heart but mine;*
> *And in my breast the imperfect joys expire;*
> Yet morning smiles the busy race to cheer,
> And new-born pleasure brings to happier men;
> The fields to all their wonted tribute bear;
> To warm their little loves the birds complain.
> *I fruitless mourn to him that cannot hear,*
> *And weep the more because I weep in vain.*"

It will easily be perceived, that the only part of this Sonnet which is of any value is the lines printed in Italics; it is equally obvious, that, except in the rhyme, and in the use of the single word "fruitless" for fruitlessly, which is so far a defect, the language of these lines does in no respect differ from that of prose.

By the foregoing[2] quotation it has been shown that the language of Prose may yet be well adapted to Poetry; and it was previously asserted, that a large portion of the language of every good poem can in no respect differ from that of good Prose. We will go further.

[1] To illustrate *so* 1836: I have not space for much quotation, but to illustrate 1800–32

[2] By the foregoing . . . composition *so* 1802: Is there then, it will be asked, no essential difference between the language of prose and metrical composition? I answer that there neither is nor can be any essential difference. 1800

It may be safely affirmed, that there neither is, nor can be, any *essential* difference between the language of prose and metrical composition.[1] We are fond of tracing the resemblance between Poetry and Painting, and, accordingly, we call them Sisters: but where shall we find bonds of connection sufficiently strict to typify the affinity betwixt metrical and prose composition ? They both speak by and to the same organs ; the bodies in which both of them are clothed may be said to be of the same substance, their affections are kindred, and almost identical, not necessarily differing even in degree ; Poetry[2] sheds no tears "such as Angels weep",[3] but natural and human tears ; she can boast of no celestial ichor that distinguishes her vital juices from those of prose ; the same human blood circulates through the veins of them both.

If it be affirmed that rhyme and metrical arrangement of themselves constitute a distinction which overturns what has just been said on the strict affinity of metrical language with that of prose, and paves the way for other artificial[4] distinctions which the mind voluntarily admits, I answer[5] that the language of such Poetry as is here recommended is, as far as is possible, a selection of the language really spoken by men ; that this selection, wherever it is made with true taste and feeling, will of itself form a distinction far greater than would at first be imagined, and will entirely separate the composition from the vulgarity and meanness of ordinary life ; and, if metre be superadded thereto, I believe that a dissimilitude will be produced altogether sufficient for the gratification of a rational mind. What other distinction would we have ? Whence is it to come ? And where is it to exist ? Not, surely, where the Poet speaks through the mouths of his characters: it cannot be necessary here, either for elevation of style, or any of its supposed ornaments: for, if the Poet's subject be judiciously chosen, it will naturally, and upon fit occasion, lead him to passions the language of which, if selected truly and judiciously, must necessarily be dignified and variegated, and alive with metaphors and figures. I forbear to speak of an incongruity which would shock the intelligent Reader, should the Poet inter-

---

[1] See footnote 2, page 391.

[2] I here use the word "Poetry" (though against my own judgment) as opposed to the word Prose, and synonymous with metrical composition. But much confusion has been introduced into criticism by this contradistinction of Poetry and Prose, instead of the more philosophical one of Poetry and Matter of Fact, or Science. The only strict antithesis to Prose is Metre ; nor is this, in truth, a *strict* antithesis, because lines and passages of metre so naturally occur in writing prose. that it would be scarcely possible to avoid them, even were it desirable. W. W. footnote 1802 ; 1800 *stops at* Metre.

[3] *Paradise Lost*, i. 619   [4] artificial *not in* 1800

[5] *The whole passage from* I answer *to* remind the reader *on p.* 398 (*middle*) *was added in* 1802

weave any foreign splendour of his own with that which the passion naturally suggests: it is sufficient to say that such addition is unnecessary. And, surely, it is more probable that those passages, which with propriety abound with metaphors and figures, will have their due effect, if, upon other occasions where the passions are of a milder character, the style also be subdued and temperate.

But, as the pleasure which I hope to give by the Poems now presented to the Reader must depend entirely on just notions upon this subject, and, as it is in itself of high importance to our taste and moral feelings, I cannot content myself with these detached remarks. And if, in what I am about to say, it shall appear to some that my labour is unnecessary, and that I am like a man fighting a battle without enemies, such persons may be reminded, that, whatever be the language outwardly holden by men, a practical faith in the opinions which I am wishing to establish is almost unknown. If my conclusions are admitted, and carried as far as they must be carried if admitted at all, our judgments concerning the works of the greatest Poets both ancient and modern will be far different from what they are at present, both when we praise, and when we censure: and our moral feelings influencing and influenced by these judgments will, I believe, be corrected and purified.

Taking up the subject, then, upon general grounds, let me ask, what is meant by the word Poet ? What is a Poet ? To whom does he address himself ? And what language is to be expected from him ?— He is a man speaking to men: a man, it is true, endowed[1] with more lively sensibility, more enthusiasm and tenderness, who has a greater knowledge of human nature, and a more comprehensive soul, than are supposed to be common among mankind ; a man pleased with his own passions and volitions, and who rejoices more than other men in the spirit of life that is in him ; delighting to contemplate similar volitions and passions as manifested in the goings-on of the Universe, and habitually impelled to create them where he does not find them. To these qualities he has added a disposition to be affected more than other men by absent things as if they were present ; an ability of conjuring up in himself passions, which are indeed far from being the same as those produced by real events, yet (especially in those parts of the general sympathy which are pleasing and delightful) do more nearly resemble the passions produced by real events, than anything which, from the motions of their own minds merely, other men are accustomed to feel in themselves:—whence, and from practice, he has acquired a greater readiness and power in expressing what he thinks and feels, and especially those thoughts and feelings which, by his own choice, or from the structure of his own mind, arise in him without immediate external excitement.

[1] endowed 1836: endued 1802–32

But whatever portion of this faculty we may suppose even the greatest Poet to possess, there cannot be a doubt that[1] the language which it will suggest to him must often, in liveliness and truth, fall short of that which is uttered by men in real life, under the actual pressure of those passions, certain shadows of which the Poet thus produces, or feels to be produced, in himself.

However exalted a notion we would wish to cherish of the character of a Poet, it is obvious, that while he describes and imitates passions, his employment is in some degree mechanical,[2] compared with the freedom and power of real and substantial action and suffering. So that it will be the wish of the Poet to bring his feelings near to those of the persons whose feelings he describes, nay, for short spaces of time, perhaps, to let himself slip into an entire delusion, and even confound and identify his own feelings with theirs; modifying only the language which is thus suggested to him by a consideration that he describes for a particular purpose, that of giving pleasure. Here, then, he will apply the principle of selection which has been already insisted upon. He will depend upon this for removing what would otherwise be painful or disgusting in the passion; he will feel that there is no necessity to trick out or to elevate nature: and, the more industriously he applies this principle, the deeper will be his faith that no words, which *his* fancy or imagination can suggest, will be to be compared with those which are the emanations of reality and truth.

But it may be said by those who do not object to the general spirit of these remarks, that, as it is impossible for the Poet to produce upon all occasions language as exquisitely fitted for the passion as that which the real passion itself suggests, it is proper that he should consider himself as in the situation of a translator, who does not scruple to substitute[3] excellencies of another kind for those which are unattainable by him; and endeavours occasionally to surpass his original, in order to make some amends for the general inferiority to which he feels that he must submit. But this would be to encourage idleness and unmanly despair. Further, it is the language of men who speak of what they do not understand; who talk of Poetry as of a matter of amusement and idle pleasure; who will converse with us as gravely about a *taste* for Poetry, as they express it, as if it were a thing as indifferent as a taste for rope-dancing, or Frontiniac or Sherry. Aristotle, I have been told, has said, that Poetry is the most philosophic of all writing: it is so: its object is truth, not individual and local, but general, and operative; not standing upon external

---

[1] that 1836: but that 1802-32

[2] *so* 1845: his situation is altogether slavish and mechanical 1802-32: 1836 *omits* altogether

[3] does not ... substitute 1836: deems himself justified when he substitutes 1802-32

testimony, but carried alive into the heart by passion;[1] truth which is its own testimony, which gives competence and confidence[2] to the tribunal to which it appeals, and receives them from the same tribunal. Poetry is the image of man and nature. The obstacles which stand in the way of the fidelity of the Biographer and Historian, and of their consequent utility, are incalculably greater than those which are to be encountered by the Poet who comprehends[3] the dignity of his art. The Poet writes under one restriction only, namely, the necessity of giving immediate pleasure to a human Being possessed of that information which may be expected from him, not as a lawyer, a physician, a mariner, an astronomer, or a natural philosopher, but as a Man. Except this one restriction, there is no object standing between the Poet and the image of things; between this, and the Biographer and Historian, there are a thousand.

Nor let this necessity of producing immediate pleasure be considered as a degradation of the Poet's art. It is far otherwise. It is an acknowledgment of the beauty of the universe, an acknowledgment the more sincere, because not formal, but indirect; it is a task light and easy to him who looks at the world in the spirit of love: further, it is a homage paid to the native and naked dignity of man, to the grand elementary principle of pleasure, by which he knows, and feels, and lives, and moves. We have no sympathy but what is propagated by pleasure: I would not be misunderstood; but wherever we sympathise with pain, it will be found that the sympathy is produced and carried on by subtle combinations with pleasure. We have no knowledge, that is, no general principles drawn from the contemplation of particular facts, but what has been built up by pleasure, and exists in us by pleasure alone. The Man of science, the Chemist and Mathematician, whatever difficulties and disgusts they may have had to struggle with, know and feel this. However painful may be the objects with which the Anatomist's knowledge is connected, he feels that his knowledge is pleasure; and where he has no pleasure he has no knowledge. What then does the Poet ? He considers man and the objects that surround him as acting and re-acting upon each other, so as to produce an infinite complexity of pain and pleasure; he considers man in his own nature and in his ordinary life as contemplating this with a certain quantity of immediate knowledge, with certain convictions, intuitions, and deductions, which from habit acquire the quality of intuitions; he considers him as looking upon this complex scene of ideas and sensations, and finding everywhere

---

[1] its object is truth . . . passion: Cf. Davenant's prefatory letter to *Gondibert*: "Truth narrative and past is the idol of historians, (who worship a dead thing), and truth operative, and by effects continually alive, is the mistress of poets."

[2] competence and confidence 1836: strength and divinity 1802–32

[3] comprehends 1836: has an adequate notion of 1802–32

objects that immediately excite in him sympathies which, from the necessities of his nature, are accompanied by an overbalance of enjoyment.

To this knowledge which all men carry about with them, and to these sympathies in which, without any other discipline than that of our daily life, we are fitted to take delight, the Poet principally directs his attention. He considers man and nature as essentially adapted to each other, and the mind of man as naturally the mirror of the fairest and most interesting properties[1] of nature. And thus the Poet, prompted by this feeling of pleasure, which accompanies him through the whole course of his studies, converses with general nature, with affections akin to those, which, through labour and length of time, the Man of science has raised up in himself, by conversing with those particular parts of nature which are the objects of his studies. The knowledge both of the Poet and the Man of science is pleasure; but the knowledge of the one cleaves to us as a necessary part of our existence, our natural and unalienable inheritance; the other is a personal and individual acquisition, slow to come to us, and by no habitual and direct sympathy connecting us with our fellow-beings. The Man of science seeks truth as a remote and unknown benefactor; he cherishes and loves it in his solitude: the Poet, singing a song in which all human beings join with him, rejoices in the presence of truth as our visible friend and hourly companion. Poetry is the breath and finer spirit of all knowledge; it is the impassioned expression which is in the countenance of all Science. Emphatically may it be said of the Poet, as Shakspeare hath said of man, "that he looks before and after."[2] He is the rock of defence for human nature; an upholder and preserver, carrying everywhere with him relationship and love. In spite of difference of soil and climate, of language and manners, of laws and customs: in spite of things silently gone out of mind, and things violently destroyed; the Poet binds together by passion and knowledge the vast empire of human society, as it is spread over the whole earth, and over all time. The objects of the Poet's thoughts are everywhere; though the eyes and senses of man are, it is true, his favourite guides, yet he will follow wheresoever he can find an atmosphere of sensation in which to move his wings. Poetry is the first and last of all knowledge—it is as immortal as the heart of man. If the labours of Men of science should ever create any material revolution, direct or indirect, in our condition, and in the impressions which we habitually receive, the Poet will sleep then no more than at present; he will be ready to follow the steps of the Man of science, not only in those general indirect effects, but he will be at his side, carrying sensation into the midst of the objects of the science itself. The remotest discoveries of the Chemist, the Botanist, or

[1] properties 1836: qualities 1802–32   [2] *Hamlet*, IV. iv. 37.

Mineralogist, will be as proper objects of the Poet's art as any upon which it can be employed, if the time should ever come when these things shall be familiar to us, and the relations under which they are contemplated by the followers of these respective sciences shall be manifestly and palpably material to us as enjoying and suffering beings. If the time should ever come when what is now called science, thus familiarised to men, shall be ready to put on, as it were, a form of flesh and blood, the Poet will lend his divine spirit to aid the transfiguration, and will welcome the Being thus produced, as a dear and genuine inmate of the household of man.—It is not, then, to be supposed that any one, who holds that sublime notion of Poetry which I have attempted to convey, will break in upon the sanctity and truth of his pictures by transitory and accidental ornaments, and endeavour to excite admiration of himself by arts, the necessity of which must manifestly depend upon the assumed meanness of his subject.

What has been thus far said applies to Poetry in general; but especially to those parts of composition where the Poet speaks through the mouths of his characters; and upon this point it appears to authorise the conclusion[1] that there are few persons of good sense, who would not allow that the dramatic parts of composition are defective, in proportion as they deviate from the real language of nature, and are coloured by a diction of the Poet's own, either peculiar to him as an individual Poet or belonging simply to Poets in general; to a body of men who, from the circumstance of their compositions being in metre, it is expected will employ a particular language.

It is not, then, in the dramatic parts of composition that we look for this distinction of language; but still it may be proper and necessary where the Poet speaks to us in his own person and character. To this I answer by referring the Reader to the description before given of a Poet. Among the qualities there enumerated as principally conducing to form a Poet, is implied nothing differing in kind from other men, but only in degree. The sum of what was said is, that the Poet is chiefly distinguished from other men by a greater promptness to think and feel without immediate external excitement, and a greater power in expressing such thoughts and feelings as are produced in him in that manner. But these passions and thoughts and feelings are the general passions and thoughts and feelings of men. And with what are they connected? Undoubtedly with our moral sentiments and animal sensations, and with the causes which excite these; with the operations of the elements, and the appearances of the visible universe; with storm and sunshine, with the revolutions of the seasons, with cold and heat, with loss of friends and kindred, with injuries and resentments, gratitude and hope, with fear and sorrow. These, and the like, are the sensations and objects which the Poet describes, as they are the sensa-

[1] authorise the conclusion 1836: have such weight that I will conclude 1802–32

tions of other men, and the objects which interest them. The Poet thinks and feels in the spirit of human passions. How, then, can his language differ in any material degree from that of all other men who feel vividly and see clearly ? It might be *proved* that it is impossible. But supposing that this were not the case, the Poet might then be allowed to use a peculiar language when expressing his feelings for his own gratification, or that of men like himself. But Poets do not write for Poets alone, but for men. Unless therefore we are advocates for that admiration which subsists[1] upon ignorance, and that pleasure which arises from hearing what we do not understand, the Poet must descend from this supposed height ; and, in order to excite rational sympathy, he must express himself as other men express themselves. To this it may be added, that while he is only selecting from the real language of men, or, which amounts to the same thing, composing accurately in the spirit of such selection, he is treading upon safe ground, and we know what we are to expect from him. Our feelings are the same with respect to metre ; for, as it may be proper to remind the Reader, the distinction of metre[2] is regular and uniform, and not, like that which is produced by what is usually called POETIC DICTION, arbitrary, and subject to infinite caprices upon which no calculation whatever can be made. In the one case, the Reader is utterly at the mercy of the Poet, respecting what imagery or diction he may choose to connect with the passion ; whereas, in the other, the metre obeys certain laws, to which the Poet and Reader both willingly submit be-cause they are certain, and because no interference is made by them with the passion, but such as the concurring testimony of ages has shown to heighten and improve the pleasure which co-exists with it.

It will now be proper to answer an obvious question, namely, Why, professing these opinions, have I written in verse ? To this, in addition to such answer as is included in what has been already said, I reply, in the first place, Because, however I may have restricted myself, there is still left open to me what confessedly constitutes the most valuable object of all writing, whether in prose or verse ; the great and universal passions of men, the most general and interesting of their occupations, and the entire world of nature before me—to supply endless combina-tions of forms and imagery. Now, supposing[3] for a moment that whatever is interesting in these objects may be as vividly described in prose, why should I be condemned for attempting to superadd to such description the charm which, by the consent of all nations, is acknow-ledged to exist in metrical language ? To this, by such as are yet un-convinced[4] it may be answered that a very small part of the pleasure given by Poetry depends upon the metre, and that it is injudicious to

[1] subsists 1836: depends 1802–32
[2] metre 1802: rhyme and metre 1800
[3] supposing 1802: granting 1800
[4] by such . . . unconvinced *not in* 1800

write in metre, unless it be accompanied with the other artificial distinctions of style with which metre is usually accompanied, and that, by such deviation, more will be lost from the shock which will thereby be given to the Reader's associations than will be counterbalanced by any pleasure which he can derive from the general power of numbers. In answer to those who still contend for the necessity of accompanying metre with certain appropriate colours of style in order to the accomplishment of its appropriate end, and who also, in my opinion, greatly underrate the power of metre in itself, it might, perhaps, as far as relates to these Volumes[1] have been almost sufficient to observe, that poems are extant, written upon more humble subjects, and in a still more naked and simple style, which have continued to give pleasure from generation to generation. Now, if nakedness and simplicity be a defect, the fact here mentioned affords a strong presumption that poems somewhat less naked and simple are capable of affording pleasure at the present day; and, what I wished *chiefly* to attempt, at present, was to justify myself for having written under the impression of this belief.

But various causes might be pointed out why, when the style is manly, and the subject of some importance, words metrically arranged will long continue to impart such a pleasure to mankind as he who proves[2] the extent of that pleasure will be desirous to impart. The end of Poetry is to produce excitement in co-existence with an overbalance of pleasure; but, by the supposition, excitement is an unusual and irregular state of the mind; ideas and feelings do not, in that state, succeed each other in accustomed order. If the words, however, by which this excitement is produced be in themselves powerful, or the images and feelings have an undue proportion of pain connected with them, there is some danger that the excitement may be carried beyond its proper bounds. Now the co-presence of something regular, something to which the mind has been accustomed in various moods[3] and in a less excited state, cannot but have great efficacy in tempering and restraining the passion by an intertexture of ordinary feeling[4], and of feeling not strictly and necessarily connected with the passion. This is unquestionably true; and hence, though the opinion will at first appear paradoxical, from the tendency of metre to divest language, in a certain degree, of its reality, and thus to throw a sort of half-consciousness of unsubstantial existence over the whole composition, there can be little doubt but that more pathetic situations and sentiments, that is, those which have a greater proportion of pain connected with them, may be endured in metrical composition, especially in rhyme, than in prose. The metre of the old ballads is very artless; yet they contain many passages which would illustrate

[1] as far . . . Volumes *not in* 1800   [2] proves 1836: is sensible of 1800–32
[3] in various moods and 1802: when in an unexcited or 1800
[4] and of . . . in them *not in* 1800

this opinion; and, I hope, if the following Poems be attentively perused, similar instances will be found in them.[1] This opinion may be
further illustrated by appealing to the Reader's own experience of the
reluctance with which he comes to the re-perusal of the distressful
parts of Clarissa Harlowe, or the Gamester;[2] while Shakspeare's
writings, in the most pathetic scenes, never act upon us, as pathetic,
beyond the bounds of pleasure—an effect which, in a much greater
degree than might at first be imagined[3] is to be ascribed to small, but
continual and regular impulses of pleasurable surprise from the
metrical arrangement.—On the other hand (what it must be allowed
will much more frequently happen) if the Poet's words should be in-
commensurate with the passion, and inadequate to raise the Reader
to a height of desirable excitement, then, (unless the Poet's choice of
his metre has been grossly injudicious) in the feelings of pleasure
which the Reader has been accustomed to connect with metre in
general, and in the feeling, whether cheerful or melancholy, which he
has been accustomed to connect with that particular movement of
metre, there will be found something which will greatly contribute to
impart passion to the words, and to effect the complex end which the
Poet proposes to himself.

If I had undertaken a SYSTEMATIC defence of the theory here maintained, it would have been my duty to develope the various causes
upon which the pleasure received from metrical language depends.
Among the chief of these causes is to be reckoned a principle which
must be well known to those who have made any of the Arts the object
of accurate reflection; namely, the pleasure which the mind derives
from the perception of similitude in dissimilitude. This principle is
the great spring of the activity of our minds, and their chief feeder.
From this principle the direction of the sexual appetite, and all the
passions connected with it, take their origin: it is the life of our
ordinary conversation; and upon the accuracy with which similitude
in dissimilitude, and dissimilitude in similitude are perceived, depend
our taste and our moral feelings. It would not be a useless employment to apply this principle to the consideration of metre, and to
show that metre is hence enabled to afford much pleasure, and to
point out in what manner that pleasure is produced. But my limits
will not permit me to enter upon this subject, and I must content
myself with a general summary.

I have said that poetry is the spontaneous overflow of powerful
feelings: it takes its origin from emotion recollected in tranquillity:
the emotion is contemplated till, by a species of re-action, the tranquillity gradually disappears, and an emotion, kindred to that which was

[1] See footnote 4, p. 399.

[2] the Gamester] A domestic tragedy by Edward Moore, first performed
in 1753 by Garrick, who contributed some passages to it.

[3] which . . . imagined 1802: which is in a great degree 1800

before the subject of contemplation, is gradually produced, and does itself actually exist in the mind. In this mood successful composition generally begins, and in a mood similar to this it is carried on ; but the emotion, of whatever kind, and in whatever degree, from various causes, is qualified by various pleasures, so that in describing any passions whatsoever, which are voluntarily described, the mind will, upon the whole, be in a state of enjoyment. If Nature be thus cautious to preserve in a state of enjoyment a being so employed, the Poet ought to profit by the lesson held forth to him, and ought especially to take care, that, whatever passions he communicates to his Reader, those passions, if his Reader's mind be sound and vigorous, should always be accompanied with an overbalance of pleasure. Now the music of harmonious metrical language, the sense of difficulty over come, and the blind association of pleasure which has been previously received from works of rhyme or metre of the same or similar construction,[1] an indistinct perception perpetually renewed of language closely resembling that of real life, and yet, in the circumstance of metre, differing from it so widely[1]—all these imperceptibly make up a complex feeling of delight, which is of the most important use in tempering the painful feeling always found intermingled with power-ful descriptions of the deeper passions. This effect is always produced in pathetic and impassioned poetry ; while, in lighter compositions, the ease and gracefulness with which the Poet manages his numbers are themselves confessedly a principal source of the gratification of the Reader. All that it is *necessary* to say, however, upon this subject, may be effected by affirming, what few persons will deny, that, of two descriptions, either of passions, manners, or characters, each of them equally well executed, the one in prose and the other in verse, the verse will be read a hundred times where the prose is read once.[2]

Having thus explained a few of my reasons for writing in verse, and why I have chosen subjects from common life, and endeavoured to bring my language near to the real language of men, if I have been too minute in pleading my own cause, I have at the same time been treating

---

[1] an . . . widely *not in* 1800

[2] once./Having] We see that Pope by the power of verse alone, has con-trived to render the plainest common sense interesting, and even frequently to invest it with the appearance of passion. In consequence of these con-victions I related in metre the Tale of GOODY BLAKE and HARRY GILL which is one of the rudest of this collection. I wished to draw attention to the truth that the power of the human imagination is sufficient to produce such changes even in our physical nature as might almost appear miraculous. The truth is an important one ; the fact (for it is a *fact*) is a valuable illustra-tion of it. And I have the satisfaction of knowing that it has been com-municated to many hundreds of people who would never have heard of it, had it not been narrated as a Ballad, and in a more impressive metre than is usual in Ballads. 1800–36

a subject of general interest; and for this reason a few words shall be added with reference solely to these particular poems, and to some defects which will probably be found in them. I am sensible that my associations must have sometimes been particular instead of general, and that, consequently, giving to things a false importance[1], I may have sometimes written upon unworthy subjects; but I am less apprehensive on this account, than that my language may frequently have suffered from those arbitrary connections of feelings and ideas with particular words and phrases, from which no man can altogether protect himself. Hence I have no doubt, that, in some instances, feelings, even of the ludicrous, may be given to my Readers by expressions which appeared to me tender and pathetic. Such faulty expressions, were I convinced they were faulty at present, and that they must necessarily continue to be so, I would willingly take all reasonable pains to correct. But it is dangerous to make these alterations on the simple authority of a few individuals, or even of certain classes of men; for where the understanding of an Author is not convinced, or his feelings altered, this cannot be done without great injury to himself: for his own feelings are his stay and support; and, if he set them aside in one instance, he may be induced to repeat this act till his mind shall lose all confidence in itself, and become utterly debilitated. To this it may be added, that the critic[2] ought never to forget that he is himself exposed to the same errors as the Poet, and, perhaps, in a much greater degree: for there can be no presumption in saying of most readers, that it is not probable they will be so well acquainted with the various stages of meaning through which words have passed, or with the fickleness or stability of the relations of particular ideas to each other; and, above all, since they are so much less interested in the subject, they may decide lightly and carelessly.

Long as the Reader has been detained, I hope he will permit me to caution him against a mode of false criticism which has been applied to Poetry, in which the language closely resembles that of life and nature. Such verses have been triumphed over in parodies, of which Dr. Johnson's stanza is a fair specimen:—

> "I put my hat upon my head
> And walked into the Strand,
> And there I met another man
> Whose hat was in his hand."

Immediately under these lines let us place one of the most justly-admired stanzas of the *Babes in the Wood*.

> "These pretty Babes with hand in hand
> Went wandering up and down;
> But never more they saw the Man
> Approaching from the Town."

[1] importance,/I: sometimes from diseased impulses 1800–32
[2] critic 1836: Reader 1800–32

In both these stanzas the words, and the order of the words, in no respect differ from the most unimpassioned conversation. There are words in both, for example, "the Strand", and "the Town", connected with none but the most familiar ideas; yet the one stanza we admit as admirable, and the other as a fair example of the superlatively contemptible. Whence arises this difference? Not from the metre, not from the language, not from the order of the words; but the *matter* expressed in Dr. Johnson's stanza is contemptible. The proper method of treating trivial and simple verses, to which Dr. Johnson's stanza would be a fair parallelism, is not to say, this is a bad kind of poetry, or, this is not poetry; but, this wants sense; it is neither interesting in itself, nor can *lead* to anything interesting; the images neither originate in that sane state of feeling which arises out of thought, nor can excite thought or feeling in the Reader. This is the only sensible manner of dealing with such verses. Why trouble yourself about the species till you have previously decided upon the genus? Why take pains to prove that an ape is not a Newton, when it is self-evident that he is not a man?[1]

One request I must make of my reader, which is, that in judging these Poems he would decide by his own feelings genuinely, and not by reflection upon what will probably be the judgment of others. How common is it to hear a person say, I myself do not object to this style of composition, or this or that expression, but, to such and such classes of people it will appear mean or ludicrous! This mode of criticism, so destructive of all sound unadulterated judgment, is almost universal: let the Reader then abide, independently, by his own feelings, and, if he finds himself affected, let him not suffer such conjectures to interfere with his pleasure.

If an Author, by any single composition, has impressed us with respect for his talents, it is useful to consider this as affording a presumption, that on other occasions where we have been displeased, he, nevertheless, may not have written ill or absurdly; and further, to give him so much credit for this one composition as may induce us to review what has displeased us, with more care than we should otherwise have bestowed upon it. This is not only an act of justice, but, in our decisions upon poetry especially, may conduce, in a high degree, to the improvement of our own taste; for an *accurate* taste in poetry[2] and in all the other arts, as Sir Joshua Reynolds has observed, is an *acquired* talent, which can only be produced by thought and a long-continued intercourse with the best models of composition. This is mentioned, not with so ridiculous a purpose as to prevent the most inexperienced Reader from judging for himself, (I have already said that I wish him to judge for himself;) but merely to temper the

[1] Cf. Pope, *Essay on Man*, ii. 34.

[2] for an *accurate* . . . *end of paragraph*] from the *Preface* to *L. B.* 1798 (*v.* p. 384).

rashness of decision, and to suggest, that, if Poetry be a subject on which much time has not been bestowed, the judgment may be erroneous; and that, in many cases, it necessarily will be so.

Nothing would, I know, have so effectually contributed to further the end which I have in view, as to have shown of what kind the pleasure is, and how that pleasure is produced, which is confessedly produced by metrical composition essentially different from that which I have here endeavoured to recommend: for the Reader will say that he has been pleased by such composition; and what more can be done for him? The power of any art is limited; and he will suspect, that, if it be proposed to furnish him with new friends, that can be only upon condition of his abandoning his old friends. Besides, as I have said, the Reader is himself conscious of the pleasure which he has received from such composition, composition to which he has peculiarly attached the endearing name of Poetry; and all men feel an habitual gratitude, and something of an honourable bigotry, for the objects which have long continued to please them: we not only wish to be pleased, but to be pleased in that particular way in which we have been accustomed to be pleased. There is in these feelings enough to resist a host of arguments; and I should be the less able to combat them successfully, as I am willing to allow, that, in order entirely to enjoy the Poetry which I am recommending, it would be necessary to give up much of what is ordinarily enjoyed. But, would my limits have permitted me to point out how this pleasure is produced, many obstacles might have been removed, and the Reader assisted in perceiving that the powers of language are not so limited as he may suppose; and that it is possible for poetry to give other enjoyments, of a purer, more lasting, and more exquisite nature. This part of the subject has not been altogether neglected, but it has not been so much my present aim to prove, that the interest excited by some other kinds of poetry is less vivid, and less worthy of the nobler powers of the mind, as to offer reasons for presuming, that if my purpose were fulfilled, a species of poetry would be produced, which is genuine poetry; in its nature well adapted to interest mankind permanently, and likewise important in the multiplicity and quality of its moral relations.

From what has been said, and from a perusal of the Poems, the Reader will be able clearly to perceive the object which I had in view: he will determine how far it has been attained; and, what is a much more important question, whether it be worth attaining: and upon the decision of these two questions will rest my claim to the approbation of the Public.

APPENDIX[1]

See page 398—"by what is usually called POETIC DICTION".

PERHAPS, as I have no right to expect that attentive perusal, without which, confined, as I have been, to the narrow limits of a preface, my meaning cannot be thoroughly understood, I am anxious to give an exact notion of the sense in which the phrase poetic diction has been used; and for this purpose, a few words shall here be added, concerning the origin and characteristics of the phraseology, which I have condemned under that name.

The earliest poets of all nations generally wrote from passion excited by real events; they wrote naturally, and as men: feeling powerfully as they did, their language was daring, and figurative. In succeeding times, Poets, and Men ambitious of the fame of Poets, perceiving the influence of such language, and desirous of producing the same effect without being animated by the same passion,[2] set themselves to a mechanical adoption of these figures of speech, and made use of them, sometimes with propriety, but much more frequently applied them to feelings and thoughts[3] with which they had no natural connection whatsoever. A language was thus insensibly produced, differing materially from the real language of men in *any situation*. The Reader or Hearer of this distorted language found himself in a perturbed and unusual state of mind: when affected by the genuine language of passion he had been in a perturbed and unusual state of mind also: in both cases he was willing that his common judgment and understanding should be laid asleep, and he had no instinctive and infallible perception of the true to make him reject the false; the one served as a passport for the other. The emotion[4] was in both cases delightful, and no wonder if he confounded the one with the other, and believed them both to be produced by the same, or similar causes. Besides, the Poet spake to him in the character of a man to be looked up to, a man of genius and authority. Thus, and from a variety of other causes, this distorted language was received with admiration; and Poets, it is probable, who had before contented themselves for the most part with misapplying only expressions which at first had been dictated by real passion, carried the abuse still further, and introduced phrases composed apparently in the spirit of the original figurative language of passion, yet altogether of their own invention, and characterised[5] by various degrees of wanton deviation from good sense and nature.

It is indeed true, that the language of the earliest Poets was felt to differ materially from ordinary language, because it was the language

[1] APPENDIX. *not in* 1800
[2] *so* 1836: without having the same animating passion 1802–32
[3] thoughts 1836: ideas 1802–32
[4] emotion 1836: agitation and confusion of mind 1802–32
[5] characterised 1836: distinguished 1802–32

of extraordinary occasions; but it was really spoken by men, language which the Poet himself had uttered when he had been affected by the events which he described, or which he had heard uttered by those around him. To this language it is probable that metre of some sort or other was early superadded. This separated the genuine language of Poetry still further from common life, so that whoever read or heard the poems of these earliest Poets felt himself moved in a way in which he had not been accustomed to be moved in real life, and by causes manifestly different from those which acted upon him in real life. This was the great temptation to all the corruptions which have followed: under the protection of this feeling succeeding Poets constructed a phraseology which had one thing, it is true, in common with the genuine language of poetry, namely, that it was not heard in ordinary conversation; that it was unusual. But the first Poets, as I have said, spake a language which, though unusual, was still the language of men. This circumstance, however, was disregarded by their successors; they found that they could please by easier means: they became proud of modes of expression[1] which they themselves had invented, and which were uttered only by themselves.[2] In process of time metre became a symbol or promise of this unusual language, and whoever took upon him to write in metre, according as he possessed more or less of true poetic genius, introduced less or more of this adulterated phraseology into his compositions, and the true and the false were inseparably interwoven until, the taste of men becoming gradually perverted, this language was received as a natural language: and at length, by the influence of books upon men, did to a certain degree really become so. Abuses of this kind were imported from one nation to another, and with the progress of refinement this diction became daily more and more corrupt, thrusting out of sight the plain humanities of nature by a motley masquerade of tricks, quaintnesses, hieroglyphics, and enigmas.

It would not be uninteresting[3] to point out the causes of the pleasure given by this extravagant and absurd diction.[4] It depends upon a great variety of causes, but upon none, perhaps, more than its influence in impressing a notion of the peculiarity and exaltation of the Poet's character, and in flattering the Reader's self-love by bringing him nearer to a sympathy with that character; an effect which is accomplished by unsettling ordinary habits of thinking, and thus assisting the Reader to approach to that perturbed and dizzy state of mind in which if he does not find himself, he imagines that he is *balked* of a peculiar enjoyment which poetry can and ought to bestow.

[1] modes of expression 1836: a language 1802–32
[2] themselves./In process] and, with the spirit of a fraternity, they arrogated it to themselves as their own. 1815–32
[3] *so* 1836: be highly interesting 1802–32
[4] diction 1836: language, but this is not the place 1802–32

The sonnet quoted from Gray, in the Preface, except the lines printed in Italics, consists of little else but this diction, though not of the worst kind ; and indeed, if one may be permitted to say so, it is far too common in the best writers both ancient and modern. Perhaps in no way, by positive example, could more easily be given a notion of what I mean by the phrase *poetic diction* than by referring to a comparison between the metrical paraphrase which we have of passages in the Old and New Testament, and those passages as they exist in our common Translation. See Pope's "Messiah" throughout; Prior's "Did sweeter sounds adorn my flowing tongue", &c. &c. "Though I speak with the tongues of men and of angels", &c. &c. 1st Corinthians, chap. xiii. By way of immediate example take the following of Dr. Johnson:—

"Turn on the prudent Ant thy heedless eyes,
Observe her labours, Sluggard, and be wise;
No stern command, no monitory voice,
Prescribes her duties, or directs her choice;
Yet, timely provident, she hastes away
To snatch the blessings of a plenteous day;
When fruitful Summer loads the teeming plain,
She crops the harvest, and she stores the grain.
How long shall sloth usurp thy useless hours,
Unnerve thy vigour, and enchain thy powers?
While artful shades thy downy couch enclose,
And soft solicitation courts repose,
Amidst the drowsy charms of dull delight,
Year chases year with unremitted flight,
Till Want now following, fraudulent and slow,
Shall spring to seize thee, like an ambush'd foe."

From this hubbub of words pass to the original. "Go to the Ant, thou Sluggard, consider her ways, and be wise: which having no guide, overseer, or ruler, provideth her meat in the summer, and gathereth her food in the harvest. How long wilt thou sleep, O Sluggard? when wilt thou arise out of thy sleep? Yet a little sleep, a little slumber, a little folding of the hands to sleep. So shall thy poverty come as one that travelleth, and thy want as an armed man." Proverbs, chap. vi.[1]

[1] chap. vi/One more quotation] In order further to point out some of the ordinary and less disgusting shapes which Misdiction puts on at the present day, I will transcribe a poem published a few years ago, which, though of great merit, is crowded with these defects.

Could then the Babes from yon *unshelter'd* cot
Implore thy *passing charity* in vain?
Too thoughtless Youth! what though *thy happier lot*
Insult their life of poverty and pain.
What though their Maker doom'd them thus forlorn
To brook the mockery of the *taunting throng*
Beneath the *Oppressor's iron scourge* to mourn
To *mourn but not to murmur at his wrong!*

One more quotation, and I have done. It is from Cowper's Verses supposed to be written by Alexander Selkirk:—

> "Religion! what treasure untold
> Resides in that heavenly word!
> More precious than silver and gold,
> Or all that this earth can afford.
> But the sound of the church-going bell
> These valleys and rocks never heard,
> Ne'er sighed at the sound of a knell,
> Or smiled when a sabbath appeared.
>
> "Ye winds, that have made me your sport
> Convey to this desolate shore
> Some cordial endearing report
> Of a land I must visit no more.
> My Friends, do they now and then send
> A wish or a thought after me?
> O tell me I yet have a friend,
> Though a friend I am never to see."

This passage is quoted as an instance of three different styles of composition. The first four lines are poorly expressed; some Critics would call the language prosaic; the fact is, it would be bad prose, so bad, that it is scarcely worse in metre. The epithet "church-going" applied to a bell, and that by so chaste a writer as Cowper, is an instance of the strange abuses which Poets have introduced into their language, till they and their Readers take them as matters of course, if they do not single them out expressly as objects of admiration. The two lines "Ne'er sighed at the sound", &c., are, in my opinion, an instance of the language of passion wrested from its proper use, and, from the mere circumstance of the composition being in metre, applied upon an occasion that does not justify such violent expressions; and I should condemn the passage, though perhaps few Readers will agree with me, as vicious poetic diction. The last stanza is throughout admirably expressed: it would be equally good whether in prose or verse, except that the Reader has an exquisite pleasure in seeing such natural language so naturally connected with metre. The beauty of this stanza tempts me to conclude[1] with a principle which

> Yet when their *last late* evening shall decline,
> Their evening chearful though their day distrest,
> A Hope perhaps more *heavenly bright* than thine,
> A Grace by thee unsought, and unpossest,
> A Faith more fix'd, a rapture more divine
> Shall gild their passage to eternal rest.—RUSSEL.

The Reader has only to translate this sonnet into such language as any person of good sense and lively sensibility, one, I mean, who does not talk out of books—would use upon such an occasion in real life, and he will at once perceive in what manner the passages printed in italics are defective.

Longman MS. [1] See footnote 1, p. 409

ought never to be lost sight of, and which has been my chief guide in all I have said,—namely, that in works of *imagination and sentiment*, for of these only have I been treating, in proportion as ideas and feelings are valuable, whether the composition be in prose or in verse, they require and exact one and the same language. Metre is but adventitious to composition, and the phraseology for which that passport is necessary, even where it may be graceful at all, will be little valued by the judicious.[1]

ESSAY, SUPPLEMENTARY TO THE PREFACE[2]

WITH the young of both sexes, Poetry is, like love, a passion; but, for much the greater part of those who have been proud of its power over their minds, a necessity soon arises of breaking the pleasing bondage; or it relaxes of itself;—the thoughts being occupied in domestic cares, or the time engrossed by business. Poetry then becomes only an occasional recreation; while to those whose existence passes away in a course of fashionable pleasure, it is a species of luxurious amusement. In middle and declining age, a scattered number of serious persons resort to poetry, as to religion, for a protection against the pressure of trivial employments, and as a consolation for the afflictions of life. And, lastly, there are many, who, having been enamoured of this art in their youth, have found leisure, after youth was spent, to cultivate general literature; in which poetry has continued to be comprehended *as a study*.

[1] conclude . . . *end, so* 1836: add a sentiment which ought to be the pervading spirit of a system, detached parts of which have been imperfectly explained in the Preface, namely, that in proportion as ideas and feelings are valuable, whether the composition be in prose or in verse, they require and exact one and the same language. 1802–32. *Longman MS. adds:* The Reader, I hope, will believe that it is with great reluctance I have presumed, in this note, to censure so freely the writings of other Poets, and that I should not have done this, could I otherwise have made my meaning intelligible. The passages which I have condemned I have condemned upon principle, and I have given my reasons, else I should have been inexcusable. Without an appeal to laws and principles there can be no criticism. What passes under that name is, for the most part, little more than a string of random extempore judgments, a mode of writing more cheap than any other, and utterly worthless. When I contrast these summary decisions with the pains and anxiety of original composition, especially in verse, I am frequently reminded of a passage of Drayton on this subject, which, no doubt, he wrote with deep feeling:

> Detracting what laboriously we do
> Only by that which he but idly saith.

[2] Printed in 1815 as supplementary to the Preface of that volume. In 1820 placed in Vol. III, in 1827 in Vol. II, in 1832 in Vol. I, but in 1837 Vol. III, p. 315; and thereafter Wordsworth decided that in its subject-matter and main tendency it was supplementary rather to the *Lyrical Ballads*. v. N & Q, 26 May 1951.

Into the above Classes the Readers of poetry may be divided; Critics abound in them all; but from the last only can opinions be collected of absolute value, and worthy to be depended upon, as prophetic of the destiny of a new work. The young, who in nothing can escape delusion, are especially subject to it in their intercourse with Poetry. The cause, not so obvious as the fact is unquestionable, is the same as that from which erroneous judgments in this art, in the minds of men of all ages, chiefly proceed; but upon Youth it operates with peculiar force. The appropriate business of poetry, (which, nevertheless, if genuine, is as permanent as pure science,) her appropriate employment, her privilege and her *duty*, is to treat of things not as they *are*, but as they *appear;* not as they exist in themselves, but as they *seem* to exist to the *senses*, and to the *passions*. What a world of delusion does this acknowledged obligation[1] prepare for the inexperienced! what temptations to go astray are here held forth for them whose thoughts have been little disciplined by the understanding, and whose feelings revolt from the sway of reason!—When a juvenile Reader is in the height of his rapture with some vicious passage, should experience throw in doubts, or common-sense suggest suspicions, a lurking consciousness that the realities of the Muse are but shows, and that her liveliest excitements are raised by transient shocks of conflicting feeling and successive assemblages of contradictory thoughts—is ever at hand to justify extravagance, and to sanction absurdity. But, it may be asked, as these illusions are unavoidable, and, no doubt, eminently useful to the mind as a process, what good can be gained by making observations, the tendency of which is to diminish the confidence of youth in its feelings, and thus to abridge its innocent and even profitable pleasures ? The reproach implied in the question could not be warded off, if Youth were incapable of being delighted with what is truly excellent; or, if these errors always terminated of themselves in due season. But, with the majority, though their force be abated, they continue through life. Moreover, the fire of youth is too vivacious an element to be extinguished or damped by a philosophical remark; and, while there is no danger that what has been said will be injurious or painful to the ardent and the confident, it may prove beneficial to those who, being enthusiastic, are, at the same time, modest and ingenuous. The intimation may unite with their own misgivings to regulate their sensibility, and to bring in, sooner than it would otherwise have arrived, a more discreet and sound judgment.

If it should excite wonder that men of ability, in later life, whose understandings have been rendered acute by practice in affairs, should be so easily and so far imposed upon when they happen to take up a new work in verse, this appears to be the cause ;—that, having

---

[1] obligation 1837: principle 1815–32

discontinued their attention to poetry, whatever progress may have been made in other departments of knowledge, they have not, as to this art, advanced in true discernment beyond the age of youth. If, then, a new poem fall in their way, whose attractions are of that kind which would have enraptured them during the heat of youth, the judgment not being improved to a degree that they shall be disgusted, they are dazzled; and prize and cherish the faults for having had power to make the present time vanish before them, and to throw the mind back, as by enchantment, into the happiest season of life. As they read, powers seem to be revived, passions are regenerated, and pleasures restored. The Book was probably taken up after an escape from the burden of business, and with a wish to forget the world, and all its vexations and anxieties. Having obtained this wish, and so much more, it is natural that they should make report as they have felt.

If Men of mature age, through want of practice, be thus easily beguiled into admiration of absurdities, extravagances, and misplaced ornaments, thinking it proper that their understandings should enjoy a holiday, while they are unbending their minds with verse, it may be expected that such Readers will resemble their former selves also in strength of prejudice, and an inaptitude to be moved by the unostentatious beauties of a pure style. In the higher poetry, an enlightened Critic chiefly looks for a reflection of the wisdom of the heart and the grandeur of the imagination. Wherever these appear, simplicity accompanies them; Magnificence herself when legitimate, depending upon a simplicity of her own, to regulate her ornaments. But it is a well-known property of human nature, that our estimates are ever governed by comparisons, of which we are conscious with various degrees of distinctness. Is it not, then, inevitable (confining these observations to the effects of style merely) that an eye, accustomed to the glaring hues of diction by which such Readers are caught and excited, will for the most part be rather repelled than attracted by an original Work, the colouring of which is disposed according to a pure and refined scheme of harmony? It is in the fine arts as in the affairs of life, no man can *serve* (*i.e.* obey with zeal and fidelity) two Masters.

As Poetry is most just to its own divine origin when it administers the comforts and breathes the spirit of religion, they who have learned to perceive this truth, and who betake themselves to reading verse for sacred purposes, must be preserved from numerous illusions to which the two Classes of Readers, whom we have been considering, are liable. But, as the mind grows serious from the weight of life, the range of its passions is contracted accordingly; and its sympathies become so exclusive, that many species of high excellence wholly escape, or but languidly excite, its notice. Besides, men who read from religious or moral inclinations, even when the subject is of that kind which they approve, are beset with misconceptions and mistakes.

peculiar to themselves. Attaching so much importance to the truths which interest them, they are prone to overrate the Authors by whom those truths are expressed and enforced. They come prepared to impart so much passion to the Poet's language, that they remain unconscious how little, in fact, they receive from it. And, on the other hand, religious faith is to him who holds it so momentous a thing, and error appears to be attended with such tremendous consequences, that, if opinions touching upon religion occur which the Reader condemns, he not only cannot sympathise with them, however animated the expression, but there is, for the most part, an end put to all satisfaction and enjoyment. Love, if it before existed, is converted into dislike; and the heart of the Reader is set against the Author and his book.—To these excesses, they, who from their professions ought to be the most guarded against them, are perhaps the most liable; I mean those sects whose religion, being from the calculating understanding, is cold and formal. For when Christianity, the religion of humility, is founded upon the proudest faculty[1] of our nature, what can be expected but contradictions? Accordingly, believers of this cast are at one time contemptuous; at another, being troubled, as they are and must be, with inward misgivings, they are jealous and suspicious;—and at all seasons, they are under temptation to supply by the heat with which they defend their tenets, the animation which is wanting to the constitution of the religion itself.

Faith was given to man that his affections, detached from the treasures of time, might be inclined to settle upon those of eternity;—the elevation of his nature, which this habit produces on earth, being to him a presumptive evidence of a future state of existence; and giving him a title to partake of its holiness. The religious man values what he sees chiefly as an "imperfect shadowing forth" of what he is incapable of seeing. The concerns of religion refer to indefinite objects, and are too weighty for the mind to support them without relieving itself by resting a great part of the burthen upon words and symbols. The commerce between Man and his Maker cannot be carried on but by a process where much is represented in little, and the Infinite Being accommodates himself to a finite capacity. In all this may be perceived the affinity between religion and poetry; between religion—making up the deficiencies of reason by faith; and poetry—passionate for the instruction of reason; between religion—whose element is infinitude, and whose ultimate trust is the supreme of things, submitting herself to circumscription, and reconciled to substitutions; and poetry—ethereal and transcendent, yet incapable to sustain her existence without sensuous incarnation. In this community of nature may be perceived also the lurking incitements of kindred error;—so that we shall find that no poetry has been more subject to distortion, than

---

[1] faculty 1820: quality 1815

that species, the argument and scope of which is religious; and no lovers of the art have gone farther astray than the pious and the devout.

Whither then shall we turn for that union of qualifications which must necessarily exist before the decisions of a critic can be of absolute value ? For a mind at once poetical and philosophical; for a critic whose affections are as free and kindly as the spirit of society, and whose understanding is severe as that of dispassionate government ? Where are we to look for that initiatory composure of mind which no selfishness can disturb ? For a natural sensibility that has been tutored into correctness without losing anything of its quickness; and for active faculties, capable of answering the demands which an Author of original imagination shall make upon them, associated with a judgment that cannot be duped into admiration by aught that is unworthy of it ?—among those and those only, who, never having suffered their youthful love of poetry to remit much of its force, have applied to the consideration of the laws of this art the best power of their understandings. At the same time it must be observed—that, as this Class comprehends the only judgments which are trust-worthy, so does it include the most erroneous and perverse. For to be mistaught is worse than to be untaught; and no perverseness equals that which is supported by system, no errors are so difficult to root out as those which the understanding has pledged its credit to uphold. In this Class are contained censors, who, if they be pleased with what is good, are pleased with it only by imperfect glimpses, and upon false principles; who, should they generalise rightly, to a certain point, are sure to suffer for it in the end; who, if they stumble upon a sound rule, are fettered by misapplying it, or by straining it too far; being incapable of perceiving when it ought to yield to one of higher order. In it are found critics too petulant to be passive to a genuine poet, and too feeble to grapple with him; men, who take upon them to report of the course which *he* holds whom they are utterly unable to accompany, confounded if he turn quick upon the wing, dismayed if he soar steadily "into the region";—men of palsied imaginations and indurated hearts; in whose minds all healthy action is languid, who therefore feed as the many direct them, or, with the many, are greedy after vicious provocatives;—judges, whose censure is auspicious, and whose praise ominous! In this Class meet together the two extremes of best and worst.

The observations presented in the foregoing series are of too ungracious a nature to have been made without reluctance; and, were it only on this account, I would invite the Reader to try them by the test of comprehensive experience. If the number of judges who can be confidently relied upon be in reality so small, it ought to follow that partial notice only, or neglect, perhaps long continued, or attention wholly inadequate to their merits—must have been the fate of most

works in the higher departments of poetry; and that, on the other
hand, numerous productions have blazed into popularity, and have
passed away, leaving scarcely a trace behind them: it will be further
found, that when Authors shall have at length raised themselves
into general admiration and maintained their ground, errors and
prejudices have prevailed concerning their genius and their works,
which the few who are conscious of those errors and prejudices would
deplore; if they were not recompensed by perceiving that there are
select Spirits for whom it is ordained that their fame shall be in the
world an existence like that of Virtue, which owes its being to the
struggles it makes, and its vigour to the enemies whom it provokes;—
a vivacious quality, ever doomed to meet with opposition, and still
triumphing over it; and, from the nature of its dominion, incapable
of being brought to the sad conclusion of Alexander, when he wept
that there were no more worlds for him to conquer.

Let us take a hasty retrospect of the poetical literature of this
Country for the greater part of the last two centuries, and see if the
facts support these inferences.

Who is there that now reads[1] the "Creation" of Dubartas? Yet
all Europe once resounded with his praise; he was caressed by Kings;
and, when his Poem was translated into our language, the Faery
Queen faded before it. The name of Spenser, whose genius is of a
higher order than even that of Ariosto, is at this day scarcely known
beyond the limits of the British Isles. And if the value of his works
is to be estimated from the attention now paid to them by his
Countrymen, compared with that which they bestow on those of
some other writers, it must be pronounced small indeed.

> "The laurel, meed of mighty conquerors
> And poets *sage*"—[2]

are his own words; but his wisdom has, in this particular, been his
worst enemy: while its opposite, whether in the shape of folly or
madness, has been *their* best friend. But he was a great power, and
bears a high name: the laurel has been awarded to him.

A dramatic Author, if he write for the stage, must adapt himself
to the taste of the audience, or they will not endure him; accordingly
the mighty genius of Shakspeare was listened to. The people were
delighted: but I am not sufficiently versed in stage antiquities to
determine whether they did not flock as eagerly to the representation
of many pieces of contemporary Authors, wholly undeserving to
appear upon the same boards. Had there been a formal contest for
superiority among dramatic writers, that Shakspeare, like his predecessors Sophocles and Euripides, would have often been subject
to the mortification of seeing the prize adjudged to sorry competitors,

---

[1] *so* 1845: can now endure to read 1815–36
[2] *The Faerie Queene*, I. i. 9.

becomes too probable, when we reflect that the admirers of Settle and Shadwell were, in a later age, as numerous, and reckoned as respectable in point of talent, as those of Dryden. At all events, that Shakspeare stooped to accommodate himself to the People, is sufficiently apparent; and one of the most striking proofs of his almost omnipotent genius, is, that he could turn to such glorious purpose those materials which the prepossessions of the age compelled him to make use of. Yet even this marvellous skill appears not to have been enough to prevent his rivals from having some advantage over him in public estimation; else how can we account for passages and scenes that exist in his works, unless upon a supposition that some of the grossest of them, a fact which in my own mind I have no doubt of, were foisted in by the Players, for the gratification of the many?

But that his Works, whatever might be their reception upon the stage, made but[1] little impression upon the ruling Intellects of the time, may be inferred from the fact that Lord Bacon, in his multifarious writings, nowhere either quotes or alludes to him.[2] His dramatic excellence enabled him to resume possession of the stage after the Restoration; but Dryden tells us that in his time two of the plays of Beaumont and Fletcher were acted for one of Shakspeare's. And so faint and limited was the perception of the poetic beauties of his dramas in the time of Pope, that, in his Edition of the Plays, with a view of rendering to the general reader a necessary service, he printed between inverted commas those passages which he thought most worthy of notice.

At this day, the French Critics have abated nothing of their aversion to this darling of our Nation: "the English, with their bouffon de Shakspeare", is as familiar an expression among them as in the time of Voltaire. Baron Grimm is the only French writer who seems to have perceived his infinite superiority to the first names of the French Theatre; an advantage which the Parisian Critic owed to his German blood and German education. The most enlightened Italians, though well acquainted with our language, are wholly incompetent to measure the proportions of Shakspeare. The Germans only, of foreign nations, are approaching towards a knowledge and feeling of what he is. In some respects they have acquired a superiority over the fellow-countrymen of the Poet: for among us it is a current, I might say, an established opinion, that Shakspeare is justly praised when he is pronounced to be "a wild irregular genius,

---

[1] but *not in* 1815–32

[2] The learned Hakewill (a third edition of whose book bears date 1635), writing to refute the error "touching Nature's perpetual and universal decay", cites triumphantly the names of Ariosto, Tasso, Bartas, and Spenser, as instances that poetic genius had not degenerated; but he makes no mention of Shakspeare.—W. W.

in whom great faults are compensated by great beauties". How long may it be before this misconception passes away, and it becomes universally acknowledged that the judgment of Shakspeare in the selection of his materials, and in the manner in which he has made them, heterogeneous as they often are, constitute a unity of their own, and contribute all to one great end, is not less admirable than his imagination, his invention, and his intuitive knowledge of human Nature ?

There is extant a small Volume of miscellaneous poems, in which Shakspeare expresses his own feelings in his own person. It is not difficult to conceive that the Editor, George Steevens, should have been insensible to the beauties of one portion of that Volume, the Sonnets; though in no part of the writings of this Poet is found, in an equal compass, a greater number of exquisite feelings felicitously expressed. But, from regard to the Critic's own credit, he would not have ventured to talk of an[1] act of parliament not being strong enough to compel the perusal of those little pieces,[2] if he had not known that the people of England were ignorant of the treasures contained in them: and if he had not, moreover, shared the too common propensity of human nature to exult over a supposed fall into the mire of a genius whom he had been compelled to regard with admiration, as an inmate of the celestial regions—"there sitting where he durst not soar ".[3]

Nine years before the death of Shakspeare, Milton was born; and early in life he published several small poems, which, though on their first appearance they were praised by a few of the judicious, were afterwards neglected to that degree, that Pope in his youth could borrow[4] from them without risk of its being known. Whether these poems are at this day justly appreciated, I will not undertake to decide: nor would it imply a severe reflection upon the mass of readers to suppose the contrary; seeing that a man of the acknow-ledged genius of Voss, the German poet, could suffer their spirit to evaporate; and could change their character, as is done in the trans-lation made by him of the most popular of those pieces. At all events, it is certain that these Poems of Milton are now much read, and loudly praised; yet were they little heard of till more than 150 years after their publication; and of the Sonnets, Dr. Johnson, as appears from Boswell's Life of him, was in the habit of thinking and speaking as contemptuously as Steevens wrote upon those of Shakspeare.

[1] This flippant insensibility was publicly reprehended by Mr. Coleridge in a course of Lectures upon Poetry given by him at the Royal Institution. For the various merits of thought and language in Shakspeare's Sonnets, see Numbers, 27, 29, 30, 32, 33, 54, 64, 66, 68, 73, 76, 86, 91, 92, 93, 97, 98, 105, 107, 108, 109, 111, 113, 114, 116, 117, 129, and many others.—W. W.

[2] *so* 1837: of these, or any production of Shakspeare 1815

[3] *Paradise Lost*, iv. 839   [4] borrow 1837: pilfer 1815

About the time when the Pindaric odes of Cowley and his imitators, and the productions of that class of curious thinkers whom Dr. Johnson has strangely styled metaphysical Poets, were beginning to lose something of that extravagant admiration which they had excited, the Paradise Lost made its appearance. "Fit audience find though few," was the petition addressed by the Poet to his inspiring Muse. I have said elsewhere that he gained more than he asked; this I believe to be true; but Dr. Johnson has fallen into a gross mistake when he attempts to prove, by the sale of the work, that Milton's Countrymen were "*just* to it" upon its first appearance. Thirteen hundred Copies were sold in two years; an uncommon example, he asserts, of the prevalence of genius in opposition to so much recent enmity as Milton's public conduct had excited. But, be it remembered that, if Milton's political and religious opinions, and the manner in which he announced them, had raised him many enemies, they had procured him numerous friends; who, as all personal danger was passed away at the time of publication, would be eager to procure the master-work of a man whom they revered, and whom they would be proud of praising. Take, from the number of purchasers, persons of this class, and also those who wished to possess the Poem as a religious work, and but few I fear would be left who sought for it on account of its poetical merits.[1] The demand did not immediately increase; "for," says Dr. Johnson, "many more readers," (he means persons in the habit of reading poetry) "than were supplied at first the Nation did not afford." How careless must a writer be who can make this assertion in the face of so many existing title-pages to belie it! Turning to my own shelves, I find the folio of Cowley, seventh edition, 1681. A book near it is Flatman's Poems, fourth edition, 1686; Waller, fifth edition, same date. The Poems of Norris of Bemerton not long after went, I believe, through nine editions. What further demand there might be for these works I do not know; but I well remember, that, twenty-five years ago, the booksellers' stalls in London swarmed with the folios of Cowley. This is not mentioned in disparagement of that able writer and amiable man; but merely to show—that, if Milton's work were not more read, it was not because readers did not exist at the time. The early editions of the Paradise Lost were printed in a shape which allowed them to be sold at a low price, yet[2] only three thousand copies of the Work were sold in eleven years; and the Nation, says Dr. Johnson, had been satisfied from 1623 to 1664, that is, forty-one years, with only two editions of the Works of Shakspeare; which probably did not together make one thousand Copies; facts adduced by the critic to prove the "paucity of Readers."—There were readers

---

[1] *so* 1837: Take . . . merits *not in* 1815–32
[2] *so* 1837: The early editions . . . yet *not in* 1815–32

in multitudes; but their money went for other purposes, as their admiration was fixed elsewhere. We are authorised, then, to affirm, that the reception of the Paradise Lost, and the slow progress of its fame, are proofs as striking as can be desired that the positions which I am attempting to establish are not erroneous.[1]—How amusing to shape to one's self such a critique as a Wit of Charles's days, or a Lord of the Miscellanies or trading Journalist of King William's time, would have brought forth, if he had set his faculties indus- triously to work upon this Poem, everywhere impregnated with *original* excellence.

So strange indeed are the obliquities of admiration, that they whose opinions are much influenced by authority will often be tempted to think that there are no fixed principles[2] in human nature for this art to rest upon. I have been honoured by being permitted to peruse in MS. a tract composed between the period of the Revo- lution and the close of that century. It is the work of an English Peer of high accomplishments, its object to form the character and direct the studies of his son. Perhaps nowhere does a more beautiful treatise of the kind exist. The good sense and wisdom of the thoughts, the delicacy of the feelings, and the charm of the style, are, through- out, equally conspicuous. Yet the Author, selecting among the Poets of his own country those whom he deems most worthy of his son's perusal, particularises only Lord Rochester, Sir John Denham, and Cowley. Writing about the same time, Shaftesbury, an author at present unjustly depreciated, describes the English Muses as only yet lisping in their cradles.

The arts by which Pope, soon afterwards, contrived to procure to himself a more general and a higher reputation than perhaps any English Poet ever attained during his life-time, are known to the judicious. And as well known is it to them, that the undue exertion of those arts is the cause why Pope has for some time held a rank in literature, to which, if he had not been seduced by an over-love of immediate popularity, and had confided more in his native genius, he never could have descended. He bewitched the nation by his melody, and dazzled it by his polished style, and was himself blinded by his own success. Having wandered from humanity in his Eclogues with boyish inexperience, the praise, which these compositions ob- tained, tempted him into a belief that Nature was not to be trusted, at least in pastoral Poetry. To prove this by example, he put his

---

[1] Hughes is express upon this subject: in his dedication of Spenser's Works to Lord Somers, he writes thus. "It was your Lordship's encouraging a beautiful edition of Paradise Lost that first brought that incomparable Poem to be generally known and esteemed."—W. W.

[2] This opinion seems actually to have been entertained by Adam Smith, the worst critic, David Hume not excepted, that Scotland, a soil to which this sort of weed seems natural, has produced.—W. W.

friend Gay upon writing those Eclogues which their author intended
to be burlesque. The instigator of the work, and his admirers, could
perceive in them nothing but what was ridiculous. Nevertheless,
though these Poems contain some detestable[1] passages, the effect, as
Dr. Johnson well observes, "of reality and truth became conspicuous
even when the intention was to show them grovelling and degraded."
The Pastorals, ludicrous to such as prided themselves upon their
refinement, in spite of those disgusting passages, "became popular,
and were read with delight, as just representations of rural manners
and occupations."

Something less than sixty years after the publication of the Paradise Lost appeared Thomson's Winter; which was speedily followed
by his other Seasons. It is a work of inspiration; much of it is written
from himself, and nobly from himself. How was it received? "It
was no sooner read," says one of his contemporary biographers,
"than universally admired: those only excepted who had not been
used to feel, or to look for anything in poetry, beyond a *point* of
satirical or epigrammatic wit, a smart *antithesis* richly trimmed with
rhyme, or the softness of an *elegiac* complaint. To such his manly
classical spirit could not readily commend itself; till, after a more
attentive perusal, they had got the better of their prejudices, and
either acquired or affected a truer taste. A few others stood aloof,
merely because they had long before fixed the articles of their poetical
creed, and resigned themselves to an absolute despair of ever seeing
anything new and original. These were somewhat mortified to find
their notions disturbed by the appearance of a poet, who seemed to
owe nothing but to nature and his own genius. But, in a short time,
the applause became unanimous; every one wondering how so many
pictures, and pictures so familiar, should have moved them but
faintly to what they felt in his descriptions. His digressions too,
the overflowings of a tender benevolent heart, charmed the reader
no less; leaving him in doubt, whether he should more admire the
Poet or love the Man."

This case appears to bear strongly against us:—but we must distinguish between wonder and legitimate admiration. The subject of
the work is the changes produced in the appearances of nature by
the revolution of the year: and, by undertaking to write in verse,
Thomson pledged himself to treat his subject as became a Poet.
Now, it is remarkable that, excepting the nocturnal Reverie of Lady
Winchilsea, and a passage or two in the Windsor Forest of Pope,[2]
the poetry of the period intervening between the publication of the
Paradise Lost and the Seasons does not contain a single new image

[1] *so* 1837: odious and even detestable 1815–32
[2] *so* 1837: excepting a passage or two in the Windsor Forest of Pope, and
some delightful pictures in Poems of Lady Winchilsea 1815–32

of external nature; and scarcely presents a familiar one from which it can be inferred that the eye of the Poet had been steadily fixed upon his object, much less that his feelings had urged him to work upon it in the spirit of genuine imagination. To what a low state knowledge of the most obvious and important phenomena had sunk, is evident from the style in which Dryden has executed a description of Night in one of his Tragedies, and Pope his translation of the celebrated moonlight scene in the Iliad. A blind man, in the habit of attending accurately to descriptions casually dropped from the lips of those around him, might easily depict these appearances with more truth. Dryden's lines are vague, bombastic, and senseless[1]; those of Pope, though he had Homer to guide him, are throughout false and contradictory. The verses of Dryden, once highly cele-brated, are forgotten; those of Pope still retain their hold upon public estimation,—nay, there is not a passage of descriptive poetry, which at this day finds so many and such ardent admirers. Strange to think of an enthusiast, as may have been the case with thousands, reciting those verses under the cope of a moonlight sky, without having his raptures in the least disturbed by a suspicion of their absurdity!—If these two distinguished writers could habitually think that the visible universe was of so little consequence to a poet, that it was scarcely necessary for him to cast his eyes upon it, we may be assured that those passages of the elder poets which faithfully and poetically describe the phenomena of nature, were not at that time holden in much estimation, and that there was little accurate attention paid to those appearances.

Wonder is the natural product of Ignorance; and as the soil was *in such good condition* at the time of the publication of the Seasons, the crop was doubtless abundant. Neither individuals nor nations become corrupt all at once, nor are they enlightened in a moment. Thomson was an inspired poet, but he could not work miracles; in cases where the art of seeing had in some degree been learned, the teacher would further the proficiency of his pupils, but he could do little *more;* though so far does vanity assist men in acts of self-deception, that many would often fancy they recognized a likeness when they knew nothing of the original. Having shown that much of what his biographer deemed genuine admiration must in fact have been blind wonderment—how is the rest to be accounted for ?—

[1]   CORTES *alone in a night-gown.*
All things are hush'd as Nature's self lay dead;
The mountains seem to nod their drowsy head.
The little Birds in dreams their songs repeat,
And sleeping Flowers beneath the Night-dew sweat:
Even Lust and Envy sleep; yet Love denies
Rest to my soul, and slumber to my eyes."
                    DRYDEN'S *Indian Emperor.*—W. W.

Thomson was fortunate in the very title of his poem, which seemed to bring it home to the prepared sympathies of every one: in the next place, notwithstanding his high powers, he writes a vicious style; and his false ornaments are exactly of that kind which would be most likely to strike the undiscerning. He likewise abounds with sentimental common-places, that, from the manner in which they were brought forward, bore an imposing air of novelty. In any well-used copy of the Seasons the book generally opens of itself with the rhapsody on love, or with one of the stories (perhaps Damon and Musidora); these also are prominent in our collections of Extracts, and are the parts of his Work which, after all, were probably most efficient in first recommending the author to general notice. Pope, repaying praises which he had received, and wishing to extol him to the highest, only styles him "an elegant and philosophical Poet;" nor are we able to collect any unquestionable proofs that the true characteristics of Thomson's genius as an imaginative poet[1] were perceived, till the elder Warton, almost forty years after the publication of the Seasons, pointed them out by a note in his Essay on the Life and Writings of Pope. In the Castle of Indolence (of which Gray speaks so coldly) these characteristics were almost as conspicuously displayed, and in verse more harmonious, and diction more pure. Yet that fine poem was neglected on its appearance, and is at this day the delight only of a few!

When Thomson died, Collins breathed forth his regrets in an Elegiac Poem, in which he pronounces a poetical curse upon *him* who should regard with insensibility the place where the Poet's remains were deposited. The Poems of the mourner himself have now passed through innumerable editions, and are universally known; but if, when Collins died, the same kind of imprecation had been pronounced by a surviving admirer, small is the number whom it would not have comprehended. The notice which his poems attained during his lifetime was so small, and of course the sale so insignificant, that not long before his death he deemed it right to repay to the bookseller the sum which he had advanced for them, and threw the edition into the fire.

Next in importance to the Seasons of Thomson, though at considerable distance from that work in order of time, come the Reliques of Ancient English Poetry; collected, new-modelled, and in many instances (if such a contradiction in terms may be used) composed by the Editor, Dr. Percy. This work did not steal silently into the world, as is evident from the number of legendary tales, that appeared

---

[1] Since these observations upon Thomson were written, I have perused the second edition of his "Seasons," and find that even *that* does not contain the most striking passages which Warton points out for admiration; these, with other improvements, throughout the whole work, must have been added at a later period.—W. W. 1820 (*not in* 1815)

not long after its publication ; and had been modelled, as the authors persuaded themselves, after the old Ballad. The Compilation was however ill suited to the then existing taste of city society; and Dr. Johnson, 'mid the little senate to which he gave laws, was not sparing in his exertions to make it an object of contempt. The critic triumphed, the legendary imitators were deservedly disregarded, and, as undeservedly, their ill-imitated models sank, in this country, into temporary neglect; while Bürger, and other able writers of Germany, were translating or imitating these Reliques, and composing, with the aid of inspiration thence derived, poems which are the delight of the German nation. Dr. Percy was so abashed by the ridicule flung upon his labours from the ignorance and insensibility of the persons with whom he lived, that, though while he was writing under a mask he had not wanted resolution to follow his genius into the regions of true simplicity and genuine pathos (as is evinced by the exquisite ballad of Sir Cauline and by many other pieces), yet when he appeared in his own person and character as a poetical writer, he adopted, as in the tale of the Hermit of Warkworth, a diction scarcely in any one of its features distinguishable from the vague, the glossy, and unfeeling language of his day. I mention this remarkable fact[1] with regret, esteeming the genius of Dr. Percy in this kind of writing superior to that of any other man by whom in modern times it has been cultivated. That even Bürger (to whom Klopstock gave, in my hearing, a commendation which he denied to Goethe and Schiller, pronouncing him to be a genuine poet, and one of the few among the Germans whose works would last) had not the fine sensibility of Percy, might be shown from many passages, in which he has deserted his original only to go astray. For example,

> "Now daye was gone, and night was come,
> And all were fast asleepe,
> All save the Lady Emeline,
> Who sate in her bowre to weepe:
>
> "And soone she heard her true Love's voice
> Low whispering at the walle,
> Awake, awake, my dear Ladye,
> 'Tis I thy true-love call."

---

[1] Shenstone, in his "Schoolmistress," gives a still more remarkable instance of this timidity. On its first appearance, (see D'Israeli's 2nd Series of the "Curiosities of Literature") the Poem was accompanied with an absurd prose commentary, showing, as indeed some incongruous expressions in the text imply, that the whole was intended for burlesque. In subsequent editions, the commentary was dropped, and the People have since continued to read in seriousness, doing for the Author what he had not courage openly to venture upon for himself.—W. W. 1827 (*not in* 1815–20)

Which is thus tricked out and dilated:

> "Als nun die Nacht Gebirg' und Thal
> Vermummt in Rabenschatten,
> Und Hochburgs Lampen überall
> Schon ausgeflimmert hatten,
> Und alles tief entschlafen war;
> Doch nur das Fräulein immerdar,
> Voll Fieberangst, noch wachte,
> Und seinen Ritter dachte:
> Da horch! Ein süsser Liebeston
> Kam leis' empor geflogen.
> 'Ho, Trudchen, ho! Da bin ich schon!
> Frisch auf! Dich angezogen!'"

But from humble ballads we must ascend to heroics.

All hail, Macpherson! hail to thee, Sire of Ossian! The Phantom was begotten by the snug embrace of an impudent Highlander upon a cloud of tradition—it travelled southward, where it was greeted with acclamation, and the thin Consistence took its course through Europe, upon the breath of popular applause. The Editor of the Reliques had indirectly preferred a claim to the praise of invention, by not concealing that his supplementary labours were considerable! how selfish his conduct, contrasted with that of the disinterested Gael, who, like Lear, gives his kingdom away, and is content to become a pensioner upon his own issue for a beggarly pittance!— Open this far-famed Book!—I have done so at random, and the beginning of the "Epic Poem Temora", in eight Books, presents itself. "The blue waves of Ullin roll in light. The green hills are covered with day. Trees shake their dusky heads in the breeze. Grey torrents pour their noisy streams. Two green hills with aged oaks surround a narrow plain. The blue course of a stream is there. On its banks stood Cairbar of Atha. His spear supports the king; the red eyes of his fear are sad. Cormac rises on his soul with all his ghastly wounds." Precious memorandums from the pocket-book of the blind Ossian!

If it be unbecoming, as I acknowledge that for the most part it is, to speak disrespectfully of Works that have enjoyed for a length of time a widely-spread reputation, without at the same time producing irrefragable proofs of their unworthiness, let me be forgiven upon this occasion.—Having had the good fortune to be born and reared in a mountainous country, from my very childhood I have felt the falsehood that pervades the volumes imposed upon the world under the name of Ossian. From what I saw with my own eyes, I knew that the imagery was spurious. In nature everything is distinct, yet nothing defined into absolute independent singleness. In Macpherson's work, it is exactly the reverse; everything (that is not stolen) is in this manner defined, insulated, dislocated, deadened,—yet nothing distinct. It will always be so when words are substituted for things. To say that the characters never could exist, that the manners are impossible, and that a dream has more substance than the whole state of society, as there depicted, is doing nothing more than pronouncing a censure which Macpherson defied; when, with the steeps of Morven before his eyes, he could talk so familiarly of his Car-borne heroes;—of Morven, which, if one may judge from its appearance at the distance of a few miles, contains scarcely an acre of ground sufficiently accommodating for a sledge to be trailed along its surface.—Mr. Malcolm Laing has ably shown that the diction of this pretended translation is a motley assemblage from all quarters; but he is so fond of making out parallel passages as to call poor Macpherson to account for his "*ands*" and his "*buts!*" and he has weakened his argument by conducting it as if he thought that every striking resemblance was a *conscious* plagiarism. It is enough that the coincidences are too remarkable for its being probable or possible that they could arise in different minds without communication between them. Now as the Translators of the Bible, and Shakspeare, Milton, and Pope, could not be indebted to Macpherson, it follows that he must have owed his fine feathers to them; unless we are prepared gravely to assert, with Madame de Staël, that many of the characteristic beauties of our most celebrated English Poets are derived from the ancient Fingallian; in which case the modern translator would have been but giving back to Ossian his own.—It is consistent that Lucien Buonaparte, who could censure Milton for having surrounded Satan in the infernal regions with courtly and regal splendour, should pronounce the modern Ossian to be the glory of Scotland;—a country that has produced a Dunbar, a Buchanan, a Thomson, and a Burns! These opinions are of ill omen for the Epic ambition of him who has given them to the world.

Yet, much as those pretended treasures of antiquity have been admired, they have been wholly uninfluential upon the literature of the Country. No succeeding writer appears to have caught from them a ray of inspiration; no author, in the least distinguished, has ventured formally to imitate them—except the boy, Chatterton, on their first appearance. He had perceived, from the successful trials which he himself had made in literary forgery, how few critics were able to distinguish between a real ancient medal and a counterfeit of modern manufacture; and he set himself to the work of filling a magazine with *Saxon Poems*,—counterparts of those of Ossian, as like his as one of his misty stars is to another. This incapability to amalgamate with the literature of the Island, is, in my estimation, a decisive proof that the book is essentially unnatural; nor should I require any other to demonstrate it to be a forgery, audacious as worthless.—Contrast, in this respect, the effect of Macpherson's publication with the Reliques of Percy, so unassuming, so modest in their pretensions!—I have already stated how much Germany is indebted to this latter work; and for our own country, its poetry has been absolutely redeemed by it. I do not think that there is an able writer in verse of the present day who would not be proud to acknowledge his obligations to the Reliques; I know that it is so with my friends; and, for myself, I am happy in this occasion to make a public avowal of my own.

Dr. Johnson, more fortunate in his contempt of the labours of Macpherson than those of his modest friend, was solicited not long after to furnish Prefaces biographical and critical for the works of some of the most eminent English Poets. The booksellers took upon themselves to make the collection; they referred probably to the most popular miscellanies, and, unquestionably, to their books of accounts; and decided upon the claim of authors to be admitted into a body of the most eminent, from the familiarity of their names with the readers of that day, and by the profits, which, from the sale of his works, each had brought and was bringing to the Trade. The Editor was allowed a limited exercise of discretion, and the Authors whom he recommended are scarcely to be mentioned without a smile. We open the volume of Prefatory Lives, and to our astonishment the *first* name we find is that of Cowley!—What is become of the morning-star of English Poetry? Where is the bright Elizabethan constellation? Or, if names be more acceptable than images, where is the ever-to-be-honoured Chaucer? where is Spenser? where Sidney? and, lastly, where he, whose rights as a poet, contra-distinguished from those which he is universally allowed to possess as a dramatist, we have vindicated,—where Shakspeare?—These, and a multitude of others not unworthy to be placed near them, their contemporaries and successors, we have *not*. But in their stead, we have (could better be expected when precedence was to be settled by an abstract of reputation at any given period made, as in this case before us?) Roscommon, and Stepney, and Phillips, and Walsh, and Smith, and Duke, and King, and Spratt—Halifax, Granville, Sheffield, Congreve, Broome, and other reputed Magnates—metrical writers utterly worthless and useless, except for occasions like the present, when their productions are referred to as evidence what a small quantity of brain is necessary to procure a considerable stock of admiration, provided the aspirant will accommodate himself to the likings and fashions of his day.

As I do not mean to bring down this retrospect to our own times, it may with propriety be closed at the era of this distinguished event. From the literature of other ages and countries, proofs equally cogent might have been adduced, that the opinions announced in the former part of this Essay are founded upon truth. It was not an agreeable office, nor a prudent undertaking, to declare them; but their importance seemed to render it a duty. It may still be asked, where lies the particular relation of what has been said to these Volumes?—

The question will be easily answered by the discerning Reader who is old enough to remember the taste that prevailed when some of these poems were first published, seventeen years ago; who has also observed to what degree the poetry of this Island has since that period been coloured by them; and who is further aware of the un-remitting hostility with which, upon some principle or other, they have each and all been opposed. A sketch of my own notion of the constitution of Fame has been given; and, as far as concerns myself, I have cause to be satisfied. The love, the admiration, the indiffer-ence, the slight, the aversion, and even the contempt, with which these Poems have been received, knowing, as I do, the source within my own mind, from which they have proceeded, and the labour and pains, which, when labour and pains appeared needful, have been bestowed upon them, must all, if I think consistently, be received as pledges and tokens, bearing the same general impression, though widely different in value;—they are all proofs that for the present time I have not laboured in vain; and afford assurances, more or less authentic, that the products of my industry will endure.

If there be one conclusion more forcibly pressed upon us than another by the review which has been given of the fortunes and fate of poetical Works, it is this,—that every author, as far as he is great and at the same time *original*, has had the task of *creating* the taste by which he is to be enjoyed: so has it been, so will it continue to be. This remark was long since made to me by the philosophical Friend for the separation of whose poems from my own I have previously expressed my regret. The predecessors of an original Genius of a high order will have smoothed the way for all that he has in common with them;—and much he will have in common; but, for what is peculiarly his own, he will be called upon to clear and often to shape his own road:—he will be in the condition of Hannibal among the Alps.

And where lies the real difficulty of creating that taste by which a truly original poet is to be relished? Is it in breaking the bonds of custom, in overcoming the prejudices of false refinement, and dis-placing the aversions of inexperience? Or, if he labour for an object which here and elsewhere I have proposed to myself, does it consist in divesting the reader of the pride that induces him to dwell upon those points wherein men differ from each other, to the exclusion of those in which all men are alike, or the same; and in making him ashamed of the vanity that renders him insensible of the appropriate excellence which civil arrangements, less unjust than might appear, and Nature illimitable in her bounty, have conferred on men who may stand below him in the scale of society? Finally, does it lie in establishing that dominion over the spirits of readers by which they are to be humbled and humanised, in order that they may be purified and exalted?

If these ends are to be attained by the mere communication of *knowledge*, it does *not* lie here.—Taste, I would remind the reader, like Imagination, is a word which has been forced to extend its services far beyond the point to which philosophy would have confined them. It is a metaphor, taken from a *passive* sense of the human body, and transferred to things which are in their essence *not* passive,—to intellectual *acts* and *operations*. The word, Imagination, has been overstrained, from impulses honourable to mankind, to meet the demands of the faculty which is perhaps the noblest of our nature. In the instance of Taste, the process has been reversed; and from the prevalence of dispositions at once injurious and discreditable, being no other than that selfishness which is the child of apathy,—which, as Nations decline in productive and creative power, makes them value themselves upon a presumed refinement of judging. Poverty of language is the primary cause of the use which we make of the word, Imagination; but the word, Taste, has been stretched to the sense which it bears in modern Europe by habits of self-conceit, inducing that inversion in the order of things whereby a passive faculty is made paramount among the faculties conversant with the fine arts. Proportion and congruity, the requisite knowledge being supposed, are subjects upon which taste may be trusted; it is competent to this office;—for in its intercourse with these the mind is *passive*, and is affected painfully or pleasurably as by an instinct. But the profound and the exquisite in feeling, the lofty and universal in thought and imagination; or, in ordinary language, the pathetic and the sublime;—are neither of them, accurately speaking, objects of a faculty which could ever without a sinking in the spirit of Nations have been designated by the metaphor—*Taste*. And why? Because without the exertion of a co-operating *power* in the mind of the Reader, there can be no adequate sympathy with either of these emotions: without this auxiliary impulse, elevated or profound passion cannot exist.

Passion, it must be observed, is derived from a word which signifies *suffering*; but the connection which suffering has with effort, with exertion, and *action*, is immediate and inseparable. How strikingly is this property of human nature exhibited by the fact, that, in popular language, to be in a passion, is to be angry!—But,

> "Anger in hasty *words* or *blows*
> Itself discharges on its foes."

To be moved, then, by a passion, is to be excited, often to external, and always to internal, effort; whether for the continuance and strengthening of the passion, or for its suppression, accordingly as the course which it takes may be painful or pleasurable. If the latter, the soul must contribute to its support, or it never becomes vivid,—and soon languishes, and dies. And this brings us to the point. If every great poet with whose writings men are familiar, in the highest exercise of his genius, before he can be thoroughly enjoyed, has to call forth and to communicate *power*, this service, in a still greater degree, falls upon an original writer, at his first appearance in the world.—Of genius the only proof is, the act of doing well what is worthy to be done, and what was never done before: Of genius, in the fine arts, the only infallible sign is the widening the sphere of human sensibility, for the delight, honour, and benefit of human nature. Genius is the introduction of a new element into the intellectual universe: or, if that be not allowed, it is the application of powers to objects on which they had not before been exercised, or the employment of them in such a manner as to produce effects hitherto unknown. What is all this but an advance, or a conquest, made by the soul of the poet? Is it to be supposed that the reader can make progress of this kind, like an Indian prince or general— stretched on his palanquin, and borne by his slaves? No; he is invigorated and inspirited by his leader, in order that he may exert himself; for he cannot proceed in quiescence, he cannot be carried like a dead weight. Therefore to create taste is to call forth and bestow power, of which knowledge is the effect; and *there* lies the true difficulty.

As the pathetic participates of an *animal* sensation, it might seem— that, if the springs of this emotion were genuine, all men, possessed of competent knowledge of the facts and circumstances, would be instantaneously affected. And, doubtless, in the works of every true poet will be found passages of that species of excellence, which is proved by effects immediate and universal. But there are emotions of the pathetic that are simple and direct, and others—that are complex and revolutionary; some—to which the heart yields with gentleness; others—against which it struggles with pride; these varieties are infinite as the combinations of circumstance and the constitutions of character. Remember, also, that the medium through which, in poetry, the heart is to be affected, is language; a thing subject to endless fluctuations and arbitrary associations. The genius of the poet melts these down for his purpose; but they retain their shape and quality to him who is not capable of exerting, within his own mind, a corresponding energy. There is also a meditative, as well as a human, pathos; an enthusiastic, as well as an ordinary, sorrow; a sadness that has its seat in the depths of reason, to which the mind cannot sink gently of itself—but to which it must descend by treading the steps of thought. And for the sublime,—if we consider what are the cares that occupy the passing day, and how remote is the practice and the course of life from the sources of sublimity, in the soul of Man, can it be wondered that there is little existing preparation for a poet charged with a new mission to extend its kingdom, and to augment and spread its enjoyments?

Away, then, with the senseless iteration of the word, *popular*, applied to new works in poetry, as if there were no test of excellence in this first of the fine arts but that all men should run after its productions, as if urged by an appetite, or constrained by a spell!— The qualities of writing best fitted for eager reception are either such as startle the world into attention by their audacity and extravagance; or they are chiefly of a superficial kind, lying upon the surfaces of manners; or arising out of a selection and arrangement of incidents, by which the mind is kept upon the stretch of curiosity, and the fancy amused without the trouble of thought. But in everything which is to send the soul into herself, to be admonished of her weakness, or to be made conscious of her power;—wherever life and nature are described as operated upon by the creative or abstracting virtue of the imagination; wherever the instinctive wisdom of antiquity and her heroic passions uniting, in the heart of the poet, with the meditative wisdom of later ages, have produced that accord of sublimated humanity, which is at once a history of the remote past and a prophetic enunciation of the remotest future, *there*, the poet must reconcile himself for a season to few and scattered hearers. —Grand thoughts (and Shakspeare must often have sighed over this truth), as they are most naturally and most fitly conceived in solitude, so can they not be brought forth in the midst of plaudits, without some violation of their sanctity. Go to a silent exhibition of the productions of the sister Art, and be convinced that the qualities which dazzle at first sight, and kindle the admiration of the multitude, are essentially different from those by which permanent influence is secured. Let us not shrink from following up these principles as far as they will carry us, and conclude with observing —that there never has been a period, and perhaps never will be, in which vicious poetry of some kind or other, has not excited more zealous admiration, and been far more generally read, than good; but this advantage attends the good, that the *individual*, as well as the species, survives from age to age; whereas, of the depraved, though the species be immortal, the individual quickly *perishes;* the object of present admiration vanishes, being supplanted by some other as easily produced; which, though no better, brings with it at least the irritation of novelty,—with adaptation, more or less skilful, to the changing humours of the majority of those who are most at leisure to regard poetical works when they first solicit their attention.

Is it the result of the whole, that, in the opinion of the Writer, the judgment of the People is not to be respected? The thought is most injurious; and, could the charge be brought against him, he would repel it with indignation. The People have already been justified, and their eulogium pronounced by implication, when it was said, above—that, of *good* poetry, the *individual*, as well as the species, *survives*. And how does it survive but through the People ? What preserves it but their intellect and their wisdom ?

"—Past and future, are the wings
On whose support, harmoniously conjoined,
Moves the great Spirit of human knowledge—" *MS.*[1]

The voice that issues from this Spirit, is that Vox Populi which the Deity inspires. Foolish must he be who can mistake for this a local acclamation, or a transitory outcry—transitory though it be for years, local though from a Nation. Still more lamentable is his error who can believe that there is anything of divine infallibility in the clamour of that small though loud portion of the community, ever governed by factitious influence, which, under the name of the PUBLIC, passes itself, upon the unthinking, for the PEOPLE. Towards the Public, the Writer hopes that he feels as much deference as it is entitled to: but to the People, philosophically characterised, and to the embodied spirit of their knowledge, so far as it exists and moves, at the present, faithfully supported by its two wings, the past and the future, his devout respect, his reverence, is due. He offers it willingly and readily ; and, this done, takes leave of his Readers, by assuring them—that, if he were not persuaded that the contents of these Volumes, and the Work to which they are subsidiary, evince something of the "Vision and the Faculty divine ;" and that, both in words and things, they will operate in their degree, to extend the domain of sensibility for the delight, the honour, and the benefit of human nature, notwithstanding the many happy hours which he has employed in their composition, and the manifold comforts and enjoyments they have procured to him, he would not, if a wish could do it, save them from immediate destruction ;—from becoming at this moment, to the world, as a thing that had never been.

1815.

DEDICATION
PREFIXED TO THE EDITION OF 1815
TO SIR GEORGE HOWLAND BEAUMONT, BART.

MY DEAR SIR GEORGE,

Accept my thanks for the permission given me to dedicate these Volumes to you. In addition to a lively pleasure derived from general considerations, I feel a particular satisfaction ; for, by inscribing these Poems with your Name, I seem to myself in some degree to repay, by an appropriate honour, the great obligation which I owe to one part of the Collection—as having been the means of first making us personally known to each other. Upon much of

[1] *Prelude*, vi. 448–50

the remainder, also, you have a peculiar claim,—for some of the best pieces were composed under the shade of your own groves, upon the classic ground of Coleorton; where I was animated by the recollection of those illustrious Poets of your name and family, who were born in that neighbourhood; and, we may be assured, did not wander with indifference by the dashing stream of Grace Dieu, and among the rocks that diversify the forest of Charnwood.—Nor is there any one to whom such parts of this Collection as have been inspired or coloured by the beautiful Country from which I now address you, could be presented with more propriety than to yourself—to whom it has suggested so many admirable pictures. Early in life, the sublimity and beauty of this region excited your admiration; and I know that you are bound to it in mind by a still strengthening attachment.

Wishing and hoping that this Work, with the embellishments it has received from your pencil,[1] may survive as a lasting memorial of a friendship, which I reckon among the blessings of my life,

I have the honour to be,

My dear Sir George,

Yours most affectionately and faithfully,

WILLIAM WORDSWORTH.

RYDAL MOUNT, WESTMORELAND,
    February 1, 1815.

PREFACE TO THE EDITION OF 1815

[2]THE powers requisite for the production of poetry are: first, those of Observation and Description,—*i.e.* the ability to observe with accuracy things as they are in themselves, and with fidelity to

---

[1] The state of the plates has, for some time, not allowed them to be repeated.—W.

[2] 1815 *begins thus:* The observations prefixed to that portion of these Volumes, which was published many years ago, under the title of "Lyrical Ballads", have so little of a special application to the greater part, perhaps, of this collection, as subsequently enlarged and diversified, that they could not with any propriety stand as an Introduction to it. Not deeming it, however, expedient to suppress that exposition, slight and imperfect as it is, of the feelings which had determined the choice of the subjects, and the principles which had regulated the composition of those Pieces, I have transferred it to the end of the second Volume, to be attended to, or not, at the pleasure of the Reader.

In the Preface to that part of "The Recluse", lately published under the title of "The Excursion", I have alluded to a meditated arrangement of my minor Poems, which should assist the attentive Reader to perceiving their connection with each other, and also their subordination to that Work. I shall here say a few words explanatory of this arrangement, as carried into effect in the present Volumes. *So, with slight verbal variant in first sentence,* 1820–36

describe them, unmodified by any passion or feeling existing in the mind of the describer; whether the things depicted be actually present to the senses, or have a place only in the memory. This power, though indispensable to a Poet, is one which he employs only in submission to necessity, and never for a continuance of time: as its exercise supposes all the higher qualities of the mind to be passive, and in a state of subjection to external objects, much in the same way as a translator or engraver ought to be to his original. 2ndly, Sensibility,—which, the more exquisite it is, the wider will be the range of a poet's perceptions; and the more will he be incited to observe objects, both as they exist in themselves and as re-acted upon by his own mind. (The distinction between poetic and human[1] sensibility has been marked in the character of the Poet delineated in the original preface.) 3rdly, Reflection,—which makes the Poet acquainted with the value of actions, images, thoughts, and feelings; and assists the sensibility in perceiving their connection with each other. 4thly, Imagination and Fancy,—to modify, to create, and to associate. 5thly, Invention,—by which characters are composed out of materials supplied by observation; whether of the Poet's own heart and mind, or of external life and nature; and such incidents and situations produced as are most impressive to the imagination, and most fitted to do justice to the characters, sentiments, and passions, which the Poet undertakes to illustrate. And, lastly, Judgment,—to decide how and where, and in what degree, each of these faculties ought to be exerted; so that the less shall not be sacrificed to the greater; nor the greater, slighting the less, arrogate, to its own injury, more than its due. By judgment, also, is determined what are the laws and appropriate graces of every species of composition.[2]

The materials of Poetry, by these powers collected and produced, are cast, by means of various moulds, into divers forms. The moulds may be enumerated, and the forms specified, in the following order. 1st, The Narrative,—including the Epopœia, the Historic Poem, the Tale, the Romance, the Mock-heroic, and, if the spirit of Homer will tolerate such neighbourhood, that dear production of our days, the metrical Novel. Of this Class, the distinguishing mark is, that the Narrator, however liberally his speaking agents be introduced, is himself the source from which everything primarily flows. Epic Poets, in order that their mode of composition may accord with the elevation of their subject, represent themselves as *singing* from the inspiration of the Muse, "Arma virumque *cano;*" but this is a fiction, in modern times, of slight value: the Iliad or the Paradise Lost would gain little in our estimation by being chanted. The other

[1] *for* human *read* common: emendation of N. C. Smith.
[2] **As** sensibility to harmony of numbers, and the power of producing it, are invariably attendants upon the faculties above specified, nothing has been said upon those requisites.—W. W. 1836

poets who belong to this class are commonly content to *tell* their tale;—so that of the whole it may be affirmed that they neither require nor reject the accompaniment of music.

2ndly, The Dramatic,—consisting of Tragedy, Historic Drama, Comedy, and Masque, in which the Poet does not appear at all in his own person, and where the whole action is carried on by speech and dialogue of the agents; music being admitted only incidentally and rarely. The Opera may be placed here, inasmuch as it proceeds by dialogue; though depending, to the degree that it does, upon music, it has a strong claim to be ranked with the lyrical. The characteristic and impassioned Epistle, of which Ovid and Pope have given examples, considered as a species of monodrama, may, without impropriety, be placed in this class.

3rdly, The Lyrical,—containing the Hymn, the Ode, the Elegy, the Song, and the Ballad; in all which, for the production of their *full* effect, an accompaniment of music is indispensable.

4thly, The Idyllium,—descriptive chiefly either of the processes and appearances of external nature, as the Seasons of Thomson; or of characters, manners, and sentiments, as are Shenstone's Schoolmistress, The Cotter's Saturday Night of Burns, The Twa Dogs of the same Author; or of these in conjunction with the appearances of Nature, as most of the pieces of Theocritus, the Allegro and Penseroso of Milton, Beattie's Minstrel, Goldsmith's Deserted Village. The Epitaph, the Inscription, the Sonnet, most of the epistles of poets writing in their own persons, and all loco-descriptive poetry, belong to this class.

5thly, Didactic,—the principal object of which is direct instruction; as the Poem of Lucretius, the Georgics of Virgil, The Fleece of Dyer, Mason's English Garden, &c.

And, lastly, philosophical Satire, like that of Horace and Juvenal; personal and occasional Satire rarely comprehending sufficient of the general in the individual to be dignified with the name of poetry.

Out of the three last has been constructed a composite order, of which Young's Night Thoughts, and Cowper's Task, are excellent examples.

It is deducible from the above, that poems, apparently miscellaneous, may with propriety be arranged either with reference to the powers of mind *predominant* in the production of them; or to the mould in which they are cast; or, lastly, to the subjects to which they relate. From each of these considerations, the following Poems have been divided into classes; which, that the work may more obviously correspond with the course of human life, and for the sake of exhibiting in it the three requisites of a legitimate whole, a beginning, a middle, and an end, have been also arranged, as far as it was possible, according to an order of time. commencing with Childhood, and terminating with Old Age, Death, and Immortality. My guiding wish was, that the small pieces of which these volumes consist, thus discriminated, might be regarded under a two-fold view; as composing an entire work within themselves, and as adjuncts to the philosophical Poem, "The Recluse." This arrangement has long presented itself habitually to my own mind. Nevertheless, I should have preferred to scatter the contents of these volumes at random, if I had been persuaded that, by the plan adopted, anything material would be taken from the natural effect of the pieces, individually, on the mind of the unreflecting Reader. I trust there is a sufficient variety in each class to prevent this; while, for him who reads with reflection, the arrangement will serve as a commentary unostentatiously directing his attention to my purposes, both particular and general. But, as I wish to guard against the possibility of misleading by this classification, it is proper first to remind the Reader, that certain poems are placed according to the powers of mind, in the Author's conception, predominant in the production of them; *predominant*, which implies the exertion of other faculties in less degree. Where there is more imagination than fancy in a poem, it is placed under the head of imagination, and *vice versâ*. Both the above classes might without impropriety have been enlarged from that consisting of "Poems founded on the Affections;" as might this latter from those, and from the class "proceeding from Sentiment and Reflection." The most striking characteristics of each piece, mutual illustration, variety, and proportion, have governed me throughout.[1]

[1] throughout. / None] It may be proper in this place to state, that the Extracts in the 2nd Class entitled "Juvenile Pieces," are in many places altered from the printed copy, chiefly by omission and compression. The slight alterations of another kind were for the most part made not long after the publication of the Poems from which the Extracts are taken.[a] These Extracts seem to have a title to be placed here as they were the productions of youth, and represent implicitly some of the features of a youthful mind, at a time when images of nature supplied to it the place of thought, sentiment, and almost of action; or, as it will be found expressed, of a state of mind when

> "the sounding cataract
> Haunted me like a passion: the tall rock,
> The mountain, and the deep and gloomy wood,
> Their colours and their forms were then to me
> An appetite, a feeling and a love,
> That had no need of a remoter charm,
> By thought supplied, or any interest .
> Unborrowed from the eye."——

I will own that I was much at a loss what to select of these descriptions, and perhaps it would have been better either to have reprinted the whole, or suppressed what I have given. 1815–36

a These poems are now printed entire.—W. W. 1820–36.

None of the other Classes, except those of Fancy and Imagination, require any particular notice. But a remark of general application may be made. All Poets, except the dramatic, have been in the practice of feigning that their works were composed to the music of the harp or lyre: with what degree of affectation this has been done in modern times, I leave to the judicious to determine. For my own part, I have not been disposed to violate probability so far, or to make such a large demand upon the Reader's charity. Some of these pieces are essentially lyrical; and, therefore, cannot have their due force without a supposed musical accompaniment; but, in much the greatest part, as a substitute for the classic lyre or romantic harp, I require nothing more than an animated or impassioned recitation, adapted to the subject. Poems, however humble in their kind, if they be good in that kind, cannot read themselves; the law of long syllable and short must not be so inflexible,—the letter of metre must not be so impassive to the spirit of versification,—as to deprive the Reader of all[1] voluntary power to modulate, in subordination to the sense, the music of the poem;—in the same manner as his mind is left at liberty, and even summoned, to act upon its thoughts and images. But, though the accompaniment of a musical instrument be frequently dispensed with, the true Poet does not therefore abandon his privilege distinct from that of the mere Proseman;

"He murmurs near the running brooks,
A music sweeter than their own."[2]

Let us come now to the consideration of the words Fancy and Imagination, as employed in the classification of the following Poems. "A man," says an intelligent author, "has imagination in proportion as he can distinctly copy in idea the impressions of sense: it is the faculty which *images* within the mind the phenomena of sensation. A man has fancy in proportion as he can call up, connect, or associate, at pleasure, those internal images (φαντάζειν is to cause to appear) so as to complete ideal representations of absent objects. Imagination is the power of depicting, and fancy of evoking and combining. The imagination is formed by patient observation; the fancy by a voluntary activity in shifting the scenery of the mind. The more accurate the imagination, the more safely may a painter, or a poet, undertake a delineation, or a description, without the presence of the objects to be characterised. The more versatile the fancy, the more original and striking will be the decorations produced."—*British Synonyms discriminated, by W. Taylor.*

Is not this as if a man should undertake to supply an account of a building, and be so intent upon what he had discovered of the

[1] all 1836: a 1815–32
[2] *A Poet's Epitaph* (*Poems of Sentiment and Reflection*, viii).

foundation, as to conclude his task without once looking up at the superstructure ? Here, as in other instances throughout the volume, the judicious Author's mind is enthralled by Etymology; he takes up the original word as his guide and escort, and too often does not perceive how soon he becomes its prisoner, without liberty to tread in any path but that to which it confines him. It is not easy to find out how imagination, thus explained, differs from distinct remembrance of images; or fancy from quick and vivid recollection of them: each is nothing more than a mode of memory. If the two words bear the above meaning, and no other, what term is left to designate that faculty of which the Poet is "all compact;"[1] he whose eye glances from earth to heaven, whose spiritual attributes body forth what his pen is prompt in turning to shape; or what is left to characterise Fancy, as insinuating herself into the heart of objects with creative activity ?—Imagination, in the sense of the word as giving title to a class of the following Poems, has no reference to images that are merely a faithful copy, existing in the mind, of absent external objects; but is a word of higher import, denoting operations of the mind upon those objects, and processes of creation or of composition, governed by certain fixed laws. I proceed to illustrate my meaning by instances. A parrot *hangs* from the wires of his cage by his beak or by his claws; or a monkey from the bough of a tree by his paws or his tail. Each creature does so literally and actually. In the first Eclogue of Virgil, the shepherd, thinking of the time when he is to take leave of his farm, thus addresses his goats:

> "Non ego vos posthac viridi projectus in antro
> Dumosa *pendere* procul de rupe videbo."
> ———"half way down
> *Hangs* one who gathers samphire,"[2]

is the well-known expression of Shakspeare, delineating an ordinary image upon the cliffs of Dover. In these two instances is a slight exertion of the faculty which I denominate imagination, in the use of one word: neither the goats nor the samphire-gatherer do literally hang, as does the parrot or the monkey; but, presenting to the senses something of such an appearance, the mind in its activity, for its own gratification, contemplates them as hanging.

> "As when far off at sea a fleet descried
> *Hangs* in the clouds, by equinoctial winds
> Close sailing from Bengala, or the isles
> Of Ternate or Tidore, whence merchants bring
> Their spicy drugs; they on the trading flood
> Through the wide Ethiopian to the Cape
> Ply, stemming nightly toward the Pole: so seemed
> Far off the flying Fiend."[3]

[1] *A Midsummer Night's Dream*, v. i. 7–17.   [2] *King Lear*, iv. vi. 16.
[3] *Paradise Lost*, ii. 636–43.

Here is the full strength of the imagination involved in the word *hangs*, and exerted upon the whole image: First, the fleet, an aggregate of many ships, is represented as one mighty person, whose track, we know and feel, is upon the waters; but, taking advantage of its appearance to the senses, the Poet dares to represent it as *hanging in the clouds*, both for the gratification of the mind in contemplating the image itself, and in reference to the motion and appearance of the sublime objects to which it is compared.

From impressions[1] of sight we will pass to those of sound; which, as they must necessarily be of a less definite character, shall be selected from these volumes:

"Over his own sweet voice the Stock-dove *broods*;"[2]

of the same bird,

"His voice was *buried* among trees,
Yet to be come at by the breeze;"[3]

"O, Cuckoo! shall I call thee *Bird*,
Or but a wandering *Voice?*"[4]

The stock-dove is said to *coo*, a sound well imitating the note of the bird; but, by the intervention of the metaphor *broods*, the affections are called in by the imagination to assist in marking the manner in which the bird reiterates and prolongs her soft note, as if herself delighting to listen to it, and participating of a still and quiet satisfaction, like that which may be supposed inseparable from the continuous process of incubation. "His voice was buried among trees," a metaphor expressing the love of *seclusion* by which this Bird is marked; and characterising its note as not partaking of the shrill and the piercing, and therefore more easily deadened by the intervening shade; yet a note so peculiar and withal so pleasing, that the breeze, gifted with that love of the sound which the Poet feels, penetrates the shades in which it is entombed, and conveys it to the ear of the listener.

"Shall I call thee Bird,
Or but a wandering Voice?"

This concise interrogation characterises the seeming ubiquity of the voice of the cuckoo, and dispossesses the creature almost of a corporeal existence; the Imagination being tempted to this exertion of her power by a consciousness in the memory that the cuckoo is almost perpetually heard throughout the season of spring, but seldom becomes an object of sight.

Thus far of images independent of each other, and immediately

---

[1] impressions 1836: images 1815–32
[2] *Resolution and Independence*, 5 (*supra*, p. 235).
[3] 'O Nightingale! Thou surely art' 13–14 (*supra*, p. 214).
To the Cuckoo, 3–4 (*supra*, p. 207).

endowed by the mind with properties that do not inhere in them, upon an incitement from properties and qualities the existence of which is inherent and obvious. These processes of imagination are carried on either by conferring additional properties upon an object, or abstracting from it some of those which it actually possesses, and thus enabling it to re-act upon the mind which hath performed the process, like a new existence.

I pass from the Imagination acting upon an individual image to a consideration of the same faculty employed upon images in a conjunction by which they modify each other. The Reader has already had a fine instance before him in the passage quoted from Virgil, where the apparently perilous situation of the goat, hanging upon the shaggy precipice, is contrasted with that of the shepherd contemplating it from the seclusion of the cavern in which he lies stretched at ease and in security. Take these images separately, and how unaffecting the picture compared with that produced by their being thus connected with, and opposed to, each other!

> "As a huge stone is sometimes seen to lie
> Couched on the bald top of an eminence,
> Wonder to all who do the same espy
> By what means it could thither come, and whence,
> So that it seems a thing endued with sense,
> Like a sea-beast crawled forth, which on a shelf
> Of rock or sand reposeth, there to sun himself.
>
> Such seemed this Man; not all alive or dead
> Nor all asleep, in his extreme old age.
>   .   .   .   .
> Motionless as a cloud the old Man stood,
> That heareth not the loud winds when they call,
> And moveth altogether if it move at all."[1]

In these images, the conferring, the abstracting, and the modifying powers of the Imagination, immediately and mediately acting, are all brought into conjunction. The stone is endowed with something of the power of life to approximate it to the sea-beast; and the sea-beast stripped of some of its vital qualities to assimilate it to the stone; which intermediate image is thus treated for the purpose of bringing the original image, that of the stone, to a nearer resemblance to the figure and condition of the aged Man; who is divested of so much of the indications of life and motion as to bring him to the point where the two objects unite and coalesce in just comparison. After what has been said, the image of the cloud need not be commented upon.

Thus far of an endowing or modifying power: but the Imagination also shapes and *creates;* and how? By innumerable processes; and

---

[1] *Resolution and Independence*, 57–65, 75–7 (*supra*, p. 237).

in none does it more delight than in that of consolidating numbers into unity, and dissolving and separating unity into number,—alternations proceeding from, and governed by, a sublime consciousness of the soul in her own mighty and almost divine powers. Recur to the passage already cited from Milton. When the compact Fleet, as one Person, has been introduced "sailing from Bengala," "They," *i.e.* the "merchants," representing the fleet resolved into a multitude of ships, "ply" their voyage towards the extremities of the earth: "So," (referring to the word "As" in the commencement) "seemed the flying Fiend;" the image of his Person acting to recombine the multitude of ships into one body,—the point from which the comparison set out. "So seemed," and to whom seemed? To the heavenly Muse who dictates the poem, to the eye of the Poet's mind, and to that of the Reader, present at one moment in the wide Ethiopian, and the next in the solitudes, then first broken in upon, of the infernal regions!

"Modo me Thebis, modo ponit Athenis."[1]

Hear again this mighty Poet,—speaking of the Messiah going forth to expel from heaven the rebellious angels,

"Attended by ten thousand thousand Saints
He onward came: far off his coming shone,"—[2]

the retinue of Saints, and the Person of the Messiah himself, lost almost and merged in the splendour of that indefinite abstraction "His coming!"

As I do not mean here to treat this subject further than to throw some light upon the present Volumes, and especially upon one division of them, I shall spare myself and the Reader the trouble of considering the Imagination as it deals with thoughts and sentiments, as it regulates the composition of characters, and determines the course of actions: I will not consider it (more than I have already done by implication) as that power which, in the language of one of my most esteemed Friends, "draws all things to one; which makes things animate or inanimate, beings with their attributes, subjects with their accessories, take one colour and serve to one effect[3]." The grand store-houses of enthusiastic and meditative Imagination, of poetical, as contra-distinguished from human and dramatic Imagination, are the prophetic and lyrical parts of the Holy Scriptures, and the works of Milton; to which I cannot forbear to add those of Spenser. I select these writers in preference to those of ancient Greece and Rome, because the anthropomorphitism of the Pagan religion subjected the minds of the greatest poets in those countries too much to the bondage of definite form; from which the Hebrews

---

[1] Horace, *Epistles*, II. i. 213. [2] *Paradise Lost*, vi. 767–8.
[3] Charles Lamb upon the genius of Hogarth.—W. W.

were preserved by their abhorrence of idolatry. This abhorrence was almost as strong in our great epic Poet, both from circumstances of his life, and from the constitution of his mind. However imbued the surface might be with classical literature, he was a Hebrew in soul; and all things tended in him towards the sublime. Spenser, of a gentler nature, maintained his freedom by aid of his allegorical spirit, at one time inciting him to create persons out of abstractions; and, at another, by a superior effort of genius, to give the universality and permanence of abstractions to his human beings, by means of attributes and emblems that belong to the highest moral truths and the purest sensations,—of which his character of Una is a glorious example. Of the human and dramatic Imagination the works of Shakspeare are an inexhaustible source.

> "I tax not you, ye Elements, with unkindness,
> I never gave you kingdoms, call'd you Daughters!"[1]

And if, bearing in mind the many Poets distinguished by this prime quality, whose names I omit to mention; yet justified by recollection of the insults which the ignorant, the incapable, and the presumptuous, have heaped upon these and my other writings, I may be permitted to anticipate the judgment of posterity upon myself, I shall declare (censurable, I grant, if the notoriety of the fact above stated does not justify me) that I have given in these unfavourable times, evidence of exertions of this faculty upon its worthiest objects, the external universe, the moral and religious sentiments of Man, his natural affections, and his acquired passions; which have the same ennobling tendency as the productions of men, in this kind, worthy to be holden in undying remembrance.[2]

To the mode in which Fancy has already been characterised as

---

[1] *King Lear*, III. ii. 16–17.

[2] remembrance. / To the mode] I dismiss this subject with observing— that, in the series of Poems placed under the head of Imagination, I have begun with one of the earliest processes of Nature in the development of this faculty. Guided by one of my own primary consciousnesses, I have presented a commutation and transfer of internal feelings, co-operating with external accidents, to plant, for immortality, images of sound and sight, in the celestial soil of the Imagination. The Boy, there introduced, is listening, with something of a feverish and restless anxiety, for the recurrence of those riotous sounds which he had previously excited; and, at the moment when the intenseness of his mind is beginning to remit, he is surprised into a perception of the solemn and tranquillizing images which the Poem describes.—The Poems next in succession exhibit the faculty exerting itself upon various objects of the external universe; then follow others, where it is employed upon feelings, characters, and actions;[a] and the Class is concluded with imaginative pictures of moral, political and religious sentiments. 1815–36

[a] Such of these as were furnished by Scottish subjects have since been arranged in a class, entitled "Memorials of Tours in Scotland."—W.W

the power of evoking and combining, or, as my friend Mr. Coleridge has styled it, "the aggregative and associative power," my objection is only that the definition is too general. To aggregate and to associate, to evoke and to combine, belong as well to the Imagination as to the Fancy; but either the materials evoked and combined are different; or they are brought together under a different law, and for a different purpose. Fancy does not require that the materials which she makes use of should be susceptible of change in their constitution, from her touch; and, where they admit of modification, it is enough for her purpose if it be slight, limited, and evanescent. Directly the reverse of these, are the desires and demands of the Imagination. She recoils from everything but the plastic, the pliant, and the indefinite. She leaves it to Fancy to describe Queen Mab as coming,

> "In shape no bigger than an agate-stone
> On the fore-finger of an alderman."[1]

Having to speak of stature, she does not tell you that her gigantic Angel was as tall as Pompey's Pillar; much less that he was twelve cubits, or twelve hundred cubits high; or that his dimensions equalled those of Teneriffe or Atlas;—because these, and if they were a million times as high it would be the same, are bounded: The expression is, "His stature reached the sky!" the illimitable firmament!—When the Imagination frames a comparison, if it does not strike on the first presentation, a sense of the truth of the likeness, from the moment that it is perceived, grows—and continues to grow—upon the mind; the resemblance depending less upon outline of form and feature, than upon expression and effect; less upon casual and outstanding, than upon inherent and internal, properties: moreover, the images invariably modify each other.—The law under which the processes of Fancy are carried on is as capricious as the accidents of things, and the effects are surprising, playful, ludicrous, amusing, tender, or pathetic, as the objects happen to be appositely produced or fortunately combined. Fancy depends upon the rapidity and profusion with which she scatters her thoughts and images; trusting that their number, and the felicity with which they are linked together, will make amends for the want of individual value: or she prides herself upon the curious subtilty and the successful elaboration with which she can detect their lurking affinities. If she can win you over to her purpose, and impart to you her feelings, she cares not how unstable or transitory may be her influence, knowing that it will not be out of her power to resume it upon an apt occasion. But the Imagination is conscious of an indestructible dominion;—the Soul may fall away from it, not being able to sustain its grandeur; but, if once felt and acknowledged, by no act of any

[1] *Romeo and Juliet*, I. iv. 55–6.

other faculty of the mind can it be relaxed, impaired, or diminished. —Fancy is given to quicken and to beguile the temporal part of our nature, Imagination to incite and to support the eternal.—Yet is it not the less true that Fancy, as she is an active, is also, under her own laws and in her own spirit, a creative faculty. In what manner Fancy ambitiously aims at a rivalship with Imagination, and Imagination stoops to work with the materials of Fancy, might be illustrated from the compositions of all eloquent writers, whether in prose or verse; and chiefly from those of our own Country. Scarcely a page of the impassioned parts of Bishop Taylor's Works can be opened that shall not afford examples.—Referring the Reader to those inestimable volumes, I will content myself with placing a conceit (ascribed to Lord Chesterfield) in contrast with a passage from the Paradise Lost:—

> "The dews of the evening most carefully shun,
> They are the tears of the sky for the loss of the sun."[1]

After the transgression of Adam, Milton, with other appearances of sympathising Nature, thus marks the immediate consequence,

> "Sky lowered, and, muttering thunder, some sad drops
> Wept at completion of the mortal sin."[2]

The associating link is the same in each instance: Dew and[3] rain, not distinguishable from the liquid substance of tears, are employed as indications of sorrow. A flash of surprise is the effect in the former case; a flash of surprise, and nothing more; for the nature of things does not sustain the combination. In the latter, the effects from the act, of which there is this immediate consequence and visible sign, are so momentous, that the mind acknowledges the justice and reasonableness of the sympathy in nature so manifested; and the sky weeps drops of water as if with human eyes, as "Earth had before trembled from her entrails, and Nature given a second groan."[4]

Finally, I will refer to Cotton's "Ode upon Winter," an admirable composition, though stained with some peculiarities of the age in which he lived, for a general illustration of the characteristics of Fancy. The middle part of this ode contains a most lively description of the entrance of Winter, with his retinue, as "A palsied king,"

---

[1] Chesterfield, *Advice to a Lady in Autumn.*
[2] *P. L.* ix. 1000–3. [3] and] 1836: or 1815
[4] groan." / Finally: Awe-stricken as I am by contemplating the operations of the mind of this truly divine Poet, I scarcely dare venture to add that "An address to an Infant", which the Reader will find under the Class of Fancy in the present Volumes, exhibits something of this communion and interchange of instruments and functions between the two powers; and is, accordingly, placed last in the class, as a preparation for that of Imagination which follows. 1815–36 (*An Address to an Infant* [*supra*, p. 174] *is not the last poem in the Class of Fancy after ed.* 1832).

and yet a military monarch,—advancing for conquest with his army; the several bodies of which, and their arms and equipments, are described with a rapidity of detail, and a profusion of *fanciful* comparisons, which indicate on the part of the poet extreme activity of intellect, and a correspondent hurry of delightful feeling. Winter[1] retires from the foe into his fortress, where

> —————"a magazine
> Of sovereign juice is cellared in;
> Liquor that will the siege maintain
> Should Phœbus ne'er return again."

Though myself a water-drinker, I cannot resist the pleasure of transcribing what follows, as an instance still more happy of Fancy employed in the treatment of feeling than, in its preceding passages, the Poem supplies of her management of forms.

> "'Tis that, that gives the poet rage,
> And thaws the gelly'd blood of age;
> Matures the young, restores the old,
> And makes the fainting coward bold.
>
> "It lays the careful head to rest,
> Calms palpitations in the breast,
> Renders our lives' misfortune sweet;
>
> .   .   .   .
>
> "Then let the chill Sirocco blow,
> And gird us round with hills of snow,
> Or else go whistle to the shore,
> And make the hollow mountains roar,
>
> "Whilst we together jovial sit
> Careless, and crowned with mirth and wit,
> Where, though bleak winds confine us home
> Our fancies round the world shall roam.
>
> "We'll think of all the Friends we know,
> And drink to all worth drinking to;
> When having drunk all thine and mine,
> We rather shall want healths than wine.
>
> "But where Friends fail us, we'll supply
> Our friendships with our charity;
> Men that remote in sorrows live,
> Shall by our lusty brimmers thrive.
>
> "We'll drink the wanting into wealth,
> And those that languish into health,
> The afflicted into joy; th' opprest
> Into security and rest.

[1] Winter 1836: He 1815

"The worthy in disgrace shall find
Favour return again more kind,
And in restraint who stifled lie,
Shall taste the air of liberty.

"The brave shall triumph in success,
The lover shall have mistresses,
Poor unregarded Virtue, praise,
And the neglected Poet, bays.

"Thus shall our healths do others good,
Whilst we ourselves do all we would;
For, freed from envy and from care,
What would we be but what we are ?"[1]

When I sate down to write this Preface, it was my intention to have made it more comprehensive; but, thinking that I ought rather to apologise for detaining the reader so long, I will here conclude.[2]

POSTSCRIPT[3]

1835

In the present volume, as in those that have preceded it,[4] the reader will have found occasionally opinions expressed upon the course of public affairs, and feelings given vent to as national interests excited them. Since nothing, I trust,[5] has been uttered but in the spirit of reflective patriotism, those notices are left to produce their own effect; but, among the many objects of general concern, and the changes going forward, which I have glanced at in verse, are some especially affecting the lower orders of society; in reference to these, I wish here to add a few words in plain prose.

[1] are ?" / When] It remains that I should express my regret at the necessity of separating my compositions from some beautiful Poems of Mr. Coleridge, with which they have been long associated in publication. The feelings, with which that joint publication was made, have been gratified; its end is answered, and the time is come when considerations of general propriety dictate the separation. Three short pieces (now first published) are the work of a Female Friend; and the Reader, to whom they may be acceptable, is indebted to me for his pleasure; if any one regard them with dislike, or be disposed to condemn them, let the censure fall upon him, who, trusting in his own sense of their merit and their fitness for the place which they occupy, *extorted* them from the Authoress. 1815–32

[2] but . . . conclude *so* 1845: but as all that I deem necessary is expressed, I will here detain the reader no longer:—what I have further to remark shall be inserted, by way of interlude, at the close of this Volume. 1815 (introduced . . . in some other part of these Volumes. 1820–36)

[3] *v.* Vol. iv, p. 426 *infra* for opening paragraphs in MS.

[4] as in the author's previous poems 1835

[5] I trust] he trusts: 1835 *has third person for first throughout the Postscript*

Were I conscious of being able to do justice to those important topics, I might avail myself of the periodical press for offering anonymously my thoughts, such as they are, to the world; but I feel that, in procuring attention, they may derive some advantage, however small, from my name, in addition to that of being presented in a less fugitive shape. It is also not impossible that the state of mind which some of the foregoing poems may have produced in the reader, will dispose him to receive more readily the impression which I desire to make, and to admit the conclusions I would establish.

I. The first thing that presses upon my attention is the Poor-Law Amendment Act. I am aware of the magnitude and complexity of the subject, and the unwearied attention which it has received from men of far wider experience than my own; yet I cannot forbear touching upon one point of it, and to this I will confine myself, though not insensible to the objection which may reasonably be brought against treating a portion of this, or any other, great scheme of civil polity separately from the whole. The point to which I wish to draw the reader's attention is, that *all* persons who cannot find employment, or procure wages sufficient to support the body in health and strength, are entitled to a maintenance by law.

This dictate of humanity[1] is acknowledged in the Report of the Commissioners; but is there not room for apprehension that some of the regulations of the new act have a tendency to render the principle nugatory by difficulties thrown in the way of applying it? If this be so, persons will not be wanting to show it, by examining the provisions of the act in detail,—an attempt which would be quite out of place here; but it will not, therefore, be deemed unbecoming in one who fears that the prudence of the head may, in framing some of those provisions, have supplanted the wisdom of the heart, to enforce a principle which cannot be violated without infringing upon one of the most precious rights of the English people, and opposing one of the most sacred claims of civilized humanity.

There can be no greater error, in this department of legislation, than the belief that this principle does by necessity operate for the degradation of those who claim, or are so circumstanced as to make it likely they may claim, through laws founded upon it, relief or assistance. The direct contrary is the truth: it may be unanswerably maintained that its tendency is to raise, not to depress; by stamping a value upon life, which can belong to it only where the laws have placed men who are willing to work, and yet cannot find employment, above the necessity of looking for protection against hunger and other natural evils, either to individual and casual charity, to despair and death, or to the breach of law by theft, or violence.

And here, as in the Report of the Commissioners the fundamental

---

[1] dictate of humanity] principle 1835

principle has been recognised, I am not at issue with them any farther than I am compelled to believe that their "remedial measures" obstruct the application of it more than the interests of society require.

And, calling to mind the doctrines of political economy which are now prevaient, I cannot forbear to enforce the justice of the principle, and to insist upon its salutary operation.

And first for its justice: If self-preservation be the first law of our nature, would not every one in a state of nature be morally justified in taking to himself that which is indispensable to such preservation, where, by so doing, he would not rob another of that which might be equally indispensable to *his* preservation? And if the value of life be regarded in a right point of view, may it not be questioned whether this right of preserving life, at any expense short of endangering the life of another, does not survive man's entering into the social state; whether this right can be surrendered or forfeited, except when it opposes the divine law, upon any supposition of a social compact, or of any convention for the protection of mere rights of property?

But, if it be not safe to touch the abstract question of man's right in a social state to help himself even in the last extremity, may we not still contend for the duty of a christian government, standing *in loco parentis* towards all its subjects, to make such effectual provision, that no one shall be in danger of perishing either through the neglect or harshness of its legislation? Or, waiving this, is it not indisputable that the claim of the state to the allegiance, involves the protection, of the subject? And, as all rights in one party impose a correlative duty upon another, it follows that the right of the state to require the services of its members, even to the jeoparding of their lives in the common defence, establishes a right in the people (not to be gainsaid by utilitarians and economists) to public support when, from any cause, they may be unable to support themselves.

Let us now consider the salutary and benign operation of this principle. Here we must have recourse to elementary feelings of human nature, and to truths which from their very obviousness are apt to be slighted, till they are forced upon our notice by our own sufferings or those of others. In the Paradise Lost, Milton represents Adam, after the Fall, as exclaiming, in the anguish of his soul—

> "Did I request Thee, Maker, from my clay
> To mould me man; did I solicit Thee
> From darkness to promote me?
> .   .   .   .   .   .   My will
> Concurred not to my being."[1]

Under how many various pressures of misery have men been

[1] *P.L.* x. 743–7.

driven thus, in a strain touching upon impiety, to expostulate with the Creator! and under few so afflictive as when the source and origin of earthly existence have been brought back to the mind by its impending close in the pangs of destitution. But as long as, in our legislation, due weight shall be given to this principle, no man will be forced to bewail the gift of life in hopeless want of the necessaries of life.

Englishmen have, therefore, by the progress of civilisation among them, been placed in circumstances more favourable to piety and resignation to the divine will, than the inhabitants of other countries, where a like provision has not been established. And as Providence, in this care of our countrymen, acts through a human medium, the objects of that care must, in like manner, be more inclined towards a grateful love of their fellow-men. Thus, also, do stronger ties attach the people to their country, whether while they tread its soil, or, at a distance, think of their native land as an indulgent parent, to whose arms, even they who have been imprudent and undeserving may, like the prodigal son, betake themselves, without fear of being rejected.

Such is the view of the case that would first present itself to a reflective mind; and it is in vain to show, by appeals to experience, in contrast with this view, that provisions founded upon the principle have promoted profaneness of life, and dispositions the reverse of philanthropic, by spreading idleness, selfishness, and rapacity: for these evils have arisen, not as an inevitable consequence of the principle, but for want of judgment in framing laws based upon it; and, above all, from faults in the mode of administering the law. The mischief that has grown to such a height from granting relief in cases where proper vigilance would have shown that it was not required, or in bestowing it in undue measure, will be urged by no truly enlightened statesman, as a sufficient reason for banishing the principle itself from legislation.

Let us recur to the miserable states of consciousness that it precludes.

There is a story told, by a traveller in Spain, of a female who, by a sudden shock of domestic calamity, was driven out of her senses, and ever after looked up incessantly to the sky, feeling that her fellow-creatures could do nothing for her relief. Can there be Englishmen who, with a good end in view, would, upon system, expose their brother Englishmen to a like necessity of looking upwards only; or downwards to the earth, after it shall contain no spot where the destitute can demand, by civil right, what by right of nature they are entitled to?

Suppose the objects of our sympathy not sunk into this blank despair, but wandering about as strangers in streets and ways, with the hope of succour from casual charity; what have we gained by such

a change of scene ? Woeful is the condition of the famished Northern
Indian, dependent, among winter snows, upon the chance-passage
of a herd of deer, from which one, if brought down by his rifle-gun,
may be made the means of keeping him and his companions alive.
As miserable is that of some savage Islander, who, when the land
has ceased to afford him sustenance, watches for food which the
waves may cast up, or in vain endeavours to extract it from the
inexplorable deep. But neither of these is in a state of wretchedness
comparable to that, which is so often endured in civilised society:
multitudes, in all ages, have known it, of whom may be said:—

> "Homeless, near a thousand homes they stood,
> And near a thousand tables pined, and wanted food."[1]

Justly might I be accused of wasting time in an uncalled-for
attempt to excite the feelings of the reader, if systems of political
economy, widely spread, did not impugn the principle, and if the
safeguards against such extremities were left unimpaired. It is
broadly asserted by many, that every man who endeavours to find
work, *may* find it: were this assertion capable of being verified, there
still would remain a question, what kind of work, and how far may
the labourer be fit for it ? For if sedentary work is to be exchanged
for standing; and some light and nice exercise of the fingers, to
which an artisan has been accustomed all his life, for severe labour
of the arms; the best efforts would turn to little account, and occasion
would be given for the unthinking and the unfeeling unwarrantably
to reproach those who are put upon such employment, as idle,
froward, and unworthy of relief, either by law or in any other way!
Were this statement correct, there would indeed be an end of the
argument, the principle here maintained would be superseded. But,
alas! it is far otherwise. That principle, applicable to the benefit of
all countries, is indispensable for England, upon whose coast families
are perpetually deprived of their support by shipwreck, and where
large masses of men are so liable to be thrown out of their ordinary
means of gaining bread, by changes in commercial intercourse, subject mainly or solely to the will of foreign powers; by new discoveries
in arts and manufactures; and by reckless laws, in conformity with
theories of political economy, which, whether right or wrong in the
abstract, have proved a scourge to tens of thousands, by the abruptness with which they have been carried into practice.

But it is urged,—refuse altogether compulsory relief to the able-
bodied, and the number of those who stand in need of relief will
steadily diminish through a conviction of an absolute necessity for
greater forethought, and more prudent care of a man's earnings.
Undoubtedly it would, but so also would it, and in a much greater
degree, if the legislative provisions were retained, and parochial

---

[1] *Guilt and Sorrow*, 368–9.

relief administered under the care of the upper classes, as it ought to be. For it has been invariably found, that wherever the funds have been raised and applied under the superintendence of gentlemen and substantial proprietors, acting in vestries, and as overseers, pauperism has diminished accordingly. Proper care in that quarter would effectually check what is felt in some districts to be one of the worst evils in the poor law system, viz. the readiness of small and needy proprietors to join in imposing rates that seemingly subject them to great hardships, while, in fact, this is done with a mutual understanding, that the relief each is ready to bestow upon his still poorer neighbours will be granted to himself, or his relatives, should it hereafter be applied for.[1]

But let us look to inner sentiments of a nobler quality, in order to know what we have to build upon. Affecting proofs occur in every one's experience, who is acquainted with the unfortunate and the indigent, of their unwillingness to derive their subsistence from aught but their own funds or labour, or to be indebted to parochial assistance for the attainment of any object, however dear to them. A case was reported, the other day, from a coroner's inquest, of a pair who, through the space of four years, had carried about their dead infant from house to house, and from lodging to lodging, as their necessities drove them, rather than ask the parish to bear the expense of its interment:—the poor creatures lived in the hope of one day being able to bury their child at their own cost. It must have been heart-rending to see and hear the mother, who had been called upon to account for the state in which the body was found, make this deposition. By some, judging coldly, if not harshly, this conduct might be imputed to an unwarrantable pride, as[2] she and her husband had, it is true, been once in prosperity. But examples, where the spirit of independence works with equal strength, though not with like miserable accompaniments, are frequently to be found even yet among the humblest peasantry and mechanics. There is not, then, sufficient cause for doubting that a like sense of honour may be revived among the people, and their ancient habits of independence restored, without resorting to those severities which the new Poor Law Act has introduced.

But even if the surfaces of things only are to be examined, we have a right to expect that law-givers should take into account the various tempers and dispositions of mankind: while some are led, by the existence of a legislative provision, into idleness and extravagance, the economical virtues might be cherished in others by the knowledge that, if all their efforts fail, they have in the Poor Laws

---

[1] with an understanding, which prepares the way for the relief . . . neighbours being granted to . . . relatives, when it shall be applied for. 1835
[2] By some . . . as *not in* 1835

a "refuge from the storm and a shadow from the heat." Despondency and distraction are no friends to prudence: the springs of industry will relax, if cheerfulness be destroyed by anxiety; without hope men become reckless, and have a sullen pride in adding to the heap of their own wretchedness. He who feels that he is abandoned by his fellow-men will be almost irresistibly driven to care little for himself; will lose his self-respect accordingly, and with that loss what remains to him of virtue?

With all due deference to the particular experience, and general intelligence of the individuals who framed the Act, and of those who in and out of parliament have approved of and supported it; it may be said, that it proceeds too much upon the presumption that it is a labouring man's own fault if he be not, as the phrase is, beforehand with the world. But the most prudent are liable to be thrown back by sickness, cutting them off from labour, and causing to them expense: and who but has observed how distress creeps upon multitudes without misconduct of their own; and merely from a gradual fall in the price of labour, without a correspondent one in the price of provisions; so that men who may have ventured upon the marriage state with a fair prospect of maintaining their families in comfort and happiness, see them reduced to a pittance which no effort of theirs can increase? Let it be remembered, also, that there are thousands with whom vicious habits of expense are not the cause why they do not store up their gains; but they are generous and kind-hearted, and ready to help their kindred and friends; moreover, they have a faith in Providence that those who have been prompt to assist others, will not be left destitute, should they themselves come to need. By acting from these blended feelings, numbers have rendered themselves incapable of standing up against a sudden reverse. Nevertheless, these men, in common with all who have the misfortune to be in want, if many theorists had their wish, would be thrown upon one or other of those three sharp points of condition before adverted to, from which the intervention of law has hitherto saved them.

All that has been said tends to show how the principle contended for makes the gift of life more valuable, and has, it may be hoped, led to the conclusion that its legitimate operation is to make men worthier of that gift: in other words, not to degrade but to exalt human nature. But the subject must not be dismissed without adverting to the indirect influence of the same principle upon the moral sentiments of a people among whom it is embodied in law. In our criminal jurisprudence there is a maxim, deservedly eulogised, that it is better that ten guilty persons should escape, than that one innocent man should suffer; so, also, might it be maintained, with regard to the Poor Laws, that it is better for the interests of humanity among the people at large, that ten undeserving should partake of the funds provided, than that one morally good man, through want of relief, should either have his principles corrupted, or his energies destroyed; than that such a one should either be driven to do wrong, or be cast to the earth in utter hopelessness. In France, the English maxim of criminal jurisprudence is reversed; there, it is deemed better that ten innocent men should suffer, than one guilty escape: in France, there is no universal provision for the poor; and we may judge of the small value set upon human life in the metropolis of that country, by merely noticing the disrespect with which, after death, the body is treated, not by the thoughtless vulgar, but in schools of anatomy, presided over by men allowed to be, in their own art and in physical science, among the most enlightened in the world. In the East, where countries are overrun with population as with a weed, infinitely more respect is shown to the remains of the deceased; and what a bitter mockery is it, that this insensibility should be found where civil polity is so busy in minor regulations, and osten-tatiously careful to gratify the luxurious propensities, whether social or intellectual, of the multitude! Irreligion is, no doubt, much concerned with this offensive disrespect, shown to the bodies of the dead in France; but it is mainly attributable to the state in which so many of the living are left by the absence of com-pulsory provision for the indigent so humanely established by the law of England.

Sights of abject misery, perpetually recurring, harden the heart of the community. In the perusal of history, and of works of fiction, we are not, indeed, unwilling to have our commiseration excited by such objects of distress as they present to us; but, in the concerns of real life, men know that such emotions are not given to be indulged for their own sakes: there, the conscience declares to them that sympathy must be followed by action; and if there exist a previous conviction that the power to relieve is utterly inadequate to the demand, the eye shrinks from communication with wretchedness, and pity and compassion languish, like any other qualities that are deprived of their natural aliment. Let these considerations be duly weighed by those who trust to the hope that an increase of private charity, with all its advantages of superior discrimination, would more than compensate for the abandonment of those principles, the wisdom of which has been here insisted upon. How discouraging, also, would be the sense of injustice, which could not fail to arise in the minds of the well-disposed, if the burden of supporting the poor, a burden of which the selfish have hitherto by compulsion borne a share, should now, or hereafter, be thrown exclusively upon the benevolent.

By having put an end to the Slave Trade and Slavery, the British people are exalted in the scale of humanity; and they cannot but feel so, if they look into themselves, and duly consider their relation to God and their fellow-creatures. That was a noble advance; but a retrograde movement will assuredly be made, if ever the principle, which has been here defended, should be either avowedly abandoned or but ostensibly retained.

But after all, there may be little reason to apprehend permanent injury from any experiment that may be tried. On the one side will be human nature rising up in her own defence, and on the other prudential selfishness acting to the same purpose, from a conviction that, without a compulsory provision for the exigencies of the labouring multitude, that degree of ability to regulate the price of labour, which is indispensable for the reasonable interest of arts and manufactures, cannot, in Great Britain, be upheld.[1]

II. In a poem[2] of the foregoing collection. allusion is made to the state of the workmen congregated in manufactories. In order[2] to relieve many of the evils to which that class of society are subject and to establish a better harmony between them and their employers, it would be well to repeal[3] such laws as prevent the formation of joint-stock companies. There are,[4] no doubt, many and great obstacles to the formation and salutary working of these societies, inherent in the mind of those whom they would obviously benefit. But[3] the combinations of masters to keep down, unjustly, the price of labour would be fairly checked by them, as far as they were practicable; they would encourage economy, inasmuch as they would enable a man to draw profit from his savings, by investing them in buildings or machinery for processes of manufacture with which he was habitually connected. His little capital would then be working for him while he was at rest or asleep; he would more clearly perceive the necessity of capital for carrying on great works; he would better learn to respect the larger portions of it in the hands of others; he would be less tempted to join in unjust combinations; and, for the sake of his own property, if not for higher reasons, he would be slow to promote local disturbance, or endanger public tranquillity; he would, at least, be loth to act in that way *knowingly*: for it is not to be denied that such societies might be nurseries of opinions unfavourable to a mixed constitution of government, like that of Great Britain. The democratic and republican spirit which they might be apt to foster would not, however, be dangerous in itself, but only as it might act without being sufficiently counterbalanced, either by landed proprietorship, or by a Church extending itself so as to embrace an ever-growing and ever-shifting population of mechanics

[1] But after all . . . upheld *not in* 1835   [2] *v.* 'Humanity', vol. iv, p. 102.

[3] In order . . . repeal.] May the author be permitted to say, that, after much reflection on the subject, he has not been able to discover a more effectual mode of alleviating the evils to which that class are liable, and establishing . . . employers than by a repeal of 1835

[4] There are . . . But *not in* 1835

and artisans. But if the tendencies of such societies would be to make the men prosper who might belong to them, rulers and legislators should rejoice in the result, and do their duty to the state by upholding and extending the influence of that Church to which it owes, in so great a measure, its safety, its prosperity, and its glory.

This, in the temper of the present times, may be difficult, but it is become indispensable, since large towns in great numbers have sprung up, and others have increased tenfold, with little or no dependence upon the gentry and the landed proprietors; and apart from those mitigated feudal institutions, which, till of late, have acted so powerfully upon the composition of the House of Commons. Now it may be affirmed that, in quarters where there is not an attachment to the Church, or the landed aristocracy, and a pride in supporting them, *there* the people will dislike both, and be ready, upon such incitements as are perpetually recurring, to join in attempts to overthrow them. There is no neutral ground here: from want of due attention to the state of society in large towns and manufacturing districts, and ignorance or disregard of these obvious truths, innumerable well-meaning persons became zealous supporters of a Reform Bill, the qualities and powers of which, whether destructive or constructive, they would otherwise have been afraid of; and even the framers of that bill, swayed as they might be by party resentments and personal ambition, could not have gone so far, had not they too been lamentably ignorant or neglectful of the same truths both of fact and philosophy.

But let that pass; and let no opponent of the bill be tempted to compliment his own foresight, by exaggerating the mischiefs and dangers that have sprung from it: let not time be wasted in profitless regrets; and let those party distinctions vanish to their very names that have separated men who, whatever course they may have pursued, have ever had a bond of union in the wish to save the limited monarchy, and those other institutions that have, under Providence, rendered for so long a period of time this country the happiest and worthiest of which there is any record since the foundation of civil society.

III. A philosophic mind is best pleased when looking at religion in its spiritual bearing; as a guide of conduct, a solace under affliction, and a support amid the instabilities of mortal life: but the Church having been forcibly brought by political considerations to my notice, while treating of the labouring classes, I cannot forbear saying a few words upon that momentous topic.

There is a loud clamour for extensive change in that department. The clamour would be entitled to more respect if they who are the most eager to swell it with their voices were not generally the most ignorant of the real state of the Church, and the service it renders to the community. *Reform* is the word employed. Let us pause and consider what sense it is apt to carry, and how things are confounded by a lax use of it. The great religious Reformation, in the sixteenth century, did not profess to be a new construction, but a restoration of something fallen into decay, or put out of sight. That familiar and justifiable use of the word seems to have paved the way for fallacies with respect to the term reform, which it is difficult to escape from. Were we to speak of improvement, and the correction of abuses, we should run less risk of being deceived ourselves, or of misleading others. We should be less likely to fall blindly into the belief, that the change demanded is a renewal of something that has existed before, and that, therefore, we have experience on our side; nor should we be equally tempted to beg the question, that the change for which we are eager must be advantageous. From generation to generation, men are the dupes of words; and it is painful to observe, that so many of our species are most tenacious of those opinions which they have formed with the least consideration. They who are the readiest to meddle with public affairs, whether in church or state, fly to generalities, that they may be eased from the trouble of thinking about particulars; and thus is deputed to mechanical instrumentality the work which vital knowledge only can do well.

"Abolish pluralities, have a resident incumbent in every parish," is a favourite cry; but, without adverting to other obstacles in the way of this specious scheme, it may be asked what benefit would accrue from its *indiscriminate* adoption to counterbalance the harm it would introduce, by nearly extinguishing the order of curates, unless the revenues of the church should grow with the population, and be greatly increased in many thinly peopled districts, especially among the parishes of the North.

The order of curates is so beneficial, that some particular notice of it seems to be required in this place. For a church poor as, relatively to the numbers of people, that of England is, and probably will continue to be, it is no small advantage to have youthful servants, who will work upon the wages of hope and expectation. Still more advantageous is it to have, by means of this order, young men scattered over the country, who being more detached from the temporal concerns of the benefice, have more leisure for improvement and study, and are less subject to be brought into secular collision with those who are under their spiritual guardianship. The curate, if he reside at a distance from the incumbent, undertakes the requisite responsibilities of a temporal kind, in that modified way which prevents him, as a new-comer, from being charged with selfishness: while it prepares him for entering upon a benefice of his own, with something of a suitable experience. If he should act under and in co-operation with a resident incumbent, the gain is mutual. His studies will probably be assisted; and his training, managed by a superior, will not be liable to relapse in matters of prudence, seemliness, or in any of the highest cares of his functions; and by way of return for these benefits to the pupil, it will often happen that the zeal of a middle-aged or declining incumbent will be revived, by being in near communion with the ardour of youth, when his own efforts may have languished through a melancholy consciousness that they have not produced as much good among his flock as, when he first entered upon the charge, he fondly hoped.

Let one remark, and that not the least important, be added. A curate, entering for the first time upon his office, comes from college after a course of expense, and with such inexperience in the use of money, that, in his new situation, he is apt to fall unawares into pecuniary difficulties. If this happens to him, much more likely is it to happen to the youthful incumbent; whose relations, to his parishioners and to society, are more complicated; and, his income being larger and independent of another, a costlier style of living is required of him by public opinion. If embarrassment should ensue, and with that unavoidably some loss of respectability, his future usefulness will be proportionably impaired: not so with the curate, for he can easily remove and start afresh with a stock of experience and an unblemished reputation; whereas the early indiscretions of an incumbent being rarely forgotten, may be impediments to the efficacy of his ministry for the remainder of his life. The same observations would apply with equal force to doctrine. A young minister is liable to errors, from his notions being either too lax or overstrained. In both cases it would prove injurious that the error should be remembered, after study and reflection, with advancing years, shall have brought him to a clearer discernment of the truth, and better judgment in the application of it.

It must be acknowledged that, among the regulations of ecclesiastical polity, none at first view are more attractive than that which prescribes for every parish a resident incumbent. How agreeable to picture to one's self, as has been done by poets and romance-writers, from Chaucer down to Goldsmith, a man devoted to his ministerial office, with not a wish or a thought ranging beyond the circuit of its cares! Nor is it in poetry and fiction only that such characters are found; they are scattered, it is hoped not sparingly, over real life, especially in sequestered and rural districts, where there is but small influx of new inhabitants, and little change of occupation. The spirit of the Gospel, unaided by acquisitions of profane learning and experience in the world,—that spirit, and the obligations of the sacred office may, in such situations, suffice to effect most of what is needful. But for the complex state of society that prevails in England, much more is required, both in large towns, and in many extensive districts of the country. A minister there should not only be irreproachable in manners and morals, but accomplished in learning, as far as is possible without sacrifice of the least of his pastoral duties. As necessary, perhaps more so, is it that he should be a citizen as well as a scholar; thoroughly acquainted with the structure of society, and the constitution of civil government, and able to reason upon both with the most expert; all ultimately in order to support the truths of Christianity, and to diffuse its blessings.

A young man coming fresh from the place of his education, cannot have brought with him these accomplishments; and if the scheme of equalising church incomes, which many advisers are much bent upon, be realised, so that there should be little or no secular inducement for a clergyman to desire a removal from the spot where he may chance to have been first set down; surely not only opportunities for obtaining the requisite qualifications would be diminished, but the motives for desiring to obtain them would be proportionably weakened. And yet these qualifications are indispensable for the diffusion of that knowledge, by which alone the political philosophy of the New Testament can be rightly expounded, and its precepts adequately enforced. In these times, when the press is daily exercising so great a power over the minds of the people, for wrong or for right as may happen, *that* preacher ranks among the first of benefactors who, without stooping to the direct treatment of current politics and passing events, can furnish infallible guidance through the delusions that surround them; and who, appealing to the sanctions of Scripture, may place the grounds of its injunctions in so clear a light, that disaffection shall cease to be cultivated as a laudable propensity, and loyalty cleansed from the dishonour of a blind and prostrate obedience.

It is not, however, in regard to civic duties alone, that this knowledge in a minister of the Gospel is important; it is still more so for softening and subduing private and personal discontents. In all places, and at all times, men have gratuitously troubled themselves, because their survey of the dispensations of Providence has been partial and narrow; but now that readers are so greatly multiplied, men judge as they are *taught*, and repinings are engendered everywhere, by imputations being cast upon the government; and are prolonged or aggravated by being ascribed to misconduct or injustice in rulers, when the individual himself only is in fault. If a Christian pastor be competent to deal with these humours, as they may be dealt with, and by no members of society so successfully, both from more frequent and more favourable opportunities of intercourse, and by aid of the authority with which he speaks; he will be a teacher of moderation, a dispenser of the wisdom that blunts approaching distress by submission to God's will, and lightens, by patience, grievances which cannot be removed.

We live in times when nothing, of public good at least, is generally

acceptable, but what we believe can be traced to preconceived intention, and specific acts and formal contrivances of human understanding. A Christian instructor thoroughly accomplished would be
a standing restraint upon such presumptuousness of judgment, by
impressing the truth that—

> "In the unreasoning progress of the world
> A wiser spirit is at work for us,
> A better eye than ours."—*MS*.[1]

Revelation points to the purity and peace of a future world; but
our sphere of duty is upon earth; and the relations of impure and
conflicting things to each other must be understood, or we shall be
perpetually going wrong, in all but goodness of intention; and goodness of intention will itself relax through frequent disappointment.
How desirable, then, is it, that a minister of the Gospel should be
versed in the knowledge of existing facts, and be accustomed to a
wide range of social experience! Nor is it less desirable for the purpose of counterbalancing and tempering in his own mind that ambition with which spiritual power is as apt to be tainted as any other
species of power which men covet or possess.

It must be obvious that the scope of the argument is to discourage
an attempt which would introduce into the Church of England an
equality of income, and station, upon the model of that of Scotland.
The sounder part of the Scottish nation know what good their
ancestors derived from their church, and feel how deeply the living
generation is indebted to it. They respect and love it, as accommodated in so great a measure to a comparatively poor country, through
the far greater portion of which prevails a uniformity of employment; but the acknowledged deficiency of theological learning among
the clergy of that church is easily accounted for by this very equality.
What else may be wanting there, it would be unpleasant to inquire,
and might prove invidious to determine: one thing, however, is
clear; that in all countries the temporalities of the Church Establishment should bear an analogy to the state of society, otherwise it
cannot diffuse its influence through the whole community. In a
country so rich and luxurious as England, the character of its clergy
must unavoidably sink, and their influence be everywhere impaired,
if individuals from the upper ranks, and men of leading talents, are
to have no inducements to enter into that body but such as are
purely spiritual. And this "tinge of secularity" is no reproach to
the clergy, nor does it imply a deficiency of spiritual endowments.
Parents and guardians, looking forward to sources of honourable
maintenance for their children and wards, often direct their thoughts
early towards the church, being determined partly by outward circumstances, and partly by indications of seriousness, or intellectual

[1] *Prelude*, v. 359–61.

fitness. It is natural that a boy or youth, with such a prospect before him, should turn his attention to those studies, and be led into those habits of reflection, which will in some degree tend to prepare him for the duties he is hereafter to undertake. As he draws nearer to the time when he will be called to these duties, he is both led and compelled to examine the Scriptures. He becomes more and more sensible of their truth. Devotion grows in him; and what might begin in temporal considerations, will end (as in a majority of instances we trust it does) in a spiritual-mindedness not unworthy of that Gospel, the lessons of which he is to teach, and the faith of which he is to inculcate. Not inappositely may be here repeated an observation which, from its obviousness and importance, must have been frequently made, viz. that the impoverishing of the clergy, and bringing their incomes much nearer to a level, would not cause them to become less worldly-minded: the emoluments, howsoever reduced, would be as eagerly sought for, but by men from lower classes in society; men who, by their manners, habits, abilities, and the scanty measure of their attainments, would unavoidably be less fitted for their station, and less competent to discharge its duties.

Visionary notions have in all ages been afloat upon the subject of best providing for the clergy; notions which have been sincerely entertained by good men, with a view to the improvement of that order, and eagerly caught at and dwelt upon, by the designing, for its degradation and disparagement. Some are beguiled by what they call the *voluntary system*, not seeing (what stares one in the face at the very threshold) that they who stand in most need of religious instruction are unconscious of the want, and therefore cannot reasonably be expected to make any sacrifices in order to supply it. Will the licentious, the sensual, and the depraved, take from the means of their gratifications and pursuits, to support a discipline that cannot advance without uprooting the trees that bear the fruit which they devour so greedily? Will *they* pay the price of that seed whose harvest is to be reaped in an invisible world? A voluntary system for the religious exigencies of a people numerous and circumstanced as we are! Not more absurd would it be to expect that a knot of boys should draw upon the pittance of their pocket-money to build schools, or out of the abundance of their discretion be able to select fit masters to teach and keep them in order! Some, who clearly perceive the incompetence and folly of such a scheme for the agricultural part of the people, nevertheless think it feasible in large towns, where the rich might subscribe for the religious instruction of the poor. Alas! they know little of the thick darkness that spreads over the streets and alleys of our large towns. The parish of Lambeth, a few years since, contained not more than one church and three or four small proprietary chapels, while dissenting chapels, of every denomination were still more scantily found there; yet the inhabi-

tants of the parish amounted at that time to upwards of 50,000.
Were the parish church and the chapels of the Establishment existing
there, an *impediment* to the spread of the Gospel among that mass
of people ? Who shall dare to say so ? But if[1] any one, in the face
of the fact which has just been stated, and in opposition to authentic
reports to the same effect from various other quarters, should still
contend, that a voluntary system is sufficient for the spread and
maintenance of religion, we would ask, what kind of religion ? wherein
would it differ, among the many, from deplorable fanaticism ?[1]

For the preservation of the Church Establishment, all men,
whether they belong to it or not, could they perceive their true
interest, would be strenuous: but how inadequate are its provisions
for the needs of the country! and how much is it to be regretted
that, while its zealous friends yield to alarms on account of the
hostility of dissent, they should so much over-rate the danger to be
apprehended from that quarter, and almost overlook the fact that
hundreds of thousands of our fellow-countrymen, though formally
and nominally of the Church of England, never enter her places of
worship, neither have they communication with her ministers!
This deplorable state of things was partly produced by[2] a decay of
zeal among the rich and influential, and partly by[3] a want of due
expansive power in the constitution of the Establishment as regulated by law. Private benefactors, in their efforts to build and
endow churches, have been frustrated, or too much impeded by
legal obstacles: these, where they are unreasonable or unfitted for
the times, ought to be removed; and, keeping clear of intolerance
and injustice, means should be used to render the presence and
powers of the church commensurate with the wants of a shifting and
still-increasing population.

This cannot be effected, unless the English Government vindicate
the truth, that, as her church exists for the benefit of all (though not
in equal degree), whether of her communion or not, all should be
made to contribute to its support. If this ground be abandoned,[4]
cause will be given to fear that a moral wound may be inflicted upon
the heart of the English people, for which a remedy cannot be
speedily provided by the utmost efforts which the members of the
Church will themselves be able to make.[4]

But let the friends of the church be of good courage. Powers are
at work, by which, under Divine Providence, she may be strengthened
and the sphere of her usefulness extended; not by alterations in her
Liturgy, accommodated to this or that demand of finical taste, nor

[1] But if . . . fanaticism ? *not in* 1835
[2] seems partly owing to 1835   [3] by] to 1835
[4] the not remote consequence will be, the infliction of a wound upon the
moral heart of the English people, from which, till ages shall have gone by,
it will not recover. 1835

by cutting off this or that from her articles or Canons, to which the scrupulous or the overweening may object. Covert schism, and open nonconformity, would survive after alterations, however promising in the eyes of those whose subtilty had been exercised in making them. Latitudinarianism is the parhelion of liberty of conscience, and will ever successfully lay claim to a divided worship. Among Presbyterians, Socinians, Baptists, and Independents, there will always be found numbers who will tire of their several creeds, and some will come over to the Church. Conventicles may disappear, congregations in each denomination may fall into decay or be broken up, but the conquests which the National Church ought chiefly to aim at, lie among the thousands and tens of thousands of the unhappy outcasts who grow up with no religion at all. The wants of these cannot but be feelingly remembered. Whatever may be the disposition of the new constituencies under the reformed parliament, and the course which the men of their choice may be inclined or compelled to follow, it may be confidently hoped that individuals acting in their private capacities, will endeavour to make up for the deficiencies of the legislature. Is it too much to expect that proprietors of large estates, where the inhabitants are without religious instruction, or where it is sparingly supplied, will deem it their duty to take part in this good work; and that thriving manufacturers and merchants will, in their several neighbourhoods, be sensible of the like obligation, and act upon it with generous rivalry?

Moreover, the force of public opinion is rapidly increasing: and some may bend to it, who are not so happy as to be swayed by a higher motive; especially they who derive large incomes from lay-impropriations, in tracts of country where ministers are few and meagrely provided for. A claim still stronger may be acknowledged by those who, round their superb habitations, or elsewhere, walk over vast estates which were lavished upon their ancestors by royal favouritism or purchased at insignificant prices after church-spoliation; such proprietors, though not conscience-stricken (there is no call for that) may be prompted to make a return for which their tenantry and dependents will learn to bless their names. An impulse has been given; an accession of means from these several sources, co-operating with a *well*-considered change in the distribution of some parts of the property at present possessed by the church, a change scrupulously founded upon due respect to law and justice, will, we trust, bring about so much of what her friends desire, that the rest may be calmly waited for, with thankfulness for what shall have been obtained.

Let it not be thought unbecoming in a layman, to have treated at length a subject with which the clergy are more intimately conversant. All may, without impropriety, speak of what deeply concerns all; nor need an apology be offered for going over ground which has been trod before so ably and so often: without pretending, however, to anything of novelty, either in matter or manner, something may have been offered to view, which will save the writer from the imputation of having little to recommend his labour, but goodness of intention.

It was with reference to thoughts and feelings[1] expressed in verse, that I entered upon the above notices, and with verse I will conclude. The passage is extracted from my MSS. written above thirty years ago: it turns upon the individual dignity which humbleness of social condition does not preclude, but frequently promotes. It has no direct bearing upon clubs for the discussion of public affairs, nor upon political or trade-unions; but if a single workman—who, being a member of one of those clubs, runs the risk of becoming an agitator, or who, being enrolled in a union, must be left without a will of his own, and therefore a slave—should read these lines, and be touched by them, I should indeed rejoice, and little would I care for losing credit as a poet with intemperate critics, who think differently from me upon political philosophy or public measures, if the sober-minded admit that, in general views, my affections have been moved, and my imagination exercised, under and *for* the guidance of reason.

> "Here might I pause, and bend in reverence
> To Nature, and the power of human minds;
> To men as they are men within themselves.
> How oft high service is performed within,
> When all the external man is rude in show;
> Not like a temple rich with pomp and gold,
> But a mere mountain chapel that protects
> Its simple worshippers from sun and shower!
> Of these, said I, shall be my song; of these,
> If future years mature me for the task,
> Will I record the praises, making verse
> Deal boldly with substantial things—in truth
> And sanctity of passion, speak of these,
> That justice may be done, obeisance paid
> Where it is due. Thus haply shall I teach,
> Inspire, through unadulterated ears
> Pour rapture, tenderness, and hope; my theme
> No other than the very heart of man,
> As found among the best of those who live,
> Not unexalted by religious faith,
> Nor uninformed by books, good books, though few,
> In Nature's presence: thence may I select
> Sorrow that is not sorrow, but delight,
> And miserable love that is not pain
> To hear of, for the glory that redounds
> Therefrom to human kind, and what we are.

[1] and feelings *not in* 1835

Be mine to follow with no timid step
Where knowledge leads me; it shall be my pride
That I have dared to tread this holy ground,
Speaking no dream, but things oracular,
Matter not lightly to be heard by those
Who to the letter of the outward promise
Do read the invisible soul; by men adroit
In speech, and for communion with the world
Accomplished, minds whose faculties are then
Most active when they are most eloquent,
And elevated most when most admired.
Men may be found of other mould than these;
Who are their own upholders, to themselves
Encouragement and energy, and will;
Expressing liveliest thoughts in lively words
As native passion dictates. Others, too,
There are, among the walks of homely life,
Still higher, men for contemplation framed;
Shy, and unpractised in the strife of phrase;
Meek men, whose very souls perhaps would sink
Beneath them, summoned to such intercourse.
Theirs is the language of the heavens, the power,
The thought, the image, and the silent joy:
Words are but under-agents in their souls;
When they are grasping with their greatest strength
They do not breathe among them; this I speak
In gratitude to God, who feeds our hearts
For his own service, knoweth, loveth us,
When we are unregarded by the world."[1]

[1] *Prelude*, xiii. 224–78.

APPENDIX

POEMS EITHER NOT REPRINTED BY WORDSWORTH OR HITHERTO UNPUBLISHED

I. ANDREW JONES

[Composed 1798.—Published 1800, 1802, 1805 (*Lyrical Ballads*); ed. 1815; omitted from edd. 1820 to 1849–50.]

I HATE that Andrew Jones: he'll breed
His children up to waste and pillage,
I wish the press-gang or the drum
Would, with its rattling music, come,
And sweep him from the village!   5

I said not this, because he loves
Through the long day to swear and tipple;
But for the poor dear sake of one
To whom a foul deed he had done,
A friendless Man, a travelling Cripple!   10

For this poor crawling helpless wretch
Some Horseman who was passing by,
A penny on the ground had thrown;
But the poor Cripple was alone
And could not stoop—no help was nigh.   15

Inch-thick the dust lay on the ground
For it had long been droughty weather;
So with his staff the Cripple wrought
Among the dust till he had brought
The halfpennies together.   20

It chanc'd that Andrew pass'd that way
Just at the time; and there he found
The Cripple in the mid-day heat
Standing alone, and at his feet
He saw the penny on the ground.   25

1–10   And now he sees a shallow stream
Across the highway fret and ripple
And he bethinks him then of one
To whom a foul deed he had done,
A helpless Man, a travelling Cripple! MS.
12 It chanced some traveller passing by MS   21, 28 Andrew] Peter MS.

He stooped and took the penny up:
And when the Cripple nearer drew,
Quoth Andrew, "Under half-a-crown,
What a man finds is all his own,
And so, my Friend, good-day to you."   30

And *hence* I say, that Andrew's boys
Will all be train'd to waste and pillage;
And wish'd the press-gang, or the drum
Would, with its rattling music, come,
And sweep him from the village!   35

II

I LOVE upon a stormy night
To hear those fits of slender song
Which through the woods and open plains,
Among the clouds or in the rains,
The loud winds bear along.   5

Then do I love to stand alone
By some huge rock or tree defended,
To stand like one that's blind, and catch
Of those small strains the last faint snatch
For human ears intended.   10

But sweeter when the moon shines bright
And the clear sky in calm blue weather
With rocks and woods and with the green
Of a small meadow makes a scene
Of earth and heaven together.   15

But sweeter then when you could hear,
Almost could hear a falling feather,
To listen to that music small
Prolonged through many a madrigal
For half an hour together.   20

But you will say how can this be?
I'll tell you, for the truth I know;
Above the ocean's foaming waves,
Through hollow woods and gloomy caves,
A thousand beings come and go.   25

I've heard them many and many a time,
A thing you'll say that's past conceiving,
Over the green and open lands,
And o'er the bare and yellow sands,
Their airy dances weaving.   30

31–5 *not in* MS.

'Tis not for one like me to tell
Their shape, their colour, and their size,
But they are thin and very spare,
Beings far thinner than the air,
And happier than the summer flies.   35

And often too by lake or grove
Have I beheld, from time to time,
A troop of tiny spirits fair,
All glistening like the moonlight air
Or sparkles in the frosty rime.   40

Oft have I seen in glade or bower
Sweet shapes upon the moonlight ground,
Some here, as little fairies small,
Some there, as human beings tall,
All dancing round and round.   45

III. ALCÆUS TO SAPPHO

How sweet, when crimson colours dart
Across a breast of snow,
To see that you are in the heart
That beats and throbs below.

All heaven is in a maiden's blush,   5
In which the soul doth speak,
That it was you who sent the flush
Into the maiden's cheek.

Large steadfast eyes! eyes gently rolled
In shades of changing blue,   10
How sweet are they, if they behold
No dearer sight than you!

And can a lip more richly glow,
Or be more fair than this ?
The world will surely answer, No!   15
I, SAPPHO, answer, Yes!

Then grant one smile, tho' it should mean
A thing of doubtful birth;
That I may say these eyes have seen
The fairest face on earth!   20

IV   [THE GLOW WORM]

[Composed April 12, 1802.—Published 1807; never reprinted by W.]

AMONG all lovely things my Love had been;
Had noted well the stars, all flowers that grew
About her home; but she had never seen
A Glow-worm, never one, and this I knew.

While riding near her home one stormy night   5
A single Glow-worm did I chance to espy;
I gave a fervent welcome to the sight,
And from my Horse I leapt; great joy had I.

Upon a leaf the Glow-worm did I lay,
To bear it with me through the stormy night: 10
And, as before, it shone without dismay;
Albeit putting forth a fainter light.

When to the Dwelling of my Love I came,
I went into the Orchard quietly;
And left the Glow-worm, blessing it by name,   15
Laid safely by itself, beneath a Tree.

The whole next day, I hoped, and hoped with fear;
At night the Glow-worm shone beneath the Tree:
I led my Lucy to the spot, "Look here!"
Oh! joy it was for her, and joy for me!   20

5-8   While I was riding on a stormy night
              Not far from her abode, I chanc'd to spy
              A single Glow-worm once; and at the sight
              Down from my horse *etc.*   *MSS.*
9-12   I laid the Glow-worm gently on a leaf
              And bore it *etc.*
              In my left hand without dismay or grief
              Shining, albeit with *etc.*   MS. *letter*
19 Lucy] Emma MSS.   spot] place MS. *letter*

NOTES

POEMS FOUNDED ON THE AFFECTIONS

p. 1. I. THE BROTHERS. "1800. This poem was composed in a grove at the north-eastern end of Grasmere Lake, which grove was in a great measure destroyed by turning the high-road along the side of the water. The few trees that are left were spared at my intercession. The poem arose out of the fact, mentioned to me at Ennerdale, that a shepherd had fallen asleep upon the top of the rock called The Pillar, and perished as here described, his staff being left midway on the rock."—I. F.

This Poem was intended to be the concluding poem of a series of pastorals, the scene of which was laid among the mountains of Cumberland and Westmoreland. I mention this to apologise for the abruptness with which the poem begins.—W. W. *note* 1800–32.

W. heard the incident on which *The Brothers* is based during his tour in the Lake country with Coleridge in Oct.–Nov. 1799. In Coleridge's diary, under date Nov. 12, when they were at Ennerdale, Coleridge tells of a youth named Bowman who "broke his neck by falling off a crag. He is supposed to have lain down and slept—walked in his sleep, and so came to this crag and fell off. (This was at Proud Knot on the mountain called Pillar up Ennerdale.) His pike staff struck midway and stayed there till it rotted away."

The poem was begun in Dec. 1799, *v. E.L.*, 237. A few lines of it in W. W.'s hand are in D. W.'s *Journal*, Oct. 1801–Feb. 1802.

57. blue] altered from "green" on the suggestion of Barron Field who wrote in Sept. 1837: "Read *blue* wave. The sea far from shore is blue—in soundings only is it green."

65 (note). William Gilbert (1760–1825); his poem *The Hurricane; a Theosophical and Western Eclogue*, was published in 1796. At Bristol, where he lived, he made the acquaintance of Southey and Coleridge, who both regarded him as a man of genius and eloquence, but of a deranged mind. W. quotes from a note to *The Hurricane* in *Excursion*, III. 931 (note).

143–5. The impressive circumstance here described, actually took place some years ago in this country, upon an eminence called Kidstow Pike, one of the highest of the mountains that surround Hawes-water. The summit of the Pike was stricken by lightning; and every trace of one of the fountains disappeared, while the other continued to flow as before.—W. W. 1800–5. This actually took place upon Kidstow Pike at the head of Haweswater.—W. W. 1815–36.

182–3. There is not anything more worthy of remark in the manners of the inhabitants of these mountains, than the tranquility, I might say indifference, with which they think and talk upon the subject of death. Some of the country churchyards, as here described, do not contain a single tombstone, and most of them have a very small number.—W. W. *note* 1800.

369–74. W.'s alteration of the text was due to Coleridge's criticism of this passage as an example of *prosaism* in the poem—"that model of English pastoral, which I have never yet read with unclouded eye" (*Biog. Lit.* ch. xviii, ed. Shawcross, ii. 62).

p. 14. II. ARTEGAL AND ELIDURE. "Rydal Mount. This was written in the year 1815, as a token of affectionate respect for the memory of Milton. 'I have determined,' says he, in his preface to his History of England, 'to bestow the telling over even of these reputed tales, be it for nothing else but in favour of our English Poets and Rhetoricians, who by their art will know how to use them judiciously.' "—I. F. (The quotation comes not from the Preface, but Bk. I, end of paragraph 2. E. Q.'s copy of the I. F. note, the only one known to be extant, has "wit" for "art".)

The "reputed tale" is thus told by Milton: "Gorbonian, the eldest of his [Morindus'] five sons, than whom a juster man lived not in his age, was a great builder of temples, and gave to all what was their due: to his gods, devout worship: to men of desert, honour and preferment: to the commons, encouragement in their labours and trades, defence and protection from injuries and oppressions: so that the land flourished above her neighbours: violence and wrong seldom were heard of. His death was a general loss: he was buried in Trinovant.

"Archigallo, the second brother, followed not his example: but depressed the ancient nobility: and, by peeling the wealthier sort, stuffed his treasury, and took the right way to be deposed.

"Elidure, the next brother, surnamed the Pious, was set up in his place: a mind so noble, and so moderate, as almost is incredible to have been ever found. For, having held the sceptre five years, hunting one day in the forest of Calater, he chanced to meet his deposed brother, wandering in a mean condition: who had been long in vain beyond the seas, importuning foreign aids to his restorement; and was now, in a poor habit, with only ten followers, privately returned to find subsistence among his secret friends. At the unexpected sight of him, Elidure himself also then but thinly accompanied, runs to him with open arms; and after many dear and sincere welcomings, conveys him to the city Alclud: there hides him in his own bedchamber. Afterwards feigning himself sick, summons all his peers, as about greatest affairs, where admitting them one by one, as if his weakness endured not the disturbance of more at once, causes them, willing or unwilling, once more to swear allegiance to Archigallo. Whom, after reconciliation made on all sides, he leads to York: and, from his head, places the crown on the head of his brother. Who thenceforth, vice itself dissolving in him, and forgetting her firmest hold, with the admiration of a deed so heroic, became a true converted man; ruled worthily ten years, died, and was buried in Caerleir. Thus was a brother saved by a brother, to whom love of a crown, the thing that so often dazzles and vitiates mortal men, for which thousands of nearest blood have destroyed each other, was in respect of brotherly dearness, a contemptible thing." The theme of "brotherly dearness" which attracted W. to the story, accounts for his placing the poem next to *The Brothers*.

Three MSS. of the poem are known to me; (1) an incomplete rough draft in W. W.'s hand, (2) one begun by S. H., but completed by W. W.; (3) by M. W. (probable date 1817).

13–18. "This island . . . was desert and inhospitable; kept only by a remnant of giants, whose excessive force and tyranny had consumed the rest. Them Brutus destroys, and to his people divides the land. . . . To Corineus, Cornwall, as we now call it, fell by lot; the rather by him liked, for that the hugest giants in rocks and caves were said to lurk still there; which kind of monsters to deal with was his old exercise." Milton.

16. From *Faerie Queene*, II. x. 7

hideous Giants . . .
That never tasted grace nor goodnesse felt.

33–40. The story of Guendolen's revenge on Locrine, her faithless lord, is told both by Milton and by Spenser (*F.Q.* II. x. 17–19).

50 (MS.). England's darling: a reminiscence of Gray's *Progress of Poesy* where Shakespeare is called "Nature's Darling".

92. "poorly provided, poorly followed"] probably, as Nowell Smith suggests, not a verbally accurate quotation, but adapted from Milton's words, quoted *supra*, "in a poor habit, with only ten followers".

195. passed: W.'s texts all read "past", giving eye-rhyme with "cast"—but an impossible form for the preterite. That the spelling here is merely an oversight is shown by *The Pass of Kirkstone* 44 where "passed" rhymes with "blast", and by *Duddon Sonnet* xv, l. 14, *infra*, Vol III, p. 252, where *past* is corrected to *pass'd*.

218–25. Note that the MS. version of these lines (*v. app. crit.*) is much closer to Milton than the published text.

p. 22. III. To A BUTTERFLY. "1801. Written in the Orchard, Town-End Grasmere."—I. F. But the correct date of composition is fixed by an entry in D. W.'s *Journal* for Apr. 20, 1802. "Wm wrote a conclusion to the poem of the Butterfly—I've watched you now a full half-hour."—D. W.'s words are usually interpreted as meaning that this poem was written as a conclusion to the poem *To a Butterfly* written on March 14 ("Stay near me"; *v.* Vol. I, p. 226); but it is quite as probable that she means that on April 20 W. wrote the conclusion of this poem, to which she refers by its first line to distinguish it from the other and earlier poem on the same subject.

Certainly it expresses a wholly different mood, a fact which W. emphasized on their first publication (1807) by placing one at the beginning and the other at the end of the section entitled *Moods of my own Mind*.

p. 23. IV. A FAREWELL. "1802. Composed just before my Sister and I went to fetch Mary from Gallow-hill, near Scarborough."—I. F. D. W.'s *Journal* for May 29 reads "Wm finished his poem on going for Mary. I wrote it out". But on June 13 is the entry "Wm has been altering the poem to Mary this morning", and W.'s letter to M. H. on the 14th (*E.L.*, pp. 304–5, *q.v.*) shows that ll. 33–40 had just been added, and that other changes had been made from the text as "finished" on May 29. On the 17th D. W. wrote: "When I came home I found Wm at work attempting to alter a stanza in the poem to Mary, which I convinced him did not need altering." It is interesting to note that in the letter W. speaks of *A Farewell* as a "Spenserian" poem.

18 two months] They were actually away from July 9 to October 6.

22 gowan] a word used commonly in N. English for the common daisy, but clearly not so here. The O.E.D. says that with the qualification "yellow" [*v.* "saffron coat" of previous line] it is used for any species of ranunculus, that the "open" gowan signifies the globe flower and the "witch" gowan the globe flower or the dandelion. W. probably here means the globe flower.

56. one song that will not die] *The Sparrows Nest* (*v.* Vol. I, p. 227).

p. 25. V. STANZAS WRITTEN IN MY COPY OF THOMSON'S "CASTLE OF INDOLENCE". "Composed in the Orchard, Grasmere, Town-End. Coleridge was living with us much at the time; his son Hartley has said, that his father's character and habits are here preserved in a livelier way than anything that has been written about him."—I. F. D. W.'s *Journal*, May 9, 1802: "After tea he wrote two stanzas in the manner of Thomson's *Castle of Indolence* and was tired out." May 11: "Wm finished the stanzas about C. and himself."

Matthew Arnold, in his Selection of the Poems published in the *Golden Treasury Series*, was responsible for circulating the error, which he afterwards admitted, that the first 4 stanzas referred to C. and the next three to W. But the evidence is overwhelming, that the reverse is the case. Cf. the Personal Reminiscences of Justice Coleridge, quoted M. ii. 309: "Oct. 10 1836. I have passed a great many hours to day with W., in his house. . . . He read me nearly all the sweet stanzas written in his copy of *The C. of I.*, describing himself and my uncle, and he and Mrs W. both assured me the description of the latter at that time was perfectly accurate: that he was almost as a great boy in feelings, and had all the tricks and fancies there described. Mrs W. seemed to look back on him, and those times, with the fondest affection." Mr. Thomas Hutchinson was the first to notice the resemblance between W.'s portrait of himself in these stanzas and the hero of Beattie's *Minstrel*, especially i. 16, 17, 20–2, ii. 6; and D. W. herself, as early as 1793, had noted the likeness of her brother to "Edwin" (*v. E.L.*, pp. 97–8): "In truth he was a strange and wayward wight etc. That verse of Beattie's *Minstrel* always reminds me of him, and indeed the whole character of Edwin resembles much what W. was when first I knew him—after my leaving Halifax—'and oft he traced the uplands, etc.'" W. has skilfully adapted the style of his poem to that of Thomson in *The C. of I.*

27. like a naked Indian] Cf. *Prelude* (1805), i. 301–4; for the description of the shed in which he lay as an "Indian shed" cf. *A Farewell*, 26.

35–6. Shelley seems to have been indebted to these lines in *Adonais* xxxi:

> And his own thoughts, along that rugged way,
> Pursued, like raging hounds, their father and their prey.

W. develops the same idea in *Prelude* (1850), i. 145–54.

43. (MS.) A face divine of heaven born idiotcy] Despite W.'s somewhat abnormal tolerance for idiocy, he wisely excised this line from the printed version of the poem. But its vivid truth is attested by Coleridge himself. In an unpublished version of *Happiness* (1791) he had alluded to his "fat vacuity of face", and in Nov. 1796 he had written to Thelwall: "My face, unless when animated by immediate eloquence, expresses great sloth, and great, indeed, almost idiotic good-nature. 'Tis a mere carcass of a face; fat, flabby, and expressive chiefly of inexpression. . . . I cannot breathe through my nose, so my mouth, with sensual thick lips, is almost always open."

47. For the "gamesome"-ness of Coleridge cf. D. W.'s account of his romps with little Dora W. in 1808. (*M.Y.*, p. 256.)

p. 28. VI. LOUISA. "Town-End 1805."—I. F. This date is clearly wrong, for in the I. F. note to "Dear Child of Nature" (p. 522) W. states that that poem, which appeared in the *Morning Post* of Feb. 11, 1802, was "written at the same time and designed to make one piece" with this one. There has been much discussion as to the identity of Louisa. Hutchinson and Hale White, chiefly on the grounds that W. usually chose a synonym metrically equivalent to the name of his original, suggest Joanna Hutchinson, and note that the epithets "ruddy, fleet and strong" apply more fitly to her than to D. W. But there is no evidence of this, nor that she fits in either with ll. 7–12 of the poem or with the other poem, "Dear Child of Nature", which may be a reference to the rebuke received by D. W. from her aunt Crackenthorp in 1794 (*v. E.L.*, p. 113), now recalled by W., as was his wont, "from hiding-places ten years deep". It is most probable that both poems are in part fancy pictures, but that Dorothy was chiefly in W.'s thoughts as he wrote.

7–12. This stanza, omitted in 1845 and 1849, I restore to the text in the conviction that its omission was accidental. The suggestions that it was omitted because of Joanna's death in 1845 (if the lady *is* Joanna), or because of Dorothy's pathetic illness (which would apply equally in 1836) seem to be quite untenable. On the latter supposition W. would have to have omitted from the latest editions of his poems many other lines of equal beauty.

19. "beneath the moon "]. *King Lear* iv. vi. 26–7, "for all beneath the moon Would I not leap upright ".

p. 29. VII. *Strange fits of passion.* "The next three poems were written in Germany, 1799."—I. F. The MS. readings of this and the following poem are from the joint letter of W. W. and D. W. to Coleridge, Dec. 1798–Jan. 1799 (*v. E.L.*, pp. 204–5). "Lucy" in this poem is probably Dorothy, and the incident, like that in *The Glow-worm* (*v.* p. 466) may well have occurred at Racedown. As a poem it may be the better for the omission of the last stanza in the MS., but the conclusion recorded in it is both natural and probable, and is eminently Wordsworthian.

6. Fresh as a rose in June] Professor Beatty compares Percy's *Reliques*, "Dulcina", l. 17, "And cheekes as fresh as rose in June ", and reminds us that W. had just bought a copy of the *Reliques* at Hamburg (*v.* D. W.'s *Hamburgh Journal* for Oct. 2).

p. 30. VIII. *She dwelt among the untrodden ways.* There has been much discussion as to the identity both of the springs of Dove and of Lucy. Wordsworth knew a river Dove in Derbyshire, in Yorkshire, and in Westmorland; and it is impossible to say of which he was thinking. If Coleridge is right in saying that "A slumber did my spirit seal" was written to suggest what W. would have felt on the death of his sister, this poem had probably a similar source. And the fact that it was written at Goslar, when he was in her company, supports the conclusion.

8/9 (MS. 1799) the broom that flowers on Carron's side] a purely literary allusion, as W. had not yet been to Scotland. He owed it to his favourite poet Langhorne, who had a poem on *Owen of Carron* which begins "On Carron's side the primrose pale ", and refers later on to the yellow leaf of the broom.

p. 30. IX. *I travelled among unknown men.* It seems certain that this poem was not written, as W. stated, in Germany in 1799, but some time after his return. It is significant that it did not appear with the other "Lucy" poems in *Lyrical Ballads*, 1800, but that a copy of it was sent to the printer for the 1802 ed., with instructions that it should be inserted after "A slumber did my spirit seal" (the printer omitted to carry out this instruction), and that in 1801 W. sent it in a letter to M. H. as "a short poem to be read after 'She dwelt among'". If it had been written in 1799, M. H. would already have known it (*v. E.L.*, pp. 275–6). The MS. variants are found in that letter, and in MS. M.

p. 31. X. *Ere with cold beads of midnight dew.* "Rydal Mount 1826. Suggested by the condition of a friend."—I. F., probably a suitor for the hand of his daughter Dora. She had more than one proposal about this time. (*v. L.Y.*, p. 239.)

p. 31. XI. To——. "Rydal Mount, 1824. Prompted by the undue importance attached to personal beauty by some dear friends of mine."—I. F. Dowden plausibly suggests that it was addressed to Dora, comparing it with *The Longest Day*, ll. 61–4.

20–2. From Spenser, *Hymne in Honour of Beautie*, 211–15:

> But they which love indeede, looke otherwise,
> With pure regard and spotlesse true intent,
> Drawing out of the object of their eyes
> A more refyned forme which they present
> Unto their mind, voide of all blemishment.

p. 32. XII. THE FORSAKEN. "This was an overflow from the 'Affliction of Margaret——,' and was excluded as superfluous there, but preserved in the faint hope that it may turn to account by restoring a shy lover to some forsaken damsel. My poetry has been complained of as deficient in interests of this sort,—a charge which the piece beginning, 'Lyre! though such power do in thy magic live,' will scarcely tend to obviate. The natural imagery of these verses was supplied by frequent, I might say intense, observation of the Rydal torrent. What an animating contrast is the ever-changing aspect of that, and indeed of every one of our mountain brooks, to the monotonous tone and unmitigated fury of such streams among the Alps as are fed all the summer long by glaciers and melting snows. A traveller observing the exquisite purity of the great rivers, such as the Rhine at Geneva, and the Reuss at Lucerne, when they issue out of their respective lakes, might fancy for a moment that some power in nature produced this beautiful change, with a view to make amends for those Alpine sullyings which the waters exhibit near their fountain heads ; but, alas ! how soon does that purity depart before the influx of tributary waters that have flowed through cultivated plains and the crowded abodes of men."—I. F.

Dated by W. 1804, but the existence in the *Longman MSS.* of some lines introductory to the poem (*v.* p. 476 *infra*), with an appended note "Written for the Lyrical Ballads", makes a slightly earlier date probable. No additions were made to the 1802 and 1805 edd. of the *L.B.*, and it is unlikely that W. contemplated any as late as 1804.

p. 34. XIV. A COMPLAINT. "Town-End 1806. Suggested by a change in the manner of a friend."—I. F. In the I. F. note "Town-End" is crossed out and "Coleorton" written beneath it, and "Coleridge S. T." is written in the margin. The author of this emendation is unknown, but it is almost certainly correct. Coleridge stayed with the W.s at Coleorton, Dec. 1806–Jan. 1807, and for evidence of the

change that had come over him *v.* D. W.'s letters. and my *Life of
D. W.*, pp. 210–12.

p. 35. XV. To——(Let other bards) "Rydal Mount, 1824. On
Mary Wordsworth".—I. F.

p. 36. XVII. *How rich that forehead's calm expanse.* "Rydal Mount,
1824. Also on M. W."—I. F. Dowden, K., and Nowell Smith all
quote the following as an I. F. note, but I have not found it: "Mrs
Wordsworth's impression is that the Poem was written at Coleorton:
it was certainly suggested by a Print at Coleorton Hall." Mrs W.
was very likely right; W. was staying at Coleorton in April–May of
that year.

7–8. So looked Cecilia, *etc.*] an obvious allusion to Dryden's
Alexander's Feast, 161, 170. At last divine Cecilia came. . . . She
drew an angel down.

p. 36. XIX. To——(O dearer far) "Rydal Mount, 1824. To M. W."
—I. F. The poem was prompted by W.'s emotions on the imminent
death of Thomas Monkhouse, Mrs. W.'s cousin, of whom he speaks
as "one of my most valued friends". Monkhouse died in Feb. 1825,
but all through the latter months of 1824 his friends had little hope
of his recovery.

8. "sober certainties"] from *Comus* 263. "Such sober certainty of
waking bliss I never heard till now."

p. 37. XX. LAMENT OF MARY QUEEN OF SCOTS. "This arose out
of a flash of moonlight that struck the ground when I was approaching
the steps that lead from the garden at Rydal Mount to the front of
the house. 'From her sunk eye a stagnant tear stole forth' is taken,
with some loss, from a discarded poem, 'The Convict', in which
occurred, when he was discovered lying in the cell, these lines:

> But now he upraises the deep-sunken eye,
>   The motion unsettles a tear;
> The silence of sorrow it seems to supply
>   And asks of me—why I am here."—I. F.

For "The Convict", *v.* Vol. I, p. 312.

p. 40. XXI. THE COMPLAINT OF A FORSAKEN INDIAN WOMAN.
"Written at Alfoxden in 1798, where I read Hearne's Journey with
deep interest. It was composed for the volume of Lyrical Ballads."—
I. F. Referring in the Preface 1800–5 to the purpose of the *Lyrical
Ballads*—"to follow the fluxes and refluxes of the mind when
agitated by the great and simple affections of our nature", W. speaks
of "accompanying [in this poem] the last struggles of a human being,
at the approach of death, cleaving in solitude to life and society".

The book referred to by W. in his preparatory note (and still in his
library at the time of his death) is *A Journey from Prince of Wales's
Fort in Hudson's Bay to Northern Ocean 1769–1772, by order of the
Hudson's Bay Company* by Samuel Hearne, 4to, 1795. Dowden

points out that in chap. vii Hearne tells of a woman left behind by her Indian companions, who three times succeeded in coming up to them. "At length, poor creature! she dropt behind, and no one attempted to go back in search of her."

In the note-book containing D. W.'s *Journal* for 1800 the following lines are preserved, obviously an overflow from this poem:

> The snow-tracks of my friends I see
> Their foot-marks do not trouble me
> For ever left alone am I
> Then wherefore should I fear to die?
> Me to the last my friends did cherish
> And to the last were good and kind;
> Methinks 'tis strange I did not perish
> The moment I was left behind.
>
> Why do I watch those running deer,
> And wherefore wherefore come they here?
> And wherefore do I seem to love
> The things that live, the things that move?
> Why do I look upon the sky?
> I do not live for what I see;
> Why open thus mine eyes? To die
> Is all that now is left for me.
> If I could smother up my heart
> My life would then at once depart.
>
> My Friends, you live and yet you seem
> To me the people of a dream,
> A dream in which there is no love,
> And yet, my friends, you live and move.
> And can one hour to me remain,
> One moment, one, to me arrive
> When I could live without a pain
> And feel no wish to be alive?
> In quiet hopelessness I sleep
> Alas! how quiet and how deep!
>
> Oh no! I do not, cannot rue,
> I did not strive to follow you.
> I might have dropp'd, and died alone
> On unknown snows, a spot unknown.
> This spot to me must needs be dear,
> Of my dear Friends I see the trace.
> You saw me, friends, you laid me here,
> You know where my poor bones shall lie,
> Then wherefore should I fear to die?

Alas that one beloved, forlorn,
Should lie beneath the cold starlight;
With them I think I could have borne
The journey of another night,
And with my friends now far away
I could have lived another day.

p. 43. XXII. THE LAST OF THE FLOCK: "Produced at the same time
and for the same purpose. The incident occurred in the village of
Holford, close by Alfoxden."—I. F. Written in revulsion from
Godwin's attack on property in his *Political Justice*. "The man who
holds with Godwin that property is the cause of every vice and the
source of all the misery of the poor is naturally astonished to find
that this so-called evil, the offspring of human institutions, is a
vigorous instinct closely interwoven with the noblest feelings. It
represents familiar and dearly-loved fields, a hereditary cottage, and
flocks every animal of which has its own name." Legouis, *Early Life
of W.*, tr. Matthews, p. 310.

p. 46. XXIII. REPENTANCE. "Town-End, Grasmere. 1804. Suggested by the conversation of our next neighbour, Margaret Ashburner."—I. F. For the "conversation" *v.* D. W.'s *Journal* for
Nov. 24, 1801. The poem has the same theme as *The Last of the
Flock.*

7. Allan] Ashburner's real name was Thomas, as given in the MSS.
of the poem.

p. 47. XXIV. THE AFFLICTION OF MARGARET. "Town-End,
Grasmere. 1804. This was taken from the case of a poor widow who
lived in the town of Penrith. Her sorrow was well known to Mary, to
my Sister, and, I believe, to the whole town. She kept a shop, and
when she saw a stranger passing by, she was in the habit of going out
into the street to inquire of him after her son."—I. F. On the correct
date *v.* note to XII. *The Forsaken, supra.* The *Longman* MS. gives the
following introductory lines, which, however, W. wisely cancelled
before publication:

This Book, which strives to express in tuneful sound
The joys and sorrows which through life abound,
(Some great, some small, some frequent, and some rare,
Yet all observ'd or felt and truly there)
May in the following pages, which are penn'd
From general motives, gain a private end:
This little wandering Book (for who can say
Into what coverts it shall find its way)
May reach, perchance, the very Man, whose ear
Knows nothing of what many Strangers hear,
Whether through his mishap or his neglect:
A doleful plaint it is, to this effect.

p. 50. XXV. The Cottager to her Infant. "(by my sister). Suggested to her while beside my sleeping children."—I. F.

p. 51. XXVI. Maternal Grief. "This was in part an overflow from the Solitary's description of his own and his wife's feelings upon the decease of their children, and, I will venture to add *for private notice only*, is faithfully set forth from my Wife's feelings and habits after the loss of our two children within half a year of each other."— I. F. Catharine W. died on June 4, 1812, and Thomas on Dec. 1: the poem can therefore be dated Dec.–Jan. 1812–13. The variants quoted in the *app. crit.* are from a draft of *The Excursion*, Book III. For D. W.'s account of Mrs. W.'s grief, *v. M.Y.* 529–36, 542.

17. celestial light] For the thought cf. Ode: *Intimations, etc.*, where, however, the Christian idea of sinfulness has no place.

p. 54. XXVII. The Sailor's Mother. "Town-End, 1800. I met this woman near the Wishing-Gate, on the high-road that then led from Grasmere to Ambleside. Her appearance was exactly as here described, and such was her account, nearly to the letter."—I. F. For the correct date of the poem *v.* D. W.'s *Journal* for March 11–12, 1802, where it is named *The Singing Bird.* On the next two days W. wrote *Alice Fell* and *Beggars,* all three of them in his homeliest style, to be criticized by Coleridge, with *Simon Lee* and *Anecdote for Fathers,* as poems which "notwithstanding the beauties which are to be found in each of them where the poet interposes the music of his own thoughts, would have been more delightful to me in prose " (*Biog. Lit.,* chap. xviii). It was to meet this objection that W. made several attempts to improve the text.

19–36. Coleridge says of these stanzas (*loc. cit.*) that they "furnish the only fair instance that I have been able to discover in all Mr W.'s writings of an *actual* adoption, or true imitation, of the *real* and *very* language of low and rustic life, freed from provincialisms." For W.'s reply to Barron Field's objection to some of his alterations of the text *v. L.Y.,* p. 309.

p. 55. XXVIII. The Childless Father. "Town-End, 1800. When I was a child at Cockermouth, no funeral took place without a basin filled with sprigs of boxwood being placed upon a table covered with a white cloth in front of the house. The huntings on foot, in which the Old Man is supposed to join as here described, were of common, almost habitual, occurrence in our vales when I was a boy; and the people took much delight in them. They are now less frequent."—I. F.

p. 56. XXIX. The Emigrant Mother. " 1802. Suggested by what I have noticed in more than one French fugitive during the time of the French Revolution. If I am not mistaken, the lines were composed at Sockburn, when I was on a visit to Mary and her brother." —I. F. The poem is in MS. M; the (K) variant of ll. 87–8 is from a MS. that I have not seen.

The correct date is fixed by D. W.'s *Journal* for March 16–17, 1802.

11. endeavouring in our English tongue] Cf. Milton, *At a Vacation Exercise*, 2 "my first endeavouring tongue".

p. 59. XXX. VAUDRACOUR AND JULIA: "Town-End, 1805. Faithfully narrated, though with the omission of many pathetic circumstances, from the mouth of a French Lady, who had been an eye-and-ear-witness of all that was done and said. Many long years after, I was told that Dupligne was then a monk in the Convent of La Trappe."—I. F.

For a discussion of the source of the story, and its possible autobiographical significance, *v.* my edition of *The Prelude*, pp. 572–3.

p. 67. XXXI. THE IDIOT BOY. "Alfoxden 1798. The last stanza —'The Cocks did crow to-whoo, to-whoo, And the sun did shine so cold'—was the foundation of the whole. The words were reported to me by my dear friend, Thomas Poole; but I have since heard the same repeated of other Idiots. Let me add that this long poem was composed in the groves of Alfoxden, almost extempore; not a word, I believe, being corrected, though one stanza was omitted. I mention this in gratitude to those happy moments, for, in truth, I never wrote anything with so much glee."—I. F.

The importance that Wordsworth attached to *The Idiot Boy* is shown by the fact that in the *L.B.* 1800 it and *The Ancient Mariner* are the only poems which are given a separate title-page, and that in *The Prelude*, where he recounts the companionship with Coleridge "on Quantock's grassy hills" he only mentions it and *The Thorn* of his own and *The Ancient Mariner* and *Christabel* of Coleridge. In May 1802 John Wilson, then seventeen years old, had written Wordsworth an appreciative letter on the *L.B.*, but criticizing *The Idiot Boy*: for W.'s reply defending the poem, *v. E.L.*, pp. 294–8.

338. these fourteen years] This dates back W.'s poetic life to 1784, when he was fourteen years old. His first extant poem is dated 1785 (*v.* Appendix to Vol. I).

p. 80. XXXII. MICHAEL. "Town-End, 1801. Written about the same time as *The Brothers*. The Sheepfold, on which so much of the poem turns, remains, or rather the ruins of it. The character and circumstances of Luke were taken from a family to whom had belonged, many years before, the house we lived in at Town-End, along with some fields and woodlands on the eastern shore of Grasmere. The name of the Evening Star was not in fact given to this house but to another on the same side of the valley more to the north."—I. F. In 1836 W. told Mr. Justice Coleridge that "Michael was founded on the son of an old couple having become dissolute and run away from his parents; and on an old shepherd having been seven years in building up a sheepfold in a solitary valley" (M. ii. 305). To Thomas Poole he wrote on April 9, 1801: "I have attempted to give a picture of a man, of strong mind and lively sensibility, agitated by two of the most powerful affections of the human heart;

the parental affection, and the love of property, *landed* property, including the feelings of inheritance, home, and personal and family independence. . . . I had a still further wish that this poem should please you because in writing it I had your character often before my eyes, and sometimes thought I was delineating such a man as you yourself would have been under the same circumstances" (*E.L.*, p. 266). Cf. also W.'s letter to Charles James Fox, where he speaks of *Michael* as an "attempt to draw a picture of the domestic affections as I know they exist among . . . the statesmen, men of respectable education who daily labour on their own little properties" (*E.L.*, p. 261).

The exact date of the poem's composition is fixed by D. W.'s *Journal*. On Oct. 11 is the entry: "After dinner we walked up Greenhead Gill in search of a sheepfold. . . . The sheepfold is falling away. It is built nearly in the form of a heart unequally divided," and several subsequent entries record W. at work on the poem, often unsuccessfully: on Dec. 9 is the entry "Wm finished his poem to-day".

Two note-books preserve drafts of lines which either occur in *Michael* or were originally intended for it. (1) is a defective interleaved copy of Coleridge's *Poems*, 1796, used by W. at an early stage of composition: (2) is the book used by D. W. for her *Journal* of Feb. 1802–Jan. 1803, obviously used by W. later than (1). (K.'s statement that the entries are in D. W.'s hand is incorrect.) MS. 1 contains early versions of ll. 61–73 and 151–76, and four other stray lines; its variants are quoted as MS. in my *app. crit.* It has also early drafts of passages found in MS. 2—i.e. MS. 2 (*b*) 22–8, (*d*) 1–26, and of some lines of the episode included in *The Prelude*, Bk. VIII; as well as others intended to form part of that episode, but rejected. Thus, after ll. 237–43 of *Prelude*, VIII it runs on:

> Then onwards to the verge of Greenside Fell
> Towards Glenridding Screes and low Glencoin,
> Places forsaken now, yet loving still
> The Muses as they loved them in the day
> Of the old Minstrels and the Border Bards.
> Far went these shepherds in their devious quest,
> And far did they look forth, and many a sheep[1] *etc. as* MS. 2, (*d*).

MS. 1 also contains the following lines not found elsewhere:

> (α)   For me,
> When it has chanced that having wandered long
> Among the mountains, I have waked at last
> From dream of motion in some spot like this,
> Shut out from man, some region—one of those
> That hold by an inalienable right

---

[1] The first five of these lines were afterwards incorporated in *Musings near Aquapendente* (1837), 47–52.

An independent Life, and seem the whole
Of nature and of unrecorded time;
If, looking round, I have perchance perceived
Some vestiges of human hands, some stir
Of human passion, they to me are sweet
As lightest sunbreak, or the sudden sound
Of music to a blind man's ear who sits
Alone and silent in the summer shade.
They are as a creation in my heart;
I look into past times as prophets look
Into futurity, a [?] of life runs back
Into dead years, the [?] of thought
The [   ] spirit of philosophy
Leads me through moods of sadness to delight.

These lines may have been intended as part of an Introduction to *Michael* (cf. especially ll. 21–3 of the poem) or they may be merely an "Extempore Effusion" on a theme dear to W. The train of thought bears obvious connexion with passage (*e*), *infra*.

(β) When in the open space behind the ho[use]
A tawny bunch of withered [   ],[1]
Scarcely to be distinguished from a kite
Or yellow falcon, wheel'd itself about
On the invisible whirlwind, while the boy
Shouted and shouted at the plant to see
The playful life it led among the [   ]
[   ] I guess it was
Delight for which a happy man [?]
When they have stood above the [?]
Some blustering day of winter, while below
In the deep hollow of the mountain vale,
[   ]

(γ) In soft warm winter mornings, when the snow
Had fallen through the whole night, and up they went
Into the heights, at such a busy time
The dear beloved Boy would sometimes [? win]
Forgetfulnesses through the father's thought;
And he would stand beside him like a man
Robb'd of all purpose,—when the boy by chance,
Or wilfully, had on some steep descent
Unsettled with his foot a tuft of snow
Small as a sparrow's egg, which, sliding down
Inch after inch, before a yard were gone,
Had gathered up a small round mass that split

[1] Grass or fern? MS. blank. But cf. *Hint from the Mountains*, p. 151 and I. F. note.

With its own weight and made a hundred tufts
Which, branching each his several way, did each
Collect his separate mass which, one and all,
Went bounding on, till in its turn each broke
Into a thousand fragments which branch'd off,
Splitting and gathering, till the mountain seemed
Raced over by a thousand living things,
Ten thousand snow-white rabbits of the cliffs;
At sight whereof the lad would whoop for joy;
And when the race was ended he would point
Down to the fork of that gigantic tree,
Which far beneath them, by the devious track
Left by the runners in that elfin race,
Had been impressed upon the snow, and lay
With track beginning at the Lad's own feet,
And branches covering half the mountain side.
There, with a mingled sentiment of love,
Authority and sympathy and blame,
The old man stood spectator of the sight;
Meanwhile that princely Dog of which I spake
Eagerly following his peculiar work,
While every echo slept among the snow,
As if defrauded of his voice, unheard,
Barked restlessly among the sullen rocks.

(δ) But I am loitering even as if I thought
     That all my hearers had one heart, and loved
     Such matter as I love it

(ε)   Among the hills
     Moreover, shepherds' children, when they play
     In those wild places, seem almost to lose
     The quality of childhood, for their sports
     Are sanctified by such collateral aid
     Of majesty as fits them for the hearts
     Of men made grave by years. And thus it is
     That in such regions, by the sovereignty
     Of forms still paramount, to every change
     Which years can bring into the human heart
     Our feelings are indissolubly bound
     Together, and affinities preserved
     Between all stages of the life of man;
     Hence with more pleasure far than others feel,
     Led by his son, this shepherd now went back
     Into the years which he himself had lived;
     And natural feelings coming from within
     And from without, he to the present time

Link'd the dear memory of old histories,
Not with the loose and garrulous tongue of age,
But even as with a young man's eloquence,
Adding thereto the tenderness of years.
Hence may you guess the joy of Michael's heart
When with his son he clomb on Fairfield side.

(ζ)   I will relate
One incident, and then will close a strain
Which I have lengthened out as if I thought
That all my hearers had one heart, and loved
Such matter as I love it

[*Here follows draft of lines beginning the story told in "The Prelude".*
(1805) viii. 221–310.]

The following passages are found in MS. 2:

(*a*) There is a shapeless crowd of unhewn stones
That lie together, some in heaps, and some
In lines, that seem to keep themselves alive
In the last dotage of a dying form.
At least so seems it to a man who stands
In such a lonely place.

(*b*) No doubt if you in terms direct had ask'd
Whether he lov'd the mountains, true it is
That with blunt repetition of your words
He might have stared at you, and said that they
Were frightful to behold, but had you then   5
Discours'd with him in some particular sort
Of his own business, and the goings on
Of earth and sky, then truly had you seen
That in his thoughts there were obscurities,
Wonders and admirations, things that wrought   10
Not less than a religion in his heart.
And if it was his fortune to converse
With any who could talk of common things
In an unusual way, and give to them
Unusual aspects, or by questions apt   15
Wake sudden recognitions, that were like
Creations in the mind, and were indeed
Creations often, then, when he discoursed
Of mountain sights, this untaught shepherd stood
Before the man with whom he so convers'd   20
And look'd at him as with a Poet's eye.
But speaking of the vale in which he dwelt
And those bare rocks, if you had asked if he
For other pastures would exchange the same

And dwell elsewhere, I will not say indeed   25
What wonders might have been perform'd by bribes
And by temptations, but you then had seen
At once what Spirit of Love was in his heart.

(c) I have related that this Shepherd loved
The fields and mountains, not alone for this,
That from his very childhood he had lived
Among them, with a body hale and stout,
And with a vigorous mind, but furthermore   5
From circumstance peculiar to himself.
For as you have been told his bodily frame
Was of unusual strength, and in his mind
There was an active and propelling power
Which finding objects in his daily gains   10
And in the [? love] of gain in special sort
Attach'd him to his calling. But exclude
Such reasons, and he had less cause to love
His native vale and patrimonial fields
Or pleasure which is in the common earth   15
Than others have, for Michael had liv'd on
Childless, until the time when he began
To look towards the shutting in of life.
Strenuous the Shepherd still had been, still was
To further without stop or one stray thought   20
The business of the present hour, but now,
When they were both upon the heights, the freaks
And pastimes of the boy would intersperse
Short fits of idleness which meeting still
Habitual opposition or thrown off   25
With termination sudden and abrupt

(d)   Many a sheep
On height, in bottom did they see in flocks
Or single, and although it needs must seem
Hard to believe, yet could they well discern
Ev'n at the utmost distance of two miles—   5
Such strength of vision to the Shepherd's eye
Doth practice give, that neither in the flocks
Or in the single sheep was what they sought.
So to Helvellyn's eastern side they went
Down looking on that hollow, where the pool   10
Of Thirlmere flashes like a Warriour's shield
His light high up among the gloomy rocks
With gift of now and then a straggling gleam
To Armath's pleasant fields. And now they came
To that high spring which bears the human name   15

Of one unknown by others, aptly called
The fountain of the mists. The Father stoop'd
To drink of the clear water, laid himself
Flat on the ground even as a Boy might do,
To drink of the cold well; when in like sort   20
His son had drunk, the old Man said to him
That now he might be proud, for he that day
Had slak'd his thirst out of a famous well
The highest fountain known on British Land.
Thence journeying on a second time they pass'd   25
Those small flat stones which, rang'd by Travellers' hands
In cyphers on Helvellyn's highest ridge,
Lie loose on the bare turf, some half o'ergrown
By the grey moss, but not a single stone
Unsettled by a wanton blow from foot   30
Of Shepherd, man or Boy. They have respect
For strangers who have travell'd far perhaps
For men who in such places feeling there
The grandeur of the earth have left inscrib'd
Their epitaph which rain and snow   35
And the strong wind have reverenced.

(e) His hair was bushy, curling locks and long
Of a dark grey; these often as he stoop'd
Fell forward on his face, and at his work
They would so teaze and fret him that his face
Grew red as with a youthful bloom, and then,
Say they, he was a beautiful old man.

In this note-book also is found the episode at the time intended for
inclusion in *Michael*, but afterwards incorporated in the 1805 text
of *The Prelude*, viii. (*v. supra*).

For textual irregularities in *Michael v.* J. Edwin Wells, *P.M.L.A.*,
March 1938, 'Lyrical Ballads, 1800: Cancel Leaves.'

23–4. Shepherds . . . loved] cf. *Prel.* (1805), viii. 74–119, 178–82.

40. forest-side] the eastern side of the lake, between Greenhead
Ghyll and Town End.

258. Richard Bateman] The story alluded to here is well known
in the country. The chapel is called Ings Chapel and is on the road
leading from Kendal to Ambleside. W. W. *note*, 1802–5. "Richard"
is an error of W.'s for "Robert", as is shown by the stone tablet
over the west door of the Chapel at Ings, which reads: "This Chapel
was begun to be rebuilt Anno Domini 1743 at ye sole expense of
Mr. Robert Bateman, merchant at Leghorn, born in this hamlet.
But he dying suddenly the same year the work was ordered and
appointed to be finished by his executors."

324. a sheepfold] It may be proper to inform some readers that a sheepfold in these mountains is an unroofed building of stone walls, with different divisions. It is generally placed by the side of a brook, for the convenience of washing the sheep; but it is also useful as a shelter for them, and as a place to drive them into, to enable the shepherds conveniently to single out one or more for any particular purpose. W. W. *note*, 1802–5.

p. 94. XXXIII. THE WIDOW ON WINDERMERE SIDE. "The facts recorded in this Poem were given me, and the character of the person described, by my friend the Rev. R. P. Graves, who has long officiated as curate at Bowness, to the great benefit of the parish and neighbourhood. The individual was well known to him. She died before these verses were composed. It is scarcely worth while to notice that the stanzas are written in the sonnet form, which was adopted when I thought the matter might be included in 28 lines."— I. F. The poem was dated 1837 by Graves.

p. 96. XXXIV. THE ARMENIAN LADY'S LOVE. "Rydal Mount, 1830."—I. F. "The subject of the following poem is from the *Orlandus* of the author's friend, Kenelm Henry Digby; and the liberty is taken of inscribing it to him as an acknowledgment, however unworthy, of pleasure and instruction derived from his numerous and valuable writings, illustrative of the piety and chivalry of the olden time." W. W. 1835. W. first met Digby on Nov. 1830 (*v. L.Y.*, p. 539), but he was already acquainted with Digby's *Broadstone of Honour*, a book of Chivalry. Several MSS. of the poem are extant.

p. 102. XXXV. LOVING AND LIKING. "Rydal Mount, 1832. It arose, I believe, out of a casual expression of one of Mr. Swinburne's children."—I. F. In 1837 W. appended the note: "In the former editions of the author's Miscellaneous Poems are three pieces, addressed to Children—the following, a few lines excepted, is by the same Writer; and, as it belongs to the same unassuming class of compositions, she has been prevailed upon to consent to its publication."

p. 104. XXXVI. FAREWELL LINES. "These lines were designed as a farewell to Charles Lamb and his sister, who had retired from the throngs of London to comparative solitude in the village of Enfield." I. F.

Lamb retired to Enfield in Sept 1827, and W. visited him there in May 1828; this poem was probably written soon afterwards.

1. "High bliss" *etc.*] l. 10 of Thomson's poem *To the Rev. Patrick Murdoch* (K.)

p. 105. XXXVII. THE REDBREAST. "Rydal Mount, 1834. All our cats having been banished the house, it was soon frequented by redbreasts. Two or three of them, when the window was open, would come in, particularly when Mary was breakfasting alone. My Sister being then confined to her room by sickness as, dear creature, she still is, had one that without being caged, took up its abode with her, and at night used to perch upon a nail from which a picture had hung. It used to sing and fan her face with its wings in a manner that was very touching."—I. F.

38. pale faced Child] but, as the previous note shows, the invalid was not a child, but the poet's sister.

70. *lilt*] Italicized by W. because he is using the word in the dialect (Lakeland) sense of "walk with a light and springing step".

p. 107. XXXVIII. HER EYES ARE WILD. "Alfoxden, 1798. The subject was reported to me by a Lady of Bristol who had seen the poor creature."—I. F.

Legouis notes that the poem was written, in revulsion from Godwin's tenet that the feelings should be subservient to the intelligence, to show the pathos of unreasoning affection. Hutchinson notes "the obvious debt to the Scottish ballad *Lady Anne Bothwell's Lament* in Percy's *Reliques*".

10. And it was in the English tongue] For W. W.'s defence of this line *v*. his letter to Kenyon, *L.Y.*, p. 812.

21. a fire was once within my brain] Perhaps suggested by the *Mad Song* of "The Frantic Lady" in Percy's *Reliques, Second Series*, II. xxii:

> I burn, my brain consumes to ashes,
> Within my breast there glows a solid fire.

Cf. also *The Thorn* 120–1, written about the same time.

POEMS ON THE NAMING OF PLACES

In MS. M is found this *Motto for Poems on the Naming of Places*:

> Some minds have room alone for pageant stories,
> Some for strong passion flesh'd in action strong;
> Others find tales and endless allegories
> By river margins, and green woods among.

It is significant of their spirit and intention that W. placed them immediately after the *Poems founded on the Affections*.

p. 111. I. "*It was an April morning*." "Grasmere 1800. This poem was suggested on the banks of the brook that runs through Easedale, which is, in some parts of its course, as wild and beautiful as brook can be. I have composed thousands of verses by the side of it."—I. F.

39. My EMMA] said by Hutchinson and others to be a pseudonym for "the poet's sister Dora". But though the poem is unquestionably addressed to Dorothy, there is no evidence that she was ever called Dora: Emma may, however, be used as the metrical equivalent for "Dolly", a name by which she was known in her youth.

47. The Dell can be identified as by Easedale Beck, a little above Goody Bridge.

p. 112. II. TO JOANNA. "Grasmere, 1800. The effect of her laugh is an extravagance; though the effect of the reverberation of voices in some parts of the mountains is very striking. There is, in the Excursion, an allusion to the bleat of a lamb thus re-echoed, and described without any exaggeration, as I heard it, on the side of Stickle Tarn, from the precipice that stretches on to Langdale Pikes." —I. F.

In a note-book chiefly devoted to *Peter Bell*, MS. 2, is the following comment on *To Joanna*: "The poem supposes that at the Rock something had taken place in my mind either then, or afterwards in thinking upon what then took place which, if related, will cause the Vicar to smile. For something like this you are prepared by the phrase 'Now by those dear immunities', *etc.* I begin to relate the story, meaning in a certain degree to divert or partly play upon the Vicar. I begin— my mind partly forgets its purpose, being softened by the images of beauty in the description of the rock, and the delicious morning, and when I come to the 2 lines 'The Rock like something' *etc.*, I am caught in the trap of my own imagination. I entirely lose sight of my first purpose. I take fire in the lines 'that ancient woman'. I go on in that strain of fancy 'Old Skiddaw' and terminate the description in tumult 'And Kirkstone' *etc.*, describing what for a moment I believed either actually took place at the time, or when I have been reflecting on what did take place I have had a temporary belief, in some fit of imagination, did really or might have taken place. When the description is closed, or perhaps partly before I waken from the dream and see that the Vicar thinks I have been extravagating, as I intended he should, I then tell the story as it happened really; and as the recollection of it exists permanently and regularly in my mind, mingling allusions suffused with humour, partly to the trance in which I have been, and partly to the trick I have been playing on the Vicar. The poem then concludes in a strain of deep tenderness."

Joanna Hutchinson (1780–1843) was Mary W.'s youngest sister. The poem must not be taken literally; (1) Joanna was not brought up "amid the smoke of cities", (2) the W.s had only settled at Grasmere in the previous December, and if she had visited them before the poem was written D. W.'s *Journal* is evidence that it could not have been after May 14, and therefore not in the summer, when the broom was "full-flowered".

19–20. those lofty firs that overtop . . . the old steeple-tower] The firs were cut down during the W.'s absence at Coleorton 1806–7. On July 19, 1807, D. W. wrote to Mrs. Clarkson: "On our arrival our spirits sank, our first walk in the evening was very melancholy. . . . All the trees in Bainriggs are cut down, and even worse, the giant sycamore near the parsonage house and all the finest firtrees that overtopped the steeple tower.' ' The W.s had intimate experience of the "gloom" of the rectory when they lived there (May 1811–April 1813).

53–65. Coleridge speaks of these lines (*Biog. Lit.*, chap. xx) as "that noble imitation of Drayton, (if it be not a coincidence):

> Which Copland scarce had spoke, but quickly every hill,
> Upon her verge that stands, the neighbouring vallies fill;
> Helvillon from his height, it through the mountains threw,
> From whom as soon again, the sound Dunbalrase drew,
> From whose stone-trophied head, it on to Wendross went,
> Which tow'rds the sea again, resounded it to Dent,
> That Brodwater therewith within her banks astound,
> In sailing to the sea, told it to Egremound
> Whose buildings, walks, and streets, with echoes loud and long,
> Did mightily commend old Copland for her song."—
>
> *Polyolbion. Song* xxx.

p. 115. III. *There is an eminence* "1800. It is not accurate that the Eminence here alluded to could be seen from our orchard-seat. It rises above the road by the side of Grasmere lake, towards Keswick, and its name is Stone-Arthur."—I. F.

p. 115. IV. *A narrow girdle of rough stones and crags*, "1800. The character of the eastern shore of Grasmere Lake is quite changed, since these verses were written, by the public road being carried along its side. The friends spoken of were Coleridge and my Sister, and the fact occurred strictly as recorded."—I. F.

p. 118. V. *To M. H.* "To Mary Hutchinson, two years before our marriage. The pool alluded to is in Rydal Upper Park."—I. F. In the note-book afterwards used by D. W. for her *Journal*, Feb. 1802–Jan. 1803 is a MS. of this poem, of which half the page is torn away. It is dated Sat. Dec. 28, 1799.

p. 118. VI. *When, to the attractions of the busy world.* "1805. The grove still exists, but the plantation has been walled in, and is not so accessible as when my brother John wore the path in the manner here described. The grove was a favourite haunt with us all while we lived at Town-End."—I. F.

The poem was dated 1802 by W. in edd. 1815 and 1820, but 1805 in 1836 and I. F. An entry in D. W.'s *Journal* for Sept. 1, 1800: "W. read Joanna and The Firgrove to Coleridge", suggests that an early draft of ll. 1–83 was in existence at that date, though the view of Dowden and Hutchinson that this is the poem to which she refers on Aug. 30 as the *Inscription of the Pathway* is made unlikely by the discovery, in the *Longman* MS., of six lines, headed *The Orchard Pathway*, and intended as the motto for a group of poems:

> Orchard Pathway, to and fro,
> Ever with thee, did I go,
> Weaving Verses, a huge store!
> These, and many hundreds more,
> And, in memory of the same,
> This little lot shall bear thy name!

It seems probable that the poem was complete in the form given in the extant MSS. (one of which is found in MS. M, in the hand of D. W. and the other in the hand of S. H.) in 1802, when John was on a voyage to China; the revision into something like its first published form may have been the work of 1805. But it is clear, from the note appended to the poem in 1815 and subsequently, that it was not substantially altered after Feb. 11, 1805, the day on which the news of John W.'s death reached Grasmere. John W.'s sojourn at Town End had been from Jan. or Feb. to May 14, and from June 8 to Sept. 29, 1800.

The "Firgrove" is situated in Ladywood, above and almost exactly opposite to the Wishing Gate. From the reference to Silver How in l. 91, it has been conjectured that this is the poem D. W. refers to on March 26, 1802, as "his Silver How poem".

p. 123. VII. *Forth from a jutting ridge.* The two heathclad Rocks are situated in Bainriggs, high above the main road between Grasmere and Rydal Lakes.

16. now are they parted] S. H. died on June 23, 1835.

POEMS OF THE FANCY

p. 124. I. A MORNING EXERCISE. "Rydal Mount, 1825. I could wish the last five stanzas of this to be read with the poem addressed to the Skylark."—I. F. Dated 1828 by W. in edd. of his poems, but his statement in the I. F. note is more likely to be correct, from the poem's affinity to *The Skylark* ("Ethereal Minstrel", etc.) which was written in 1825. ll. 43–8 were transferred in 1845 from that poem to their present place.

60. singing as they shine] from the last stanza of Addison's *Ode* "The spacious firmament on high".

p. 126. II. A FLOWER GARDEN. "Planned by my friend Lady Beaumont in connexion with the garden at Coleorton."—I. F.

p. 127. III. *A whirl-blast from behind the hill.* "Observed in the holly grove at Alfoxden, where these verses were written in the spring of 1799. I had the pleasure of again seeing, with dear friends, this grove in unimpaired beauty, 41 years after."—I. F. The poem was written in 1798 not 1799; W. revisited Alfoxden in June, 1841, i.e. 43 "years after". A rough draft of the poem is to be found in the Alfoxden MS.

p. 128. IV. THE WATERFALL AND THE EGLANTINE. "Suggested nearer to Grasmere [i.e. nearer than *The Oak and the Broom q.v.*] on the same mountain track. The eglantine remained many years afterwards, but is now gone."—I. F.

15. tyrannous and strong] This phrase has been supposed to be an "unconscious echo" of *The Ancient Mariner* 40–1, "And now the storm blast came and he Was tyrannous and strong", but as this

reading in the *A. M.* did not appear till the ed. of 1817, and W. wrote
his poem in 1800, the borrowing is Coleridge's.

p. 130. V. THE OAK AND THE BROOM. "1800. Suggested upon the
mountain pathway that leads from Upper Rydal to Grasmere. The
ponderous block of stone, which is mentioned in the poem, remains,
I believe, to this day, a good way up Nab-Scar. Broom grows under
it and in many places on the side of the precipice."—I. F.

p. 134. VI. To A SEXTON. Written in Germany, 1799.—I. F.

p. 135. VII–IX. To THE DAISY; To THE SAME FLOWER; and THE
GREEN LINNET. "All composed in Town End Orchard, where the
Bird was often seen as here described."—I. F.

This Poem, and two others to the same Flower, . . . were written
in the year 1802; which is mentioned, because in some of the ideas,
though not in the manner in which those ideas are connected, and
likewise even in some of the expressions, there is a resemblance to
passages in a Poem (lately published) of Mr. Montgomery entitled
A Field Flower. This being said, Mr. Montgomery will not think any
apology due to him; I cannot, however, help addressing him in the
words of the Father of English Poets.

> "Though it happe me to rehersin—
> That ye han in your freshe songis saied,
> Forberith me, and beth not ill apaied,
> Sith that ye se I doe it in the honour
> Of Love, and eke in service of the Flour."
>
> W. W. 1807.

In a footnote to VIII W. writes (*ed.* 1807): The two following poems
[i.e. this poem and "Bright Flower whose home is everywhere",
Poems of Sent. and Refl. ix.] were overflowings of the mind in composing the one which stands first in the first volume." [i.e. VII].

Hutchinson points out that this poem is one of the first fruits of
W.'s study of the Elizabethans, whom "he had begun to study
diligently in Robert Anderson's *Corpus* of the British Poets, 1795".
In Feb.–March 1802 D. and W. W. were reading Ben Jonson (*v.
Journal*) and the metre of the Daisy poems is imitated from Ben
Jonson's *Underwoods, Eupheme*, Song i; though whereas ll. 4 and 8
in *Eupheme* have 4 syllables in *The Daisy* they have normally 5,
(but l. 4 of the first stanza, 7.) He notes also the influence of Drayton's *Nymphidia*, the metre of which is used for *The Green Linnet*,
written about the same time. *Nymphidia* has 7 syllables in ll. 4 and
8 of its stanzas, and st. i of *The Daisy* contains an obvious reminiscence of st. ii of *Nymphidia*:

> Another sort there be that will
> Be talking of the Fayries still,
> Nor never can they have their fill,
> As they were wedded to them;

No tales of them their thirst can slake
So much delight therein they take,
And some strange thing they faine would make,
Knew they the way to doe them.
The quotation which heads the poem is from Wither's *The Shepherd's Hunting, Eclogue* 4. (but Wither reads in l. 3 "invention" for "instruction" and in l. 4 "her" for "the") and was perhaps, as Dykes Campbell suggested, prompted by Lamb's admiration of that Eclogue (*v.* his essay *On the Poetical Works of George Wither*).

1–4. Cf. *Prelude* (1805). XI. 190–5, and *Lines composed a few miles above Tintern Abbey* 65–85.

22. remote] for the North country rhyme with "nought", and "thought" cf. Vol. I, p. 367.

25. secret mews] Miss Darbishire notes the debt to Spenser. *F.Q.* II. vii. 19: "But safe I have them kept in secret mew."

34–6. Cf. W. W.'s Letter to Lady Beaumont, Feb. 3, 1807: "I can say with truth that in the month of April I have passed many an hour under the shade of a green holly, glad to find it in my walk, and unwilling to quit it because I had not courage to face the sun." (*M.Y.*, p. 113.)

p. 139. IX. THE GREEN LINNET. On date of composition and metre *v.* notes to *The Daisy, supra.* The changes in the text in both the first and last stanzas were probably due in part to the strictures of the *Edinburgh Review* and *The Simpliciad*, both of which mocked at "the *toy* that doth my fancy *tether*" (7–8) and the word *teems.* Of the last stanza W. wrote to Barron Field in 1828: "The stanza, as you have been accustomed to quote it, is very faulty. 'Forth he teems' is a provincialism. As Johnson says, 'A low word, when used in this sense'. But my main motive for altering this stanza was the wholly unjustifiable use of the word *train* as applied to leaves attached to a tree. A train of *withered* leaves, driven by the wind along the gravel, as I have often seen them, sparkling in April sunshine, might be said" (*L.Y.*, p. 310).

p. 141. X. TO A SKYLARK. Dated by W. 1805, but Hutchinson thinks that both the tone and style of the poem suggest an earlier date, probably 1802; and W.'s statement (quoted *infra*) of Coleridge's habitual attitude to it rather points to the period, before his departure for Malta, when they were in constant literary communion. The drastic treatment of the text in 1827 and after (*v. app. crit.*) is explained in W.'s letter to Barron Field Oct. 1828: "After having succeeded in the second *Skylark* [i.e. 'Ethereal Minstrel', *etc.*] and in the conclusion of the poem entitled *A Morning Exercise*, in my notice of this bird, I became indifferent to this poem, which Coleridge used severely to condemn and to treat contemptuously. I like, however, the beginning of it so well that, for the sake of that, I tacked to it the respectably-tame conclusion. I have no objection,

as you have been pleased with it, to restore the whole poem. Could
you improve it a little ?"

p. 142. XI. To the Small Celandine. "Grasmere, Town-End,
1805. It is remarkable that this flower, coming out so early in the
Spring as it does, and so bright and beautiful, and in such profusion,
should not have been noticed earlier in English verse. What adds
much to the interest that attaches to it is its habit of shutting itself
up and opening out according to the degree of light and temperature
of the air."—I. F. The correct date is April 30, 1802, as is proved by
D. W.'s *Journal* of that day.

p. 144. XII. To the Same Flower. **50.** beneath our shoon]
probably, as K. notes, an imperfect recollection of *Comus*, 634–5 :
"and the dull swain Treads on it daily with his clouted shoon."

p. 146. XIII. The Seven Sisters. The story of this poem is
from the German of Frederica Brun.—W. W. 1807. The Ballad is
entitled *Die Sieben Hügel*. W. took the name Binnorie from the
refrain of the old Scots ballad *The twa Sisters*, of which the first two
lines run :

> There were twa sisters lived in a bouir ;
> Binnorie, O Binnorie!

The poem is dated by the entry in D. W.'s *Journal* for Aug. 17, 1800 :
"William read us *The Seven Sisters*."

p. 148. XIV. *Who fancied what a pretty sight.* In 1807 printed as
one of the *Moods of my own Mind*.

p. 149. XV. The Redbreast Chasing the Butterfly. "Observed
as described in the then beautiful Orchard at Town-End."—I. F.
Misdated by W. 1806, but cf. D. W.'s *Journal*: "April 17, 1802, I saw
a robin chasing a scarlet butterfly this morning. April 18. William
wrote the poem on The Robin and the Butterfly."

10 *and* **30.** (1807) The author of *The Simpliciad* burlesques

> "Poets, [who]
> With brother lark or brother robin fly
> And flutter with half-brother butterfly,"

adding the note "The relationship of the Butterfly is not so easily
settled, but in virtue of his being brother to the robin,

> a brother he seems of thine own,

I have ventured to give his genealogy as above".

There are MS. copies of the poem in the *Longman* MSS. and in MS. M.

2. The pious bird] K. compares Cowley

> And Robin redbreasts whom men praise
> For pious birds.

But cf. note to l. 23.

2–14. Father Adam] W.'s footnote was added on the suggestion
of De Quincey (*v. Works*, ed. Masson, iii. 26–9).

23. Cf. *The Children in the Wood* (Percy's *Reliques*)

No burial this pretty pair
Of any man receives,
Till Robin Redbreast piously
Did cover them with leaves.

p. 150. XVI. SONG FOR THE SPINNING WHEEL. "1806. The belief on which this is founded I have often heard expressed by an old neighbour of Grasmere."—I. F. But dated 1812 by W. in edd. of his poems. Probably addressed to Sara H. (cf. *Misc. Sonnets*, I, xx).

p. 151. XVII. HINT FROM THE MOUNTAINS. "Bunches of fern may often be seen, wheeling about in the wind as here described. The particular bunch which suggested these verses was noticed in the Pass of Dunmail-Raise. The verses were composed in 1817, but the application is for all times and places."—I. F. Cf. the lines originally written for inclusion in *Michael*, p. 480 *supra*.

p. 152. XVIII. ON SEEING A NEEDLECASE, *etc.* E. M. S.: Edith May Southey b. 1804. m. Rev. J. J. Warter, 1834. She was the intimate friend of Dora W.

p. 153. XIX. TO A LADY, *etc.*: First printed according to T. Wise (*Two Lake Poets*, a Catalogue, *etc.*, p. 31) in a privately issued quarto brochure, entitled *Verses, Composed at the Request of Jane Wallas Penfold*, by William Wordsworth, Esq. Poet Laureate, with the date Jan. 1, 1843, and followed by *Song of the Madeira Flowers*, composed at the request of Jane Wallas Penfold by Mrs. Calverley Bewicke.

p. 155. XXI. THE CONTRAST. "*The Parrot and the Wren.* The Parrot belonged to Mrs. Luff while living at Fox Ghyll. The Wren was one that haunted for many years the Summerhouse between the two terraces of Rydal Mount."—I. F.

46. darkling] Mr. Nowell Smith calls attention to the fact that this word, used as a noun, must be a coinage of W.'s; the only previously recorded instance of it is in a MS. poem by J. Ross, called *Fratricide* (1773) (*v. O.E.D.*).

p. 156. XXII. THE DANISH BOY. "Written in Germany 1799. It was entirely a fancy, but intended as a prelude to a ballad poem never written."—I. F. These stanzas were designed to introduce a Ballad upon the Story of a Danish Prince who had fled from Battle, and, for the sake of the valuables about him, was murdered by the Inhabitant of a Cottage in which he had taken refuge. The House fell under a curse, and the Spirit of the Youth, it was believed, haunted the Valley where the crime had been committed.—W. W. *ed.* 1827.

Mr. Nowell Smith notes the similarity in "rhythm and metre to *The Thorn*, the only difference being the absence of rhyme in ll. 1 and 3 of the Stanza in *The Thorn*". He notes too the similarity of style, especially between *The Thorn* and the stanza which stood last but one in 1800, but was afterwards omitted.

p. 160. XXIV. STRAY PLEASURES. "Suggested on the Thames by the sight of one of those floating mills that used to be seen there. This I noticed on the Surrey side between Somerset House and Blackfriars Bridge. Charles Lamb was with me at the time; and I thought it remarkable that I should have to point out to *him*, an idolatrous Londoner, a sight so interesting as the happy group dancing on the platform. Mills of this kind used to be, and perhaps still are, not uncommon on the Continent. I noticed several upon the river Saone in the year 1790, particularly near the town of Chalons, where my friend Jones and I halted a day when we crossed France, so far on foot: there we embarked and floated down to Lyons."—I. F.

33–5. Hutchinson and other critics have noted W.'s debt here to Drayton's *The Muses' Elysium*, sixth Nymphal, 4–7:

> The wind had no more strength than this,
> That leisurely it blew,
> To make one leaf the next to kiss,
> That closely by it grew.

p. 161. XXV. THE PILGRIM'S DREAM. "I distinctly recollect the evening on which these verses were suggested in 1818. I was on the road between Rydal and Grasmere where glow-worms abound. A star was shining above the ridge of Loughrigg Fell just opposite. I remember a blockhead of a critic, in some Review or other, crying out against this piece. 'What so monstrous,' said he, 'as to make a star talk to a Glow-worm?' Poor fellow, we know well from this sage observation what the primrose on the river's brim was to him."—I. F.

p. 163. XXVI. THE POET AND THE CAGED TURTLEDOVE. "Rydal Mount 1830. This Dove was one of the pair that had been given to my daughter by our excellent friend Miss Jewsbury, who went to India with her husband, Mr. Fletcher, where she died of cholera. The Dove survived its mate many years, and was killed to our great sorrow by a neighbour's cat that got in at the window and dragged it partly out of the cage. These verses were composed *ex tempore*, to the letter, in the Terrace Summer House before spoken of. It was the habit of the bird to begin cooing and murmuring whenever it heard me making my verses."—I. F. The manuscript is a fair copy by D. W.; it is headed "'Twenty minutes exercise upon the Terrace last night (at the beginning of December)' but the scene is within doors".

p. 164. XXVII. A WREN'S NEST. "Rydal Mount. This nest was built, as described, in a tree that grows near the pool in Dora's field next the Rydal Mount garden."—I. F.

There is a fair copy of the poem, in M. W.'s hand (cited in *app. crit.* as MS. A) which preserves an earlier and shorter version. Later additions, and variants (cited as MS.), are written over the fair copy and on the verso, by W. W.

p. 167. XXVIII. LOVE LIES BLEEDING. "It has been said that
the English, though their country has produced so many great Poets,
is now the most unpoetical nation in Europe. It is probably true; for
they have more temptation to become so than any other European
people. Trade, commerce, and manufactures, physical science, and
mechanic arts, out of which so much wealth has arisen, have made
our countrymen infinitely less sensible to movements of imagination
and fancy than were our Forefathers in their simple state of society.
How touching and beautiful were, in most instances, the names they
gave to our indigenous flowers, or any other they were familiarly
acquainted with! Every month for many years have we been
importing plants and flowers from all quarters of the globe, many of
which are spread through our gardens, and some perhaps likely to
be met with on the few Commons which we have left. Will their
botanical names ever be displaced by plain English appellations,
which will bring them home to our hearts by connection with our
joys and sorrows? It can never be, unless society treads back her
steps towards those simplicities which have been banished by the
undue influence of Towns spreading and spreading in every direction,
so that city-life with every generation takes more and more the lead
of rural. Among the ancients, Villages were reckoned the seats of
barbarism. Refinement, for the most part false, increases the desire
to accumulate wealth; and while theories of political economy are
boastfully pleading for the practice, inhumanity pervades all our
dealings in buying and selling. This selfishness wars against disinterested imagination in all directions, and, evils coming round in a
circle, barbarism spreads in every quarter of our Island. Oh for the
reign of justice, and then the humblest man among us would have
more power and dignity in and about him than the highest have
now."—I. F.

In a MS. note-book dated 1833, and placed between XLVII and
XLVIII of *Itinerary Poems of 1833*, is the following Sonnet:

They call it Love *lies* bleeding, rather say
That in this crimson flower Love bleeding *droops*,
A flower how rich in sadness! thus it stoops
With languid head unpropped from day to day,
From month to month, life passing not away;
Even so the dying Gladiator leans
On Mother earth, and from his patience gleans
Relics of tender thought, regrets that stay
A moment and are gone. O fate-bowed flower,
Fair as Adonis bathed in sanguine dew
Of his death wound, *that* Lover's heart was true
As heaven, who pierced by scorn in some lone bower
Could press thy semblance of unpitied smart
Into the service of his constant heart.

The poem is clearly a development from this sonnet, and may have been written specially for the 1842 volume, any time after 1833. In June 1835 Dora W. sent Quillinan a different version of both these poems. *The first begins*:

> What keeps this flower reclined upon its bed,
> With unchanged aspect, when the rose is fled,
> And files of stateliest plants have ceased to bloom,
> Each in its turn submitting to like doom ?
> Never enlivened *etc. as* XXIX, 1–6, *but* 4–5 (cf. xxix. 67)
> This lovely one that once was summer's guest
> Preserves her beauty among falling leaves,

The MS. *then goes on as* XXVIII, 1–6, *followed by*

> The dying Gladiator ; thus he leans
> Alone, with hanging brow, and body bent
> Earthward in uncomplaining languishment, (*cf.* sonnet *supra*)
> Yet not unblest while he from patience gleans
> Relics of tenderest thought. O fate-bowed Flower
> So drooped Adonis *etc. as* 13–14
> His softest sweetest respirations drew,
> Till Venus *etc. as* 15–16 (17 *omitted*)
> She suffered *etc. as* 18
> But keener pangs that gentle Lover knew
> *etc. as* 20–2, *omitting* 23, *and for* 24
> And gave, sad Flower, the name that thou will ever bear!

The second poem (corresponding to XXIX) *begins*:

> Narcissus cherishing a downcast mien
> The Laurel glittering with immortal green
> The spotted hyacinth, and poplars dank
> Sighing in concert on a river's bank
> Speak and remind the Intelligent how free
> Were Poets once—how strong in sympathy
> They touched the heart with lapse of fountain clear
> Or moved with impulses of viewless air (cf. 14–15)

etc. as 16–27, *but* 16 found *for* sought, 19 classic *for* Grecian, 21 Youth by Hope betrayed, 23 melancholy *for* undeparting *and* 26 And with this parallel his passion feeding

p. 168. XXX. RURAL ILLUSIONS. "Rydal Mount 1832. Observed a hundred times in the grounds at Rydal Mount."—I. F. There are at least four manuscripts of the poem, the earliest entitled *Innocent Illusions*. It is not everywhere possible to determine the relative dates of the corrections in the MSS., but the earliest preserved version of the poem is cited in the *app. crit.* as MS. 1, and the others as MS. 2.

p. 170. XXXI. THE KITTEN AND FALLING LEAVES. "1805. Seen at Town-End Grasmere. The Elder-bush has long since disappeared : it hung over the wall near the cottage, and the kitten continued to

leap up catching the leaves as here described. The infant was Dora."
—I. F. In edd. of his poems W. gives the date as 1804. It is worth
noting that the name Dora was substituted in the poem for Laura,
only after Dora's death in 1847, and that at the same time her name
was added to the title of the next poem. The variants given in the
app. crit. are from the *Longman* MS.

p. 174. XXXII. ADDRESS TO MY INFANT DAUGHTER, DORA.
Towards the end of the Preface of 1815, after discussing the difference
between the Fancy and the Imagination and illustrating his point
from Milton, W. has the following paragraph (omitted 1845): "Awe-
stricken as I am by contemplating the operations of the mind of this
truly divine Poet, I scarcely dare venture to add that 'An address to
an Infant', which the Reader will find under the Class of Fancy in
the present Volumes, exhibits something of this communion and
interchange of instruments and functions between the two powers,
and is, accordingly, placed last in the class, as a preparation for that
of Imagination which follows."

Two MSS. of this poem survive.
15. "heaven's eternal year"] Dryden *To the pious Memory of
. . . Mrs. Anne Killigrew*, 15. "Since Heaven's eternal year is thine."

p. 176. XXXIII. THE WAGGONER. "Written at Town-End,
Grasmere. The characters and story from fact."—I. F.

"Several years after the event that forms the subject of the poem,
in company with my friend, the late Mr. Coleridge, I happened to fall
in with the person to whom the name of Benjamin is given. Upon
our expressing regret that we had not, for a long time, seen upon the
road either him or his waggon, he said:—"They could not do without
me; and as to the man who was put in my place, no good could come
out of him; he was a man of no *ideas*."

"The fact of my discarded hero's getting the horses out of a great
difficulty with a word, as related in the poem, was told me by an eye-
witness."—W. 1836.

K. is responsible for the current error which identifies Benjamin
with Jackson, Southey's landlord at Greta Hall. Jackson was not
the hero of W.'s poem, but was Benjamin's employer.

The Waggoner was a great favourite with Southey, and with Lamb,
who acknowledged its dedication to him in a letter dated June 7,
1819: "My dear Wordsworth, you cannot imagine how proud we are
here of the dedication. We read it twice for once that we do the poem
—I mean all through—yet Benjamin is no common favorite—there
is a spirit of beautiful tolerance in it—it is as good as it was in 1806—
and will be as good in 1829 if our dim eyes shall be awake to peruse it.

"Methinks there is a kind of shadowing affinity between the subject of the narrative and the subject of the dedication—but I will not
enter into personal themes—else, substituting * * * * * * * * * *
for Ben, and the Honble United Company of Merch^ts trading to the

East Indies for the Master of the misused Team, it might seem by no far fetched analogy to point its dim warnings hitherward—but I reject the omen—especially as its import seems to have been diverted to another victim. . . . The Waggoner is very ill put up in boards, at least it seems to me always to open at the dedication—but that is a technical fault. . . ."

For W.'s own criticism of it *v*. note on III, 28/9, *infra*.

There are three manuscripts of the poem, all in the hand of S. H., but with corrections by the poet. The first two probably date from about 1805–6 and represent the first completed form of the poem; they are identical in texts and have many of the same corrections, though MS. 1 has been used more often for inserting later drafts.

MS. 3 is in a volume with *Peter Bell* and *Artegal and Elidure*, and seems to have been copied when publication was already contemplated. MS. 1 is in the British Museum, the others at Dove Cottage.

On the top of the first page of MS. 1 W. has written "This poem was at first thrown off under a lively impulse of feeling during the first fortnight of 180[6][1] and has since at several times been carefully revised and with the Author's best efforts retouched and inspirited."

In 1820 *The Waggoner* was the first of the *Poems of the Fancy*; in 1827–36 it was placed between *Poems of the Affections* and *Poems of the Fancy*; in 1845 it was placed last of the *Poems of the Fancy*.

The mottoes of 1819 (employed in 1827 for *Peter Bell* where they have more propriety) are from *Romeo and Juliet* II, ii. 43 and *Julius Caesar*, I. i. 147; the motto adopted in 1845 is from Thomson's *Seasons; Summer* 977–9: it was suggested by Barron Field.

I. 3. The buzzing dor-hawk, *etc.*] "When the poem was first written the note of the bird was thus described:

> The Night-hawk is singing his frog-like tune,
> Twirling his watchman's rattle about—

but from unwillingness to startle the reader at the outset by so bold a mode of expression, the passage was altered as it now stands."— W. 1836.

I. 53. the Dove and Olive Bough] W.'s cottage at Town-End, Grasmere, formerly an Inn, and later known as Dove Cottage.

I. 171. Sidrophel] the astrologer in Butler's *Hudibras* (II. iii).

I. 210. King Dunmail's bones] the tradition still survives that Dunmail, the last king of Cumberland, deposed 945 A.D., is buried under the cairn at the summit of Dunmail Raise, which marks the boundary between Cumberland and Westmorland.

II. 128–34. K. notes the similarity of this passage with Corporal Trim's exposition of the siege of Namur in *Tristram Shandy* (Bk. IX, ch. xxviii): "And this," said he, "is the town of *Namur*—and this

---

[1] "6" added later in pencil.

the citadel—and there lay the *French*—and here lay his honour and myself." Doubtless W. had this passage at the back of his mind.

III. **28/9.** "After the line, *"Can any mortal clog come to her"*, followed in the MS. an incident which has been kept back. Part of the suppressed verses shall here be given as a gratification of private feeling, which the well-disposed reader will find no difficulty in excusing. They are now printed for the first time.

Can any mortal clog come to her ?
It can : . . .

.   .   .   .   .   .

But Benjamin, in his vexation,
Possesses inward consolation ;
He knows his ground, and hopes to find   5
A spot with all things to his mind,
An upright mural block of stone,
Moist with pure water trickling down.
A slender spring ; but kind to man
It is, a true Samaritan ;   10
Close to the highway, pouring out
Its offering from a chink or spout ;
Whence all, howe'er athirst, or drooping
With toil, may drink, and without stooping.

Cries Benjamin "Where is it, where ?   15
Voice it hath none, but must be near."
—A star, declining towards the west,
Upon the watery surface threw
Its image tremulously imprest,
That just marked out the object and withdrew,   20
Right welcome service ! . . .

.   .   .   .   .   .

ROCK OF NAMES !
Light is the strain, but not unjust
To Thee and Thy memorial-trust
That once seemed only to express
Love that was love in idleness ;   25
Tokens, as year hath followed year
How changed, alas, in character !
For they were graven on thy smooth breast
By hands of those my soul loved best ;
Meek women, men as true and brave   30
As ever went to a hopeful grave :
Their hands and mine, when side by side
With kindred zeal and mutual pride,
We worked until the Initials took
Shapes that defied a scornful look.—   35

Long as for us a genial feeling
Survives, or one in need of healing,
The power, dear Rock, around thee cast,
Thy monumental power, shall last
For me and mine! O thought of pain,   40
That would impair it or profane!
Take all in kindness then, as said
With a staid heart but playful head;
And fail not Thou, loved Rock! to keep
Thy charge when we are laid asleep."—W. 1836   45

The complete suppressed passage, as given in MSS., is as follows:

Can any mortal clog come to her?
It can—if chance a strong desire
Such as did soon lay hold of these
Should rise, and set the throat on fire
And nothing by to give us ease.
What wish you, with that spacious mere
And all its weight of water near,
What nobler cup would you require
To slake a thousand throats on fire?
But wise are they; and self-denial
Prefer to such a desperate trial—
Once in (I put the question plain)
Who is to help them out again?

Here follow ll. 3–16 *as above, with slight variants*—7 monumental
stone   8 with purest waters
            8/9 A spring that doth but faintly bleed
                    And yet sufficient for their need,
10 A cordial true Samaritan, *After* 16, Voice it hath none, but must
be near, *the* MSS. *go on*:

A star declining in the West
Its image faintly had impress'd
Upon the smooth and dewy block,
The surface of the upright rock;
And he espies it by this sign
And both there take a draught divine.
Could happier more convenient place
Be given in fortune's utmost grace?
They have a comfort in their madness
And feel that this is sober gladness.
            Ah[1] dearest Spot! dear Rock of Names
From which our Pair thus slaked their flames,

[1] *Against the following passage W. has written in the margin of MS. 1:*
Checks I think the interest as it stops the progress; therefore better out,
do as you think best. Let the lines however be put in the Margin.

NOTES 501

Ah! deem not this light strain unjust
To thee and to thy precious trust,
That file which gentle brave and good,
The near in friendship and in blood,
The hands of those I love the best
Committed to thy faithful breast.
Their hands and mine, dear Rock! when we
Have rested by the side of thee;
No, long as I've a genial feeling
Or one that stands in need of healing
Thy power shall last—Oh thought of pain
That would impair it or profane.
Take all in kindness then, as said
With a fond heart though playful head;
And thou thy record duly keep
Long after we are laid asleep.

As winds by pausing do grow stronger
How fierce when they can pause no longer!
So back again the tempest rush'd
That for a moment had been hush'd;
No notion have they, not a thought,
Not one that is not highly wrought
Beside the spring and silent lake.

The Hon. Justice Coleridge recorded on Oct. 10, 1836, how W. "read me some lines which formed part of a suppressed portion of *The Waggoner*, but which he is now printing 'on the Rock of Names', so called because on it they had carved out their initials: W. W., M. H., D. W., S. T. C., J. W., S. H. This rock was about a mile beyond Wythburn Chapel, to which they used to accompany my uncle, in going to Keswick from Grasmere, and where they would meet him when he returned. This led him to read much of *The Waggoner* to me. It seems a very favourite poem of his, and he read me splendid descriptions from it. He said his object in it had not been understood. It was a play of the fancy on a domestic incident and lowly character: he wished by the opening descriptive lines to put his reader into the state of mind in which he wished it to be read. If he failed in doing that, he wished him to lay it down. He pointed out, with the same view, the glowing lines on the state of exaltation in which Ben and his companion are under the influence of liquor. Then he read the sickening languor of the morning walk, contrasted with the glorious uprising of Nature, and the songs of the birds. Here he has added about six most exquisite lines." (M. ii. 310.)

III. **92.** foundrous] The word is in the *O.E.D.* under founderous (cf. "founderous passages" in W.'s letter to a friend of R. Burns): the *Dialect Dictionary* gives it as used in Lancs. for "causing to founder, boggy, swampy".

917·17 II K k

IV. **12.** scents the morning air] *Hamlet*, I. v. 58.

IV. **21.** Ghimmer Crag, his tall twin brother] the only rock now known by this name in the district is situated below the Langdale Pikes. K., by a quotation from *A Description of Sixty Studies from Nature* by William Green of Ambleside, 1810, proves that W. is referring to Fisher Crag: "The margin of the Lake on the Dalehead side has its charms of wood and water, and Fisher Crag, twin brother to Raven Crag, is no bad object." That W. was indebted to Green in this passage is rendered more probable by the fact that it is not found in MSS. 1 and 2 (1806), but is introduced later, *v. app. crit.*

IV. **47–8.** Sir Lancelot gave a safe retreat To noble Clifford] cf. *Feast of Brougham Castle*, 95–101.

IV. **71–82.** The passage referred to at the close of Justice Coleridge's note, quoted *supra*.

IV. **123.** pricked] a Spenserian word; *v. F.Q.* I. i. 1.

IV. **198.** adventurous song] *Paradise Lost* I. 13. "Invoke thy aid to my adventrous song."

IV. **207–8.** For what I have and what I miss
I sing of these! It makes my bliss:

obviously reminiscent of Chaucer in both spirit and phrasing. Cf. *Hous of Fame*, vii. 789–90.

For what I drye or what I thinke
I wol my-selven al hit drinke;

and the word "bliss", a favourite with Chaucer.

POEMS OF THE IMAGINATION

p. 206. I. THERE WAS A BOY: incorporated in *The Prelude*, v. 389–422. (1805). For notes *v.* my edition, pp. 530–1, 608, D.

p. 207. II. To THE CUCKOO. "Composed in the Orchard at Town End, 1804."—I. F. The correct date is 1802, *v.* D. W 's *Journal* March 23, 1802, "Wm worked at the Cuckoo poem", and on May 14 "Wm teased himself with seeking an epithet for the cuckoo". Cf. also the entry on June 3, "We walked into Easedale . . . the cuckoo sang . . . we have been reading the life and some of the writings of poor Logan since dinner". Logan was the reputed author of the *Ode*: *To the Cuckoo*, now ascribed to Michael Bruce, to which W. was obviously indebted in his poem; *v.* especially the stanza:

The schoolboy, wand'ring in the wood
To pull the flow'rs so gay,
Starts, thy curious voice to hear,
And imitates thy lay.

As a commentary on the poem Dowden aptly quotes from W.'s *Guide to the Lakes*: "There is also an imaginative influence in the voice of the cuckoo, when the voice has taken possession of a deep mountain valley." Cf. also W.'s *Preface*, 1815 (*supra*, p. 437).

An autograph MS. of the poem, given to Thomas Wilkinson, and now in the W. Museum, is identical with the 1807 text, but reads "*Bird*" for "bird" in l. 15.

5–8. An interesting example of felicity attained after repeated efforts. The alteration in l. 8 of "At once far off and near" (1815–20) to the reading of 1827 "As loud far off as near" was due, W. told Barron Field, to "my noticing one day that the voice of the cuckoo, which I heard from a tree at a great distance, did not seem any louder when I approached the Tree." (*L.Y.*, p. 311.)

18–19. W. added in pencil to the MS. the reading of the text, but with the comment "I like the other better. W. W."

p. 208. III. A NIGHT PIECE. "Composed on the road between Nether Stowey and Alfoxden, extempore. I distinctly recollect the very moment when I was struck, as described "He looks up at the clouds, etc."—I. F.

Two MSS. of the poem are preserved in note-books of the Alfoxden period. The entry in D. W.'s *Journal* of Jan. 25, 1798, must be indebted to W.'s "extempore" poem: "The sky spread over with one continuous cloud, whitened by the light of the moon, which, though her dim shape was seen, did not throw forth so strong a light as to chequer the earth with shadows. At once the clouds seemed to cleave asunder, left her in the centre of a black-blue vault. She sailed along, followed by multitudes of stars, small and bright, and sharp. Their brightness seemed concentrated (half-moon)."

24. Not undisturbed by the delight (MS. deep joy) it feels] A significant experience which was recurrent to W. at this period. Cf. ll. 93–5 of *Tintern Abbey*, written a few months later:

I have felt
A presence that disturbs me with the joy
Of elevated thoughts.

p. 209. IV. AIREY-FORCE VALLEY. The W. Museum has several MSS. of this poem: one of them, in the hand of Dora W., gives its date as Sept. 1836. For correct date, Sept. 1835, *v. M.L.R.*, vol. 35.

Aira Force, which is also the scene of W.'s poem *The Somnambulist*, is on the western shore of Ullswater, about half-way between the head and foot of the lake.

p. 209. V. YEW-TREES. "Grasmere, 1803. These yew-trees are still standing, but the spread of that at Lorton is much diminished by mutilation. I will here mention that a little way up the hill, on the road leading from Rosthwaite to Stonethwaite, lay the trunk of a yew-tree, which appeared as you approached, so vast was its diameter, like the entrance of a cave, and not a small one. Calculating upon what I have observed of the slow growth of this tree in rocky situations, and of its durability, I have often thought that the one I am describing must have been as old as the Christian era. The tree lay in the line of a fence. Great masses of its ruins were strewn about, and some had been rolled down the hillside and lay near the road at the bottom. As you approached the tree, you were struck with the number of shrubs and young plants, ashes, etc., which had found a bed upon the decayed trunk and grew to no inconsiderable height, forming, as it were, a part of the hedgerow. In no part of England, or of Europe, have I ever seen a yew-tree at all approaching this in magnitude, as it must have stood. By the bye, Hutton, the old Guide, of Keswick, had been so impressed with the remains of this tree that he used gravely to tell strangers that there could be no doubt of its having been in existence before the flood."—I. F.

The MS. readings quoted in the *app. crit.* are from a note-book in which the entries are, with three exceptions, poems written after 1812. The exceptions are: (1) two stanzas of *The Cuckoo*, one of which preserves a reading of 1807, the other one of 1815; (2) the first four lines of the Sonnet "I grieved for Buonaparte", with the readings of 1815; (3) *Repentance*, not published till 1820, copied first in the original version, with which W. was obviously dissatisfied, for the note-book contains many corrections which show him at work upon it. It seems highly probable, therefore, that the date 1803 for *Yew Trees* is too early. Its attribution by W. to that year was not made till 1836. If *Yew Trees* had been written by 1803 it would almost certainly be found in MS. M.

20–3. Cf. *Poems on the Naming of Places*, vi. 10–12.

22–8. Probably suggested by Virgil, *Aen.* vi. 273–84 (Dowden).

p. 211. VI. NUTTING. "Written in Germany; intended as part of a poem on my own life, but struck out as not being wanted there. Like most of my schoolfellows I was an impassioned nutter. For this pleasure, the vale of Esthwaite, abounding in coppice-wood, furnished a very wide range. These verses arose out of the remembrance of feelings I had often had when a boy, and particularly in the extensive woods that still stretch from the side of Esthwaite Lake towards Graythwaite, the seat of the ancient family of Sandys."—I. F. A MS. copy of the poem is found in a letter from D. W. to Coleridge dated Dec.–Jan. 1798–9, which speaks of it as "the conclusion of a poem of which the beginning is not written". Lines which are clearly an overflow from *Nutting*, written in the previous summer, when the poem was first conceived, will be found in my edition of *The Prelude*, pp. 591, 592–4, 596. To the same date belongs the following passage, which preserves a "beginning" to the poem already discarded when it was sent to Coleridge, and also contains lines afterwards incorporated in *The Prelude*:

Nutting

Ah! what a crash was that! with gentle hand
Touch these fair hazels—My beloved Friend!
Though 'tis a sight invisible to thee

From such rude intercourse the woods all shrink
As at the blowing of Astolpho's horn. 5
Thou, Lucy, art a maiden "inland bred"
And thou hast known "some nurture"; but in truth
If I had met thee here with that keen look
Half cruel in its eagerness, those cheeks
Thus [   ] flushed with a tempestuous bloom, 10
I might have almost deem'd that I had pass'd
A houseless being in a human shape,
An enemy of nature, hither sent
From regions far beyond the Indian hills—
Come rest on this light bed of purple heath, 15
And let me see thee sink into a dream
Of gentle thoughts, protracted till thine eye
Be calm as water when the winds are gone
And no one can tell whither.—See those stems
Both stretch'd along the ground, two brother trees 20
That in one instant at the touch of spring
Put forth their tender leaves, and through nine years,
In the dark nights, have both together heard
The driving storm—Well! blessed be the powers
That teach philosophy and good desires 25
In this their still Lyceum, hand of mine
Wrought not this ruin—I am guiltless here—
For, seeing little worthy or sublime
In what we blazon with the pompous names
Of power and action I was early taught 30
To look with feelings of fraternal love
Upon those unassuming things which hold
A silent station in this beauteous world.

Ye gentle Stewards of a Poet's time!
Ye Powers! without whose aid the idle man 35
Would waste full half of the long summer's day,
Ye who, by virtue of its dome of leaves
And its cool umbrage, make the forenoon walk,
When July suns are blazing, to his verse
Propitious, as a range o'er moonlight cliffs 40
Above the breathing sea—And ye no less!
Ye too, who with most necessary care
Amid the concentration of your groves
Restore the springs of his exhausted frame,
And ye whose general ministry it is 45

15–19. These lines, which recur in several MSS., were finally utilized in the sequel to *Lycoris* ll. 42–5.
28–33. Cf. *Prelude*, 1805, xii. 47–52. 45–52. Cf. *Prelude*. 1805, xi. 15–22.

To interpose the covert of these shades,
Even as a sleep, betwixt the heart of man
And the uneasy world, 'twixt man himself,
Not seldom, and his own unquiet heart,
Oh! that I had a music and a voice   50
Harmonious as your own, to tell the world
What ye have done for me. It seems a day

etc. as MS. Letter *down to* l. 32 *but* ye . . . your *for* They . . . their *in* l. 3:
the remainder of the poem is cut away.

p. 212. VII. THE SIMPLON PASS. An extract from *The Prelude*
(vi. 553–72), *q.v.* W. dated the lines 1799, but the part of *The Prelude*
in which they occur belongs to 1804.

p. 213. VIII. *She was a phantom of delight*: "1804 Town-End.
The germ of this poem was four lines composed as a part of the verses
on the Highland Girl. Though beginning in this way, it was written
from my heart, as is sufficiently obvious." I. F.

Written, as W. informed Justice Coleridge and others, "on my
dear wife". The lines upon her in *The Prelude* (xiv. 266–74), not in
the A text but added later, were obviously indebted to this poem.
v. my notes to *Prelude*, p. 607.

22. machine] K. aptly compares *Hamlet*, II. ii. 124, "Thine evermore, most dear lady, whilst this machine is to him". Nowell Smith
adds, from the *O.E.D.*, a quotation from Garth's *Dispensary*, v. 54:

And shall so useful a machin as I
Engage in civil Broyls, I know not why?

but, as Dowden has pointed out, the collocation of "pulse" and
"machine" is perhaps due to a subconscious recollection of a passage
in Bartram's *Travels*, a book with which W. was very familiar—
"At the return of the morning, by the powerful influence of light, the
pulse of nature becomes more active, and the universal vibration of
life insensibly and irresistibly moves the wondrous machine."

p. 214. IX. *O Nightingale! thou surely art*: "Town-End, 1806."
—I. F. (which M. W. has corrected in pencil "at Coleorton"). Included in 1807 among the *Moods of my own Mind*.

2. fiery heart] altered by W. to "ebullient" because of the jibes
in the *Simpliciad* at his "drunken larks and fiery nightingales". But
he had taken the epithet from Shakespeare, *Henry VI, Pt.* 3, I. iv. 87,
and it was restored in 1820, with the addition, in 1845, of quotation
marks.

p. 214. X. *Three years she grew*: "1799. Composed in the Hartz
Forest."—I. F.

p. 216. XI. *A slumber did my spirit seal*: "1799. Written in
Germany."—I. F. "Some months ago Wordsworth transmitted to me
a most sublime epitaph. Whether it had any reality I cannot say.

Most probably, in some gloomier moment he had fancied the moment in which his sister might die." Coleridge to T. Poole, April 6, 1799.

XII. *I wandered lonely as a cloud*: "Town-End, 1804. The two best lines in it are by Mary. The daffodils grew and still grow on the margin of Ulswater and probably may be seen to this day as beautiful in the month of March, nodding their golden heads beside the dancing and foaming waves."—I. F. (a pencil note added to I. F. identifies the two lines as 21, 22).

The occasion which inspired the poem was on April 15, 1802, when W. and his sister "were in the woods beyond Gowbarrow Park", returning to Grasmere from Eusmere; and it is clearly indebted to D. W.'s *Journal* of that date: "We saw a few daffodils close to the water-side. We fancied that the lake had floated the seeds ashore, and that the little colony had so sprung up. But as we went along there were more and yet more; and at last, under the boughs of the trees, we saw that there was a long belt of them along the shore, about the breadth of a country turnpike road. I never saw daffodils so beautiful. They grew among the mossy stones about and about them; some rested their heads upon these stones, as on a pillow, for weariness; and the rest tossed and reeled and danced, and seemed as if they verily laughed with the wind, that blew upon them over the lake; they looked so gay, ever glancing, ever changing." In 1807 W. placed it among the *Moods of my own Mind*; in 1815 he appended the note: " The subject of these Stanzas is rather an elementary feeling and simple impression (approaching to the nature of an ocular spectrum) upon the imaginative faculty, than an *exertion* of it. The one which follows ['Poor Susan'] is strictly a Reverie; and neither that, nor the next after it in succession, 'The Power of Music,' would have been placed here [*i.e.* among 'Poems of the Imagination'] except for the reason given in the foregoing note."

p. 217. XIII. THE REVERIE OF POOR SUSAN. "Written 1801 or 1802. This arose out of my observation of the affecting music of these birds hanging in this way in the London streets during the freshness and stillness of the Spring morning."—I. F.

As the poem was published in 1800 the I. F. note is clearly wrong. In 1836 W. assigned the poem to 1797, and this can probably be accepted. The fifth stanza, which only appears in the 1800 ed., was probably dropped owing to a protest of Lamb's: "The last verse of Susan was to be got rid of at all events. It threw a kind of dubiety upon Susan's moral conduct. Susan is a servant maid. I see her trundling her mop, and contemplating the whirling phenomenon through blurred optics; to term her a poor outcast seems as much as to say that poor Susan is no better than she should be, which I trust was not what you meant to express."

p. 217. XIV. POWER OF MUSIC. "Taken from life, 1806."—I. F.

p. 219. XV. STAR-GAZERS. "Observed by me in Leicester Square

as here described, 1806."—I. F. An early MS. copy of the poem was
included in a letter to Lady Beaumont of Nov. 14, 1806.

p. 220. XVI. WRITTEN IN MARCH: "Extempore, 1801. This little
poem was a favourite with Joanna Baillie."—I. F. The correct date
is April 16, 1802; cf. D. W.'s *Journal* of that day: "When we came
to the foot of Brother's Water I left William sitting on the bridge.
. . . When I returned I found William writing a poem descriptive of
the sights and sounds we saw and heard. There was the gentle
flowing of the stream, the glittering, lively lake, green fields without
a living creature to be seen on them; behind us, a flat pasture with
forty-two cattle feeding . . . The people were at work ploughing,
harrowing, and sowing; lasses working, a dog barking now and then;
cocks crowing, birds twittering; the snow in patches at the top of
the highest hills. . . . William finished his poem before we got to the
foot of Kirkstone." Published in 1807 among the *Moods of my own
Mind*. A MS. of the poem survives in a letter to Coleridge of April
16, 1802 (*E.L.*, p. 288), and another in MS. M.

p. 221. XVII. *Lyre! though such power etc.*: *v.* I. F. note to *The
Forsaken* (*v.* p. 473).

p. 222. XVIII. BEGGARS. "Town-End, 1802. Met, and described
to me by my Sister, near the quarry at the head of Rydal Lake, a
place still a chosen resort of vagrants travelling with their families."
—I. F. Cf. D. W.'s *Journal* for March 13 and 14: "Wm finished
Alice Fell, and then he wrote the poem of the Beggar Woman, taken
from a woman whom 1 had seen in May (now nearly two years ago)
when John and he were at Gallow Hill. I sate with him at intervals
all the morning, took down his stanzas, etc. . . . After tea I read to
Wm that account of the little boy belonging to the tall woman, and
an unlucky thing it was, for he could not escape from those very
words, and so he could not write the poem. He left it unfinished and
went tired to bed." [June 14] "Wm had slept badly; he got up at
nine o'clock, but before he rose he had finished *The Beggar Boys*."
The account to which D. W. refers runs: "On Tuesday May 27th
[1800] a very tall woman, tall much beyond the measure of tall
women, called at the door. She had on a very long brown cloak and
a very white cap, without bonnet. Her face was excessively brown,
but it had plainly once been fair. She led a little bare-footed child
about two years old by the hand, and said her husband, who was a
tinker, was gone before with the other children. I gave her a piece
of bread. Afterwards on my road to Ambleside, beside the bridge
at Rydal, I saw her husband sitting by the roadside, his two asses
feeding beside him, and the young children at play upon the grass.
The man did not beg. I passed on and about a quarter of a mile
further I saw two boys before me, one about 10, the other about 8
years old, at play chasing a butterfly. They were wild figures, not
very ragged, but without shoes and stockings. The hat of the elder

was wreathed round with yellow flowers; the younger, whose hat
was only a rimless crown, had stuck it round with laurel leaves. They
continued at play till I drew ɛvery near, and then they addressed me
with the begging cant and the whining voice of sorrow. I said 'I
served your mother this morning' (the boys were so like the woman
who had called at the door that I could not be mistaken). 'O!' says
the elder, 'you could not serve my mother, for she's dead, and my
father's on at the next town—he's a potter.' I persisted in my
assertion, and that I would give them nothing. Says the elder,
'Come, let's away,' and away they flew like lightning."

In a letter to Barron Field dated Oct. 24, 1828, W. explains his
reasons for changes made in the text (*L.Y.*, pp. 307–8, *q.v.*).

18. weed of glorious feature] from Spenser, *Muiopotmos*, 213.

p. 225. XIX. SEQUEL TO THE FOREGOING. **2.** the daedal earth]
daedal, a favourite word of Shelley's, is nowhere else used by W.:
he owed it, probably, to the *Faerie Queene*, IV. x. 45:

> Then doth the daedale earth throw forth to thee
> Out of her fruitful lap aboundant flowers.

p. 226. XX. GIPSIES. "Composed at Coleorton, 1807. I had observed
them, as here described, near Castle Donnington, on my way to and
from Derby."—I. F. This is one of the poems criticized by Coleridge
(*Biog. Lit.*, chap. xxii) for mental bombast, or thoughts and images
too great for the subject: W. attacks the gipsies, says Coleridge, in words
which "would have been rather above than below the mark, had it
been applied to the immense empire of China improgressive for thirty
centuries". W. attempted to meet this by adding in 1820 a somewhat
lame apology for their indolence. But surely Miss Darbishire is right
in pointing out that "The original poem suggests nothing more than
the sublime poetic expression of a mood in which the poet, active
in mind and body, feeling himself consciously at one with the activi-
ties of the universe, is impressed by the spectacle of stagnant life,
so picturesquely presented to his imagination by the gipsies". W.
was therefore right in telling Barron Field (*L.Y.*, p. 311) that "the
concluding apology should be cancelled", though he forgot to do so.
On the phrase "goings-on", l. 23 ed. 1807, a favourite with both him
and his sister and Coleridge, and unfortunately dropped, he wrote:
"'Goings-on' is precisely the word wanted, but it makes a weak and
apparently prosaic line, so near the end of a poem. I fear it cannot
be altered, as the rhyme must be retained, on account of the concluding verse."

p. 227. XXI. RUTH. "Written in Germany 1799. Suggested by
an account I had of a wanderer in Somersetshire."—I. F. Placed
in 1815–20 among *Poems of the Affections*. The poem was revised in
1802; *v.* D. W. *Journal* for March 7; "I wrote out *Ruth*; read it with
the alterations . . . Wm brought two new stanzas of *Ruth*." Four

MS. stanzas of the poem are preserved in one of the notebooks used by D. W. for her *Journal*.

In one of his notes to the poem, quoted *infra*, W. acknowledges a debt to Bartram's *Travels through North and South Carolina, Georgia, etc.* Mr. E. H. Coleridge points out that the whole passage describing the flora of Georgian scenery is a close rendering of Bartram's narrative, and that the frontispiece of the book depicts a chieftain, whose feathers nod in the breeze just as did the military casque of the youth from Georgia's shore.

61. magnolia] *Magnolia grandiflora.*—W. W. 1800.

64. flowers that with one scarlet gleam] the splendid appearance of these scarlet flowers, which are scattered with such profusion over the hills in the southern parts of North America, is frequently mentioned by Bartram in his Travels.—W. W. 1800.

197. She fearfully caroused] W. told Barron Field (*L.Y.*, p. 309) that this stanza was altered, "Lamb having observed that it was not English. I liked it better myself, but certainly 'to carouse cups',—that is to empty them—is the genuine English." But both Lamb and W. are mistaken; the word "carouse" can be used both transitively and intransitively.

214. Banks of Tone] The Tone is a river of Somersetshire at no great distance from the Quantock Hills. These hills, which are alluded to a few stanzas below, are extremely beautiful, and in most places richly covered with Coppice woods.—W. W. 1800.

p. 235. XXII. RESOLUTION AND INDEPENDENCE. "Town-End, 1807. This old man I met a few hundred yards from my cottage at Town-End, Grasmere; and the account of him is taken from his own mouth. I was in the state of feeling described in the beginning of the poem, while crossing over Barton Fell from Mr. Clarkson's, at the foot of Ullswater, towards Askam. The image of the hare I then observed on the ridge of the Fell."—I. F. The correct date of composition is May–July 1802; *v.* D. W.'s *Journal*: May 4, "I wrote *The Leech Gatherer* for him, which he had begun the night before, and of which he wrote several stanzas in bed this morning". May 7: "Wm feeling himself strong, fell to work at *The Leech Gatherer*; he wrote hard at it till dinner time, then he gave over, tired to death—he had finished the poem." May 9: "Wm worked at *The Leech Gatherer* almost incessantly from morning till tea-time. I copied *The Leech Gatherer*. . . . I was oppressed and sick at heart, for he wearied himself to death." July 2: "transcribed the alterations in *The Leech Gatherer*." July 4. "Wm. finished *The Leech Gatherer* to-day." For the incident on which the poem was founded *v. Journal*, Oct. 3, 1800: "When Wm and I returned from accompanying Jones, we met an old man almost double. He had on a coat, thrown over his shoulders above his waistcoat and coat. Under this he carried a bundle, and had an apron on and a nightcap. His face was interesting. He had dark eyes and a long nose. John, who afterwards met him at Wytheburn, took him for a Jew. He was of Scotch parents, but had been born in the army. He had had a wife, and 'a good woman, and it pleased God to bless us with ten children'. All these were dead but one, of whom he had not heard for many years, a sailor. His trade was to gather leeches, but now leeches are scarce, and he had not strength for it. He lived by begging, and was making his way to Carlisle, where he should buy a few godly books to sell. He said leeches were very scarce, partly owing to the dry season, but many years they have been scarce. He supposed it owing to their being much sought after, that they did not breed fast, and were of slow growth. Leeches were formerly 2s. 6d. per 100; now they are 30s." Coleridge criticized the poem for "inconstancy of style", and regarded it as "especially characteristic of the author. There is scarcely a defect or excellence in his writings of which it would not present a specimen." (*Biog. Lit.*, chap. xxii). Many of the changes in the text were prompted by Coleridge's strictures. For a defence of the poem *v.* W.'s Letter to Sara H., June 14, 1802 (*E.L.*, pp. 305–6). Four MSS. of the poem survive, the *Longman* MS., a copy in a letter from S. T. C. to Sir George Beaumont (1802), one in MS. M., and that in Sara H.'s "Poets", see Appendix *infra*, p. 539.

4–7. Cf. D. W.'s *Journal* for May 29, 1802: "We went to John's Grove and . . . lay . . . listening to the waterfalls and the birds. There was no one waterfall above another—it was the sound of waters in the air—the voice of the air."

5. Cf. Preface to *ed.* of 1815: "The Stock-dove is said to coo, a sound well imitating the note of the bird; but by intervention of the metaphor *broods*, the affections are called in by the imagination to assist in marking the manner in which the bird reiterates and prolongs her soft note, as if herself delighting to listen to it, and participating of a still and quiet satisfaction, like that which may be supposed inseparable from the continuous process of incubation."

43. I thought of Chatterton] It is significant that this poem is written in the metre of Chatterton's *Excellent Ballade of Charitie*, which, moreover, deals with a kindred theme.

57–65. Quoted by W. in the Preface to his edition of 1815 "to illustrate the conferring, the abstracting, and the modifying powers of the imagination" (*q.v. supra*, p. 437).

p. 240. XXIII. THE THORN. "Alfoxden. 1798. Arose out of my observing, on the ridge of Quantock Hill, on a stormy day, a thorn which I had often passed in calm and bright weather without noticing it. I said to myself, 'Cannot I by some invention do as much to make this Thorn permanently an impressive object as the storm has made it to my eyes at this moment?' I began the poem accordingly, and composed it with great rapidity. Sir George Beaumont painted a picture from it which Wilkie thought his best. He gave it to me;

though, when he saw it several times at Rydal Mount afterwards, he said, 'I could make a better, and would like to paint the same subject over again'. The sky in this picture is nobly done, but it reminds one too much of Wilson. The only fault, however, of any consequence is the female figure, which is too old and decrepit for one likely to frequent an eminence on such a call."—I. F.

Cf. D. W.'s *Journal* for March 19, 1798 : "William wrote some lines describing a stunted thorn," and April 20: "Came home the Crookham way, by the thorn, and the little muddy pond." In the Preface to *L.B.* 1798 W. wrote: "The poem of The Thorn, as the reader will soon discover, is not supposed to be spoken in the author's own person ; the character of the loquacious narrator will sufficiently show itself in the course of the story," and to edd. 1800–5 he appended the following note: "This Poem ought to have been preceded by an introductory Poem, which I have been prevented from writing by never having felt myself in a mood when it was probable that I should write it well. The character which I have here introduced speaking is sufficiently common. The Reader will perhaps have a general notion of it, if he has ever known a man, a Captain of a small trading vessel, for example, who being past the middle age of life, had retired upon an annuity or small independent income to some village or country town of which he was not a native, or in which he had not been accustomed to live. Such men, having little to do, become credulous and talkative from indolence ; and from the same cause, and other predisposing causes by which it is probable that such men may have been affected, they are prone to superstition. On which account it appeared to me proper to select a character like this to exhibit some of the general laws by which superstition acts upon the mind. Superstitious men are almost always men of slow faculties and deep feelings ; their minds are not loose, but adhesive ; they have a reasonable share of imagination, by which word I mean the faculty which produces impressive effects out of simple elements ; but they are utterly destitute of fancy, the power by which pleasure and surprise are excited by sudden varieties of situation and an accumulated imagery.

"It was my wish in this poem to show the manner in which such men cleave to the same ideas ; and to follow the turns of passion, always different, yet not palpably different, by which their conversation is swayed. I had two objects to attain ; first, to represent a picture which should not be unimpressive, yet consistent with the character that should describe it ; secondly, while I adhered to the style in which such persons describe, to take care that words, which in their minds are impregnated with passion, should likewise convey passion to Readers who are not accustomed to sympathize with men feeling in that manner or using such language. It seemed to me that this might be done by calling in the assistance of Lyrical and rapid Metre. It was necessary that the Poem, to be natural, should in reality move slowly; yet I hoped that, by the aid of the metre, to those who should at all enter into the spirit of the Poem, it would appear to move quickly. The Reader will have the kindness to excuse this note, as I am sensible that an introductory Poem is necessary to give this Poem its full effect.

"Upon this occasion I will request permission to add a few words closely connected with 'The Thorn' and many other Poems in these volumes. There is a numerous class of readers who imagine that the same words cannot be repeated without tautology: this is a great error: virtual tautology is much oftener produced by using different words when the meaning is exactly the same. Words, a Poet's words more particularly, ought to be weighed in the balance of feeling, and not measured by the space which they occupy upon paper. For the Reader cannot be too often reminded that Poetry is passion: it is the history or science of feelings; now every man must know that an attempt is rarely made to communicate impassioned feelings without something of an accompanying consciousness of the inadequateness of our own powers, or the deficiencies of language. During such efforts there will be a craving in the mind, and as long as it is unsatis-fied the speaker will cling to the same words, or words of the same character. There are also various other reasons why repetition and apparent tautology are frequently beauties of the highest kind. Among the chief of these reasons is the interest which the mind attaches to words, not only as symbols of the passion, but as *things,* active and efficient, which are of themselves part of the passion. And further, from a spirit of fondness, exultation, and gratitude, the mind luxuriates in the repetition of words which appear successfully to communicate its feelings. The truth of these remarks might be shown by innumerable passages from the Bible, and from the impassioned poetry of every nation. 'Awake, awake, Deborah!' &c. Judges, chap. v., verses 12th, 27th, and part of 28th. See also the whole of that tumultuous and wonderful Poem."

The Thorn, together with *Peter Bell,* which was written immediately after it, may be regarded as the extreme example of W.'s experiment "to ascertain how far the language of conversation in the middle and lower classes of society is adapted to the purposes of poetic pleasure" (*Preface,* 1798). The alterations in the text, most of them unfortunate even if more conventionally poetic, were occasioned by Coleridge's criticism of its pseudo-dramatic quality and inconsistency of style. (*Biographia Literaria,* chap. xxii.) For further criticism *v.* Hutchin-son's *ed.* of *L.B.* pp. 238–43.

William Taylor's version of Bürger's ballad *Des Pfarrer's Tochter von Taubenheim* printed under the title of *The Lass of Fair Wone* in the *Monthly Magazine,* 1796, has been suggested by Barron Field and others as a source of *The Thorn.* Hutchinson points to a more probable source in a Scots ballad printed in Johnson's *Musical*

514 NOTES

Museum, 1787–1803. In a Commonplace Book of Extracts with "Wm Wordsworth, Grasmere, Jan. 1800" on the title-page (it may, however, have been in use earlier), W. has copied the following from Herd's *Ancient and Modern Scottish Songs* (Edinburgh, 1776):

> And there she's lean'd her back to a thorn
> Oh! and alas—a day oh, *etc.*
> And there she has her baby born
> Ten thousand times good night, and be' wi' thee.
> She has honked a grave ayont the sun
> Oh! *etc.*
> And there she has buried the sweet babe in.
> Ten *etc.*
> And she has gane back to her Father's ha'
> Oh! *etc.*
> She's counted the leelest maid o' them a'.
> Ten *etc.*
> O look not sae sweet, my bonny babe,
> Oh! *etc.*
> Gin ye smyle sae ye'll smyle me dead;
> Ten *etc.*

A rough draft of the first two stanzas of the poem is found in the Alfoxden MS.

105. Martha Ray] It is strange that W. should have given his heroine the name of Basil Montague's mother. Martha Ray was the mistress of the fourth Earl of Sandwich; she was shot by the Rev. James Hackman on April 7, 1779. For a full account of the incident, which created much stir at the time, *v.* letter of Horace Walpole to the Countess of Upper Ossory, April 8, 1779 (ed. Paget Toynbee, x. 396–9).

p. 249. XXIV. HART-LEAP WELL. "Town-End. 1800. *Grasmere*. The first eight stanzas were composed extempore one winter evening in the cottage; when, after having tired myself with labouring at an awkward passage in 'The Brothers', I started with a sudden impulse to this to get rid of the other, and finished it in a day or two. My sister and I had past the place a few weeks before in our wild winter journey from Sockburn on the banks of the Tees to Grasmere. A peasant whom we met near the spot told us the story so far as concerned the name of the well, and the hart, and pointed out the stones. Both the stones and the well are objects that may easily be missed; the tradition by this time may be extinct in the neighbourhood: the man who related it to us was very old."—I. F.

In MSS. A and B of *The Recluse*, written soon after *Hartleap Well* occur the following lines which form an interesting commentary on the spirit in which he composed the poem:

when the trance
Came to us, as we stood by Hartleap Well,
The intimation of the milder day
Which is to be, the fairer world than this,
And rais'd us up, dejected as we were,
Among the records of that doleful place,
By sorrow for the hunted beast, who there
Had yielded up his breath, the awful trance,
The vision of humanity, and of God
The Mourner, God the Sufferer, when the heart
Of his poor Creatures suffers wrongfully—
Both in the sadness and the joy we found
A promise and an earnest that we twain,
A pair seceding from the common world,
Might in that hallow'd spot to which our steps
Were tending, in that individual nook
Might, even thus early, for ourselves secure,
And in the midst of these unhappy times,
A portion of the blessedness which love
And knowledge will, we trust, hereafter give
To all the vales of earth and all mankind.

97. moving accident] From *Othello*, i. iii. 97, "Of moving accidents by flood and field".

98. curl the blood (1800)] Probably a misprint for "curd the blood"; cf. *Hamlet* i. v. 69, and *All's Well*, &c. i. iii. 155.

p. 254. XXV. SONG AT THE FEAST OF BROUGHAM CASTLE: "See the note attached. This poem was composed at Coleorton while I was walking to and fro along the path that led from Sir George Beaumont's Farm-house, where we resided, to the Hall which was building at that time."—I. F.

Henry Lord Clifford, etc., etc., who is the subject of this poem, was the son of John, Lord Clifford, who was slain at Towton Field, which John, Lord Clifford, as is known to the Reader of English history, was the person who after the battle of Wakefield slew, in the pursuit, the young Earl of Rutland, son of the Duke of York, who had fallen in the battle, "in part of revenge" (say the Authors of the "History of Cumberland and Westmorland"); "for the Earl's Father had slain his." A deed which worthily blemished the author (saith Speed); but who, as he adds, "dare promise anything temperate of himself in the heat of martial fury? chiefly, when it was resolved not to leave any branch of the York line standing; for so one maketh this Lord to speak." This, no doubt, I would observe by the bye, was an action sufficiently in the vindictive spirit of the times, and yet not altogether so bad as represented; "for the Earl was no child, as some writers would have him, but able to bear arms, being sixteen or seventeen

years of age, as is evident from this (say the Memoirs of the Countess
of Pembroke, who was laudably anxious to wipe away, as far as could
be, this stigma from the illustrious name to which she was born);
that he was the next child to King Edward the Fourth, which his
mother had by Richard Duke of York, and that King was then
eighteen years of age : and for the small distance betwixt her children,
see Austin Vincent, in his 'Book of Nobility', p. 622, where he writes
of them all." It may further be observed that Lord Clifford, who was
then himself only twenty-five years of age, had been a leading man
and commander two or three years together in the Army of Lancaster,
before this time ; and, therefore, would be less likely to think that the
Earl of Rutland might be entitled to mercy from his youth.—But
independent of this act, at best a cruel and savage one, the family of
Clifford had done enough to draw upon them the vehement hatred of
the House of York : so that after the Battle of Towton there was no
hope for them but in flight and concealment. Henry, the subject of
the poem, was deprived of his estate and honours during the space of
twenty-four years ; all which time he lived as a shepherd in Yorkshire,
or in Cumberland, where the estate of his father-in-law (Sir Lancelot
Threlkeld) lay. He was restored to his estate and honours in the first
year of Henry the Seventh. It is recorded that, "when called to
Parliament he behaved nobly and wisely ; but otherwise came seldom
to London or the Court ; and rather delighted to live in the country,
where he repaired several of his Castles, which had gone to decay
during the late troubles". Thus far is chiefly collected from Nicholson
and Burn ; and I can add, from my own knowledge, that there is a
tradition current in the village of Threlkeld and its neighbourhood,
his principal retreat, that, in the course of his shepherd-life, he had
acquired great astronomical knowledge. I cannot conclude this note
without adding a word upon the subject of those numerous and noble
feudal edifices, spoken of in the poem, the ruins of some of which are,
at this day, so great an ornament to that interesting country. The
Cliffords had always been distinguished for an honourable pride in
these Castles ; and we have seen that, after the wars of York and
Lancaster, they were rebuilt ; in the civil wars of Charles the First
they were again laid waste, and again restored almost to their former
magnificence by the celebrated Lady Anne Clifford, Countess of
Pembroke, etc., etc. Not more than twenty-five years after this was
done, when the estates of Clifford had passed into the family of
Tufton, three of these Castles, namely, Brough, Brougham, and
Pendragon, were demolished, and the timber and other materials
sold by Thomas Earl of Thanet. We will hope that, when this order
was issued, the Earl had not consulted the text of Isaiah, 58th chap.
12th verse, to which the inscription placed over the gate of Pendragon
Castle, by the Countess of Pembroke (I believe his grandmother), at
the time she repaired that structure, refers the reader :—"*And they*

*that shall be of thee shall build the old waste places: thou shalt raise up
the foundations of many generations; and thou shalt be called the repairer
of the breach, the restorer of paths to dwell in.*" The Earl of Thanet, the
present possessor of the Estates, with a due respect for the memory of
his ancestors, and a proper sense of the value and beauty of these
remains of antiquity, has (I am told) given orders that they shall be
preserved from all depredations.—W. W. 1807.

For a further note on the hero of this poem *v.* W.'s note to *The
White Doe of Rylstone*, Canto I, l. 267, ed. 1815; also Addenda, p. 532.

p. 259. XXVI. LINES, COMPOSED A FEW MILES ABOVE TINTERN
ABBEY: "July 1798. No poem of mine was composed under circumstances more pleasant for me to remember than this. I began it upon
leaving Tintern, after crossing the Wye, and concluded it just as I
was entering Bristol in the evening, after a ramble of 4 or 5 days,
with my sister. Not a line of it was altered, and not any part of it
written down till I reached Bristol. It was published almost immediately after in the little volume of which so much has been said in
these notes. (The Lyrical Ballads, as first published at Bristol by
Cottle)."—I. F.

In a letter to the Rev. T. S. Howson in Sept. 1848, the Duke of
Argyle wrote: "He told us he had written *Tintern Abbey* in 1798,
taking four days to compose it, the last 20 lines or so being composed
as he walked down the hill from Clifton to Bristol;—he read the
introductory lines descriptive of the scenery in a low clear voice.
But when he came to the thoughtful and reflective lines his tones
deepened, and he poured them forth with a fervour and almost
passion of delivery which was very striking and beautiful. I observed
that Mrs. W. was deeply affected by the reading. The strong emphasis
that he put on the words addressed personally to the person to whom
the poem is addressed struck me as almost unnatural at the time—
'My dear, *dear* friend' ran the words,—'in thy wild eyes'. It was
not till after the reading was over that we found out that the old
paralytic and *doited* woman we had seen in the morning was the
sister to whom *T.A.* was addressed, and her condition accounted for
the fervour with which the old Poet read lines which reminded him
of their better days. But it was melancholy to think that the vacant
silly stare which we had seen in the morning was from the 'wild
eyes' of 1798."

"I have not ventured to call this Poem an Ode; but it was written
with a hope that in the transitions, and the impassioned music of the
versification, would be found the principal requisites of that species
of composition."—W. W. 1800.

1. Five years have passed] Cf. I. F. note to *Guilt and Sorrow*
(Vol. I, p. 330). W. visited Tintern in 1793, after leaving the Isle of
Wight, and on his way to Salisbury Plain.

33. that best portion of a good man's life] Cf. Milton's Preface to

The Judgment of Martin Bucer concerning Divorce : "whereby good men in the best portion of their lives and in that ordinance of God which entitles them from the beginning to most just and requisite content-ments, are compelled to civil indignities."

106. Young's *Night Thoughts*, vi. 424, "And half-create the won-drous world they see".

p. 263. XXVII. *It is no Spirit who from heaven hath flown* : "1803. Town-End. I remember the instant my sister, S. H., called me to the window of our Cottage, saying, 'Look how beautiful is yon star! It has the sky all to itself'. I composed the verses immediately."—I. F.

9–17. Dowden compares these lines with the poem, "If thou indeed derive thy light from Heaven" (Vol. I, p. 1), which, in 1845, W. placed "as a sort of Preface" to his poems.

p. 264. XXVIII. FRENCH REVOLUTION. "An extract from the long poem on my own poetical education. It was first published by Coleridge in his 'Friend', which is the reason of its having had a place in every edition of my poems since."—I. F.

From *The Prelude*, xi. 105–44 (1805, x. 690–728); for notes *v.* my ed., p. 584.

p. 265. XXIX. *Yes, it was the mountain Echo* ; "Town-end. 1805 The echo came from Nab-Scar, when I was walking on the opposite side of Rydal Mere. I will here mention, for my dear Sister's sake, that, while she was sitting alone one day high up on this part of Loughrigg Fell, she was so affected by the voice of the Cuckoo heard from the crags at some distance that she could not suppress a wish to have a stone inscribed with her name among the rocks from which the sound proceeded. On my return from my walk I recited these verses to Mary, who was then confined with her son Thomas, who died in his 7th year, as is recorded on his head-stone in Grasmere Church-yard."

4/5. (1807.) Whence the voice *etc.*] This stanza was probably omitted after 1807 because of the ridicule directed at it by both Jeffrey and *The Simpliciad*.

p. 266. XXX. To A SKYLARK. "Rydal Mount 1825. (Where there are no skylarks, but the poet is everywhere. *pencil addition*)"—I. F. Barron Field noted the parallel with Cowley :

> The wise example of the heavenly lark
> My fellow poet, Cowley, mark.
> Above the clouds let thy proud music sound,
> Thy humble nest build on the ground.

p. 267. XXXI. LAODAMIA. "Rydal Mount, 1814. Written at the same time as *Dion* and *Artegal and Elidure*. The incident of the trees growing and withering put the subject into my thoughts, and I wrote with the hope of giving it a loftier tone than, so far as I know, has been given to it by any of the Ancients who have treated of it.

NOTES 519

It cost me more trouble than almost anything of equal length I have ever written."—I. F.

In 1815–20 the poem was placed among those *"founded on the Affections"*, and according to Crabb Robinson (*Diary*, May 1, 1815) was "not much esteemed" by W. as belonging to this "inferior" class. On April 7, 1815, Lamb wrote to W.: *"Laodamia* is a very original poem. I mean original with reference to your own manner. You have nothing like it. I should have seen it in a strange place, and greatly admired it, but not suspected its derivation." But W.'s knowledge of classical literature and his affection for it dates from his school days, and had always been stronger than is usually recognized (*v.* my essay on *The Early Wordsworth*, English Assoc., 1936, and the Appendix to Volume I of this edition). *Laodamia* is primarily based on Virgil, *Aeneid* vi, but is also indebted to Ovid, *Heroides* xiii, and to Euripides, *Iphigenia in Aulis*. For a detailed account of this debt *v.* the essay by Dr. Heard in K. vi. 10–14.

The only MS. of the poem known to me is an extended draft of the opening of the poem (ll. 1–13), quoted in the *app. crit.* But in a copy of the 1815 ed. now in the library of Wellesley College, U.S.A., is a cancelled sheet (quoted in *app. crit.* as 1815 *Wel.*) which preserves a few earlier readings. (But *v.* Addendum, p. 532.)

1–6. The early reading of these lines was attacked by Landor in his *Imag. Conversation; Southey and Porson*: "I do not see the necessity of *Performed*, which is dull and cumbersome. The second line and the fourth terminate too much alike, and express to a tittle the same meaning; *have I required* and *have I desired* are worse than prosaic; beside which there are four words of equal length in each." W. admitted these faults in his letter to Landor, Jan. 21, 1824 (*L.Y.*, p. 134), and said that he had made many attempts to alter the passage. But his final reading did not satisfy Landor.

58. Thou should'st elude] This reading was adopted owing to the criticism of Barron Field, who pointed out, in a letter of Nov. 1839, that "'should'st cheat' is hardly utterable".

101–2. The original reading of these lines was attacked by Landor as "stinking and reeking from the conventicle". W. defended them in his letter above cited, but nevertheless altered them.

112. To this line W., in 1815, appended the note: "For this feature in the character of Protesilaus, see the *Iphigenia in Aulis* of Euripides."

115–20. This stanza was added to the text in the proofs, *v.* Letter to De Quincey, Feb. 1815 (*M.Y.*, p. 629). In that letter the last word, enchained, is followed by a comma, which is obviously correct. The reading "enchained." is an error of 1815 which persisted through all subsequent editions.

158–63. For W.'s changes in the text of this stanza *v.* his letter to John W. 1831 (*L.Y.*, p. 582). W.'s last reading is a compromise

between the positions taken up in the previous two ; if the second was
too severe upon his heroine, the first was clearly both un-Virgilian
and also inconsistent with the ethos of the poem.

p. 272. XXXII. Dion. This poem began with the following
stanza, which has been displaced on account of its detaining the
reader too long from the subject, and as rather precluding, than
preparing for the due effect of the allusion to the genius of Plato :
[For stanza v. app. crit.].—W. 1837.

"This poem was first introduced by a stanza that I have since
transferred to the Notes, for reasons there given, and I cannot comply
with the request expressed by some of my friends that the rejected
stanza should be restored. I hope they will be content if it be, hereafter, immediately attached to the poem, instead of its being degraded
to a place in the Notes."—I. F. But this was not done in either 1845
or 1849. Before 1845 *Dion* was classed among *Poems of Sentiment and
Reflection.* A fair copy in W.'s hand is found towards the end of a
manuscript notebook of which the first page is dated 1817 ; it represents an early stage of the text, and is quoted in the *app. crit.* as MS.
It has been much corrected in places, and is followed by several
redrafts of some passages, not all of which found a place in the final
text. These are quoted as MS. x.

For an exhaustive account of W.'s debt to Plutarch v. Dr. Heard's
essay, printed in K. vi. 126–9.

In the I. F. note to *An Evening Walk* W. stated that he owed the
picture of the swan, with which *Dion* originally opened, to his
recollection of the swans on Windermere when he was a schoolboy
(v. Vol. I, p. 319).

13. self-sufficing solitude] Cf. *Prelude,* ii. 77: The self-sufficing
power of Solitude.

49. Wisdom dwelt retired] Cf. Collins, *Ode to Passions* 58: Pale
Melancholy sate retired.

p. 278. XXXIII. The Pass of Kirkstone. "Rydal Mount, 1817.
Thoughts and feelings of many walks in all weathers by day and
night over this pass, alone and with beloved friends."—I. F. A
note in a copy preserved at Coleorton states that the poem was composed "chiefly in a walk from the top of Kirkstone to Patterdale",
and on the back of the MS. is written "Mr. Wordsworth's verses,
June 27, 1817".

In edd. 1820–32 it is entitled Ode : The Pass of Kirkstone. The
variants quoted in the *app. crit.* are from a MS. dated 1817.

19. raised] the ed. of 1859 and some subsequent editions read
"razed", but the MS. and all edd. revised by W. have "raised",
which is quite intelligible.

p. 280. XXXIV. To Enterprise. Before 1845 included among the
Memorials of a Tour on the Continent, with a note appended to
the effect that it arose from a train of thought started in the poem

The Italian Itinerant. (Hence its date is probably 1821 and not, as often stated, 1820.) "Nothing can be conceived more poetical than the *Ode to Enterprise.* If your enemies had hearts it would break them. I wish Porson were alive. Although in the latter part of his days I believe he did retract the sillier of his observations, both on your poetry and on Southey's, he would now be forced to acknowledge that you had beaten his own trained bands at their own weapons." (Landor to W. W., April 23, 1822.)

77–82. Dowden compares these lines on the steamship, added 1832, with Coleridge: *Youth and Age* (1828):

> Like those trim skiffs, unknown of yore,
> On winding lakes and rivers wide,
> That ask no aid of sail or oar,
> That fear no spite of wind or tide!

114–15. a living hill *etc.*] Awhile the living hill
Heaved with convulsive throes, and all was still.
Dr. Darwin describing the destruction of the army of Cambyses. —W. W. 1822.

145. Sweet Bird, misnamed the melancholy] cf. *Il Penseroso, 61,* "Sweet bird . . . most musical most melancholy", and Coleridge, *The Nightingale,* 13–15

> "Most musical, most melancholy" bird!
> A melancholy bird? Oh! idle thought!
> In Nature there is nothing melancholy.

p. 286. XXXV. To ——. On her first ascent to the summit of Helvellyn. "Rydal Mount. 1816. The lady was Miss Blackett, then residing with Mr. Montagu Burgoyne at Fox-Ghyll. We were tempted to remain too long upon the mountain; and I, imprudently, with the hope of shortening the way, led her among the crags and down a steep slope, which entangled us in difficulties that were met by her with much spirit and courage."—I. F.

25. choral] the reading "coral", which appears in 1832 and after, I regard, with Dowden and Hutchinson, as a misprint. For Hutchinson's defence of "choral" *v.* Oxford W., *Preface,* viii.

29. Niphates' top] The reference is to *Paradise Lost,* iii. 736–42.

> Satan, bowing low,
>
> . . .
>
> Took leave, and toward the coast of Earth beneath,
> Down from th' Ecliptic, sped with hop'd success,
> Throws his steep flight in many an Aerie wheele,
> Nor staid, till on *Niphates* top he lights.

p. 287. XXXVI. To a Young Lady, *etc.* "Composed at the same time and on the same view as 'I met Louisa in the shade'. Indeed they were designed to make one piece."—I. F. *v.* my note on that poem, *supra*, p. 471. From 1807–32 placed among *Poems of Senti-ment and Reflection*.

p. 288. XXXVII. WATER FOWL. "Observed frequently over the Lakes of Rydal and Grasmere."—I. F. In 1836 W. dated these lines 1812, but they are found in the first draft of *Recluse* Bk. I.—*Home at Grasmere*, which belongs to March 1800. The first line, however, with its "poetic diction", may well date from 1812. Elsewhere there is much in the phrasing reminiscent of Milton—e.g., "inferior to angelical", "orb after orb", cf.

> Thus when in Orbes
> Of *circuit* inexpressible they stood
> Orb *within* orb (*P.L.*, v. 594–6).

"progress intricate" cf. "mazes intricate" (*P.L.*, v. 622), and "indefatigable flight" cf. "spread his aerie flight Upborn with indefatigable wings" (*P.L.*, ii. 407–8).

p. 289. XXXVIII. VIEW FROM THE TOP OF BLACK COMB. "1813. Mary and I, as mentioned in the 'Epistle to Sir G. Beaumont', lived for some time under its shadow."—I. F. i.e. in August 1811, when they stayed at Bootle, Cumberland. Three MSS. of the poem survive, showing different stages in its composition.

p. 290. XXXIX. THE HAUNTED TREE. "1819. This tree grew in the park of Rydal, and I have often listened to its creaking as described."—I. F. Dowden calls attention to the variants of this poem as an example of W.'s "fastidious correction".

p. 292. XL. THE TRIAD. "Rydal Mount, 1828. The girls Edith May Southey, my daughter Dora and Sara Coleridge."—I. F. A letter to M. and Dora W., which encloses some additional lines to the poem, shows it to have been completed by early March 1828 (*L.Y.*, 294–7). It was originally called *The Promise*; W. explains the title *The Triad* by reference to Johnson's *Dictionary*—"The Triad, three united." The poem was a favourite with W. "I think", he wrote to Barron Field on Dec. 20, 1828, "a great part of it as elegant and spirited as anything I have written—but I was afraid to trust my judgment, as the aery Figures are all sketched from living originals that are dear to me" (*L.Y.*, 340; cf. also pp. 335, 339).

41–79. Edith Southey.

79/80 (*app. crit.*) Cf. *On the Power of Sound*, xii, and note.

89–173. Dora W. The allusion in l. 137 is to her supposed likeness in contour of face to the Memnon head in the British Museum.

174–211. Sara Coleridge. Commenting on the poem in her *Memoir and Letters* Sara C. wrote "There is no truth in the Poem as a whole, although bits of truth, glazed and magnified, are embodied in it".

p. 299. XLI. THE WISHING-GATE "Rydal Mount, 1828. See also 'Wishing Gate Destroyed'."—I. F. In 1832 placed among *Poems of*

Sentiment and Reflection. The gate, which still stands on the middle road between White Moss Common and Town End, was known in the Wordsworth family as Sara's Gate. *v.* D. W. *Journal* for Oct. 31, 1802.

p. 301. XLII. THE WISHING-GATE DESTROYED. "In the vale of Grasmere, by the side of the old highway leading to Ambleside, is a gate which, time out of mind, has been called the Wishing-gate."

Having been told, upon what I thought good authority, that this gate had been destroyed, and the opening, where it hung, walled up, I gave vent immediately to my feelings in these stanzas. But going to the place some time after, I found, with much delight, my old favourite unmolested.—W. W.

p. 303. XLIII. THE PRIMROSE OF THE ROCK. "Rydal Mount 1831. It stands on the right hand a little way leading up the middle road from Rydal to Grasmere. We have been in the habit of calling it the Glow-worm Rock from the number of glow-worms we have often seen hanging on it as described. The tuft of primrose has, I fear, been washed away by the heavy rains."—I. F.

Cf. D. W.'s *Journal* for April 24, 1802. "We walked in the evening to Rydal. . . . We [i.e. W. and D. W. and Coleridge] all stood to look at the Glow-worm Rock—a primrose that grew there, and just looked out on the road from its own sheltered bower."

A fair copy of the poem in hand of M. W. (cited in *app. crit.* as MS. 1) preserves its earlier and shorter version, which omits ll. 25–42. In the same notebook is a rough draft, in W.'s hand, of the completed poem, cited as MS. 2; in another a fair copy, as text, by D. W.

p. 305. XLIV. PRESENTIMENTS. "1830, Rydal Mount."—I. F. There are several manuscripts of this poem. MS. 1 is an early draft of a few stanzas; MS. 2 a fair copy by Dora W. of an early and shorter version; it omits stanzas 6, 9, 11, and 12, i.e. ll. 31–6, 49–54, 61–72, and places stanza 3 (ll. 13–18) before the last stanza. MSS. 3 and 4 are in the hands of D. W. and W. W. and provide some other variants; MS. 5, by D. W., corresponds with text.

p. 308. XLV. VERNAL ODE. "Rydal Mount, 1817. Composed to place in view the immortality of succession where immortality is denied, as far as we know, to the individual creature."—I. F. In the collective editions of 1820 and 1836–49 it was placed among *Poems of Imagination*; in 1827–32 among *Poems of Sentiment and Reflection.* Two manuscripts are extant, both apparently of the year 1817; one of them heads the poem *ODE*: April 17, 1817.

p. 313. XLVI. DEVOTIONAL INCITEMENTS. "Rydal Mount, 1832." —I. F. The quotation which heads the poem is from *Paradise Lost*, v. 77–80

> Taste this, and be henceforth among the Gods
> Thy self a Goddess, not to Earth confind,
> But somtimes in the Air, as wee, somtimes
> Ascend to Heav'n.

p. 315. XLVII. The Cuckoo-Clock. "Of this clock I have nothing further to say than what the poem expresses, except that it must be here recorded that it was a present from the dear friend for whose sake these Notes were chiefly undertaken, and who has written them from my dictation."—I. F. Two manuscripts in M. W.'s and Dora W.'s hands, supply the date of composition—"W. W. April 7, his 70th birthday".

33. *wandering* voice] A quotation from l. 4 of *To the Cuckoo*, hence the MS. reading is really preferable to that of the text.

34–44. K. found this last stanza on p. 429 of Crabb Robinson's copy of the 1845 ed., in the blank space following *Animal Tranquillity and Decay*; he mistook it for an independent and hitherto unpublished poem, and printed it as such (K. viii. 308). In l. 39 he reads "points" for "founts", probably an error of transcription.

p. 316. XLVIII. To the Clouds. "These verses were suggested while I was walking on the foot-road between Rydal Mount and Grasmere. The clouds were driving over the top of Nab Scar across the vale; they set my thoughts agoing, and the rest followed almost immediately."—I. F.

There are at least five manuscripts of this poem. MS. 1 is a rough copy entered on the versos of MS. 1 of *Peter Bell*, but much later than the rest of that MS. MS. 2 contains also a discursive blank verse poem entitled *The Tuft of Primroses* of which portions were adapted to *The Prelude* and *The Excursion*, and a blank verse poem, *The Vision of St. Paul's*, described in a letter to Sir George Beaumont of April 8, 1808. This fact, together with a reference in *The Tuft of Primroses* to the death of Mr. Sympson (June 27, 1807) and to their distress on returning from Coleorton (July 1807) to find that the fir trees and sycamore by the church had been cut down, and to the illness of S. H. (March–April 1808), prove that the poem was written in the spring of that year, for all the entries in this notebook were clearly made at the same time. MS. 3 is a revised copy by M. W. of MS. 2. MSS. 3 and 4 probably date from 1842, and were revisions made with a view to publication in the 1842 volume.

p. 320. XLIX. Suggested by a Picture of the Bird of Paradise. "This subject has been treated of in another Note. I will here only by way of comment direct attention to the fact that pictures of animals and other productions of nature as seen in conservatories, menageries, museums, etc., would do little for the national mind, nay they would be rather injurious to it, if the imagination were excluded by the presence of the object, more or less out of a state of nature. If it were not that we learn to talk and think of the lion and the eagle, the palm-tree and even the cedar, from the impassioned introduction of them so frequently into Holy Scripture and by great poets, and divines who write as poets, the spiritual part of our nature, and therefore the higher part of it, would derive no benefit from such intercourse with such subjects."—I. F.

7. Glendoveers] "A race of beautiful sprites in Southey's artificial quasi-Hindu mythology. ' *Kehama* VI. ii 'The Glendoveers. The loveliest race of all of heavenly birth'."—O. E. D.

p. 321. L. A JEWISH FAMILY. "Coleridge, my daughter, and I, in 1828, passed a fortnight upon the banks of the Rhine, principally under the hospitable roof of Mr. Aders of Gotesburg, but two days of the time we spent at St. Goar in rambles among the neighbouring vallies. It was at St. Goar that I saw the Jewish family here described. Though exceedingly poor, and in rags, they were not less beautiful than I have endeavoured to make them appear. We had taken a little dinner with us in a basket, and invited them to partake of it, which the mother refused to do, both for herself and children, saying it was with them a fast-day; adding diffidently, that whether such observances were right or wrong, she felt it her duty to keep them strictly. The Jews, who are numerous on this part of the Rhine, greatly surpass the German peasantry in the beauty of their features and in the intelligence of their countenances. But the lower classes of the German peasantry have, here at least, the air of people grievously opprest. Nursing mothers, at the age of seven or eight and twenty often look haggard and far more decayed and withered than women of Cumberland and Westmoreland twice their age. This comes from being underfed and overworked in their vineyards in a hot and glaring sun."—I. F.

There are at least four fair copies of this poem. The first, in Dora's hand, is entitled "A Jewish Child", and preserves some earlier readings. The others are by Dora, D. W., and S. H.

In Dora W.'s Journal of her Tour on the Continent (1828) is the entry "St. Goar, Monday [July] 14th... such a family—I will not anticipate Father's Poem by transcribing my thoughts and feelings; one affecting thing only will I note. When Mr. Coleridge told this Rachel how much he admired her child, 'Yes', said she, 'she is beautiful' (adding with a sigh) 'but see these rags and misery'—pointing to its frock which was made up of a thousand patches."

p. 323. LI. ON THE POWER OF SOUND. "Rydal Mount, 1828. I have often regretted that my tour in Ireland, chiefly performed in the short days of October in a carriage and four (I was with Mr. Marshall) supplied my memory with so few images that were new, and with so little motive to write. The lines, however, in this poem, 'Thou too be heard, lone Eagle etc.' were suggested near the Giants' Causeway, or rather at the promontory of Fairhead where a pair of eagles wheeled above our heads and darted off as if to hide themselves in a blaze of sky made by the setting sun."—I. F. The poem was developed from some lines, "There is a world of spirit etc." which were written originally for *The Triad*, and rejected from it. (*v. app.*

crit., p. 294.) On Dec. 15 W. wrote to G. H. Gordon, "During the last week I wrote some stanzas on the *Power of Sound*, which ought to find a place in my larger work if aught should ever come of that." If his dating is correct he must in that month have finished his first version of the poem, of which a fair copy survives written by S. H. I quote this version as MS. A; it will be noted that it opens with the stanza published as XII, and does not include stanzas I, IV, V, VII–X, and XIII. In its present form the poem must be dated after September 1829, when (not in October as W. states, *supra*) he visited the Giants' Causeway. In addition to MS. A there are several fair copies and rough drafts of separate passages: the variants from these I quote as MS.

W. himself ranked *On the Power of Sound* very high among his own compositions; in several of the MSS. the title is followed by the words *Paulo majora canamus*, and to Dyce who wrote to him "Perhaps I am wrong in thinking that the Ode contains some passages as magnificent as any you have ever written", he replied "I cannot call to mind a reason why you should not think some passages in it equal to anything I have produced; when first printed in 'Yarrow Revisited' I placed it at the end of the Volume, and in the last ed. of my Poems, at the close of the Poems of the Imagination, indicating thereby my own opinion of it." (*L.Y.*, p. 906.) Barron Field, also, rated the poem highly. On Dec. 17, 1836 he wrote to W.: "Never was sound made so much of before. Milton should have written it when blind. . . . Truly are sounds things, as much as sights; for the purposes of imagination perhaps more so. Even in versification, how deeply you have studied the sound as well as the sense of poetry will one day be acknowledged."

14. pealing down the long-drawn aisle] K. points out the debt to Gray, *Elegy*, 39–40.

Where through the long-drawn aisle and fretted vault
The pealing anthem swells the note of praise.

Both Gray and W. had, probably, Milton's "pealing organ" (*Il Pens.* 160) at the back of their minds.

76. Lydian airs] *L'Allegro* 136.

134–6. the dulcet sound . . . listening dolphins] cf. *A Midsummer-Night's Dream*, II. i. 150–1

And heard a mermaid, on a dolphin's back,
Uttering such dulcet and harmonious breath.

150–1. beat the ground In cadence] K. compares Gray, *The Progress of Poesy*, 34, "To brisk notes in cadence beating".

204–5. Deep to Deep . . . calls] *Psalms* xlii. 7.

217–18. O Silence! are Man's noisy years *etc.*] an echo of the famous lines in the *Ode: Intimations of Immortality*, 158–9:

Our noisy years seem moments in the being
Of the eternal silence;

Both are reminiscent of lines which occur in an *Address to Silence* published in the *Weekly Entertainer*, and copied by Dorothy, who appends the initials W. W., into a note-book in 1798.

> Eternity of calmness is thy joy,
> Immensity of space is thine abode,
> The rolling planets own thy sacred power ;
> Our noisy years are moments of thy life,
> Our little world is lost amid thy spheres,
> The harmony serene of mind is thine. *v.* Add., p. 532.

p. 331. PETER BELL. "Alfoxden. 1798. Founded upon an anecdote, which I read in a newspaper, of an ass being found hanging his head over a canal in a wretched posture. Upon examination a dead body was found in the water and proved to be the body of its master. The countenance, gait, and figure of Peter, were taken from a wild rover with whom I walked from Builth, on the river Wye, downwards nearly as far as the town of Hay. He told me strange stories. It has always been a pleasure to me through life to catch at every opportunity that has occurred in my rambles of becoming acquainted with this class of people. The number of Peter's wives was taken from the trespasses in this way of a lawless creature who lived in the county of Durham, and used to be attended by many women, sometimes not less than half a dozen, as disorderly as himself, and a story went in the country that he had been heard to say while they were quarrelling, 'Why can't you be quiet ? there's none so many of you'. Benoni, or the child of sorrow, I knew when I was a school-boy. His mother had been deserted by a gentleman in the neighbourhood, she herself being a gentlewoman by birth. The circumstances of her story were told me by my dear old Dame, Anne Tyson, who was her confidante. The lady died broken-hearted.—In the woods of Alfoxden I used to take great delight in noticing the habits, tricks, and physiognomy of asses ; and I have no doubt that I was thus put upon writing the poem out of liking for the creature that is so often dreadfully abused. The crescent-moon, which makes such a figure in the prologue, assumed this character one evening while I was watching its beauty in front of Alfoxden House. I intended this poem for the volume before spoken of, but it was not published for more than 20 years afterwards.—The worship of the Methodists or Ranters is often heard during the stillness of the summer evening in the country with affecting accompaniments of rural beauty. In both the psalmody and the voice of the preacher there is, not unfrequently, much solemnity likely to impress the feelings of the rudest characters under favourable circumstances."—I. F.

Six manuscripts of *Peter Bell* are known to me. On April 20. 1798, is the entry in D. W.'s *Journal*, "William all the morning engaged in wearisome composition. The moon crescent. *Peter Bell* begun." It was finished within two months, for in the following June Hazlitt, on a visit to Coleridge at Nether Stowey, came over to Alfoxden and "W. read to us the story of Peter Bell in the open air: the comment on it by his face and voice was very different from that of some later critics! Whatever might be thought of the poem 'his face was as a book where men might read strange matters', and he announced the fate of his hero in prophetic tones" (*My first Acquaintance with Poets*). MS. 1, on paper with the watermark 1795, a carefully written fair copy by D. W., represents the first stage of the poem, as read to Hazlitt. In its present state it is fragmentary, only ll. 96–105, 111–15, 165–215, and 326–500 surviving. Many corrections and erasures by W. indicate that it was used in preparation for MS. 2.

On Feb. 27, 1799, W. wrote to Coleridge from Goslar, "I have lately been employed in hewing down *Peter Bell*—with another dressing I think he will do"; and on Dec. 25, from Grasmere, "As to the Tragedy [i.e. *The Borderers*] and *Peter Bell*, D. will do all in her power to put them forward". MS. 2, chiefly in D. W.'s hand, was the result. It can be dated 1799–1800 from the fact that between Parts II and III some pages are filled, among other things, with a note on *Joanna* and a few lines of *The Brothers*, which were both written early in 1800. Part III is partly copied by W. From this MS. ll. 206–390 are missing.

MS. 3 is contemporary with MS. 2. On the first page is written "Mary Hutchinson, Gallow Hill". The text is practically identical with that of MS. 2, and it was probably written during W.'s visit to Gallow Hill in May–June 1800. Most of it is in M. H.'s hand, but some in W.'s and some in a hand now unidentifiable. Ll. 610–700 have been cut out.

MS. 4, a careful fair copy by D. W., is dated by a note on the title-page—"Grasmere, Sunday ½ past 5 o'clock by the gold watch, now hanging above the fire, a rainy coldish day, snow on the ground, but there is a thrush singing. Feb. 21, 1802". And in her *Journal* for that year we find the entries: "Feb, 17: I copied the second part of *Peter Bell*. Feb. 18: I copied third part of *Peter Bell* in W.'s absence. Feb. 20: I wrote the first part of *Peter Bell*. Sunday Feb. 21: I wrote the 2nd prologue to *Peter Bell*. . . . After dinner I wrote the 1st prologue." This manuscript is preserved in a vellum-bound notebook known as M. (*v.* my ed. of *Prelude*, pp. xx, xxi). The other contents of M. comprise work written in or before 1804, but not yet published, and all copied in 1804. That *Peter Bell* was not recopied with a view to inclusion in this volume is shown by the fact that its pages are longer than those of the rest of the book, and have, each of them, been carefully folded back so as not to obtrude beyond the binding. MS. 4 represents a development of the text from MSS. 2 and 3.

MS. 5 is a fair copy by S. H. From its similarity in paper, binding, and handwriting to MS. 2 of *The Waggoner* I should judge that its

date is 1805–6, and that it is the copy from which W. read the poem
to the Beaumonts (*v. M.Y.*, p. 167). On the verso of one page appear
for the first time the famous lines 130–55. It would be interesting to
know the date of their composition; they may have been added
any time between the writing of this manuscript and the poem's
publication.

MS. 6, copied by S. H. into a notebook which also contains *The
Waggoner* and *Artegal and Elidure*, was probably prepared shortly
before publication.

All the manuscripts contain corrections in W.'s hand. When, as is
usual, these corrections are incorporated in the next MS., or in the
printed text, I have recorded them as belonging to the text of which
they first form an integral part, for they were obviously made when
the text was being revised and do not belong to the date of the MS. in
which they appear only as a correction.

W. justly regarded *Peter Bell* as one of his great imaginative poems
and spent endless pains in its improvement. It was written at first,
like some of the *Lyrical Ballads* with which it is contemporary, as
"an experiment, with a view to ascertain how far the language of
conversation in the middle and lower classes of society is adapted to
the purposes of poetic pleasure"; and in no poem, not even in *The
Thorn* or *The Idiot Boy*, is the diction so daringly commonplace, and
the style so clearly a realistic attempt to convey the idea of a simple
but profoundly imaginative tale told as it might be told in a village
circle. This characteristic of the poem was progressively toned down
in succeeding revisions, though to the end much remained which
represents W.'s most defiant challenge to literary convention.

Mr. T. Hutchinson has pointed out the affinity of *Peter Bell* with
other poems written by W. W. and Coleridge in 1798—*The Three
Graves, The Ancyent Marinere, Cain*, and *Goody Blake and Harry Gill*,
as all of them studies in mental pathology, and having a common
psychological basis. "Each in its own fashion illustrates the tremendous effect on the imagination (and through it on the physical
organism) of a painful idea suddenly and vividly impressed on the
mind. The idea is the same in all five cases—that of a curse." He
further notes the similarity of scenic background in *Cain* and *Peter
Bell*, both of which are influenced by the Valley of Rocks near Lynton,
Devon, though W. places the scene of *Peter Bell* by the river Swale
and near Leeming Lane in Yorkshire.

128. ambitious Youth] i.e. Coleridge, who in *The Ancient Mariner*
and *Christabel* had taken as his province poetry in which "the incidents and agents were to be, in part at least, supernatural".

515/16. Is it a party in a parlour] "This stanza I omitted, though
one of the most imaginative in the whole piece, not to offend the
pious."—W. to Barron Field (*M.Y.*, p. 312). Crabb Robinson in his
Diary records that he "ventured to beg W. to expunge it" and that

Lady Beaumont also advised its omission; Lamb, however, regarded
it as "full of imagination". Mrs. Basil Montagu claimed that she had
suggested the image to W. by relating to him an anecdote: "A person
walking in a friend's garden, looking in at a window, saw a company
of ladies sitting at a table near the window with countenances fixed.
In an instant he was aware of their condition and broke the window.
He saved them from incipient suffocation." The chief objection to
accepting Mrs. Montagu's claim is that the stanza was written in
1798, and it is extremely unlikely that W. had met her before her
marriage to Montagu in 1808. Moreover it is quite unnecessary to
suppose that the party were physically asphyxiated; the stanza is a
vivid picture of the intellectual vacuity of a dull country tea-party,
such as W. may sometimes have been driven to attend among his
neighbours in Somersetshire.

The stanza was prefixed by Shelley to his *Peter Bell the Third*.

573. resigned] i.e. absorbed in, a use of the word current in the
Lake district. *v.* D. W. *Journal* for April 30, 1802, "I lay with half-
shut eyes, looking at the prospect as on a vision almost, I was so
resigned to it."

578–80. These lines owe something, doubtless, to the incident of
W.'s boyhood related in *Prelude* v. 448–50.

675–80. Opposite these lines MS. 2 has preserved two stanzas, not
incorporated in any text of the poem, but of some autobiographical
interest (cf. I. F. note, *supra*):

> Now Peter do I call to mind
> That eventide when thou and I
> Over ditch and over stile
> Were fellow travellers many a mile
> Near Builth on the banks of Wye.
> Oh Peter who could now forget
> That both hung back in murderer's guize?
> 'Twas thou that wast afraid of me.
> And I that was afraid of thee,
> We'd each of us a hundred eyes.

885/6. made by the God that made us all] a reminiscence both in
conception and phrasing of *The Ancient Mariner*, 616–17:

> For the dear God who loveth us
> He made and loveth all.

973–4. "The notion is very general, that the Cross on the back and
shoulders of this Animal has the origin here alluded to."—W. W. 1819.

976. "I cannot suffer this line to pass, without noticing that it was
suggested by Mr. Haydon's noble picture of Christ's Entry into Jerusalem."—W. W. 1820. It will be noted that the passage does not
occur in the MSS. of the poem. The picture alluded to, now at

NOTES   531

Cincinnati, contains portraits of Wordsworth, Voltaire, Keats, and
Hazlitt; that of Wordsworth, according to Hazlitt, "the most like his
drooping weight of thought and expression".

APPENDIX

p. 463. I. ANDREW JONES. Lines 6–30 of this poem, found in the
Alfoxden notebook and in the book which contains MS. 2 of *Guilt and
Sorrow, etc.* (*v.* Vol. I, p. 331), were clearly written as an incident in the
career of Peter Bell, but later rejected and made into a separate poem
by the addition of the first and last stanzas. For a similar incident
in Peter Bell's career *v. Peter Bell* 885–6.

p. 464. II. *I love upon a stormy night*: This poem, in the same
metre, and found in the same MS. notebook as the above, was probably written at the same time as *Peter Bell*, and is, perhaps, a rejected
first draft of its Prologue, or an overflow from it. With the first two
stanzas cf. *Prelude*, ii. 306–10.

p. 465. III. ALCÆUS TO SAPPHO. Sent by Coleridge to Stuart in
Oct. 1800, for inclusion in the *Morning Post*, where it appeared on
Nov. 24; and included in editions of Coleridge's *Poems*. But W., in a
letter to Coleridge from Goslar in 1798, refers to "How sweet when
crimson colours etc." as a recent composition of his own, for which, he
adds, "I do not care a farthing". It was thus written by W. at the
same time as he was writing "Strange fits of passion", "She dwelt
among the untrodden ways", and "Three years she grew"; and it is
highly probable that it is a poem that he had rejected from the series
of poems to Lucy. We do not know how far Coleridge rehandled it,
but it is safe to assume that he is responsible for the title, and for the
introduction of the name "Sappho" into the penultimate stanza.

In the first volume of this edition I failed to point out that W.'s
juvenile poem *Beauty and Moonlight* is the original from which Coleridge developed his *Lewti*. The only important variant from *Beauty
and Moonlight* in the first draft of *Lewti* is in Coleridge's substitution
of "Tamaha's stream" for "Winander's stream", thus giving to the
poem a remoteness of scene which is the first stage in its transformation into a "Circassian Love Chant". By a similar transformation the
lines "How sweet when crimson colours etc.", which W. rightly
deemed unworthy to be offered to "Lucy", were palmed off on
readers of the *Morning Post* as the address of Alcæus to Sappho.

p. 466. IV. THE GLOW-WORM. Included in this volume as it is
obviously "founded on the Affections", and is especially related to
nos. vi–ix of that series. The date of composition is stated in D. W.'s
Journal. On April 16, 1802, W. wrote to Coleridge: "I parted with
Mary on Monday afternoon about six o'clock. . . . Between the beginning of Lord Darlington's park at Raby and two or three miles beyond
Staindrop, I wrote the Poem which you will find on the opposite

page." After the poem he adds: "The incident of this Poem took place about seven years ago between Dorothy and me." It thus records an incident of their life together at Racedown. W. may have dropped it from his collected editions because he was peculiarly sensitive to ridicule directed against a poem of which the setting and the feeling are so intimately personal. The *Simpliciad* made mock of poets who

> With fervent welcome greet the glow-worm's flame,
> Put it to bed, and bless it by its name.

In addition to the MS. preserved in the letter to Coleridge, the poem is found in MS. M.

W. published the poem without a title, but D. W. refers to it more than once as *The Glow-worm*.

ADDENDUM

pp. 271-2. LAODAMIA, **158-63**. Mr. M. Buxton Forman sends me another version of this stanza, which he has found copied by W. on to the back of a letter to Haydon (n.d.). It runs

> She whom a trance of passion thus removed
> As she departed not without the crime
> Of Lovers who *etc. as* 1827, *but* joyless *for* grosser, *and* in

Elysian *for* 'mid unfading

ADDENDA TO NOTES, 1951

p. 517. SONG AT THE FEAST OF BROUGHAM CASTLE. *The following notes should be added*:

27. "Earth helped him with the cry of blood." This line is from *The Battle of Bosworth Field* by Sir John Beaumont (Brother to the Dramatist), whose poems are written with so much spirit, elegance, and harmony, that it is supposed, as the Book is very scarce, a new edition of it would be acceptable to Scholars and Men of taste, and accordingly, it is in contemplation to give one. W. W. 1807.

123. "And both the undying Fish that swim
Through Bowscale-Tarn," etc.

It is imagined by the people of the Country that there are two immortal Fish, Inhabitants of this Tarn, which lies in the mountains not far from Threlkeld.—Blencathara, mentioned before, is the old and proper name of the mountain vulgarly called Saddle-back.—W. W. 1807.

p. 527. ON THE POWER OF SOUND.

Note **217-18**. *add*: When D. W. copied the lines of which the first and last lines follow she wrote at the end the initials W. W.

Eternity of calmness . . .
The harmony serene of mind is thine.

This, in conjunction with the fact that the factotum at Racedown,
Joseph Gill, noted in his *Diary*, Jan. 1st, 1797, "Mr. P. of Blackdown
to send Mr. W.'s poem to the Entertainer" led me to find in *The
Weekly Entertainer* the whole poem in the number for March 6, 1797.
It stands as follows:

ADDRESS TO SILENCE
[Read at a Literary Club]

SILENCE! calm, venerable majesty:
Guardian of contemplation and of love.
Thy voice, in marv'llous words of nature, speaks
Not to the ear, but to the eye of man;
Thy placid mien restores the ruffled heath
Or shattered forests, where the storm is past;
And calms the ocean wave without a shore.
Sometimes, when not a single leaf is wav'd;
When no mild breeze sweeps o'er the smiling vale;
When, in the lake, each undulation sleeps;
When heaven is full serene; and grove, and hill,
And mother earth are stript of herb and flower
By winter's hand, laying in deep repose
Whole islands; heav'nly musing silence reigns.
Round Iceland's coast the frozen sea its base,
Its top the sky, lit by the polar star,
Thy throne is fixt. Thy palace, now and then,
Is to the center shook, by falling rocks
Of glittering ice; or the enormous whale;
Or by the roar of Hecla's flaming mouth
Loud thundering o'er thy widely echoing realms.

Silence! I would not visit thy domains,
In north and south, for the most precious ore,
The gold and gems which Afric, Asia hold;
Or rivers wash into the eastern main:
No: Not for the sweet beauties of our earth;
Nor the proud glories of the light of day.
Sceptres and thrones, imperial crowns and stars,
Fade in the shadowy mansions of the dead,
Where Kings, lords, slaves, without distinction lie
Beneath thy sway.
            Thy peaceful sceptre scorns
The triumphs of the throng'd metropolis,

And exclamations of the multitude.
Floods; cataracts o'er precipices huge;
The mighty sounds of Ganges and of Nile,
Have not a charm for thee; nor thunder's voice,
Nor dire convulsions, which the mountains shake.
Far, far remote from noise, thy presence dwells.
The sleeping infant, and his mother's eye;
The smiling picture, and the breathless bust;
The rest of ages, and the mourner's face;
The mould'ring abbey and the quiet grave;
The lonely tower upon a desart rock;
The shining valley, with the full orb'd moon,
Are thy delights: With them thou art well pleas'd.
With thee 'tis peace: peace now; peace evermore!

Eternity of calmness is thy joy;
Immensity of space is thine abode;
The rolling planets own thy sacred power;
Our little years are moments of thy life;
Our little world is lost amid thy spheres.

The harmony serene of mind is thine;
And human thought, that wings its boundless way
From earth to heaven, is led through air by thee;
With solitude and thee our God resides!
Hush winds! be still: Cease flood! thy tedious voice,
The monotonous music of thy streams;
Or I must leave you, and with silence stray
To the deep forest, or the deeper grave,
Where neither winds nor waves disturb repose.

Yet, silence! let me once review the haunts
Of men. Once more let me enjoy the scene
Of social hearts; and view sweet friendship's smiles,
Ere I be seen no more!
                    Then have thy sway,
    Silence!
                                            W. C.

The initials W. C., not W. W., suggest the possibility that Coleridge
may have had a hand in the poem. I am convinced, however, that the
main composition is W. W.'s. *v.* my lecture "An approach to Wordsworth's Genius" in *English Studies Today,* 1951.

APPENDIX II TO VOL. II

In a small note-book of Sara Hutchinson now in the possession of Miss Joanna Hutchinson, I find transcripts of twenty-four poems of Wordsworth all except one of which were, as it appears, composed between the end of 1801 and June 1802, and sent to Mary and Sara Hutchinson at Gallow Hill, perhaps in batches, as they were composed. The dates, as we follow the poems through, are nearly all clearly confirmed by entry in Dorothy Wordsworth's *Journal* or by reference in letters. Clinching, and most interesting, evidence of date is found in the transcription by Sara here of an early version, unfortunately mutilated by the tearing out of a page, of *The Leech-gatherer* later called *Resolution and Independence*. Between May 3 and 9, as Dorothy records in her *Journal*, W. composed his first draft of *The Leech-gatherer*. On June 14 he writes to Sara (*v. Early Letters* edited by E. de S., pp. 305-6) rebuking her with severity for her failure to understand his main purpose in the poem, of which he must have sent this first draft to her and Mary in the interval:

My dear Sara,

I am exceedingly sorry that the latter part of the Leechgatherer has displeased you, the more so because I cannot take to myself (that being the case) much pleasure or satisfaction in having pleased you in the former part. I will explain to you in prose my feeling in writing that poem and then you will be better able to judge whether the fault be mine or yours or partly both. I describe myself as having been exalted to the highest pitch of delight by the joyousness and beauty of Nature; and then as depressed, even in the midst of those beautiful objects, to the lowest dejection and despair. A young Poet in the midst of the happiness of Nature is described as overwhelmed by the thought of the miserable reverses which have befallen the happiest òf all men, viz. Poets. I think of this till I am so deeply impressed with it, that I consider the manner in which I was rescued from my dejection and despair almost as an interposition of Providence. Now whether it was by peculiar grace, A leading from above—A person reading this Poem with feelings like mine will have been awed and controuled, expecting almost something spiritual or supernatural. What is brought forward ? 'A lonely place, a Pond', 'by which an old man *was*, far from all house or home': not *stood*, not *sat*, but *was*—the figure presented in the most naked simplicity possible. This feeling of spirituality or supernaturalness is again referred to as being strong in my mind in this passage. *How came he here?* thought I, or what can he be doing ? I then describe him, whether ill or well is not for me to judge with perfect confidence ; but this

I can *confidently* affirm, that though I believe God has given me a strong imagination, I cannot conceive a figure more impressive than that of an old Man like this, the survivor of a Wife and ten children, travelling alone among the mountains and all lonely places, carrying with him his own fortitude, and the necessities which an unjust state of society has entailed upon him. . . . You speak of his speech as tedious: everything is tedious when one does not read with the feelings of the Author. *The Thorn* is tedious to hundreds; and so is *The Idiot Boy* to hundreds. It is in the character of the old man to tell his story, which an *impatient* reader must necessarily feel as tedious. But, Good God! Such a figure, in such a place; a pious, self-respecting, miserably infirm and [ ] Old Man telling such a tale!

It will be seen that W. here quotes phrases from the poem which do not appear in any printed version, viz. "A lonely place, a Pond, by which an old man *was*", "far from all house or home;" and "How came he here? thought I." Now Sara's version holds the lines

> I to the borders of a Pond did come,
> By which an Old Man was, far from all house or home.

"How came he here? thought I" must have been on the torn-out page. Sara had evidently expressed feelings of tedium in reading the second part of the poem which gave the old man's tale of his loss of wife and ten children and details of his travels and his difficulties in his unlucrative occupation.

In her transcript of the early version of the poem the stanza immediately following the line quoted,

"By which an Old Man was, far from all house or home" opens thus:

> He seem'd like one who little saw or heard
> For chimney nook, or bed, or coffin meet.

This suggestion of the sort of dead-alive old figure often seen in a cottage chimney-corner did not invoke in Sara that sense of "spirituality or supernaturalness" which W. meant to give to his vision of the old man.

It is much to Wordsworth's credit that he digested Sara's criticism, at first unpalatable, but found later to be sound and even stimulating. He cut out the stanza of which I have just quoted the beginning, and put in its place that stanza which is surely the imaginative core of the poem; setting the old man in a wild desolate landscape, and making him partake of its strangeness:

> As a huge stone is sometimes seen to lie
> Couch'd on the bald top of an eminence, &c.

Further he cut out from the Leech-gatherer's speech his account of his family losses, and some at least of his difficulties over the leeches. Sara's copy is clearly that first version which W. completed on May 9, and which is not found in any other known MS.

The revision was done as D. W. records in her *Journal*, by July 4th. For full record of the variants *v. infra* pp. 539–41.

To read that first version, patched together as well as we can from what remains of Sara's transcript, is to realize most sharply the move forward that W. was making in the spring of 1802 from the matter-of-fact descriptive style of the *Lyrical Ballads*, of which some examples survive in the volumes of 1807 (e.g. in *Alice Fell* and *The Sailor's Mother*) to the freer imaginative art which finds its release in those volumes (e.g. in *The Solitary Reaper*).

Thirteen of the poems transcribed by Sara appear in the present volume, as I have noted in my Preface. I deal with these first, but for completeness I have added from the same notebook, variants in the few other poems which appear in the present edition, Vols. I, III, and IV. In "I griev'd for Buonaparte", III p. 110, there are no variants to record. Throughout I give only the variants which are independent of those quoted in *app. crit.* of the present edition.

To a Butterfly, p. 22 *supra*.
  8 Shall find
  9 And call
 13 And feed
 18 And childish summer days as long [altered to text of 1807–49].

A Farewell, p. 23 *supra*.
  This version was transcribed after receiving W.'s letter of June 14, 1802: it embodies corrections and additions there made. The text corresponds with that of the MS. quoted in *app. crit.*, pp. 23–5 *supra* except:
  3 Of Fairfield's mighty temple
 13   distant chattels
 26   love this Bower
 33 Dear Spot whom

[*Stanzas written in my pocket-copy of Thomson's "Castle of Indolence"*: no title in transcript.]
      "Within our happy Castle . . ." p. 25 *supra*.
  Text identical with MS. quoted in *app. crit.*, pp. 25–7 *supra*, except:
 39   large dark
 46 Ah God forefend!
 62 And leaves & flowers, & herbage green & gold
 69 Most happy livers

Repentance, p. 46 *supra*.
  1 O Fools that we were etc. as MSS. quoted in *app. crit.*, p. 46.
  2 Half a dozen snug fields, fat, contented and gay;
  For the rest the transcript corresponds with the MSS. (generally with MS. 3) except:
  6 Let him come, let him come with his bags

15 Sometimes when I lift up the latch of a gate
31   on the fields and the cows & the sheep.

[*The Sailor's Mother*: no title in transcript.] p. 54 *supra*.
 1 The day was cold and rain [clearly a slip of the pen for *raw*] and wet
 5 —Majestic seem'd she as a mountain storm;
 6 A Roman matron's gait—like feature & like form
11   of low estate
13–16 When from my lofty thoughts I woke,
       With the first word I had to spare
       I said to her 'Beneath your cloak
       What is it you are carrying there ?'
19–24 "My eldest son, a Sailor, sail'd
       "With God's good blessing many a day
       "But at the last, his fortune fail'd—
       "—In Denmark he was cast away:
       "At Hull he liv'd where I have been to see
       "What Clothes he might have left, or other property.
 24/5 "The room in which he lodg'd was small,
       "And few effects were in it, when
       "I reach'd the place; I sold them all,
       "And now am travelling home again.
       "I live at Mary-port, a weary way!
       "And scarcely what I have will for my journey pay.
29–34 *om.*
    For the last stanza, MS. reads first four lines as 25–8 of text;
followed by:
       "And I, God help me! for my little wit
       "Trail't with me, Sir! he took so much delight in it!"

The Emigrant Mother, p. 56 *supra*.
    The first 14 lines, also the last two stanzas, of the printed edd. are
missing. The poem begins after the title:
15   Dear Babe! thou daughter of another
45   My own dear Harry he
48   his day
63–4 *as* 1807–15 *but* those two *for* those smiles
74   any Babe
75–95 *om.*

To a Skylark[1], p. 141 *supra*.
 5   With all the clouds about us ringing

    [1] W. dated the poem 1805, but Mr. T. Hutchinson suggested that from
its style it belonged to 1802, and further that it was probably conceived on
W.'s visit on foot to Scotland in 1801. W. went by the same route that he
and D. W. followed in 1803, on which D. W. notes, in her *Journal*, of their
journey through Solway Moss, "the dreary waste cheered by the endless
singing of sky larks." *v.* lines 8–9.

6–7 We two will sail along [This line provides a rhyme to line 2,
which in the printed version ends with a blind rhyme.]

8–9 I have sung in wildernesses dreary
But today

14 Up with me, up with me powerfully
I will yoke myself to thee
And we'll travel merrily ;
Up with me, up with me high and high

18 nest, which thou lov'st best ;

The Redbreast chasing the Butterfly, p. 149 *supra*.

6 the Charles of Swedish Boors

8/9 In Germany their little Hans,
The Frederick whom they love in France,

24 ails . . . must pursue

To a Cuckoo, p. 207 *supra*.

The text is identical with that of 1807 except:

6 hollow *for* restless

18–19 I listen'd to, whom I
Look'd for a thousand, thousand ways

*Written while resting upon the Bridge near the foot of Brother's Water—
at noon Ap. 15th. 1802*, p. 220 *supra*.

The correct date is given both in W.'s letter to S. T. C. 16th April,
1802, and in D. W.'s *Journal* "April 16th, Good Friday'. [April 16,
1802 was Good Friday].

6–7 The horse and his marrow
Drag the plough and the harrow,

[*Beggars*: no title in transcript.] p. 222 *supra*.

16 Such woes thought I can

17–18 —"And yet some small assistance you shall have
And for your beauty's sake—you are a woman brave."

A line is drawn here, and below stands the heading *Second part*.

20 did I spy

25–36 *om.*

37 They spied me all at once—and lo!

41 "That could not be," said one, "my mother's dead."

47 said one

The Leech-gatherer (*title in transcript*): *Resolution and Independence,*
1807, p. 235 *supra*.

This version of the poem was composed between May 3 and 9,
(*v.* D. W.'s *Journal*) and sent to Sara and Mary some days before
June 14, when W. writes the letter answering Sara's criticism
(*v. supra* p. 536–7). The revision made in response to Sara's objections
was done between July 2 and 4. (*v.* D. W.'s *Journal*.) Unfortunately
Sara tore out the page containing most of the early version cancelled
by W., but a good deal of it can be reconstructed from the remaining

stub which on the recto sometimes gives the first letters of the lines,
and on the verso in one instance the last two words, making identification possible.

38–9   Who will not wade to seek a bridge or boat,
          How can he ever hope to cross the flood ?
after 53–4 *as in* 1807, *v. app. crit.* p. 237 *supra*
          I to the borders of a Pond did come
          By which an Old Man was, far from all house or home.

57–60   He seem'd like one who little saw or heard
          For chimney-nook, or bed, or coffin meet.
          A stick was in his hand wherewith he stirr'd
          The waters of the pond beneath his feet.

The torn-out page follows, and the stub shows the following words at
the beginning of the next three lines:

          How [
          But [
          How [

I suggest that the last line began "How came he here, thought I . . .".
Of the next stanza little can with confidence be reconstructed, but its
4th, 5th, and 6th lines, judging from the stub, seem to have been

67–9   Com[ing together in life's pilgrimage]
          As if [some dire constraint of pain, or rage]
          Of [sickness had by him in times long past]

for "had by him", the early reading, *v.* W.'s letter to Mary, May 14,
1802.

The next stanza is indicated by the stub quite clearly as that
which occurs in the copy sent to Longman for printing in 1807.
[MSS. formerly in the possession of Mr. T. Norton Longman, now in
that of Mr. E. H. W. Meyerstein.]

84/5   He [wore a Cloak, the same as women wear]
          As [one whose blood did needful comfort lack:]
          His [face look'd pale as if it had grown fair]
          An[d, furthermore, he had upon his back,]
          Ben[eath his cloak, a round and bulky Pack;]
          A l[oad of wool or raiment, as might seem;]
          [That on his shoulders lay as if it clave to him].[1]

Two more stanzas should follow but the stub gives no help in
identification. This brings us to the bottom of the torn-out page.
On the verso the stub makes it possible to identify the first stanza
as lines 99–105, 1807, or stanza XIV, p. 238 *supra*: the word on the

----

[1] This stanza was withdrawn at the last moment, perhaps in response
to the criticism of Coleridge, who remarked as a characteristic defect in
Wordsworth's poetry, "the insertion of accidental circumstances in order
to the full explanation of his living characters." (*v. Biog. Lit.* ch. xxii).
"This accidentality," he urged, "contravenes the essence of poetry."

stub at the end of the first line is "chest", at the end of the last, "dues."

Three stanzas and the first five lines of a fourth, telling of his loss of wife and ten children and his struggle for a living, must have followed on the verso. The next page (not torn out) is as follows:

124–6 I yet can gain my bread, tho' in times gone
     I twenty could have found where now I can find one.
om. 1807 Feeble I am in health these hills to climb
 and all Yet I procure a living of my own
  edd. This is my summer work, in winter time
     I go with godly Books from Town to Town.[1]
     Now I am seeking Leeches up & down
     From house to house I go, from Barn to Barn
     All over Cartmell Fells & up to Blellan Tarn.[2]
134–40 With this the Old Man other matter blended
     Which he deliver'd with demeanour kind
     Yet stately in the main—*etc. as text of* 1807, lines 143–7.

"Among all lovely things my Love had been" p. 466 *supra.*

The chief variations are those recorded in *app. crit.*, p. 466 *supra*, except:

19 *For* Lucy *read* Mary. The copy sent to S. T. C. reads Emma.

For date of composition and of the incident of the poem *v. supra* p. 531.

"My Heart leaps up" I, p. 226 *ante.*

The heading in transcript is *Extempore*

8 And I should wish that all my days may be

To a Butterfly, I, p. 226 *ante.*

2 A little moment
3 Much reading
4 Thou Bible
12 My sister Dorothy
18 his wings

The Sparrow's Nest, I, p. 227 *ante.*

W. dates the poem 1801, but it must surely belong to Spring 1802.

1–4 *as* 1807 *but* line 4 this simple
6 and little bed
9 My Sister Dorothy

[*Foresight*: No title in transcript.] I, p. 227 *ante.*

16 Spare the little
21 Daisies must *as* 1807 *v. app. crit.*

---

[1] *v.* D. W.'s *Journal.* Oct. 3, 1800.

[2] For W.'s elimination of local names and details in later versions cf. *A Farewell* p. 537 *supra* and *The Prelude passim.*

Alice Fell, I, p. 232 *ante.*

The top of the page is torn off so that at least one stanza is wanting from the beginning of the poem. Sara's transcript starts thus:

> The sky grows wild—a storm is near
> Clouds gather and the moon is drown'd—
> What is it that strange sound I hear ?
> What is the meaning of that sound ?
>
> As if the wind blew many ways
> I hear the noises more and more ;
> —Down go the windows of the chaise,
> And the noise follows as before.
>
> "Hola! what noise is that," said I,
> The Post Boy halted at the word
> I listened, neither voice nor cry
> Nor aught else like it could be heard.
>
> The Post Boy smack'd his whip, and fast
> The horses scamper'd through the rain ;
> And as before between the blast
> I heard the self-same sound again.

Two stanzas are now missing from the verso of the page of which the top was torn off. The transcript continues:

25-28   "'Tis torn in pieces look!—look here."
> Entangled in the wheel it hung,
> A weather-beaten rag, as e'er
> Upon a murderer's gibbet hung.

29 'Twas twisted, *etc., as text.*
The rest of the poem corresponds with the text of 1807 with very slight variations.

"The Sun has long been set", IV, p. 9 *post.*
    Text identical with 1807 *v. app. crit.* except:
4   and the trees
5 There's the Cuckoo.

"These chairs they have no words" *Half an hour afterwards.* (one poem in two parts.) IV, p. 365 *post.*
    Text as in IV, p. 365, except that it omits the penultimate line "Be but thou ever as now."

The Tinker: in *Longman* MSS. but not printed in 1807, nor ever by W. W. IV, p. 366, *post.*

The text is identical with that of *Longman* MSS. except:
42 Not doubting of her dread
  Like a Bullfinch black and red

Travelling, IV, p. 423 *post.*
  Text identical with MS. M (with same title) except:
  2 these fading leaves.

INDEX OF TITLES AND FIRST LINES

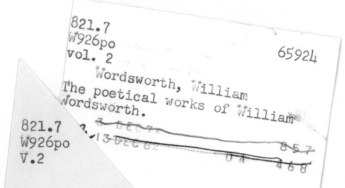